D0070112

ALEXANDER KERENSKY

The First Love. Kerensky salutes the navy, Sebastapol, May 1917.

ALEXANDER KERENSKY

THE FIRST LOVE OF THE REVOLUTION

Richard Abraham

COLUMBIA UNIVERSITY PRESS

NEW YORK 1987

Library of Congress Cataloging-in-Publication Data

Abraham, Richard, 1941–
Alexander Kerensky: the first love of the revolution.

Bibliography: p.
Includes index.
1. Kerensky, Aleksandr Fyodorovich, 1881–1970.
2. Prime ministers—Soviet Union—Biography.
3. Soviet Union—History—February Revolution, 1917.
I. Title.
DS254.K3A64   1987   947.084′1′0924 [B]   86–17548
ISBN 0–231–06108–0

Columbia University Press
New York   Guildford, Surrey
Copyright © 1987 Columbia University Press
All rights reserved

Printed in the United States of America

c 10 9 8 7 6 5 4 3 2

Book design by Ken Venezio

BARRY HOLLINGSWORTH

1935–1975

Contents

Illustrations appear as groups
after pages 80 and 272

Preface

The first light of dawn revealed the huddled, gray figures, chewing their cheap tobacco. Around them were the hills and valleys of Galicia, dotted with tree stumps and isolated wattle and thatch cottages, once so neat with their fences and orchards, but now unkempt and roofless. The hedgeless fields of wheat and rye looked equally forlorn, disfigured by the shallow, sinister zigzags of the trenches and the random gashes of shell craters. The larks were heard no more. The men tensed themselves for the whistles and thuds of shrapnel, while those at the command post stared at the thirty-six-year-old Minister of War who had come to urge them on. His famous brush cut now concealed by a flat military cap, he clenched his gloved fist against his plain but well-cut tunic as he paced nervously back and forth.

They remembered how he had spoken up for them in courthouse and parliament when the whole country had been silenced by the now vanished gendarmes. Their new subalterns, fresh out of grammar schools, worshipped him as the "Leader of the Intelligentsia." For the hidebound careerists, he was something else, a socialist waffler, an upstart, perhaps even a "Yid." He himself knew otherwise. A socialist intellectual he had been, but he had the blood of a general as well. His grandfather had served in the armies of the ill-fated Tsar Nicholas I, who had been humiliated by the English and French in the Crimea. But he had another dream, the dream of Themistocles that free men might fight harder to defend their liberty than enemy slaves would to extinguish it. The future of the world hung on this moment, on the Russian front in June of 1917.[1]

Fifty years later I met Alexander Kerensky, but time was short and I never got to know him. I did not then know what an irreparable loss this was. There is one compensation: my resolve to tell his story unvarished might not have survived a friendship with him. Even his closest friends admit that he gave little away. As Elena Izvolskaya, his friend for four decades, put it, "he has told in his books all that he has ever told me."[2] He lived and died a conspirator, whose real gift eluded the literati who recorded his failures. One can fail to be a "Great Man" but still be a great human being. To many, Alexander Kerensky was an irresistibly lovable person. Those who accepted their affection for him could never escape the web of loyalty he wove. Others were blinded to his quality by patriarchal prejudice and intellectual snobbery. No one who knew him well has ever published an objective account of him.

In 1966, Professor Werner Mosse suggested Kerensky as a topic for research, though the initial work was supervised by Dr. Lionel Kochan. It was an almost full-time occupation during the three years I spent at the University of East Anglia. By the early seventies, I had visited Paris, Helsinki, New York, Austin, Stanford—and briefly Leningrad—and *a* book was nearly complete. As the burdens of career and family mounted, the work ground to a halt. It was rescued in the mid-seventies by Kerensky's grandson, Oleg Kerensky, the ballet critic, who found readers sufficiently encouraging to justify the disruption of our normal existence. The support of Walter Deakin and Raymond Long secured the generosity of the Inner London Education Authority, which released me for a term on full pay in 1982 to take up an Education Fellowship at Keble College, Oxford. The Warden, Fellows, and first year politics students gave me the stimulus I needed to get re-started. It has still taken another three years to complete.

Oleg Kerensky prodded me into finishing the book and followed up some important leads in New York. John D. Moore, President and Director of Columbia University Press, repeatedly urged me to overcome the practical obstacles to its completion. Börje Thilman, Director of Yritystieto Oy. of Helsinki and occasional contributor to *Hufvudstadsbladet*, extended his unstinting hospitality, contacts, and resources purely *amore scientiae*. Kerensky's sons, the late Dr. Oleg Kerensky, CBE, FRS, and Gleb Kerensky bore my endless and sometimes impertinent questions with patient courtesy and, eventually, with unexpected frankness. Both of them spent hours correcting my drafts and searching for odd documents and photographs for me. I came to know Olga Lvovna Kerenskaya well in her Southport refuge, her lovable spirit unquenched by five decades of bitterness. Her friend, Tatiana Alexeyevna Ossorgina, has been unfailingly supportive and helpful. Professor Marc Ferro and Professor Tuomo Polvinen suggested lines of inquiry in Paris and Helsinki and Mme. A. Laurent kindly allowed me to consult the papers of her uncle, M. Eugène Petit. Professor Nina Berberova, Gladys Edds, Asher Gransby, Kirill Grigorkoff, Elena Ivanoff, the late Elena Izvolskaya, and Professor Barbara T. Norton were generous with information, advice, and materials. Barbara Norton shared her perceptions of freemasonry and interviewed Professor Sergei Utekhin on my behalf, and I was blessed by meticulous research assistance from Robert S. Call, Mark Cornwall, and Inga Offerberg.

Many of those who helped me cannot afford to offend the Soviet government and cannot be acknowledged here. I am grateful to the following for assistance which ranged from indispensable hospitality to the provision of information and translation and technical services:

Dr. Kurt Aaron OBE, Jessie Andrews, A. N. Artemoff, Stella Auchter, Dr. Christopher Barnes, D. Bartkiw, Ruth Boski, Stephen Boski, Anna Bourguina-Nicolaevsky, Dr. Roy Bridge, Helen Bristow, Professor Robert P. Browder, Ronald Bulatoff, Andy Burgess, Mary Burgum, Noel Busch, Hélène Cagan, Jacques Cagan, Professor Wilhelm Carlgren, Dr. Clem Christesen, Nina Christesen, Dr. John Coates, Anna Collingwood, Lawrence Collingwood, Grace Copp, Dr. Stephen Corrsin, Venetia Cross, Richard Davies, Mary Durbrow, Eeva Ede, Evelyn Egerton, Boris Elkin, Michael Elliott, Pirkko Elliott, Ted Fletcher, Mrs. A. D. Foam, Michael Fontenet, Dr. J. P. Fox, Orma Fry, Connell Gallagher, William Garnett, Syd Greenberg, Max Hayward, Cathy Henderson, Mary Hirth, Malcolm Howard, Colin Hughes, Countess Fira Ilinska, Jessie Jackson, Lorraine Jarrett, Dr. Osmo Jussila, Professor Simon Karlinsky, Dr. George Katkov, Denis Kensit, Kathleen Kensit, Michael Kettle, Mary Louise King, Hilja Kukk, Dr. J. L. C. Laahz, Carol A. Leadenham, Donna De Luca, Eugene Lyons, N. N. Martianoff, Mr. and Mrs. John McGinley, Professor V. D. Medlin, Judge Aarne Nuutilainen, Morris S. Ochert, Paul V. Olferiev, Professor Temira Pachmuss, Matti Pasanen, Robert Payne, Kerstin Petersson, Morgan Philips-Price, Tatiana Pollock, Joan Priest, Angela Retchford, Pirkko Ritvala, Reino Ritvala, C. Easton Rothwell, Professor Leonard Schapiro, Dr. Harold Shukman, Collette De Silvers, Professor Nathan

Smith, Dr. Boris Sokoloff, Mrs. John Somers, Oliver Soskice, Victor Sos-kice, Lord and Lady Stow Hill (Frank Søskice and Susan Soskice), Professor Ilmar Talve, Heather Tritton, J. Cyril Tritton, Professor Sergei Utekhin, Ewing S. Walker, Ludmila Weidlé, Ella Wolfe, and N. B. Yarrow.

I am indebted to the following institutions:

In England: Battersea District Library, Battersea Labour Party, BBC Sound Archives, Bodleian Library, British Library, British Library of Po-litical and Economic Science, Cambridge University Library, *The Evening Standard*, the Library and Records Department of the Foreign & Common-wealth Office, Gloucester Ukrainian Club, House of Lords Record Office, Keble College Library, New College (the Milner Papers), Public Record Office, St. Antony's College, School of Slavonic & East European Studies, University of East Anglia, Messrs. A. P. Watt (The Maugham Estate).

In the United States: Bailey/Howe Library, University of Vermont; Co-lumbia University Libraries; the Hoover Institution on War, Revolution and Peace, Stanford, California; the Harry Ransom Humanities Research Center, University of Texas in Austin; the *New Canaan Advertiser*; New Canaan Historical Society; New York Public Library; Norwalk Land Rec-ords; Radio Free Europe/Radio Liberty.

In France: Archives Nationales, Bibliothèque de Documentation Inter-nationale Contemporaine, Bibliothèque Nationale, École Nationale des Langues Orientales Vivantes, Institut d'Histoire Sociale, Archive du Min-istère des Relations Étrangères.

In Finland: Åbo Akademis Bibliotek, Brage Urklipssamverket, Helsingin Kirurgien Sairaala, Helsingin Yliopiston Kirjasto, *Hufvudstadsbladet*, Sotain-valiidienveljenliitto, *Suomen Kuvalehdet*, Työväen Arkisto, Valtion Arkisto.

In Australia: *The Courier-Mail*, Brisbane, Somerville House Old Girls Association.

In Austria: Haus-, Hof-, und Staatsarchiv.

In Sweden: Kungliga Biblioteket, Riksarkivet.

I am grateful to the following for permission to reproduce illustrations: Åbo Akademis Bibliotek; Peter Benenson; *The Courier-Mail*, Brisbane; Brit-ish Library Newspaper Collection, Colindale; Century Hutchinson Limited; Mrs. Gladys Edds; Asher Gransby; The Harry Ransom Humanities Re-search Center, University of Texas in Austin; The Kerensky Family; *The New York Times*; The Slavonic Division, The New York Public Library; *Suomen Kuvalehdet*; UPI/Bettmann Newsphotos; Valtion Arkisto, Helsinki (The National Archives of Finland).

I have profited over many years from discussions with Marion

Berghahn, Volker Berghahn, John Biggart, James Jacob, Margaret C. Jacob, Lionel Kochan, Miriam Kochan, Werner Mosse, Peter Reddaway and my colleagues at Battersea County. I owe a lot to the assertive humanity of Battersea young people, especially Tom Hill, Lizzie Clegg, Mark Pearce, Ore Okosi and Sonia Roach. Had asthma not brought his life to an untimely close, Barry Hollingsworth would have saved me many an error. The stimulation provided by P. J. Abraham, and the critical forbearance of Wendy Abraham can never be repaid.

Richard Abraham
Battersea, June 1985.

Note on Dates

The text employs prevailing Russian usage. In the nineteenth century, the Russian calendar was twelve days behind our own, in the twentieth century, thirteen. On February 1 (14), 1918, the Soviet Government adopted the Western calendar—Dates in the notes are as they appear in the sources.

Spring Rain
Whose is this heart ? Why all the blood drained
   from cheeks, flooding him to fame ?
It beats away: the hands of the minister
   have bound mouths and hearts in a love-knot.

This is no night, no rain, no choral recital,
   exploding: "Kerensky, hurrah !"
It is the blinding march into the forum
   from the locked catacombs of yesterday.

These aren't roses, nor lips, nor the murmur
   of crowds, this by the theatre is the breaking
Surf of the night of Europe's trembing,
   proud of ourselves on our own asphalt streets.
                              —Boris Pasternak.

Bent over the map, unsleeping,
   There stoops a man.
A Bonaparte breath goes sweeping
   Across my land.

For someone the thunder rages:
   —Come, bridegroom, come !
Hot hurricane, young dictator,
   He tears along.
            —Marina Tsvetaeva,
            trans. Robert Kemball.★

★Reprinted with permission of Ardis Publishers from *The Demesne of the Swans/ Lebedinnyi stan*, Ann Arbor: Ardis, 1980.

I

Inspector Kerensky's Career

About 300 miles southeast of Moscow in the region of Penza lies the small town of Vadinsk.[1] The name is a hybrid, a Russified form of the old Mordva name of the river Vad, which passes through it. When Ivan the Terrible conquered the Islamic Khan of Kazan in 1552, he acquired his pagan Mordva subjects. The sword and the miracle were employed to persuade the Mordva to love Orthodoxy and pay taxes. Their place names were replaced by good Russian Orthodox ones, so the Vad became the Kérenka, and the settlement on it, Kérensk. Tsar Peter dragooned the lethargic Mordva and Russian nobility into European methods of fighting and accounting. Catherine the Great demanded higher standards of thought and manners. Napoleon's armies rekindled Russian patriotism on their way to the burning Kremlin, but his liberation of the serfs of East and Central Europe doomed Russia's antiquated social system. Tsar Alexander liberated Europe but vacillated at home. His Quixotic successor, Nicholas I, attempted in vain to resurrect the methods of Peter the Great without compromising Russia's greatness. Peasant resentments and a ferment of European ideas were followed by the national disaster of the Crimean War.

During the stifling reign of Nicholas I, an insignificant village priest called Father Mikhail served his parishioners in Kerensky District, Penza Province. A parish priest was a member of an hereditary closed caste, the son of a village priest himself. His education, marriage, benefice—even his surname should he need one—were at the whim of his bishop. He could not even aspire to become a bishop himself, as the hierarchy was recruited exclusively from the "White" monastic clergy, celibate offspring of influential families.[2] His hopes for the future were thus focused, on the world to come, and on his children, two of whom were boys.

Fyodor Mikhailovich was born in 1842. He had a brother, probably born later and perhaps called Alexander. At nine years old, they went to the parish school at which their father taught them Church history, Russian grammar, arithmetic, chanting the psalms, reading, and writing. At eleven, they went to a district school, probably in Kerensk itself, now a town of some 5000 inhabitants. There they learnt Greek, Latin, Russian, and Old Church Slavonic, the language of the Orthodox Bible and Missal. Both Father Mikhail's sons did well enough to proceed to Theological Seminary, probably soon after the death of Nicholas I. This was a landmark in the life of the country youths, and probably the moment at which the Bishop of Penza gave the young seminarians the family name Kerensky, after their place of origin. The name, with its unusual stress on the first syllable, is both memorable and immune to satire.[3]

Penza seminary was a much more intense place than the district school. The prior and inspector, who took themselves seriously—perhaps too seriously—in responding to the challenge of a new age, tried to cram all they knew into the minds of their charges. They left their young charges little time for distractions. In addition to the endless round of devotions and such familiar subjects, as Old Church Slavonic and Greek, they taught such new subjects as French and agricultural science, and introduced rationalist ideas of technical innovation.

Fyodor Mikhailovich Kerensky was not the only seminarian to find the atmosphere of the seminary irksome. On June 28, 1860, two large stones shattered the inspector's windows. In the ensuing investigation, two subversive poems were discovered which described the grievances of the students with mournful eloquence:

> All his instructors are concerned with is science ancient and barren.
> With this dead knowledge, he is cut off from people
> And in society, he is a despised orphan. . . .
> Who will lighten his life with her love;
> All the maidens regard him with contempt.
> Only the servant girls sometimes look but
> There can be no life with their love.

The unknown poet remembers cameraderie in "jolly drinking," but anticipates the impending sacrifice of friendship in a desperate struggle for benefices:

> Ah! Shall we split up into our former enmity
> With bitter tears and malicious sadness?!

In the "thaw" of the early 1860s, the inspector lost this encounter. One of the witnesses was a student called Vasily Klyuchevsky, the most distinguished pupil in the seminary. In the wake of this affair, the young Klyuchevsky begged to be released from his obligations. He went on to became Russia's greatest liberal historian.[4] A year below Klyuchevsky, Fyodor Kerensky remained on friendly terms with him, a relationship consolidated by the marriage of Klyuchevsky's cousin to Kerensky's sister. Soon, he followed Klyuchevsky's example, and become a member of the Russian intelligentsia at the very moment it was becoming a vital subclass of Russian society.[5]

The new Tsar, Alexander II, was advised that a modern army could not be created until serfdom was abolished, and after several years of trying to browbeat a reluctant nobility into acquiescence, he signed the Liberation Statute on February 19, 1861. The Statute was at once too liberal for the nobility and a bitter disappointment for the peasants. All over Russia, there were angry scenes as the peasants expressed the feeling that they had been cheated yet again by the landholders (*pomeshchiki*) who had exchanged their seigneurial rights for the outright ownership of the best land and annuities from the peasants. The economic benefits of the Liberation disappointed the peasants, but they gained a good deal more personal freedom.

The liberation of the serfs implied radical changes in nearly every other department of Russian life, and in the 1860s Russia emerged hesitantly into the European nineteenth century. A new, leaner and more professional army took shape, and the construction of railroads and factories was actively fostered. Political prisoners were released and censorship relaxed. Dissenters were now to be tried in courts modeled after those of France and Belgium, defended by lawyers belonging to independent corporations and judged by a jury. A partly elective system of local government was created to improve communications, agriculture, and the health and education of the people. Railroad men, village teachers, and rural medical assistants formed the rank-and-file of an intelligentsia whose genius was creating a culture to astonish the world. Only one fatal omission marred this hopeful picture. To the intense disappointment of liberal gentry and intelligentsia, the Tsar would permit no attenuation of his autocratic rule. There would be no elected parliament.[6]

The most hopeful reform for Fyodor Kerensky was the one that freed the universities from direct ministerial control and democratized their admissions policies. His son tells us that "because of his poverty, he was forced to work for a time as an ordinary district teacher." He probably disliked this humble work, for his son calls it "drudgery." Fortunately, the fees of the nearest university, in Kazan, were very modest, and Fyodor's determination was such that he was able to save enough to realize his ambition within a year or so.[7]

Fyodor Kerensky was busy during his student years, supplementing his savings by tutoring candidates for the Classical Gymnasium, and it was there he went on graduation, first as a class teacher but quickly earning promotion as inspector responsible for discipline. Simultaneously, he taught in the Empress Marie Ladies Gymnasium, where he was remembered with affection:

> Stern and upright and strong,
> Our Russian teacher;
> He's festive and scented
> Like the King of France.[8]

One of his pupils at the Ladies Gymnasium was Nadezhda Adler, daughter of General Alexander Adler, Chief of the Topographical Section of the Kazan Military District. She was attractive, lively, and well-educated, and she married him shortly after she left school.

Russia was still desperately short of well-qualified people and a man with a good education had good prospects. An inspector in a Gymnasium was an established member of the civil service of the Russian Empire with the bureaucratic rank of Collegiate Assessor. Fyodor Kerensky's talents were also recognized by the publication, in 1874, of an article on ancient Russian sects in the journal of the Ministry of Education. His future now looked brilliant, and in 1879 he became Director of the Classical Gymnasium in the down-to-earth northern town of Vyatka. It was here that they started their family. The first three children were all girls. Elena ("Lyolya") came first, to be followed by Anna ("Nyeta") and Nadezhda ("Nadya").

After only a year in Vyatka, Fyodor Mikhailovich was given a plum appointment as Director of the Simbirsk Classical Gymnasium. His happiness increased the following spring, when Nadezhda presented him with a son. Alexander Fyodorovich Kerensky was born on April 22, 1881 and nicknamed "Sasha." A couple of years later, a second son, Fyodor ("Fedya") followed. The family was now complete.[9]

Simbirsk was that rarity, a natural fortress on the windswept Eurasian plain. Situated on a narrow ridge which separates the Volga from its errant tributary, the Sviyaga, the Tatars called it "Hill of the Winds." It defied Russia's two great peasant rebellions led by Stenka Razin and Emelyan Pugachov. Secure from attack, and with a view of the Volga that appealed to romantic sensibilities, Simbirsk became an aristocratic haven. "All these families met often and all the rest of society was attracted to them whether it was the highest provincial administration or the educational authorities." This aristocratic preeminence was clearly visible. On "The Crown," the public buildings were surrounded by the villas of the aristocrats—solid, even rambling country houses set in ample gardens planted with orchards. The merchants had their mansions on the western side facing the Sviyaga, while the hovels of the lower classes clung to the sometimes flooded slopes below. Fyodor Kerensky lived near the Crown while his brother, Father Alexander Kerensky, lived halfway down the hill, a graphic reminder of the distance he had ascended.[10]

Older, but only slightly senior in rank to Fyodor Kerensky, was Ilya Nikolaevich Ulyanov, another educational administrator, and perhaps an acquaintance, from Penza. They must have found it a relief to turn from the small talk of the aristocrats to share their hopes for the enlightenment of Russia and to discuss the impressive progress of their children. Fyodor Kerensky must have been delighted to tell Ulyanov of the successes of his sons, Alexander and Vladimir, the latter only eleven years older than Kerensky's own son, Sasha.[11]

Fyodor Kerensky soon inspired Simbirsk Gymnasium with his own enthusiasm. The last Tsarist Minister of Agriculture was one of his pupils, and he recalled that "thanks to his exceptional energy, he quickly began to improve and ginger up everything. He was an active, sympathetic Director, penetrating everything and personally supervising everything." He won the devotion of his pupils by teaching Latin and Russian literature by his own unapproved methods, encouraging boys to translate aloud from Latin without wasting hours on the dull, repetitive exercises laid down by the Ministry. He strongly discouraged the boys from loquacity, or, as he put it, *"non multa, sed multum."*[12]

Substantially older than his wife, Fyodor Kerensky embodied discipline and reason for his children, while his wife offered them warmth, imagination, and tolerance. He was a patriarch, but a liberal one. Like many of his background and generation, he associated corporal punishment with the demeaning treatment of serfs and he did not employ it on his children. His rational ethics were supplemented by the undogmatic Christianity of their mother's biblical stories and the fabulous tales of the *nyanya*, Ekaterina Suchkova, a living witness to Christian charity.[13]

The "Great Reforms" of the 1860s had jolted Russian society without settling anything. They unleashed massive and rapid social and economic changes without providing the people with adequate means to respond to them. They did not overcome the alienation of the educated who resented their continued exclusion from government. They totally failed to forestall the emergence of a virtual caste of Populist revolutionaries, consecrated to the eradication of Autocracy at all costs. They looked back to the "Decembrist" aristocrats who had plotted a botched coup in 1825. The Decembrists had included admirers of George Washington and of Maximilien Robespierre, a tension that recurred in successive generations of Russian revolutionaries, though such repulsive terrorists as Nechaev were vastly outnumbered by the thousands of young idealists of both sexes who flocked to serve "The People." Russia's first revolutionary party, *Zemlia i Volia* [Land and Freedom] appeared in the 1870s, committed to agitation and assassination, only to split in 1879, when the future Marxist, G. V. Plekhanov decided to concentrate on agitation. The majority resolved to assassinate the Tsar-Liberator himself, and on March 1, 1881 their efforts were finally successful.[14]

Toward the end of his reign, Alexander II had begun to contemplate a new series of reforms, including the addition of a small elective element to proposed consultative assemblies, but after his death even these modest measures were blocked by his son, Alexander III, whose mentor, K. P. Pobedonostsev, did not conceal his view that the Great Reforms had been a "criminal error." Under his baneful aegis, Education Minister I. D. Delyanov did his best to undo the work of men such as Ulyanov and Kerensky. Ulyanov's work in creating a network of elementary schools was jeopardized when, in 1881, they were handed over to the Holy Synod and their syllabuses emasculated.[15] Some consolation for Ulyanov's professional frustrations came two years later when his elder son, Alexander, won the gold medal as best student of the graduating class at Simbirsk Gymnasium. Armed with a glowing testimonial from Fyodor Kerensky, Alexander Ulyanov enrolled in the science faculty of St. Petersburg University. The following year his father was offered early retirement, but died soon after, in 1886.

Disillusioned by the failure of his father's "small deeds," Alexander Ulyanov joined the revolutionary Populists. On February 19, 1886, he unsuccessfully tried to organize a service of commemoration for the Liberation Statute. The *Narodnaia Volia* [People's Freedom] group, to which he belonged, resolved to take the life of the new Tsar on the sixth anniversary of the death of Alexander II. At the last moment they were betrayed. Alexander Ulyanov insisted on accepting full responsibility for the plot and refused to recant. Despite the desperate lobbying of his mother, he was executed on May 8, 1887.

Simbirsk was stunned and the Ulyanovs were ostracized by aristocrats and bourgeois alike. Alexander's younger brother, Vladimir, concentrating on his final examinations, came in on top, as usual. Despite the social pressure, Fyodor Kerensky recommended that Vladimir Ulyanov receive the gold medal, as had his brother, and wrote him a testimonial calculated to assuage any reluctance the University of Kazan authorities might feel at admitting the brother of a regicide. "Neither in the Gymnasium," wrote Kerensky, "nor outside was a single occasion remarked on which Ulyanov, by word or deed, provoked an unflattering opinion of himself among the authorities or the teachers. . . . Religion and discipline were the basis of his upbringing, the fruits of which are apparent in Ulyanov's behaviour." The Director noted the aloofness of the man who would be known as Lenin, but pointed out that his mother intended to take the family to Kazan to keep an eye on him. Even after 1917, Lenin was to remember his headmaster with affectionate respect.[16]

Friends of Alexander Kerensky would one day claim that "the first childish memories of A. F. Kerensky, were, in his own words, vague memories of the silent horror which seized Simbirsk when they heard there of the execution of the son of the local director of elementary schools, the student, Alexander Ilyich Ulyanov." Kerensky himself described his sense of awe at "the carriage with drawn blinds which mysteriously drove through the town at night and took people away into the unknown," and he remembered their *nyanya* threatening them with "The Carriage" if they misbehaved. "Of this contact," he concluded, "accidental and innocent as it was, something remained in my soul for ever."[17]

Critics pointed out that Ulyanov was arrested in St. Petersburg so Sasha Kerensky could not have seen the carriage (if any) used to arrest Ulyanov.[18] But if Alexander Kerensky had wanted to fabricate a story he could easily have checked details of this kind. Childhood memories are notoriously fallible, but we can be sure that the news of Alexander Ulyanov's attempted regicide shook Simbirsk, creating the kind of gossip among the *nyanya*s in which a mysterious carriage made an appearance. Kerensky's critics are clutching at straws; they would have done better to point out that Alexander Kerensky's attempt to appeal to the sentimentality of Lenin's supporters was pathetically misplaced.

The year of the Ulyanov tragedy was indeed critical for the six-year-old Sasha Kerensky, for he was stricken with tuberculosis of the hip. For six months he was segregated from the other children, an experience that may have contributed to his gregariousness, as well as making him slightly introspective. His mother and *nyanya* did their best, of course. His mother read him stories by Dickens, Harriet Beecher Stowe, and Tolstoy, which deeply affected his view of the poor and oppressed.

He recovered in time to appreciate the beauties of a city famous for its spring thaw. It was on one of these spring days that Sasha Kerensky found himself looking out over the huge surface of the Volga river:

Spellbound by the scene, I experienced a sense of elation that grew almost to the point of spiritual transfiguration. Then, suddenly overcome by an unaccountable feeling of terror, I ran away.

The adult Kerensky felt that this brief moment was decisive for his life, confirming a mysticism that never quite left him.

The Kerenskys were soon to leave Simbirsk, for in 1889 Fyodor Kerensky was appointed Chief Inspector of Schools for Turkestan

Territory, simultaneously becoming an "Official State Counsellor," a rank that carried him into the hereditary nobility. No one had thought of penalizing him for his magnanimity toward Vladimir Ulyanov, who had by now been expelled from Kazan University. The Russia of the later Tsars was authoritarian, but it lacked the vindictive efficiency of later totalitarian regimes.

His father's elevation removed Sasha Kerensky from Russia proper to her newest colonial possessions. He carried with him poignant images of the Russia of his infancy:

the beauty of the Volga, the chimes of evening bells, the bishop sitting solemnly in a carriage drawn by four horses, the convicts with heavy chains, the pretty little girls with whom I went to dancing lessons, the ragged, barefoot village boys with whom I played in the summer, my parents, the nursery and nyanya, the Russian epic heroes and Peter the Great.

There is no hint of social criticism in this archaic vision which stuck in his mind as the real Russia underwent rapid industrialization and many peasant families went down in ruin. He saw no peasants flogged and he grew up without the sense of personal guilt that stung so many upper-class young Russians into radical activity. Nor did he come to envy the successful vulgarity of the new bourgeois, as did revolutionary and reactionary critics of the economic policies of Alexander III's ministers. He did not see this as a gap in his education. "How glad I am," he wrote, "that my age prevented me from seeing the seamy side of Russian life in the eighties."[9]

The journey was a pageant of Imperial Russian exoticism which terminated in Tashkent, their new home. It was now a city of 150,000, only a quarter of them Russians. The ancient city was a maze of narrow alleys winding past the blank, yellow-earth walls of houses and mosques, whose minarets proclaimed the Islamic faith of its residents. Its heart was the bazaar, a raucous ramshackle place whose din could be heard for a mile. The Russian town, founded only after the conquest of 1865, was an assertion of European geometry, its broad highways lined by poplars and tropical trees and small irrigation canals, a conspicuous luxury in this thirsty land. They were a mixed blessing, increasing the summer humidity and breeding mosquitoes and crickets that preyed on skin and ears. Whenever they could, the Russians escaped the town for dachas in a cool ravine in the foothills of the nearby Pamirs. In winter, the frosts made Tash-

kent as cold as Siberia and the Russians stayed snugly in their un-
pretentious mansions playing cards, giving tea parties and dances,
sometimes visiting the theater for a break in the routine.[20]

The Russians had conquered Central Asia to pre-empt a British
advance through Afghanistan. At first they had tried to divide and
rule, ingratiating themselves with the Emir of Bokhara in his perennial feud with the Khan of Kokand. They had made vague promises
to the peasantry that they would limit the extortions of tax collectors
and irrigation officials, and they did abolish slavery; they also reduced
taxation, and justice became speedier and less corrupt. More radical
changes were wrought indirectly, as a result of the quickening of
economic activity, particularly after the introduction of new strains
of cotton from North America.

Not everyone benefited equally from the Russian presence, and
between 1885 and 1892 there were three small rebellions.[21] As the
Russian population increased, the temptation to transform the local
cultures grew. It corresponded with the Russifying policies favored
by Alexander III elsewhere in the Empire. Fyodor Kerensky found
himself in the middle of this controversy, usually in opposition
to Nikolai Ostroumov, Director of the Tashkent Classical Gymnasium, who had been acting head of the local educational administration before his arrival and who was piqued that Kerensky had
been appointed over his head. Of course both men wanted to assim-
ilate the natives to Russian culture, but they differed over the means.
Ostroumov could see little virtue in progressive language-teaching
methods, while Kerensky found Ostroumov too ready to ride roughshod over local sensibilities.

These differences were sharpened in 1898, when a local mullah
declared a *jihad* against the Russians. It was soon suppressed and six
of its leaders hanged, but the Governor-General, Baron Vrevsky,
was accused of laxity and removed. Ostroumov now argued for
Russian control of the Muslim schools attached to the Islamic med-
resas, while Kerensky's attempts at a more flexible and tolerant approach ran into greater official disapproval. The development of
Russian schooling for the natives was hampered by Russian poverty
and local pride. The first native primary school opened in 1884, but
there were only twenty-five of them by the turn of the century.
Between 1886 and 1891, the number of Muslim pupils in Russian
gymnasia declined from thirteen to nine.[22]

Turkestan still retained the atmosphere of a frontier society, a refuge for upper-class scapegraces and a starting point for adventure. In 1888, the young Grand Duke Nikolai Konstantinovich was exiled to Tashkent after stealing his mother's jewels to maintain his American mistress. During Sasha Kerensky's school days the first lady in Tashkent was the English governess of Baron Vrevsky's daughter. Just before the end of his schooldays, they were visited by Captain Lavr Kornilov, fresh from a dangerous *recce* into Persia protected by his Asiatic appearance and a gift for Asian tongues. Another visitor to Tashkent was Carl Mannerheim, a Finnish officer in Russian service and an explorer of Chinese Central Asia.[23]

Now at the zenith of his career, Fyodor Kerensky had "a commanding figure, robust and broad, . . . slightly rolling and slow in his gait, like a sailor; clean-shaven, military-style with a spare moustache." Nadezhda Kerensky was "an admirable, fine and delicate woman." For a few years, *nyanya* Suchkova was succeeded by a French governess, but as the children grew up she left their service as well. Elena was now a serious and rather plain young woman. Anna and Nadya were opposites: Anna was tall, fair, and gentle; Nadya was dark, plump, and lively. Fedya resembled his father in face and build and showed little of his elder brother's vitality. The family was successful and popular.

Alexander Kerensky may have sensed the tension between his father and his headmaster. At all events, he was an exemplary pupil: "We were not stifled by the indifferent formalism of schools in European Russia, and we rather liked our teachers and our classes." He was successful at most subjects but he excelled in everything dramatic. His recitations of patriotic poems revealed a voice of remarkable timbre, and he took the lead in several school productions, playing Khlestakov in Gogol's *Inspector-General*. His German teacher felt that "the figure of this lovable lady killer and unwitting conman might have been created for him." Sasha Kerensky dreamed of going on the stage to play Tsar Fyodor Ioannovich, the pious and emotional son of Ivan the Terrible in A. K. Tolstoy's trilogy. His rapid, light movements made a natural dancer of him and on one occasion, Herr Dukmeyer lent him the key to one of the school halls during a function, only to find the young Kerensky and friends with their girlfriends from the Ladies Gymnasium at an impromptu dance.[24]

The young Kerensky observed the tangible monuments to Russian enterprise with patriotic pride. "I have seen the effects of Russian rule in Turkestan," he wrote later, "and they seem to me to reflect nothing but credit on Russia."[25] It was not unusual for a European socialist to see imperialism in a positive light, but few Russian socialists identified personally with Russian imperialism the way he did. Never happy using foreign languages, he could see no earthly point in learning Persian or Turkish.

Fyodor Kerensky's loyalty was unshakable but not uncritical. On one occasion, Sasha Kerensky overheard his father reading Leo Tolstoy's protest against the Franco-Russian Entente to a circle of friends. This was a plea for a reduction of international tensions and greater efforts to improve the quality of Russian life by nonpolitical means. Count Witte, the architect of Russian industrialization, visited Fyodor Kerensky in Tashkent. After the interview, Fyodor Kerensky told his son that Witte was the only "real live man" in St. Petersburg and implied that only Witte really "wished Russia well."[26]

By the time Alexander Kerensky left school, his family had become acquainted with Tsarist Russia's first Prime Minister and last ministers of Agriculture and the Interior, with one of Russia's greatest historians, with the Populist regicide Alexander Ulyanov, and his brother, the future Lenin. They had met the man who would try to abort Lenin's revolutionary experiment and possibly his more successful Finnish counterpart. There was an element of chance in all this, but the coincidences become less remarkable if we consider Russia's social pyramid as measured by the 1897 census. The Tsar's subjects then numbered 125,600,000 (excluding the Finns), of whom less than half were Great Russians. Families with access to secondary or higher education numbered between 5 and 6 million. A million and a quarter were technically "noble," while a mere 2000 held ranks equal or superior to Fyodor Kerensky's. The Russian ruling class was a tiny minority, a European veneer on a largely illiterate Eurasian society on the verge of a dramatic awakening from the sleep of centuries.[27]

The eldest Kerensky, Elena, was the first to leave home. Plain, though not unattractive, there was no reason why she should not have made a good marriage and settled down to childbearing and good works. She wanted none of it. The campaign by Russian women to achieve the right to medical training is an inspiring story.

Assisted by a few men, who risked their careers to help them, they often had to qualify abroad before returning home. A few individuals were driven into secret revolutionary organizations which welcomed them as equals. Finally, in 1887, a legal Medical School for Women was opened in St. Petersburg, and it was there that Elena Kerensky began her training.[28]

Alexander Fyodorovich Kerensky was due to graduate from the Gymnasium in the summer of 1899 and his parents decided to send him to St. Petersburg University and his sister, Anna, to the Conservatoire. Sasha Kerensky was now recognizable as the Kerensky of history. His oval face, with its regular, rather amorphous features, was topped by a crew cut, which reinforced the impression of boyish eagerness suggested by his rapid movements. Some would find this unattractive, but his gaiety and enthusiasm were infectious. His voice was a rich baritone, capable of infinite modulation. He was short-sighted, but vain enough to prefer to hold a paper a few inches from his eyes rather than don spectacles. He had bad teeth, soon replaced by false teeth, and this may have added to his self-consciousness when speaking in public. He was neat, tidy, and unusually fastidious for a Russian student. If his personality left a small question mark it was perhaps because he seemed at times to be playing a role: to conceal his inner self from public scrutiny, the symptom of a detachment that protected him from the total absorption of his father's ideas. In a country at peace with itself, the future of such a charming, respectable, and well-educated young man would have been assured.[29]

2

A Hesitant Hero

This first visit to St. Petersburg was a pilgrimage for the young Kerenskys, their first chance to share the obsessive dream to which Tsar Peter had condemned so many serfs to waste their lives amidst the mosquito-infested, wind-swept marshes of the Neva. They had known of it as the city of foggy winter days and "white" summer nights, haunted by the heroes of Pushkin and Dostoyevsky, the city of uniforms and military parades, of gruff cabbies and wraithlike match girls. It was already the confection of vast palaces, endless broad boulevards, and delicate spires we know today. It had just begun its brief moment of glory as the world's leading center for music, painting, and the theatrical arts. The barometer of a society in ferment, the city was coming to respect the determination of an industrial working class impatient of exploitation. As yet, only the radical students were openly demanding a mitigation of autocracy; for their temerity, many were immediately conscripted into the army.

Cowed briefly by government threats, the student body was quiet during Alexander Kerensky's first year at university. He had intended to live in a boarding house, but when he discovered that the halls of residence were not too closely supervised, he decided to live in. "Dormitory residents enjoyed complete freedom" of discussion, he remembered, but this was quite adequate for the growth of an *esprit de corps* with distinctly oppositional overtones. Kerensky was soon elected to the committee of students from Central Asia.[1]

Fyodor Kerensky had introduced his son to his own friends, senior bureaucrats, and he soon found himself dancing with the daughters of a future police chief of the Empire. He quickly found this embarrassed him in radical student circles but he was adaptable enough to modify his manners and accept a lower standard of living to win their trust. There were compensations in the electrical atmosphere of the radical intellectual movements that, by the end of his first year, had transformed him into another "young madman."[2]

In the autumn semester of 1900, a new ordinance was introduced that prohibited study in more than one faculty, a device designed to discourage the eternal students who tended to become agitators. This forced Kerensky to choose a straight law course, though he continued to attend history lectures whenever he could. He was also upset by events at Kiev University, where students demonstrated against the expulsion of two of their fellows, arguing that they should be permitted to remove bad eggs themselves. This time the government conscripted 183 students into the army, one of them an old boy of Kerensky's Gymnasium. Unable to face the ruin of his career, the young man committed suicide.[3]

A third radicalizing influence was Kerensky's friendship with Sergei Vasiliev, a young engineering student, and his seventeen-year-old cousin, Olga Baranovskaya. When their grandfather, Academician Vasiliev, died in 1900, Sergei invited Kerensky to join the guard of honor at his funeral. When Sasha Kerensky arrived for the ceremony, his upper-class manner and stylish clothes offended the ascetically raised "Olya." He retaliated by refusing to take the principles of the pretty teenager seriously.

Olya's family had a curious history, with some bearing on Kerensky's career. Her father was a successful soldier, who had spent a few enjoyable years in the glamorous Cuirassier Life Guard Regiment before assuming more significant but less expensive postings that made him a Major General by 1914. His marriage to the daughter of Academician V. P. Vasiliev, author of Russia's first Chinese and Manchu dictionaries, was not successful. Lev Baranovsky's elder brother, Vsevolod, was already married to Maria Vasilieva's elder sister, which put them within the prohibited degrees of consanguinity. The state-controlled Orthodox Church licensed their marriage and soon there were three children, Vladimir, Olga, and Elena. Like Henry VIII, Lev Baranovsky found his conscience troubled him, so he divorced Olga's mother and quickly remarried. He took Vladimir with him but left the girls with their embittered mother, who returned to her father's official apartment. The girls were brought up in Spartan splendor, their only dress was student uniform. Chastened by his daughter's experience, the old man allowed the girls no suitors and warned them to consider a man's mind before his pocket when contemplating marriage.[4]

For nearly two years, the students of St. Petersburg had been quiet; their sullen hostility toward strikebreaking professors who supported the regime degenerated into innocuous student ragging. So confident was Bogolepov, the new Minister of Education, that he began to visit the halls of residence. He paid for this error, when on February 14, 1901, he was fatally wounded by a young terrorist belonging to the Party of Socialist Revolutionaries. Kerensky and his comrades regarded the young man as a saint, ready to lay down not just his life, but his soul as well, in the service of his fellows.[5]

Shamed out of their passivity, the students decided to demonstrate on the anniversary of the Liberation Statute. The affair passed without incident, as the police contented themselves with taking the names of over 200 demonstrators. It soon emerged that two-thirds of them were "*kursistki*," students of the unofficial women's university, the Higher Women's Courses. Russian radicals had welcomed women as equals in their struggles, but this was more than honor could bear and an unofficial student committee now appealed for a second demonstration before the Kazan Cathedral on March 4. While anxious parents urged discretion, both sides prepared for a battle. Sasha Kerensky supported Maria Baranovskaya's attempts to dissuade Olya from taking part. The young woman, insisting on attending, agreed only to be chaperoned by a male student.

When the day came, the police permitted the crowd to gather outside the Cathedral, bitter speeches were made attacking governmental repression, and stirring songs were sung in praise of Maria Vetrova (a student who had burned herself to death) and other martyrs of the liberation movement. Suddenly, a unit of mounted gendarmes rode into the crowd beating the students with their long batons. The students were thrashed and Society shocked. This did not make the parents pleased with their imprudent children. Maria Baranovskaya now decided that she had wasted enough of her limited savings on her errant daughter, so she withdrew Olya from the Higher Women's Courses and sent her to relatives in the country.

When she returned, she had to take a typing job with the Nikolaevsky Railroad Company.[6]

Kerensky had missed the demonstration for the funeral of a friend, an impeccable excuse, but this must have involved a lot of tedious explanation. The pressure on him was mounting and just before the end of the Easter semester of 1901, he cracked. Apropos of nothing, he burst into speech to a group of students who had gathered on a university staircase. His clean record was blotted at last. The Rector informed him that he owed the leniency of his punishment—a few day's rustication—to his father's eminence. Kerensky's summary of the results of this storm in a teacup is refreshingly candid:

To the youth of Tashkent I was a hero, and I basked in their admiration. Unfortunately, however, my homecoming was marred by my first serious clash with my father, who was greatly upset by the whole affair.

Fyodor Kerensky was desperately afraid his son would go the way of the unfortunate Ulyanov boys. His disapproval produced the desired effect and by the end of the summer, he had extracted a promise from his son to refrain from political activity until after graduation. At least he would then have a career to fall back on.[7]

By the time Alexander Kerensky arrived at St. Petersburg University, the Russian intelligentsia had begun to recover from the uncritical infatuation with Marxism of the previous decade. Russian Marxism was epitomized by the Monism of Plekhanov, "characterized by slavish submission to authority, together with a belief that in that submission the values of scientific thought can be preserved." Plekhanov and Struve proved that the intelligentsia could at last win its hereditary struggle with autocracy, by riding on the back of its new ally, the proletariat. As Struve put it, "on its strong shoulders the Russian working class must carry out the task of conquering political freedom."[8]

The ink was hardly dry on this statement before Struve, and many other Russian Marxists, began to see its drawbacks. Could the immature Russian working class really be relied on to preserve that modicum of European sophistication and humane culture so dear to the intelligentsia? And how could the historically necessary bourgeois phase of Russian development be achieved if Marxist class-hatreds inflamed the workers against their capitalist allies as well as their feudal opponents? In the ironic words of a civilized Menshevik:

What was necessary was an outlet to those "eternal" ethical "values," to those supreme courts of appeal, before the face of which the class contradictions of the liberation movement could disappear and the bases of a renewed liberalism could be set down.[9]

Where his future party comrade, Victor Chernov, had to battle with the Marxists at Moscow University, Kerensky was able to escape without the intellectual discipline which comes to thinkers who develop in opposition to current intellectual trends and he gave little serious consideration to the "mechanistic tendencies" which repelled him. "I sought out and found professors who confirmed for me *my own* instinctive feelings about the world." In the end, these were neither the historians of Russian pluralism, nor the academic lawyers, but the philosophers Nicholas Lossky and Leo Petrazhitsky, who offered Kerensky "a systematic framework for my intuitive views."[10]

Lossky was only 28 when he began to lecture on intuitivism, or mystical empiricism, in 1900. He was a Christian Platonist for whom God and His Kingdom were "the primary reality, where total organic wholeness exists, where all substances are welded by love, which is the basis of all positive values." Lossky's philosophy encouraged Kerensky to persist in his belief in God and in the view that most arguments were based on misunderstandings and "that the quarrelling parties, being one-sided, were partly right and partly wrong."[11] This was a striking contrast to the chilling rigor of Lenin's demand for partisanship in all aspects of thought.

Petrazhitsky took up the Chair in Legal Philosophy in 1898, earning the hero-worship of the students and the snide hostility of his peers by comparing his work to that of Copernicus, or even Galileo. This was perhaps a shot at Plekhanov, who had compared Marx to Copernicus. Petrazhitsky saw Law as a psychic entity, "in the unique form of ascribing to different beings . . . 'duties' and 'rights';. . . ." Law was therefore an extension of ethics, but where ethics merely bind individuals before their own consciences, law obliges them to desist from certain actions in the expectation that others will be similarly bound. This view corresponds closely to the Kantian Categorical Imperative: Act as if the maxim of your action were to become through your will a general natural law. The task of legislators is therefore one of discovery. Progressive Law could not be found by a priorist reasoning but by a psychology, whose methods must be introspection and analogy. With the creation of such a psychology, the politics of Law could begin. "The science of legal policy would consist in leading humanity in the direction that it had so far moved in unconsciously. . . . the ideal is the achievement of a completely social character, the total dominion of active love in mankind."[12]

Both these philosophers would join the future liberal Constitutional Democratic Party while Kerensky would become a Socialist Revolutionary. Yet neither then nor later did Kerensky acknowledge any intellectual debt to such Populist thinkers as Lavrov or Mikhailovsky. This was the period when Mikhailovsky brought together three of Kerensky's future ministerial colleagues to write for his journal *Russkoe Bogatstvo* [Russian Wealth]. Paul Milyukov was already middle-aged, an historian of distinction with an awesome presence; A. V. Peshekhonov looked like a typical *intelligent* with his thick spectacles and drooping moustache, but he had a keen mind for socioeconomic questions. Victor Chernov, with his leonine looks, became the Populist who thought he had mastered the Marxists at their own doctrine.[13] These three men marked out the parameters of Kerensky's entire political evolution, yet his mental processes differed crucially from theirs. Where they attempted to chart the political *principles* appropriate to early twentieth century Russian society, he was concerned with political *values*. He would never hesitate to sacrifice a principle where he felt a value was at risk.

To be honest, Kerensky also lacked the academic *Sitzfleisch* required to plow through the statistical studies of these political thinkers. They were altogether too practical as well. Kerensky preferred the company of the circles remembered by one of his younger comrades:

They lived entirely among ideas and ideals; they dreamed about a new world, but they wanted freedom most of all. They were unquestionably humanitarian and utterly Russian in every respect. A smoky room, a table loaded with samovar and plates of sandwiches, and groups of twelve or fifteen men and women of various ages were typical of an evening assemblage of the intelligentsia of Saint Petersburg.[14]

These young people were the direct opposite of Sergei Witte, Alexander III's finance minister, who had driven Russia headlong toward modernization and whose monument was the Trans-Siberian Railroad, completed in 1902. He had subjected the peasantry to relentless fiscal pressure to export grain and finance the importation of foreign machinery and expertise. The ex-peasant workers huddled into industrial barracks, without regard to sex or nationality, were forced to work long hours, denied maternity leave, and deprived of any form of organized representation. Naturally enough, their resentments were exploited by intellectual agitators, though the workers responded with peasant suspiciousness at first. Gradually, European methods of organization percolated through to the workers from Poland and the western provinces and in 1897 there was a massive and successful strike of textile workers in St. Petersburg itself. In 1902, this newfound militancy spread to the peasantry in the provinces of Poltava and Saratov, long the scene of Populist agitation.[15]

The time had come for the organization of political parties, whatever the law might say. In 1898, the Marxists had made an abortive attempt to create an All-Russian organization, though immediate repression left little but a memory and Struve's famous manifesto. In 1903, the first real Congress of the Russian Social-Democratic Labour Party (RSDRP) met in Brussels and London, but immediately split into Lenin's Bolshevik faction and a number of splinter groups known loosely as Mensheviks.[16]

Neither bourgeois nor peasant intelligentsias could accept the leadership of Marxists, with their insistence on "proletarian hegemony." After their release from long terms of exile in the nineties, the "grandmother" and "grandfather" of Russian Populism, Ekaterina Breshko-Breshkovskaya and Mark Natanson, tramped the countryside preaching to the peasants the message that their numbers gave them enormous strength. Soon, there were Populist groups in Kiev, Moscow, and the Volga Region, and the well-known Populist writers Peshekhonov and Myakotin began to contribute to illegal Socialist Revolutionary journals. By 1902, the Party of Socialist Revolutionaries (PSR), based in Geneva, had succeeded in gaining the affiliation of nearly all the Populist groups in Russia and in exile.[17]

The young Kerensky did not yet consider himself a socialist. He looked for leadership to the liberal gentry active in the partly elective organs of local government, the *zemstvos*, and to non-party liberal intellectuals including Milyukov and Struve, a Marxist no longer. In 1902, they created a Union of Liberation in Stuttgart and published the first number of *Osvobozhdenie* [Liberation]. Aiming itself at "those groups in Russian society which cannot find an outlet for their feelings of indignation—neither in class nor in revolutionary struggle," it demanded greater civic freedoms and political reform, including a "non-class representative body". When he caught sight of a smuggled copy of *Osvobozhdenie*, Kerensky was thrilled:

Until that moment we had been completely unaware of the secret work that had been going on since the mid–1890's to organize the movement of which this journal was the official organ. . . . We students used to scout around for copies, and whenever we found one we would read it aloud to one another until it literally fell to pieces.[18]

Kerensky was also attracted by less political movements. At a literary soirée at his sister's hall of residence, he first heard Dmitry Merezhkovsky, the most portentous contemporary figure of Russian letters and his wife, the distinguished poet Zinaida Hippius. They were then involved in an unprecedented series of religious-philosophical assemblies which brought members of the literary intelligentsia face to face with the more sophisticated leaders of the Church hierarchy. For an emotional young man, Merezhkovsky's vision of a "Third Revelation" of a "freer religion in a liberated and enlightened Church" must have seemed very attractive. The meetings were cut short when reactionary churchmen intervened in 1903 and ecclesiastical support for anti-Semitic excesses in the 1905 revolution postponed the rapprochement between Church and intelligentsia until the Church itself began to suffer the persecution it had so often inflicted on others.[19]

In 1902, Witte was displaced as principal minister of the young Tsar Nicholas II by the new Minister of the Interior Vyacheslav von Plehve. Plehve, who initially posed as a liberal, soon revealed a more vicious side when, in 1903, he encouraged anti-Jewish riots in Kishinev, Bessarabia, where the authorities stood by as hundreds of Jews were killed, raped, beaten, and robbed. Protests from the outraged intelligentsia were ineffective. In January 1904, Russia went to war with Japan in an arcane dispute over logging rights on the Sino-Korean border which intellectuals were quick to dismiss as an attempt by the cynical Plehve to mobilize Russian patriotism. *Osvobozhdenie* quoted a "young Russian scholar":

What will the Russian people lose if their army and navy are routed in the Far East? . . . if their army is victorious . . . they will lose everything. . . . They will lose the last hope of liberation.

Kerensky must have shared these views, for he began to help "on the technical side of the Union's activity—distributing copies of the journal, and so on"—his first breech of his promise to his father.[20]

Kerensky's father is unlikely to have shared this view, knowing that the defeat of Russia by an Asian power would certainly not pass unnoticed by Russia's Asian subjects. Nor did his sisters. Elena broke off her medical studies to treat the soldiers, while Anna abandoned her singing to volunteer as a nurse. This brought an abrupt halt to the reconciliation between Olga Baranovskaya and her brother Vladimir, about to graduate as a Guards' artillery officer. Many years later, Kerensky remembered:

The years of the Japanese war were a cruel spiritual torture, because the . . . attitude towards it brought strife into the most friendly relations and divided nearly every family into two hostile camps. . . . the memories of those long, sleepless nights, spent in frenzied arguments about the war, poisoned with anger and hatred towards each other, are still painful to me, to this day.[21]

It was now that Kerensky had to choose a career. "My childhood dream of becoming an actor or musician gave way to a decision to serve my people, Russia and the state, as my father had done all his life." He had hoped to be a professor, one of those academics who had played an honorable and conspicuous part in the liberation movement from their sheltered platforms. This idea was now abandoned. "Deep inside I already felt that this was not to be, and that my place was among the active opponents of the autocracy." This feeling may have resulted in a deterioration in the quality of his work; Olga remembered a row he had with Petrazhitsky at the time. Petrazhitsky did not like Kerensky's final essay and felt unable to back his hopes for postgraduate study. Kerensky's experience echoed Milyukov's, since it was Klyuchevsky's surely less justified doubts about Milyukov's academic qualities that drove Milyukov into politics.[22]

Many decades later, Alexander Kerensky reminded Olga that "I never met on my life's path a more intense and beautiful woman than you."[23] At twenty, "Olya," with her graceful figure, pale oval face with its fine, regular features framed in curtains of shiny jet-black hair, was strikingly beautiful. The word "intense" (or "concentrated," i.e., *pristal'nee*) is less obvious but equally appropriate. Olya shared Kerensky's impatience, his rapidity of speech and movements, and there was a kind of purity about her that inhibited levity. She was won over by the strength of Kerensky's commitment to their common ideals and his irresistible bubbling humor.

Olga was still earning a living as a typist with the railroad, but she took extra typing home for P. E. Shchegolev, the historian of the liberation movement. Kerensky subsisted on his father's allowance, generous enough for a student but inadequate to support a family, so his parents were horrified when, in the spring of 1904, he wrote to announce his forthcoming marriage to Olga. Fyodor Kerensky and the girls regarded Alexander as far too young, and they affected to see Olga as a wanton revolutionary leading their beloved Sasha to ruin. In desperation, they even wrote to Olga, asking her to postpone the wedding. These appeals went unheeded, and after his graduation in the late spring of 1904, Kerensky broke with family custom to join Olga's family on their small estate, rather than joining his own family in Tashkent. After three days on the train, they arrived in Kazan. A small boat took them up the Volga to Sviyazhsk, and a two-horse carriage took them on the remaining two-hour journey to Kainki.

Olga never forgot Kainki. Her grandfather's house stood in the middle of the village, next to the church. It was big and solidly built. They shared the extensive premises with the family who looked after the place when they were absent. Her grandfather had given away most of the land but he retained an arable plot and three small hills covered with cherry trees, wild strawberries, and nut trees. Kainki had an unforgettable aroma:

We usually came in the middle of May and gathered lilies of the valley. We had huge lilac-trees, ally [sic] of lime-trees, jasmine. They blossomed one after the other and their fragrance filled the air. It sounds funny but when you approached [the] house there was such a strong, fresh, healthy smell of manure. . . . And all around the village were fields and meadows and every step brought a different smell. Even the hemp which peasants cultivated for their different needs had a sharp, pungent, peculiar smell.

From the beginning A[lexander] was "under the spell of Kainki and its simple charm." The pain he felt in breaking his ties with his family was partly assuaged by this opportunity to reforge his ties with the Volga region and its historic townships.

One day Alexander and Olga walked past the graves of her grandparents and into the little church, where they were married by the village priest before a congregation of peasants. This was probably the happiest moment they had ever known—or would ever know. "We slept with windows wide open and woke up to the fresh air and sun." When, regretfully, they tore themselves away, Olga was carrying their first child.[24]

They arrived in St. Petersburg at the end of August 1904 and were struck by the changed atmosphere. They had left their friends fearful that Plehve would succeed in turning the masses against the radical intelligentsia by winning a short war against Japan. The workers seemed to have been tamed by the police unions devised by the ingenious General Zubatov to "protect" them from the influence of socialist intellectuals. All this had been changed by the series of Japanese victories in the East and the success of the young Socialist Revolutionary (SR) terrorist, Yegor Sazonov, in assassinating Plehve. The new Minister of the Interior, Prince Svyatopolk-Mirsky, went out of his way to placate the liberal opposition, even permitting the Union of Liberation to organize public banquets to commemorate the Great Reforms of the 1860s. He spoke warmly of the *zemstvos* in interviews with the press, much to the irritation of the Tsar. This autumnal "Spring" reached its apogee in December, when the government promised more religious toleration, greater freedom for the press, and a review of labor legislation.[25]

In the autumn of 1904, Kerensky applied to join the Bar. For references, he listed a former Governor, a former Public Prosecutor, and an admittedly very liberal judge of Imperial Russia's supreme court, the Senate. The Council of Assistant Lawyers was appalled at his "bureaucratic" friends and turned him down flat. Kerensky's first reaction was one of fury, but eventually he calmed down and found more appropriate references. "I did not succeed at once in entering the fairly tight-knit organization of political defenders since in this milieu, linked in the main with the left-wing parties I then had no contacts and apart from that I bore the label of a 'bureaucratic background.'"[26] This incident shows just how remote he still was from revolutionary modes of thinking.

If he was not yet trusted to defend the victims of the regime in open court, Kerensky could at least offer them free advice on their rights. A number of legal aid organizations already existed in the larger cities but Kerensky wanted to found his own. He and a young Social Democrat colleague went to see Countess Sofia Panina, a distinguished liberal feminist, who had created a recreational center or "People's House" on Ligovskaya Street, to ask her to let them run their center in her institution. She found them a niche on the strict understanding that they did not use it for political propaganda. They accepted this condition, and for two years this was Kerensky's principal occupation. There, he got to know "the lowest strata of the urban population, in particular the working class."[27]

Kerensky could easily have made his fortune in the well-paid branches of the legal system.[28] Instead he worked for virtually nothing in the hope that the political defenders would one day take him seriously. He suffered both material privation and the moral discomfort of living off an allowance from a disapproving father and the earnings of the pregnant wife he adored, and who, sharing his views, accepted her share of the sacrifices with real enthusiasm.

The Kerenskys were supported in their resolve by the friends who had replaced his early contacts in "bureaucratic" society. The moving spirit of the group was still Olga's cousin, Sergei Vasiliev. A graduate engineer working for the Ministry of Transport, Vasiliev was already a committed SR sympathizer. Another of Olga's cousins who moved in their circle was Evgenia (Zhenya) Moiseenko, sister of Boris Moiseenko, the number three in the PSR's Fighting Organization, popularly called the "Central Terror." Zhenya managed furtive meetings with her brother on his visits to the capital. Alexander (Shura) Ovsyannikov and Viktor Somov, a school friend from Tashkent, were two of Kerensky's friends from law school, both of them SR sympathizers. A. F. Yanovsky was the only Social Democrat in the group and he lacked the chronic sectarianism of many of his comrades.

Despite the war and his marriage, Kerensky kept in close contact with his sister, Elena, now an intern at the Obukhov hospital. When his brother, Fyodor, arrived to study at the university, Sasha and Olya offered him lodgings with them. "Fedya" was much more conservative than his elder brother and they avoided talking politics.[29]

On January 5, 1905, Prime Minister Kokovtsev reported to the Tsar that nearly 90,000 men, women, and children had gone on strike. Father George Gapon and his colleagues in the leadership of the major police-sponsored trade union, in an attempt to regain control of the movement, petitioned the Tsar. The militancy of the workers was reflected in the radicalism of the petition's demand for a Constituent Assembly, democratically elected by secret ballot. "That is our most important request, everything rests in it and on it, it is the chief and sole remedy for our septic wounds, without it these wounds will bleed terribly and drive us to our deaths." On January 6, Nicholas II attended the blessing of the waters of the Neva at the Winter Palace. Somehow a live shell was loaded into one of the saluting canon in the Peter-Paul Fortress and it just missed the Imperial party. It was widely rumored that this was an assassination attempt.[30]

The capital was now humming with the news that on Sunday January 9 the workers would march to the Winter Palace to present the petition to the "Little Father" in person. The government's response was to post a few proclamations reminding the workers that demonstrations were illegal and to deploy a vast force of troops and police to meet the threat of revolution. The night before the scheduled demonstration, a delegation of distinguished socialist and liberal intellectuals, including Gorky and Peshekhonov, toured the homes of the ministers imploring them to avert a massacre and begging that the Tsar receive the demonstrators. They were told to mind their own business, and briefly arrested on suspicion of forming a revolutionary Provisional Government. When the word went round about the arrests, scores of the intelligentsia signed protests. One of them was Alexander Kerensky, who thereby earned himself a secret file in the offices of the *Okhrana*, the Security Section of the Police Department.[31]

The morning of January 9 dawned fine and cold, there was a thin layer of ice on the Neva and ice on the streets. Kerensky and Ovsyannikov went down to Nevsky to get a good view of the workers' march. In his memoirs, Kerensky repeated the myth that the demonstrating workers were all innocent monarchists. The truth was more complex. Gapon himself, who had set off with one of the many feeder processions from the Narva suburb, never reached Nevsky. His march was stopped by eight volleys of shots fired when it reached the Narva Triumphal Arch nearly three miles away. Nearly all those workers who got through to Nevsky had already come under fire and had made their way to the Winter Palace by side streets. By then, the innocents were the middle-class bystanders who were as amazed at the actions of the troops as any of the workers.[32] There was nothing mythical about Kerensky's anger, however. Some of the workers had tried to shame the soldiers by urging them to join them or fight the Japanese, and these pleas may have suggested Kerensky's response. When he reached home, he sat down and wrote letters to the young guards officers he knew, including Vladimir Baranovsky. "I reminded them that at a time when the army was fighting for Russia, they at home, with all Europe looking on, had shot down defenceless workers and had thereby greatly harmed the country's prestige abroad."[33] This combination of moral censure and patriotism was typical of the man.

After "Bloody Sunday," as January 9 became known, Kerensky redoubled his work for the oppressed, visiting the homes of the victims' families on behalf of the Bar Council. This was the first time he had entered the shacks, tenements and barracks of the workers, though he found no "class-conscious" proletarians among them. But how could they explain their plight to this kind, young *barin* (gentleman)? And how could he avoid a note of condescention as he offered them the benefits of his university education?

Even Nicholas II was shocked by the massacre and he invited a hand-picked workers' delegation to hear a little homily from him at Tsarskoe Selo.[34] This gesture was ineffective. The liberal "banquets" were the occasion for increasingly radical speeches by the liberal opposition. The government itself gave the socialists their chance by offering the workers an opportunity to elect representatives to serve on a commission of inquiry into their grievances. The workers elected revolutionary socialists who ignored the commission but set about creating new, free trade unions which set about the capitalists with vigor. On February 4, the SR terrorists struck again. This time they assassinated the Tsar's reactionary uncle, Sergei Alexandrovich, the Governor-General of Moscow. Even the cautious Milyukov, active in the leadership of the intelligentsia unions, kept an eye on the secret military organizations that the SRs and Social Democrats (SDs) were trying to form in the army. In mid-February, Nicholas II appealed for support in his struggle against rebellion, but promised the convocation of a consultative assembly, or *Duma*, and offered to accept petitions from all sections of the population in the future. This offer failed to still the demand for a democratic Constituent Assembly, on which the opposition had set its heart. Only a decisive victory against Japan could now save the government further humiliation.[35]

When Kerensky was not assisting the victims of Bloody Sunday, he attended meetings of young SR sympathizers at the apartment opposite Olga's workplace, the Nikolaevsky Railroad Station, which Ovsyannikov and Vasiliev shared. His shyness at public speaking was slow to dissipate. As his comrade Chernilov remarked to Sergei one day, "You know I liked that school-boy Kerensky very much— obviously he's a very bright lad." He was taken aback to be told that the "schoolboy" was an assistant lawyer and university graduate.[36]

Vasiliev himself had already begun conspiratorial work, duplicating nearly a thousand copies of Father Gapon's curse on the Tsar. Frustrated by the difficulty of joining the SR party in the conspiratorial fog imposed by the government, he, Ovsyannikov and one other student decided to form their own organization with the grandiloquent title of Organization of Armed Rebellion. In the 1950s, Vasiliev would remind Kerensky that he had also joined the group, though Kerensky himself left contradictory accounts of the episode. At all events, he was right to dub these activities "revolutionary romanticism," and Vasiliev himself admitted as much, calling his group "semi-mythological." The organization's sole serious action was to duplicate appeals for a rising, which Zhenya Moiseenko and Kerensky's peasant best man handed out to the peasants.[37]

The Spring and summer of 1905 brought no relief to the Tsar. His army surrendered at Mukden, and after an epic journey round the world his navy was sunk in the Tsushima Strait. More workers and some peasants joined revolutionary disturbances, and in June, the newest battleship of the Black Sea Fleet, *Potëmkin of the Taurida*, hoisted the red flag. For one who had realized "for some time" that his place was "among the active opponents of the autocracy," Kerensky was curiously quiescent.

Easter 1905 should have been a time of rejoicing for the Kerensky family. Oleg Alexandrovich, their first son, was born on April 4, 1905. The joy of the occasion, which might have brought Kerensky closer to his parents, turned into a time for further remorse, for Nadezhda Kerenskaya died. This was such a painful memory that neither Alexander nor Olga Kerensky could even recall how long she had been ill or what she died of, yet she was barely fifty. Emotional difficulties were added to the financial distress of the young family, and this may have held Kerensky back from revolutionary activity for a while.[38]

By the summer of 1905, the Tsar realized that he could not defeat the Japanese and the revolution at the same time. There was a ceasefire in Manchuria and a promise that the forthcoming *Duma* would have some legislative powers and a pledge that gentry, peasantry, and upper bourgeoisie would be represented in it. This was, of course, an insult to the majority of the intelligentsia and the industrial workers. The reestablishment of university autonomy provided enclaves within which they could organize themselves. Trotsky remembered that "completely free popular gatherings were taking place within the walls of the universities while Trepov's unlimited terror reigned in the streets" as "one of the most astonishing political paradoxes of the autumn months of 1905." Vasiliev's group provided teams of speakers to put forth the SR view at these meetings. On one occasion, Vasiliev spoke right after Trotsky to an audience that included Kerensky, his sister Elena, Olga, and her cousin Zhenya Moiseenko. It was now that Kerensky first heard his future SR comrades Nikolai Avksentiev and Ilya Bunakov-Fondaminsky.[39]

On October 8, 1905, the Moscow railroadmen went on strike; four days later their Petersburg colleagues joined them and on October 10, the Petersburg Soviet of Workers' Deputies was born in the building of the Imperial Free Economic Society. It rapidly became the coordinating center for a general strike. Its nominal head was the left-liberal Nosar, but its two vice-chairmen, Trotsky and Avksentiev, exercised far more influence. The Tsar, advised that disaffection was spreading within the armed forces, finally gave way to Witte, and issued a manifesto conceding civic freedoms and a representative assembly, promising as "an unshakeable rule" that no law would be passed without the endorsement of this Duma. He closed with an appeal to "all true sons of Russia . . . to help to stop this unheard-of trouble and together with Us to concentrate all their forces on the reestablishment of quiet and peace in our native land."[40]

Kerensky said of that night that he had "heard someone urgently ringing my doorbell. I thought it was the police but it turned out to be my friend Ovsyannikov in a state of great excitement." Despite all his previous disappointments, Kerensky's reactions were monarchist rather than revolutionary; he was elated by the news and confident that Tsar and People would now be reconciled. Many more seasoned contemporaries shared this brief moment of euphoria. It was soon dissipated as news came in of the response of the "true sons of Russia," who went on another orgy of murder and destruction of Jewish lives and property in the Ukraine and who assassinated the Bolshevik Baumann in Moscow. The ties between the proto-fascist "Black Hundreds" and the police were all too clear. As a current joke had it, "scratch a Black Hundred and you'll find a police constable or gendarme."[41]

Kerensky's group decided to test the promised freedom of the press for themselves. Their comrade Mironov had money in the family, though not much was required, as many businessmen were anxious to take out insurance in case the revolution triumphed while the printers were usually delighted to help. They called their paper *Burevestnik* [Stormy Petrel], a reference to Gorky's poem but not to be confused with Gorky's own later publication of the same title. This was no hectographed sheet but a well-produced newspaper on eight sides of quarto. Its masthead suggested coyly that it was a "political popular-socialist newspaper" but it carried the PSR motto, the full text of speeches by leading PSR members, and the notes of the assassin of Grand Duke Sergei. Its first issue carried the draft program of the PSR; subsequently it admitted to "sharing the views of the PSR in all matters," and Kerensky claims that by its fifth biweekly issue, it had been recognized as an official PSR publication.

The editors of *Burevestnik* did not trust the Tsar's promises and signed all their articles with pseudonyms, though Kerensky could not resist the temptation to print their real names in an advertisement for their legal advice center. The only other genuine name that appears is the name of the so-called "responsible editor," a volunteer figurehead, whose only qualification was his willingness to go to prison when the authorities pounced. So who was the real editor? Mironov and Vasiliev were largely organizers and fundraisers. This leaves Kerensky and Ovsyannikov, and on one occasion, Kerensky admitted that he had been *the* editor.[42]

Many years later, Kerensky suggested that *Burevestnik* had pursued two main aims. One was to prosecute the revolution. An example of this kind of writing is an article by 'Alov' (Kerensky ?) in issue no. 5, blaming the pogroms of Jews and opposition leaders on the government. "Revenge!" it thundered. "May this slogan become universal and may the great citizen of Russia multiply his efforts tenfold to attain the new regime under which alone this revenge will become possible."[43]

Kerensky's second alleged aim was "to combat the absurd decision of both the Social Democrats and the Socialist Revolutionaries to boycott the elections to the first Duma. I felt very strongly that this policy only played into the hands of the enemies of democracy and was, moreover, contrary to the mood of the people." There is no contemporary evidence for this at all, and Kerensky was probably confusing the feelings he held in the autumn of 1905 with those he held the following spring or even later. None of the surviving issues of *Burevestnik* so much as hint at supporting participation in the Duma elections and the paper was suppressed before Witte enlarged the proposed franchise to offer workers limited representation. It was only with the defeat of the risings in Latvia, Estonia, and Moscow that the mass of the industrial workers resigned themselves to a further period of semi-legal activity within a modified Tsarist system. Though the parties had not yet taken binding decisions, the overwhelming majority of SD and SR activists were hotly opposed to legitimizing undemocratic elections.[44]

In November 1905 it was armed rebellion that beckoned to the youthful editors of *Burevestnik*, filling "Alov" with "a feeling of anxiety, of the anxiety not of fear but triumph." This may have been the "bloody article" written by Kerensky which landed the unfortunate "editor" in prison for two or three years.[45] Despite his bloodthirsty articles, Kerensky suffered no ill effects from this publishing venture. The *Okhrana* had its hands full with much bigger fish and, but for a tragicomic circumstance culled straight from the pages of Bely's *Petersburg*, Kerensky might have got through the 1905 revolution completely unscathed.

During the late summer of 1905, Sergei Vasiliev began to feel the police uncomfortably close on his tracks. The time had come to move his hectographic equipment, his newly acquired Browning pistol, and the remaining undistributed appeals of the Organization of Armed Rebellion to Kerensky's apartment on Grodnensky Pereulok. Even Vasiliev, by now a co-opted member of the Petersburg Committee of the PSR, did not know that a "Military Group" of the party was holding its meetings in another apartment in the same building. Serafima Klitchoglu, a member of the group, was tailed

to the meetings. The investigator asked the concierge which apartment she had gone to, but the conspirators had foreseen this and had
bribed the concierge, probably by outbidding their "tail." The concierge told them that Klitchoglu came to visit Kerensky.[46]

Unaware that he was already under surveillance, Kerensky tried
to get into even deeper water in December 1905. This is one of
several mysterious incidents in his life of which he never told Olga,
and for which we have only his word. Outraged by Nicholas II's
public patronage of the anti-Semitic "Union of the Russian People,"
Kerensky decided to assassinate him. He therefore asked Zhenya
Moiseenko to arrange a rendezvous for him with her brother Boris.
Zhenya was at first reluctant to help; she was fond of Olga and baby
Oleg was only eight months old. Still, her revolutionary duty was
clear, and she arranged what proved to be the first of two meetings
between Moiseenko and Kerensky. At the first, Kerensky explained
his motives for wanting to join the Fighting Organization. At the
second, Moiseenko informed him that his offer had been rejected in
view of his inexperience. Kerensky was chagrined to find himself
regarded in the same condescending light in which he saw the "revolutionary romantics" around him.[47]

Many years later, Moiseenko is alleged to have told Kerensky that
he had been rejected at the behest of the Head of the Fighting Organization, Yevno Azef. This version was much more flattering to
Kerensky's *amour propre*, since Azef had by then been shown up as
a double agent. It may also be true. The Fighting Organization was
overwhelmed by volunteers at this time (only the *Okhrana* itself
received more offers of collaboration from the perennially destitute
Russian intelligentsia). Azef *always* tried to put off recruits on principle (as a police agent) and for reasons of efficiency and security (as
a terrorist). On this occasion, he and Moiseenko were also carrying
out the policy of the PSR Central Committee, which had decided
that following the October Manifesto "terrorist acts were now in-
admissible." Asked by the CC to assume all the risks of underground
work without the psychological incentive of real terrorist acts, Azef
had refused, dissolving the organization on his own authority.

Kerensky had therefore volunteered to join an organization that
was being wound down and which would not be reformed until
after the First Congress of the PSR, which met in Finland at the turn
of the year. Moiseenko may not have wanted to admit to a situation

of which he strongly disapproved. Boris Savinkov remembered him as a believer "only in terror" and a sympathizer with anarchists even in Western democracies.[48] Moiseenko would have discovered Kerensky's family circumstances and also his brief enthusiasm for the October Manifesto from his sister. Their meetings must have confirmed his view that Kerensky loved life too much to be a good martyr.

On the night of December 23, 1905, Kerensky heard a loud knocking at their door. His subsequent recollections of the thoughts that passed through his mind at this ominous sound tell their own story:

"This time I went to answer it without a thought of the police" (1934). "It could only be the police" (1965).

The apartment was thoroughly searched, though the police were careful to avoid waking Oleg. Vasiliev's incriminating paraphernalia was soon unearthed, and Kerensky was taken off to the main remand prison, the Vyborg One-Night Prison (more popularly and accurately known as *Kresty* [The Crosses] because of its ground plan.) Vasiliev was "liquidated" at the same time (In those innocent days the word meant simply "arrested.") Ovsyannikov actually witnessed Vasiliev's arrest and rushed round to warn Kerensky, only to find him gone. The prisoners were soon able to reestablish contact by tapping on the walls. They could receive visitors in the presence of a guard, as well as food parcels and letters, and could borrow books from the prison library.[49]

The authorities had their hands full and it is hardly surprising that they failed to charge Kerensky within the legal time limit. He became sufficiently indignant at this to go on hunger strike. After a few days, the authorities gave way, to the extent of charging him with the preparation of the violent overthrow of the government, an offense carrying a maximum penalty of perpetual hard labor. the counterproductive nature of this "victory" did not disturb him: "My hunger strike had been motivated by the desire to draw to the attention of the public the fact that the law continued to be violated despite the October Manifesto."

His friends let him down, suppressing news of his action to avoid worrying Olga—a misjudgement as she would certainly have publicized his gesture immediately.[50] The capital's press was full of the indignities suffered by libertarian young people of good family. In fact they got almost as much attention as the massacres of rebellious workers and peasants.

Kerensky was released "under the special surveillance of the police" on April 5, 1906, the day after Oleg's first birthday. He was to be banished from the capitals for several years while Vasiliev and the others were allowed to resume their normal occupations. Kerensky was livid: "I, who had done nothing but store some of their pamphlets in my apartment, was to have my whole life distorted." It is just possible that this discrimination was due to his approach to the fighting organization. After a period of noncollaboration with the police department in the latter part of 1905, Azef resumed his former role in 1906. In due course, he would betray Klitchoglu and many others. One official is alleged to have mocked Kerensky with the taunt: "This one dreams of killing the Tsar." Even more intriguing is the allegation of *Okhrana* General Gerasimov that Kerensky was the "head of the fighting group of the Socialist Revolutionaries of the Alexander-Nevsky District."[51]

Strings were pulled to enable Kerensky to meet the nominal director of the police department, with whose daughters he had once danced. Kerensky pointed out that exile would wreck his career and insisted that imprisonment would be preferable. Eventually it was agreed that he spend a long holiday with his father in Tashkent, less a compromise than a capitulation by the professional policemen, who retained their suspicions of him, to the pressure exercised by Kerensky's father's connections in society. In September 1906, after their return to St. Petersburg, the case was finally laid to rest.

On hearing of his son's arrest, Fyodor Kerensky had written a vitriolic letter to Olga, accusing her of ruining his son and predicting that should would ruin his grandson. The distraught Olga showed the letter to Elena, who told her to destroy it and never to mention it to Kerensky. Olga burnt it, but she could not quite follow her sister-in-law's advice to forget it, and she always retained bitter memories of the summer in Tashkent that followed. The old man's normally impeccable manners had deserted him and he barely managed to say "good morning" and "good night." Even the presence of his grandchild failed to mollify him.[52]

By the autumn of 1906, Kerensky was out of danger. His own verdict on his activities was modest and accurate: "My revolutionary spurs were earned—though, truth to say, without great risk. The stigma of "bureaucratic descent" was removed under the shower-bath of the common wash-house in prison. I was now 'one of them' in the radical and socialist circles." This was certainly true of those who remained at liberty in the capitals, though some of those sent to fester in Siberian exile would prove harder to convince. Kerensky needed this minimal baptism of repression to win the trust of the socialists his career required, so his occasional claims that storing Vasiliev's leaflets cost him and his wife dear cannot be taken seriously. Anxiety and family friction there was, but the long-term results were entirely to his advantage.[53]

There were brief moments in 1905 when Kerensky was overcome by a desire for reconciliation with patriarchal authority, and there was an occasional hint of bourgeois self-indulgence in his reactions. He was still inspired in part by those feelings of caste that made it inconsistent with the personal honor of a humanitarian Mikhailovsky or a terrorist Savinkov to tolerate autocracy.[54] Impelled into revolutionary activity and membership of the Socialist Revolutionary Party by youthful impetuosity and a desire to impress his peers, he came to despise the government for more mature reasons. Nicholas II persistently preferred proto-fascist policies to democratic ones with bloody consequences, some of which Kerensky witnessed. He would not rest until the Tsar's authoritarian and parasitical regime was removed.

3

Against the Tide

The Revolution had brought Kerensky some disappointments. The SR terrorists had failed to uproot that *radix malorum*, Nicholas II. The military organizations of the socialist parties had failed to win the armed forces for the revolution. Many SRs had neglected the organization of the industrial workers, leaving the field free for the Marxist Social Democrats. Sadly, some of the "dark masses," especially in the southwest, had been persuaded to take part in vile attacks on Jews. Milyukov and his new liberal Constitutional Democratic ("Kadet") Party, had shown a willingness to abandon the masses, provided they were allowed to participate in politics themselves. The defeat of the December risings meant that the struggle would prove longer and more painful than he had hoped.[1]

Yet these negative phenomena were insignificant by comparison with the revelation of mass power and capacity for disciplined revolutionary activity. Now that they knew they could shake the autocracy, surely the masses would not revert to their former apathetic obedience. They had ignored the appeals of the anarchist left, and few had followed the anti-Semitic right, overwhelmingly showing their confidence in such democratic and socialist intellectuals as Georgii Nosar, Leon Trotsky, and Nikolai Avksentiev. The workers had supported the campaign of the Petersburg Soviet for the eight-hour day with discipline and without unnecessary violence. The peasants had supported the All-Russian Peasant Union's leadership of liberals and populists in their campaign for a peaceful boycott of bad landlords. Only when the government smashed their organization had the peasants resorted to the more barbaric methods of the age of Pugachov.[2]

Kerensky was also encouraged by the poor showing of the theoreticians. Georgii Plekhanov did not even make it back to Russia. Lenin and Chernov arrived only after the October Manifesto, remaining for a few weeks each. Chernov made a pathetic appearance before the Petersburg Soviet to argue unsuccessfully *against* the campaign for an eight-hour day, while Lenin's chief contribution was to persuade his comrades to drop their ludicrous demand that the Petersburg Soviet submit to their control or disband. Struve's penitential journey toward the right in politics had removed him from mass support.[3] Both Trotsky and Milyukov were intellectuals, but their successes seemed to owe as much to their abilities as orators and organizers, fields in which Kerensky would have something to offer.

Despite his recent promise that "no law may receive force without the ratification of the State Duma," the Tsar created a State Council to share this power, comprising his own nominees and representatives of the Church, nobility, zemstvos, education, trade, and industry. He endorsed budgetary rules restricting the Duma's right to debate national finances, and a law "legalizing" some forms of trade union activity, which actually limited the promised "freedom of assembly and association." On the eve of the opening of the Duma in April 1906, Prime Minister Witte published new Fundamental Laws of the Empire, which restated the principle of autocracy and established a mechanism for circumventing the Duma, should the need arise. Witte had been brought in to pacify educated society and negotiate a French loan to tide the autocracy over its crisis. In this he was successful. But when he failed to overcome Kadet hostility to continued repression, he was brusquely sacked.[4]

Witte's concession of limited franchise for the workers did not immediately weaken socialist objections to participation in an undemocratic electoral system, except in Georgia, where the Mensheviks had become the standard bearers of an overwhelmingly popular progressive movement. Elsewhere both Marxists and Populists boycotted the elections. There was virtually no disagreement about this, though Peshekhonov unsuccessfully urged the Party of Socialist Revolutionaries to participate in the official closed meetings of registered electors, to urge them not to elect. (The "Maximalist" left wing of the PSR wanted to bomb these assemblies!) As a result, the election was a walkover for the Kadets and the Polish, Ukrainian and Muslim parties aligned with them.[5]

On April 27, 1906, the Tsar received the Duma in the Winter Palace and greeted them as those "best persons, whom I instructed my beloved subjects to elect from amongst themselves," a phrase he would come to regret. They then traveled by barge to the Tauride Palace, once the home of Catherine the Great's favorite, Prince Potemkin, and now the home of the Duma. They were cheered by huge crowds who took advantage of the occasion to demand a total amnesty for all political prisoners. Even the inmates of Kresty prison demonstrated by waving their bed linen through the bars and shouting for an amnesty.[6]

The convocation of the Duma presented the Populists of the capital with an unpalatable dilemma. Boycotting the elections was all very well, but could they ignore the ninety-odd ill-educated and politically unlettered men sent, despite official attempts to influence the elections, by the peasantry and poorer workers to speak for them? This offended against the sense of obligation they bore "The People." As an SR paper admitted later: "the peasantry believed that the Duma could give them both land and freedom, that the Duma could do everything the working people needed."[7] If the Populist intellectuals denied the Duma's "Trudovik" (Labor) group their cooperation, it would simply be led by the nose by Milyukov, fast emerging as the stage manager of the Duma. Peshekhonov had now split from the PSR and his Popular Socialists soon made up their minds. The PSR leaders reluctantly followed suit and Vasiliev's group began working for the *Gazeta Trudovikov* [Trudovik Gazette].[8]

Both Kadets and socialists were adamant that old scores must now be laid to rest, but their demand for an unconditional amnesty played a key part in ensuring that there would be no cooperation between Tsar and opposition. The bill to abolish the death penalty was carried unanimously, an unprecedented event. When Trudovik deputies arrived with this news at a meeting of Populist intellectuals the meeting broke into frenzied applause. This unforgettable moment would come back to haunt the intelligentsia in 1917.[9]

On July 4, the Duma reaffirmed its view that the solution to the land question lay in the compulsory redistribution of noble land. The Tsar, determined not to compromise on this issue, dissolved the Duma, whereupon 178 of its members traveled to Vyborg in Finland

and issued a Manifesto appealling to the population to refuse taxes and military conscription until the government recalled the Duma. The illusion that they alone stood between the government and popular retribution was soon exposed. A few mutinies and some agrarian disturbances did not suffice to conceal the embarrassment of the Kadet authors of the Vyborg Manifesto.[10]

Nicholas II now appointed as Prime Minister the notorious hardliner Peter Stolypin. On the day the Kerenskys returned to St. Petersburg, the SR "Maximalists" tried to assassinate him. The massive explosion destroyed his house and killed 32 people. It also injured two of his children. Two days later, the Fighting Organization killed General Min, the butcher of the Moscow Rising, and the following day Polish socialists killed the Governor-General of Warsaw. The Tsar's response was fierce. On August 20, he established new field courts-martial. Their verdicts were not subject to review or appeal. Executions were to be carried out in 24 hours, and military lawyers could not be judges in these courts. In the two months before the new law, 102 people were executed; in the two months that followed, there were 387. This was a time of moral darkness for the intelligentsia, equal to "the darkest period before the 1905 Manifesto."[11]

Oppressed by a sense of failure, by the political reaction, by the poverty of his young family and his dependence on the earnings of his wife and father, it was with elation that Kerensky responded to a phone call in October from Nikolai Sokolov, a leading Social Democratic lawyer. Sokolov asked him to take over the defense of a group of rebellious Estonian peasants, while he went to Kronstadt to defend Ilya Bunakov-Fondaminsky from an incitement to mutiny charge. For Kerensky, this was a lucky break. Instead of beginning his career as the junior member of a team, he was able to start as leading counsel. The local luminary, Jaan Poska, a future prime minister of independent Estonia, kindly allowed Kerensky to take over, a shrewd move in view of Kerensky's command of Russian and the judges' dislike of better-known lawyers.[12]

The trial involved an incident that had occurred in December 1905, when a peasant uprising had erupted in the Estonian countryside (following the general revolt that had broken out in Latvia). Some of the German-speaking gentry had already abandoned their estates to their stewards. Others, less prudent, had been imprisoned in their manor houses by baying mobs, armed with flintlocks, axes, pitchforks, and clubs, and forced to watch as their estates were ransacked. The peasants demolished and burnt two dozen houses, several distilleries, and the Kappa-Kohila railroad station, reigning unchallenged until a detachment of dragoons arrived. The troops, who had been promised they would not be punished for overzealousness, killed two of the marauders, wounded at least twenty more, and flogged a large number on the spot.[13]

Over twenty of these peasants came before the Reval (Tallinn) District Court on October 30, 1906. For four days, Kerensky said little, allowing the local defense counselors to clarify the details. He reserved the concluding oration for himself, however. It seems to have been a direct appeal to the hearts of the judges. He reminded them of the socially sanctioned and habitual violence of the landlords and the ferocity of their military "pacifiers." Some of the cases were dismissed outright, and seven defendants were acquitted. None of the accused received more than three years' imprisonment. The grateful Estonians presented Kerensky with an engraved silver chalice that would sit proudly on his mantlepiece.[14] Although not always so successful, his commitment and discretion made him popular in Tallinn and Young Estonian socialists on the run knew that they could turn to him with confidence.[15]

In December 1906, Kerensky was in Riga for the mass trial of the leaders of the so-called "Tukkum Republic" of 1905. Trouble had flared in November 1905, when the Governor-General had attempted to suppress revolutionary organizations. The Latvian socialists had responded by organizing their own democratic local administrations and replacing the city police forces with their own militias. In Tukkums, a thousand armed revolutionaries besieged a small force of dragoons in their barracks, setting trip wires to prevent a breakout and then setting fire to the building. Half the dragoons were killed as they tried to escape. Their commander was shot when captured, and someone cut off his finger as a grisly momento. The relieving force, under General Khorunzhenkov, shot 45 men and women as a reprisal. The General was dissuaded from an even more drastic purge of the town only by townsmen who claimed that the culprits had fled and offered to search for arms themselves. He also had to rescue other isolated detachments. This clemency was more than the Tsar could stand. In a marginal note on the Governor-General's report, he wrote: "That's no reason, he should have destroyed the town."[16]

Kerensky's pleading was less successful this time and of the 75 accused, only 12 were acquitted, while 17 were sentenced to death. The sentences were promptly carried out. Even in failure, however, he had won friends, as one remembered:

Kerensky had defended my friends and fellow-revolutionaries impassionately [sic] reminding the tribunal of the fact that the reason for the Latvian unrest was the oppression and lack of freedom which they had to suffer under the rule of the local German Balt nobility and the Russian Czar.[17]

Kerensky, who had spent long enough in Riga for his wife and infant son to have joined him, plunged back into party work on his return home. The elections to the Second Duma were imminent and this time all the socialist parties took part, though the PSR was still at a disadvantage. The Bolsheviks, Mensheviks, and Popular Socialists could all participate legally in the official pre-election meetings, but the PSR which had resumed its campaign of assassinations, could not. Their answer was a "front" organization for electoral agitation called *Zemlia i Volia* [Land and Freedom], whose leading members were all second-rank SRs, known to the *Okhrana* but not currently under investigation. They included Prince G. D. Sidamon-Eristov, a Georgian lawyer; a city councilor; the aristocratic ex-guards' officer S. D. Mstislavsky, who had organized a secret SR group in the armed forces before his transfer to the General Staff Library, and the charming Dr. Zhikharyov.

Kerensky joined this group, while Olga worked with Chernov's ex-wife, Anastasia Slyotova, on the secretarial side.[18] V. V. Kiryakov, one of the organizers of the All-Russian Peasant Union and Kerensky's first biographer, was also a member, and he recorded Kerensky's continuing defects as an orator:

At that time, he did not possess the self-control required of an orator. He often exploded into the speech of another orator and sputtered objections. . . . Then, recollecting himself suddenly, he at once broke off in mid-word, apologized to his opponent, and slightly embarrassed, shut up.

Kiryakov did pay tribute to Kerensky's tactical sense, and it was probably a tactical agreement that enabled the socialist parties to rob the Kadets of three of the nine Petersburg seats they had won in the First Duma. The PSR controlled three of the largest factories in the capital and were able to insist on one of these seats, with the rest going to the Bolsheviks.[19]

By the spring of 1907, Sasha and Olya Kerensky were only 26 and 21 years old respectively. Their second child was conceived the same spring. There were times when they needed some relief from anxiety, some encouragement, some hope for a better future for themselves and their country. Sometimes they found this in the theater. Olga Kerenskaya remembered that they had seen Wagner's *Ring*, a tremendous hit with the Petersburg intelligentsia in those dark days. This was not just because of the grandeur of Wagner's music. The story of a patriarchal authority willing to break any promise to hang on to power could not have failed to remind them of recent Russian history. The fearless heroes and heroines of the cycle, their lives manipulated and brought to premature conclusions by the "capitalist" Alberich, were all too like the young heroes of 1905.[20]

Kerensky preferred Rimsky-Korsakov's new opera, *The Legend of the Invisible City of Kitezh and the Maid Fevronia*. The action takes place in the legendary medieval city of Kitezh, an earthly paradise, protected from the advancing Tatar hordes by a divine gift of invisibility, though its reflection could sometimes be seen in Lake Svetloyara and its bells heard by those with a conscience. The central character is Grishka Kuterma, a peasant so degraded by abuse and exploitation that he will sell his country to the Tatars for money. He is finally returned to the path of virtue leading to Kitezh by the purity and self-sacrifice of the Maid Fevronia.[21] This view of a simple abused people, who might be manipulated by those who should know better but who would infallibly return to their true mentors was shared by Kerensky and many other SRs. At the First SR Congress, Chernov had assured his comrades that should "anarchizing elements" call on the workers to expropriate the factories during the revolution, they would soon return, chastened, to the leadership of the PSR.[22] *Kitezh* was no great box-office hit but Kerensky loved it and hummed its tunes to himself for months.

Theatrical diversions were good for morale but the progress of reaction seemed inexorable. Breshkovskaya and other PSR leaders implored and almost cursed the peasants to save the day:

woe to you, peasants, if you now remain indifferent to these appeals, if you once more carry your mortal shame in silence and once more hand over your children to the trials of hunger, ignorance and slavery.[23]

But it was not the peasants who acted but Stolypin. The elections to the Second Duma had resulted in a strengthening of the far right, but the fulcrum remained with the Kadets. This time matters were precipitated by the government, which accused 55 of the Duma Social Democrats of sedition. When the Duma majority refused to hand over the deputies without examining the evidence itself, it was dissolved on June 3, 1907. Simultaneously, new electoral regulations were published, radically reducing the representation of the Russian peasantry and all the national minorities in future Dumas.

This was a clear breach of both the October Manifesto and the Fundamental Laws. Even within the Kadet party, there were now voices calling for a boycott of future elections. Once more the PSR imposed a boycott, while the newly reunited Social Democrats split over the issue. This time Lenin sided with the Mensheviks, while most of his erstwhile Bolshevik following maintained the boycott. It took Lenin five years of financial manipulation and philosophical debate before he could recover control of the Bolshevik faction. Meanwhile, Stolypin was able to proceed with the implementation of agrarian "reforms" which, he hoped, would result in the emergence of "strong" individual peasant farmers opposed to revolution and the destruction of the peasant communes idealized by the Populists.[24]

The opposition seemed powerless. The Government had denied even the liberal Kadets formal registration. Executions and exiles of revolutionaries were followed by dismissals and proscriptions of professors, actors, and teachers. In 1905, there were some 100,000 members of underground revolutionary groups. By 1910, there were only a tenth the number, and they were working at a much less intense level. Many of the workers and peasants came to feel that they had been deserted by the intelligentsia, and totally failed to understand their sudden preoccupation with sexuality.[25]

Squeezed between an upper class which paid lip service to Christian ideals while practicing a double standard, and a peasantry that looked up to Christian marriage as an almost unattainable ideal, the Russian intelligentsia usually refused to admit the importance of sexuality in

human affairs. Whenever an audacious radical, such as Chernysh-
evsky or Kollontai, dared to speculate about sexual relations based
on love rather than convention, smutty reactionaries would seek to
undermine their influence over the ethically conservative people by
suggesting that they were promiscuous purveyors of "free love."[26]

At meetings of the Religious-Philosophical Society, Kerensky
must have heard Vasily Rozanov, an erudite and charming speaker,
the husband of Dostoyevsky's mistress, Apollinaria Suslova. He had
done valuable sociological work on the appalling consequences for
working-class Russians of the inability of the Orthodox Church to
minister for their new needs in the working class barracks of the
cities. Rozanov found Orthodox Christianity anti-sexual and sought
a new dispensation in which people could love Christ and enjoy a
natural sexual life. As the revolution ebbed, he was opposed with
increasing acerbity by Nicholas Berdyaev, who insisted instead on
the "thirst of the individual for perfect immortality." Zinaida Hippius, the moving spirit behind these meetings, was struggling to
express a complex sexual identity, in a high-minded Sartrean *huits
clos* with her husband Merezhkovsky and D. S. Filosofov.[27]

These earnest discussions of sexuality were swamped by the *succès
de scandale* which now attended the younger generation of "Sym-
bolist" or "Decadent" writers, and which permanently inhibited
Russian intellectuals from further discussion of them. After soaking
up garbled versions of Freud's theories, these young men launched
a sacrilegious assault on the most holy values of socialism and democracy. The "hero" of Sologub's *Spellbinders* was a revolutionary
Social Democrat and sadist, while in *Darkness*, Andreev's SR "Hero"
finds his higher truth in a whorehouse.[28] The most successful of these
iconoclastic works was Artsybashev's *Sanin*, a more serious and substantial work than the others. Its anti-hero exposes the superficiality
of Bazarov's nihilism, taking pleasure in his own incestuous feelings.
Kerensky might have recognized himself as he had been a few years
earlier in the person of Yuri Svarovich, a revolutionary exiled to his
conservative father's house, who finds the admiration of the local
librarian more important than a free constitution for Russia. Kerensky himself disapproved strongly of the wave of semi-pornogra-
phy which emerged in these years, titillating its readers with
"neutral" descriptions of sadism, homosexuality, paedophilia and
incest.[29]

By contrast, Kerensky's own career took him into the ranks of a profession which insisted on the strictest possible ethics, and into membership of the sub-caste of political defenders for whom service to the people and a relentless sense of duty were paramount. These ethics were cultivated by the Bar Councils, established at the Petersburg, Moscow, and Kiev Chambers of Justice by the reform of 1864. They insisted, successfully, that defense counsel serve their clients and not the state.

To begin with, assistant lawyers were attached to a patron specializing in criminal, civil, or administrative law. To gain admittance to the bar, an assistant lawyer had to wait five years (the government usually forced Jews to wait longer), attend "conferences" for two successive years, and provide three testimonials. They must also have defended at least ten cases. Kerensky was attached to N. A. Oppel, a criminal lawyer not noted for his political work. However, he was in sympathy with his protégé.[30]

Kerensky's true patron was Nikolai Sokolov, whose *Okhrana* nickname, "The Beard," referred to his black patriarchal whiskers. The son of a court priest and author of theological textbooks, Sokolov retained something of the puritanism and scholasticism of his forefathers. (He once walked out of a fairly innocent display of Gipsy dancing to which Alexander and Olga had taken him.) As a student, he was already a rather doctrinaire Menshevik Marxist, but he distinguished himself during the 1905 Revolution by his outspoken attacks on anti-Semitism and by his representation of the lawyers on the Central Bureau of the Union of Unions. Sokolov used his impressive appearance to good account with witnesses, and his revolutionary contacts kept him busy with cases. As a Social Democrat city councilor, he became the unofficial convenor of the Social-Democratic intelligentsia of St. Petersburg.[31]

Sokolov supplied Kerensky with cases on a regular basis until he had established an independent practice. Kerensky's last professional contact with Oppel came when he completed his five-year apprenticeship and became a full member of the St. Petersburg bar in 1909. These were a grueling five years. O. O. Gruzenberg, one of the leaders of the bar, wrote later; "No other profession, even the medical, knew such a huge percentage of unpaid assistance: legal aid cases from the courts, permanent consultations, unpaid advice at home."[32] Until Kerensky became a full member of the bar, he played a supporting role in most of his cases, acting as junior to such greater names as Berenshtam and Sokolov. Arising as they did from the recent history of Russia, these cases enabled him to observe the leaders of the opposition at first hand. He helped defend the Trudovik signatories of the Vyborg Manifesto, the All-Russian Peasant Union, and leaders of the Petersburg Social-Democrat military organization and of the Northern Flying Column of the SR Military Organization.[33]

The more Kerensky discovered about the administration of justice, the more he came to equate political reaction with the most cynical manipulation of the law. Some of his clients were acquitted after spending up to three years in prison. The defense was frequently prevented from calling witnesses. The accused were often prevented from describing their motives lest they pillory the government. When evidence for the prosecution was lacking, it could be created. "The Arabian Nights of Nikifor Patsyuk" was the apt label applied by one of Kerensky's colleagues to the evidence of a witness who had postponed his own execution for three years by offering prosecution evidence in trial after trial. Kerensky had helped defend Patsyuk himself and he went on to defend the unhappy man's victims. Press reporting was often slanted by the simple expedient of threatening all but the papers of the right with contempt proceedings.[34]

The courtroom orator was a distinct type in pre-Revolutionary Russia. One of the greatest described his task as follows: "I thought it was necessary—even essential—to learn to master the law with its own iron tail, to stimulate the impartiality of the forgetful judge and to confute the drunken prosecutor with his own slander." Distinguished liberal judges, such as Koni and Manukhin, ensured that official tolerance for such tactics survived until 1905.

After the revolution, fear stilled the scruples of many judges. The most notorious was Senator Krasheninnikov, senior president of the St. Petersburg Chamber of Justice, who made no bones about the fact that he was fighting a political battle. Exemplary sentences often "provoked weeping and hysterical cries on the part of the many relatives filling the courtroom," driving a little iron into even Kerensky's charitable soul.[35] Unlike some socialists, Kerensky never became cynical about law as such. On the contrary, he became more and more determined to see a just and legally administered social system established in Russia.

At the turn of 1907, Kerensky defended one of the leaders of the

All-Russian Peasant Union, who included Peshekhonov and Kiryakov. He argued that his client had been morally obliged to discuss
a possible Constituent Assembly and the land question with peasants:

for at this meeting, he was one of the few representatives of the intelligentsia,
and to be silent, when the dark mass seeks a way to the light, would be to
break that eternal tradition, which distinguishes the Russian intelligentsia
and which consists in an especially acute sensitivity to popular misery.

He admitted that his clients had defied a police ban to visit a peasants'
meeting,

but is it right during a storm to keep the masts up when they might be
dismantled and used as fuel for the halting engines to avert an impending
wreck? So much the more virtuous is it to sacrifice the insignificant demands
of the police in the interests of the preservation of the essence of state power
(*sostav gosudarstvennago stroia*).[36]

Kerensky firmly believed that only the guidance of the intelligentsia
could ensure that the Russian Revolution would be culturally progressive and not slide through anarchism to reaction.

Kerensky was gradually finding his proper place in politics, demonstrating great moral courage and ensuring that however ambiguous his relations with the parties might be, his central allegiance to
humanitarian values would not waver. If there had ever been a hint
of Artsybashev's Yuri Svarovich in him, it was now banished. He
quickly earned the respect of what remained of the Russian legal left
in these years. Sokolov kept him in contact with the Marxists and
he became a close associate of Vodovozov, Peshekhonov, and Bramson. His work in the courts brought into contact with the Anglo-
Russian David Soskice.[37] They, like his clients Kiryakov and Kozmin, would reappear to serve him in 1917. The network of friends
and comrades he built up soon spanned Russia.

In November 1907, SRs everywhere were shattered by the news
that the entire Northern Fighting Organization of the PSR had been
arrested. Suspicions had been growing that a traitor was active within
the councils of the party and these arrests were the last straw for a
group of young SRs—friends of Sergei Vasiliev—exiled in France.
They demanded action by the Central Committee (CC) to investigate
"provocation in the centre of the Party." Their suspicions focused
on Yevno Azef, head of the "Central Terror," who had been denounced to the CC by SR sympathizers, and by disgruntled careerists

within the *Okhrana* itself. Just before the arrests, they were joined by Vladimir Burtsev, editor of an historical journal devoted to the liberation movement, who tipped off the CC. When they took no action he publicly accused Azef of working for the *Okhrana*.

The SR Central Committee in Paris refused to accept the allegations and convened a court of honor of veteran revolutionaries to try Burtsev. In the end, Azef was exposed by a former Director of the Police Department, who was anxious to get back at Azef for inadvertently ruining his career and keen to ingratiate himself with liberal society. The Central Committee, which had ordered the execution of lesser spies without a qualm, now permitted Azef to sneak off with his mistress to a life of bourgeois comfort in Berlin.[38]

Azef's exposure was a world sensation. For young SRs it was a crushing blow. Azef had betrayed Boris Moiseenko, whom Kerensky had met in December 1905, and Serafima Klitchoglu, who had put the police on to Kerensky's leaflets. He had betrayed the Northern Fighting Organization, which Kerensky had gotten to know in court before seven of them were hanged. The terror tactic was discredited without providing any alternative. The Central Committee ceased to command the respect of young SRs, and SR cells in Russia fell apart from mutual suspiciousness. The *Okhrana*, who probably derived more benefit from this fearful atmosphere of distrust than from the information offered by Azef and his like, decided that the time had come to disrupt the Petersburg SR front group. They had Mstislavsky and Zhikharyov arrested and then released, so that their comrades would assume that one of them had been a police spy—but would not know which one. The group collapsed and *Okhrana* General Gerasimov was jubilant. "During the entire winter of 1908–9," he remembered, "not a single revolutionary organization was working."[39]

Given this state of things, it was a relief for Kerensky to contemplate the uncomplicated virtues of his own household. Olga remained an affectionate and supportive partner, acting as receptionist at the Legal Advice Center and visiting the prisons with gifts and messages as a member of the Political Red Cross, an organization of which she eventually became secretary. Despite this, his tendency to leave her in the dark about his own political involvements grew. He handled their financial affairs on his own, though he was often away for long periods. Both of them admired the revolutionary veterans Vera

Figner and Ekaterina Breshkovskaya—women who had left husbands and children to serve the Revolution. It is hard to believe that Kerensky would have been pleased had Olga left him and the boys. In this respect, as in many others, Kerensky's attitudes were not really revolutionary at all. This was a weakness he shared with many of his comrades.

It was motherhood that did most to divide them. Oleg Alexandrovich was born in April 1905 and Gleb followed on November 24, 1907. After Gleb's birth, Olga gave up paid work, and as time went on Kerensky's work brought in enough to make good the deficit. The boys missed their father when he went off on his exhausting train journeys in search of the oppressed. Yet when he was in Petersburg, he did his best to dine with them every evening. He would then go to meetings, returning very late and often bringing home a friend, who might end up sleeping on the sofa in the early hours. By Edwardian standards, he was quite a good father. He helped the boys celebrate birthdays and name days with presents and candles, brought them fine Christmas trees, and painted Easter eggs. When they were little, he would lie on the floor and rock on his back, using his arms and legs as the sides of a "boat" for them. Kerensky appealed to Olga to bring the boys up in the Orthodox faith. This she refused; she was no militant atheist, but she had no use for Orthodoxy.

Throughout their life in St. Petersburg (or Petrograd as it was renamed in 1914), the Kerensky family lived in the eastern half of the left bank of the Neva. In the early days, they endured a small apartment in Grodnensky Pereulok, near the Preobrazhensky barracks. In 1906, they moved to a cheaper apartment behind the Nikolaevsky Railroad Station, where the walls were slimy and the water froze. When they returned from Riga after the Tukkums case, they did not even have fuel to heat the apartment.

By 1908, however, Kerensky's increasing success meant that they could move to a more pleasant apartment over a funeral parlor on Basseynaya. In 1912, they moved from there into the apartment at 23 Zagorodny. Even this was not luxurious, as they had to climb five flights of stairs to reach it. It was still very small for Alexander and Olga Kerensky, who had been brought up in spacious official apartments. As a rule, they had two bedrooms, a small kitchen, a living room and a study and the odd storeroom. The study contained

Kerensky's law books and one or two items of weighty furniture. It was decorated with mementoes of his trials and a relic of Lieutenant Schmidt's mutiny in 1905. With their large ceramic stoves, these apartments were typical of the kind then found in central or Eastern Europe. Usually, the family employed a servant who cooked for them, and from time to time, they hired a Baltic German *au pair* to look after the boys.

Winter in Petersburg was cold and damp and the doctors were always afraid that the children would contract tuberculosis. The acknowledged remedy for this was to provide them with seaside holidays. The Baltic coast was close at hand and they could rent cheap dachas at the resorts that dotted the coast. Kerensky himself stayed with them for a couple of weeks, but Olga and the boys stayed for the whole summer, soaking up the sun and sea air. Whenever they could, they also went to Kainki, which they all adored.[40]

When, in 1911, Alexander Kerensky finally became a man of property, it was not in Petersburg, but in the little town of Volsk, hundreds of miles away on the middle Volga. The house he acquired was valued at twice the 200 rubles he paid for it, but this was no property speculation. He was qualifying himself for election to the Fourth Duma. Some months earlier, he had been approached by leading members of the Trudovik Group in the Third Duma, and by leading Popular Socialists, including Bramson and Peshekhonov, who suggested that he stand as a Trudovik candidate in the forthcoming elections. He warned them that "in my convictions I stand closer to the SR," but this did not deter his sponsors, who were anxious to reunite the various Populist factions. Other SRs were nominated by the Trudoviks in the same way.[41]

The Trudovik Group in the First Duma had been constituted by peasant deputies wary of socialist jargon and fearful of the reprisals they would meet in their villages if they openly joined the socialist parties. Their political legacy was the Bill of the 104 on land reform, which Chernov took as evidence of peasant support for the SR land program. It included the socialization of all land and its redistribution according to the so-called labor-equalization norm. "They long for an equalised distribution of the land," mocked Lenin, "but they forget the power of capital, about the power of money, about commodity economy, which even under the 'fairest' division will inevitably again give rise to inequality and exploitation." Lenin was aiming at a straw man. The peasant deputies themselves recognized that a new exploiting class might arise from their own ranks and therefore provided for periodic redistribution, a traditional practice in many areas of Russia.[42]

Hard hit by Stolypin's revision of the franchise, only thirteen Trudoviks survived in the Third Duma, where they were practically ignored.[43] The answer seemed to lie in the recruitment of reinforcements. It no longer made sense to stand aloof from the support proffered by the intellectuals in the Popular Socialist Party and by undercover SRs. It was against SR policy to stand for the Duma; SRs were even supposed to urge nonmembers to resign from it, so Kerensky was running the risk of expulsion from his party. Fortunately for him, the only deviations from party policy which carried an automatic penalty of expulsion were such "Maximalist" excesses as unauthorized bank raids, or preaching the irreconcilability of intellectual and worker interests.[44] Kerensky also benefited from the demise of the Petersburg SR organization. In a plea to Paris, intercepted by the *Okhrana* in 1910, the Petersburg group "begs for the sending of new active party workers." Nor was the party in exile in a position to take up Kerensky's conduct. Many of the young SRs critical of the Central Committee had been drawn to Avksentiev's view that the PSR should now participate in local government and Duma elections in Russia. Avksentiev had all SR groups in Russia canvassed on the issue. Most were still in favor of a boycott, though the Petersburg faction did not even reply. The CC therefore resolved once more on a boycott of "the fraudulent constitutional comedy of elections." Avksentiev, and Bunakov-Fondaminsky refused to accept the decision and began to publish their own paper, *Pochin* [The Initiative], calling for a clean break with terror and for the "use of the State Duma, as an All-Russian tribune."[45]

The opponents of terror received unexpected encouragement from Boris Savinkov, formerly Azef's deputy and subsequent head of the Fighting Organization. In his novel *The Pale Horse*, prepared in collaboration with Zinaida Hippius, Savinkov suggested that the isolation and remoteness from democratic control of the SR terrorists had presented devilish temptations as well as the heroism and spirituality familiar from the letters of the party's martyrs. The novel's anti-hero absconds from the cause for an affair which concludes when he shoots his lover's husband out of jealousy. This undeniably authentic portrayal of the professional fatigue of the terrorist forced the intelligentsia to think once more about the ethics of the Revolution. (Such a reappraisal was already underway following the publication of the anthology *Vekhi* [Signposts] in 1910, by a group of right-wing Kadets, who now included Berdyaev and Struve).[46] The novel was an abomination for Lenin, who had always preached the superiority of conspiratorial organizations, but he nevertheless failed in his attempts to embarrass Chernov into the expulsion of Savinkov. While Lenin fought his way from isolation within his Bolshevik faction to a reconstitution of it under his sole control, Chernov did nothing at all to reassert the moral supremacy of his Central Committee.[47]

In January 1913, the head of the Paris Agency of the *Okhrana* wrote to the Director of the Police Department, claiming that Kerensky was a member of the Central Committee of the PSR. The letter alleged that Kerensky had joined the party in 1903, that he had belonged to the Petersburg Committee in 1906, and—most startling of all—that he had some connection with Bogrov, who assassinated Stolypin following the Premier's loss of Imperial favor in 1911. It concluded:

in the autumn of 1911, when a split occurred in the PSR, three different currents were formed and *Pochin* began to appear, Kerensky announced his departure from the Central Committee, but was obliged to remain until the calling of a council or congress of the party.[48]

This fantastic picture of Kerensky's conspiratorial achievements is as much an exaggeration as Chernov's contrary suggestion that Kerensky only "called himself a Socialist Revolutionary". It was a retrospective attempt to explain the importance that Kerensky quite suddenly assumed in 1912 by men who had failed to forsee such a development. Stolypin's assassination had been facilitated by police negligence, and the *Okhrana* had good reasons for wanting to place the blame on the opposition. At all events, they were bolting the stable door after the horse had fled.[49]

4

Tribune of the People

In January 1912, a total of 159 Armenians were charged with membership in the revolutionary Dashnaktsutyun Party before Russia's supreme court, the Senate. Kerensky was one of the lawyers for the defense. Founded around 1890 to defend the Armenians against Turkish massacres, the Dashnaks had turned against Russia in 1903, when Prince Golitsyn insisted on the Russification of the Armenian educational system. During the Revolution, the Dashnaks had split into Old Dashnaks, allied with the Kadets and Young Dashnaks, aligned with the SRs. Determined to prove that all forms of Armenian nationalism were equally culpable for revolutionary excesses, the Russian authorities put "the entire Armenian intelligentsia, including writers, physicians, lawyers, bankers, and even merchants" on trial. Only fifteen or twenty spectators were allowed in the gallery and the newspapers were forbidden to describe the evidence.

The original investigators had been encouraged by the local administration to use any available means to get convictions. The defense challenged much of their evidence. Kerensky, despite warnings from the court as to his fate should he be mistaken, insisted on an expert examination of the pre-trial deposition of one of his clients. Kerensky was entirely vindicated. It emerged that the magistrate had altered his client's words "cannot recognize" to read "and also recognizes," and "unlike" to "very like." While the court was still sitting, other controversial documents disappeared.

Kerensky and other counsellors made openly contemptuous declarations to the press about this incident, but got away unscathed.

The Senators, now bent on reestablishing their tarnished authority, instituted proceedings against the magistrate. The unlucky man was finally certified insane, and 94 of the accused were acquitted, while the remainder received terms of imprisonment or exile, none exceeding six years.[1]

Foreign interest in the Dashnak trial was prompted by a condescending fascination with Russian exoticism and barbarism. Such interest in the next major story to emerge from Russia was related to a more tangible interest of readers of the Western press. In March 1912, *The Times* of London announced that the miners of Lenzoto, the Russian subsidiary of the Lena Goldfields Company Ltd., had gone on strike. Lenzoto produced over 90 percent of the gold then mined in Russia and was one of the world's major producers. On the following day, *The Times* reported that 5000 men were now on strike demanding "an eight hour day and 30 per cent increase of wages."[2] Four thousand miles away, in the frozen wastes of the Siberian taiga, miners and administration braced themselves for a bitter struggle. The firm's position looked impregnable. They had alternative sources of labor and promises of military assistance from friends in high places. They had only to deny the strikers credit in the shops, all of which they owned in this remote locality, for the strikers to be forced to default on their rents. They could then be evicted in groups until the strike collapsed.

The Governor of Irkutsk ordered the arrest of the strike committee and its chairman, a Menshevik exile. On April 4, as the news spread, several thousand miners milled about discussing their next move. Mining Inspector Tulchinsky, the only official the miners respected, begged them not to do anything violent. He succeeded in persuading one group to disperse, but only managed to slow down another group which was rapidly approaching a detachment of gendarmes. The front ranks turned to listen to him but were pushed forward by the pressure of those behind them. No one heard any warning. There was a volley of shots. In the mêlée that followed, 373 men were shot; 170 died on the spot while six died later from their wounds.[3]

The shock felt by a still superstitious Russian people was reinforced by an eclipse of the sun, which had occurred the same day. The Minister of the Interior, A. A. Makarov, expressed his sorrow at the deaths but blamed the agitation on the exiled Social Democrats. "When a crowd, which has lost its reason under the influence of malicious agitators, throws itself on troops, they have no other resort but to shoot. Thus it has been and so it will be in the future."[4]

The brutality and insensitivity of the government shook Russia's working classes out of their apathy. In April alone, half a million went on sympathy strikes, five times more than the entire number striking in the previous year. Soon the Bolshevik *Pravda* and the SR *Mysl'* [Thought] were able to appear semi-openly in Russia. Desperate to find some means of calming the situation, the Tsar personally entrusted the investigation of the affair to Senator Manukhin, one of the least partisan judges in Russia. The miners themselves had already appealed for legal aid. Public subscriptions soon gathered enough money for five lawyers to travel to the Lena. Patushinsky and Tyushevsky arrived from Irkutsk, Kobyakov and Nikitin from Moscow, and Alexander Kerensky from St. Petersburg.[5]

This tragic journey to the Siberian taiga was one of the most unforgettable experiences in Kerensky's life. It was there he met Ekaterina Breshkovskaya, still a member of the PSR Central Committee. So began one of the most enduring affections of his life. He was deeply moved by the strange, wild beauty of the Lena valley and impressed by the decency of Manukhin and Inspector Tulchinsky. These were the bright spots in a very somber picture.[6]

Kerensky's radicalism often lacked social content but the operations of Lenzoto excited his contempt for "a capitalist utopia in which the government served as the handmaiden of capital." The company had failed to observe even the legal minimum standards of housing, diet, and medical welfare; it had paid its workers in arrears and in coupons for its own shops. Their wives were forced to work as domestics for administrators who subjected them to sexual harassment and sentenced objecting husbands to freezing work with inadequate clothing. Manukhin found that Lenzoto "showed no good will" toward the workers while the ministry responsible had rapped Tulchinsky's knuckles for drawing attention to these abuses, implying untruthfully that the rigorous enforcement of the law might force the company into liquidation. (In the year of the strike, the London parent company passed a vote of confidence in Lenzoto and voted itself a 20 percent dividend).[7]

Manukhin's unavailing attempts to secure justice demonstrated just how frail a plant the law still was in Tsarist Russia, but he did enough to ensure that the name of the gendarme captain responsible for the

shooting became an object of detestation to all civilized Russians—
and to earn the hostility of his master, the Tsar.[8]

Kerensky's work was not limited to factfinding. He knew that the
Tsar would bow only to irresistible force; he might recall Manukhin
without warning and replace him with a man of iron. A miner
recorded that "Batyushka Alexander Fyodorovich pressed on the
meetings of us Feodosiev miners, until his tearful voice had persuaded
the majority to return to work." He was moved by empirical hu-
manitarianism: the strikers were running out of money; the government was intact; the revolutionary movement was as yet unable to
render decisive assistance.[9]

Manukhin did at least force Lenzoto to negotiate for a new contract
for the workers with Kerensky and the other lawyers, committing
it to increased expenditure on their welfare. Despite this modest
success, most of the strikers left the mines at the end of the summer,
so that it was a new generation of miners who benefited. Still, Kerensky felt that "the great Lena strike has finished with a victory for
the mass of the workers." Lenin described the Lena massacre as "a
most exact reflection of the whole regime," and for once Kerensky
agreed, echoing a Menshevik comrade: "Thus it has been and thus
it will be, as long as these people are in power."[10]

Kerensky reported back to his comrades in St. Petersburg and took
a brief rest with the family on the Estonian coast before returning
to Saratov Province for the election campaign. This was not a campaign as we understand one. The electoral regulations had been devised expressly to avert the risk of open politics. Instead, there were
"special preparatory assemblies" allowed only during the month preceding the elections. Their purpose was discuss "persons worthy of
election." They were restricted to registered electors, and there was
always a police representative in attendance, who had the power to
disperse the assembly.[11]

On August 29, 1912, Kerensky—now an expert on the Dashnak
trial and the Lena massacre—addressed his first meeting in Volsk.
He began with a review of events since 1906, when "the best representatives [of the people] were sent to the Duma, who stood firmly
for the political freedoms promised by the Manifesto of 17 October
[1905], which had promised a bright future." When he moved from
self-recommendation to a comparison of the programs of the various
parties, the police representative had the pretext he required and the

meeting was closed. This must have irritated his listeners, well-educated professionals in the main. Kerensky remembered that "at pre-electoral meetings I was able to speak freely, for here my ideas were understood, and there was no need to resort to revolutionary clichés." Here, as in the capitals, there was a strong feeling among the intelligentsia that the Kadets and socialists should pull together and not engage in polemic.[12]

In the first stage of the electoral process, the urban electors nominated a candidate who also became one of their electors at the Provincial Electoral Assembly, where the landowners had a majority. The administration had intended to browbeat the urban electors into voting for their nominee, but this time social pressure worked the other way and the Governor's nominee disappeared at the last moment. The second stage might have taxed Kerensky's reserves of "bureaucratic" charm to the limit, as the Saratov landowners were still bitter over peasant violence in the revolution. Fortunately for Kerensky, the urban electors were entitled to a single uncontested nomination and they chose him. On October 21, 1912, the Kadet paper *Rech'* [Speech] announced his election to the Duma.[13]

Thanks to the Electoral Law of June 3, 1907, the Fourth Duma, which gathered in November 1912, was an overwhelmingly conservative body. Of its 436 members, about 150 supported the anti-Semitic far right. The center, was occupied by 130 Octobrists and their allies, moderate conservatives who wanted no truck with revolution. The left included some 55 Kadets and 20 representatives of the national minorities. Coerced by the power of numbers, the socialists accepted the label 'extreme left' for themselves. They numbered 13 nominally united Social Democrats and 9 Trudoviks, though more joined during the life of the Duma. Numbers were not everything. Stolypin's demise had discredited his Octobrist allies, who had lost 30 of the seats they had held in the Third Duma, while the Lena protest strikes had given new confidence to the socialists.[14]

The Trudovik Central Committee had hoped to secure the re-election of Mikhail Berezin, who had been the leader of the group in the Second Duma. He and other leading Populists were disenfranchised by administrative chicanery so the surviving Trudoviks initially chose the elderly Siberian Vladimir Dzyubinsky as their leader. Also elected was his fellow Siberian, Vasily Vershinin, the owner of a press and publisher of a newspaper in Tomsk. Aleksei

Sukhanov, a city councilor from Tobolsk and Prince Varlaam Gelovani, a Georgian lawyer, were also important members of the
group. There were two peasants from Kovno in the West, one Orthodox, one Catholic. Kerensky was the only Trudovik elected from
the Great Russian heartland. The Trudoviks aspired to an alliance of
the intelligentsia with the whole of the working classes. In practice,
they were a party of the comfortable peasants of the borderlands and
the Populist intelligentsia of Great Russia.[15]

Kerensky now had to accomplish the disagreeable necessity of
signing an oath of loyalty to "His Imperial Majesty, Our Sovereign
Emperor."[16] Not that Kerensky felt bound by an enforced oath to
a monarch who broke his own promises by subjecting nine-tenths
of his citizens to a series of exceptional laws, a matter debated early
in the life of the new Duma. The debate was concluded by statements
from the party leaders or their deputies, and on December 3, 1912,
Kerensky mounted the mahogany rostrum to make his maiden
speech. As he looked out over the semicircular sea of portly faces,
with their whiskers and expressions of complacency and condescension, he sensed the hostility they bore him. With his bright eyes,
rapid gestures, and slender frame, he was physically and emotionally
the antithesis of all they stood for.

Conceding that a Duma elected on Stolypin's restricted franchise
was bound to throw out his protest, Kerensky declared:

So long as that exists that exists now; so long as that Duma exists in which
we are present, and of whose illegality we speak, until then, there will not
be an hour in Russia, when people will not die on the gallows or be destroyed
in forced labour.

The record states that there was noise and laughter from the right.

"For those to whom life is precious," he tried to continue—but
this just provoked another outburst of hilarity on the right. His rage
and indignation were boundless:

I say to those who laugh at this moment: I am happy and glad because
between you and us there can be no communication: it is either you, or
us . . .

He was called to order, but he persisted in nailing the circular logic
of reaction:

In a country ruled by violence, where the masses in their millions are excluded from legislation, are not allowed [*sic*] in it, where at any moment any police inspector—to say nothing of the governors—can throw any citizen into jail or arrest him, there can be no strong people, there can be no national security.

Reminded by the chair that his time was up, Kerensky concluded:

but I believe that she [Russia] will turn to a better life, and not by those methods indicates by Messrs. Octobrists here.[17]

Five days later, Kerensky replied to Prime Minister Kokovtsev's program with a more considered statement. Pressure for change was building up, he argued. "The country says: it can't go on like this, we can't live like this." The overriding need was for democracy. "A question can not be decided by naked force, but should be decided by a decision of the whole popular mass." All classes demanded "the summoning of popular representation on the basis of a universal, direct and equal franchise and the secret ballot. . . . There is no way out for Russia apart from democracy, there is no salvation for Russia apart from democracy." He challenged the rightists to seek a democratic mandate and accused them of seeking to restore unrestrained Autocracy.

Kerensky bitterly attacked Stolypin's agrarian laws for breaking up peasant communes in the interests of the "titled aristocracy." They had "wanted to destroy the peasant commune, they had wanted to found in its place a strong peasant, who could oppose the elemental urge and consciousness of the peasant masses that the land is God's and every toiler should be able to subsist on this land . . . but they did not achieve their goal." The government's claim to be the defender of property rights was hypocritical. "When each person wishing to leave the commune and grab the best land, has the right to do this against the will of his commune, when to this end, all the means of administrative coercion are used, isn't that the expropriation of the land? Isn't that the same principle against which you claim to fight?"[18]

Kerensky rarely prepared his speeches in advance. They lacked rigorous organization and contrived rhetorical decoration. Not for him the relentless logic of a Lenin, or the elegant sarcasm of a Trotsky: He depended on "pure" emotion, avoiding the foreign jargon beloved of intellectuals. He would begin nervously. "He gulps air," a friend reported, "like a fish taken out of water." There were familiar rhythms to his speeches:

His first phrase is always loud, short, like a shot from a Browning. Then, a pause, also short. Then, a stormy passionate speech, emotional and emotive and reaching the depths of the hearts of his listeners.

Never a polished speaker, he did learn to control his emotions sufficiently to achieve a certain kind of effectiveness.

What sort of orator am I? . . . I don't know what to say. That which must be said, that which ought to be said, that I say . . . . An imperative, an order what to say comes from somewhere within, from the depths: An order that one can't ignore, a stern, insistent order. I only collect together words at the beginning, before I begin. The order must be expressed in exact and clear language. But when I begin, the prepared words disappear somewhere. Other, new words appear, necessary, exact and clear. One must only say them as quickly as possible for other words are hurrying, pushing, hustling each other.

Uttered at the "white heat of passion," these speeches, accompanied by furious gestures, left him apparently exhausted and he would descend from the tribune "with his whole body trembling and with perspiration pouring down his pale cheeks."[19]

Kerensky was not popular in the smoking room and lobby where his vanity and precocious ambition were resented. His colleagues were used to the moralizing of socialists, but "their monotony was that of the babbling brook, his that of a railway whistle." His style contrasted sharply with the "flat, mumbling delivery and strong Georgian accent" of the Social Democrat [Menshevik] leader Chkheidze, who was less disliked in the Duma. The reverse was true in the gallery, where working-class groups gathered. For them, Kerensky's only peer was the sturdy, red-faced, excitable Polish workman, Roman Malinovsky. Entrusted by Lenin with the delicate task of splitting the Duma Social Democrats and asserting Bolshevik leadership over the reviving worker's movement, Malinovsky was simultaneously a police spy, submitting drafts of his Duma speeches first to Lenin and then to the Director of the Police Department.[20]

It was in the Duma that Kerensky first confronted Paul Milyukov, the leader of the Constitutional-Democratic Party. Milyukov, at 47, was an impressive personality, a historian and journalist widely admired in Western Europe and North America. The man Witte had vainly courted in his attempt to legitimize the "pacification" of popular disturbances in 1906 had turned his back on revolution since the failure of the Vyborg Manifesto. Henceforth, he would follow strictly constitutional paths, trying to convince Nicholas II and the intelligentsia of their common interest in a peaceful, bourgeois Russia, commanding international respect. Milyukov's "doctrinaire" insistence on strict constitutionalism soon disabused the intelligentsia of the illusion that the Fourth Duma would resume the struggle with the government that had broken off in 1907.[21]

After 1905, a furious debate broke out within each of the opposition parties about the political methods best suited to the quasi-legal political system that had come into being. Lenin coined the term "liquidators" to label those who argued that the conspiratorial organizations must now submit to the control of open political parties. His opponents paid him back in his own coin, suggesting that his support for participating in undemocratic elections was a compromise with autocracy. Within the SR Party, Avksentiev was accused of "liquidationism" for similar views.[22] This kind of tension existed even within the "bourgeois" parties. Within the Kadet party, Nikolai Nekrasov, a handsome young Siberian professor of statistics, whose ambitions were not satisfied by his Vice-Chairmanship of the Duma, led a left-wing group which jibed at Milyukov's leadership. Nekrasov shared Lenin's view that the Tsarist police state had to be challenged by a conspiratorial organization. Unlike Lenin, he wanted an organization that would serve as a liaison between all those opposed to autocracy, irrespective of party.[23]

In his very first speech, Kerensky had signaled his willingness to cooperate with anyone willing to lead Russia in a progressive direction, or work for the triumph of democracy. Shortly afterward, he was approached by either Chkheidze or Nekrasov and asked to join a secret organization dedicated to the struggle for democracy. Kerensky found this combination of "above party" politics and mysticism irresistible, and he was soon inducted into the Russian political freemasonry, the Masonry of the Peoples of Russia.[24]

Freemasonry was no newcomer to Russia. The movement patronized by Catherine the Great and suppressed by her grandson inspired the Decembrists, while many Russian liberals, in exile, joined the French Masonic movement. After the October Manifesto, an independent Russian section was formed by Professor Kovalevsky and Vasily Maklakov, which fed the Tsar's fears that Russian disorders were the result of "Judaeo-Masonic" plotting. The membership was split by a scandal when the *Okhrana* infiltrated its Moscow Lodge, but not all the Masons were discouraged. Nekrasov was one of the initiators of a purged organization unconnected with French freemasonry.[25]

The political freemasonry emphasized its break with Masonic tradition by abolishing all ritual and admitting women. The only vestige of mysticism was the oath of absolute silence, which the *Okhrana* failed to break. It was organized in lodges or cells of five, which were not supposed to know of each other's existence, though some idea of the scale of the movement could be gathered at its biennial congresses. There was a lodge in the Duma, a lodge for writers, and lodges in other institutions. As its title implies, the movement co-opted leading members of the national minorities. It was frankly élitist. As Ekaterina Kuskova put it: "It was raw material with which it was necessary to work and with just such organizations." By the summer of 1912, the movement had established a national network and a secretariat.[26] By joining this movement, Kerensky gained an entrée to political, industrial and military circles, which might otherwise have ostracized him.

The essence of the organization is still debated. Was it a centralized, disciplined body whose instructions took precedence over the decisions of the political parties to which its members belonged? Or was it a looser, more tolerant forum for the exchange of information and the transfer of funds? Nekrasov would later tell the NKVD, the Soviet secret police, that "the Masonry was above-party, i.e. representatives of various political parties entered it, but they gave an undertaking to place the directives of the Masonry above those of the parties."[27] In a statement prepared to calm speculation by Russian emigrés, Kerensky's friends, the SR Mikhail Ter-Pogosian and the Menshevik Yakov Rubinshtein, gave a quite different impression of the organization, claiming that it "did not demand subordination from its members, that it did not give them political orders or commissions," and that "its members retained complete freedom of political activities and could therefore remain loyal members of various political parties."[28]

Kuskova's letters and V. A. Obolensky's memoirs were written under less pressure, but they contradict one another. Kuskova was categoric in stating that "there was no cabal (*konvent*) but merely "a moral bond and a demand for *actions* without party feuds and all those pathological symptoms of Russian partisanship," but she also claimed that the organization *had* taken political decisions and had informed Milyukov, a non–Mason, of them, and that it had threatened to expel Alexander Guchkov, when he tried to organize a coup d'état. Obolensky, who left the organization's Supreme Council at about the time Kerensky assumed high office within it, gave a more modest assessment. "I cannot imagine that it played a large role in revolutionary events because its members came from various mutually hostile political parties whose internal cohesion was very much stronger than masonic fraternity."[29] One thing is clear: Kerensky's seniority in the organization was the reflection, not the cause, of his eminence in Russian politics. There is no suggestion that Kerensky ever did anything under Masonic orders with which he disagreed.

In 1912, Kerensky was not yet formally leader of the Trudoviks, but this was just a matter of time and etiquette. As the sole SR in the Duma, he was the focus for future Populist agitation, crucially poised to benefit from any movement toward democracy in Russia. Colleagues like Nekrasov saw in the young advocate an energetic, industrious, businesslike, and tactful colleague. His Masonic connection gave him access to nonsocialist circles. The government appreciated that Kerensky was a dangerous adversary and kept him under constant surveillance.[30]

Time had not stood still for the family. The ever-loyal Lyolya was still working at the Obukhov hospital, but Fedya was back in Tashkent as a public prosecutor, while Nyeta was being courted by a dashing diplomat. It was while Kerensky was away on the Lena, that his father died, after a long and debilitating cancer. On this occasion, Kerensky's sadness was mitigated by the fact that they had been fully reconciled, a process begun during a visit to Tashkent to defend some Central Asian comrades. When the old man's illness became chronic, he came to their Petersburg apartment to die.

The boys were growing up and he was anxious for their future in an increasingly militaristic Europe. When Vladimir Baranovsky presented Oleg with a sword, Kerensky broke it over his knee. He was determined that his children should have a schooling at least as tolerant and progressive as his own. This was hard to find in government gymnasia, which had been purged of progressive teachers after

1905. The answer to their prayers was provided by a pupil of Froebel, Maria Shidlovskaya, who registered her private school as a "commercial school," a fiction that fooled no one. It quickly became *the* school for Petersburg's progressives. Oleg started there in 1913, in the same class as the composer Dimitri Shostakovich. Later on, a number of famous Bolsheviks sent their children there. In this progressive paradise, there were no punishments and boys and girls sewed together. Its gifted staff included Zinaida Hippius' younger sister, Tatiana, an artist who became Gleb's form tutor.[31]

Kerensky began 1913 in fine fettle with an attack from the Duma tribune on official malpractice during the Duma elections. Even the Octobrists were smarting over the activities of the governors, so Kerensky was assured of the sympathy of the majority. The irregularities were blandly denied by N. E. Markov, the leader of the ultra-right, who would make a habit of capping Kerensky's speeches. "The Trudoviks, and even the socialists, are becoming quite successful," he quipped.[32]

Kerensky could also wither the Octobrists with scorn, as for example when they demanded stiffer penalties for land seizures. "This bill is an echo of that split and that struggle which is growing bigger and bigger in the countryside," he noted, and blamed the right for this. Markov pointed out that aristocrats as well as peasants could be prosecuted under the proposed legislation, and concluded on an ironic note, "so the most talented deputy Kerensky is not quite right, impetuously charging at a gallop against the gentry-estate owners as if defending the peasants." Even democracies had to deal with violent crime and they often imposed heavy penalties, too.

Kerensky was not lost for a spirited reply: "if one can make mistakes in one's youth, then it must be very unpleasant to live until one's hairs are grey and still not understand what the discussion is about." He had not sought to distinguish between Russia and the west. "Reaction also exists everywhere," he declared, "it's just as much an international union, as is the union of worker-peasant democracy."[33]

These public jousts were good for morale, letting Russia know that Populism had acquired a new resonant voice and earning Kerensky a mass following. Equally portentous were his relations with the socialist parties as they emerged after the dark years of reaction. Lenin had seized the initiative in January 1912, when he had formed a self-styled 'Central Committee of the RSDLP' at a conference of carefully selected Bolsheviks in Prague. In April 1912, the Bolsheviks began to publish the daily *Pravda*. The next step was a foothold in the Duma. In the Fourth Duma elections, the Bolsheviks had taken all the workers' seats for the Russian heartland, while the Mensheviks were successful in the borderlands. Lenin had no intention of permitting his six Bolsheviks to be outvoted by the seven Mensheviks but he did not want to be identified as the author of a split against which so many worker electors had expressed themselves.

The Mensheviks were never a cohesive faction, and such famous figures as Plekhanov and Trotsky openly followed their own paths. In September 1912, the Mensheviks followed the Bolsheviks by publishing their own daily *Luch* [The Ray] and reforming their own conspiratorial organizations. This did nothing to blunt Lenin's attacks on "liquidationists," allegedly prepared to abandon conspiracy for such forms of open organization as were acceptable to the extreme right "Black Hundreds." Throughout 1913, the polemic between Bolsheviks and Mensheviks grew more intense, and in the autumn the Bolshevik deputies finally broke with the Mensheviks to form their own Duma fraction.[34]

Okhrana agents in Paris reported a revival of the SR party inside Russia during 1912. By the end of that year, three separate SR committees, a "Petersburg Committee," a workers' committee, and a committee of intellectuals, existed in the capital. Early in 1913, they began to forge links with one another, a process facilitated by the amnesty to honor the tercentennial of the Romanov dynasty. Literary crimes were now forgiven and on March 25, 1913, Kerensky took part in an assembly of the "Petersburg Collective," of the PSR which met to consider the revival of party work. There were proposals for a demonstration to commemorate the Lena massacre and sabotage the Tercentennial celebrations, and for a conference of SRs, Social Democrats, and Anarchists. Since 1912, the SRs had also possessed their own periodical, the intellectual monthly *Zavety* [Precepts]. They now established the biweekly *Mysl'* [Thought] in direct competition with the Marxist papers. Like them, it suffered repeated persecution; it was shut down on ten occasions, and met its demise in July 1914. After each closure it would reappear under an altered, but recognizable title, such as *Zhivaia Mysl'* [Living Thought] or *Volnaia Mysl'* [Free Thought].[35]

Ideologically and personally, the leading SRs were closer to the Mensheviks and Kerensky found the high-minded, if doctrinaire, Chkheidze more congenial than the swashbuckling Malinovsky. However, the SRs, Kerensky included, tried to keep out of the "controversies among the Marxists," which they put down to the ills of conspiratorial life:

We openly declare . . . that the claim of the Bolshevik faction that it alone embraces the entire working-class movement is as unreasonable and absurd as the efforts of the two Social Democratic factions to incorporate the entire socialist movement in Russia. The future belongs only to the unification of all the socialist trends in a single party.[36]

The Trudoviks were therefore receptive to both Menshevik and Bolshevik overtures for regular consultations in the Duma. In a defensive account of them, the Bolshevik Badayev recalled:

Notwithstanding its "Left" tendencies, this group was very unstable and vacillated from the Social Democrats on the one side to the Cadets and Progressives on the other. Precisely for this reason we thought it necessary to establish closer relations with the Trudoviks in order to win them over from the Cadets and bring them under our influence.[37]

On May 3, 1913, the Duma got its first limited opportunity to debate the Lena massacre. It was Kerensky who opened the attack. Thirteen months had now passed and the government had still to report to the Duma. It could not do so without incriminating itself, he charged, and he singled out S. I. Timashev, the Minister of Trade and Industry, Baron G. E. Gintsburg, the chief shareholder, and I. I. Belozerov, chief administrator of Lenzoto, as the guilty parties. He described the miners' feelings in popular idiom:

They searched for God's truth everywhere; the Tsar's truth was not to be found! When Manukhin went there, the workers said: 'Look, the Tsar's messenger is coming, he will tell the truth, he will punish the murderers of our brothers. but Manukhin came, Manukhin went and the murderers were not punished, and the workers at the mines know that the truth that they sought is not to be found on earth!

Nor did he flinch from the conclusion that "people are sitting even here who have got blood on their hands." The right roared its disapproval as Kerensky was hustled from the tribune.[38]

Autocratic Russia now hid behind Gintsburg's Jewish race as Markov came up with his usual patronizing irony. He excused "the impetuosity of the deputy's nature and the strong feelings experienced by him on the subject." Markov affected equal indignation. "We are dismayed that in our state, which is under the virtuous administration of the All-Russian Autocrat, signs are beginning to be observed, which are characteristic and usual and even obligatory for parliamentary countries, for countries ruled by the Yiddish kahal, for republics, especially democratic ones." Nothing was to be permitted to spoil the tercentenniel and for the time being, Markov had the last word.[39]

Hopes for a more radical Duma were dashed in the first few weeks of 1913, when the right blackmailed the Duma into suspending Chkheidze, after a row with the proto-fascist Vladimir Purishkevich. Two weeks after the short debate on the Lena massacre, the Duma showed what it thought of Kerensky by excluding him for three sessions, for defending Chkheidze's supposedly blasphemous comments on the Holy Synod. But nothing could inhibit Kerensky from bombarding the ears of the Duma with anecdotes of official chicanery drawn from his experience in the courts, and the unwilling respect he was beginning to inspire was reflected in the frequency with which Markov replied in person to his charges. "When member of the State Duma Kerensky speaks," he chuckled, "you see in front of you a sincere—young it's true—but all the same, sincere chap." But, he continued, "gentlemen, if all that deputy Kerensky says were true, if it were all correct, it really would be impossible to live in Russia, but we know that in reality, nothing of the sort is true."[40]

In June 1913, Kerensky went to Moscow for the Fourth All-Russian Conference of Employees of Trade and Industry, representing just over a tenth of Russia's clerks and shop assistants. The conference was ostensibly to discuss the social welfare of the workers, measures to deal with occupational illness and hours of work, and methods of forcing employers to observe existing labor legislation. This agenda might have been drawn up by the legally minded Kadet and right-Menshevik members of the industry, but Lenin claimed that nearly half the delegates turned out to be Bolsheviks. The feud with the Mensheviks was then at its height and Lenin was anxious to limit their influence. The Bolsheviks therefore offered the "Left-Narodniks," as the still illegal SRs euphemistically called themselves, a voting bloc. This must have been accepted for it was Kerensky

who was elected chairman of the conference, which he described as
"the greatest honor of my life."[41] Thanks to the Bolsheviks, Kerensky was now an accredited leader of a working-class organization.

Kerensky did his best to keep the conference orderly and pragmatic
but the Bolshevik Malinovsky insisted on speaking in a more militant
vein. The Governor intervened, telling Kerensky that he did not care
whether militants or moderates came out on top. When Malinovsky
was later exposed as a police agent, the closure of the conference
looked like a police provocation. However, the Ministry of Trade
and Industry, which had originally sanctioned the conference, had
now passed into the hands of Minister Timashev, whom Kerensky
had savaged over the Lena massacre. Kerensky's chairmanship was
probably just as obnoxious to him as Malinovsky's pretended
militancy.[42]

The reopening of the Duma in the autumn of 1913 coincided with
the climax to sinister proceedings in the city of Kiev, sometimes
called the Russian Dreyfus affair. In March 1911, Andrei Yushchin-
sky, a Kiev teenager, was found murdered. He had been stabbed 47
times. Anti-semitic groups immediately alleged that he was the victim of ritual murder by Orthodox Jews. (According to medieval
Christian legend, Jews need the blood of a Christian boy to bake in
their matzos at Passover in celebration of the murder of Christ.) Such
accusations were a routine annoyance to Kiev's Jews, but matters
took a far more serious turn when, in August 1911, Mendel Beilis,
foreman of a nearby brickworks, was officially charged with the
murder. Beilis was a working-class Jew of no great piety as Zionists
were quick to note. The investigation dragged on for two years
largely because it was difficult for Justice Minister Shcheglovitov to
find investigators villainous enough to perform their roles in this
macabre farce, especially as this involved shielding the criminals actually responsible for the murder.

The case became an international scandal, drawing protests from
such august personages as the Archbishop of Canterbury. The defense succeeded in demonstrating the means employed to frame
Beilis, and even the conservative Shulgin denounced the case as
claptrap.

In October 1913, Beilis was acquitted of murder, though the jury
of unlettered Russians and Ukrainians opined that the crime might
have been a case of ritual murder.[43] On October 23, Kerensky de-

nounced the whole case to the Duma, declaring that "the very act of writing such an indictment is a state crime." That same evening, the St. Petersburg Bar convened for its annual general meeting. Sokolov and Kerensky insisted on putting a motion protesting the Beilis case. There was some reluctance to this unprecedented action, though even the Octobrist lawyers agreed with its sentiments. An amended version was finally adopted, protesting

against the distortions of . . . justice evident in the staging of the Beilis trial, against the slander of the Jewish people in court, a slander which is rejected by the entire cultured world, and against entrusting the court with the inappropriate task of propagating ideas of racial and national animosity. This outrage against the foundation of human society debases and disgraces Russia before the whole world, and we raise our voice in defence of Russia's dignity and honour.[44]

Though it was immediately picked up by the foreign press, the resolution was rather overwhelmed inside Russia by the wave of protests that poured in from all over the country. Not for many years had so much of educated society been so united against the government. Shcheglovitov now compounded his error by prosecuting the lawyers, and in December 1913 Senator Krashenninikov asked the Duma to lift Kerensky's immunity. The protest had been lifted out of obscurity and carried to the furthest corners of Russia, "escorted by Articles 13 and 279 of the Criminal Code." "Now, every intelligent man knows this resolution," recorded one commentator.[45]

The protest at the Beilis affair enhanced Kerensky's reputation, but it was no substitute for the grass-roots work the Bolsheviks had begun with the Petersburg workers. Malinovsky and his comrades had begun to articulate the mundane demands of the workers, sending out questionnaires to trade union branches and factory groups throughout the country on such issues as health and safety and hours of work. In defending himself against criticism by Rosa Luxemburg at the Socialist International, Lenin collected an impressive set of data to demonstrate that these tactics had secured the Bolsheviks "hegemony" in working-class circles. Some of this evidence was endorsed by Emile Vandervelde, the Chairman of the International. Equally impressive testimony to Bolshevik vitality was given by SRs who bemoaned their own failure to make working-class demands the center of their work. As late as May 1914, Avksentiev was admitting that the SRs had remained "behind the starting flag." Sukhanov criticized Kerensky for spending too little time on the shop floor and Avksentiev felt that the SRs lacked a "crystal," such as Malinovsky, "who could organize public opinion and the activity of the workers around himself."[46]

Bolshevik demands at this time were for a democratic republic in contrast to the Kadet ambivalence on the future form of government. They also advocated the confiscation of landed estates and the eight-hour day. There was nothing here that Kerensky could not endorse, though some of his Trudovik comrades were more cautious in the words they chose. In February 1914, Kerensky copied the Bolsheviks. He sent out questionnaires throughout the country, asking for detailed information on abuses of authority, on the working conditions of white and blue collar workers and peasant reactions to Stolypin's agrarian legislation.[47] Lenin's appraisal of these activities was actually more positive than Avksentiev's. Whereas, he argued, the Menshevik following among the workers had stagnated since 1913, the 'Left-Narodniks' had doubled theirs. "By their opportunism and renunciation of the Party," he thundered, "the liquidators [Mensheviks] are pushing their working-class supporters toward the *other*, more "radical" (in word) bourgeois group."[48]

Early in 1914, the government countered with proposals for a further reduction in the rights of the Duma to question ministers, and an increase in the power to limit debate, censor Duma reports and lift the immunity from deputies responsible for "false statements." For the time being, a plan to strip the Duma of *all* its legislative powers was shelved. The restrictions were yet another retreat from the Tsar's promises of October 1905. They would have prevented the socialists from acting as popular tribunes, since their speeches would barely have reached the people before they found themselves in Siberia. (By the summer of 1914, the Duma was sitting on demands for the lifting of the immunity of all three socialist fraction leaders.)[49]

On April 22, 1914, Prime Minister Goremykin, the 75-year-old cipher Nicholas II had settled on to carry out his will, appeared before the Duma. As he ascended the rostrum, the socialist deputies began to shout and hoot. One after another, they were excluded from the Duma for the maximum fifteen sessions. The expulsions took a long time, for each of the 21 socialist deputies had to be given ten minutes to defend himself before the Prime Minister was able to speak. This was the occasion for a verbal onslaught on the government, though Chairman Rodzyanko cut many of the speeches short for fear they would draw even greater wrath on the head of the Duma. The Kadets refused to condone such ungentlemanly tactics and voted with the majority or abstained. Some of the protestors had to be forcibly removed by soldiers, and as Kerensky was escorted out of the Catherine Hall he warned the commandant, "you have power now but another day will come after this."

In the two days that followed, over 50,000 workers in Petersburg went out on sympathy strikes. Lenin normally referred in caustic terms to the "petty-bourgeois" Kerensky, but now he espied a "left bloc" of Trudoviks and Mensheviks against both the far Right and "treacherous bourgeois liberalism."[50]

In the end, the "bourgeois liberals" softened to the extent of reducing the sentence of exclusion. The socialist factions decided on a joint statement on their return to the Duma. Malinovsky was in an irascible mood, but he acquiesced in Kerensky's nomination as joint spokesman—he was better than a Menshevik after all. All the returning socialists arranged to learn the same speech so that it could be completed even if Kerensky was again debarred. When they returned to the Duma on May 7, Rodzyanko repeatedly interrupted them, though Kerensky did manage to blurt out the warning that "the government has decided that the end has come, the time to strike a final blow and destroy the last shadow of popular representation." The other socialists, especially Malinovsky, tried to complete the statement, but the government frustrated this ingenious tactic by simply censoring the record.[51]

The next day, Rodzyanko was astonished when Malinovsky visited him to announce his resignation, and thunderstruck when Assistant Minister of the Interior Dzhunkovsky arrived to tell him that Malinovsky had been a police agent all along. Dzhunkovsky had no obvious personal axe to grind and the reasons for Malinovsky's exposure have never been established. However, it may be that the *Okhrana* though this the easiest way of terminating an experiment that had gotten out of hand. Malinovsky was supposed to split the Social Democrats, not win them a mass following. Lenin refused to accept that his Duma favorite had been a police agent and, though this discredited him in some quarters, it may have been a lesser evil than the demoralization that afflicted the SRs after Azef's exposure. The major beneficiary of the episode was Alexander Kerensky. As a percipient English journalist recorded:

The mysterious disappearance of the Okhrana spy, Malinovski, who had been the leader of the Bolsheviks in the Duma, removed the only man who could rival Kerensky in appeal to the masses.[52]

In June 1914, Kerensky, Sokolov, and their 23 colleagues, were finally brought to trial for their protest against the Beilis affair. Sokolov received eight months' imprisonment and Kerensky six. That evening, they were guests of honor at a dinner given by the Chairman of the Bar Council and on the following day, they were fêted at a "solidarity dinner" by 200 Duma deputies and fellow lawyers. Telegrams poured in from all over Russia and from such political opponents as the Octobrist leader Guchkov and the Kadet Kokoshkin. The Bolshevik Badayev records that 30,000 workers went out on another sympathy strike. When Kerensky next entered the Duma

The Progressists, the Kadets, the Trudoviks and the Social Democrats gave him a stormy ovation, for a period of several minutes the hall shook with applause. A. F. Kerensky was touched and bowed silently. The Rights tried to drown the applause with hissing and booing, but the applause grew louder still.[53]

Kerensky and Sokolov appealed and the case was eventually deferred. Now the most popular socialist in the Duma, Kerensky was still protected by his immunity. Five days later, the Duma was prorogued and Kerensky and Nekrasov went off on a tour of the Russian interior.[54]

Kerensky's writings are usually persuasive rather than concise or analytical, but he left one unpublished analytical fragment, a seven-page typescript analysis of his own role in Russian history in note form entitled "My Work for the Sake of My Russia." It notes that despite the "Stolypin reaction" and the growing influence of Rasputin, Russia was making great cultural, political, and economic strides by 1914, a view that is generally shared today. This progress was of course the result of the introduction of market relations extolled by Struve in his Marxist phase rather than the abolition of the division of labor anticipated by the Populist Mikhailovsky. Kerensky's endorsement of this process justifies the contention of some Marxists that "Populism" had become "Revisionism" by 1914.[55]

All that remained was politics, and here Kerensky felt that

the final skirmish of the country with the degenerate regime had become inevitable. It had become clear that on the agenda was not a struggle over party programmes, but a struggle with the remains of Autocracy in the name of a radical reform of the very state order. This STRUCTURAL crisis had to be decided by the establishment of a democratic parliamentary regime, with a government responsible to popular representation.

The view is partly supported by both Soviet and Western historians who write of a "new revolutionary upsurge" in 1912–14, though their views on the destination of this movement differ.[56]

Kerensky's faith in a progress that was both material and moral was illustrated by his frequent references to the supposed incongruity of reaction in the twentieth century. This "Whig interpretation" anticipated that all countries would eventually be governed by representative institutions. As he once declared to the Duma:

nowhere, never have any attempts to annihilate those duties of a popular representative [institution] freely and openly to fight for the rights of the people against the malpractices of the government led to any results at all.[57]

His understandable hostility to those "artificially" impeding Russia's progress was no vengeful hatred. As a loyal student of Professors Lossky and Petrazhitsky, he offered his enemies a bloodless revolution: "Hatred and malice, hatred to the end towards political opponents is incomprehensible to us." He warned the right that "we will never allow ourselves in connection with you to depart from those basic principles of righteousness, truth and love."[58]

He was not impressed by the threats posed toward his attractive vision by the extremes in Russian society. Nicholas II had been obstinate in 1905, yet he had been forced to grant the October Manifesto. He might be removed by a military conspiracy and replaced by his more malleable brother. Kerensky's contacts in the army assured him that the military would not oppose such a peaceful "surgical operation." The political freemasonry was well placed to ensure the orderly transfer of power. By 1914, Kuskova claims it had come to embrace aristocrats and high-ranking officers, leading capitalists, and the intellectual élite. Even future Bolsheviks were Masons, and

Kerensky could later claim that "the main points of the programs of
the future republican government were settled."[59]

Kerensky was perfectly well aware of the Bolsheviks' popularity
with the workers, but he attached quite a different significance to it
than historians blessed with hindsight. The danger that exercised him
in 1914 was not the "anarchizing" Lenin of 1917, but the gulf between
intellectual socialists and the masses that had reopened after 1907. In
that context, the efforts of *all* socialist parties to put down roots
among the people were viewed positively. Lenin might huff and puff
about "liquidationists," but it was precisely in the sphere of open
politics that his party had scored its greatest successes since 1912.
The policies they advanced were acceptable to Kerensky, and the
"hegemony" they had acquired could be dismissed as the result of
a police intrigue. In a democratic Russia, Lenin's control of half a
dozen deputies would mean much less than in an Autocratic police
state. A revolution in 1914 would not have been dependent on millions of half-trained peasant conscripts, nor would its new government have had to face an economy devastated by three years of war.
Neither then nor later did Kerensky face the economic problems that
beset a successful land reform, nor the problems posed by the conflicting ambitions of the Russian intelligentsia. How could Russian
democrats continue to live a European lifestyle, devolve power to
the localities and border nationalities, and yet enforce rates of rein-
vestment adequate to ensure that Russia did not fall further behind
the dynamic capitalist economies of the West?[60]

Kerensky was often irritated by Paul Milyukov, yet he approved
of Milyukov's sincere efforts to preserve the peace of Europe during
these years. He himself felt the 1914 Russian Army Law to be a threat
to peace, since it provided for the erosion of Germany's military
supremacy within two years. The only way to avert conflict, he felt,
was to install a democratic government which would concentrate on
Russia's internal needs. The censorship prevented any agitation
against the Army Law, but at a small socialist conference in Petersburg, his comrades approved the line they would take in the event
of a war. It seemed remote: "Outside the city boundary of St. Petersburg one was in a land which had no idea that a complicated and
bitter diplomatic struggle was being waged in Europe."[61]

The day after the Duma was prorogued on July 14, the Austrian
Archduke Franz Ferdinand was assassinated by a partisan of Russia's

Balkan ally, Serbia, but when Kerensky spoke in Samara's City Theater, all thoughts were on Russia's peaceful progress. "Thousands
assembled—literally all the people, from top to bottom."[62]

The popular tribune had little time to spare his family, and Olga
took the boys on her own to the rocky shores and woods of Hanko
in Finland. Kerensky and Nekrasov heard the news of Austria's ultimatum in Samara. Sensing that war was imminent, they were both
troubled and excited. On the Volga steamer they took from Samara,
Kerensky met one of Lenin's sisters. "Look now," he said, "you'll
see your brother Vladimir soon."

"Why?" she asked. "The war will change everything in Russia
and he will return home, he replied."

In the meantime, it was Olga and the boys who were forced home
as their holiday home at Hanko was within easy range of German
naval guns.[63]

5

Terribly Little Time

When Kerensky thought about the Beilis trial, he was overcome by shame, "burning shame for myself and for our culture. . . . All the peoples loved and respected Russia, chaotic and materially negligible, as the land of Tolstoy and Pushkin, as a brilliant seat of spiritual culture." Under a democratic regime, anti-Semitism would wither and there would be no foreign adventures by cliques anxious to distract attention from their own redundancy. "We say that a democratic government alone could really achieve a peaceful solution of international questions."[1] As a patriot and a democrat, Kerensky seems to fit the epithet "social-chauvinist," which Lenin shortly bestowed upon him. As so often, the Leninist label obscures as much as it enlightens, for until 1917–18, Kerensky remained a staunch humanitarian, who loathed war on principle. Nor was he such a "chauvinist" as to seek advantage for Russia over Germany or Austria in the war. On the contrary, he remained a consistent supporter of proposals to end the war without prejudice to the interests of the Central Powers. Still a revolutionary, by 1915, his radicalism was such that even the Petrograd Bolsheviks would write to Lenin, asking his permission for "joint revolutionary work" with Kerensky and Chkheidze.[2]

In exile, Kerensky would suggest that his own reaction to the war had been purely patriotic. "All internal struggle," he wrote, "should be stopped, all forces in the country concentrated on the war." He would cite with approval the Petrograd workers who went back to their jobs when war was declared.[3] This was not what he had felt at the time, however. In 1916, he had used far less flattering words to describe the patriotic mood:

The war provoked a peculiar kind of atavism in a large part of Russian society. All the non-democratic classes of Russian society from the first shot on the Western frontier did in fact "unite," slithering down immediately into a sort of trench of social and state Muscovitism.[4]

Zinaida Hippius met him on August 2, 1914 and observed, "it's clear that he has not yet entirely found his position. The military contagion cannot touch him, simply because he doesn't have that physiology [*sic*], he's too much the revolutionary." This was an overstatement. The Latvian Populist, Vladimir Stankevich, felt Kerensky considered that his duty lay in the "service of the war by way of criticism of the government, warning it against mistakes threatening the success of the war or the purity of its principles." Kerensky was not lacking in patriotism; he just did not let it override his commitment to democracy. In the autumn of 1914, Stankevich met him again at the Imperial Free Economic Society:

after my warm speech about the necessity to subordinate all interests to the war, Kerensky remarked that if I wished to be consistent, I would got to war myself.

"Don't worry," I answered with irritation, "you'll soon see me in military uniform."[5]

The Tsar convened a special session of the Duma on July 26. Hastily, the *senyoren konvent*, or steering committee, met to decide on the agenda. A right-wing deputy suggested that the Duma should simply demonstrate its patriotism by shouting "hurrah" three times after the reading of the Imperial Manifesto. Kerensky ridiculed this proposal and, with Menshevik and Bolshevik backing, he demanded that each faction be permitted to explain its attitude to the war.

We, like genuine "doctrinaires," did not appreciate in the same way all the grandeur of this picture of a "speechless people." Thus, against the will of the "patriotic block" (from Markov II to Milyukov) the historic sitting of 26 July was brought about by our "partisan obstinacy."[6]

Milyukov had come to aspire to the role of Leader of the Opposition, and he haughtily explained that a "union sacrée" was as obligatory in Russia as in the western democracies, despite the political and constitutional differences between them. Kerensky asked Rodzyanko to inform the Tsar that everyone was ready to unite, but only if the government ceased persecuting the Finns, Poles, Jews and socialist leaders. Most party leaders refused to set a price on their patriotism and supported Milyukov. Kerensky's only supporters were the liberal Moscow industrialist, A. I. Konovalov, Nekrasov, and Chkheidze—all masons—and the Bolshevik Petrovsky.

Kerensky was so angry over this episode that he applied to Milyukov the motto of that infamously brutal nineteenth-century reactionary, Arakcheev, "*bez lesti predan*" [devoted without flattery], which—by the alteration of a single letter—became *bes, lesti predan* [a devil addicted to flattery]. It did not prevent him from making a final gesture to the "Supreme Power," for he jotted down his terms for unity and asked Rodzyanko to transmit them to the Tsar. Rodzyanko later assured him he had done so. "Naturally," concluded Kerensky, "my opinion had no significance at all at that time at Court, but I could not refrain from doing it."[7]

At the same time, Kerensky found himself at loggerheads with his socialist comrades. At the Basel Congress in 1912, the Socialist International had agreed to prevent the ruling classes from dragging the workers into a fratricidal war. When the time came to translate these brave words into action, few could withstand the jingoism of July 1914. Jaurès' assassination stilled the most powerful voice of French pacifism, while only Karl Liebknecht refused to vote for war credits in the Reichstag. This was a tremendous shock for the Russian socialists, who had always looked to the German socialists as their mentors. The socialist leaders in Russia had to make up their minds before news arrived of the "betrayal" of the German socialists, and in the absence of their major theoreticians. At first they agreed on a joint statement, but at the last moment Chkheidze told Kerensky that the German Social Democrats had opposed the war and that the Russian Social Democrats would echo their position in a pacifist statement. Kerensky thought the news was false and found Chkheidze's attitude "very depressing."

The socialists did at least agree to boycott the Imperial reception at the Winter Palace which preceded the Duma sitting on July 26.[8] Rodzyanko opened the proceedings with the Imperial Manifesto, his plummy presence the ideal vehicle for its paternal cadences: "Let the union between the Tsar and His people be stronger than ever, and let Russia, rising like one man, repel the insolent assault of the enemy."

Kerensky was the first to reply. Stressing the evils of warfare, he expressed the hope that the people of Russia would develop the unity required to liberate themselves from their internal enemies as a result of the war. He blamed *all* Europe's governments for the war:

Russians, citizens! Remember, that you have no enemies among the working classes of the belligerent countries. . . . remember that this frightful war would never have happened if the great ideals of democracy,—liberty, equality and fraternity,—had directed the activities of the rulers of Russia and the governments of all countries.

He referred to the continuing distress of the victims of the struggle for democracy and the oppressed nationalities, and he concluded:

Peasants and workers, all who desire the happiness and welfare of Russia, in the great trials harden your spirits, collect all your forces, and *when you have defended the country, liberate it.* [My italics—RA]

Kerensky would stick to this view of the war for the next eight months. The vote on war credits was uncontested. The Social Democrats walked out to avoid voting while the Trudoviks abstained.[9]

The war gave the Russian government a golden opportunity to repress the burgeoning opposition. Newspapers and journals were now subjected to rigorous censorship, militant workers were drafted into the army, and Jewish communities near the front were handed over to the rough justice of martial law. Even the Kadet *Rech'* was banned on one occasion until the government realized that it contained an unconditionally patriotic appeal from the Kadet Central Committee. Ever since the First World War, Russians of right and left have accused one another of having been unwilling to subordinate all other interests to those of "Russia." The truth is that in 1914, as in 1878 and 1904, the Tsar was not prepared to allow the war to become the occasion for a diminution of his powers, while the opposition was not prepared to see patriotism used to buttress autocracy.[10]

The suggestion that *all* Russia's workers abandoned all hope for revolution and a rapid peace in 1914 is, of course, a myth. There were still spirits bold enough to hand out antiwar leaflets and shout antiwar slogans; but, by comparison with the months before July, they were a small and increasingly demoralized minority. The mobilization of 18 percent of the workers, intense police activity, and anti-German sentiment in factories controlled or managed by German capitalists, helped to secure a rapid reduction in the incidence of strikes. There were isolated incidents where peasant conscripts refused to accept call-up in the middle of the harvest and the *Okhrana* even found a few peasants percipient enough to speculate that the war might provide an opportunity for getting rid of the landlords. They posed no threat to the government.[11]

The would-be leaders of the masses were bitterly divided. The Social Democrats were split four ways. On the right, Plekhanov, the 'Father of Russian Marxism' argued for unconditional opposition to German aggression. The Menshevik fraction of the Duma now assumed the direction of the Menshevik Organizing Committee, "accepting" the war but opposing the government until it made concessions. As the war went on, a third current—that of Menshevik-Internationalists—made its appearance, arguing for an immediate peace, but anxious to take advantage of the damage done by this war to the fabric of "bourgeois" society. Leon Trotsky and Julius Martov found their different ways into this tendency, as did Kerensky's war-time associate, Nikolai Sukhanov. Finally, Lenin and his supporters demanded the conversion of the war between nations into a war between classes.

These groupings were highly unstable. The Bolshevik Kamenev announced his opposition to Lenin's views, while the originally "defencist" Sukhanov became an "internationalist."[12]

The Socialist Revolutionaries were equally divided. In Paris, Vladimir Burtsev joined Boris Savinkov in the publication of *Prizyv* [The Call], whose patriotic fervor exceeded Plekhanov's. Most of the former SR terrorists and Avksentiev rallied to this position. The SR equivalent of the Menshevik Organizing Committee was the Foreign Delegation, founded by Chernov in 1915, though its views were closer to Martov's than Chkheidze's. Few of the SR exiles supported Chernov, and his delegation had only tenuous contact with SRs in Russia. One result was that left-wing SRs increasingly looked to the Bolsheviks for leadership. There were also a number of anarchist-communist groups which were inspired by pacifist or quasi-Leninist ideas. Altogether, party allegiances became less im-

САРАТОВСКАЯ губернія.

КЕРЕНСКІЙ

КЕРЕНСКІЙ,
АЛЕКСАНДРЪ ѲЕДОРОВИЧЪ.

Родился въ 1881 г.   Трудъ

Above. Olga Lvovna (née Baranovskaya), with Gleb and Oleg kneeling, about 1912. Inset: A.F. Kerensky in boyhood. (Suomen Kuvalehdet)

Below. The unofficial Lena Commission, Bodaibo, Siberia, summer 1912. Kerensky is second from right.

„БУРЕВѢСТНИКЪ“ ◆

№ 1. **ПОЛИТИЧЕСКАЯ НАРОДНО-СОЦІАЛЬНАЯ ГАЗЕТА.** № 1.

Выходитъ по Воскресеньямъ и Четвергамъ.

Въ борьбѣ обрѣтешь ты право свое! ✚ Воскресенье, 20 Ноября 1905 г.

Подписная цѣна съ доставкой и пересылкой по всей Россіи: на годъ—**3 р.**; на 6 м.—**1 р. 75 к.**; 3 м.—**1 р.**; 1 м.—**40** г. Отдѣльные номера—**5 к.** Рукописи, присланныя въ редакцію, подлежатъ въ случаѣ надобности сокращенію. Контора газеты—**Невскій, 110, кв. 28.** Открыта отъ 11—3 ч. Редакторъ принимаетъ отъ 5—6 ч. в. ежедневно—Загородный, 30, кв. 15.

ПРОГРАММА ГАЗЕТЫ.

Программа газеты партійная. *Въ политической и правовой области* наша газета будетъ стоять за установленіе демократической республики съ широкой автономіей областей и общинъ, какъ городскихъ, такъ и сельскихъ; за возможно болѣе широкое примѣненіе федеративнаго начала къ отношеніямъ между національностями; признаніе между ними безусловнаго права на самоопредѣленіе: прямое, тайное, равное, всеобщее право голосованія для всякаго гражданина не моложе 20 лѣтъ,—безъ различія пола, религіи и національности; пропорціональное представительство; прямо-народное законодательство (референдумъ и иниціатива); выборность, смѣняемость во всякое время и подсудность всѣхъ должностныхъ лицъ; полная свобода совѣсти, слова, печати; собраній, рабочихъ стачекъ и союзовъ; полное и всеобщее гражданское равноправіе; неприкосновенность личности и жилища; полное отдѣленіе церкви отъ государства и объявленіе религіи частнымъ дѣломъ; ажданго; установленіе обязательнаго, равнаго для всѣхъ общаго свѣтскаго образованія на государственный счетъ; ра..норавіе языковъ; безплатность судопроизводства; уничтоженіе постоянной арміи и замѣна ея народнымъ ополченіемъ.

1) *Въ народно-хозяйственной области:*

Въ вопросахъ рабочаго законодательства газета ставитъ свсею цѣлью охрану духовныхъ и физическихъ силъ рабочаго класса, для чего будетъ отстаивать возможно большее сокращеніе рабочаго времени въ предѣлахъ прибавочнаго труда; установленіе законодательнаго максимума рабочаго времени сообразно нормамъ, указываемымъ научной гигіеной (въ ближайшее время—8 часовая норма для большинства отраслей производства, и соотвѣтственно меньшая въ болѣе опасныхъ и вредныхъ для здо..овья); установленіе минимума заработка по соглашенію между органами самоуправленія и профессіональными союзами рабочихъ; государственное страхованіе во всѣхъ его видахъ (отъ несчастныхъ случаевъ, отъ безработицы, на случай болѣзней, старости и т. д.) на счетъ государства и хозяевъ и на началахъ самоуправленія страхуемыхъ; законодательная охрана труда во всѣхъ отрасляхъ производства и торговли, сообразно требованіямъ научной гигіены, подъ наблюденіемъ фабричной инспекціи, избираемой рабочими (нормальная обстановка труда, гигіеничность устройства помѣщеній, запрещеніе работы малолѣтнихъ до 16 лѣтъ, ограниченіе работы несовершеннолѣтнихъ, запреще-

..нскаго и дѣтскаго труда въ извѣстныхъ отрасляхъ производства и въ извѣстные періоды, достаточный непрерывный еженедѣльный отдыхъ и т. п.; профессіональная организація рабочихъ и. ихъ прогрессивно расширяющееся участіе въ установленіи внутренняго распорядка въ промышленныхъ заведеніяхъ.

2) *Въ вопросахъ аграрной политики и поземельныхъ отношеній* газета ставитъ себѣ цѣлью использовать, въ интересахъ соціализма и борьбы противъ буржуазно-собственническихъ началъ, какъ общинныя, такъ и вообще трудовыя воззрѣнія, традиціи и формы жизни русскаго крестьянства, и въ особенности взглядъ на землю, какъ на общее достояніе всѣхъ трудящихся. Въ этихъ видахъ газета будетъ стоять за соціализацію всѣхъ частно-владѣльческихъ земель, т. е. за изъятіе ихъ изъ частной собственности отдѣльныхъ лицъ и переходъ въ общественное владѣніе и въ распоряженіе демократически организованныхъ общинъ на началахъ уравнительнаго пользованія. Въ случаѣ если это главное и основное требованіе аграрной программы-минимумъ не будетъ осуществлено сразу, въ качествѣ революціонной мѣры, въ дальнѣйшей аграрной политикѣ она будетъ руководиться соображеніями о возможномъ приближеніи къ осуществленію этого требованія во всей его полнотѣ, выступая за возможныя переходныя къ нему мѣры, какъ напр.: расширеніе правъ общинъ и т.-рриторіальныхъ ихъ союзовъ по экспропріаціи частно-владѣльческихъ земель; конфискація земель монастырскихъ, удѣльныхъ, кабинетскихъ и т. п., и обращеніе ихъ, равно какъ и государственныхъ имуществъ, на то же дѣло обезпеченія общинъ достаточнымъ количествомъ земли, а также на нужды разселенія и переселенія; ограниченіе платы за пользованіе землею размѣрами чистаго дохода и издержекъ производства и нормальнаго вознагражденія за трудъ); вознагражденіе за произведенныя улучшенія въ землѣ при переходѣ пользованія ею отъ одного лица къ другому; обращеніе ренты путемъ спеціальнаго налога въ доходную статью общинъ и органовъ самоуправленія.

3) *Въ вопросахъ финансовой политики* газета будетъ агитировать за введеніе прогрессивнаго налога на доходы и наслѣдства, при совершенномъ освобожденіи отъ налога мелкихъ доходовъ ниже извѣстной нормы; за уничтоженіе косвенныхъ налоговъ (исключая обложенія предметовъ роскоши), покровительственныхъ пошлинъ и всѣхъ вообще налоговъ, падающихъ на трудъ.

Revolutionary Activism. *Burevestnik,* No. 1, 20 November 1905.
(Slavonic Division, The New York Public Library)

White Nights. Elena ('Lyolya') and Sasha Kerensky, St. Petersburg, 1900. (Kerensky Family Papers)

Sasha Kerensky on his mother's lap. (Kerensky Family Papers)

Fyodor Kerensky, just inside the pavilion at the right, at a meeting with Central Asian notables. (Harry Ransom Humanities Research Center, University of Texas in Austin)

Kerensky's parents: Nadezhda (née Adler) and Fyodor
Kerensky, in the 1890s. (Kerensky Family Papers)

Opposite top. Kerensky's clients. Lena miners after the massacre, 1912.

Opposite bottom. The cover of Kerensky's *Okhrana* file. The photo was crudely added, cut out of the issue of the Kadet paper, *Rech,* with the 1912 election results. (Suomen Kuvalehdet)

Top. Nikolai Nekrasov, Kerensky's closest political collaborator.

The last summer holiday. Kerensky with Oleg and Gleb, Kainki, Kazan
Province, 1913. (Kerensky Family Papers)

portant as "defencist" SRs worked with "defencist" Social Democrats and "defeatists" of all parties were drawn together.[13]

One of the key differences between the Marxist Social Democrats, who were mainly intellectuals and factory workers, and the radical Socialist Revolutionary intellectuals and ex-peasants was their attitude to ideology. The Marxist factions were cemented, and sometimes split, by ideology. The SRs were bound more by ties of kinship, the intangible fellowship of conspiracy, and the comradeship of struggle. In the absence of Chernov, Kerensky was able to exploit these features of the SR subculture to consolidate an SR organization inside Russia far stronger than the party had been since 1907. This story has been ruthlessly suppressed since 1917 not only by a Bolshevik government determined to deny Kerensky any revolutionary credentials, but also by Alexander Kerensky himself. Not a word of it appears in any of the memoirs Kerensky would publish after his emigration. Only in 1961, during a recorded conversation with a friend, Elena Ivanoff, did Kerensky make the following incoherent remark: "There, in Petersburg, I had worked simultaneously in the [Trudovik] group and restored the S-R organization in Petersburg, because... And I won during this time, because then, in the S-R milieu, after the Zimmerwald Manifesto, there began to filter in and permeate... "[14] Even this distorts his reaction to the conference of anti-war socialists in Zimmerwald, Switzerland, in the summer of 1915, as we shall see.

The Marxist intellectual Sukhanov spent many a night during the war arguing with Kerensky and he remembered that:

Kerensky took the most direct part in SR Party affairs; in so doing he so far abused his position as a deputy and his popularity, that living under the most thorough, unceasing and comprehensive observation by the police, he considered the rules of conspiracy obligatory only for others and, refusing to be restricted, entangled himself in countless possible pretexts for the most serious... judicial political trials.[15]

Toward the end of August 1914, Kerensky convened the Populists of the capital for a meeting. They agreed on the creation of a single, authoritative voice for Populism by merging *Russkoe Bogatstvo*, the mouthpiece of Mikhailovsky and Peshekhonov, with the less prestigious *Zavety* [Precepts]. The police retaliated by closing both. Only *Severnyia Zapiski* [Northern Notes] survived. Undeterred, the "non-party radical intelligentsia" of the capital met under Kerensky's chairmanship in the Free Economic Society to set up a so-called "Information Bureau." Kerensky, Ekaterina Kuskova, Professor L. I. Lutugin, A. A. Potresov, V. Ya. Bogucharsky and V. A. Myakotin were all members and Kuskova identifies most of them as Masons. They soon found SRs work in the hospital and library commissions of the Free Economic Society, while the Information Bureau used the Society's legitimate provincial ties for its own purposes. Kerensky was probably using his Masonic ties and abusing the immunity of an Imperial institution to foster the development of the PSR in his own image. This was not immediately obvious to the *Okhrana*, but they did notice that Kerensky and his comrades censored the reading material donated for convalescent soldiers, weeding out the contributions from right-wing organizations and from the Holy Synod, except for the Gospels. On the other hand, they forwarded opposition publications with a will.[16]

The government's decision to do without the Duma for as long as possible allowed Kerensky to tour the provinces "to counteract the right-wing tendency [*popravnenie*] in society, which had then just begun under the influence of military events." In Saratov, he urged small groups of comrades to mobilize the radical intelligentsia for struggle against the government, both underground and open. Agrarian cooperatives and workers' welfare organizations should be infiltrated. The government should be attacked for doing nothing to restrain the appetites of the rich, who were responsible for inflating the prices of essentials. This message should be passed on to the peasants, zemstvo employees, and soldiers about to return to the front. He assured them that a Petrograd Committee would soon finance an underground newspaper and direct the activities of provincial groups. The police record cites the resurrection of groups as far away as Irkutsk as a result of his agitation. When an active Moscow SR went to Petrograd, it seemed natural for him to visit both Kerensky, and the Bolshevik deputy Petrovsky.[17]

Shortly after the beginning of the war, the police had broken up an underground Bolshevik conference just outside Petrograd, arresting a number of leading Bolsheviks including Lev Kamenev. The arrest of the Bolshevik Duma fraction soon followed. When the Duma reconvened for a three-day session in January 1915, it did so in the absence of the Bolshevik deputies, who were awaiting trial. Only the Trudoviks and Mensheviks remained to denounce the illusion of harmony created by the other speakers. Kerensky attacked the delay in summoning the Duma, the harrassment of national minorities and internal repression. The government's charges against the Bolsheviks were "slander against our comrades." Again, he looked forward to "undoubted liberation from that power which has caused endless sufferings and endless unhappiness to our people."[18] This time, Rodzyanko took the initiative in censoring Kerensky's speech in the Duma record, but this did not save the Duma, which was prorogued on January 29. The following day, the police took their revenge on Kerensky by closing the Imperial Free Economic Society, and with it Kerensky's "Information Bureau."[19] This setback did nothing to deter him.

It was all very well for Lenin to take a principled stand against "social chauvinism." Safe in neutral Switzerland from Imperial gendarmes and patriotic demonstrators, he could accept the idea of Russia's defeat with perfect equanimity in the conviction that a European revolution was imminent. His comrades at home were uncomfortably aware that the penalty for treason was death and unsure how far their peacetime followers were prepared to follow Lenin's appeals. Emile Vandervelde, Chairman of the Socialist International and now a Belgian minister, begged them to give the Russian government their unconditional support. They refused this request but it was not until November 1914 that they were able to convene the meeting to discuss Lenin's views on the war, at which they were arrested. To the immense relief of all the Russian left, the Bolsheviks were charged not with treason but merely with membership in an organization dedicated to the overthrow of the state. Kerensky, Sokolov, and the other socialist lawyers came forward to defend them.

The stage was set for a show trial and the creation of martyrs. What followed was a bad case of funk. Under interrogation, the deputies had denied being at the Bolshevik conference; alternatively, they suggested it had been a wedding anniversary or birthday party. They had nothing to do with Lenin's organization in Switzerland. Kamanev denied that he was Kamenev and dissociated himself from Lenin's views on the war in court. Soviet accounts suggest that these tactics were simply "to make the legal examination more difficult," while admitting that the same result could have been achieved with greater dignity had Kamenev and all the deputies refused to testify—as one of them had.

Soviet historians asserted that all the Bolsheviks "entirely endorsed" Lenin's views, though this was denied at the trial by deputy Petrovsky, who pointed out that he had amended Lenin's Manifesto in his own handwriting. Petrovsky claimed that one of these alterations softened the impact of Lenin's "defeatism," by describing the defeat of "the Tsarist monarchy and its armies" as merely "the lesser evil" for the working class. Kerensky took this up in court, imploring the judges to consider that this substantially altered the content of the manifesto. He asserted that his clients' consciences had prevented them from following the directives of Lenin's Central Committee abroad. If the prosecution's case had been true, he averred, "many of us would not have occupied the defense benches in this case." In vain, he asked the judges to consider that the absence of national unity was the government's fault.[20] The deputies were sentenced to the deprivation of all civil rights and perpetual exile in Siberia.[21]

A piquant note in Petrovsky's diary helps to explain his behavior.

Illegal work ruins life, it requires an iron character, cold logic, unbreakable faith amongst all the suspiciousness of external and internal enemies. It is a blessing that my position saves me from this evil Russian lot.[22]

In the end, his position failed to save him, but he reminds us of the immense value of the immunity normally extended to members of the Duma, an immunity that was rapidly making Chkheidze Russia's leading Menshevik, and Kerensky Russia's leading SR. Lenin quantified the advantages conferred by the immunity of deputies. The exile of the Bolshevik deputies had made "the work of our party . . . 100 times more difficult," he wrote.[23]

Socialist intellectuals found the conduct of the Bolsheviks shameful. Working men and women, accustomed to evading arbitrary violence, may have taken a less censorious view. Still, the Bolshevik leaders had gone, and they were soon followed by several dozen Bolshevik activists in Petrograd. For some months the Bolshevik Petrograd Committee and many district committees ceased to exist and Bolshevik influence declined sharply. Veterans of pre-war strikes were replaced by women, youths, and old men, often straight from the land, who flooded into the factories. During the elections to the

Central War Industries Committee in autumn 1915, there were many factories where the Bolsheviks could not find a single worker sufficiently respected to carry their banner.

To whom could the Petrograd workers look for leadership? The answer was clear to E. H. Wilcox, the astute correspondent of the London *Daily Telegraph*:

> The arrest and sentence of the rest of the Bolshevik group in the Duma left . . . [Kerensky] the spokesman of the urban proletariat. The natural political heirs of the Bolsheviki would have been the Mensheviki; but there was no one in that party who could stir the artisans in the public galleries of the Tauride Palace as Kerensky did, and his word soon became law to the masses of Petrograd. In the industrial quarters on "the Viborg side," and in the ship yards and iron works at the mouth of the Neva, "What has Alexander Feodorovitch said?" or "What will Alexander Feodorovitch say?" were the final standards on all political questions.

Sukhanov also confirms his exceptional popularity.[24]

Kerensky did not forget the debt he owed the exiled Bolsheviks. In the summer of 1915, he sought an audience with the new Minister of Justice, threatening to cause a scene in the Duma unless the deputies were released within three days. Whatever the Bolsheviks may have said in private, he argued, they had renounced Lenin's 'defeatism' in open court. Minister Khvostov examined Kerensky's notes but he could not agree. Of course, they had only to denounce 'defeatism' for him to petition the Tsar for their pardon. Even Milyukov thought this was tantamount to asking the Bolsheviks to commit political suicide.[25]

★   ★   ★

Russia's advances into East Prussia in 1914 probably saved Paris, but the Germans stemmed the tide at Tannenberg in August 1914, and by early 1915, the Russians were retreating along the whole of the front with Germany. By midsummer, they began to retire from Galicia as well, in the face of an Austro-Hungarian army stiffened with German heavy artillery. Defeat brought a rapid decline in the prestige of the high command and the whole government. Competing cliques began to look for scapegoats and rumors were put about that the defeats were caused by espionage by officers close to General Sukhomlinov, the Minister of War. A scapegoat was found in the fussy and venal ex-gendarme, Colonel Myasoedov, formerly a protégé of Sukhomlinov's, who was executed after a summary trial in March 1915. Myasoedov had offended too many people in high places during his years in the gendarmerie. He had once fought a duel with Guchkov, the leader of the Octobrists, who had scores to settle with Sukhomlinov. No real evidence has ever been found for Myasoedov's guilt, but his execution provided all the evidence Society needed.[26]

Milyukov still refused to rock the boat, but Kerensky and Nekrasov were quick to turn the scandal to advantage. On February 25, 1915, Kerensky wrote to Rodzyanko alleging that leading figures in the Ministry of Internal Affairs, "in the interests of reaction, whose bulwark is Germany, regard a speedy conclusion of the war as necessary and for this purpose had allowed espionage which had been exposed by the military authorities," but not before the destruction of two army corps. "The Russian public knows quite well in which Ministries sit the patrons of the hope, still alive here, of coming to an understanding with the Berlin Government as quickly as possible, and thus of restoring the firmest and most indispensable support of internal reaction." Only the Duma, he concluded, could "protect the nation from the stabs in the back with which it is threatened." Thousands of copies of the letter soon appeared all over Russia, even reaching troops of the Moscow garrison—impressive testimony to the conspiratorial links forged by the masonic and SR networks.[27]

Kerensky must have received information from a very authoritative source to identify himself quite so closely with this demagogic campaign. Guchkov himself is an obvious possibility. Kerensky's own brother-in-law, Vladimir Baranovsky, is also a possible candidate. Some time during the war, Baranovsky wrote to Kerensky admitting that he had been partly right about the monarchy. Perhaps the most likely informant was Count A. A. Orlov-Davydov, an aristocratic landowner and deputy, with whom Kerensky became remarkably close during the war.[28]

The anti-Semitic right had no intention of taking this campaign lying down. Their revenge took the form of a campaign of slander against the Jewish inhabitants of the little town of Kuzhi in Kovno Province, who were alleged to have hidden German soldiers in their cellars so that they could surprise Russian units at night. Between April 27 and May 5, 1915, there were wholesale deportations of Jews from their homes in Kovno and Courland provinces. J. G. Frumkin and A. I. Braudo of the Jewish Political Bureau contacted I. V. Hessen, the editor of *Rech'*, who referred them to Milyukov. Milyukov refused to help on the grounds that "we are at war. This is not the time to criticize the military"; and at a subsequent meeting, he repeated that he "had no wish to please Berlin." *Rech'* failed to report the pogrom. The Jewish leaders then contacted Kerensky, who went to Kuzhi in person, examined the supposed hiding places, and concluded that the allegations were slanders. The Jews were delighted: "In his speeches at the Duma, Kerensky consistently disproved the slanderous, fabricated charges, citing the incontrovertible evidence he had obtained. Again and again, he protested vigorously the anti-Jewish measures introduced by the military."[29]

Not all his time was spent so arduously. Sometime before the war, Kerensky had been invited to join the Sunday night soirées at the famous Muruzi House of the Merezhkovskys. The Merezhkovskys had been virtually ostracized by the political leadership of the intelligentsia for their patronage of 'decadent' literature. In 1911, *Sovremennik* [Contemporary] omitted *all* poetry since, it opined, *all* Russian "poeziia" since 1900 had been an abuse of the term. Following their return from Paris, Dmitrii Merezhkovsky tried to mend fences, even penitently comparing the Populist balladeer Nekrasov to Pushkin, a comparison that left doubts as to his taste as well as his sincerity. Nevertheless, the barriers slowly came down and later editions of *Sovremennik* carried verses by Bunin and Khodasevich.[30] Zinaida Hippius, Merezhkovsky's wife, enjoyed the "delightful company of schoolboys and young poets" and found the courtly Kerensky very much to her taste. "Kerensky is not very clever, in that respect he has always been specially understandable and pleasant to me with all his boyish-brave ardour."[31] Since the 1905 Revolution, Hippius had been drawn to such right-SRs as Bunakov-Fondaminsky and Savinkov. As the only SR in the Duma, Kerensky was a natural candidate for the patronage of this charming but enigmatic woman.[32]

On May 15, 1915, Kerensky, Sokolov, Kartashev, and Dmitrii Merezhkovsky signed a declaration that unless there were revolutionary upheavals during the war, they would certainly occur at its conclusion, so Russians interested in liberty should organize themselves. Only the fear that the future of Russian liberty was now in doubt could have persuaded the puritan rationalist, Sokolov, to sign this document. Liberalism was in a state of crisis, with such ostensible liberals as Milyukov unable to grasp what was happening. Those Russians who loved liberty had to look within themselves for the spiritual resources to face the future.[33]

Olga and the boys had gradually gotten used to seeing less of Alexander Kerensky. Their sense of loss was tempered by their pride in his selfless and courageous work for civilized values and Russian freedom. His intense friendship with a woman with a notorious reputation (however misplaced) for bringing out the decadent inclinations of others was another matter, and Olga must have wondered whether this was strictly necessary. Relations between them were cooler but still respectful, and he was as good a father as time allowed, but he told her almost nothing about the things that mattered most to him.

War has a cruel way of revealing the emptiness of lives that seemed full. Olga had the love of her sons, but they were growing up. Her work for the Political Red Cross did not quite meet her need for emotional commitment. It was the war that brought this out, as it did for millions of women in all the belligerent countries. Thousands of educated Russian women, from grand duchesses to Lenin's sisters, volunteered to nurse the victims of the war. Olga did relief work with dependents of men at the front, but became "unsatisfied with this work," and became a nurse in the King Albert Hospital instead. This was "one of the happiest periods of my life," she remembered:

When I knelt over the filthy feet of the soldiers and washed them, or washed and re-washed their stinking, rotten wounds, I felt an almost religious ecstasy. I knelt before all the soldiers who had given up their lives for Russia. I never again experienced such ecstasy in life.[34]

A number of "Voluntary organizations" were now established to coordinate this widespread desire to help, and to steer it in politically desirable directions. The liberal leaders of these organizations were confident that they would demonstrate their superior competence over the government, thereby facilitating a smooth transition to constitutional government at the end of the war—or even sooner. Under the presidencies of Prince G. E. Lvov and M. V. Chelnokov, the Mayor of Moscow, an All-Russian Union of Zemstvos and a Union of Towns were formed to distribute relief among the soldiers. In May 1915, another organization was created by a much tougher-minded group. This was the Central War Industries Committee, and its local offshoots. Its leaders were Guchkov, the Octobrist leader, with interests in banking, insurance, and publishing; P. P. Ryabushinsky, the banker; Konovalov, a leading Progressist, banker, and director of insurance companies and owner of a cotton mill, and Mikhail Tereshchenko, a "sugar-king," whose factories employed 5500 workers. In August 1915, the government was obliged to give legal sanction to these organizations and concede them representation on new "Special Councils," with wide powers over various aspects of the economy.[35]

The Moscow industrialists knew that if they wanted to oust the Tsar's bureaucrats without disrupting the economy they would have to achieve a rapprochement with the workers. To this end, they organized a conference in Moscow, ostensibly to discuss inflation. When it opened in July 1915, some 900 delegates attended, representing industrial management, the cooperatives, and workers elected to the boards of sick benefit associations. Characteristically, the Social Democrats present objected to Kerensky's admission as a representative of the working classes, rather than an "expert"; but this was soon resolved.

Kerensky was now convinced that time for unity on Milyukov's terms was fast running out and confident that the military reverses were certain to provide political benefits. As he laconically put it, "Peremyshl fell: Maklakov resigned; Lvov fell: Sukhomlinov resigned; Warsaw will fall: Goremykin will resign."[36] He was also well informed about working-class anger at the shooting of striking textile workers in Kostroma. His speech in Moscow began with a militant denunciation of ritual invocations of "unity":

... gentlemen, these words, which we have heard throughout the last ten months ... what have they given us of substance? ... They call on you, representatives of the working classes, for cooperative work, and in the interests of the motherland. But I ask you, what is the motherland? Isn't it perhaps those same millions of peasants or workers? This is not the time to declaim old words. We must establish a new Russia and a new freedom.

And he lectured the liberals:

Those who turn to the workers and peasants must show by their actions that they have understood that a reconciliation is impossible with those who are leading Russia to destruction, not only internal but external.

At another of the sessions, he came close to demanding immediate revolution. "Gradualism is fine at other times . . . [but] now powerful demands must be achieved by a panther's leap."

Kerensky's attempt to re-create an SR organization under the aegis of the Free Economic Society had been checked by the police, but he was now more determined than ever to rebuild a viable national SR organization and to use it, in alliance with parallel Social Democrat organizations, to put so much pressure on the 'bourgeois' leaders of Duma and industry that they would themselves break with Tsarism. According to the Chief of the Petrograd *Okhrana*, Kerensky was "the central figure and initiator of the re-creation of the local organization of the SR Party, broken up by previous arrests." For this purpose, he toured Southern Russia and the Volga Region in the early summer of 1915, while the Populist writer, V. V. Vodovozov, toured the north. Kerensky was not simply trying to rebuild the PSR that Chernov had led from 1906 to 1914. He wanted to reunite the SRs with the other legatees of revolutionary Populism, the Trudoviks and the Popular Socialists. In words of rare generosity, even a Soviet historian acknowledged "the energetic attempts of A. F. Kerensky to unite all these tendencies in a single organization."[37]

The Moscow capitalists provided a tougher shield than the Petersburg intellectuals, and it was in Moscow that Kerensky was able to canvas SRs from all over Russia on his tactical and organizational ideas. The majority of SRs present supported him ("I won," he remembered), but a minority dissented, objecting to his position on the war and demanding an immediate revolution, "thereby demonstrating the revolutionary adventurism characteristic of the SRs."[38] This Soviet verdict on the future left-SRs is rather harsh considering the opinion of many Soviet historians that there was indeed a "revolutionary situation" in the summer of 1915. It is also misleading, since it implies that Kerensky did *not* want a revolution.

Armed with this support, Kerensky summoned a congress of all three Populist parties to his apartment in Petrograd on July 16–17. Thirty representatives from eleven cities attended, including such famous names as N. V. Chaikovsky, V. M. Zenzinov, S. L. Maslov, A. V. Peshekhonov and Vodovozov. A central bureau of populist organizations was established, with three representatives from each party. Given their diverse backgrounds, it is not surprising that their views on the war were rather eclectic. They accepted the Marxist view that it was caused by a struggle "for hegemony over economic markets," but as libertarians, they also blamed "the inadequate influence of democracy on the administration of the state." They demanded an immediate peace but urged the participation of the workers in the defense of the country from "external aggression," though they renounced foreign conquests in favor of plebiscites in contested areas. They also demanded a general amnesty, full human rights and "the democratization of the state structure from top to bottom," and the overthrow of the government and its replacement by a democratically elected government. Pending the convocation of a Constituent Assembly, the Duma might be used as a platform.[39]

Some radical SRs were still unhappy. P. A. Alexandrovich wrote to Alexandra Kollontai to complain (in a letter that Lenin found rather too undiscriminating), while Lenin himself received a letter from an SR, who said he was "waving goodbye" to the PSR. Lenin himself felt that those around Kerensky had done enough to justify their elevation in the hierarchy of Marxist terminology from the ranks of "social chauvinists" to "revolutionary chauvinists."[40] This was surely correct in view of the statement made by the July Populist Congress that "the moment for determined struggle for power has arrived." An SR leaflet distributed to the Volga Region gives some impression of what the Populists were saying to the people:

Citizens! For the sake of victory over the enemy, for the sake of the happiness of Russia, for the protection of the lives of millions of our brothers and sons, who stand there on the western frontier, unarmed, plundered, betrayed by their leaders, let us arise and overthrow this government, where stupidity is in close harmony with treason.[41]

Despite these rumblings from below, or perhaps because of them, Milyukov refused to bend to pressures from the left. On the contrary, he was encouraged by a government reshuffle—in which the Tsar had dismissed some of his most reactionary ministers—to believe that the arrival of parliamentary politics was imminent.

On July 19, 1915, Goremykin made the most friendly speech ever made by an Imperial Prime Minister to the opening session of the Duma. He announced no program, but hinted favorably at autonomy for Poland. Milyukov regarded this as a major concession, though most of Poland was already in German hands. Milyukov argued for an end to "cruel methods of police repression," but he also expressed himself emotionally in favor of the annexation of the Dardanelles, an "imperialist" demand that divided him from the socialists.[42]

Kerensky attacked Milyukov for choosing a Duma majority over a majority in the country, for preferring a pact with the *pays légal* to a mobilization of the *pays réel*. He himself demanded "that all the belligerent governments should renounce annexationist tasks in this war." He specifically demanded plebiscites in Poland and Eupen-Malmédy and even in Alsace-Lorraine, despite the Allied etiquette that defined Alsace-Lorraine as French territory rather than a French annexation. He gave notice that he and his comrades would not wait upon the success of Milyukov's efforts:
"I call not upon you, but upon the population itself to take into its hands the salvation of the country and whatever happens, to achieve the right to the administration of the state."[43]

The summer of 1915 witnessed divergent, yet interrelated, developments. One was the organization of a majority of the *pays légal* in the so-called Progressive Block. The other was the culmination of a wave of mass popular discontent, which began in the spring with the first major expressions of unhappiness over the war. This second development has been endlessly studied in Soviet historiography, though there is an understandable coyness about revealing the identity of the leaders of this movement, a coyness fully shared by Kerensky himself. (It is quite clear that it owed nothing to systematic German subversion, which was only just being planned.) There was a relationship between the two developments. Popular unrest impelled the Duma liberals to act, while liberal opposition suggested to the masses that successful mass action might succeed. In fact, Milyukov, who took himself for the master of the hour, could succeed only with the indirect backing of social forces he professed to abhor. "*Du glaubst zu schieben.*"[44]

Soviet historians accuse the moderate socialists of greeting the Progressive Block "with . . . wishes for successful work" and Kerensky later claimed that the block had "a program consistent with my own ideas about the future of the country." However, in an unpublished fragment, he points out that the note he had penned for Nicholas II in 1914 had become the program of the block, "only with/an irremed./delay" [*sic*]. When, in 1916, a Bolshevik suggested that the Trudoviks had been offended at being left out of the block, Kerensky replied that this was a lie: the block had been concocted in the greatest secrecy from the Trudoviks.[45] While technically true, this disclaimer is unconvincing in view of Kerensky's Masonic ties with some of the block's leaders.

The Progressive Block was an alliance of conservative liberals in the Duma, the State Council, and some of the ministries; it was designed to persuade the Tsar to appoint a "ministry of public confidence," which would seek the approval of the Duma. The question assumed greater urgency when, against the advice of most of his ministers, Nicholas II personally assumed the supreme command of the army on August 23, 1915. Nicholas II had more courage, and less sense, than Alexander I or Stalin, and the chief result of this rash action was to hand control of the government to the politically incompetent Tsarina and her friends, while making the Tsar himself responsible for defeat as well as victory. As a condition for their collaboration, the Duma liberals demanded an end to the persecution of national minorities and working class organizations. The program of the block was finally published on August 26, 1915 as a "loyal suggestion" to the Sovereign Emperor.

Prime Minister Goremykin had other ideas. He knew that the Tsar was irritated at his liberal ministers for opposing his assumption of the high command and he now maneuvered them into offering their resignations. The Tsar was easily persuaded to reject the resignations and prorogue the Duma. The Progressive Block,—and Russian liberalism,—had been dealt a blow from which it never recovered.[46]

All this was grist to Kerensky's mill. He and Chkheidze had been calling groups of workers (they would often entertain the workers at Kerensky's apartment) to urge them to create "factory commissions and collectives," under the pretext of resolving possible conflicts between workers and management, but in reality to create firm organizational units, whose delegates could proclaim themselves a "Soviet of workers' deputies," as in 1905. Kerensky told them that he and his friends were simultaneously creating a national network of committees of the intelligentsia. At the vital moment, they would appear in Petrograd and, together with the nascent Soviet, constitute a Constituent Assembly.[47]

The workers themselves recognized that their renewed militancy required coordination. In June, 80,000 had gone on strike, some in protest at the shootings in Kostroma. There was a lull in July, but August saw a massive strike of textile workers in Ivanovo-

Voznesensk, a Bolshevik stronghold. This time 100 strikers were killed and 40 wounded. Between August 17 and 19, 20,000 Petrograd workers in twenty factories struck in protest. Worried at this growing politicization of industrial disputes, the gendarmerie arrested the thirty most active workers of the giant Putilov factory. Between September 2 and 5, over 80,000 workers in Petrograd and 68,000 in Moscow went out on strikes and demonstrated against the government. Their demands were both political and economic. Resolutions passed demanded the release of the Bolshevik deputies, the democratization of the state, and civic freedoms, and also protested at the prorogation of the Duma.[48]

Underground Bolsheviks, Mensheviks, and SRs were all involved in this activity, but Kerensky, and to a lesser extent Chkheidze, played a crucial part in it. When the *Okhrana* archives were opened in 1917, the alert E. H. Wilcox discovered a police department letter, dating from late August or early September 1915, and asking for instructions on how to deal with Kerensky:

The strikes with a political background which are at present occurring among the workmen, and also the ferment among them, are the result of the revolutionary activity of members of the Social Democratic and Labor fractions of the Duma, and especially of the leader of the latter, the lawyer Kerensky. The revolutionary propaganda of Kerensky has expressed itself in the watchword "Struggle for power and for a constituent assembly," and had led to a systematic discrediting of the government party in the eyes of the masses. For the success of these demands Kerensky has recommended the workmen to establish impromptu factory groups for the formation of councils of workmen's and soldiers' delegates on the model of 1905, with the object of impelling the movement in a definite direction at the given moment, with the cry for a Constituent Assembly which should take into its hand the defense of the country. For the greater success of his agitation Kerensky is circulating among the workmen rumors that he is receiving from the provinces numbers of letters with the demand that he overthrow the Romanoff dynasty and take power into his own hands.

It describes Kerensky's relations with the Bolsheviks and Mensheviks and begs for directions on dealing with "the chief ringleader of the present revolutionary movement, the member of the Imperial Duma, Kerensky."[49]

Despite the later conspiracy of silence between Soviet historians and Kerensky to conceal Kerensky's pivotal organizational role within Russian socialism in the summer of 1915, some indication of the dilemma this posed the Petrograd Bolsheviks emerged from the publication in 1964 of Lenin's reply to a letter from A. G. Shlyapnikov, his representative in Petrograd. (Shlyapnikov's letter, now in the Institute of Marxism-Leninism in Moscow, has never been published.) Shlyapnikov had asked Lenin whether or not to *support* Kerensky, and Lenin replied in headmasterly fashion: "Our relations towards revolutionary chauvinists (such as Kerensky and parts of the SD-liquidators or patriots), can not in my opinion be expressed in the formula 'support'."

Lenin had no objections, however, to 'using . . . the revolutionary work' of the chauvinists, nor to "joint activities," nor even to reciprocal technical services, provided each side understood one another's position of principle on the war. In another letter, written on the same day to the SR "defeatist" Alexandrovich, Lenin confirmed that he regarded the activities of Kerensky and his associates as "revolutionary."[50] An even more curious tribute to Kerensky's prominence at this time was provided by the arrival of Count Paul Tolstoy, allegedly at the behest of the Tsar's brother Michael, to discover Kerensky's attitude toward the possibility that Michael might displace his brother on the throne.[51]

When the formal prorogation of the Duma was fixed for September 3, Kerensky and Chkheidze lobbied the other leaders in the vain hope that they might make a vigorous protest; but when the day came, only Kerensky's cry of "Long live the Russian People!" disturbed the funereal calm of the proceedings. The Duma was far too valuable a sounding board for him not to regret its dismissal and when he rang up Hippius, Kerensky blamed the government for consequences he considered inevitable. "What will happen now?" she asked.

"There will be that which begins with A . . . " he replied.

"Kerensky is right," she commented in her diary, "and I understand him; there will be anarchy. In any case, it is impossible to discount the clear possibility of *unorganized* revolution, called forth by the mad actions of the government to answer to the mistakes of the politicians."[52]

Unfortunately, neither soldiers nor peasants were yet ready to follow the workers of the capitals, and it fell to Kerensky and Chkheidze to know when to end a strike without losing their influence over the workers. They resolved this problem with some ingenuity. For example, they visited the Putilov factory and cut short a demonstration there by suggesting that the government had itself provoked the strikes in order to put them down, to which end it was even ready to conclude a separate peace with Germany! Kerensky warned a deputation of Putilov workers that came to his apartment not to protest over trifles, but to form their own unofficial organizations and then demand a Constituent Assembly. Once more, he referred to the letters he had received, urging him to take power himself.[53]

This was not quite the end of Kerensky's hopes for a revolution in wartime but it was the apogee of his influence over the industrial working class. Much is still vague, yet the evidence is unmistakable: In the summer of 1915, assisted by Nikolai Nekrasov, Nikolai Chkheidze, Vladimir Zenzinov, and many more, Alexander Kerensky came close to precipitating a revolution of the masses around "bourgeois" leadership. This attempt failed, as did a very different attempt by German-funded networks early in 1916. Yet it demonstrated quite remarkable audacity and outstanding organizational talent. Kerensky's attempted revolution does not deserve to be forgotten.

In trying to comprehend exactly what Kerensky was trying to achieve in 1915, we must put aside the prejudice that there is something unpatriotic about a revolution in wartime. Kerensky really did believe that an effete government was *losing* the war and that only the creative energies of the people could save Russia, a view that had sound historical precedents in 1610 and 1812. He himself compared this view to the attitudes generated by the Second World War:

the totalitarian psychology has poisoned even the consciousness of democracy. The assertion that a softening of a bureaucratic or a terrorist regime, the liberation of social initiative, can assist a war, can divert a country from a frightful dead-end,—such an assertion seems old-fashioned and naive. In 1915 we/they thought otherwise and we/they were right.[54]

The Progressive Block and the strike movement had failed, and an atmosphere of depression settled on the Russian intelligentsia, best articulated by the right-wing Kadet and Duma member, Vasily Maklakov. Using the "Aesopian language" devised by generations of Russian intellectuals he described a family being driven along a cliff

edge by a "mad chauffeur." The only possible course of action seems
to be to sit tight and pray,

But how will you feel when you realize that your self-restraint might still
be of no avail and that even with your help the chauffeur will be unable to
cope? How will you feel when your mother, having sensed the danger,
begs you for help, and misunderstanding your conduct, accuses you of
inaction and indifference?[55]

Kerensky and Chkheidze spoke for "mother" in this tragic scenario.

When the congress of the Union of Towns opened in Moscow on
September 7, Kerensky was still hoping that it might be induced to
rally the workers and proclaim itself a Constituent Assembly. Again
he was disappointed. The congress leaders conceded that the government might have been taken over by pro-German cliques but
refused to do anything overtly illegal. Sixty workers' delegates tried
to gain admission to the congress, enough perhaps to create a plausible "constituent," but the door was closed to them. When Kerensky
and Chkheidze asked to observe the proceedings as "correspond-
ents," that too was refused. In their own ad hoc meeting with the
workers, they discussed the strikes in Petrograd and passed resolutions censuring the Union of Towns for not admitting them and
demanding a Constituent Assembly. They warned the workers not
to strike, but to devote themselves to organizational problems. When
these had been resolved, Kerensky assured them no one would dare
ignore them.[56]

Conflict with the bourgeoisie also arose over the election of worker
representatives to the War Industries Committees. Guchkov, Konovalov, Tereshchenko and their colleagues were keen to co-opt
workers on to their committees to limit strikes, to marshal the support of the workers for their own struggle against the bureaucracy,
and as a kind of insurance against excesses of working-class militancy.
As bait they offered the workers an interval of almost total political
freedom in the factories for the duration of the elections, an alluring
prospect after months of repression.[57]

Some right-wing Mensheviks greeted this opportunity for an air-
ing of working-class grievances enthusiastically, but the Bolsheviks
and their allies vehemently opposed anything that smacked of collaboration in the war effort and set out to sabotage the elections. As
the principal members of the CWIC were Kerensky's Masonic breth-

ren, it comes as a shock to discover that he aligned himself with the Bolsheviks, advising his SR comrades to explain their nonpartici-pation in the elections as follows: "The workers can not consider themselves as expressing the opinions of the whole working class of Russia, for which a workers' congress is necessary." Such a congress would not be permitted, said Kerensky, and two advantages would follow: Society would be convinced that the workers did want to assist the defense of the country, while it would blame the govern-ment for its lack of sincerity in appealing to the workers to join the CWIC. [58] On September 27, 1915, the first meeting of the Petrograd worker-electors took place. A Bolshevik-SR block was victorious, though some right-wing SRs supported the Menshevik defencists. The defencist worker Kuzma Gvozdev then wrote a letter to the press alleging Bolshevik malpractice, a drastic breach of revolution-ary etiquette that must have appalled Kerensky. This provided the organizers with a pretext for annulling the first meeting and calling another one. This time the Bolsheviks and some SRs walked out of the meeting and Gvozdev's group was elected. [59]

Shortly after the prorogation of the Duma, delegates of the left-wing oppositions of a number of European socialist parties had gath-ered in the Swiss village of Zimmerwald to try to revive the Inter-national and define a socialist policy on the war. The Russians were represented by Lenin, Trotsky, Martov and Chernov, who described "Kerensky and his Duma group" as "patriotic" at the conference. The conference eventually adopted a manifesto, analyzing the origins of the war on Marxist terms, but it failed to embrace Lenin's call for transforming the war between nations into a war between classes. On the contrary, it demanded a "fight for peace—for peace without annexations or indemnities." It was signed by Lenin, by the Men-shevik Axelrod, and the left-wing SR Natanson. Chernov, who had proposed an amendment that was not accepted, did not sign. [60]

The *Okhrana* had no doubt that the Zimmerwald Manifesto was much better received by the Petrograd SRs than the simultaneous declaration issued by a conference of defencists, including Plekhanov and Savinkov, in Geneva. On October 17, 1915, an assembly of SRs gathered in Kerensky's apartment, though some left early because of police surveillance. They set up a commission to prepare an SR declaration on the war for preliminary discussion by local groups and cells before its ratification at a conference in December, at which a new Petrograd Committee of the PSR would be elected.

Kerensky prepared a draft for circulation to the groups whose radicalism shocked even the *Okhrana*. They had no hesitation in ascribing Kerensky's radicalism to the influence of the Zimmerwald Conference. "This is no war of liberation," Kerensky wrote, "no war for law and culture; both sides are merely struggling for world mastery." The government had to be totally destroyed: "Victory over the Rasputinite Autocracy of Nicholas II—this is our first and inescapable duty." The *Okhrana* also reported that this was no longer a matter of oratory or peaceful organization. Kerensky had founded a military organization called the Army of Popular Salvation and had joined it himself.

In reporting to the Trudovik group on November 10, Kerensky went a step farther, reporting that the country, "having lost all hope in a successful outcome of the war . . . wants peace and peace must be given to it." Even these views failed to satisfy some SR factory cells, which criticized his draft as "a compromise, permitting diverse interpretations," while the Petrograd district SRs objected that "it distinguished its point of view from the Plekhanovites . . . with in-sufficient sharpness and clarity." No doubt there were equally sharp criticisms from defencist SRs. At the Petrograd SR conference on December 8, Kerensky defended his draft precisely on the grounds that in excluding both victory and defeat it would have the widest resonance in all the belligerent countries. The aim was not sabotage and disorganization, but organization for the purpose of seizing power, "our immediate task." With some amendments, his draft was accepted. A proposal to expel the defencists was lost only on the formal grounds that this was a matter for an All-Russian SR conference.[61]

On November 20, 1915, a conference of opposition leaders met at Konovalov's Moscow apartment. Kerensky was there, still de-manding strikes or demonstrations. According to Kerensky, "there are no grounds for fearing that once begun, they will not stop when necessary thereby causing general disorganization . . . at the moment the popular mass is sufficiently disciplined."

A few days later, he, Vodovozov, and Maxim Gorky were guests of honor at a dinner of the "Fraternal Echo" society at the Petrograd lawyers' club. Kerensky's terms of reference were now very close to Lenin's. The Progressive Block had been doomed to failure since it combined the feudal-reactionary nobility and the bourgeoisie. He mocked society for underestimating the strength of the socialist masses organized in "democracy," and he appealed for a "Red Block" of the discontented.[62] Despite these optimistic appraisals of socialist organization, Shlyapnikov felt that the Petrograd SRs had been unable to create a strong organization, while Kerensky himself told the SR conference in December that "not a single one of the parties is in such a state of disorganization as ours."[63]

Kerensky's police file for 1915–16 presents a staggering picture of activity. The *Okhrana* reported him at fifteen major meetings over the winter,—and that only lists those penetrated by their collaborators such as the SR worker Yakov Surin. There were dozens they failed to penetrate. The *Okhrana* claimed that he controlled the personnel of the Petrograd employment exchange and the budding military organization. His "golden hands" obtained money to finance SR publications in Petrograd, Moscow, and Saratov. He traveled constantly to and from Moscow and he conducted a tour of the Volga that took him back to Samara, Saratov, and on to Tsaritsyn. He also fitted in work for the political freemasonry. Nor did he neglect the Merezhkovskys.[64]

In February 1916, Kerensky explained his reasons for an increasingly negative view of the war to his Trudovik colleagues in the Duma. Zimmerwald was a positive development, but the attitude of many socialists had changed not because of the conference, but "under the influence of fatigue, a conviction of the uselessness of further struggle and the consciousness of the proletariat that it was fighting for alien ideals." Two days later, he discussed the war with an outright defencist at the Merezhkovskys. Hippius sympathized with Kerensky.

the arguments get confused. A notable Russian characteristic: incomprehension of precision, blindness towards anything moderate. If I don't "thirst for victory," it means I "thirst for defeat." The slightest general criticism of the "victory-ites" simply ends in . . . if we are not nationalists, it means we are for Germany. Either be a "defeatist" openly and sit in prison as the fanatic Rosa Luxemburg sat there, or shut your eyes and shout "hurrah" without reflection.[65]

The beginning of 1916 saw a renewed explosion of working-class militancy and an increasing tendency for society to blame the government's failings on Rasputin and his pro-German friends. But Kerensky had run out of the short time granted to him to lead the revolutionary movement. Since June 1915, he had been suffering from tuberculosis of the kidney. As Hippius recalled, "Kerensky is ill all the time, white, like paper, claims he has 'tuberculosis'. However, he doesn't calm down but bounces about." Dr. Boris Sokolov found him immersed in work, "pale and feverish, yet smiling at his visitors and full of vitality." He seemed to feel he could defy both Tsar and Death with impunity, yet in the end his friends insisted on a period of rest in Finland. On February 12, 1916, he left for Bad Grankulla, the sanatorium run by Dr. Einar Runeberg, just outside Helsinki. Chkheidze was also unwell, so the Duma socialists were anxious for Kerensky to return quickly. They were disappointed. Not for seven months would Kerensky be fit to resume his responsibilities.[66]

Dr. Elena Kerenskaya accompanied her brother to Bad Grankulla, but it was probably Dr. Runeberg who referred him to Professor Frans Krogius. Krogius was appalled at his condition. For ten years, Kerensky had not spared his health and Krogius doubted whether his life could be saved. It all hinged on whether one or both kidneys was infected. On March 16, Krogius operated in the Surgical Hospital in Garrison street. One kidney was saved. Kerensky would suffer no further serious illnesses until advanced old age. This was not immediately apparent, and on April 9, he returned to Grankulla for convalescence.[67]

Kerensky's sudden departure for Finland had unnerved the *Okhrana*, who feared he was planning to contact the Finnish "Activists" who had formed battalions to fight for Finnish independence within the German army. They were relieved to discover that he was only ill, though his stay in such a small village proved embarrassing for them all the same. The police "tails" were ludicrously conspicuous and all the residents were soon aware that a prominent person was at the sanatorium. Kerensky made little attempt to contact Finnish politicians, but on his arrival he had given an interview to the press. In it he criticized the Progressive Block for including former supporters of the "Stolypin reaction" and attacked Milyukov's legalism, this time over Finland. Milyukov had just prevented a discussion of Finnish affairs in the Duma on the grounds that they were the exclusive concern of the Supreme Power.[68]

A few days after Kerensky's return to Grankulla, Hippius' play *The Green Ring* opened at the Alexandrinsky Theater in Petrograd. For once, Hippius employed a deliberately naturalistic dialogue to plead the cause of the nonsectarian youth who had grown up between revolution and war. A group of young people seeks relief from fatal emptiness in a mystical but informal association which assumes a collective responsibility for its members in a spirit of liberty, equality, and fraternity, somewhat like the political freemasonry. The young people felt that their doctrinaire elders treated them with a terrible mental cruelty, but they were determined to return good for evil.[69] Kerensky knew this play, as Hippius had taken him to some of its rehearsals. He, too, had suffered from the mental cruelty of the doctrinaires, Plekhanov and Lenin, Natanson and Chernov, Struve and Milyukov. Like Sergei, the play's protagonist, he would forgive them all.

Kerensky's initial frustration at the erosion of his leadership was mitigated by good company, as the spring of 1916 advanced. His host was a nephew of the compiler of Finland's national epic, *Kalevala*.[70] A frequent visitor to Bad Grankulla was Olga's cousin, Elena, née Baranovskaya. (Their mothers were sisters and their fathers were brothers.) Kerensky soon got to know her as "Lilya." She was a younger, less serious and more carefree version of Olga, and as his convalescence advanced, he found her visits more and more welcome.

6

Citizen Brutus

On January 9, 1916, massive strikes broke out in Petrograd and quickly spread to the naval shipyards of the Black Sea. This time the *Okhrana* found no evidence Kerensky was influencing the striking workers. It has since emerged that the renegade Polish-German socialist, Alexander Helphand, had received a million rubles from the German Foreign Ministry in December 1915, after promising that he could instigate a wave of strikes and precipitate a revolution in Russia. By the time Kerensky returned to Petrograd at the end of May, the strikes had been put down and the workers subjected to martial law. Once more the *Okhrana* rounded up working-class militants, to the relief of most of educated society. Only the workers' group of the Central War Industries Committee was spared.[1]

The second serious clash with the working classes had been decided to the government's advantage, and its morale was much improved. The army was in much better shape, too. It was considerably superior in morale and materiel to the army of 1915, as it proceeded to demonstrate in the "Brusilov offensive" in June. This improvement was not without its risks for the government, since it was partly the result of closer ties between the Special Councils, the War Industries Committees, and the Army High Command. The Allied Military Missions, intolerant of Russian inefficiency, may also have infected the military with attitudes more critical of the government.[2]

The Tsar now acted to exploit the gulf between the liberals and the socialists. He visited the Duma for the very first time, in order to congratulate Milyukov. The Foreign Ministry facilitated a visit to the Western allies by a Duma delegation, nominally headed by the moderate Octobrist Protopopov but led in fact by Milyukov. He was able to indulge an old ambition by speaking to heads of state and government in the West as an accredited representative of Russia. Milyukov hoped that this would have practical consequences when the war ended and when, he hoped, Russia's creditors would insist that the Duma retain control of Russian finances. The Trudoviks and Mensheviks were also offered places on this delegation, but it offended their democratic and their internationalist principles, so they declined.[3]

The government pressed its advantage by using the Duma itself to suggest to the peasant soldiers that the socialists were not really their friends at all. It used demagogic agitation against Russia's German and Jewish subjects and offered the peasants "civic equality." Kerensky claimed that the bill on peasant rights contained nothing that had not been conceded under duress in October 1906, but he could not prevent it from dividing the Kadets from the socialists. Maklakov commented ironically, "I think that Member of the Duma Kerensky would even be happy if this bill were rejected. True, the peasants would not get anything, but on the other hand, they would read an attractive and beautiful speech."[4]

Kerensky made twelve speeches attacking the bill in sixteen days. On June 3,—his first appearance since his operation,—he spoke for so long he had to pause for an early lunch so that he could regain his strength. He did his best to demolish the government's credentials as friends of the peasantry, asserting that all Russian cabinets since 1906 had been "cabinets for the defense of the nobility." He sneered at the patriotism of a government which had used German expertise in its agrarian "reforms." If the nobility really wanted to forget "their caste greatcoats" and go to the peasantry, they should follow the example of the Decembrists. Some days later, Kerensky became even more worked up when right-wing deputies referred to "Jewish espionage." There might be Jewish spies, but this gave no one the right to call espionage "Jewish," he insisted. "If, after Myasoedov and Sukhomlinov, anyone dared to call all Russians spies, in my presence, he would perhaps, not leave the spot." Did all this vehemence stem from physical weakness and nervous exhaustion, or did he fear that Tsarism would successfully exploit its victories to evade the nemesis he and his comrades had prepared for it?[5]

As Kerensky pointed out in that first speech on June 3, the revolution that had seemed so imminent in 1915, was now apparently remote. "We will struggle for freedom, law and justice for all ... the ideals laid down by the movement of 1905 will arise and those ideals will be taken up by the movement *after the war*" [My italics— RA].[6] In the steering committee on June 20, he called once more on the other factions to demonstrate against the prorogation of the Duma, but once more he was ignored. When Rodzyanko later remonstrated with him for his "irresponsible" behavior, Kerensky allegedly replied, "the platform is one thing, where obedience to party slogans is required; the substance of the matter, considered impartially, is another." This is the first recorded incident suggesting that he was beginning to find the discipline of the reconstituted SR Party a trifle irksome.[7]

In private meetings with the Trudovik deputies, he now proposed a reversion to the agitational-organizational tactics of 1913–14, advising them to gather information on all aspects of the welfare of the people, on abuses committed by the authorities, attempts by the right to discredit the Duma, and on corruption in the administration. He was anxious for Trudovik speeches on peasant rights and the Jewish question to be printed and distributed among the people.[8]

Kerensky had left Bad Grankulla only two months after the operation, and before his right kidney had fully adjusted to the extra activity required of it. This was not a long period of convalescence in those pre-antibiotic days. At any rate, he returned to the sanatorium for a further six weeks. He arrived in time for the Midsummer Festival, a time of fragrant woodland smells, evening calm, and haunting midnight light. He was closely observed by Alma Söderhjelm, Finland's first woman professor, who remembered:

We were really good friends; he used to read aloud from Russian papers for me and comment on military events and then translate into French as he read. . . . I sat outside and chatted with Kerensky and his admiring coterie. Their table was furthermore always loaded with all that which the Russians like to eat between meals: caviar and chocolate and other things. Kerensky had a mass of good things sent daily by his male and female admirers in Petersburg.

It was in this slightly sybaritic atmosphere that Kerensky fell in love with Elena Baranovskaya.[9]

Elena (Lilya) Vsevolodovna Baranovskaya was born in 1892. Her father, Vsevolod Baranovsky, and his brother, Lev, Olga's father, had gone to school in Helsinki. Like his brother, Vsevolod served in a glamorous guards' regiment and in the 1878 Turkish war. He secured a brilliant future for himself by graduating in 1883 from the Academy of Military Law. He then married Lydia Vasilieva, Olga's aunt. Vsevolod and Lydia's first child, Vera, was born in 1885. A brilliant actress, Vera's debut at the Moscow Arts' Theatre came in 1906, in a production of A. K. Tolstoy's *Tsar Fyodor Ioannovich*. Eventually, she would become one of the most famous film stars in Russian cinema history, playing the title role in Pudovkin's production of Gorky's *Mother*.[10]

In 1894, Lilya's family moved to Turkestan and it is just possible that she saw Kerensky portray Khlestakov in his school's production of *The Inspector General*. By 1912, Lilya had met and married Nikolai Biryukov, a successful soldier some years her senior. In 1913, she gave birth to a son, who was named after his grandfather. In the same year Vsevolod Baranovsky was appointed to the Imperial Finnish Senate, the Finnish cabinet appointed by the Tsar. When the war came, Lilya began to study medicine while her husband was promoted to the rank of Colonel. Her marriage was not too restricting for she commuted freely between the sumptuous official apartment of her parents in Helsinki and her husband's apartment in Petrograd.

Unlike Olga, Lilya was brought up by a couple who enjoyed a successful marriage, who had no reason to share the puritan attitudes of the ascetic Academician Vasiliev and his disappointed younger daughter. Lilya probably shared the "bureaucratic" charm Olga eschewed and she had the resources to indulge in cosmetics and the trappings of femininity for which Olga had neither time, money, nor interest. As the Empire crumbled, she found her way from the protection of a leading Tsarist official, her father, to that of a leading revolutionary.[11]

Was this an egotistical and self-indulgent symptom of revolutionary exhaustion of the kind fictionalized in Andreyev's *Darkness* or Savinkov's *Pale Horse*? Kerensky's simultaneous friendship with the patroness of "decadent" literature invites such speculation, but the evidence suggests that Kerensky spent the minimum time required for his convalescence at Bad Grankulla. Nor did he deceive his wife. He asked for a divorce.[12]

Kerensky's confession came as a double betrayal for Olga, who had met Lilya as a friend as recently as 1914. In her anguish, she turned to Dr. Elena Kerenskaya. "Lyolya" begged her to refuse the divorce. "He needs you and the boys," she said. Olga found mitigating circumstances: his incessant work, his ill health, her own absorption in the upbringing of the boys and the nursing of the wounded, but she could not fully condone what he had done. Their new apartment on Tverskaya offered her greater privacy, but she allowed him to live under the same roof so that he could see the boys. She extracted no pledges of good behavior and it was he who insisted the boys be told, even though there was to be no divorce.

Unfortunately, this compromise was all too characteristic of the Russian intelligentsia,—a high-minded attempt to reconcile the irreconcilable. When he continued to visit Lilya, there were acrimonious scenes between him and Olga. They were acutely unhappy together, an unhappiness for which Kerensky always assumed full responsibility.[13]

Kerensky's romantic convalescence was rudely interrupted by horrifying news of rebellion in Central Asia. On August 13, 1916, he left Bad Grankulla on a four-day train journey through Russia and the Kazakh Steppe to Tashkent. What he found there shocked him beyond measure and probably contributed to his growing antipathy to "Zimmerwaldist ideas."[14]

The Russian army had begun to feel a severe shortage of manpower in 1916. The answer seemed to lie in the recruitment of Russia's colonial subjects to build fortifications behind the front line. The recruitment was inefficient, tactless, and corrupt, and on July 6, riots broke out which soon broadened into full-scale revolt and intercommual massacres. The Central Asian paradise of Kerensky's youth had been transformed into what he called the Turkestan Front. Thousands of Russians and tens of thousands of Central Asians had been killed. Women had been raped, bodies mutilated, huts and crops burnt down. Kerensky was able to see for himself the mass burials, the tearful widows and children, and the famine-stricken survivors. He must have been haunted by the memory of his father's efforts to make this place an example of civilized progress. His own monarchist younger brother, "Fedya," who resembled their father in face and manner, was there to inquire whether this was what he planned for the whole of Russia.[15]

Kerensky visited Samarkand, Dzhizak, Fergana, and Tashkent with the Islamic deputy, Kutlug-Mukhamed Tevkelev. They were cordially received by Governor-General Kuropatkin, and soon satisified themselves that right-wing allegations that the rebellion had been provoked by Turkish agents were untrue.

It was strange and surprising, gentlemen, for me to see how deep was their naïve faith, the naïve enthusiasm immanent in that dark mass and directed not to the Sultan of Turkey, not to foreign agents, but to us, to that very Russian state to which they have bound themselves;[16]

The blatant historical untruth of this last claim suggests that, as usual, Kerensky agitated as he investigated.

Kerensky told the Duma that the revolt was caused by "the criminal activity of the central power." The instructions to the Central Asian authorities had been illegal in form and content, and had been drawn up without reference to the local authorities. The conscription of 250,000 Central Asians during the *Ramadan*, which happened to coincide with the harvest, among a population previously exempt from military service, was bound to cause trouble. In the absence of records of age, young men bought exemptions, while poor men of sixty had been conscripted. The army had employed barbaric methods to quell the revolt, including summary executions, the confiscation of property, and the destruction of entire villages. The damage to Dzhizak surpassed any Kerensky had seen on the front with Germany. Curiously, he went as far as a socialist possibly could to exempt Kuropatkin, "the white crow," from this criticism.[17]

Soviet critics charge that Kerensky criticized only "individual shortcomings and methods of the administration by Tsarism of a colonial policy, which he really supported."[18] Of course, he wanted Russia to hold on to Central Asia, just as his Soviet critics do, but his attack on the administration went further than they imply. In denying that only Asian officials were corrupt, Kerensky argued that "they were only agents in the hands of the Russian administration, which even earlier, in close union with and through those same agents enriched themselves, blackmailing and exploiting the population."

these Russian administrators, who rule in the name of a great European country, are not better, but worse than those satraps of Bukhara and Turkey, for they do not have such refined methods for exterminating the population.[19]

Kerensky's failure to mention atrocities committed by some of the Central Asians left some of the Duma liberals unsatisfied. Kerensky replied: "For what the dark masses, Kirgiz or Russian did, they are not to blame; no-one taught them anything, no-one ever inculcated the principles of law and justice into them." When pressed, however, Kerensky admitted that political etiquette inhibited him from describing the excesses of ordinary Central Asians and Russians. It was simply "too painful" to describe such horrors.[20]

Nor did Kerensky analyze the economic and social consequences of colonialism. Was the treatment of the Kirgiz not uncomfortably like American treatment of the Indians? What difference would it make if Russia had an American-style constitution? Did the Central Asians have the right to secede and, if not, how were nationalist mutinies to be dealt with? For a man who was by turns a Russian nationalist, a democratic socialist, and an opponent of the death penalty, these were uncomfortable questions.

Embarrassing questions of a different kind were put to Kerensky in autumn 1916 over a comic-opera scandal surrounding his close friend, Count Orlov-Davydov. The Count was a caricaturist's gift, obese and short-sighted, aristocrat enough to spend the night with a French singer, but enough of a Tolstoyan to make an honest woman of her and save his child from bastardy when Mlle. Poiret announced her pregnancy. Kerensky had read and admired *Resurrection* and he could never refuse a noble gesture, so he accepted the invitation to be the Count's best man with alacrity. Unhappily, the butler found evidence that the child provided by the new Countess had been bought for the purpose. Kerensky was thus called as a witness in a divorce case that delighted and titillated wealthy socialites bored by the war. Not even Olga could understand why Kerensky should court such ridicule for the sake of a titled millionaire. The right-wing Zamyslovsky baited Kerensky in the Duma: "Let him tell how he became the best man," but Kerensky found no difficulty in ignoring one of the instigators of the Beilis trial.[21]

In the early autumn, Kerensky had returned to the Volga region in the wake of a rash of strikes, which had taken the underground socialist organizations by surprise. This had not prevented the police from rounding up another swathe of militants and dispatching them to join the members of Kerensky's underground networks picked up during his illness.[22] Denied permission for a public meeting in Saratov, he gave a private gathering of comrades his view of the "Brusilov offensive." The government was torn between its financial dependence on the Allies and its political leanings towards Germany, so it would order offensives to please the Allies and then undermine their success by limiting the operations of the Voluntary Organizations.

From Saratov, Kerensky proceeded to his "home" in Volsk, where his police shadows were mistaken for supporters and arrested by the local gendarmerie. By the time they had resumed their duties, Kerensky was delivering a report to another group of supporters over tea. He was scathing about the Kadets, who had moved to the right to patch up the Progressive Block and he warned that the coming winter would be decisive, as food supplies were becoming increasingly unreliable. He expressed his satisfaction that the halting of the Brusilov offensive had lowered government morale once more and at "the nervousness of Society."[23]

On the steamer to Samara, Kerensky had a moment of melancholy. He was suddenly afraid that he might never see the grand old Mother-River of Russia again. His Samara comrades greeted him joyfully and dissuaded him from going straight on to Petrograd to lobby for the release of his comrades in Saratov. "No", Kiryakov told him, "you must stay. The lecture has been permitted and the seats have been sold already."

"How's that?" Kerensky laughed, "In Saratov the Governor forbade me to hold a lecture. . . . "

"We are in another state and with us the states are disunited, not United," Kiryakov joked. "For once it's turned out for the best." After a moment's silence to honor fallen comrades, Kerensky launched into a ferocious attack on Milyukov and the Progressive Block. During an interval, he wondered if he had not been too harsh. "Are we ourselves doing all that is needed?" he asked. After the break, he returned with a more expansive and optimistic message.

"I can already hear the march of the people distinctly," he declared. "Prepare to meet it ... Prepare yourselves to walk with the people step by step and hand in hand." His listeners were ecstatic and crowds of young people thronged the main entrance to cheer his departure. For once, he disappointed them by leaving by a side door.[24]

By the onset of winter 1916, police repression and divisions over the war had radically undermined Kerensky's position in the PSR. Chernov's emissary, P. A. Alexandrovich, was now at the helm of the Petrograd SRs, while the Moscow SRs were issuing violently anti-war leaflets. "We can only avoid famine by overthrowing the autocratic government, by stopping the war," they declared. "Down with the war! Down with Autocracy! Long live the Russian Revolution!"[25] Kerensky and Zenzinov responded by organizing "a small group, mostly of workers," who passed a resolution in favor of continuing the war on a defensive footing, since a defeated Russia would be dependent on either Germany or the West. Kerensky had come down in favor of defencism at last, and it is not surprising that he began to collaborate with the workers' groups of the war industries committees. Even in conspiratorial meetings, he was now urging Populist intellectuals to press for a "responsible ministry, which can be achieved by the pressure of all social forces on the government." These were Milyukov's objectives, though Kerensky was prepared to use more radical means to achieve them.[26]

The first "bourgeois" party to accept Kerensky's overtures was the quintessentially capitalist Progressist party, which on the eve of the autumn session of the Duma, finally withdrew from the Progressive Block, a gesture of no confidence in Milyukov.[27] But if Kerensky seriously hoped to create an alliance of all democratic forces, he would have to persuade the party representing most of Russia's best educated citizens, the Kadets themselves, to desert their Octobrist allies. Nekrasov had repeatedly challenged Milyukov's tactics, but just as often, Milyukov, supported by Struve, Izgoev and Tyrkova, beat off the challenge. In his frustration, Kerensky publicly mocked Milyukov's policies. "What poor, miserable activity," he wrote, "what a hopeless undertaking; to perform the task executed by Hercules in the famous stables with white gloves on!"[28]

Almost all educated Russians now harbored the fear that the government would soon make a separate peace with Germany. They felt they had to prove that any separate peace would be tantamount to treason. Spy-mania gripped factory workers, intellectuals, generals, and ministers alike. Suspicion focused on three key figures. Boris Stürmer, appointed Premier in January 1916, was a gray-haired nonentity cursed with a German name, who aroused Allied hostility by protecting Sukhomlinov and sacking Foreign Minister Sazonov. A. D. Protopopov had reneged on his Octobrist comrades to accept the Ministry of the Interior. He had also been incautious enough to talk peace terms with a German banker in Stockholm on his way back from Paris and London. There was also Rasputin, whose intimacy with the Imperial Family was now public knowledge; the Tsarina's dependence on him was often given the grossest interpretation. Rasputin had secured the dismissal of Minister of Justice Khvostov, who retaliated by telling everyone he met (including Kerensky) that he had seen evidence to prove that Rasputin was a German spy.[29]

Milyukov now decided that the only way to prevent a further attrition of his influence would be to make these accusations his own. If "Zimmerwaldism" could be identified with Rasputin's friends, any change of government would reinforce rather than weaken the commitment of the Russian people to the war.[30]

The Duma reopened on November 1, 1916, with a declaration by the Progressive Block which was sharply hostile to the government without mentioning the word "treason." Chkheidze wondered whether the Block had lost the courage of their convictions. His own Marxist analysis of the war ended with a demand for the "liquidation of this frightful war." Chkheidze had been less opposed to the war than Kerensky in 1915; he was now the greater pacifist.

Kerensky tried to bridge the gap between patriotism and socialist internationalism demanding that "the bloody whirlwind into which the democracy of Europe was drawn at the instigation of the ruling classes, must be ended; a term must be set to it!" On the other hand, he now described the patriotic unity of 1914 in much warmer terms. "Hasn't everything possible been done, gentlemen, all the time, to destroy the enthusiasm and buoyancy that was in the Russian state?" The government was demoralizing the people and then setting them at one another's throats in the search for scapegoats. He himself was the first to name names. This campaign had been "directed by the whisperings and instructions of irresponsible circles, guided by the contemptible Grishka Rasputin!"

The acting president cautioned Kerensky when he called the ministers "hired assassins" and "cowards," but Kerensky repeated that there was no greater enemy than the enemy within. He urged the people: "before you . . . finish off this fratricidal war between the peoples, before you . . . conclude a peace worthy of international democracy, you must yourselves achieve the right to direct and participate in the affairs of state." He invited the Progressive Block to "fulfill your fundamental duty before the country: you must destroy the power of those who are not conscious of their duty. They must depart, they are traitors to the interests of the country." Too late, he was ordered off the tribune. He had called for the overthrow of the government in wartime.

Milyukov's speech was more than three times as long as Kerensky's and much less fiery. This time, however, its moderate language made it more deadly than Kerensky's passion. For the most part, it consisted of circumstantial attacks on the government, punctuated by the rhetorical question: "Is this stupidity or treason?" Stürmer was attacked for frustrating the Duma's attempt to impeach Sukhomlinov. Allied suspicions of the reasons for Stürmer's appointment and Sazonov's dismissal were related. Milyukov read out comments on the German and Austrian press on Stürmer's appointment, which came down to the speculation that since Stürmer was bound by no personal pledge to the Allies, he might opt for a separate peace. For the first time, Milyukov was bolder than Kerensky. Where Kerensky had named Rasputin, he aimed even higher. Exploiting the acting president's ignorance of German, he read out the verdict of a Viennese newspaper on Stürmer's appointment: "*Das ist der Sieg der Hofpartei, der sich um die junge Zarin gruppiert.*" [That is the victory of the court party assembled round the young Tsarina.][31]

Milyukov's provocative use of the phrase "stupidity or treason," and the government's failure to make a convincing response, "created a sensation in the Duma," Hippius recorded, "They simply shut the mouths of Chkheidze and Kerensky." The Duma record was not printed immediately, but in the meantime the speeches circulated in millions of typed and handwritten copies. Even the Bolshevik Shlyapnikov had to admit that "all the institutions . . . of all Pieter were occupied with the copying of those speeches, and they had probably never been distributed in such quantities as they were then." The reaction was exactly what Milyukov had counted on, as the

Okhrana reported: "The sitting of 1 November 1916 inclined the broad masses to turn more confidently to the Duma, in which they suddenly began to see 'the best representatives of the people,' 'the representatives of All the Russias,' etc." Telegrams of congratulation poured in from all over Russia, and Milyukov became the darling of the officers at the front, whose failings he had effectively excused.[32]

The government forced the acting president to resign and introduced military censorship for Duma speeches, but Nicholas II felt he had no option but to dismiss Stürmer, the first and last time the Duma secured the dismissal of a Tsarist Prime Minister. The new Prime Minister, A. F. Trepov, was little improvement. The socialists saw him as the younger brother of the butcher of the 1905 Revolution and when the Duma reconvened on November 19, they banged on their desks and shouted "Down with Trepov!" and "Away with him!" The Duma majority was still not ready to condone such caddish tactics, but they showed their sympathy by excluding the socialists for only eight sittings, half the penalty imposed for the similar demonstration in 1914. Even this enraged Kerensky, who threatened hyperbolically, "Exclude us and tell the country that between the people and you there is nothing in common." Some days later, Rodzyanko was approached by a delegation of workers, appealing for a lifting of the suspension of the socialist deputies. He told them unctuously that he might have done so but for their petition, but he would not do so under duress.[33]

In the end the Duma majority found a way of making amends by the unprecedented gesture of electing two Trudoviks (including Kerensky) and two Mensheviks to the Commissions on Military and Naval Affairs. This did not satisfy the socialists. On December 8, they clashed with the Progressive Block in the debate on local government, arguing that "the patient needed an operation rather than a change of sheets." Kerensky's anxiety for Kadet support emerged when Shingaryov accused him of talking like the extreme right.

Gentlemen, it is necessary for the whole mass to rise up as one man, for the whole country to be fired by enthusiasm, to push towards the great cause for the whole nation, forgetting its differences to throw itself into the creative work of saving the state in one impulse, by its joint efforts!

This was probably the speech that provoked Milyukov to take the unusual step of congratulating Kerensky on a fine performance.[34]

An additional reason for Kerensky's increasingly "above-party" tone was his increasing eminence within the political freemasonry. According to I. Ya. Halpern, Kerensky became Secretary of the Grand Council of the Masonry of the Peoples of Russia at this time. This is corroborated inferentially by Blodnieks' recollection that at its congress, Kerensky delivered a speech, "historical at least by its length—full six hours."[35] This may also be seen as a symptom of the radicalization of Russian society that was everywhere apparent. On December 9–11, 1916, the Congress of Zemstvos met in Moscow without police permission and passed a resolution demanding the creation of a government responsible to the country and the Duma. On December 16, the ultraconservative United Nobility passed a final resolution demanding the elimination of "dark forces in the affairs of state," and the conservative Duma unanimously accepted the report of the socialist Kerensky on Central Asia.[36]

Not everyone kept pace with these portents. The right-wing Kadet Izgoev was still accusing Kerensky and Konovalov of forming an anti-Progressive "Red-Black" block with the right, but by mid-December even Milyukov was telling the Duma that "the social struggle is leaving the framework of strict legality and the illegal forms of 1905 are being reborn." He warned that lightning was about to strike. Kerensky chided the left-Octobrist Shidlovsky for saying that he was no revolutionary, comparing him to Molière's hero who does not know he has been speaking prose all his life. "The process in which Sergei Iliodorovich Shidlovsky is participating *is* a revolutionary process." He concluded with a shocking parable:

No long ago a policeman raped a seamstress who was going home at night. Another representative of authority ran up to render him assistance, and did the same . . . (interruption from the chair) . . . What would have been the situation if a citizen who, instead of carrying away the victim from the rapist and throwing the latter to one side, had said that "according to the law" he would report the matter tomorrow to the appropriate agency?! Wouldn't that have been worse conduct than a simple "failure to oppose evil"? If the government uses the law and the apparatus of state administration solely to rape the country, to drag her to ruin, it is the obligation of the citizens not to obey the law.[37]

The following day, Rasputin was murdered by Duma deputy V. M. Purishkevich, Price Felix Yusupov and the young Grand Duke Dmitrii Pavlovich. The lightning heralded by Milyukov had struck once. Where would it strike next?

Rasputin's murder was greeted euphorically by society and condoned by the grand dukes in a collective letter to Nicholas II, but it did nothing to bolster the monarchy, and it alienated the Tsar even further from the Duma. It had not been the only plot under consideration at the time. Since the autumn of the previous year, chatter about plots to rid the country of Rasputin, the Empress, or even the Tsar had become commonplace, though Rodzyanko and Milyukov disowned such talk, at least in the their official capacities. Such soundings compromised large numbers of public figures and senior army officers and gradually loosened their commitment to their oaths of loyalty.[38]

The most significant plot involved Kerensky's Masonic brethren, Nekrasov and Guchkov. It arose from a discussion in September 1916 between the leaders of the Octobrist, Progressist, and Kadet parties. Milyukov had invited them to consider how best to avert a revolution "from below," though most felt that nothing could be done until the Tsar himself appointed a "ministry of confidence." Should a revolution from below occur, the leaders of society would have to intervene. Guchkov was unconvinced. Why should those who made the revolution hand power to Milyukov? Only Nekrasov supported him. Later, he saw Guchkov privately and they decided that a coup d'état was the only way to save Russia.[39]

The conspirators co-opted Tereshchenko, Price Vyazemsky, and General Krymov onto their staff. They planned to surround the Imperial train between Petrograd and Army GHQ and force the Tsar to abdicate in favor of his young son. The plot incurred the disapproval of most freemasons and there were moves to expel Guchkov, another example of the movement's lack of cohesion. Kerensky was not involved in the plot but was kept informed of its progress "since we did not want at any cost to allow a revolution in the form of an elemental explosion." He was allowed, however, to brief the other socialists, including the Bolsheviks, on what was planned.[40]

Kerensky's relations with Lilya now took precedence over the family Christmas and they spent about ten days in Bad Grankulla, while Olga's family arranged for her to take the boys to Kainki. Isaac Babel met Kerensky in Bad Grankulla and he later wrote a slightly fictionalized account for Soviet readers. It is, in fact, a skillful example of the use of art in the service of untruth. As they walked through the snow together, Babel was surprised to discover that Kerensky could not recognize a young woman skating on a nearby lake. He implored Kerensky to buy spectacles so that he could enjoy "the line," the divine forms of nature. Kerensky was unmoved:

I don't need your line which is base like reality. You live no better than a teacher of trigonometry, while I am surrounded by wonders . . . Why do I need the freckles in fröken Kirsti's face when I can divine in that girl all I wish without seeing her clearly? Why do I need the clouds in this Finnish sky when I can see the tossing ocean above my head? Why do I need line when I have colour? The whole world is a gigantic theatre in which I am the only member of the audience without opera-glasses . . . and you want to blind me with spectacles for fifty kopecks.[41]

Kerensky was, of course, a Platonist, but Babel was not acute enough to spot an even simpler truth: he had left his spectacles at home for reasons of vanity. The implication is that Kerensky was out of touch as compared with such realists as Lenin. Such a view is not borne out by Lenin's writings at this time, which oscillate between the belief that the revolution was imminent and the fear that it would not happen in his lifetime. So "acute" were Lenin's powers of analysis, that he had persuaded himself that Nicholas II and Wilhelm II had *already* concluded a separate peace in secret. It was not the superiority of "Marxist" analysis over neo-Kantian intuition, but the correlation of social forces that would decide the issue.[42]

On January 4, 1917, Kerensky traveled directly from Finland to Moscow, probably to find out how plans for the coup were developing. If so, he returned to Petrograd unsatisfied, as the plot was constantly being postponed. If there was little action, there was no dearth of gossip. Shulgin found "the sparrows . . . chirping over coffee in every hotel" over the coup. Meanwhile, General Krymov was talking to politicians in Rodzyanko's apartment. The situation of the army was catastrophic and only a coup could revive morale. "The state of mind of the army is such that it will accept with joy the news of a coup d'état . . . if you decide on this extreme measure, we will support you." Shidlovsky, Shingaryov, and Tereshchenko agreed, but why was he telling them? As Shingaryov lamely put it, "who will decide to accomplish it?"[43]

At the end of January 1917, Stankevich met Kerensky in a "very intimate circle" for a discussion of a coup d'état:

Everyone reacted determinedly in the negative to the possibility of a popular outbreak, fearing that once provoked, a popular mass movement could turn in an extreme left direction and this would create extraordinary difficulties for the conduct of the war. Even . . . a transition to a constitutional regime provoked serious reservations and the conviction that the new government would be unable to manage without harsh measures for the maintenance of law and the prohibition of defeatist propaganda. But this did not shake the general determination to finish with the indecencies of court circles and to depose Nicholas.[44]

The ripples spread wider and wider. Sokolov told Shlyapnikov that people in liberal circles were preparing a coup and that Chkheidze and Kerensky were in touch with the plotters. One wonders what the *Okhrana* was doing. Despite what Kerensky has written since 1917, he was probably becoming increasingly skeptical about the likelihood of a successful coup. In the event, the "guards" tradition of the eighteenth and early nineteenth centuries would remain dormant in 1917, as it had in 1905.[45]

During this fraught winter, Kerensky agonized over the accusation by Izgoev that he was guilty of trying to form a 'Red-Black' block and over the attacks of the SR internationalist Alexandrovich for his association with the Workers' Group of the CWIC. He answered attacks of this kind in the January issue of the SR journal, *Severnyia Zapiski* [Northern Notes]:

the process of "darkening" of the cultural consciousness at the beginning of the war as a consequence of the frightful pressure of horror and the scale of events on human reason took place everywhere, seizing hold of the most cultured countries of Europe. . . . The old conception of the permissible and impermissible in polemic is disappearing and those who ought to concentrate all the force of their minds on assisting the masses to orientate themselves to events . . . submit themselves more and more to the dark horror of the crowd and introduce new temptations and chaos into the public consciousness.

He felt it was time to stop seeing conspiracies and return to a more serious analysis and explanation of events. This was rather disingenuous coming from a member of at least two conspiratorial organizations, though Kerensky had identified a problem of vital importance for the destiny of civilization. Later on, he would criticize Trotsky for his assertion that the Imperial regime had sought a separate peace, but he was hardly guiltless himself.[46] Did he know that his attacks on Myasoedov and Rasputin lacked any basis in evidence? Probably not. What, after all, was he to think when told by an ex-Minister of Justice that Rasputin was a German spy? The conduct of Kerensky and Milyukov demonstrated the sheer impossibility of standing aloof from this demeaning process.

On his brief visit to Moscow, Kerensky had told Moscow's leading liberals that "we are in the revolution." "My words were greeted with total disbelief", he remembered. "With all my being, I felt and KNEW that the time for a successful coup d'état had been passed by and that to stop the country on the road to revolution 'from below' was already completely impossible." On January 22, the acting British Consul-General, Robert Bruce Lockhart, also reported that "the general belief in a Court revolution seems to have disappeared."[47]

Kerensky's conviction that the plotters had missed the boat led him to undertake another characteristically bold move early in 1917. Again, Kerensky never wrote a line about this highly portentous event, and when I pressed him about it at our sole meeting in 1967, he claimed to have forgotten all about it. "There were so many demonstrations," he said. Yet this eleventh-hour attempt to guide Russia into a peaceful revolution permits a glimpse of relations between the socialist parties in January and February 1917.

January 9, 1917 was the twelfth anniversary of Bloody Sunday and 100,000 workers struck to commemorate it. Gvozdev and the right-Mensheviks on the CWIC Workers' Group could see that they would have to do something very radical to regain the prestige they were losing to the Bolsheviks and SR-internationalists. On January 24, they appealed to the workers in unprecedented terms. "The liquidation of the war and the peace for which the exhausted country yearns will not lead the people out if its appalling circumstances unless the people itself, and not the present autocratic government, liquidates the war." They urged the workers to gather outside the Tauride Palace when the Duma reconvened to demand that the Duma take power. As Kuzma Gvozdev himself expressed it: "Through the Duma to the Revolution." An agitator for the Workers' Group recalled that the aim of the demonstration was to "embrace [the Tauride Palace] in a ring of iron and to force the deputies of the Duma to go with the people against the government of Nicholas II." These tactics were strikingly similar to those pursued by Kerensky in 1915.[48]

On January 26, the Workers' Group was arrested, incarcerated in the *Kresty* prison, and charged with plotting to bring about a social democratic republic. Their appeal to the workers not to strike in sympathy was suppressed. Kerensky visited Gvozdev in Prison to warn him that he might get a fifteen-year sentence, as the authorities were considering turning him over to a field court-martial. Guchkov felt this was a challenge to his own power base and he and his industrialist friends decided to do all they could to save their working-class allies. Milyukov was cooler, insisting that only the Duma had the right to undertake political initiatives. Kerensky and Chkheidze attacked him bitterly, warning that he might soon find himself "on the tail of events."[49]

S. P. Beletsky, the Director of the Police Department, said later that A. D. Protopopov had made a mistake in arresting the Workers' Group rather than their mentors, Kerensky and Chkheidze. He felt that Protopopov had been reluctant to arrest his former Duma colleagues, hoping for a reconciliation with the Duma, and even with Kerensky personally—not inconceivable considering their common links with Simbirsk. Despite this setback, Kerensky continued to canvas the demonstration outside the Duma on February 14, when it reopened. Alarmed at the prospect of serious trouble, the government declared Petrograd an independent military district, giving General Khabalov special powers to put down disturbances. On February 9, Khabalov issued a stern warning against the planned demonstration, which *Rech'* printed alongside one by Milyukov. The Kadet leader claimed that an agitator masquerading as "P. N. Milyukov" has appealed to the workers to join the demonstration. "I will only direct the attention of the workers to the fact that the bad and dangerous advice which has been distributed in their midst by such contemptible means, apparently emanates from a very murky source."[50]

Being associated with a murky source was the last straw for Kerensky and when he visited Hippius, he was "boiling, was beside himself." She was more philosophical, shrugging her shoulders and commenting "Milyukov and his Block are true to themselves." Nor would the Bolsheviks support a demonstration designed to pull other people's chestnuts out of the fire, and they were supported, much to Kerensky's chagrin, by Alexandrovich and even the Menshevik Organizing Committee, controlled by Chkheidze for most of the

war. The Bolsheviks went so far as to organize a counterdemonstration for February 10, the second anniversary of the exile of their
five deputies. In the event, both demonstrations flopped. More workers came out on February 14, but they did not go to the Duma as Kerensky had hoped. Kerensky flared up at Shlyapnikov, "You have destroyed the democratic movement prepared with such difficulty."[51]

The Duma gathered in an atmosphere of extreme tension. Rows
of police and soldiers prepared to ward off any demonstrators who
might try to put pressure on the deputies, while their presence was
itself an effective counterdemonstration. Within the Duma, relations
between socialists and liberals were at an all-time low. In answer to
Chkheidze's accusations of spinelessness, Milyukov declared that
"our word is already our deed. The word and the vote are so far the
essence, our sole weapon. But look, gentlemen, even this weapon
is not blunt." Words could also stir and organize. He was optimistic
that the country would win the war despite its government. As
Milyukov left the tribune, Rodzyanko heaved himself out of the
chair and handed the gavel over to Nekrasov, a diplomatic move as
the next speaker was Kerensky.

In his most outspoken and dangerous speech, Kerensky set about
the government and the Progressive Block with almost equal fervor,
though he made it plain that he desired an alliance with the Kadets
as strongly as he desired the destruction of the status quo. He did
not entirely share their views on the war. A reasonable government
would now seek peace in view of the rate at which Russia's resources
were being squandered. The war should not be prolonged for such
"utopian" annexations as Constantinople or Bohemia, which the
people did not support. These points were badly taken, and when
he mentioned peace, he was accused of being an "assistant of Wilhelm," while Shingaryov indignantly denied that the people did not
want to conquer the Dardanelles.

The Kadets agreed that the government was sabotaging the economy, social structure, and political life of Russia, but the sacking of
individual ministers made little difference. What then was the answer?
Kerensky now proclaimed his membership in the SR Party and his
support for its use of terror, "the possibility of armed struggle with
the individual representatives of the government, a party which
openly recognized the necessity of the killing of tyrants. We were
persecutors of those people." Even Nekrasov was now squirming

and he begged Kerensky not to expose the Duma to reprisals. Kerensky was not to be stopped as he praised "what citizen Brutus did in classical times." The task of the moment was "the destruction of the medieval regime immediately at any cost." For such a task, he lamented, the Duma majority was too selfish:

You don't simply not want to break—you cannot break—with the old government, all the way; you can't because, as I have already said, up to now you do not want to subordinate your economic and social interests, the interests of one group of the population to the interests of the whole.

The Duma majority was unmoved, seeing themselves to the last as the principal players, and Kerensky and Chkheidze as the hooligans on the sidelines.[52]

Just three days after the unsuccessful demonstration of February 14, a strike broke out in the massive Putilov factory, and on February 22, the management declared a lockout. The workers had just been warned by the liberal leaders of the Duma that food shortages were imminent. Now, the management was telling them that even if food supplies lasted, they would have no money to buy any.

The Putilov workers elected a strike committee and sent deputations to persuade workers in other factories to support them. They also lobbied the socialist fractions in the Duma.[53] Zenzinov described later how he was approached by a deputation of five or six men from the Putilov plant, demanding to speak to Deputy Kerensky on a matter of importance. When Kerensky arrived, the workers told him rather defensively that they had done all they could to avoid the closure of the factory, even withdrawing their demands for an increase in wages. Before the lockout, they claimed, the dominating mood had been opposed to an immediate assertion of mass militancy, but the lockout had changed all that.

Entirely concisely, and very seriously, the workers delegates declared to A. F. Kerensky that the strike that had begun did not bear a partial character and that the question was not one of economic demands, nor difficulties over food supply. The workers were conscious that it was the beginning of some sort of major political movement and they considered it their duty to warn the Deputy about it. How this movement would finish, they didn't know, but to judge by the mood of the workers around them, it was clear to them that something very serious could happen.[54]

The following day, February 23, was International Women's Day and the main thoroughfares of Petrograd were invaded by large groups of working-class women. As Kerensky told the Duma,

what has overrun Petersburg in the form of a wave of starving women on the streets is already collapse. This is already a situation in which it is almost impossible to organize, almost impossible to administer. For this mass, this elemental force, for whom hunger is becoming the only tsar, whose reason is eclipsed by a desire to chew a crust of black bread, for whom, in place of reflection there is a bitter hatred of everything that prevents them from being sated; with this mass, this elemental force, it is already impossible to discuss, it will not submit to persuasion and words any more.

He demanded the immediate transfer of food distribution to elected local committees, in which he probably saw the nuclei of a new, democratic state order. The Duma must assert itself to maintain the cohesion of the state in the face of the "organized enemy," Germany.[55]

Kerensky was now fully committed to the revolution. Any recovery of control by the Tsarist government might have been followed by fatal consequences for him in view of his poor health. The head of the Petrograd *Okhrana* wanted Kerensky arrested for treason, but Beletsky found the evidence insufficiently conclusive to justify this. Protopopov promised Beletsky that he would not hesitate to apply "measures of determined character" to Kerensky, but hesitate is exactly what he did. Kerensky's suggestion that someone do "what Brutus did in classical times" was widely circulated, though it was excised from the Duma record. Prime Minister Golytsin was told that "Kerensky had made a speech practically appealing for the murder of the Sovereign," but Rodzyanko refused to give him the uncut record of the speech. Empress Alexandra hoped that "Kedrinsky [*sic*] would be hanged," but no one was listening any more. The Imperial Government had ceased to believe in itself.[56]

Kerensky's politics of the emotions never commanded much respect among the more rationalist politicians, but even they were having to take him seriously. Milyukov claimed that the lists of members of a possible "ministry of public confidence" that had been circulating since the summer of 1915 never included Kerensky's name; but times were changing. Early in 1917, Shingaryov suggested to Shulgin that the Block would have to open its ranks to the left should it suddenly find itself in power. When Shulgin asked how, he was told, "I would call on Kerensky." "Kerensky? As what?" "Let's say as minister of justice. . . . At the moment the post has no significance, but we must detach from the revolution one of its leaders. . . . Of them Kerensky is the only one. . . . Much better to have him with you than against you."[57]

The Marxist Nikolai Sukhanov was coming to a similar conclusion. He pointed out to Kerensky that, in the event of a change of regime, he would occupy a crucially important position. Kerensky did not demur.[58] His conspiratorial talents enabled him to keep a straight face at this "discovery" by a Marxist intellectual of a matter long settled by the political freemasonry. In Switzerland, Lenin had come to the same conclusion, arguing that the Tsarist government had already concluded a secret peace with Germany, but could not say so openly for fear it would be replaced by "a government of Milyukov and Guchkov, if not of Milyukov and Kerensky." Lenin's insight may have come from a list of members of a "Committee of Public Safety" comprising Prince Lvov, Guchkov, and Kerensky, dating from 1916, since the Estonian nationalist who passed it on to the German Foreign Ministry was also in touch with Lenin. This was probably less important than Lenin's habitual use of people as ciphers for class interests.[59] In February 1917, it was obvious to all thoughtful Russians that Alexander Kerensky would soon play a vital role in the future of his country.

7

Fires of Hope and Aspiration

By the evening of February 23, 1917, 100,000 strikers had joined the starving women on the streets of Petrograd, milling around, stopping trams, and beating up policemen. The Populist teacher Kryukov felt "a ripple that would not die down." Policemen and cossacks drew their clubs but made few arrests. The conscript soldiers showed an ominous friendliness to the crowds, listening intently to the women who begged them not to fire on innocent people who simply wanted food. Socialist militants hurriedly stitched together banners with the slogans "Give us bread" and "Down with the war."[1]

By Friday, February 24, 200,000 men and women were on strike, and many of them marched down Nevsky Prospect. General Khabalov tried to explain that any possible food shortages were the result of misunderstandings, but no one believed him. The authorities also began to cordon off the city to prevent the junction of demonstrators from different suburbs. The day was "sunny, clear, and warm." Middle-class shoppers and students watched the marching workers with benevolence and the troops exchanged jokes with the women. The cordons were sloppy affairs permitting civilians to pass through almost at will. Ordered to prevent workers from the Vyborg Side from crossing the river, the soldiers allowed themselves to be pushed back across the Liteiny Bridge before resuming control. "The revolution was fun."[2] There were exceptions, as the normally speechless Father Krylov reported to the Duma. He had seen a crowd,

shouting "hurrah . . . accompanying the cossacks and the regiments which were passing by with their bands. When I asked "What does that mean?

Why are they shouting 'hurrah' to the cossacks and the marching regiments with their bands? What sort of demonstration is that?" the first person I met explained that one of the policemen had been hitting a woman with a whip . . . but the cossacks immediately intervened and chased away the police.[3]

Kerensky's mood was still bleak as he reiterated his warnings of "collapse, catastrophe, and anarchy when the country's mind will be extinguished; when it will be overcome by a wave of hunger and hate." He might not understand all that was passing through the minds of the workers, but "the question of further bloodshed, the question of further sacrifices at the front is not a matter of indifference to that mass which is giving up its sons and brothers and which is starving here." The Duma should not put the pacifism of the masses down to German subversion but assume their leadership. The majority ignored him, merely asking the government to clarify its intentions on food supply, while Rodzyanko warned of "undesirable phenomena . . . impermissible in the grave times of war." Kerensky then came back to urge the masses to "recognize your duty to yourselves and to the state . . . You must systematically and regularly organize yourselves and then say fearlessly and bravely: we want this and we shall do it."[4]

The Minister of War had the speeches of Rodichev, Chkheidze, and Kerensky cut from the newspapers and at GHQ, to which Nicholas II had just returned, the official military historian recorded,

25 Saturday. Mogilev. From Petrograd disturbing news; hungry workers demand bread, cossacks disperse them; factories and works on strike; State Duma sitting very noisy; social-democrats [*sic*] Kerensky and Skobelev call for the overthrow of autocratic power, but there is no power.[5]

That night it froze hard and the ships on the Neva were gripped firmly by the ice, but it was long into the morning of the new day before the lights went out in restless Petrograd.[6]

On Saturday, February 25, the incipient hatred of which Kerensky had warned began to surface. The strike was now general and the workers threw themselves into the city center with increasing determination, shouting "Down with Autocracy!" On one occasion, cossacks allowed a crowd to beat up a police inspector, while another cossack was reported as having wounded another inspector with his sabre. The more prosaic observers lost their bearings in the grandeur of panoramic events. Police repression was meeting fierce retaliation, while the soldiers were failing to back up the policemen. In the evening, Olga Kerensky witnessed the first use of firearms on Nevsky. Meanwhile, the horrified ministers had omitted to keep the Tsar abreast of the gravity of the situation, for fear of losing their commissions. They were thunderstruck to receive a telegram ordering them to "stop tomorrow disorders in the capital impermissible in grave period of war with Germany and Austria."[7]

The demonstrators still ignored the Duma. For the last time, Kerensky urged the Duma to lead the revolution and establish "a government subordinated to the control of the whole people," by demanding freedom of expression and organization. Rodzyanko ruled Kerensky's motion out of order. That would prove to be his last substantive action as Chairman of the Fourth State Duma.[8]

Kerensky went straight to Sokolov's apartment, where he found the inevitable gathering of socialist intellectuals. Peshekhonov, Sukhanov and Zenzinov were there, Shlyapnikov was absent. Sukhanov found Kerensky excited and "somewhat pathetic and . . . theatrical". Kerensky ridiculed the panic of the Duma majority, but when Sukhanov asked him whether any views were beginning to crystallize on a new form of government, Kerensky found the question irrelevant and the two fell to wrangling.[9]

Early that evening, the Menshevik fraction of the Duma and the Petrograd Union of Workers' Consumer Societies held a meeting under Chkheidze's chairmanship at which a Menshevik "defencist" raised the question of forming a Soviet of Workers' Deputies. Most of the Mensheviks went on to a meeting organized by a few members of the Workers' Group of the CWIC who had evaded arrest. They were joined by several leading Populists, including Kerensky, and later by Guchkov and Tereshchenko. By then, the police had already removed the workers, but they went cheerfully, confident that they had little to fear.[10]

Kerensky and the Menshevik deputy Skobelev went directly to the Petrograd City Duma, which was still chattering about food supply. The intellectuals were gradually conscious of the infiltration of "gray people," who crowded in from Nevsky, bringing a number of wounded demonstrators into the chamber. Shingaryov, Kerensky, and Skobelev demanded a change of government and freely elected food distribution committees, and Kerensky told the meeting of the arrest of the remaining members of the Workers' Group. The City Duma requested Mayor Lelyanov and Shingaryov to intercede for them. The meeting had no practical results, but it demonstrated the increasing militancy of socialists and liberals and the first signs that the workers on the streets might look to them for leadership.[11]

This was the last opportunity for those Imperial ministers who wanted compromise with Milyukov to stave off the revolution. Foreign Minister Pokrovsky and the acting Minister of Agriculture contacted Milyukov, Maklakov, and Savich for talks. The liberals insisted that a "ministry of public confidence" be formed, attaching great importance to the smooth transfer of authority, without which a new government might be unable to rely on the civil service and army. Maklakov, a perennial pessimist, confided to Maurice Paléologue, the French Ambassador, that "if they don't grant rapid reforms to the country, the movement will degenerate into a mutiny and from mutiny into revolution; it is not far off."[12]

Kerensky was excited and optimistic the next day and this partly explains the unpleasant impression he made on Shulgin when they met in the Tauride Palace. "As usual, he was rushing somewhere, head bent and furiously rubbing his hands. After him, trying to keep up; Skobelev." Kerensky could not suppress his amusement when this conservative solicited his advice. Power must pass into other, nonbureaucratic hands, and he added that lack of experience did not matter in a minister. "What are all those offices and undersecretaries for?" he asked.

"What else?" echoed Shulgin ironically.

"Now, well then," and Kerensky boyishly, flippantly and jovially rubbed his hands, "a few freedoms. Well, there's the press, assembly and so on."

"Is that all?" "All so far", said Kerensky, "but hurry . . . hurry . . ."[13]

Sunday, February 26 began with deceptive calm and General Khabalov telegraphed the Tsar to say that since the morning all was quiet in the city. "A bright sun, a pleasant light frost, a blue sky and a recent light fall of snow gave rise to a holiday atmosphere." Many of the workers who reached the center of the city came in their Sunday best, though numbers did not really build up until the early afternoon. This time the authorities were prepared. Nevsky was strictly cordoned off into sections and the troops were given instructions to shoot all demonstrators who refused to disperse after the firing of warning rounds. It says a lot for the tenacity of the workers that many defied the blank rounds and stood their ground. The police counted 50 dead and another 48 wounded after they had opened fire on Znamensky Square. There was a rumor that the number of victims would have been greater had not many soldiers preferred to aim over the heads of the crowd. Then came news of a mutiny in a company of the Life-Guard Pavlovsky Regiment. It spread rapidly, thus playing a large part in convincing the socialist intellectuals that victory was in sight. Kerensky phoned Sukhanov from the Tauride Palace to assure him that "the Pavlovsky Regiment has risen," though this proved an exaggeration.[14]

That night a motley gathering of socialist militants met for their fourth, and final, exchange of information. Kerensky, Zenzinov, Sokolov, Ehrlich of the Jewish Socialist Workers' Party (the *Bund*), Alexandrovich of the SR-internationalists and Yurenev, chairman of the Trotskyite Interdistrict Committee were present. The majority tried to persuade Alexandrovich and Yurenev to get their comrades to withdraw the slogan "Down with the War!" which threatened to divide the movement by offending the Kadets. The meeting turned into a personal duel between Kerensky and Yurenev. Yurenev ridiculed Kerensky's "usual characteristic hysteria," while Kerensky remembered Yurenev asserting that "the reaction is gaining strength. The unrest in the barracks is subsiding. Indeed, it is clear that the working classes and the soldiery must go different ways. We must not rely on day-dreams and preparations for a revolution, but on systematic propaganda at the works and the factories, in store for better days." Kerensky's suggestion for the distribution of leaflets to influence the mass movement was premature.[15]

Kryukov was not at this meeting, but from a political position close to Kerensky's, he had also come to the conclusion that "the cause is played out". These appraisals say more about the temperaments of their exponents than their politics. "In the end," wrote Kryukov, "the nerves were harassed and exhausted, there was no sleep and nothing to give rest to the soul."[16]

Rodzyanko's morale was also shattered that night, for when he got home, he found waiting for him an Imperial decree proroguing the Duma. Who would now stand between the anarchy of the street and the "practical anarchists" in the government? Kerensky knew nothing of this until the following morning, but spent the late evening comparing notes with his comrades on the phone.[17]

The intellectuals had made their appeals and the working men and women had shown as much courage and determination as can be asked of an unarmed people facing a mighty military machine. The issue now rested with the capital's garrison, which consisted mainly of training battalions, whose officers were an unstable mixture of teenage sons of the intelligentsia and elderly or injured careerists, and whose ranks were composed of members of oppressed national minorities and working-class socialists (often conscripted to stop them from agitating in the factories). The reserves had fallen so low that they included youths of seventeen and family men of nearly forty.[18]

There were intense nocturnal debates in the barracks. Soldiers resented the gendarmes, who looked fit but stayed in Petrograd while they were sent off to freezing trenches with unhealed wounds. They were in sympathy with workers' protests against the food shortages and inflation (which also afflicted their own families) and hoped for a fair peace that would allow them to go home. Xenophobic peasants wondered what was the point of fighting Germany when 'Germans' already ruled the Motherland, while class-conscious workers denounced the "frightful war, started by the capitalists . . . for our enslavement." There were more personal grievances as well. Early the next morning, soldiers of the Volynsky Regiment refused to perform any more police duties. When one of them killed an unpopular major the die was cast.[19]

The elements blessed the February Revolution. The sun drove the mist from the endless vistas of the Petrograd prospects, and the dream of six generations of Russian intelligentsia came to life. A regiment of the Imperial Russian Army, led by a sergeant, marched out in parade order, its band playing, to join the revolution. "Never, even in slumber, had I dreamt such a marvellous, grandiose, magical symphony," recalled Kryukov.[20]

At 8:00 A.M., Kerensky was wakened by Olga, who told him, "Nekrasoff is on the telephone. He says the Duma has been dissolved, the Volinsk Regiment has mutinied and is leaving its barracks. You are wanted at the Duma at once." Kerensky took a moment to take in the news. "It came to me with a jolt, but I soon perceived, or rather felt, that the decisive hour had struck. I jumped up, dressed quickly and hurried to the Duma—a five minute walk." He was probably so abstracted that he forgot to say goodbye to his family. Olga wrote later that "when he left the flat that day, A. F. never returned to live with us. That was the final breach in our family life."[21] He would, however, return for a short time on March 2.

Kerensky and his friends then did what they could to turn the new development to advantage. He asked his wife to contact his comrades to persuade the mutineers of the Volynsky Regiment to rally round the Duma. Stankevich received this message but he had little success with the soldiers, but others may have been more successful. Kuzma Gvozdev was released from Kresty that morning, and he had the same idea. The order proroguing the Duma may also have reminded the soldiers of the Duma's importance. Unfortunately for Kerensky, it was another four hours before the soldiers began to arrive at the Tauride Palace.[22]

Kerensky approached the Palace in a mood of "tense anxiety"; no troops were yet to be seen and he had made so many vain appeals for audacity to the Duma majority. His anxieties were fully justified:

On the morning of 27 Febr., I in the name of the p[arties] Progressist, S-D, and Trud.[ovik] Group proposed to the Council of Elders to empower Rodzyanko to open a regular sitting of the S[tate] D[uma], not submitting itself to the Ukase about the prorogation of the session. If such a proposal had been accepted the S[tate] D[uma] would undoubtedly have become the real source and concentration of state power and the regulating centre of the revolution. However, my proposal was rejected by a majority . . . under the pressure of Rodzyanko and Milyukov.

Rodzyanko was still hoping that Nicholas II would appoint a new government, while Milyukov felt that the Duma's undemocratic franchise made it an implausible and even undesirable institution in time of revolution. A decade later, Kerensky remembered this tragic abdication: "The Duma died on the morning of" February 27, "the day when its strength and influence were at the highest."[23]

Kerensky rang the Duma bell to convoke the deputies to a private session in the semicircular hall (not the Catherine Hall where official sittings took place). He took no effective part in the sporadic discussions that continued there, though several deputies ribbed him about the nonarrival of "his" troops. Nekrasov called for a dictatorship under a popular general, while Chkheidze called for a revolutionary government. The prudent majority contented themselves with the constitution of a Provisional Committee of Members of the Duma "for the restoration of order and for liaison with persons and institutions," a title calculated to save their necks if the Tsar regained control. Rodzyanko chaired this body, which also included the leaders of all the center and socialist factions.[24]

For Kerensky and Chkheidze, there were lies and white lies. With the regular Duma reporters, they set about creating a newspaper to fill the gap created by the striking printers. This *Izvestiia Petrogradskikh Zhurnalistov* [News of the Petrograd Journalists] did not report the Duma's demise but claimed, on the contrary, that "The Council of Elders, having met in special session and having familiarized itself with the ukase of prorogation has resolved: The State Duma shall not disperse. All deputies shall remain at their places." This fictitious "Tennis Court Oath" aligned the Duma with the revolution; later it would confer a mythical legitimization on the Provisional Government. Nor was this the only example of exaggeration by the Petrograd Journalists, whose influence went uncontested for a day.[25]

About 1:00 P.M., the soldiers finally began to arrive. Kerensky was quite literally dressed for the occasion, "in the black jacket which I wore during the entire Revolution, without hat or overcoat, I ran through the main entrance to the soldiers for whom we had waited and wished so long."

This was the moment of transfiguration. He now became "the leader [*vozhd*] of the Revolution." "His figure suddenly grew into that of a 'notability' at that moment . . . He spoke decisively, powerfully, as though he had not panicked . . . His words and gestures were sharp, measured, his eyes burned." He posted a "revolutionary guard" at the entrances to the Duma but this frail barrier proved no match for the crush of soldiers, workers, students, and intelligentsia who began to pour into the Tauride Palace. A couple of hours later, soldiers brought in Shcheglovitov, once the author of the Beilis trail and now Chairman of the State Council. Rodzyanko offered his protection, finding it improper for the Duma to be converted into a prison for the Chairman of the "upper house." Kerensky overruled him, arresting Shcheglovitov loudly "in the name of the people." It would have been all too easy to have this hated figure battered to death, but in his most sonorous tones, Kerensky declared, "Your life is in safety . . . Know this: the State Duma does not shed blood."

Even Shulgin understood that Kerensky was appealing to the magnanimity of the men. Kerensky's experience in appealing to the better
side of Tsarist judges stood him in good stead, but he took a boyish
delight in his unwonted role as jailer, taking Zenzinov aside to show
him the key he had used to lock up Shcheglovitov. As more fallen
bureaucrats arrived, he handed their guards scribbled receipts in
pseudo-bureaucratic jargon.[26]

While the Duma majority was sitting passively in one wing of the
Palace, men of a different stamp were gathering at the other end to
discuss ways of coordinating the movement in the streets. In a room
found for them by Kerensky, a group of mainly Menshevik intellectuals and the "Gvozdevites," just released from prison, constituted
a Provisional Executive Committee of the Petrograd Soviet of Workers' Deputies. At last, the junction of Duma leaders and popular
representatives sought by Kerensky since 1915 was becoming a reality. Kerensky was himself nominated to this committee, which appealed to the workers to send their representatives to the Tauride
Palace that night, and which set up a military organization under
Kerensky's old comrade from the "Land and Liberty" days, Colonel
Mstislavsky.

At the Soviet's first meeting that night, Sokolov proposed the
election of officers and committeemen. Chkheidze was the obvious
nomination for chairman, while Kerensky and Skobelev were elected
vice-chairmen. Kerensky and Chkheidze soon left the meeting for
discussions with the other Duma leaders. Over Bolshevik objections,
they were mandated to represent the Soviet in the Duma's Provisional
Committee. The meeting also elected a permanent executive committee; with ex officio representation for all the socialist groups,
which decided to publish a daily *Izvestiia Petrogradskago Soveta Rabochikh Deputatov* [News of the Petrograd Soviet of Workers' De-
puties], usually known as *Izvestiia*. Lenin's friend Bonch-Bruevich
was deputed to see to its publication.[27]

Not all the socialists were equal to the moment. The veteran Populist Peshekhonov was now the father of a military cadet and he
tried to remonstrate with Bonch-Bruevich when he commandeered
a private printing press for *Izvestiia*, "but they didn't even listen to
me." Georgii Khrustalev-Nosar, Chairman of the 1905 Soviet, was
dragged to the Tauride Palace by people desperate for leadership. To
his relief he spied Milyukov. "Pavel Nikolaevich," he implored,

"what do they want from me?" As thieves and hooligans celebrated the absence of police by looting shops and bourgeois apartments, shooting in the air, and careering around in hijacked cars, literary socialists such as Gorky and Kryukov became thoroughly depressed.[28]

Far more alarming than the disorderly soldiers or the opportunist criminals was the total absence of the officer corps. Peshekhonov was struck by the absence of officers from the Duma on February 27, and Kerenky's first sight of men arriving with their officers did not come until the evening of the following day. The officer-socialist Stankevich admits he felt physically afraid when he heard rumors that the men were shooting their officers. This failure of nerve or judgment, or perhaps just the inertia of inculcated loyalty, had the most drastic consequences, nourishing the fears of mutinous soldiers and socialist militants that the Tsar might somehow reconquer Petrograd and shoot them all. A British diplomat reported:

It was a Revolution, and the Army within the gates of Petrograd had made it one. But of the army outside the gates? What of the rest of Russia? What forces were coming from the Tsar? Upon that Monday evening it seemed to every man possible that the next day would show the world the bloodiest civil war in history.[29]

For the wealthy, the revolution came as a Doomsday long feared. Loyal monarchists left the Duma in disgust, silently cursing "the mentally-ill Kerensky." Conservatives such as Shulgin and liberals such as Nabokov were periodically overcome by the disorder, the dirt, the smell of unwashed men, and the implicit physical threat posed by this mob they could not control. Even Kerensky's friend and colleague, Tereshchenko, looked back with horror on the "violence, disorder, and ineptitude" of those days. But there were other moments when even some monarchists felt that the revolution was somehow sublime and epoch-making. In his earliest account of the five days he spent in the Tauride Palace, Kerensky stressed the selflessness and unity of all he dealt with, in the struggle against the old regime and against anarchy. "We forgot everything that was merely personal, all that was merely a matter of class or caste, and became for the moment simply men conscious of our common humanity. It was a moment when every man came into touch with what is universal and eternally human."[30]

Kerensky saw nothing of the excesses that besmirched the revolution in the streets. During those days, he neither ate nor slept properly, though sometimes Olga or Lilya would force a piece of chicken, a glass of brandy, or a cup of black coffee down his throat. The nervous excitement affected them all. Kerensky had always sought the "universal and eternally human" in the men and women he met. This was not just a matter of myopia or self-delusion. He had an unusual power to challenge other human beings, at least for a time, to transcend their limitations. Nekrasov soon came to join the cause of the revolution with him. Gvozdev, and others in the Soviet, tried to moderate the tone of the left. The engineer Bublikov took over the railroads and used their telegraph system to inform the country that the Duma Committee had "undertaken the formation of the new government." The railroadmen, by frustrating the Tsar's planned move on Petrograd, were decisive in persuading him to abdicate peacefully. Kerensky was able to assemble a personal staff of young and old SRs, Zenzinov, Boris Flekkel, Znamensky, Zarudny, and his school friend, Somov. Lilya and her cousin joined in, organizing a buffet at the Tauride Palace for the participants.[31]

Hour after hour, wave upon wave, all the illustrious units of the Imperial Army were arriving. Rodzyanko, Milyukov, and Chkheidze spoke to them of liberation, of the new light that was dawning, and of their patriotic duty at the front. Kerensky was hoisted on the shoulders of soldiers in the great Catherine Hall. "I saw a sea of heads, of gleaming, enthusiastic faces." He spoke of freedom, of the double duty of war and revolution, of the sacrifices made by past generations of revolutionaries and the sacrifices the Motherland would now require. It seemed to him that "New fires of hope and aspiration were kindled and the masses were drawn together by mysterious bonds." Kerensky and Chkheidze talked freely of revolution and democracy and urged a fight to the finish with tsarism.[32]

Shots were heard outside the Tauride Palace and there was a moment of panic as people threw themselves to the floor anticipating a cossack counterattack. Kerensky jumped on a window ledge and shouted, "All to your posts! . . . Defend the State Duma . . . Listen: this is Kerensky speaking, Kerensky is speaking to you . . . Defend your freedom, the revolution, defend the State Duma! All to your posts! . . ." When Sukhanov suggested that he was merely adding to the panic, Kerensky replied, "I ask everyone . . . to carry out . . . their duties and not to interfere . . . when I give instructions!"[33]

The soldiers wanted to be assured that their mutiny would be forgiven. So long as they feared a Tsarist counterattack, the Duma was an indispensable shield against the possible wrath of their commanders. As it became clear that General Ivanov would never repeat his Galician triumphs on the streets of Petrograd, they began to look more critically at this Duma. Neither Milyukov nor Rodzyanko had made an unambiguous commitment to revolution. Milyukov had been shocked by the conduct of the troops and he had not yet called for the Tsar's deposition. In asking the men to return to officers who had not yet rallied to the revolution, they seemed to be preaching counterrevolution, as socialist orators were quick to point out. "The Duma was the natural rallying point of these troops," reported the British Embassy, "but, having got there accompanied by cheering working men, they naturally very soon came under the control of the Social Democrats" [socialists—RA]. Even Chkheidze told one group of soldiers that it was all very well for a rich estate owner to talk about the defense of Russia, but who would do the defending?[34]

On February 28 and March 1, the fears of the socialists increased by the hour. They responded by trying to substitute the Soviet for the Duma as the focus of the men's loyalty. The Bolsheviks and Inter-District Group prepared a leaflet warning the peasant soldiers:

Soldiers! Beware that the gentry don't deceive the people! Go to the Duma and ask it: will the people get the land, will there be freedom, will there be peace? . . . So that the gentry and officers don't fool you take power into your own hands. They're a Romanov gang."

Urging the election of officers, it concluded:

Soldiers! Now when you have arisen and won, you are approached by your friends but also by your former enemies, the officers who call themselves your friends. Soldiers! The fox's tail is worse for us than the teeth of the wolf.

Boris Flekkel showed a copy to Kerensky who, becoming infuriated, accused its authors of being agents of the *Okhrana*, bent on dividing the masses from the educated to facilitate the restoration of tsarism. He personally persuaded the Soviet Executive Committee to proscribe the leaflet. Eventually, Sukhanov confiscated the leaflets from the Bolshevik Molotov.[35]

Less hair-raising, but more effective, was Order No. 1, issued on the night of March 1–2 by the soldier section of the Soviet, apparently on its own initiative. It was apparently dictated to Sokolov, the chairman of the sitting, by soldiers, some of them Bolsheviks. Intended to apply only to the Petrograd garrison, it was soon broadcast from the Tsarskoe Selo military radio station to the army at the front. It provided for the election of committees in all units, for the subordination of the garrison to the Soviet "in all political manifestations," and for the abolition of titles of nobility in military forms of address. Otherwise it insisted on obedience to the officers. The men were not to give up their arms to the officers and they were to follow the orders of the Duma's Military Commission, provided these did not conflict with Soviet instructions. This was an authentically revolutionary document, in many ways as important a feature of the "constitution" of Russia between February and October 1917 as the agreements between the Duma Committee and Soviet Executive Committee, hammered out in another part of the Tauride Palace just as Sokolov was greeting the soldiers.[36]

On February 28, Milyukov telegraphed Prince Georgii Lvov to come from Moscow. Lvov was the nominee of the Progressive Block for a ministry of public confidence, and Milyukov was still hoping for the appointment of such a government by the Tsar when he sent the call. By the time Lvov arrived the following day, the Duma Committee was contemplating a "revolutionary" government in which Kerensky would be Minister of Justice. Chkheidze was also offered a post. However, the Soviet Executive Committee had resolved to abstain from participation in a "bourgeois" government, since, according to the orthodox Marxist theory of the Mensheviks, "objective conditions" were not ripe for socialist revolution. Kerensky found this "utterly absurd, for . . . all the real power lay in the hands of the people themselves."[37]

Rather diffidently, Kerensky asked Sukhanov whether he should ignore the resolution. Sukhanov agreed that this would be a good idea, but pointed out that Kerensky would then become a left-wing member of a "bourgeois" government while ceasing to be a member of the Soviet. In other words, by all means join the liberal bourgeoisie, but don't expect to retain your ties with socialism and the masses. Kerensky departed "more than disappointed." Sukhanov's advice must have reminded him of the cruelty of the older generation in

The Green Ring. Equally ominous for the future of SR unity was Mstislavsky's pointed refusal to offer Kerensky any advise at all.[38]

Kerensky was reassured by the support he received from the SRs Zenzinov and Demyanov, though Demyanov felt that Kerensky was merely canvassing support for a decision already taken. The Menshevik Sokolov also agreed that Kerensky should enter the government to keep an eye on the bourgeoisie. Kerensky told all those he canvassed that he was relying exclusively on their advice.[39]

Three sleepless days and nights, his growing fears of anarchy and the uncomfortable sensation that he might soon be denounced as a renegade by many old comrades took their toll of his nerves. On the morning of March 2, Kerensky exploded on hearing yet another disorganized group of soldiers arrive at the Tauride Palace:

Do you hear? The morning is beginning and again some crowd or other is creeping in; some people without any business, for no reason! Again the holiday crowd will loaf about the whole day, not working and getting in the way . . . an atmosphere of disintegration . . . And they are feeding it . . . class war! . . . Internationalists! . . . Zimmerwaldists![40]

If Kerensky had lost some of the crispness that had so impressed his Duma colleagues, Milyukov had recovered his composure and stamina and it was he who represented the Duma Committee in the negotiations with Sukhanov, Steklov, and Sokolov of the Soviet Executive Committee, which laid down the basis for the coexistence of the two revolutionary institutions. Surprisingly, Milyukov and the Soviet Marxists soon agreed on many aspects of the provisional government's program, including the abolition of racial and religious discrimination, freedom of speech and assembly, democratic local elections, an amnesty, and the convocation of a Constituent Assembly. They disagreed only over the election of officers and the ultimate form of Russia's government. Milyukov preferred a constitutional monarchy, while the Marxists insisted on a republic. Milyukov moderated Soviet demands for the democratization of the army and persuaded the socialists to moderate the language of their appeals, but the question of the monarchy was not settled until the evening of March 2, and then only by a rather untidy compromise.[41]

Kerensky objected bitterly to the "Sukhano-Milyukovite anti-historical bookish analysis" which underpinned these negotiations. He might have called it Plekhanovite, since it was Plekhanov who had insisted that Western European evolution must be repeated exactly in Russia so that the bourgeois revolution would be separate from the socialist revolution by a significant historical period. This was accepted with enthusiasm by the leading "bourgeois liberals," many of them educated in the "legal Marxism" of the 1890s. Milyukov welcomed a state of affairs in which middle classes would exercise decisive power, or what Marx called a "dictatorship of the bourgeoisie." He wanted to retain a monarch to whom the army would swear allegiance and who might be used to repress disorder.

It was precisely to obviate this kind of possibility that Plekhanov himself had argued that the proletariat must retain its autonomy. Socialist parties, trade unions, and democratic bodies such as soviets, would enable the proletariat to mitigate the evils of capitalism and prepare for socialism. The autonomy of these institutions depended, of course, on their ability to frustrate an omnipotent "dictatorship of the bourgeoisie." Hence the notion of "dual power," expressed in the famous Soviet formula *postol'ku, poskol'ku* [in so far as] which offered Soviet support for the government only *in so far as* it carried out democratic reforms.[42]

Quite apart from his exhaustion, Kerensky always found "such interminable and impractical discussions . . . repugnant to my nature." Since at least 1915, he had been trying to unite a representative selection of workers around every possible focus of "bourgeois" organization. He regarded "bourgeois hegemony" as a chimera. "Whoever knew the social map of Russia . . . had to see clearly that the universal franchise, laid down as the basis of all political and social reforms of the February Revolution, thereby made the POLITICALLY newborn fourth estate decisive in the creative, founding work of the new democratic state." Kerensky's myopia and neo-Kantian epistemology were no obstacles to a grasp of Russian reality, acquired by direct observation of "all strata of the Russian population," which was fully equal to the insights of Lenin and Trotsky. The difference between them was one of evaluation. Kerensky's emergency was Lenin's opportunity. For Kerensky, the decisive gulf lay not between the "bourgeoisie" and the "democracy" (i. e., the socialist mass organizations), but between all those with sufficient education to comprehend the interests of the state, i. e. the intelligentsia, and those new citizens of free Russia, who had still to learn what this involved. "Dual Power" was therefore a disaster, a dog-

matic division of the minority capable of responsibility into a bourgeois government with no roots in the country, and an irresponsible
caste of socialist critics.[43]

Dual Power was bad enough, but civil war would be worse. Kerensky had spent enough hours vainly arguing with Milyukov and
Sukhanov to abstain from their negotiations, but he would not let
them fail altogether. During an impasse in the talks, he jumped up
from a sofa and demanded to speak to the Soviet negotiators. He
said these words "sharply, in that definitive-Shakespearian tone
which he adopted in the following days" and led them off.

After a quarter of an hour, the door was 'dramatically' thrown open. Kerensky, pale, said with burning eyes: "The representatives of the Executive
Committee have agreed to concessions . . ." Kerensky collapsed into his
chair again and the trio became Milyukov's prey.[44]

The night of March 1–2 was a "time of long and torturing vacillations" for Kerensky, a frightfully compressed version of the dilemma which had faced him when he had entered the Duma despite
the SR boycott. No one could deny his claim to a seat in the government, yet his comrades were set on expelling him from the Soviet
if he accepted a ministry. "I felt that if the masses were to be left to
the haphazard leadership of the Soviet and had no official representative in the Provisional Government, serious danger and trouble
were ahead. I could not permit this to come to pass. However, I felt
that without a hold on the Left, without direct contact with the
masses, the Provisional Government was foredoomed to failure. Yet
the immediate and essential need of the Revolution was a strong
government, able to organize the dissolving structure of the country." Already, he had begun to identify himself with the State and
the Revolution and to see confidence in himself as identical with faith
in both.[45]

Olga was at his side that night, and she prevailed on him to come
home for a couple of hours' rest on the morning of March 2. This
short walk gave him a glimpse of the patrols of revolutionary soldiers, the excited groups of civilians who thronged the streets, and
the smoke billowing from the Gendarmerie headquarters. When he
reached home, he fainted. "One's very nerves, one's entire organism
felt extraordinarily quick and vibrant. One lived under what seemed
unendurable tension. Yet one felt strong enough to vanquish even

death. It is worth living to experience such ecstasy." When he recovered, his mind raced over the arguments for and against participation in the government. Perhaps he remembered the pledge he
had once made the Duma conservatives that "hatred ... towards
political opponents is incomprehensible to us," for he claims it was
the fate of the captured Tsarist ministers that clinched his decision.
There were the cowards; the *Okhrana* chief Beletsky, the War Minister Belayev, and the mystic Protopopov. There were the courageous; Finance Minister Bark, Shcheglovitov, whom Kerensky had
special reasons for loathing, and Makarov, who had warned the Lena
miners to expect another massacre if they followed socialist leaders.
There was the "traitor" Sukhomlinov, ostracized by his own former
colleagues, and the pathetic Goremykin, now reduced to fondling
his Imperial insignia. Kerensky would keep the revolution unsullied
by bloodshed. He leapt up, phoned his acceptance to Milyukov, and
rushed off to face the Soviet.[46]

Abandoned by the generals and grand dukes, Nicholas II prepared
to abdicate. Nothing now stood in the way of the formation of a
Provisional Government, and shortly after Kerensky's return to the
Tauride Palace, the list was read out by Milyukov. Prince G. E.
Lvov, Prime Minister; A. F. Kerensky, Justice; P. N. Milyukov,
Foreign Affairs; A. I. Guchkov, Army and Navy; A. I. Konovalov,
Trade and Industry; M. I. Tereshchenko, Finance; A. I. Shingaryov,
Agriculture; N. V. Nekrasov, Transport; A. A. Manuilov, Educa-
tion; and V. N. Lvov, Procurator of the Holy Synod. There were
four Kadets, three monarchist Octobrists, two Progressists, and one
Trudovik. With the exception of Kerensky, this was the list of the
Progressive Block, Milyukov's government.[47]

This impression was misleading. The listing of Kerensky before
Milyukov was no accident, for at least one minister had made his
acceptance conditional on Kerensky's. Tereshchenko's nomination
also surprised Milyukov, though it was not until later that he discovered that he, together with Nekrasov, Konovalov, and Kerensky,
was a member of the political freemasonry. Milyukov would also
be desperately disappointed by Guchkov, who proved quite unable
to adapt to revolutionary politics, and Prince Lvov, who seemed to
Milyukov to be a tired old Tolstoyan, meekly entrusting himself to
the "wisdom of the people."[48]

The elegant Catherine Hall was now transformed. Gone were the well-tailored, bewhiskered gentlemen, smelling of cigars and cologne. Instead, there was a crush of noisy, cheerful intellectuals, workers, and soldiers, a bazaar of warm and sweaty humanity. On the afternoon of March 2, Steklov was reading a report explaining to the Soviet why it could not participate in a coalition when Kerensky entered still clad in the worker's jacket and breeches that suggested an affinity with his audience. This time, he did not modestly walk up the steps of the tribune, but vaulted on the Chairman's desk and burst into speech. There are two versions of what he said.

"Comrades," be began, "I have a communication of extraordinary importance for you. Comrades, do you trust me?"

"We trust you, we trust you," came a score of voices.

"I am speaking from the depths of my heart, Comrades, I am ready to die, if that will be necessary."

This provoked consternation and then thunderous applause. He then announced his entry into the government, excusing his failure to obtain the prior permission of the Soviet on the grounds that he had been forced to reply immediately. "Comrades", he continued, "the representatives of the old government are in my hands and I decided not to allow them out of my hands." Again there was applause and shouts of "right." He had ordered the release of all political prisoners and had given instructions that the five Bolshevik deputies of the Duma, his clients in 1915, should be brought back to Petrograd with full honors. "In view of the fact, comrades, that I accepted the duties of minister of justice before receiving your mandate, I renounce the title of vice-chairman of the Soviet of Workers' Deputies. But for me life without the people is unthinkable, and I am ready to accept that title for myself again if you find it necessary." "We beg you," came the reply.

Kerensky promised to work for a republic and asked to be considered a "representative of democracy" in the government. The final words of the first version, which Zenzinov confirms, explain the whole purpose of the speech: "Comrades! Allow me to return to the Provisional Government and declare to it that I am entering its ranks with your agreement, as your representative." This was greeted by stormy applause, clapping and cries of "Long live Kerensky!" as he was carried from the hall in triumph.[49]

Zenzinov was surprised to find tears on his own cheeks as Kerensky finished. Stankevich felt that Kerensky had been overwhelmed by his audience rather than overwhelming them and that he had been totally sincere. This view was shared by such journalists as Wilcox and Vasily Nemirovich-Danchenko. Wilcox felt Kerensky was "fired by a fervent and profound belief in the religion of freedom," while Danchenko noted that "all impediments between himself and his audience are intolerable to him." Photographs also suggest that the self-consciousness that dogged his most intimate relations evaporated when he stood before a mass audience.[50]

Kerensky preferred a second version of his speech, as published by *Izvestiia*, a version he probably had a hand in editing. It omits the claim that he had only five minutes to decide whether or not to enter the government, a suggestion which was known to be untrue by several of his listeners. It also omits the passionate demand, "I cannot live without the people, and in that moment when you suspect me, kill me!" Could anyone but Kerensky have invented this?[51]

Both versions of the speech derive much of their effect from the impression he gave that he would deal more harshly with the tsarist ministers than his "bourgeois" ministerial colleagues. Yet he always maintained, and this is borne out by his conduct, that he had entered the government to treat them with more clemency than anyone else could have done. Despite this deliberate ambiguity, the speech was an enormous tactical success. He was the only minister elected with the acclamation of a body rapidly growing in authority and this gave him a special position in the government. It also made him a number of enemies in the Soviet, especially Yuri Steklov (Nakhamkess), whom he had upstaged. Steklov had provided Olga Kerensky with work after the breakdown of her marriage, and this insight into Kerensky's personal circumstances may have led him to take a dim view of Kerensky's ethics. So far from being overawed by Kerensky's triumph, he now put a resolution to the Soviet opposing a coalition of bourgeois and socialist forces, which was carried.[52]

Kerensky's republicanism was less ambiguous as he now showed, when a hitch occurred in the abdication of the Tsar. The Duma Committee had sent the two monarchists, Guchkov and Shulgin, to receive the Tsar's abdication, anticipating that he would abdicate in favor of his young son, nominating his brother as regent. When informed that the Tsar was abdicating on behalf of himself and his son, they were so relieved at his acquiescence that they failed to consider that this might not be legal.

Milyukov had already announced the regency of Michael Alexandrovich, but Rodzyanko warned him that many officers would
not return to their men until the monarchy was abolished. During
the night of March 2–3, Milyukov discussed the matter with Nekrasov and Kerensky, both of whom urged the proclamation of a
republic. Milyukov curtly insisted on pressing for the accession of
Grand Duke Michael and Kerensky was so alarmed that he phoned
the Grand Duke to warn him against a precipitate decision.

Early on March 3, the Government and Duma Committee visited
the Grand Duke in the sumptuous apartment of a friend of his near
the Winter Palace. Rodzyanko listed the reasons why the Grand Duke
should renounce the throne; he was seconded by Kerensky. Milyukov
made a desperate plea for the retention of the "back-bone of the
country," the only symbol around which the people could be induced
(or compelled) to rally. "Without the support of this symbol," the
Provisional Government "would not survive until the opening of
the Constituent Assembly. It would become a frail structure and
drown in an ocean of popular emotions." Apart from Shingaryov,
only Guchkov, who arrived belatedly from Pskov, gave Milyukov
even "feeble" support. Kerensky found it inconceivable that Russia
should risk a civil war while the war with Germany was still continuing. Michael Romanov took Rodzyanko and Prince Lvov aside
to ask whether his life could be guaranteed if he accepted the throne,
just as his namesake had in 1613. The advice was not encouraging
and he resigned the throne to the Constituent Assembly. The Romanov dynasty was at an end.[53]

Even Milyukov admitted that the situation in Petrograd was so
unfavorable for the accession of Michael Alexandrovich that he might
have had to bring troops from Moscow and the front to suppress
disorder in Petrograd. Both patriotism and prudence dissuaded the
Grand Duke from a move which might have precipitated civil war.
Kerensky was so suspicious of the intentions of his monarchist colleagues that he queried a phone call made by Guchkov to his wife
and warned Shulgin against private conversations. He was correspondingly relieved when the Grand Duke announced his decision.
Rushing forward, his hand outstretched, Kerensky averred, "Your
Highness, . . . you have acted nobly and like a patriot. I assume the
obligation of making this known and to defend you."[54]

During these decisive days, Kerensky had become "the central figure of the revolution." They might have ended in a civil war superimposed on the war with Germany. It was Kerensky who worked most systematically for the alternative (a coalition between "bourgeois" and socialist interests), who begged the Duma to place itself at the head of the revolution, who tried to find it military backing, who assumed responsibility for the revolutionary arrest of the Tsar's ministers, and who greeted the troops in the name of Duma *and* Revolution. It was Kerensky's supporters who told the country the Duma had made the revolution. Kerensky suppressed socialist appeals which might have led to a massacre of officers and insisted on the end of the monarchy. He did all he could to avert a breach between Milyukov and the Soviet. He was, at first, the *only* link between the new Provisional Government and the Soviet.[55]

Egalitarian intellectuals must find Kerensky's rhetoric and his assumption of command theatrical, even repellant. Zenzinov himself was shocked when Kerensky ordered him to use more ceremony when addressing a member of the government. But Zenzinov soon perceived that Kerensky was setting out to enhance the prestige of the Provisional Government by the only means at hand, his own charisma. The speeches that appear so unconvincing in cold print wrung tears of sympathy from all but the most hardened listeners, as Stankevich explained:

He was the only man, who gave himself up to the wave of the popular movement with enthusiasm and complete confidence, feeling much more and much wider than the others. He perceived the whole historical grandeur of the revolution which had been accomplished, from the very first day. Only he spoke to the soldiers as "we" believing that he was speaking the truth . . . And he believed that the mass wanted exactly what was historically necessary for the moment.[56]

Millions throughout Russia heard his name at the instant they regained their freedom and for many he became *the* leader (*vozhd*) of the revolution. He represented an almost poetic spirit of national reconciliation and it was in all innocence that one of his admirers wrote:

Russia's heart will never forget him,
Like a first love.[57]

8

The People's Minister
of Justice

The Provisional Government of free Russia promised its citizens complete equality before the law. All political crimes, save treason, would be pardoned. Freedom of assembly and the right to strike were guaranteed. Democratic elections would soon be held for local government and for the command of a new militia. Preparations for electing a democratic Constituent Assembly would begin immediately. Soldiers would be citizens in uniform, subject to military requirements, while the units that had participated in the revolution would be neither disarmed nor withdrawn from Petrograd. The government specifically promised that "it had no intention of using military circumstances for any sort of slowing down in the realization of the aforesaid reforms and measures."[1]

Democratic Russia was committed from the outset to freedoms that had been modified or abrogated in other democracies at war. (English workers, for example had no right to strike in wartime.) The government's declaration was silent on such key issues as the war, national minorities, and Russia's collossal agrarian and industrial problems. Though it failed to specify that women could vote in the forthcoming elections, it was a charter of democratic freedoms, not a program for the transformation of society. Yet the Soviet Executive Committee, Milyukov, and Colonel Wilton of the London *Times* expressed their satisfaction. In a subsequent report, Colonel Wilton was more reserved, confessing his belief that "Orthodoxy and Tsardom constitute the indissoluble bases of the mentality of all Russians" and concluding ominously, "At present therefore, we must be content to go on with the new Provisional Government until quieter days supervene in Petrograd. . . . "[2]

Not that the Allies were idle. General Poole, the British Military Attaché, buttonholed Kerensky on March 2 to ask when war production might resume.

Kerensky replied that all the new ministers realized situation but that in his view present was an unsuitable time to attempt to coerce the people as they are now within a measurable distance of Anarchy and he feared that any drastic steps might only precipitate matters . . . He hoped that by gentle persuasion and in time that Government may get situation in hand but that at present they are powerless.[3]

A few days later, Poole saw Kerensky again to complain that "the present situation with two Governments was impossible." Kerensky assured him that "the Council of workmen and soldiers' deputies was losing ground," and added that he expected the soldiers back at drill in a week. The workers would be guaranteed an eight-hour day in principle so long as they continued to work longer hours for the war effort.[4]

The government and Soviet quickly dealt with food shortages. Food was distributed to the public and retailers reduced their prices. A French journalist found the price of butter quartered overnight, while Colonel Wilton reported a tea shop charging nothing! It was the Soviet that persuaded the workers to return to work. The Bolsheviks, Interdistrict Group, SR Internationalists, and communist-anarchists were delighted at this opportunity to undercut the Menshevik-SR leaders of the Soviet, and they urged the workers to stay out until they had won the eight-hour day, wage increases, and the dismissal of oppressive foremen. Only on Tuesday, March 7, did the trams run again, and then only after the Soviet had authorized free travel for all soldiers.[5]

The Soviet was in no hurry to permit the nonsocialist press to reappear. On Sunday, March 5, the Kadet *Rech'* appeared, protesting vociferously against the censorship of nonsocialist papers. The Kadets were visibly unhappy at finding themselves the new "far right" of Russian politics. Guchkov's monarchist and formerly anti-Semitic *Novoe Vremia* [New Time] appeared with a banner headline welcom-

ing the advent of "freedom," but this was too much for the Soviet
and it was suppressed for several more days. The main factories
finally resumed work at a rather leisurely pace some ten days after
the Revolution when the manufacturers reluctantly conceded the
principle of the eight-hour day.[6]

When news of the revolution had reached the Baltic Fleet, sailors
at Kronstadt had killed Admiral Viren and other officers, while many
more had been beaten and imprisoned. Skobelev was sent to the
Sveaborg naval base in Helsinki, while Kerensky went to the naval
base in Tallinn to prevent a repetition of these tragic events. At the
conclusion of his emotional speech to the Tallinn garrison, Kerensky
was besieged by jubilant men. So many unwashed hands pressed and
scratched his hand that it required lancing. For weeks thereafter, he
walked around in a sling.[7]

On March 6, Kerensky traveled to Moscow. The atmosphere
there, captured by Pasternak in "Spring Rain," came as a relief.[8]
During the long train journey, Kerensky told Mayor Chelnokov that
he was in favor of the war and "delaying all serious political changes
until the end of the war." This was hardly in the spirit of the government's program. At a meeting of the Moscow Soviet, Kerensky
urged the workers to return to work, and achieved some success,
but the Soviet reaffirmed its opposition to socialist participation in
government.[9]

The visit to Moscow certainly improved Kerensky's mood, as he
told an AP correspondent: "If any serious disagreements existed at
the beginning between the working men and the Duma Committee,
it was only a passing symptom of the fever attending the birth of
the new nation. I can assure you that every difference has disappeared." He was satisfied that "the whole Army, from the commander down to the last soldier, is eagerly devoted to the continuance
of the war." Kerensky was telling the Allies what they wanted to
hear and what he wanted to believe. His patriotism did not impress
everyone, however, and it was probably irreconcilable monarchists
who tried to assassinate both Guchkov and Kerensky on March 5
and 6.[10]

On March 18, Kerensky and Guchkov met General Alexeyev, the
Supreme Commander- in-Chief at GHQ in Mogilev. Kerensky took
the opportunity to expand on his objections to a speedy convocation
of the Constituent Assembly "without victory over the Germans."

so long as Russia remains under the threat of invasion a Constituent Assembly could not deliberate with the requisite freedom. Moreover, the actual holding of the elections involves preliminary work requiring at least nine months. If women are also to have the vote, the electoral mechanism would be all the more complicated.

Kerensky was rapidly coming round to the view that only military victory could reduce tension in Russia to the point where social reform could be achieved by debate rather than violence.[11]

His collaboration with Octobrists and Kadets was leading in the same direction. "From the very first session of the government," he recalled, "we spoke together and considered questions with such understanding of what was necessary to be done . . . for Russia." Mikhail Tereshchenko also remembered the men of the First Provisional Government as "truly democratic, guided by patriotic motives" and "completely selfless and courageous."[12]

This spirit of understanding and self-sacrifice was exemplified by Prince Lvov and Shingaryov. Lvov was the owner of a small estate and hence a *pomeshchik* (literally a "fief-holder") in popular parlance. But he had an intimate and sympathetic view of the Russian peasantry and welcomed compulsory expropriation provided there was compensation. He was an impressive administrator and his gentility impressed even his political adversaries. Shingaryov was known as the "peasant doctor," for his investigations into peasant conditions at the turn of the century. Despite his devotion to Milyukov, he preserved a measure of faith in the possibility of a democratic Russia long after most of his colleagues were in despair. The ministers included young and old industrialists, landowners and intellectuals. It did not at first occur to anyone that with Chkheidze's refusal of a portfolio, the ministers were all men of Orthodox Great Russian background.[13]

The chaos and fatigue that marked the early meetings of the new government were vividly described by Milyukov's friend, Vladimir Nabokov, son of a Tsarist Minister of Justice and father of the writer of the same name. Meetings were held whenever there was a quorum, often not until after 1:00 A.M. Ministers came and went on other business so that the same issue was constantly rediscussed by shifting groups of people. The daily meetings coordinated policy on matters where responsibilities overlapped. They also allowed the ministers to indulge their hopes and fears and to give and receive moral encouragement. They also witnessed major explosions over differences of policy.[14]

The chiliastic expectations raised by the Revolution soon took their toll. Konovalov began to complain of the impossibility of paying increased wages and improving conditions while maintaining war production. Each time, he was sent back to reconcile the irreconcilable. Education Minister Manuilov found his task equally impossible as students demanded the wholesale purge of conservative professors, while progressive teachers, and even young children, demanded the immediate and total transformation of the educational system.[15]

The government was politically divided between Kerensky and Nekrasov on the left and Milyukov and Guchkov on the right. Nabokov truthfully records the errors of his chief, but betrays little awareness of the condescending sarcasm to which Milyukov had subjected Kerensky for years. He felt that Kerensky was simply envious of the greater man. Kerensky certainly did find Milyukov hard to stand, and despite his greater self-control, the Kadet leader fully reciprocated these feelings. Shortly after the Revolution, Milyukov wondered aloud about the part played by German agents in bringing it about. Kerensky was incensed, challenging Milyukov to repeat the offending words, and then declaring, "After Mr. Milyukov has dared to slander the sacred cause of the great Russian revolution in my presence, I do not wish to remain here for a minute more." As Kerensky stalked out, Milyukov remarked acidly, "That's Kerensky's usual style. He often played tricks like that in the Duma, extracting some phrase or other from his political opponent which he then distorted and used as a weapon." Milyukov may not have been impressed but others were and Prince Lvov was sent to smooth Kerensky's ruffled feathers.[16]

The Kadet leader was even more hostile to Nekrasov, whom he regarded as Kerensky's gray eminence. He began to notice that Tereshchenko and Konovalov also tended to support Kerensky in a rather unexpected way. "All four were very different in character, past and political role," he recalled, "but they are united not only by radical political views. Apart from that they are bound by some personal proximity, not purely political, but of a political-moral character. They are united as if by mutual obligations proceeding from one and the same source."[17]

This was not the whole story. Kerensky's standing in the Provisional Government was due mainly to his ability to inspire faith in the possibility of a happy future for Russia. Neither Milyukov nor Guchkov could share his optimism. On March 5, Milyukov muttered to Ambassador Paléologue, "the circumstances are so serious!" He fought back with the unique mixture of courage, dignity, rationalism, and integrity that never left him; but the logical end to his policies seemed to be civil war, a civil war his supporters had little confidence of winning.[18]

Guchkov was often away at GHQ and appeared inscrutable at the few meetings of the government he did attend. On March 6, he told General Poole that "there were really two Governments now in Russia, Executive Labour Committee interfering in everything that Provisional Government undertakes," but he saw no way out of the situation. The pessimism of Milyukov and Guchkov swayed V. N. Lvov and Godnev toward Kerensky. In time, Kerensky's optimism even affected Prince Lvov, as he told a friend:

To live and act in the Provisional Government without a belief in a miracle was impossible. And it seemed more likely to expect a miracle from Kerensky's enthusiasm than from Milyukov's intellectual computations.[19]

Nabokov admitted that Kerensky was the only member of the government who could speak as its "master," while Zenzinov told Hippius that Kerensky was de facto premier, a verdict echoed by less committed observers. When the Allied Ambassadors formally recognized the Provisional Government, the British Ambassador Sir George Buchanan found only Guchkov and Kerensky "really strong men." French Ambassador Paléologue was even more impressed:

Only the young minister of justice, Mr. Kerensky, gave me the impression of a man of action, by his energetic figure, by his sober words, his dry gestures, by something fanatical and clear-cut which recalls St. Just; he is certainly the real head of the Provisional Government.[20]

This optimism was rekindled whenever Kerensky spoke to the groups of soldiers, workers, civil servants, and schoolteachers who flocked to the antechambers of the Ministry of Justice. The young SR Captain F. A. Stepun took a delegation of soldiers from the front to visit Prince Lvov and Guchkov, but only Kerensky gave them hope. "It was clear that Kerensky, as the only natural son of the Revolution in the Provisional Government (the seal of adoption lay clearly on Guchkov, Lvov and Milyukov), would come to head it sooner or later." The French journalist Claude Anet found Kerensky's personality "growing in importance every day. He is the man whom the Revolution has brought forth from the ranks." On the Southern front, an English nurse of monarchist sympathies reported that "It soon became obvious that Alexander Feodorovich Kerensky, Minister of Justice, was the man of the moment."[21] Every day he received telegrams of congratulations and support from every corner of Russia and from abroad. Requests for the righting of past wrongs came to him as Minister of Justice, perhaps the most poignant from the Lena mines. Even more welcome was the telegram from the Petrograd SR conference saluting his entry into the government as "an act of statesmanlike wisdom" and promising its "cordial support."[22]

On March 4, Kerensky moved from the Tauride Palace into the Ministry of Justice. Olga and the boys were, at first, regular visitors, as was Lilya. Kerensky quickly settled into a routine that would alter little in eight months, at least when he was in Petrograd. He got up early to read a digest of the press. This was followed by breakfast, or at least coffee. Vera Figner, or, after her return from Siberia, Ekaterina Breshkovskaya, acted as hostesses at these breakfast sessions, to which Kerensky invited Allied politicians, disgruntled civil servants, and his subordinates in the ministry, who might not see him again if they did not get his instructions at breakfast. Then he received petitioners in the reception hall, pathetic dependents of servants of the old regime begging for leniency for their relatives. Even the Court Minister, Baron Fredericks, joined this sorry queue. There were endless delegations of admirers and foreign journalists, leafing through his *Okhrana* file which was proudly displayed for all to see. It was probably there that Wilcox found the *Okhrana* circulars describing his activities in 1915. In the afternoon, Kerensky attended meetings of the government. When they finally wound up late at night, there were meetings with the Soviet Excom leaders which dragged on through the early hours.[23]

On assuming ministerial office, Kerensky had summoned all his subordinates to a mass meeting to ask them to search their consciences to see whether they felt able to cooperate with his program. He wanted cooperation, not blind obedience, in a nonhierarchical ministry, and he advised the junior officials to organize a union. Their voices would be heard in appointments. In exile, Kerensky would sometimes suggest that he had been immune to the libertarian euphoria of those heady days, but an Estonian colleague recalled his request to the Petrograd Bar Council to elect his deputies for him, a radical breach with bureaucratic tradition. The gesture fell flat at a lamentable session in which the advocates punctured one another's egos but failed to agree on a single nomination.[24]

Kerensky made harsh remarks about the senators, warning them that he would remove judges who had rejected the testimony of socialists before the revolution. When A. A. Demyanov, a fellow Trudovik lawyer, took up a senior position in the ministry, Kerensky warned him not to be too soft on those Senators who had brought the law into disrepute. In practice, his power to purge was severely limited by the government's respect for legal contracts. In order to remove a particularly obnoxious judge from the Petrograd Chamber of Justice, it proved necessary to kick him upstairs and make him a senator! On the other hand, the most hated judges, including Krasheninnikov, were arrested. This did not forestall Bolshevik charges that Kerensky was collaborating with legal officials of the old regime.[25]

Kerensky's frequent absences from his Ministry impeded his work, but in the opinion of many officials, he was one of the few ministers with any really creative ideas. Kiryakov listed 60 separate items of legislation which passed through Kerensky's hands, an average of one every day. Not all of them were major acts of legislation, but all were lovingly drafted by men who had struggled for years against arbitrary injustice in the courts of the old regime and who were determined that the legal code of the new Russia would stand comparison with the U. S. Bill of Rights or the French Revolution's Declaration of the Rights of Man and Citizen. These laws regulated the courts, moderating penalties in line with humanitarian penal theory. Politically, the most important laws were those which eliminated racial and religious barriers to civic equality, set up a commission to investigate the crimes of the fallen regime, and abolished the death penalty. The abolition of ethnic discrimination gave legal expression to the liberation of the national minorities. It was received with particular satisfaction by Jewish citizens, who could now become full members of the Bar, or army officers. The setting up of an Extraordinary Investigating Commission, under N. K. Muraviev, provided some guarantee that the Rasputinites would be brought to book, though they could anticipate magnanimity under Kerensky's bloodless revolution.[26]

The intelligentsia, nurtured on Tolstoy, greeted the abolition of the death penalty with boundless enthusiasm. The Menshevik *Rabochaia Gazeta* [Workers' Paper] wrote: "How many fighters for freedom laid down their lives on the block, or perished in the hangman's noose! And the most awful thing was that these murders were being committed legally." The SR *Delo Naroda* [Cause of the People] agreed. "The most disgraceful blot on our conscience and that of all mankind has been removed." In an article prefaced by a portrait of the "First Russian people's minister of Justice," the magazine *Probuzhdenie* [Awakening] rejoiced:

The new government, true to the best traditions of the Russian intelligentsia and Russian society, felt its sacred duty to realize as positive law the law formulated by the first popular representation [the First Duma] and which corresponded to the grandeur and moral significance of the liberation of Russia which has been accomplished.

Even the conservative *Novoe Vremia* welcomed the move. At this point, Russian conservatives were more concerned with saving their old friends than eliminating the Bolsheviks. The Bolshevik *Pravda*, now edited by Stalin and Kamenev, had the grace to keep its counsels.[27]

Just two weeks after the revolution, Kerensky went back to Finland. The highly literate Finns recorded his every step with a scrupulous attention to detail that allows us to infer the rigors of his days in Russia, too. The visit was emotionally rewarding, but fraught with an undertone of the impatience that faced the government at every turn. The Provisional Government had done well by restoring the rights subverted by Russifying Governors-General since the 1890s, sacking the appointed Senate (or cabinet)—which included Lilya's father—and installing a Senate under Oskari Tokoi drawn from the democratically elected assembly.

At noon on March 16, Kerensky arrived at the Central Station in Helsinki, where he was greeted by the Deputy Governor-General and the new Senators. The band played *La Marseillaise*, the new anthem of free Russia, and Kerensky made a brief speech on the conquest of liberty. A student choir responded with the nationalist

Bjöneborg March and then Kerensky was driven to the Governor-
General's residence for lunch.

Later, Kerensky drove to the Runeberg monument to lay a wreath
at the feet of the national bard. He was then taken to the island naval
base of Sveaborg for discussions with Admiral Maximov and to
address the sailors. He opened with an inspirational passage on the
liberty of Finland and Russia, and he explained his own role in the
revolution:

Comrades! I am not simply a minister, but also vice-chairman of the Petrograd Soviet . . . I am an old socialist and democrat, a member of the
Socialist-Revolutionary Party, and believe me, that when I decided to enter
the Provisional Government I remained your hostage there too, the hostage
of the soldiers, workers, peasants, officers and republicans, of all the citizens
who want to create a free republican Russia. (stormy applause.) Believe me
and know that as long as I am minister of justice, no-one will come to
threaten you and no-one will dare to arise against the new regime and
against free Russia.

He introduced the war tactfully, mentioning Allied admiration for
the revolution and announcing his forthcoming meeting with General
Alexeyev. "Allow me to say to him that henceforth he can rely on
the whole army and on the Baltic Fleet which will be able to defend
free Russia and the new regime which we shall, with our joint efforts,
create. Can I tell him that?" he asked. "We beg you," came the reply
amidst thunderous applause.[28]

Back on the mainland, Kerensky and the Governor-General promised Finnish party leaders the greatest possible autonomy for Finland.
By mid-evening, he was at the Labour House, the citadel of Finnish
socialism and seat of the City Soviet. He was greeted by Otto Kuusinen, who thanked him crisply for what he had said about Finnish
autonomy, but warned that this was old stuff and that the Finns now
wanted more. Kerensky asked him to be more specific and the Social
Democrats gave Kerensky a memorandum setting out their demands.

After this rather stiff session, Kerensky was escorted into the
packed main hall where, in his element once more, he celebrated the
fall of Tsarism. Aware of the Germanophilia of some Finns, Kerensky
mentioned the Germans with typical adroitness:

We believe firmly and completely that the enemy that wants to oppose
Russia's freedom, the capitalist class in Germany, will finally be compelled
to enter the international community of the family of European democracy.

To the Finns he declared, "We believe that the free union of both peoples will last firmly for ever. Together with you, we will create a new sense of respect for the free citizens." And he concluded by kissing Tokoi, Russian fashion, as the normally reserved Finns roared their enthusiasm.

On the train back to Petrograd, Kerensky probably heard a quick translation of the Social Democrat demands. They were complimentary towards Kerensky personally, but imbued with a deep distrust for Russia. The Finns envisaged a formal treaty between the two countries to replace the promises made by Alexander I in 1809 and repeatedly broken by Nicholas II. The treaty must be internationally guaranteed, a demand that was bound to sound insulting to the Provisional Government. The Finnish demands amounted to a permanent and one-sided military alliance. Kerensky was appalled. It was only four days since 100,000 Ukrainians had paraded through Petrograd, not under the red banner of free Russia, but under the yellow and blue of Ukrainian separatism. They had been followed by 15,000 Estonians under their own white-black-blue flag. Were the Finns now to hoist their old lion and roses and desert the Russian peoples at the very moment when they had asserted the values the Finns claimed to cherish? What effect would this have on the other nationalities? For their part, the Finnish Social Democrats were still putting their money on Kerensky's friendship, but to be safe they "confidentially" sent a copy of their demands to the Petrograd Bolsheviks.[29]

Despite his public references to his role as hostage of democracy, Kerensky's relations with his socialist comrades were far from secure. As early as March 6, he told Kiryakov, "I'm not afraid of the right, of the counter- revolution, it's impossible. I fear ourselves, I fear the socialists; their fractional differences, the irreconcilability of their party positions." A symptom of this irreconcilability was the controversy over the treatment of the former Tsar. During his visit to the Moscow Soviet, Kerensky had been received warmly until someone demanded the deaths of Nicholas and Alexandra. The whole atmosphere became menacing. Kerensky responded with spirit:

Now Nicholas II is in my hands, the hands of the Attorney-General. And I say to you, comrades, the Russian revolution took place bloodlessly and

I don't want, I won't permit, it to be stained. I will never be the Marat of the Russian revolution . . . but in the very near future, Nicholas II under my personal supervision, will be taken to a port and from there to England.[30]

Why should the socialist lawyer, with so much at risk, have been willing to take risks for the fallen Tsar which the King of England was determined to avoid? There may be a small place for Freudian psychology here. The hostility and subsequent regret that colored the feelings of Kerensky's generation toward Nicholas II may well correspond to those of a generation of revolutionaries for their monarchist parents. Kerensky had an additional motive: it was only a few weeks since he had made the most public appeal for regicide in Russian history. It was also a matter of honor. The Provisional Government had averted bloodshed by promising the Tsar that his life would be saved. The lessons of Russian history were there to suggest that a murdered Tsar would be a more potent symbol than an exiled one. Once blood started to flow, who knew when and where it might stop?

Kerensky's commitment to the safety of the Imperial family was reinforced when, on March 21, he met Nicholas II for the first time, at the Palace at Tsarskoe Selo. The Imperial couple presented a sharp contrast with their depictions by the socialist caricaturists. "By the side of a pleasant, somewhat awkward Colonel of the Guards, very ordinary except for a pair of wonderful blue eyes, stood a born Empress, proud and unbending, fully conscious of her right to rule." He began to feel that in their own way these two were also "victims of the Tsarist system."[31]

Kerensky's promise to save the Tsar was a loyal defense of government policy, but what of his obligations to the Soviet? On March 8, the Petrograd Soviet ordered Nicholas' arrest, while Milyukov was urgently requesting the British Government to invite Nicholas II to England. For the time being, nothing happened, since the Tsar himself wanted to join his family, some of whom were ill, at Tsarskoe Selo. This allowed the government to claim that it had not bowed to Soviet demands for his arrest, but had merely "deprived him of liberty." Satisfied with his arrangement, the Soviet reiterated its intention of trying Nicholas for his crimes. Paléologue was reminded of the return of the captured Louis XVI from Varennes, with one difference: "the moderate ministers concern themselves exclusively with saving the life of their former sovereign and limit themselves to wishing privately for the institution of a constitutional monarchy."

The Russian reactionaries were less perceptive, as Kerensky had been warned by the historian Grand Duke Nikolai Mikhailovich, who paid Kerensky a clandestine nighttime visit to thank him for trying to save the Romanovs and to warn him of the undying hatred of the Guards officers.[32]

This was the first issue over which the government and the Soviet had been seen to differ. Kerensky maintained that the government was not backing down, but to outsiders it appeared that the Soviet had won. The Tsar was indeed under guard in Tsarskoe Selo, uncomfortably close to "Red Kronstadt," where Admiral Viren had so recently been dismembered.

Even more obnoxious, from Kerensky's point of view, was the decision taken by the Soviet, during his absence in Moscow, to establish a Contact Commission to act as liaison with the government and take action "for the satisfaction of the demands [of the revolutionary people] and continuous control over their realization." Skobelev, Steklov, Sukhanov, Filipovsky and Chkheidze were elected to this commission, though for sheer glibness and malice, no one could keep pace with Steklov. Evidently, Kerensky's performance as hostage of democracy was inadequate. From March 10, the commission began to meet the ministers late at night, two or three times a week. Steklov delighted in emphasizing the government's dependence on the Soviet. Kerensky bitterly resented the pretensions of the Contact Commission, but his own role precluded him from saying so and he sat through these meetings scowling, though occasionally he reproached Prince Lvov for not being ruder toward Steklov.[33]

Kerensky was also criticized by his comrades for neglecting his ties with the Soviet. He never took part in committee meetings and so he was partly to blame for failing to prevent the "bullying" of the government. To some extent, this was a matter of time. He was so busy that it would have been virtually impossible to maintain continuous contact and anything less seemed pointless. Kerensky had behind him long years of late-night discussions with Chkheidze and Sukhanov. He had neither the detachment, nor the taste, for Marxist dialectic—a role that would eventually be played by Iraklii Tsereteli. Kerensky's regular presence in the Soviet might easily have worsened relations with the government. This was a serious flaw in his fitness for revolutionary leadership but it was sensible of him to recognize it and act accordingly. Of course there were moments when Kerensky must have been grateful to the Contact Commission, particularly when it strengthened his hand against Milyukov.

Still, Kerensky's lenient treatment of the Tsar, and of General Ivanov, who had tried to put down the revolution, began to arouse unfavorable comment. He decided to make a personal appearance in the Soviet. He chose to address not the Executive Committee, nor the workers' section—now strongly imbued with Marxist ideas—but the soldiers' section. Sukhanov malevolently remarks that the soldiers, mostly peasants, were still highly patriotic and ignorant of Marxist ideas.

On March 26, Kerensky entered a sitting of the soldiers' section in his black workman's jacket and breeches. He apologized for his absences from "the milieu from which I emerged," explaining how burdened he was by work. So far, he said, there had been no misunderstandings between him and "the Democracy," but now "rumors have arisen, propagated by malevolent people." His record of opposition to the old regime should be sufficient to ensure that he knew how to deal with the enemy. He continued:

I have heard that people are appearing who dare to express their distrust of me. Reproaches are directed against me and the Provisional Government, that I am responsible for the softening [of the treatment] of the old government and the members of the Tsar's family. I warn all those who speak like this that I will not allow anyone not to trust me and I won't permit the whole of Russian Democracy to be insulted in my person. I beg you either to exclude me from your midst or to trust me unconditionally.

He informed the meeting that an old friend of his was guarding the Tsar and promised not to leave office until a democratic republic had been established. "I will work to the limits of my powers so long as I am trusted and people are frank with me." He had not come to justify himself. "I only want to declare that I will not allow myself and the whole Russian Democracy to fall under suspicion."

His charisma was still effective and the chair assured him that "the army trusts you as the leader of Russian Democracy, Alexander Fyodorovich," as cheering soldiers carried him from the hall. Such tactics irritated the Executive Committee. No one but Steklov really

wanted to challenge Kerensky yet. Others contented themselves with
the carping criticisms no self-respecting Marxist could avoid: Kerensky, they averred, was telling them to be frank toward him and
threatening to resign if they were.[34]

Toward the end of March, the atmosphere in the Soviet began to
change. There was growing impatience at the inability of the government to reduce the strains induced by the war, an impatience
most strongly articulated by the returning exiles. Understandably,
they had clung more firmly to their party programs in exile. Many
of them were also unable to repress the jealousy they felt for those,
spared by the *Okhrana*, who had assumed the leadership of a revolution for which they had suffered.

On March 19, Iraklii Tsereteli returned to Petrograd. The leader
of the Social Democrats in the Second Duma, Tsereteli had been
exiled to Siberia in 1907. A goateed Georgian with deep-set eyes in
a pale face, he radiated determination and enormous integrity. He
soon became the leader of the Soviet majority. Equally significant
was the arrival of Joseph Stalin, Lev Kamenev, and the Bolshevik
members of the Fourth Duma. All these men believed in the Zimmerwald program and regarded the Provisional Government as bourgeois and thus untrustworthy. Only the constant pressure of the
Soviets would ensure the "deepening of the Revolution." Unlike the
Bolsheviks active in the February Days, the newcomers agreed that
the new government should not be overthrown immediately. In this
Stalin, and the future Menshevik V. S. Voytinsky—another recent
returnee from Siberia—were so far agreed. Kamenev's even more
conciliatory position cut little ice. His cowardly conduct in 1915 had
not been forgotten.[35]

The returning exiles greatly reinforced the critics of the Provisional
Government. It was easy enough to find things to criticize in those
days. The immediate danger of anarchy had receded, but the less
dramatic, but ultimately more debilitating, creeping disintegration
of Russian society, continued, as citizens pursued their own dreams
with scant regard for society as whole. The Soviet leaders still felt
this "deepening of the Revolution" to be a good thing. The Petrograd
workers used their new power to hound unpopular managers and
to extort material concessions and reacted with irritation when these
advances were swallowed by the accelerating inflation. The peasants
found the new grain monopoly irksome but they observed the dis-

appearance of authority with gratification and began to repartition the land. There was a real risk that hundreds of thousands of armed peasants would rush back from the front to participate in this "black partition." The government—reluctant in any case to split up large productive farms when food was already in short supply—felt that only the Constituent Assembly would have the authority to tackle land reform. The practical difficulties facing reform were daunting, involving the valuation of lands, the assessment of compensation and peasant needs, and the distribution of land, which was plentiful in some areas and scarce in others.[36]

The national minorities were tempted to take advantage of the absence of a firm central government to press their claims to autonomy, or even independence. Were their claims to be fulfilled, economic dislocation and fratricidal conflict would be threatened, as emerging nations fought over borders. The army was a microcosm of these tensions since the Tsarist government had sanctioned the formation of national units of Poles, Latvians, and Czechs to fight for the recovery of territories under German control—an appealing precedent for the Ukrainians, Estonians, and others.[37] It was against this unstable background that the debate over war aims opened.

On March 4, Milyukov had informed Russian ambassadors abroad that the new government would honor all previous obligations and fight "until the end, invincibly and indefatigably." Two days later, he reiterated this view in a government declaration to the people of Russia, promising to fight "to a victorious conclusion." He instructed his ambassadors to confirm that Russia would stand by all the inter-Allied treaties, though the ministers already knew that these included "secret treaties" for the partition of Austria-Hungary and Turkey and punitive guarantees for the future good conduct of the Central Powers.[38]

The Zimmerwaldists were outraged, and at a ceremonial session the Soviet replied with its own foreign policy declaration, "To the Peoples of the Whole World." "The time has come," it announced, "to begin a determined struggle with the annexationist aspirations of the governments of all countries; the time has come for the peoples to take the decisions about the question of war and peace into their own hands." Lest this sound too defeatist, it added, "the Russian revolution will not retreat before the bayonets of conquerors and will not permit itself to be put down by an external military force."

This was very much what Kerensky had been saying between 1915 and January 1917, but it was no longer what he thought.[39]

Kerensky knew the horrors of the World War far better than Lenin or Trotsky. In 1915, he had gone to see his Trudovik comrade, Prince Varlaam Gelovani, who was leading a Red Cross detachment into a contested area of his native Caucasus. "Armed only with knowledge, mercy and faith in justice, protected only by their white armbands," they disappeared into the snowy mountains. Young men and women, Russians and Georgians, led by their socialist prince, fell victim to an unknown fate—perhaps only an avalanche, but perhaps another Turkish atrocity.[40] But he had also seen Dzhizak razed, a Central Asian rehearsal for that international civil war which Lenin had preached since 1914. For all its barbarism, the imperialist war still found some place for rules of conduct and when the generals finally ordered a ceasefire, it was likely to be honored.

It was a chastened Kerensky who assured General Poole of "his sympathy for England and for the necessity of going on with the war" and swallowed his distaste for the "secret treaties"; but he warned Poole that "Miliukoff was without tact and that we were not to believe him when he asserted that Russia wanted Constantinople." Kerensky "only wanted internationalization of the Straits and self government for Poland, Finland and Armenia, the latter as a separate entity from the Caucasus." War aims were unimportant in themselves; who could tell what the situation would be at the end of the war? In the meantime, Kerensky hoped for a German advance that "would at once bring officers and men together." He had always opposed imperialist war aims, and would continue to do so; but if the alternative to world war was civil war, he would choose the former. US Consul North Winship also reported that the moderate socialists, including Kerensky, "while not openly opposing" the Soviet declaration, "deprecate the bad effect it may have on the Russian soldier and workman."[41]

Kerensky's altered views were not widely understood. Ottoman and Bulgarian diplomats in Switzerland hoped that Kerensky and Chkheidze would gain the upper hand in Petrograd and open negotiations with Germany. The French Ambassador in Rome sent Prime Minister Ribot a dossier on Kerensky's pre-revolutionary activities and a German in Stockholm described Kerensky to his own Foreign Ministry as "a young and energetic man, a true national

Russian who wants the best for his country and is not to be bought by the English, a man who would like peace in any case." This coincided with a charge by Dr. Eduard David, the patriotic socialist deputy in the Reichstag, that a revolution made by Milyukov and Rodzyanko could not bring about peace.[42]

On March 24, Kerensky set out to refute such speculations:

What hopes exactly does Deputy David repose in me and N. S. Chkheidze? If he supposes that we shall facilitate the conclusion of a separate peace then he will be cruelly disappointed. If he lays his hopes on the possibility that the German people will follow our example and depose their sovereign then we can only warmly welcome such hope.

Two days later he was even more explicit at a meeting in the Mariinsky Theater, attended by the diplomatic corps, when he praised "la grande France et la grande révolution française." Soon afterward another informant of the Auswärtiges Amt reported sadly, "Kerensky is a solid Russian and *hates* Germany."[43]

This foreign speculation was fuelled by a second skirmish over foreign policy. On March 22, the Germans increased the pressure by launching an attack on the Stokhod River, from which they claimed 10,000 prisoners.

Unfortunately Kerensky had chosen this day for an interview with a journalist in which he declared his preference for the internationalization of the Dardanelles. Milyukov, not to be outsmarted, had himself interviewed by *Rech'* to reaffirm the government's intention to pursue the war aims agreed with the Allies, including the conquest of the Straits.[44]

The next day, Kerensky stormed into a meeting of the government, a copy of *Rech'* in his hand. "Look, this can't go on," he shouted. Milyukov replied that he had simply corrected comments made by Kerensky to the press. Kerensky argued that Milyukov was pursuing a foreign policy of his own for which he had no warrant. He concluded with a rhetorical comparison of the duty owed by an Imperial minister to the Sovereign with Milyukov's obligations to the Provisional Government. "We are your Sovereign Emperor," he asserted. Milyukov controlled his anger and successfully demanded confirmation that his views reflected the policy of the whole government and offered to resign if not.[45]

Tsereteli made his first appearance as a member of the Contact

Commission at the Provisional Government's next meeting on March 24. He demanded that the government publish a declaration committing itself to democratic war aims and an active campaign for a general peace. Milyukov firmly but courteously defended his position. Nekrasov and Tereshchenko were prepared to accept Tsereteli's war aims, but more to raise the morale of the soldiers than with any real hope of peace. Only Kerensky kept his mouth firmly shut, inhibited once more by the ambiguity of his position.[46]

Prince Lvov then invited representatives of the Soviet Executive Committee and the Duma to meet the government in the Mariinsky Palace to discuss the issue. The ministers tabled a draft declaration which they hoped would meet Soviet demands. "The aim of free Russia," it read, "is not mastery over other peoples, nor the taking of their national possessions, but the establishment of a firm peace on the basis of the self-determination of peoples." The Soviet leaders welcomed this terminology, but pointed out that all uncertainty could be resolved by adding a renunciation of "the forcible annexation of foreign territories." Milyukov dug in his heels, absolutely refusing this addition, even when all the other ministers deserted him.[47]

Nabokov tried desperately to induce his chief to be more pragmatic. If Russia ended on the winning side who would oppose annexations? And if she lost, the question would not arise. Why risk the overthrow of the government for a hypothetical issue? Unconvinced but weary, Milyukov consented to the offending clause at last. The preamble to the declaration left him one last hope, "Leaving to the will of the people, in close union with our Allies, the final solution of all problems connected with the World War and its conclusion." Bound, perhaps, by a silent oath to his fallen son, Milyukov would not abandon his hopes for the conquest of the Straits.[48]

Kerensky cared little for etiquette. If Milyukov would not devise a more acceptable foreign policy, he would formulate his own. On the evening of March 27, he called at the British Embassy to discuss the policy that was emerging from Tsereteli's work in the Soviet, and his own in the government, with Sir George Buchanan. The Ambassador got Kerensky to admit that democratic war aims need not involve an immediate peace, nor even a slackening of military operations. Kerensky was even obliged to concede that a democratic peace for the Poles would imply the partition of Austria-Hungary and the detachment of Poznań from Germany, adding that "Russian democracy was in favour of war of defense in a political sense but this did not exclude war of offense in a military sense." Kerensky accepted that the existing military conventions providing for a joint offensive in the spring should still be implemented. Sir George was now prepared to back him against Milyukov.[49]

It was time to mend fences with the Soviet and Kerensky asked Sokolov to arrange an informal meeting with the Executive Committee on March 28. Kerensky complained to the Soviet leaders of Steklov's constant denigration of the government. Tsereteli argued that this problem would not have arisen had Kerensky kept in touch, but Kerensky again pleaded the burdens of office. Tsereteli pressed the point: what could be more important than relations with the Committee? Kerensky, stung by this, offered to answer any criticisms the members might wish to make. This impulsive move proved very successful. Kerensky's mortal enemies were few, and they were caught unawares. The new Menshevik–SR majority was prepared to condone those few actions of his that ran counter to Soviet policies. Most members simply wanted to be consulted. He appealed to their sympathy for his burdens of office and complained about the way the Soviet was humiliating the government. But how could they put pressure on the government without it appearing humiliating? For once, Kerensky was silenced. The meeting solved nothing but it did, for a while, improve his relations with the Committee. Neither side wanted a breach and Sukhanov was silenced in turn by Stankevich: "Why attack Kerensky like that? We must protect Kerensky, protect him from everything that can compromise him, somehow or other . . . Look, you can't deny that he's now the only man who can stand in the centre of events."[50]

On March 30, Kerensky joined Carl Enckell, the Finnish Minister-State Secretary on his official train. There he was shown a translation of a statement made by the Finnish Social Democrats at the opening of the assembly on the previous day. This was in much the same vein as the demands they had shown Kerensky on his previous visit. Kerensky was annoyed, "There's no gratitude here for what the Provisional Government has done for Finland! I had intended to visit the assembly tomorrow," he added petulantly, "but naturally that cannot be considered any more." He retired to his sleeper in bad humor. Enckell was afraid he would have trouble persuading Kerensky to re-consider. He need not have worried. The night's sleep restored him and he was determined to make a good impression.[51]

On Good Friday, March 31, Kerensky greeted the Finnish assembly in the name of the peoples of Russia. He paid homage to the women of Finland who had led their Russian sisters to the franchise and he kissed the hand of one of the women deputies, though prim newspaper reports have him only shaking it. He promised the Social Democrats that the government would respond to their demands immediately after Easter. Mindful, no doubt, of the visit he had just received from the Estonian League, demanding autonomy, he warned that the question could not be rushed in view of its implications for other nationalities. Crucial developments were imminent on the front, perhaps before the Russian government had discovered the views of the British and German governments on the question of peace.[52]

Dr. Runeberg tried to ensure that Kerensky and Lilya spent a restful time at Bad Grankulla, but he was not entirely successful. Shortly after the February Revolution, Kerensky had phoned him to arrange a meeting with the Finnish Activists. The Activists were old allies of the Russian SRs from 1905, but during the Great War, some of them preached collaboration with Germany, and a number joined a special Jäger battalion of the German Army. The Activists in Helsinki were suspicious of Kerensky for excluding the Jägers from the general amnesty, but on his first visit after the revolution, he told the students that if they ceased to support Germany, their comrades in Russia would be released, and he would turn a blind eye to their activities.

During the Easter holiday, four student Activists visited. They praised his personal warmth for Finland but argued that constitutional links between the two countries were undesirable. "Independence would be the only happy solution." Kerensky listened impassively and asked then how widespread their support was. He warned them not to forget the grand principles that demanded the interests of the revolution come before those of nationalism. The government could take no definitive decisions in advance of the Constituent Assembly, which might have to be postponed until the general situation permitted. With some hesitation, Kerensky agreed to urge the Constituent Assembly to grant Finland independence, but he warned them not to mention this publicly. Russia was going to become a federal state, he said, but if the Finns demanded secession too soon, then other nationalities would do the same, wrecking revolutionary unity. These particular students honored the agreement, but soon afterward one of their less patient comrades published an article explicitly demanding independence.[53]

On April 3, Kerensky was the guest of honor at Grankulla district school. He congratulated Finland's teachers for educating "law-abiding, dutiful and honourable citizens" and he asked the young Finns to stretch out a fraternal hand to their Russian counterparts. The children were impressed by his sonorous voice which their Russian teacher did his best to imitate as he translated Kerensky's words into Swedish. Little Hillevi Heinrichs presented him with flowers and Kerensky kissed her. The flowers would be the most precious thing he had received in Finland as they came from the hand of a child. The flowers were followed by bouquets from many other admirers and his carriage was filled with them on the return trip to Petrograd. There was a comical incident on the border when a zealous guard challenged Kerensky to show the identity papers he had left behind in Petrograd. Kerensky congratulated the man on his vigilance. On April 5, 1917, Kerensky arrived at the Finland Station, just two days after Lenin.[54]

9

Ambition and Diplomacy

As the first reports of the February Revolution reached Switzerland, Lenin condemned the new government for not mentioning "the chief and basic issue of the time, peace." He argued that the Provisional Government was tied to the Russian capitalists and landlords and to English and French capitalism. This would even be true of a "democratic bourgeois republican government, were it to consist exclusively of Kerensky and other Narodnik and 'Marxist' social-patriots." On March 6, he telegraphed Bolsheviks returning to Russia: "no trust in and no support of the new government: Kerensky is especially suspect; arming of the proletariat is the only guarantee." Kerensky was the "balalaika" on which the bourgeoisie was playing "to deceive the workers and peasants." "Kerensky's *verbal* republicanism simply cannot be taken seriously, is not worthy of a statesman and *objectively* is political chicanery. . . . The appointment of the Russian Louis Blanc, Kerensky, and the appeal to support the new government [by the Soviet] is, one may say, a classical example of betrayal of the cause of the revolution and the cause of the proletariat." Lenin mocked the "illusions" of the moderate left. Urging the "government of the Guchkovs and Milyukovs . . . to conclude a democratic peace is like preaching virtue to brothel keepers." His solution was simple: arm the whole people and smash the state.[1]

Kamenev and Stalin, the new editors of *Pravda*, were horrified. Lenin's first 'Letter from Afar' was finally published on March 21–22, but heavily edited. Some Bolsheviks might have gone even further in their support for "revolutionary defencism," but the German imperialists came to Lenin's rescue, transporting him in the famous sealed train from Switzerland to Sweden, to facilitate his return to Russia. The episode still proved a serious handicap, particularly among the soldiers.[2]

Lenin's "April Theses" were expounded before more or less skeptical audiences within a day of his arrival at the Finland Station in Petrograd on April 3, 1917. The world revolution was at hand, he argued, and the Soviets should take over decisive political and economic power in Russia. The Bolsheviks were, as yet, only a minority in the soviets of even the major cities and Lenin bemoaned the "unreasoning confidence" of the masses in "the government of capitalists." This confidence could be undermined if "revolutionary defencism" was shown to be a fraud, as no capitalist government could conclude "a truly democratic peace." These views provoked a storm of protest, and it was two-and-a-half weeks before Lenin was able to overcome resistance to them within the Bolshevik party itself. He was widely accused of fomenting the civil war for which he had argued since 1914. At first he denied this energetically. The soldiers and workers to whom he appealed wanted peace, not another war.[3]

When Lenin's articles began to appear, Hippius reported that Kerensky was "in a panic" about Lenin.[4] To begin with, Kerensky took the view that direct attacks on Lenin only brought him more publicity. He probably shared the misconception that Lenin was capable of creating anarchy but not a new form of state power. Kerensky deplored the arrival of "the anarchist socialist Lenin," but added that the government had not thought it right to deny his return to Russia. A few days later, he answered Lenin by insisting that, "we have not yet entered the period of the dictatorship of the proletariat, we are now in the period of national revolution . . . there is not and there cannot be a desire to provoke civil war."[5]

The next major socialist exile to arrive at the Finland Station was Viktor Chernov, who returned on April 8. Kerensky went to the Finland Station for his first meeting with his party leader, but unfortunately, the train was late and he was called away on other business. Chernov's traveling companions included Avksentiev, Bunakov-Fondaminsky, Boris Moiseenko, and Boris Savinkov. All but Chernov had belonged to the enthusiastically defencist *Prizyv* group in Paris. Kerensky had shared Chernov's views on the war in

1915, but early in 1917, he had tried to resume contact with the SR defencists.[6]

Chernov and Kerensky were intellectual and temperamental opposites. Chernov, was a Marxisant intellectual, and theoretician, who had been a member of the SR Central Committee since its foundation. Where Kerensky's oratory was electric, Chernov's was complacent and sometimes marred by a rather juvenile sense of humour. Chernov notably lacked Kerensky's dynamism and he was emotionally unable to see enemies on the left. Chernov had remained loyal to Zimmerwald and he resented Kerensky's "usurpation" of SR leadership in 1915–1916.

In the wake of the Revolution, the Petrograd SRs had warmly endorsed Kerensky's entry into the government, while reaffirming their principled opposition to a coalition of socialist and bourgeois parties, a tortuous distinction. The party organ, *Delo Naroda*, accepted Kerensky's presence in the government as an entirely adequate guarantee of socialist interests and accepted his definition of the revolution as a 'national' one. Kerensky's comrades were victorious in the elections to the Executive of the Petrograd Committee of the PSR early in April. Zenzinov became chairman, A. R. Gotz, rapidly becoming Kerensky's personal liaison officer with the Soviet, became vice-chairman, and Boris Flekkel, secretary.[7]

Chernov found the policies of *Delo Naroda* "impermissible" and tried to radicalize the paper. He feared that the reaction to Lenin's 'April Theses' was being manipulated by the bourgeois press to discredit all socialists. Lenin was an unfortunate product of the abnormal political life of the past who would soon be tamed by present Russian realities. "I am amused by the fears that the reverse will occur, that he will destroy the new Russian life." It was in response to this slight left turn in the PSR that on April 12, Zenzinov again defended Kerensky's entry into the government in *Delo Naroda*.[8]

Kerensky, as early as March 2, had asked the British Embassy to send "a strong representation of English Labour Party." The Labour Party, the French Socialists, and Chairman Samuel Gompers, of the U. S. American Federation of Labor (AF of L) had all sent patriotic messages and soon Allied socialists began to arrive at the Soviet. On April 4, Kerensky met Ernest Lafont, Marius Moutet, and Marcel Cachin at the French Embassy. He criticized Milyukov but emphasized that he himself was no defeatist. "The minister did not conceal," wrote Paléologue, "that in his opinion a German attack on the Russian front would have the salutary effect of cutting short party controversy and would recall the parties to reality."[9]

At a reception in the Mariinsky Palace on the following day, the Frenchmen were joined by their British comrades, James O'Grady, William Sanders, and Will Thorne. Milyukov spoke first, assuring them that Russia's policy toward the Allies had been unaffected by the revolution. Kerensky followed, throwing diplomatic etiquette to the winds. The occasion was made all the more piquant as it was Milyukov himself who acted as interpreter. "I am alone in the cabinet," said Kerensky, "and my opinion does not always coincide with that of the majority." The guests had not yet heard the voice of Russian Democracy. "We have decided to forestall any attempts at imperialism and conquest by our own country," he declared. These two speeches exposed what seemed to Nabokov a basic flaw within the government, threatening the rapid disintegration of "the artificial combination of Kerensky and Milyukov."[10]

Four days later, the Finland Station hosted yet another festive reception for Albert Thomas, socialist minister of munitions in the French government. Thomas, a veteran socialist, had been called to the colors as a sergeant, but was soon released and charged with the coordination of the French railroad system. In May 1915, he became head of the newly created department of Artillery and Munitions. In this capacity he visited Russia in 1916, making a favorable impression on the Tsar, but finding time to talk to the Duma left as well.

In December 1916, Thomas was promoted to Minister of Munitions with a seat in the French war cabinet, where he warmly supported General Nivelle's ill-fated plan for an offensive in the spring of 1917. He seemed an ideal candidate to represent Allied interests in revolutionary Russia. He became the most influential resident diplomat and one of the few foreigners to play a really important part in Russian politics in 1917. It is often assumed, perhaps mistakenly, that he was a freemason, as were so many other politicians of the Third Republic. His black beard and twinkling eyes became a familiar feature at political gatherings of all sorts during the spring and summer.[11]

Kerensky tried not to neglect his traditional constituents. Early in April, the Free Economic Society elected him an honorary member. The Fifth All-Russian Congress of Trudoviks elected him its honorary chairman, unperturbed by his "defection" to the SRs. The All-Russian Teachers' conference elected him an honorary member and he attended the All-Russian Conference of Railroadmen. These bodies represented that mixture of the lower intelligentsia and the more literate and prosperous members of the working classes that Kerensky had represented as a Trudovik deputy, the leaven, he hoped, of the new, democratic Russia.

Kerensky thanked the Trudoviks for past comradeship. For them he defined socialism as "the idea of absolute reverence before one value alone: before the human being and his personality." He told the teachers that "formally and essentially the Provisional Government disposes of a plenitude of power, but we are only Russian citizens and . . . we ourselves want control over our activities so that every step may be endorsed by the whole country." He promised the railroadmen that the government would lead the country to the Constituent Assembly as promised, and he paid tribute to the great organizing work performed by the soviets. Nekrasov followed him: "Over the Provisional Government is the hand of democracy," he proclaimed, and he swore a "Hannibalic oath" that Kerensky would not go unsupported in the cabinet.[12]

Kerensky did not miss Breshkovskaya's return. The "Grandmother of the Revolution" combined the appearance of a peasant *babushka* with the moral sensibility of a Russian student. Unlike her peer and comrade, Vera Figner, she was blessed with a warm and outgoing personality and some oratorical gifts. She traveled with Kerensky to revisit the garrison and soviet in Tallinn. Sadly, Kerensky's old friend Poska had now been dismissed as government commissar in Tallinn as a result of pressure from the Bolshevik influenced Reval Soviet. Kerensky professed not to believe in the disintegration of the "free Russian Empire" and he addressed the Estonians with greater confidence than the Finns: "We come towards you and say: if you want, come with us; if not, be free. And if you don't want to come with us it will hurt us but we shall bear it so as not to inflict mutual wounds." He reminded them that he had begun his career defending Estonians against national oppression; he would defend the German minority with the same ardor. Once more, he was overwhelmed by his reception.[13]

The "spring wave" that had inspired Hippius' fine lyric to *La Marseillaise* was still alive in March and April, and with it the hope that the "March poppy," the red flag, might yet chase away the curse of war. It fluttered at the grandiose funeral for the victims of the Revolution and on May Day, celebrated in Russia on April 18. Even a Frenchman who viewed all Russian events through the prism of French sufferings was carried away by the grandeur of this occasion. "It was a human sea, above the waves of which floated hundreds of red banners with gilded inscriptions which the wind tossed about, and whose gold letters shone, for a moment, in the sun." He was impressed by the calm and order that prevailed. Good humor and kindness, even toward a bourgeois, were the order of the day.[14]

That evening, meetings were held in all the theaters and arenas of Petrograd. Kerensky and 'Babushka' joined Chernov, Avksentiev, and Berezin at the Cinizelli Circus, the largest of them all. There were revolutionary songs from the choir of the Volynsky Guards, who had decided the revolution. Kerensky was at his most exhalted: Didn't the day's proceedings show that a free people could be trusted? "Since the time of the great French revolution," he said proudly, "not a single country has lived through such great days." Russia had massive problems, and discipline would be required to resolve them, but he disowned coercion: "There are those who say: 'how can you rule, you don't even have a police force?' But Comrades, we don't need one because the people are with us." He turned to the choir and led them in *La Marsellaise*. A member of the audience jumped on the stage and asked everyone to swear to follow Kerensky,. "We swear," echoed from hundreds of throats. One of the Volyntsy stood up, shouting, "Comrades, A. F. Kerensky is not bad at conducting the orchestra," there was laughter, then the soldier continued, "but he conducts the Russian revolution even better. Let's wish him the strength to remain at his responsible post much longer." There was an outburst of warm applause. Kerensky came back to ask the choir to join him in the *Internationale*, and his fine voice led them in the familiar words:

> Arise, ye branded by the curse,
> The whole world of hunger and slavery . . . [15]

How could one not have faith in such people?

And yet. In the cooler atmosphere of his ministry, the brave words about dispensing with a police force must have looked a little thin when he was asked to prosecute illegal seizures of property. Only a day or so after this great meeting, Kerensky had to direct local public prosecutors to prosecute those inciting class war.[16] Could they really be handled without a police force? The events of the week that followed seriously undermined Kerensky's confidence in the people, and made the first serious dent in his popularity. Paradoxically, it also saw the achievement of the hopes he had nurtured since 1915— hopes partly frustrated by Sukhanov and Milyukov in February— for a people's government with democratic war aims.

As the first verbal shots were exchanged in what would prove to be the final battle with Milyukov over war aims, Kerensky became the pivot of a curious alliance, embracing men of equal caliber to himself. Iraklii Tsereteli forged a new and disciplined majority in the Soviet, and Albert Thomas lent Kerensky his total support from the French Embassy. Helpful roles were played by Chernov, Prince Lvov, and Sir George Buchanan. For Milyukov, the revelation that Nekrasov, Tereshchenko and Konovalov were bound to Kerensky by "fraternal" ties was now confirmed. The defection of Prince Lvov, V. N. Lvov, and Godnev was less expected. Most shattering for him was the attitude of the Allies. He suspected, wrongly, that the initiative came from perfidious Albion, anxious to renege on her pledge to hand the Straits to Russia, a pledge that cut across generations of Foreign Office statecraft.[17]

Chernov opened the campaign, on April 10, when he urged the Soviet Executive Committee to insist that the government circulate its declaration of March 27 as a binding diplomatic note. On the following day, he went with Bunakov-Fondaminsky and Avksentiev to see Kerensky. This was the first meeting between Chernov and Kerensky; apparently they agreed on tactics for dealing with war aims. A slip by Kerensky many years later suggested that their conversations may have ranged even more widely. It is quite likely that Kerensky outlined to Chernov his hopes of a coalition of the progressive bourgeoisie and "Democracy," failing which he himself might have to withdraw from the cabinet.[18]

Reasonably enough, Soviet historians of the April Crisis seek an explanation of Kerensky's own foreign-policy views in his own later writings. Thus, they conclude, Kerensky shared Milyukov's war aims, but wished to pursue them in secret. This interpretation has the added merit of confirming Lenin's diagnosis of Kerensky as especially suspect, but it is contradicted by such witnesses as T. G.

Masaryk, who testify to Kerensky's sincere hostility to chauvinism at this time. Much of the blame for this confusion attaches to Kerensky himself. His nationalism became more marked as he got older and he had to justify himself in exile not to the workers of Petrograd, but to conservative exiles and leaders of opinion in the West.[19]

Fortunately, there are more reliable contemporary records. On the day Chernov paid his first visit to Kerensky, Albert Thomas followed for his first confidential discussion with his Russian comrade. Thomas was a meticulous diarist so we can eavesdrop upon them. Thomas expressed his anxiety lest the demand for democratic war aims turn into an excuse for a separate peace. "Kerensky replied at first very firmly that the thought of Constantinople, despite the assurances which Milyukov and Rodzyanko have given me, does not haunt the religious spirit of the muzhiks at all; this is a pure legend." He continued more positively, "the Russian masses sense in themselves the birth of a new Western sort of patriotism." Kerensky agreed that there had been some pacifist feeling during the revolution, but this was a natural reaction to the policies of the old regime. Thomas was afraid that the upsurge of patriotism anticipated by Kerensky might arrive too late to save the Allies from defeat. Kerensky reassured him, though "some time was necessary for the new sense of patriotism to develop in all of Russia, but if the German [sic] attacks, it may burst out suddenly."

Kerensky insisted that a plebiscite would have to precede the incorporation of Alsace-Lorraine by France and he expressed his suspicions of "English imperialism." Thomas reassured him in turn. "We will find a supporter in Lloyd George and in any case, the possession of a few colonies is not the same as brutal annexations which take place against the desires of the populace." (The view that non-Europeans had wishes that mattered was held by only a minority of European socialists at this date.) The French would have no trouble renouncing annexations once the Russians conceded that Alsace-Lorraine was not an annexation! Kerensky was willing to agree that a distinction should be made between tribute exacted from a defeated enemy, and reparations for specific damage caused by the German army.[20] In his desire to ingratiate himself with Thomas, Kerensky lost sight of the crucial question: would Russian soldiers unwilling to fight for a Russian 'Tsargrad' really fight for a French Alsace-Lorraine or the reconstruction of Rheims and Ypres?

That same evening, the Contact Commission of the Soviet, freshly purged of such Internationalists as Sukhanov and Steklov, met the government for a regular exchange of views. Chernov was present for the first time, and he requested the government to circulate its declaration of March 27 as a diplomatic note. He knew he could count on the support of Prince Lvov, Nekrasov, and Tereshchenko. Milyukov argued in isolation, disputing Chernov's account of changes in Allied opinion and asserting that a renunciation of annexations would be interpreted by the Allies as a first step toward a separate peace. The meeting was short and amicable and Tsereteli and Chernov left confident they had made their point.[21]

On the following day, Thomas went with an SR delegation, including Chernov, to the Ministry of Justice for lunch. Breshkovskaya acted as hostess at this repast, whose frugality disappointed the Frenchman. "There were two dishes without desert, no drink, just a little water." Kerensky was making a revolutionary virtue of his medically controlled diet. Thomas confirmed Chernov's suspicions that the Allies had ignored the declaration of March 27. Chernov tried to convince Thomas that revolution was imminent in Germany, enhancing the prospects of success for a Russian peace policy. Kerensky let the conversation flow. Milyukov naturally took exception to Thomas' personal diplomacy, reminding him that "in the capacity of a French minister" he could not possibly accept the suggestion that the Allies renounce "all annexations and contributions," a point Thomas was obliged to repeat to Kerensky.[22]

As Milyukov sadly remembered, Thomas' clarification had "no practical result," for on April 13, *Delo Naroda* announced that the government "is at present preparing a note" informing the Allies of Russia's new war aims as formulated in the declaration of March 27. Paléologue asked Milyukov whether this was true. "I'm not," he exploded, "I read it in the newspaper . . . You see how they treat me! . . . They are obviously trying to force my hand. I will take the matter to the Council of ministers this evening."[23]

Milyukov went onto the offensive. What did Kerensky mean by putting out an announcement which he knew to be false? Kerensky squirmed. Although the government had not yet considered sending the Allies such a note, he, Nekrasov, and Tereshchenko intended to raise the issue in the near future; in other words, the announcement had been improper but not intentionally dishonest. Kerensky's brethren failed to come to his rescue. Milyukov won a famous victory, and *Rech'* followed with the laconic announcement that "the government has not considered the question of war aims and is not preparing any note on this matter." Over the next few days, Milyukov received the full backing of the Kadet Central Committee and Prime Minister Ribot instructed Thomas to forestall any request for a reconsideration of Allied war aims.[24]

Kerensky was indeed trying to force developments with his announcement in *Delo Naroda*, in the hope of ousting Milyukov from the government; but Nekrasov and Tereshchenko were evidently as surprised by it as Milyukov, so who was supposed to back him up? Was it the Soviet, which, in his memoirs, he accuses of a "slippery, dualistic policy"? If he felt let down by his Masonic brethren and his Soviet comrades, they must have been very irritated by him. As Tsereteli and Chernov faced the gloating Bolsheviks in the Soviet, they must have had some uncharitable thoughts about Kerensky's tactics.[25]

When Thomas saw Kerensky shortly after this debacle, Kerensky was highly embarrassed at his defeat and bitterly resentful at the threat it posed to his policies of conciliation. "The attitude of Milyukov involves the government in great dangers," he confided. "He has around him some men of the right who are as dangerous to the government as Lenin's people on the extreme left." If Milyukov continued in this way, he would have to leave the government. "If on the other hand, and against my expectations," Kerensky continued, "he carries the day then it is I who shall have to leave the ministry . . . I have in the government a special position," he hinted darkly, "I don't make it felt often and I only use it to exert pressure in cases of absolute necessity, but I take into account the fact that if I leave then everything will collapse."[26]

Equally put out, the new Soviet leaders warned the government that they would not endorse its "Liberty Loan" until the declaration had been sent, while Chernov mocked "Milyukov-Dardanelsky" (i. e., "conqueror of the Straits") in *Delo Naroda*. Eventually, Milyukov succumbed to the pressure of his colleagues and agreed to circulate the declaration of March 27 to the Allies, but only with a covering note.[27]

On April 18, the government assembled at the bedside of Guchkov, then suffering from a heart condition, in his apartment on

Moika, a somber contrast with the jubilant May Day celebrations outside. Milyukov's draft described Allied war aims as liberating in character, and therefore acceptable to free Russia. Russia's part in the war effort would not slacken, as the people were now determined on a decisive victory over the invader and looked forward to the destruction of Germany. The government would punctiliously observe all obligations accepted by previous governments toward the Allies, and the democratic powers would together achieve "those guarantees and sanctions which are necessary for the prevention of new bloody conflicts in the future."

At first everyone was happy with the draft, "but then Kerensky began to take exceptions to isolated expressions, proposing extremely unfortunate variants; the mood began to go sour, the usual personal antagonism made itself felt in raised tones and sharp remarks." The reference to the destruction of Germany was deleted. Finally, a text was approved which, according to Kerensky, "should have satisfied the most violent critics of 'imperialism'." This view was not shared by Buchanan, who felt it breached the spirit, if not the letter, of the declaration of March 27, but Kerensky had no intimation of trouble ahead and he was in high spirits when he went to the mass meeting at the Cinizelli Circus that evening.[28]

The Soviet leaders first saw the statement on April 19. Tsereteli immediately read it aloud to Chkheidze, Skobelev, and Dan. Chkheidze muttered, "Milyukov is the evil genius of the revolution." They could foresee how the document would read to a German or Austrian socialist, anxious to end the war without ruining his or her country. The word victory excluded a negotiated peace. It did not commit Russia to the annexation of Constantinople—though it did not exclude it—but it obliged Russia to support secret treaties providing for the unconditional return of Alsace-Lorraine to France, Italian annexation of Slavonic Dalmatia, and the conquest of Germany's colonies by Britain and Japan. The final words about "guarantees and sanctions" might include the disarming and partition of Germany or punitive reparations.

So, far from meeting them halfway, it looked as though Milyukov was retracting previous concessions. This had implications far beyond the realm of foreign policy. It identified Milyukov with that political tradition in which promises to foreign powers are "sacred obligations," while promises to one's own people have no binding force. Kerensky ought to have foreseen this, and perhaps Tsereteli was right to explain his conduct as "frivolous"—another example of misjudgment arising from the enormous burdens he had to endure. Kerensky must also have felt inhibited by his previous defeat by Milyukov.[29]

When Kerensky joined other leading ministers in a reception for delegates of the Third Army, his popularity seemed as great as ever, and Lieutenant Colonel Postnikov told him how much the army appreciated the presence of the "minister-democrat" in the government. During the day, however, Kerensky received news of his comrades' reaction to the diplomatic note and that evening he told Thomas that the Soviet would condemn it. Several very unpleasant days followed. He was haunted by the spectre of a civil war in which he would be in the horribly invidious position of participating in a government willing to provoke civil conflict merely to preserve the "imperialist" war aims of the Allies and maintain Russia's option on the Straits.[30]

The evening of April 19 should have been a happy occasion. Olga, still publicly recognized as his wife, had organized a concert-meeting in the Mikhailovsky Theater in aid of returning political prisoners and exiles. Paléologue and Thomas were in attendance, atoning for the past collaboration of the French with the *Okhrana*. The meeting opened with Tchaikovsky's Fourth Symphony, followed by works of Glazunov and Cui. Milyukov, in fine fettle, opened the speechmaking "vibrant with patriotism and energy." He was followed by an aria from *Tosca*. A Siberian ex-convict—not a political prisoner—sought permission to speak to the meeting, but when he began to advocate fraternization with the Germans, he was howled off the stage.

Milyukov, whose appearances rarely evoked much enthusiasm, remarked acidly that "Kerensky always 'appeared.' " For once, Milyukov could have no complaint as Kerensky attacked fraternization, pointing out that the Germans were not fraternizing on the Western front. He was unusually depressed, however.

If the people don't wish to believe and follow me, I shall leave power. I shall never use force to make my opinion triumph. . . . When a country wants to throw itself into the abyss, no human power can prevent it and those who lead the government have only one thing to do: resign.[31]

At midnight that night, the Soviet Executive Committee met to consider Milyukov's note. No one tried to defend it. Tsereteli, Skobelev, Stankevich, and Bramson all argued that the note was Milyukov's entire responsibility; they were confident that the government as a whole would disavow it. For the left-wing minority, Yurenev and Shlyapnikov demanded immediate mass action against the government, a call echoed by Kamenev with his usual caution. The Bolsheviks, he said, would not initiate independent mass action but they would support any demonstration the committee cared to authorize.[32]

On April 20, the newspapers reappeared, with the text of Milyukov's note. One of many to react with instantaneous shock and anger was a young cadet officer, Cornet F. F. Linde of the Finland Guards, one of three members of the Soviet Executive Committee's military section. He assembled his men, harangued them about Milyukov's note, and led them onto the streets carrying banners reading "Down with Milyukov!" They canvassed support among the Kexholm Guards and the Second Marine Guards and then set off for the Mariinsky Palace, where they handed in a petition protesting against the note and demanding Milyukov's resignation.

The demonstration was cut short when Skobelev arrived to point out that their action had not been authorized by the Soviet, which was taking its own steps to secure a change of government policy. The Kadets were quick to allege that Linde was a Bolshevik. He was in fact an impractical idealist with a volatile temperament, who had once flirted with Bolshevism, but who was now an enthusiastic follower of Kerensky and who was later martyred as such. Later that day, groups of soldiers and workers from the Vyborg side also began to march into the center of the city to protest against the note. The vanguard party could not afford to find itself in the rearguard.[33]

This was the moment of truth for the new commander of the Petrograd Military District, General Lavr Kornilov. Since his visit to the Kerensky home in Tashkent in the 1890s, he had enjoyed a distinguished career in both the Japanese War and the First World War, crowning his success on the field of battle by escaping, while already a general, from an Austrian POW camp. Outspoken in politics, he had been closely associated with Guchkov's criticisms of the conduct of the war by the Imperial government. Immediately after the February Revolution, Guchkov brought him to Petrograd in the hope that his prestige and down-to-earth manner would help to calm the garrison. He made a fair impression on the Soviet, and played an active part in helping to institutionalize the new relations between officers and men, a task more reactionary officers evaded.

Throughout the day, Kornilov met groups of soldiers and appealed to them to return to their barracks, often successfully. He also suggested to the government that it use force to quell the demonstrations, but Prince Lvov and Nekrasov had already spoken to Tsereteli about ways of taking the sting out of the crisis and the last thing they wanted was blood on their hands. As Kerensky put it shortly afterward, "Our strength lies in moral influence, and to apply armed force would be to adopt the old road of compulsion, which I consider impossible."[34]

Sometime on April 20, Kerensky saw Albert Thomas once more for a brief exchange: "two dangers threaten the Russian republic," he said, "the followers of Milyukov and those of Lenin." Later that day they met again after government and the Soviet Executive Committee had agreed to meet for a full discussion of their differences. To Thomas' astonishment, Kerensky told him he intended to miss this meeting. "He does not want to be forced to speak against his comrades, [or] to remain a silent figure and hopes to be absent." Kerensky was increasingly fearful of a general revolt and aware that the Soviet leaders were out to increase their leverage over the government ·by allowing *all* the socialist parties to join its delegation. The bourgeois ministers would have to face the Bolsheviks themselves.

Kerensky told Thomas there were two conceivable ways to resolve the crisis. The government could appeal to the provinces for support, as Milyukov desired, in which case anarchy might take over. Alternatively, the provisional government could be reformed. Milyukov and most of his cabinet would depart. Kerensky would become prime minister, and only Nekrasov, Tereshchenko, and Konovalov would be retained. Thomas, genuinely shocked by this revelation of boundless ambition, objected. Such a reform would be "literally impossible"; it would amount to a new regime. Unmoved, Kerensky reproached Thomas for dissuading him from purging Milyukov sooner, a charge Thomas denied, reminding Kerensky that he himself had wanted to retain Milyukov previously. Milyukov could remain a minister now, Kerensky continued, only "on condition that he submits."

The two men ended their conversation on a friendly note as Thomas reminded Kerensky of their common interests, "not simply as a minister and a colleague . . . but above all as a comrade." For Thomas, Kerensky was still "the only one capable, by prudent and democratic policies, of re-establishing order in Russia, and reviving the war effort."[35]

While Kerensky was brooding on the reconstruction of the government, counterdemonstrations were hurriedly organized by the Kadet Party. The seat of the government was situated among the homes of the upper bourgeoisie and senior civil servants, so it was not too difficult for the Kadets to mobilize demonstrations which, from the windows of the Mariinsky Palace, appeared as impressive as those directed against Milyukov. Government supporters soon carried the day. By the time the government received the Soviet leaders to discuss their differences, the Palace was surrounded by Milyukov's cheering supporters. Both Nekrasov and Milyukov seemed equally pleased at this little victory. "Citizens," Nekrasov declared, "a little group of people cannot disturb the Provisional Government." The Government even felt strong enough to issue a statement reiterating that its note had been unanimously approved by the government, thereby twisting the knife in Kerensky's wound.[36]

At 9:00 P.M., the government opened its discussions with the Soviet. To emphasize that the very existence of the government was at stake, the Duma Committee also took part. To the surprise of the Soviet delegates, the ministers made no mention of the "Milyukov note." Instead they were lectured on the catastrophic state of the country, as Stalin laconically reported in *Pravda*:

It turned out that for the salvation of the country it is necessary 1) to curb the soldiers (Guchkov), 2) to curb the peasants (Shingaryov), 3) to curb the revolutionary workers (all the ministers), [who were] undermining the prestige of the Provisional Government. Support us in this difficult task, help us to wage a war of attack [Milyukov], and then everything will be all right. Otherwise we resign.[37]

Despite Stalin's irony, "this brief ultimatum came like a douche of cold water to the hotheads" and Kamenev showed no enthusiasm for an immediate Soviet takeover. Fortified by Soviet diffidence, the government refused to send a new note to the Allies, though it defined "victory" in such a way as to exclude the enslavement or humiliation of foreign nations and explained that by "guarantees and sanctions" it had meant limitations on armaments and international tribunals. But Milyukov knew he had overplayed his hand, as he told Paléologue: "j'ai trop vaincu."[38]

In Kerensky's absence, the other ministers had supported Milyukov out of collective solidarity. How could they carry out their mandate if they gave way to the demands of the latest mob to arrive at the Mariinsky Palace? Such feelings were stiffened by an ultimatum from the Kadet Central Committee. However, the net effect of the "April Crisis" was to complete the alienation of the ministers from Milyukov. Prince Lvov, in particular, was unhappy to see the good relations he had so painstakingly constructed with Tsereteli shattered merely so that Milyukov could indulge in dreams of Constantinople.

Nor were popular attitudes to be gauged solely by the Kadet demonstration on the night of April 20. Was Russia's fragile bourgeoisie really willing to fight a civil war over the Straits? What would happen if the Soviet mobilized all its potential support for mass action? It is not surprising that many educated Russians began to feel that Milyukov—an able man no doubt—might be better suited to some other position of responsibility. Chernov's jibe that the Straits were less contentious in geography lessons, under the control of the Minister of Education, began to assume some merit.[39]

The following afternoon, armed Red Guards of workers marched into the city center. The Bolsheviks were still publicly cautious, but it is difficult to believe that they were not involved. This time shots were exchanged and there were a few serious casualties. The Soviet Executive Committee was shocked into action, instructing all citizens to "maintain peace, order and discipline," prohibiting the bearing of arms at demonstrations, and asserting its right to prevent the emergence of soldiers from barracks. This last point was aimed both at Cornet Linde and General Kornilov. He envied them:

Yes, these gentlemen have got authority all right. They have been elected by the soldiers and their propaganda work is increasing. I have a few good regiments, but there are others over which I have no control at all, unless I am actually on the spot. My position is intolerable. . . . I was happy enough at the front, in command of a fine Army Corps! . . . and here I am in Petrograd, a hotbed of anarchy, with a mere shadow of authority.

Eventually he was allowed to' resign and return to the front, where he nursed his grievances. For the time being, most people were glad that order was returning and had few qualms at the thought that it was the Soviet that had done most to calm the atmosphere.[40]

Kerensky was virtually eclipsed by the April Crisis and for several days he hid from public view. The crisis had put an enormous strain on his relations both with his masonic brethren and with his Soviet comrades. For the first time, the far left had been able to attack him personally, proposing that he be stripped of his Soviet vice-chairman-ship for agreeing to the "Milyukov note." Tsereteli had been able to parry this proposal only by suggesting that he had agreed to the note in a moment of frivolity. Gorky also spoke up for him, alleging, mistakenly, and to the fury of the Kadets, that Kerensky had voted against the note in the government.[41]

When Kerensky met Thomas next on April 21 he was still not certain that he could avoid resignation, but his thoughts were focused on the isolation and elimination of Milyukov. He mentioned the idea of an inner cabinet to "concern itself with foreign affairs and control the execution by the minister of foreign affairs of the decisions of the government," evidently a lever by which to push Milyukov out. Kerensky begged Thomas to intervene with Prince Lvov and Guch-kov in favor of this proposal; perhaps his own voice no longer carried so much weight. Later that day, Guchkov told Thomas that Mil-yukov had been obliged to agree to the constitution of an inner cabinet.[42]

After April 21, Kerensky, Nekrasov and Tereshchenko began to urge the "broadening" of the cabinet to include representatives of the Soviet. The forces in favor of coalition grew stronger daily. Few ministers felt that a government which insisted on a legalistic exe-cution of its mandate would long survive, while Prince Lvov and Kerensky were ideologically disposed to seek an organic and dem-ocratic relationship between government and people which excluded repression.

On April 26, the government published an appeal for support which became known as the "political testament" of the First Provisional Government. It reviewed all the government's achievements in the realms of civic and social legislation, the defense of the country, and preparations for the Constituent Assembly. It also advanced a theory of its relations with its subjects that seemed excessively utopian, even then:

The Provisional Government . . . believes that the power of a state should be based not on violence and coercion, but on the consent of free citizens to submit to the power which they themselves created. . . . Not a single drop of blood has been shed through its fault, nor have restrictive measures been established against any trend of public opinion.

Sadly, the destructive forces unleashed by the old regime were working more effectively than the creative ones released by the new one. It warned of the path, "well known to history, leading from freedom, through civil war and anarchy to reaction and the return of despotism," and it appealed to all Russian citizens to unite "around the government which you created."[43]

At the same time, Kerensky wrote to the Central Committee of the PSR, the Petrograd Soviet, the Trudovik fraction of the Duma, and the Duma Committee, reminding them of the circumstances in which he had entered the government and indicating his reasons for believing that they had changed. "I think that representatives of labouring democracy have the right to assume the burden of power only through direct election and official authorization by the organizations to which they belong." Milyukov described this as a letter of resignation and remarked that, like Boris Godunov, Kerensky always resigned upward.[44]

Chernov would later claim to have drafted this letter for Kerensky, a claim Kerensky indignantly denied. At all events, both men were working closely together for a coalition government. As was Prince Lvov. On the day after the publication of Kerensky's letter, Lvov formally asked the Soviet Executive Committee to reconsider the question of coalition. Chkheidze and Tsereteli still opposed the idea of Soviet participation in a coalition for fear that it would awaken unrealizable hopes among the people. The victims of the subsequent disillusion would be not only the Menshevik ministers but also the government they had supported. Most SRs wanted a coalition. Avksentiev was strongly in favor, as was Gotz, but they felt unable to enter a coalition without the Mensheviks. Some left-wing SRs were opposed, as were the Bolsheviks. The proposal was narrowly defeated, but not before Stalin had asked the Mensheviks the pertinent question, "Isn't it all the same entering the government yourselves as carrying this government on your shoulders?"[45]

On April 29, Guchkov addressed the first congress of delegates from the front at the Tauride Palace. He was more optimistic than in his speech to the combined Dumas two days earlier. He described the measures taken to improve army morale and reaffirmed the view that democratization must continue so long as the personal responsibility of the officers was not infringed. As Kerensky entered the hall, Guchkov had to pause for the applause to subside. When Kerensky's turn to speak arrived, a much-decorated soldier jumped on the platform and called for cheers for Kerensky.

The week had left Kerensky with a cold premonition of disaster and he had little to say to lighten the hearts of the men.

At the present moment with the victory of new ideas and the establishment of a democratic state in Europe, we can play a colossal part in world history, if we can encourage other peoples to follow our path, if we oblige our friends and our enemies to respect our freedom. . . . If, like worthless slaves, we are not an organized strong state, then a dark and bloody period of internecine strife will ensue and our ideas will be cast under the maxim of state: might is right and not right, might.

His language betrayed emotional desperation as he warned the soldiers that his personal resources were waning.

I regret that I did not die then, two months ago: I would have died with the great dream that a new life had been kindled in Russia once and for all, that we could respect one another in the absence of whips and sticks and could administer our own state not as the former despots ruled it.

And now he adopted a tone no one had dared to use since the Tsar had been deposed. It was not the oratory of revolution, but a dressing down:

Comrades, you could be patient and silent for ten years. You were able to carry out the obligations imposed on you by the old hated government. You were even able to shoot the people when that was asked of you. Why do you have no patience now? Surely the free Russian state is not a state of rebellious slaves?

There was a moment's dead silence, followed by a hostile reaction. A non-commissioned officer stood up. For him there remained only one speaker "who understands the interests and sufferings of our brothers sitting in the trenches and that man is I. G. Tsereteli." He was loudly cheered. Tsereteli suggests that tactful journalists failed to record some even more hostile remarks. Overnight, the NCO was persuaded to "clarify" his comments. "After A. F. Kerensky's speech," he explained, "I felt I was losing my hope and my belief in the future and I could not help explaining that I believe in the Russian revolution, in the Russian people." The danger was unmistakable. Only the oratory of optimism could move the masses in revolutionary Russia. This was the resource Kerensky had once possessed in abundance. Should it desert him, popular rejection would be instantaneous. For months, the phrase "rebellious slaves" echoed round the trenches and barracks of Russia.[46]

Prince Lvov now called on Milyukov to urge him to resign his portfolio and facilitate the formation of a coalition. Milyukov refused the proferred hemlock and argued back vigorously. Since the negotiations were going on over his head, he and Shingaryov decided to pay a visit to the army GHQ, a move that aroused suspicions on the left.[47]

By the time they got to Mogilev, Guchkov had quit. In his letter of resignation, he protested against "the conditions in which the power of the government is now placed" and condemned those responsible for this "sin" against the fatherland. Milyukov, who would have fought on had anyone supported him, was furious at Guchkov's "desertion," which both he and General Alexeyev felt was based on misplaced pessimism.[48] Guchkov's resignation showed the political bankruptcy of the upper bourgeoisie. Divided and depressed, they abandoned the government to liberal intellectuals and 'statesmanlike' socialists.

Meanwhile, the pressure built up on the Mensheviks from democratic organizations all over Russia, which inundated them with telegrams pleading for coalition. Young Turks, such as Colonel Yakubovich also begged them to re-create a government commanding the respect of the army. On May 1, the Soviet Executive Committee reconsidered the question of coalition. No new exegesis of the Marxist classics emerged. The Bolsheviks still opposed the proposal, though they could scarcely conceal their glee at the prospect that their rivals were about to compromise themselves. The vote was a foregone conclusion, and by 44–19, the committee approved negotiations for a coalition.[49]

Then, as now, socialist intellectuals had a touching faith in mandates and manifestoes, so once again the negotiations began with the drafting of a program. It reiterated that political freedoms would be respected and the country led to the Constituent Assembly. The government would work for the speediest possible peace settlement, but not a separate peace. The principal task would be the democratization of the army and the restoration of its capacity for both defensive and offensive operations. More novel was the proposal for modest forays into areas of social policy. Preparations would begin for an agrarian reform based on the principle that the land should belong to those who worked it, while the government would try to see that food supplies did not suffer. The interests of industrial labor would be safeguarded and progressive taxation would be introduced.[50]

It was obvious that Milyukov could not belong to the new government, while Kerensky, so long a pacifist, was destined to be Minister of war. This extraordinary transfiguration was taken so much for granted that even Nabokov called Kerensky "the Providential Minister of War." Kerensky's elevation caused the more conservative officers to shudder inwardly, yet there was a great deal of sense to it. He had taken an active part in restoring calm and good order in the Baltic Fleet, though the Menshevik Skobelev had done even more. During his visit to GHQ, Kerensky had impressed the new Supreme Commander-in-Chief, General Alexeyev, and the front commanders as a pragmatic patriot. Despite his reference to "rebellious slaves," his speeches to the officers were generally more positive than Guchkov's, as when he told them,

It is necessary, that the officers who have accepted the decisions of the Provisional Government become imbued with the psychology of the soldier-citizen, so that discipline in the army is founded first of all on mutual understanding, on a community of views and on solidarity so that discipline is not the mechanical execution of the orders of command as it was under the old regime.

Such sentiments were the mundane wisdom of the time, though they were held against him later.[51]

Some officers welcomed Kerensky's appointment, particularly the colonels who had participated in General Polivanov's commission on military regulations, and who had urged the Soviet to join the coalition. The leading members of this group were Colonel Yakubovich, Colonel Prince Tumanov, and Kerensky's own brother-in-law, Colonel Vladimir Baranovsky. The approval of the front commanders was decisive. Prince Lvov had phoned his nephew at GHQ to ask Alexeyev for this views. The General made him wait while he consulted his colleagues, and returned with a piece of paper "on which in his small but remarkably neat handwriting was written: 1) Kerensky, 2) Palchinsky." Alexeyev added that this was the opinion of all the front commanders, since they felt a civilian to be the most appropriate choice at the moment.[52]

The negotiations over the composition of the new ministry were apprehensive and testy, with none of the euphoria that had attended the formation of the First Provisional Government. The Kadets glumly accepted Milyukov's exclusion but insisted on retaining a veto over the actions of future Kadet ministers, who would have to carry out party policy and report regularly to the Kadet Central Committee. Over SR objections, the Kadets insisted that the socialists should remain a minority. Anxious to avoid responsibility for government mistakes, the Mensheviks were glad to accept this condition. They wanted Skobelev as Naval Minister, a proposal Kerensky parried by insisting that all military affairs must remain in a single pair of hands. The socialists wanted Nekrasov as Minister of Foreign Affairs, but Nekrasov insisted that Tereshchenko was better qualified; they gave Tereshchenko an impromptu interview before accepting him. The SRs were insistent that Chernov become Minister of Agriculture and this was grudgingly accepted by the Kadets—at least this would keep him away from foreign affairs, as some left-wing SRs were demanding. When the All-Russian Peasant Union demanded that Peshekhonov become minister of food supply, Shingaryov dug his heels in, insisting that the Kadets should not be totally excluded from peasant affairs.[53]

After hours of fruitless negotiations, Kerensky appealed to his socialist comrades to make a conciliatory gesture, reminding them of the desperate plight of the country. Similar pressures were brought to bear on the Kadets. They gave ground, and Shingaryov accepted the Ministry of Finance. It was a jubilant Kerensky who announced the outcome to the socialists.[54]

The Coalition was proclaimed in the early hours of May 5. Prince Lvov remained Prime Minister and Minister of the Interior, though he accepted a Menshevik deputy. Godnev, V. N. Lvov and Konov alov kept their posts, and as agreed, Tereshchenko moved from finance to foreign affairs, Shingaryov from agriculture to finance. Apart from Shingaryov, three other ministers were mandated by the Kadet Central Committee. They were Manuilov (Education), Nekrasov (Transport) and Prince Shakhovskoy (State Control). The six socialists mandated by the Soviet included Kerensky (War and Navy), Pereverzev (Justice), Peshekhonov (Food), Chernov (Agriculture) and Tsereteli (Posts and Telegraphs). Tsereteli's portfolio was a fiction: Chernov had refused to join the government without Tsereteli, fearful of isolation in the Soviet.[55]

Despite socialist scruples about joining a bourgeois government their entry into government aroused tremendous enthusiasm, just as Tsereteli feared it would. Even Trotsky, who had just escaped from a brief internment in Canada, adopted a pedagogic rather than a subversive tone when he explained his reasons for opposing the coalition. The Soviet formula *'postol'ku . . . poskol'ku'* [in so far as], which had so offended Prince Lvov and Kerensky, was abrogated without serious dissent.[56]

Kerensky's own position was substantially altered. From the beginning, he had tried to play an "above-party" role, becoming the focus for both Soviet and bourgeois forces. As relations between them had deteriorated, he had been driven to skulk in his ministry. The "Milyukov note" and the "rebellious slaves" speech had raised the first question marks over his popularity, though at first only in Petrograd. On the other hand, the creation of the coalition was a victory for the policies he had persisted in since before the Revolution.

Kerensky was now a socialist mandated by the Soviet. In practice, he was far closer to his Masonic brethren and Prince Lvov, and his indifference to party policy soon aroused resentment among SR party members, even though the ultimate aim of the PSR had been to unite the working intelligentsia, workers, and peasants, rather than becoming a mere peasant party defending a sectional interest.

The real challenge came not from the structure of the new ministry and its irksome formal ties with other bodies, but from the central issue of war and peace. The government's cohesion depended on its ability to bring the war to an acceptable conclusion. This involved the maintenance of Russia's military power *and* the prosecution of an energetic diplomatic offensive. Kerensky and Tereshchenko now bore the responsibility for these policies.

10

Patriotism of a New Type

Ambassador Paléologue liked to remind wavering Russians that the war had been precipitated by a Slavonic cause—Austrian aggression against Russia's Serbian ally. Liberal Russian society had embraced the Allied cause as a weapon in their struggle with the Tsarist government and they could not abandon it now. The majority of the Provisional Government welcomed the opportunity for a democratic Russia to gain her spurs and assure her future. The entry of the United States into the war confirmed the democratic character of the Entente, guaranteed ultimate victory, and provided hope for a continuation of vital foreign investment, which Britain and France could no longer offer.[1]

The warring sides in the Great War were well-matched. The defection of one partner from either alliance threatened to destroy the alliance as a whole. Russia had promised to support the Nivelle offensive in the spring of 1917. To renege on this pledge was to risk the defeat of the Western allies, who might retaliate by offering the Germans a separate peace at the expense of Russia. The Germans gave no sign that they would tolerate a "no war, no peace" policy.[2]

Kerensky always denied that his offensive military tactics were imposed by Allied military agreements; he claimed they were "dictated absolutely by the inner development of events in Russia."

Having rejected the idea of a separate peace, which is always a misfortune for the country concluding it, the return to new action became unavoidable. . . . the expectancy [by the army] at all times, of impending action constitutes the fundamental condition of its existence. To say to an army in the midst of war that under no circumstances would it be compelled to fight is tantamount to transforming the troops into a meaningless mob, useless, restless, irritable and therefore capable of all sorts of excesses. For this reason, and to preserve the interior of the country from the grave wave of anarchy threatening from the front, it was incumbent upon us, . . . to make of it once more an army, i.e. to bring it back to the psychology of action, or of impending action.

This was the end of Kerensky's flirtation with Zimmerwaldism. His conversion to that "exalted patriotism" which stuck in Tsereteli's craw was now complete.[3]

By 1917, the Russian Army had grown to more than ten million men, the largest army in the world. It included men of many nationalities (some organized in national units), of many religions, of all social classes, and of a wide range in age. It even included a few female combatants. Its attitudes were correspondingly heterogeneous. The sailors at the Kronstadt naval base and the Latvian Rifleman were sympathetic to Bolshevism from the start. The Black Sea Fleet, the artillery, and the other national units were more moderate. Morale was higher among those facing the Austro-Hungarians than those facing the Germans. For some time the men at the front were intensely resentful that the Petrograd garrison was exempt from service at the front.

The officers were no more homogeneous than the men. Many monarchist officers were removed during the February Revolution, but the high command still consisted of career officers. Junior officers, increasingly recruited from the lower intelligentsia, regarded the traditional rights of officers with some ambivalence. They had in common a fear of humiliation and of death at the hands of their own men. It was, in addition, the officer corps rather than the numerically insignificant capitalist class that represented continuity with the tradition of state service. Most of them assumed that this involved the continuation of capitalism, but their vision that the state had interests independent of those of a specific class would lead many to serve the Red Army as competently as they had once served the Tsar.[4]

Most of the army had played a passive part in the Revolution. There were tense days of disjointed telegrams and denials before the final confirmation of the triumph of the revolution. Then the men responded with deep satisfaction and the oath to the new government was taken in a holiday atmosphere. The SR Captain Stepun felt that the soldiers hoped for every imaginable benefit from the Revolution, including an end to the war, without ceasing to be patriotic. Sukhanov was shocked at the patriotic sentiments of the soldier section of the Petrograd Soviet, the most politicized body of soldiers in the army. The Bolsheviks had themselves exploited anti-German feeling in the Baltic Fleet, and throughout 1917 they showed extreme touchiness when accused of action in collusion with the Germans. Russian soldiers felt some sympathy for the "Fritzes" in the trenches, but hostility to the Hohenzollerns was intense. There was, as yet, no reason to believe that the Russian army would accept a peace confirming the loss of twelve provinces and saddling Russia with a heavy debt. The Bolsheviks justified their appeals for fraternization on the grounds that this would bring about a *general* peace, and they found it difficult to argue with supporters of the government.[5] They were on much safer ground when they debated the nature of military authority.

Order No. 1 had revolutionized the army. The vain attempts of some commanders to suppress it after its unofficial distribution enhanced its reputation, and for many soldiers the "conquests of the revolution" became synonymous with the provisions of Order No. 1 and the official legislation that grew out of it. As commanders and socialist conscripts argued about its scope and authenticity, army committees sprang up all over Russia. The soldier section of the Petrograd Soviet codified the Order in a draft Declaration of Soldiers' Rights on March 9. The Tsar had abdicated a week earlier; this document was no panicky reaction to an imminent threat of counterrevolution. The following paragraph captures its essence:

Corporal punishments are to be abolished in all cases without exception. Under no circumstances should any case of inflicting corporal punishment, either in the rear zones, or on the front, remain unpenalized. . . . any officer who orders that corporal punishment be inflicted on a soldier, regardless of his rank, must be prosecuted, charged with torture of a subordinate and immediately discharged from his duties. . . . the court should designate a penalty no lighter than demotion to the rank of private.[6]

The Declaration was an affront to the honor of the officers, conflicting totally with their own, very different conceptions of relations between officers and their men. As Alexeyev explained,

The less educated the soldier, the less he is cultured, the weaker he is prepared in a military sense, the more important the officer becomes. Only he drags the inert mass after him, he alone prepares victory or defeat. Victory may not be secured without an expert and valiant officer corps, strong in spirit and enthusiasm.[7]

When the draft Declaration reached the front, it too was taken for accomplished legislation by the men, and the reluctance of some officers to accept it was given the most sinister interpretation. Few officers would agree that they should retain greater responsibility for operations without corresponding prerogatives, while fewer still had the persuasive skills required of an officer in a "democratic" army. For the men, the restoration of old forms of authority threatened flogging and, in extreme cases, shooting. Irrespective of their views on the war, they were overwhelmingly determined to hang on to these conquests of the Revolution.

At first Guchkov favored conciliation, appointing General Polivanov to a commission on new military regulations, which brought high command and Soviet delegates together. By the end of April, they had drafted a new declaration. It confirmed many of the features of Order No. 1, including the soldier's freedom off-duty, the abolition of batmen and orderlies, the abolition of condescending/deferential forms of address and the threats of severe punishment for officers using corporal punishment. It also accepted the existence of committees, while seeking to limit their powers.[8]

This official draft declaration was no more acceptable to GHQ. Alexeyev still demanded that the soldiers give "unconditional obedience to the commanders," and that the authorities "ruthlessly, without harmful concessions, suppress the disobedient." Guchkov disliked the declaration himself and gave this as a reason for his resignation. On May 2, Alexeyev met the front commanders at GHQ to consider the situation. (This was the meeting at which they were canvassed for their views on the new Minister of War.) The generals resolved to travel to Petrograd to make a last desperate appeal to the government to deny the declaration official sanction.[9]

As the military leaders were en route, Kerensky was addressing the commission for the first time. Of course the class struggle was a natural process and the state should be organized so as to facilitate the free competition of class interests, he argued, but such struggles could have no meaning if their very context had been destroyed.

This brought him to the primordial duty of national defense: "To defend that which our forefathers gave us, that which we should hand on to our children, this is the most elementary, primary obligation which no one can renounce."[10]

The next day, the generals met the new ministers and the Soviet leaders. They did not beat about the bush: the war must be fought to a victorious conclusion and discipline must therefore be restored. They were politely critical of the government. Skobelev, who spoke for the Soviet, was equally critical of the generals. Prince Lvov, Tsereteli, and Kerensky sought to paper over the cracks. "No one can level accusations at the Soviet," said Kerensky, "but no one can accuse the Commanding Staffs either." Alexeyev knew that he had failed.[11]

The Declaration of the Rights of the Soldier did not go out in quite the form Alexeyev feared. Kerensky personally insisted on the introduction of two additional clauses, which slightly improved the situation of the officers. The first reaffirmed the sole right of commanders to nominate and remove officers. The second (the contentious paragraph 14), permitted the officers to use force against mutinous subordinates *in combat*. After this, Kerensky could tell the men quite truthfully, that he had signed the declaration that Guchkov had refused to sign, and he could tell the officers that he had ameliorated the impossible situation in which Guchkov had left them. The Declaration was finally published on May 11 under a photograph of Kerensky and above his signature. The Bolsheviks immediately latched on to paragraph 14, dubbing the official declaration the "Declaration of the Deprivation of the Rights of the Soldier." Vociferous opposition was also expected from conservative officers. On Albert Thomas' advice, Kerensky headed off a mass resignation of senior officers by threatening to treat them as deserters.[12]

During his first few days as Minister of War, Kerensky assembled the staff he would retain until October. His adjutants, Captain Dementyev and Lieutenant Vinner, had SR sympathies. His brother-in-law, Colonel Baranovsky, became Chief of cabinet to the Minister of War, where he could advise Kerensky on promotions and demotions. Kerensky retained the services of Guchkov's "Young Turks," Colonel Yakubovich and Colonel Prince Tumanov, who had shown rare political sense during the April Crisis. General Polovtsev was appointed Commander-in-Chief of the Petrograd Military District, to replace Kornilov. His deputy was Ensign Kozmin, chairman of the 1905 Krasnoyarsk Soviet. Within the War Ministry, a new Political Department was established, headed at first by Stankevich, a Populist comrade of long standing. It enrolled almost the entire strength of the former SR Terror as commissars to mediate between officers and men and inspire both to bravery in combat. Other leading SRs, such as Bunakov-Fondaminsky, also became commissars, as did a number of Mensheviks, including Voytinsky, now an ex–Bolshevik.[13]

Kerensky proposed to lead by example, and on May 7, he toured the Leninist regiments of Petrograd. It was only days since soldiers of the Finland Guards had torn up General Kornilov's personal standard, an offense for which no one had yet been punished. In the event, the visit passed off better than anyone could have hoped. "The soldiers of the 180th Regiment, evidently Bolshevik, surrounded Kerensky, wouldn't let him go, raised him on their hands and carried him like this to his car." It seemed to Kozmin that the only forces at the disposal of Kerensky and his assistants were their revolutionary reputations. "Kerensky's thirteen years of public life in the Democracy, the Krasnoyarsk movement, life in exile, imprisonment, these were the forces which we possessed and which we had to use." He was too modest. To walk into the lion's den, as they had done, often required immense physical and moral courage.[14]

The coalition partners had pledged that "the strengthening of the principles of democratization in the army, and the organization and strengthening of its military power in defensive and in offensive operations, will be the most important task of the Provisional Government." With democracy consolidated in the army, attention turned to the offensive. An essential precondition was an improvement of morale at the front and it was therefore suggested that the two leading SR ministers tour the front together to whip up enthusiasm. An unintended result of this proposal was the first serious clash between Kerensky and Chernov, who flatly refused to go to the front until he had achieved some agrarian legislation to show the men. Personal and temperamental frictions had also emerged. Chernov resented Kerensky's inability to listen to him and retaliated by writing whenever Kerensky began to speak, while Kerensky regarded Chernov as a conceited pedant, incapable of urgent action. As yet, these differences were known to only a very small circle.[15]

On the eve of his tour, Kerensky appeared at the All-Russian Conference of Officers' Deputies to urge them, "go with an open face and an open heart to your soldiers and you will find the path towards the resurrection of the army." A mixed reception met him at the first meeting of his tour, in Helsinki. He made no mention of Finnish independence, but warned that "especially in Finland," it was necessary to ensure that Russian nobility and goodwill were not interpreted as signs of weakness. He was applauded when he spoke of the April Crisis, but when pressed to reveal the contents of the secret treaties, he merely promised to do so at a future peace conference. Kerensky sounded uneasy; perhaps he already suspected that the Finnish Social Democrats were about to make an alliance with Lenin.[16]

On May 10, Kerensky passed through Petrograd, where he was joined by Thomas and his old comrade, Sokolov, now famous throughout Russia as author of order No. 1. Sokolov was horrified at the unintended consequences of the order and harried by a violent campaign of defamation in the bourgeois press. He wanted to make amends by urging the men to trust their officers. They went to Kamenets-Podolsk, just inside the pre-war frontier with Austria, at the invitation of General Brusilov, Commander-in-Chief of the Southwest front. This was a logical choice. The Russian army had made gains in Galicia in 1914 and again in 1916, and the Austrians still provided weaker opposition than the Germans.[17]

Their train took two days to reach the front. Wherever it passed crowds of people waited for a glimpse of Kerensky. Even in the middle of the night, they demanded that he be woken up and shown to them. "It was a triumph. A triumphal celebration. Incessant cries spread in answer to his words of greeting." Kerensky "seemed tired and worn out in the carriage, and it was only here that one could sense how heavy was this pomp, this obligation to be before the people all the time, the object of universal attention and enthusiasm."[18]

His resilience was startling. When he faced the conference at Kamenets on the following day, he radiated "a joyful and even triumphant sense of himself as the chosen of fate and the protégé of the people." It was now that Marina Tsvetaeva wrote her poem willing him to dictatorship, yet Stepun, who saw him at first hand, rejected the suggestion that Kerensky was either an exhibitionist or a Bonapartist. Thomas agreed: "Has he any aspirations to dictatorship? I don't think so. But he savours and maintains his popularity.... There is some *artifice de campagne* but I don't believe in a will to dictatorship."

"The huge hall was filled with hundreds of soldier delegates sent from the most remote corners of the front," Kerensky remembered. "I beheld weary faces, feverish eyes, extraordinary tension." The previous day, Kerensky had asked Thomas almost resentfully why he should be "condemned to have men killed." He did not lack sympathy for the waverers. "After three years of the cruellest suffering, the millions of soldiers, exhausted to the last degree by the tortures of war, found themselves confronted suddenly with the questions: 'What are we dying for? Must we die?' " The men cheered the Bolshevik Krylenko when he demanded an immediate peace, but they also cheered Stepun and Stankevich who argued that Russia must remain at war until a general peace was concluded. The men voted for national defense, but the prospect of a rapidly concluded peace was becoming seductive. They badly needed Kerensky's encouragement.

As Kerensky, now dressed in the tunic, breeches, and boots of a common soldier, got up to speak, Thomas tried to fathom the nature of his appeal:

It is made up of short, jerky phrases, shot out in a single stream and barely linked together. It is composed of appeals to sentimentality. He gives his whole heart to it. He näively adds all his thoughts, his very own sentimentality. This allows him to descend into the sentimentality of others, to denounce the little corner of fear, the fear of death which there may be in the heart of any man. This allows him to assert his willingness to put himself at the head of a division on the day of attack if necessary, to convince them. The sacrifices he had made as a revolutionary entitle him to speak like this. . . . There is charm and grace in his eloquence. The way in which he bowed to the [Commander-in-Chief] made an impression on the men. But when, suddenly, he bowed with even greater respect to the assembly, before the enormous gray mass of soldiers, the oratorical effect was consummated. The keynote of the speech was stark: "Forward to the battle for freedom! I summon you not to a feast but to death!" He exuded faith in Russia, the Revolution, a just peace and even a successful offensive, though some observers felt he had achieved his effect by laying more stress on defense than attack. Still, he was vigorously applauded, and even Krylenko was forced on to the defensive: "I will be the first to call for the advance," he pledged, "and if my company won't follow me, I shall go alone and carry out my duty."[19]

The meeting with the delegates was followed by meetings with entire regiments. Everywhere the message was the same, as was the response. An English eyewitness noted: "When he left, they carried him on their shoulders to his car. They kissed him, his uniform, his car, the ground on which he walked. Many of them were on their knees praying; others were weeping. Some of them [were] cheering; others singing patriotic songs." She felt that had the offensive followed immediately, the men would have fought with real enthusiasm.[20]

Kerensky traveled on to the Romanian front and the Black Sea Fleet at Sebastapol. He completed his tour by visiting the Northern front, where Bolshevik influence was already considerable. Near Riga, the Bulgarian-born General Radko-Dmitriev took him to the trenches to meet a Russian regiment won over by a Bolshevik soldier. The Bolshevik was, at first, too timid to speak in the presence of the Minister, but finally he summoned up the courage to query the forthcoming offensive. Kerensky told him that this would be decided by GHQ. The soldier retorted: "If there is an offensive, then we shall all perish and a dead man needs neither freedom nor land. So the government should conclude peace sooner." The official account recorded that "A. F. Kerensky interrupted him decisively." General Gurko, no friend of Kerensky's, has him speaking in an even more traditional vein: "Hold your tongue when the Minister of War is speaking to you."

Kerensky felt that only the contempt of his comrades would overcome the egotism of this man:

Freedom does not mean license for all and everyone, and the government established by the Revolution is a real government. Over many years the best Russians perished on the scaffolds built by the Autocracy, but not so that the first passing coward should set his own personal egotistical interests higher than the interests of the whole state and the whole people.

Angrily, he turned to the regiment's commander. "Tomorrow, order this coward to be excluded from the ranks of the Russian army. He may go home but everyone will know that he is a coward who has refused to defend the Russian land." The obtuse Colonel asked whether he could cashier another five or six men, but Kerensky refused. He turned back to the men: "Perhaps you share the opinion of this coward?" A resounding "no" concluded the exchange. Kerensky claimed that the Bolshevik was so shaken that he fainted and later begged to be readmitted to the ranks, where he would become an exemplary soldier during the following weeks.[21]

On May 24, Kerensky wound up his tour with a meeting of the Soviet of the 12th Army in Riga. Latvian Bolsheviks were excluded from this meeting, but they sent him a defiant message: "A Latvian is not tired, death in the cause of an idea is not frightening to a Rifleman and a Latvian," they declared. "We don't believe that a bloody attack over the whole front at this moment will save Russia's Revolution and Freedom."

In exile, Kerensky would boast that there was no audience he could not move in the Russia of 1917. The Latvians were the exception that proved the rule, but he warned their Russian comrades once more: "When trust in me is lost, a dictator will come and then mistrust will be suppressed with bayonets and whips."[22]

Kerensky's "patriotism of a new, Western type" was no figment of his temperamental, almost professional, optimism. At the congress of the Southwest front, the Bolsheviks could muster only between 50 and 80 delegates out of a total of 700. The joint executive committee of the Romanian front and Black Sea Fleet comprised 44 Mensheviks, 22 SRs, and 3 Bolsheviks. The congress of the Western front voted its confidence in the Provisional Government without dissent. Out of 700 delegates, the Bolsheviks could persuade only twelve to abstain. Even among the Bolshevized armies of the Northern front, there was an upsurge of support for the new government's policy of diplomacy for peace and national defense, and the Latvians were obliged to agree to carry out orders that were democratically decided.[23] Thus, the spirit was there. But would the men follow career officers and socialist commissars when it came to translating national defense into offensive military action?

Kerensky was anxious to find commanders with charisma. The most promising candidate was General Brusilov, who had achieved great success in the 1916 offensive and whose command was still largely free of Bolshevik influence. Kerensky found him slightly opportunistic and even a little vain, but unlike Alexeyev he did not meddle in politics, nor persist in negative criticism. The meeting with Brusilov had important consequences. "Here, in the automobile, on the road from the front to Tarnopol, we definitely decided upon the offensive," Kerensky noted. He made up his mind to appoint Brusilov Supreme Commander-in-Chief. Another promising find was Colonel Verkhovsky. He had been expelled from the Corps of Pages, the most aristocratic school in Russia, for objecting to the massacre of workers on "Bloody Sunday" 1905. This experience had qualified him for the vice-chairmanship of the Soviet of the Black Sea Fleet. Early in June, he was transferred to the politically sensitive post of Commander-in-Chief Moscow.[24]

There were disappointments. Admiral Kolchak, whom Kerensky met on board ship from Odessa to Sebastapol, was the worst. Thoroughly demoralized, he complained about his sailors to Kerensky, "To them . . . the Central Committee means more than I do, and I no longer wish to have anything to do with them. I do not love them any more." There were also conscientious reactionaries, impervious to Kerensky's sentimentality, such as General Gurko, who finally succeeded in forcing the government to replace him.[25]

These contrasts were mirrored at lower levels. Monarchist officers gossiped about Kerensky's nonexistent Jewish origins, while others felt shamed by a Minister of War who shed tears before the men. But there was hope for the future. At a passing-out parade for cadets of the Alexandrovsky Military School in Moscow, Kerensky had to dissuade them from calling themselves the A. F. Kerensky class, advising them to call themselves merely the Class of Free Revolutionary Russia. "Remember," he warned them, "that there are no privileges for officers now except one: double work and double responsibility." For once he was not exaggerating.[26]

A symptom of the government's uncertainty over army morale was the formation of an exclusively female military unit. This was the idea of Russia's most famous woman combatant, Maria Bochkaryova, a protégée of Rodzyanko. Bochkaryova had tasted most of the humiliations attendant on her sex and status before volunteering for the army. To the incredulity of the recruiting sergeants, the Tsar accepted her petition and she served with success on the southwest front. Rodzyanko discovered her during a tour of the fronts and took her to see Kerensky, whom she asked to help her form a Women's

Battalion. Kerensky, skeptical, challenged her on her ability to maintain "a high standard of morality in the organization."

She must have satisfied him, however, for he encouraged her to address mass meetings held to recruit both male and female volunteers throughout May. Bochkaryova made no bones about her motives in forming a unit of only limited value in the narrow military sense: "It must shame those male deserters, who decline to fulfil their duty as citizens, on the eve of the final victory over the enemy." At one of these meeting, in the Cinizelli Circus, Kerensky seconded her, though without any of his usual exaltation. Deserters were not the only Russians who found it shameful that Russian women would fight when men would not. Also billed to speak was Olga Kerenskaya, but as she entered the limelight, she broke down in tears.[27]

By late May, Olga's situation had become tragically embarrassing. Ostensibly, her revolutionary eminence derived from her work for returning exiles. In reality, her prominence owed everything to her marriage, which had become a frightful embarrassment. During March, Lilya had virtually moved in with Kerensky and on one visit to the Ministry of Justice, Lilya had buttonholed Olga to ask, "Why are they making all this fuss about you?" After that, Olga and the boys visited by appointment only. The situation was fraught with potential damage for Kerensky, too. No one held it against Chernov that he and Anastasia Slyotova were divorced. But Kerensky had young children, and had taken up with his wife's cousin—herself the wife of an officer with a small child of her own. No doubt this is why those involved remained extraordinarily discreet. Still, it occasionally sounds as though the effort to suppress scandal led them to make points that would otherwise seem gratuitous. Bochkaryova's memory of Kerensky's double standard concerning the women soldiers may be an example. This is fair enough, though there were obvious pragmatic grounds for keeping a group of sexually available women away from the front.[28]

While Kerensky was in Petrograd on May 21 and 22, the projected inner cabinet "for the consideration of questions connected with the war and external affairs" was formally constituted; it consisted of Kerensky, Tereshchenko, Nakrasov, and Tsereteli; excluded were Prince Lvov, and Kadet ministers. Nor did it include the just-resigned Konovalov, whose sympathies for the impossible plight of Russian capitalists had finally overcome his Masonic solidarity.[29]

Kerensky even found time for diplomacy. The government had promised to seek a conference to revise Allied war aims, while the Soviet was planning a socialist conference in Stockholm to mobilize pacifist sentiment throughout Europe and force the belligerents to make peace. Albert Thomas was put in an invidious position when Moutet and Cachin agreed—under Soviet pressure—to go to Stockholm without imposing prior conditions on the German participants. Kerensky met with Thomas to dissuade him from saying anything that might suggest to the Russian army that the Allies were thwarting peace moves. After conferring with Henderson and Vandervelde, the senior British and Belgian socialists in Petrograd, Thomas merely dissociated himself from Moutet and Cachin, while gritting his teeth at the vitriol he would attract in the Parisian yellow press.[30]

Kerensky also visited the Soviet to answer left-wing criticism. He reported on the state of the front and explained why Finland could not be granted immediate independence. He promised that Bolshevik propaganda would not be repressed (though there had already been suggestions that the Latvian Rifle Regiments should be disbanded). "For me the freedom of propaganda and the word are sacred, and I have taken no measures and I will take no measures against them." When pressed by Lunacharsky and Kamenev, he denied that he was responsible for paragraph 14 of the Declaration of the Rights of the Soldier. The whole document had been worked out by "the entire Democracy." He left to cheers as usual.[31]

Although a Latvian socialist recalled his disappointment that Kerensky, who had once advocated "the right of all peoples to self-determination" should have been converted to "the ideas of the Russian Constitutional Democrats . . . who stood for preserving the indivisibility of the Russian Empire," Kerensky's changing attitudes toward Poland give a deeper insight into his real views on the nationalities question as well as the tactical flexibility he brought to bear on all Russia's complex problems. In the summer of 1915, when his views were most "internationalist," he had expressed the hope that all the Poles—including those in Prussia—would be reunified in a free, federal Russia. During 1916—as the Poles became more determined on independence—Kerensky, Nekrasov, Chkheidze and other comrades joined Russian Poles in a Circle of Friends of Polish Independence. Shortly after the February Revolution, Sokolov drafted an appeal to the Poles for the Petrograd Soviet. This annoyed

Milyukov but obliged the government to follow suit. On March 16, the Poles were promised "an independent Polish state, composed of all the lands in which the Polish people constitute the majority of the population." It did not quite concede Polish sovereignty, stipulating that the new state must be "united with Russia by a free military alliance."

Turning the Polish hedgehog into a cuddly rabbit has defied Russian rulers for centuries and there was nothing particularly altruistic about this pseudo-promise to a country occupied by Russia's enemies. Milyukov's "support" for Poland also provided a democratic rationale for maximalist war aims, including the detachment of Poznań from Germany and Kraków from Austria. In a truly democratic Russia, the Poles would seek to assume the leadership of other national minorities, and might even become the arbiters of an all-Russian government. Kerensky's willingness to tolerate such possibilities made him more democratic, not more chauvinist, than Milyukov.[32]

The status of Finland was now a judicial riddle. The Finns held that the rights of the Emperor-Grand Duke had devolved on their assembly, as in Russia they had devolved on the Provisional Government. The Russians denied this, asserting that only the future All-Russian Constituent Assembly had the right to alter Russo-Finish relations, a position weak in democratic terms since the Finns were not to be represented in it. Legal arguments were less important than political and strategic ones. Finland was too close to Petrograd, and too many Finns admired Germany. As Kerensky had told the Activist students, once Finland demanded independence, the other nationalities would follow suit. He hoped that Finland would remain closely linked with Russia as a sort of Western leaven, a view mocked in a Finnish nationalist song, *Kerenski se leipoi*:

> Kerensky was baking a great loaf
> And wanted to use Finland as the salt.

The Finns did not take to the idea and on May 16, the Finnish Social Democrats tabled a *Valtalaki* [Bill of Powers], providing for the assumption by the assembly of all powers of the former Grand Duke, excepting only those for defense and foreign affairs.[33]

Across the Gulf of Finland, the Estonians envied the advantages derived by the Latvians from the possession of national military units.

In March and April, they had been encouraged by Russian military officials, including Kornilov, to gather several thousand Estonian soldiers from reserve battalions in Tallinn. During the negotiations for the coalition, the Estonian Military Committee had persuaded the Petrograd Soviet to discuss the formation of Estonian units. Colonel Päts and the Estonian Trudovik, Jüri Vilms, were sent to lobby Kerensky. His decision was favorable in principle, but this unleashed a furious campaign by the Bolsheviks in the Reval Soviet and garrison. The government compromised: The Estonians could keep one regiment, though it was withdrawn to Rakvere to avert conflicts with the Russian garrison.[34]

Both Guchkov and Milyukov had strongly supported the Czech military units within the Russian Army under the aegis of the Czechoslovak National Council, but when Masaryk arrived in May to head the Petrograd Branch, he found the atmosphere transformed. On his appointment to the Ministry of War, Kerensky had ordered the disbanding of the Czechoslovak Brigade. A Czech officer remembered that Kerensky "wanted no independent Czechoslovak Army next to the unitary, socialist one, since he saw in the Czechs a reactionary, chauvinist element and saw in our uprising *an unfair way of behaving*" [My italics—RA]. Kerensky disliked the Czechs not just because the dismemberment of Austria was a Milyukovite war aim, but because the federalist views of such Austrians as Redlich and Renner complemented his hopes for a democratic, federation in Russia.[35]

It cannot have helped the Czechs that their Brigade was in the Kiev Military District, since the greatest threat to the territorial integrity of Russia came from the Ukraine. For more than a century the breadbasket of Russia, it was now also one of the chief centers of the metallurgical and mining industries. Russian workers had flooded into the grimy new towns which became a melting pot of Poles, Russians, and Tatars, as well as the formerly cossack Ukrainians. Most Russians rejected the concept of the Ukraine, preferring to think of its natives as 'Little Russians'. There were also substantial unassimilated minorities of Poles and Jews. During the February Revolution, a *Rada* (Ukrainian for Soviet) had been formed in Kiev, which gradually attracted the support of the local left-liberals, SRs, and Mensheviks and of Ukrainian peasant and military congresses. It was bitterly opposed both by the Russian landowners who dominated the Ukrainian *zemstvos*, and by the Kiev and Kharkov Soviets, who feared a conflict that would split the Ukrainian proletariat on national lines.[36]

Kerensky gave the more numerous Ukrainians a better deal than the Estonians. He agreed to the creation of a Ukrainian Bohdan Khmelnitsky Regiment. This did not solve the problem. Toward the end of May, a delegation of the *Rada* arrived in Petrograd. Its visit was marred by a row over the Second Ukrainian Military Congress, scheduled to meet in Kiev early in June. At the request of the SR Colonel Oberuchev, Kerensky banned it as untimely in view of the impending offensive (Lenin reacted with scorn—and not a little hypocrisy—in an article headed "Undemocratic Citizen Kerensky!"), and the *Rada* delegation returned from Petrograd with empty hands.

The *Rada* pushed on nevertheless and on June 10, it published its "First Universal," proclaiming the autonomy of the Ukraine, announcing the convocation of a Ukrainian national assembly, and appealing for financial support. It insisted that only Ukrainians had the right to decide on the disposition of Ukrainian land—a serious obstacle to an all-Russian land settlement in view of the vastly more favorable land–labour ratio in the Ukraine.[37]

These storm clouds were gathering as Kerensky addressed a packed meeting in the Bolshoi Theater in Moscow. Lockhart was there:

The whole theme of his speech was built around the idea that without suffering nothing that was worth having could be won. He himself looked the embodiment of suffering. The deathly pallor of his face, the restless movements of his body as he swayed backwards and forwards, the raw, almost whispering tones of his voice . . . all helped to make his appeal more terrible and more realistic. When he stated that he was ready to die for the Russia of his ideals, there was no need of words to convince the audience of the sincerity of the man. . . . And, when the end came, the huge crowd rose to greet him like one man. Men and women embraced each other in a hysteria of enthusiasm. Old generals and young praporshicks [sic] wept together over the man who all Russia feels can save the country from ruin. Women gave presents of jewelry, officers sacrificed their orders. An autograph photogravure of M. Kerensky was sold for 16,000 roubles and the whole theatre rained roses.

But was this the whole of Russia? Lockhart noticed that the box for the Soviet representatives "retained its dignity, and there the applause was more formal than enthusiastic."[38]

On June 1, the government announced the penalties for deserters.

They would lose their electoral rights, their families would be deprived of their food allowances, and their names would be published. Deserters who returned and distinguished themselves in action would have their rights restored. These penalties were laughably mild by comparison with those of all the other belligerent powers. It speaks volumes for the temper of the Russian army in 1917 that they provoked massive resentment, a resentment shared by increasing numbers of Kerensky's SR comrades.[39]

The initial enthusiasm of nearly all the SRs for the coalition soon faded. As Kerensky's intention to embark on an offensive became known, a distinct left-SR faction began to emerge, under the leadership of Alexandrovich and the returning exiles Mark Natanson, co-doyen of the PSR, the able polemicist Kamkov, and the ex-terrorist, Maria Spiridonova. Kerensky's personal following was reduced to a right-wing group, including Zenzinov, Argunov, Sorokin, and "Babushka" Breshkovskaya. Chernov occupied the middle ground, which involved making left-center speeches while leaning on Abraam Gotz of the right-center, and to a lesser extent on Avksentiev and Zenzinov, who ran the party organization.[40]

Just before the triumphal meeting in the Bolshoi Theater, Kerensky had paid a brief visit to the Third PSR Congress in Moscow. It was a fiasco. The initial applause for Kerensky provoked N. S. Rusanov a member of the Central Committee to shout angrily, "don't create idols!" Kerensky complimented the party as the "source of his strength" and his "native party"; but this cut little ice with the left, who asked whether he considered the party's sanction necessary for his ministerial career. Irritably, if reasonably, he referred them to Chernov. This sour start was compounded by the elections to the new PSR Central Committee which were held on June 1.

The absent Kerensky was endorsed by the center SRs, the largest single group, and he seemed certain of election. He had not reckoned with P. P. Dekonsky, a former police agent covering his tracks by ingratiating himself with the left-SRs, who now made an astounding announcement: Kerensky's order regarding deserters disqualified him from membership in the Central Committee. Pandemonium broke out, and after some minutes of confusion, Chernov took over the chair. Balloting was already in progress, so Chernov offered to read the offending order without comment or debate as the quickest way to restore order. Owing to some verbal infelicity, it sounded as though Kerensky was threatening a restoration of the death penalty, with the result that a large block of center SRs close to Chernov deserted Kerensky. He was defeated by 136–134.

Too late, Chernov tried to assuage the bitterness of Kerensky's friends by pointing out that he was equally responsible for the order. An official party statement made the best of a bad job, pretending that Kerensky's nonelection was because of his unavailability for party work. This fooled no one; Chernov was also a minister. For months, Kerensky said nothing, but Breshkovskaya saw no reason for such discretion. She resigned her committee membership, stating that "this congress can not be considered a good judge of the merits of those it has elected as members of the Central Committee". Relations between Chernov and Kerensky never recovered, nor would Kerensky ever forgive his "native party" for this stab in the back.[41]

The ministers were not indifferent to these assaults on their authority and integrity. On the eve of his return to France at the beginning of June, Thomas informed Paris that he had just dissuaded Kerensky from resigning. "Unfortunately, even for the best men like Prince Lvov or M. Kerensky, the moments of discouragement and pessimism are not unusual."

Sometimes a sort of fatalism moves some or others to doubt the usefulness of their efforts. But all of them have patriotism too, and enough hope already in the progress which has been recorded to keep them to their duty. . . . some new forces like those of M. Tsereteli, whose authority grows daily assist the cohesion of the government.

Thomas closed with the highest tribute a French defencist could bestow, a tribute endorsed by U.S. Senator Elihu Root (a former Secretary of War and Secretary of State) only weeks later: A separate peace had been averted forcing Germany to keep large armies in Russia.

II

"The Supreme
Persuader-in-Chief"

The rise of bolshevism

The First All-Russian Congress of Soviets brought Kerensky and Lenin face to face, for the first and last time, in a context in which they were still nominally "comrades." Conceived as a triumphant expression of socialist power, it met in an atmosphere of tension and irritation. The war continued with Allied war aims unaltered; industry was grinding to a halt; disorder was increasing in the countryside. The Bolsheviks had already swayed the Petrograd Soviet on some sensitive issues and they set the tone on many factory committees, but their representation in the Soviets was still very modest. Of the 777 delegates who declared their allegiances, 248 were for the Mensheviks, 285 were for the SRs (though some of them were increasingly tempted to follow Bolshevik leads). The Bolsheviks could muster only 105 delegates, and the Menshevik Internationalists, 25. Many of the undeclared were to the right of the socialist ministers.[1]

The Congress was ceremonially opened by Chkheidze on the evening of June 3. Almost immediately, there was a row when the old Menshevik Abramovich asked for an explanation for that morning's expulsion from Russia of the Swiss socialist Robert Grimm, who had arrived with an offer of a separate peace from Germany. The offer, expressly designed to torpedo the forthcoming Russian offensive, was an alluring prospect to the Russian troops. Some delegates objected to the expulsion as such, others to the way in which Tsereteli and Skobelev had approved it without consulting any other Soviet leaders. Martov attacked Tsereteli personally, an unprecedented event, and an uproar ensued. Trotsky leapt on to the stage shouting "Long live the upright socialist Martov!" But most of the applause that followed was for Tsereteli and Skobelev. Kerensky arrived during the debate to a "wild ovation," and the Congress approved Grimm's deportation by 640 to 121.[2]

The Congress then debated the Soviet's relations with the government. Tsereteli defended the coalition in a competent but unremarkable speech. There was one moment of real excitement when he asserted that "there is not a political party in Russia which would say: hand over power to us, resign and we will take your place. Such a party does not exist in Russia."

"It does exist!" called Lenin from the floor, in his first public warning that the Bolsheviks were prepared to demand all power for themselves if the Soviets wouldn't take it.[3]

Lenin returned to the attack on the following morning. For many of the delegates, particularly those from the front, this was their first opportunity to see him. It was also Kerensky's first chance to listen to the man whose name brought back childhood memories of Simbirsk. There stood Lenin, in the Hall of the Cadet Corps, that former haven of aristocratic privilege, attired, as usual, like an absent-minded professor, in a rather unstylish bourgeois suit. His squat figure, with its perceptible paunch, rocked occasionally as he spoke, his pudgy fingers stabbing the air. His broad face, with its slightly Asiatic eyes, radiated confidence and a slightly malicious humor over his reddish beard. His tenor voice was rather monotonous, lacking the expressiveness of the accomplished orators, and his soft *R*s sounded incongruously like the Gallic affectation popular with Polish aristocrats. But all this was soon forgotten as he cast an iron chain of Marxist logic round the minds of his listeners.

"What is this assembly?" asked Lenin, What was its class composition? Why aren't there any soviets in the West European democracies? Aren't bourgeois democracy and soviets incompatible? He asked his audience to choose one or the other. "The usual bourgeois government," he warned, "would mean that the peasants', workers', soldiers' and other Soviets are useless and will wither or be broken up by . . . the counter-revolutionary generals, who keep a hold on the armed forces and pay no heed to Minister Kerensky's fancy speeches, or they will die an inglorious death." A government of Soviets on the other hand, would mean "a transition to a republic which will establish a stable power without a police and a standing army, not in words, but in action."

"Haven't we had enough talk about programmes and drafts?" he asked, "Isn't it time to get down to business?" The cause of anarchy and economic ruin was capitalism. To the mixed applause and laughter of his listeners, he repeated that his party was "ready to take over full power at any moment." The capitalists were making profits "running as high as 500 and 800 percent."

"Make the profits of the capitalists public," he demanded, "arrest fifty or a hundred of the biggest millionaires" and reveal "the hidden springs, the fraudulent practices, the filth and greed which... are costing our country thousands and millions every day." He reminded his listeners that the "secret treaties" were still in force despite the socialist ministers and he accused Kerensky of "trying so hard to find fault" with Finland and the Ukraine, despite their reluctance to secede. Finally, he warned against any offensive. It would mean "the continuation of the imperialist slaughter and the death of more hundreds of thousands, of millions of people... with the aim of strangling Persia and other weak nations."[4]

Kerensky was relieved to note that Lenin had little impact on this audience, though he feared it might be different with the less educated. As he rose to reply, he must have struggled to master his growing hatred for Lenin. He may not have taken literally the allegations of the Russian and Allied intelligence services that Lenin was a spy, but he suspected him of working in collusion with the Germans. What could he say to undo the effect of Lenin's words? He began with restraint and some tactical delicacy. The main problem of the revolution was to hold on to the existing "conquests of the Revolution," adding ironically, so that "Comrade Lenin, who has been abroad, may have the opportunity to speak here again, and not be forced to flee back to Switzerland."

His composure broke down when he addressed Lenin's proposal to arrest the millionaires. He knew from Konovalov's reports that many Russian capitalists were facing catastrophe (and more than six decades of Soviet historiography have failed to come up with convincing examples of Lenin's 500 percent or 800 percent profits). The capitalists he knew included such patriots as Konovalov and Tereshchenko, who had subsidized the war effort and even the revolutionary movement. How could Lenin talk of abolishing coercion and arresting capitalists in the same breath?

Comrades, I am not a Social Democrat. I am not a Marxist, but I have the highest respect for Marx, his teaching and his followers. But Marxism has never taught such childlike and primitive methods. I suspect that Citizen Lenin has forgotten what Marxism is. He cannot call himself a socialist, because socialism nowhere recommends the settling of questions of economic war . . . by arresting people as is done by Asiatic despots. . . . You Bolsheviks recommend childish prescriptions—"arrest, kill, destroy." What are you: socialists or jailers of the old regime?

He warned the Congress that the Bolsheviks and the right were both embarking on a course that might result in dictatorship.

The great majority approved Kerensky's arguments and conclusions, but he could not entirely efface the impression produced by Lenin's appeals for the destruction of bourgeois society. What Lenin thought of his reply is not recorded. After watching for a few moments to see how Kerensky would be received, he quietly left the hall.[5]

A few days later, the Congress debated the war. Lenin took the opportunity to deny that the Bolsheviks wanted a separate peace:

To us, a separate peace treaty means coming to terms with the German plunderers, because they are plundering in the same way as the others. Coming to terms with Russian capital within the Russian Provisional Government is the same kind of separate peace treaty.

An anti-capitalist Russian government would have a 99 percent chance of success, and he quoted a letter written by a Bolshevik peasant: "things will turn out badly if we don't press the bourgeoisie hard enough."[6]

Kerensky replied that the government was ready for a general peace; two offers to that effect had already been made to Germany, one even before the February Revolution. The Congress should wait until the German Social Democrats overthrew the Kaiser, and he archly inquired why Lenin had not remained in Germany to help the process along.[7]

That afternoon, the alarming news reached the congress that the Bolsheviks and anarchists were preparing an armed demonstration for June 10, which might well turn into a coup. Many of the Petrograd workers and soldiers had been offended by the government's unsuccessful attempt to evict squatting anarchists from the villa of a former Tsarist minister. The Soviet Congress banned the demonstration, forcing the Bolshevik Central Committee to disavow it, much to the disgust of the Bolshevik soldiers.

On June 11, the Congress presidium met in closed session to decide what to do about the Bolsheviks. Tsereteli demanded that they be disarmed, as they had moved from criticism to armed opposition. He was supported by Kerensky, Avksentiev, and Gotz. The proposal split the Mensheviks in two. Many felt that if one socialist party disarmed another, the right would reap the profit. Finally, Dan suggested that the Congress should simply prohibit future armed demonstrations, and expel participants from the Soviets. Tsereteli and Kerensky had to make do with this tepid formula—the first serious setback to the coalition in the Soviet Congress.[8]

Sometime toward the end of May, Kerensky had met Maria Bochkaryova again at a dinner at the Astoria. He praised the beneficial influence the women were already having on the men and asked her to be prepared to bring her women out in a counterdemonstration against the Bolsheviks. Shortly after that, the first armed clash occurred between the women and the Bolshevik soldiers.

The traditional discipline enforced by Bochkaryova stood the women in good stead and the Bolshevik men were worsted. This victory also drew attention to the anomaly and illegality of Bochkaryova's refusal to tolerate a committee. Besieged by Bolshevik agitators, half the women demanded a committee. Bochkaryova retaliated by treating them to a dressing-down in barrack-room language and throwing them out of barracks at bayonet point. When Kerensky saw her again, he was distinctly less friendly, demanding that she form a committee, treat the women courteously and cease punishing them. "Otherwise I will reduce you to dust!" Kerensky banged the table with his fist, she banged back and slammed the door on him. She refused to introduce a committee into her unit, now purged of its intellectuals, and no one did anything about it.[9]

On June 13, the papers published a telegram from a regiment in Kiev appealing to Kerensky not to risk his indispensable life at the front. Despite their solicitude, Kerensky arrived at Tarnopol the following day, in time to review plans for the offensive and to draft an order of the day.[10]

The commanders begged Kerensky to spend a little more time exhorting their men to fight, so he and Stankevich went to the most unreliable sector at the village of Yankovitsy. Stankevich thought it was the biggest meeting he had ever addressed. The majority of the First Guard Corps responded well, but two regiments sat to one side, ostentatiously ignoring the proceedings. These two, the Grenadier and Pavlovsky Guards regiments, were now commanded *de facto* by Captain Dziewałtowski, a Polish aristocrat, twice wounded and eight times decorated, but a Bolshevik.

Dziewałtowski dispatched two men to declare their defiance to Kerensky and challenge him to address them on their home ground. Kerensky turned to the other regiments and asked them to decide who should move: the Bolshevik regiments or the majority? They agreed that the Bolsheviks should come to them. Kerensky barked at the abashed pair, "You have forgotten that I am the Minister of War appointed by the will of the Revolution. Bring the regiments here. March!" Stankevich noticed some resentment at Kerensky's tone, but the men departed. The rebellious regiments still refused to budge.

General Ilkevich implored Kerensky to go to the Bolshevik regiments, and despite Stankevich's fear that this would compromise his prestige, Kerensky went. Before he could even open his mouth, Dziewałtowski warned that his speeches were well known from the newspapers, so there was no point in listening to him. He then read a motion of no confidence in the Provisional Government and declared that they refused to acknowledge Kerensky as a minister.

Dziewałtowski and Grenadier Shamson cross-questioned Kerensky about relations between Government and Soviet and on the order punishing deserters. Kerensky answered that the order did not concern them, since they were not deserters, and he again pointed out that he had signed the Declaration of the Rights of the Soldier, where Guchkov had refused. The provocatively casual stances of the Bolsheviks finally got under his skin:

I ask you now: did you stand before Sukhomlinov with your arms crossed criticizing his actions? Did you dare to do so? No, because you are slaves, cowards.

The official account claims that some men cheered. He continued,

I believe in the good sense of the working masses, and I know that the soldier is a bold revolutionary, going to meet death in the name of liberty, equality and fraternity.

The debate continued, with Kerensky giving his familiar warning that if they ceased to truth him, a real dictator would appear. Some men applauded Kerensky, others Dziewałtowski. "The majority listened silently, thinking their own thoughts and probably taking no account of the disputes going on and apprehending darkly that the question was about the most important issue to each individual: to go into the offensive or not to go." Kerensky had failed, and some of the men told their comrades that "We met the Minister of War with whistles and shouts, and we saw him go with whistles. He is probably not glad that he visited the First Guard Corps." An observer who derived perverse satisfaction from this encounter was General Knox, Head of the British Military Mission. "It is well that Kerensky has had a rebuff, for it will show him the present state of things."[11]

The next morning, Kerensky set off with Boris Savinkov, now Commissar of the 7th Army, to visit smaller units. They had to speak over the thunder of the artillery barrage which was softening up the positions of the South German Army opposite. This time, Kerensky had more success. The First Trans–Amur Regiment, which had been pacifist on his previous visit, was now eager to attack. He must have wondered whether they were more or less representative than the First Guard Corps. The General Staff report on the morale of the Southwest front was cautious:

In all the armies, morale has noticeably improved and a certain uplift in spirit can be observed. However, . . . demands from the soldiers to the army committees keep arriving on the necessity of beginning the offensive so as not to allow the spirit of military exaltation to be extinguished.

Kerensky did all he could to maintain this spirit, as he recalled:

Rain and storm. At one stop regiments which had just come from the rear were awaiting us. Under the terrific downpour, to the accompaniment of thunder and lightning, drenched through and through, the thousands did not move, anxious to find in my words, faith in the justice of their coming sacrifice of death.[12]

On June 18 at 9:00 A.M., the 11th Army under General Erdeli attacked the 4th Austrian Army. Further south, General Belkovich's 7th Army advanced on the Austro-Germans around Berezhany. From the 7th Army headquarters, Kerensky and General Gutor watched as the Russian army advanced behind its new red standards. English armored cars were also in attendance. The attack was a success by contemporary standards and some 10,000 prisoners were taken. The cost was heavy; 2500 Russians were killed and some 10,000 injured. [13]

The War Ministry's *Russkii Invalid* [Russian Veteran] reported that "the success of the army wildly excited the leader of the Russian revolution," but Stankevich remembered Kerensky as embittered when he saw that the offensive was not going to be a political success. Ominously, the Grenadier and Pavlovsky Regiments put off coming up in reserve until the next day. [14]

In Petrograd, the entrances to the Ministry of War were crowded by patriotic citizens, hoping desperately for a miracle, among them the Marxist veterans Plekhanov and Deutsch. At the same time, a massive demonstration sanctioned by the Soviet Congress wound its way through the streets of the capital. The Soviet leaders had hoped to steal Bolshevik thunder by staging this demonstration but this misfired badly when the workers turned up carrying banners with Bolshevik slogans, "Down with the War!" and "Down with the ten capitalist ministers!"

Bochkaryova's women exchanged fire with Bolshevik soldiers and the next time Kerensky met her, he took a distinctly indulgent tone: "She took it into her head not to form a committee, and nothing could break her will. One must do her justice. She is a sticker, holding out all alone against us all." Nor did he forget the Czechs, who were now permitted to raise a second division. [15]

In a report to Prince Lvov for public consumption, Kerensky announced "a great triumph of the Revolution" and requested that the regiments taking part in the initial attack be renamed "June 18 Regiments." As a gesture to the men, he released all over forty from the front. As the attack continued, he traveled from unit to unit, exhorting the living and praising the dead: "Their glorious and heroic lives and deaths have given us an example of the selfless fulfillment of their duty, the ability to die for freedom and the happiness of the people, bravely and joyfully." [16]

Near Stanislavov (Ivano-Frankivsk), General Kornilov, now commanding the 8th Army, greeted Kerensky with red flags in his hands. "Under these red flags," he proclaimed, "the army will advance and carry out its duty. . . . Long live the people's leader, Kerensky!" Publicly, Kerensky continued to warn "cowards and traitors," but he also tried to counter Bolshevik accusations that he had abandoned the quest for peace. On June 22, Tereshchenko went on his behalf to ask Buchanan for help. "Nothing could I think help Kerenski so much at present moment," telegraphed Buchanan, "as announcement that Allied Governments had accepted Russian proposal for Conference early in September."[17]

On June 24 Kerensky sat down to write his confidential report on the first phase of the offensive. "The operation which has been started is developing significantly less successfully than one might have hoped in view of the strength of the preliminary bombardment and the numbers of soldiers concentrated." He put this down to German reinforcements, including some drawn from the Western front, poor organization, and Bolshevik influence. To improve the situation, there should be a purge of senior officers, "immediate and harsh legal repression" of military offenses and determined measures against anarchy in the rear, "especially in Petrograd." Psychology was not neglected and Bochkaryova's Women's Death Battalion now entrained for the front, the blessings of Metropolitan Veniamin of the Orthodox Church and Mrs. Emmeline Pankhurst, the British women's rights activist, ringing in their ears.[18]

Despite this pessimism, the following day saw the greatest success of Russian arms since 1916, as Kornilov's 8th Army advanced from Stanislavov in parallel with the Dniester. Over the next few days, General Cheremisov's right column took Kalush, a net gain of twenty miles. At the same time, the reaction of the Bolshevik soldiers became more violent. One casualty was Sokolov. A soldier Sokolov suspected of being a German agent falsely identified him as a landlord. The trick succeeded and Sokolov was injured in a hail of stones. Several regiments were now surrounded, disarmed and purged of their Bolshevik leaders.[19]

Political complications now began in Kiev. On June 23, the *Rada* had appointed a General Secretariat (or government) for the Ukraine and a conflict with the Provisional Government seemed inevitable. To head off a clash, the inner cabinet traveled to Kiev, leaving Prince Lvov to hold the fort. On June 29, they met the Ukrainian leaders. Professor Mykhaylo Hrushevsky, the President, had spent most of his life in Galicia campaigning for the Ukrainian language and his

Russian was rather rusty. V. K. Vynnychenko was the head of the General Secretariat and leader of the Ukrainian SRs. The Menshevik S. V. Petlyura was leader of the Ukrainian Military Committee.

The administrative and economic issues and the status of the Russian, Jewish and Polish minorities in the Ukraine were quickly dealt with. The most difficult source of contention was removed from the agenda when it was agreed to postpone consideration of the precise boundaries of Russia and the Ukraine. Perhaps the most difficult problem remaining was how to overcome the conflict without it appearing that either the Provisional Government or the Rada had backed down.

On June 30, the Provisional Government provisionally recognized the *Rada* and announced that it would *appoint* a General Secretariat for the Ukraine. The *Rada* noted this gesture and announced that it would *confirm* the membership of the General Secretariat. It agreed not to extend its demands before the convocation of the All-Russian Constituent Assembly.[20]

The Provisional Government's sitting of July 2 was the stormiest for a long time. In Kiev, the inner cabinet had felt empowered to conclude an agreement. The Kadet ministers, on the other hand, felt that they were being confronted with an ultimatum, since the inner cabinet had already told the *Rada* they would accept the agreements. It was obvious to the inner cabinet that the Kadet Central Committee had instructed its ministers to oppose the agreements at all costs, even though the Kiev Kadets had welcomed them. Three Kadets and one Octobrist voted against the agreements. The socialist ministers, Prince Lvov, V. N. Lvov, and Tereshchenko voted in favor. The Kadets then resigned: the "July Crisis" had begun.

As they left the Cabinet chamber, Kerensky shouted: "The blood be on your heads! There on the front our armies are carrying out an attack, tens of thousands of men are giving up their lives for the motherland. . . . And at this moment you here desert your posts and smash the government!" As a minister mandated by the Kadet Party, Nekrasov had abstained, and he now announced that he would retire temporarily from the government to sort out his relations with his party.[21]

Milyukov nicknamed the agreements with the *Rada* "The chopping-up of Russia under the slogan of self-determination." He was not out to annex the Straits and liberate the Czechs, Poles, and South

Slavs only to lose "Little Russia." Those few Kadets who admitted the existence of the Ukraine argued that it must become a German puppet. Academic historians regarded the dissolution of the Russian State with horror. Many of their supporters were civil servants with a material interest in a Russian-language bureaucracy. The liberalism of Kadet "cultural self-determination" did not go beyond allowing the border nationalities to opt for the use of their native languages in local institutions.[22]

The Kadets had broader grounds for resentment. They blamed the socialist ministers and the Soviet leaders for failing to use force against illegal actions committed by workers, students, and peasants. Konovalov had been pushed out of the government, and into the arms of the Kadet Party, by working-class militancy—aided, so he felt by Skobelev. Manuilov was bitterly attacked for not dismissing more reactionary professors and for not conceding total control over curricula to radical students and teachers. At first Shingaryov was bitterly criticized by his own party for devising a progressive income tax bill. Later, he joined the attacks on Chernov's attempts to circumvent the government veto on unofficial land seizures implemented by the land reform committees created confusingly, in parallel with the hierarchy of food supply committees, by the First provisional Government.[23]

Whenever the Kadets found legislation too radical, they invoked the omnicompetence of the Constituent Assembly. Logically, this should have made them press for the speedy convocation of the Assembly, but such was not the case. It was axiomatic for the scrupulous Kadet lawyers, who dominated the prepatory commission, that the Assembly would carry no weight unless it were elected by the last word in democratic machinery. This did not trouble them, for they assumed, as did Kerensky, that the Assembly would have to wait until the war was won. They abandoned this hope under Soviet pressure, but continued to cling to the idea that the revolutionary wave would soon pass and that it might be better not to summon the Assembly until this had happened. It was not until the early autumn that they began to fear that they had miscalculated.[24]

The departure of the Kadets left the moderate socialists in charge of the government, and they began to draw up a new, radical program. But the crisis had barely begun. On July 3, Kerensky left Petrograd for the front where Kornilov, now promoted to Commander-in-Chief of the Southwest front, was meeting stiffer German resistance. Further north, Denikin's armies were poised to attack the reinforced South German Army. Within minutes of Kerensky's departure, the streets of Petrograd began to fill with Bolshevized soldiers of the First Machine Gun Regiment and Grenadier Guards. They were joined by groups of lightly armed Bolshevik and Anarchist civilians, striking workers, and finally by 6000 armed and relatively disciplined sailors from Kronstadt. The first real trial of strength between the government and the Bolsheviks, euphemistically called the "July Days," had begun. On the same day, the Finnish Social Democrats began the final reading of the *valtalaki* in their assembly.[25]

On July 4, Kerensky stopped at GHQ to hear a report from Brusilov and General Lukomsky, his Chief-of-Staff, on the progress of the offensive. He traveled on to Kiev to meet Tsereteli and Tereshchenko for further talks with the Ukrainians. On July 3, General Polovtsev, Commander-in-Chief of Petrograd, telegraphed Kerensky about the Bolshevik mutiny in the capital, but it was not until the following day that Kerensky responded with a telegram to Prince Lvov couched in his most magisterial language:

I insist on the determined prevention of treasonable demonstrations, the disarming of mutinous detachments and the handing over to the courts of all instigators and mutineers. I demand the stopping of all further demonstrations and mutinies by armed force. The Government must take account of the impossible situation it establishes and the unbearable strain it lays on all those honourably carrying out their duty on the front, especially on all the command, the military committees and commissars. The Government must immediately publish an official communiqué on the complete liquidation of the mutiny and [stating] that the guilty will suffer ruthless punishment.

His final sentence was darkly enigmatic. "It is essential to accelerate the publication of the evidence in the hands of the Minister of Foreign Affairs." That night, P. N. Pereverzev, the Minister of Justice, summoned G. A. Alexinsky, a patriotic journalist and former Social Democrat Duma deputy, and handed him materials which seemed to show that Lenin and the Germans were in collusion. Alexinsky used them to discredit the Bolsheviks among wavering units of the Petrograd garrison.[26] The action would cost Pereverzev his job.

Kerensky stayed just one step ahead of trouble. No sooner had he left Kiev than militant Ukrainian nationalists took over the streets of Kiev. By July 5, the situation was so confused that it was rumored that Kerensky had resigned. That afternoon, he had a long telegraph conversation with Colonel Yakubovich, who acquainted him with the full seriousness of the situation in Petrograd. Even Chernov, the most radical of the ministers, had been manhandled by demonstrators, and had only been rescued by Trotsky after a severe bruising. Kerensky approved Yakubovich's suggestions for the suppression of the mutiny and thanked him for his energy. As the crisis in the capital began to subside, they began to speculate that it might end in such a way as to finish off "the criminal game with the fate of the state" and perhaps the Bolshevik party as well. Once more, Kerensky demanded "the immediate use of the Tereshchenko material." Meanwhile in Helsinki, the assembly ignored Chkheidze's desperate pleas and adopted the *valtalaki*.[27]

These exchanges with Yakubovich suggest that Kerensky had suffered an emotional conversion to a fully counterrevolutionary position. This is misleading. His own past and the pressures of the moderate left were still on his mind when he met Bochkaryova once more over lunch at Molodechno. Again, he greeted her coolly and as he left, he instructed her corps commander to "see to it that a committee be formed immediately in the Death Battalion and that she," and he pointed her out, "cease punishing the girls!" At this, Bochkaryova threw her shoulder bands in Kerensky's face, accused him of constant vacillation, and ran out of the room. Officers present told her later that in his fury, Kerensky had yelled: "Shoot her!" This was predictably softened to an order for her court-martial, which was, equally predictably, never carried out.[28]

As he traveled along the front, Kerensky's bitterness increased:

At a time when fraternal blood is flowing for the freedom and the cause of the strengthening of the Revolution, traitors and German agents in the rear are directing all their efforts to prevent the heroic offensive of the revolutionary armies.

The Government recalled him on July 6 and he arrived at Tsarskoselsky Station at six that evening. He was livid to discover that the ceremonial welcome he had ordered had been canceled by the Soviet and he sacked the hapless General Polovtsev on the spot for alleged indecisiveness in crushing the mutiny.[29] These tiffs were overshadowed by the removal of two major political figures.

The forced resignation of Minister of Justice Pereverzev soon became the object of violent controversy. Officially, Pereverzev had been dismissed on July 3 because he had released the documents on German contacts with the Bolsheviks. At the time, Kerensky was still at the front, and the decision was made in conjunction with the inner cabinet: Tsereteli, Tereshchenko, and Nekrasov (now an independent). Kerensky and Tereshchenko always claimed that his release of the documents was premature, and that having accused Lenin and his comrades of treason, Pereverzev should have arrested them. Kerensky claimed that the publication of the documents deterred Jacob Fürstenberg-Hanecki—the courier between the German Auswärtiges Amt's collaborator, Helphand-Parvus, and Lenin—from crossing into Finland, where he would have been arrested. Fürstenberg *was* apparently deterred from entering Russian territory and this seems to prove Kerensky's point. Or was he being wise after the event? Kerensky also admitted that the publication of the documents played a significant part in depriving the Bolsheviks of support at a critical moment for the government, and that the unfortunate Minister of Justice was simply unable to arrest the Bolshevik leaders during the crisis for the simple reason that they were briefly in control of more of the Petrograd garrison than he was. On the face of it, Kerensky and his closest colleagues were guilty of brutal political disloyalty.[30] What could explain such uncharacteristic behavior?

The answer is to be found in the attitudes of the Soviet leaders who had worked hard to avert an explosion, fearing that any division on the left would benefit the right. The same thinking lay behind their shocked reaction to Pereverzev's disclosures. As would shortly appear, Lenin's relations with Helphand-Parvus were not the only skeleton in the cupboard. After hurried consultations, Chkheidze and Prince Lvov had telephoned the offices of the Petrograd newspapers on the night of July 3–4, begging them not to publish documents until the case had been thoroughly investigated. Only the right-wing *Zhivoe Slovo* [Living Word] ignored this request, and on July 4, the new All-Russian Executive Committee of Soviets called on everyone to avoid making slanderous or derogatory statements about Lenin and his comrades.[31] The elimination of Pereverzev can thus be seen as a concession to the Soviets by a government which had already lost Kadet support and could not afford to antagonize the Soviets as well.

The replacement of Prince Lvov was less controversial. The Prince still inspired widespread respect and even affection, only partly eroded by his clashes with Chernov over landlords' rights. At any rate, on the train to Kiev on June 27–28, Tereshchenko and Nekrasov approached Tsereteli with a plan to make Kerensky Prime Minister and form an inner directory. Tsereteli had opposed the plan, fearing that Kerensky was too unsophisticated to handle the left, but now he changed his mind.[32]

On the evening of July 6, Kerensky stormed from the Tsarskoselsky Station to a meeting of ministers and military representatives. Before joining the meeting, he gave orders for the arrest of those Bolsheviks against whom evidence of treason could be found. To his annoyance, Soviet representatives, particularly Martov, demanded clemency on the grounds that the evidence was inconclusive. Where documents failed, circumstances succeeded, as news came in of a successful German counterattack toward Tarnopol. This seemed too great a coincidence and Soviet objections were withdrawn.

At a private meeting of ministers, Nekrasov then agreed to take over as Deputy Premier for at least the following two weeks. Kerensky went on from this meeting to Skobelev's apartment, where the so-called "Star Chamber" or the inner cabinet of the All-Russian Soviet Executive Committee was gathered. The socialist leaders there drew up a new government program which for the first time enunciated socialist policies, including the proclamation of a republic and a radical interim agrarian policy. These demands undoubtedly infringed the omnicompetence of the Constituent Assembly and Prince Lvov resigned rather than accept them. When they failed to appear in the program of the new government, published on July 8, there were immediate suspicions that they had been raised merely to push Lvov overboard.[33]

This was unfair. It was not the skulduggery of the moderate left, nor even Kerensky's admittedly unbridled ambition, that caused Lvov's resignation. The Prince was no longer up to the job. The man who gets to the top in politics must convince others that he has something unique to offer. So what was it that Kerensky offered Russia? First of all, he was still by far the most popular man in the country, even though his popularity had already begun to wane in some quarters. Secondly, Kerensky was the only available figure who seemed tough enough for the impossible task, as Kerensky himself explained. Of Lvov, he wrote, "for his gentle manner of governing the times had become too difficult. More brusqueness was required in dealing with people, more external pressure in the style of government." Lvov seemed to have realized this himself: two days after his resignation, looking terribly aged, he told an old friend, "I resigned because there was nothing left for *me* to do. To save the situation it was necessary to dissolve the Soviets and fire at the people. I could not do it. But Kerensky can."[34]

In any event, on the morning of July 7, Alexander Kerensky, while retaining the war ministry, also became Prime Minister of Russia. He had come to see the struggle he was confronted with in almost Manichaean terms, with Ludendorff and Lenin the twin faces of Lucifer. His enemies seemed to justify such thinking by their methods. Within the space of a week, a station at which he had just stopped was destroyed by artillery fire and the front part of his railroad car was destroyed by a runaway locomotive. Colonel Nikitin informed him that Steklov, a fellow intellectual once friendly with his family, had suggested to a meeting of anarchists that *they* assassinate Kerensky, as such methods conflicted with the principles of the Bolshevik party *he* had now joined.[35]

It was impossible to tell which attacks were accidents, and which the fruits of malice. The same was true of greater events. Kerensky was convinced that the Bolshevik and German offensives had been coordinated. But what of the Finns and Ukrainians? Had the Kadets precipitated the government crisis to demonstrate the government's inability to deal with the left? His routine left him less and less time for contact with ordinary people. If he assumed his foes were all in league with the devil, he might lose all sympathy for popular aspirations. The strains of his position were mounting, the risks to his still fragile constitution growing, the temptations of power increasing. He was losing his temper more often and there was little doubt that he would inject brusqueness into the language of government. The doubts remained: Could he really bring himself to shoot at the people? If so, would he know where to stop? Could any one man save Russia from defeat and disintegration?

12

No Longer an Idealist?

REPRESSION

The cabinet was now reduced to a rump consisting of socialists, freemasons and previously monarchist Octobrists. Nekrasov became Deputy Prime Minister, while Tsereteli took over the onerous Ministry of the Interior. Tereshchenko, Skobelev, Chernov, Peshekhonov, Godnev and V. N. Lvov retained their previous posts. It now formulated the first coherent body of repressive legislation since the Revolution. On July 6, it was decreed that anyone calling for murder, assault, or robbery—or "the use of force against any part of the population"—would be liable to three years' imprisonment, as would anyone who incited disobedience to government orders. Members of the armed forces found guilty of sedition would be treated as traitors. On July 7, General Kornilov was promoted to Commander-in-Chief of the Southwest front. He immediately demanded more determined action against mutineers. Kerensky agreed and ordered the purging of all unreliable units at the front. Kornilov then prohibited all meetings of front units, "in view of the gravity of the moment we are going through". Brusilov extended this order to the other fronts.

On July 11, Kornilov and Commissar Savinkov demanded that the government call off the shattered offensive and restore the death penalty. The offensive was canceled. It fell to Kerensky to propose the restoration of the death penalty at the front; that measure was carried unanimously. Kerensky remembered "with what bitterness in the soul" the inner cabinet turned their backs on the traditions of

Tolstoy, Petrazhitsky, and the First Duma. They consoled themselves by providing that such cases should be tried by elective courts-martial. Kornilov gave a stark demonstration of what lay ahead by publicly shooting fourteen men out of hand. A week later, "Kerenski boasted" to General Knox "that Korniloff had already shot 147 men including one general."[1]

The government also took measures to limit press freedom and to disarm the Bolshevik Red Guard. Denounced by Lenin for taking "the first steps toward Bonapartism," it was paradoxically, the nearest thing Russia had possessed to a socialist government. The moderate socialists now dominated the government, yet their radicalism was barely visible in the program entitled "Citizens! The dread hour has struck," published on July 8. Kerensky had returned to the front only the previous day, convinced that the program would proclaim a republic and announce the new agrarian policy. He was surprised to find that it omitted these points, though it did finally fix the date of elections to the Constituent Assembly for September 17.

Chernov later blamed Kerensky for omitting the two radical points from the program and this sounds plausible in view of Kerensky's determination to revive a coalition with some of the Kadets. Chernov certainly did have serious reservations about the government's policies and the viability of a socialist-bourgeois coalition. Under normal circumstances, he should either have forced the government to accept his policies or resign, but the circumstances were hardly normal. His own obsequiousness toward Nekrasov can be blamed on his "flabbiness and lack of political principle," but his situation was an excruciating one.

If Chernov had resigned, he would have pushed the government into the arms of the Kadets. A quiet resignation would have looked like a confession of incompetence and a betrayal of the peasantry. A scandalous resignation would have split his party, leaving him corralled with the small left-SR faction and with the Bolsheviks, whom he found too authoritarian and hostile to the peasantry.

For all his undoubted courage and integrity, Tsereteli did little better, imprisoned as he was in the Menshevik-orthodox Marxist analysis that pronounced Russia unripe for socialism. Their abandonment of radical policies marks the failure of the non-Bolshevik left in the Russian Revolution, but they did not give up without a struggle. As Tereshchenko told Buchanan, he and Nekrasov had experienced great difficulty in persuading the socialist ministers to renounce their radical policies.[2]

The negotiations with the Ukrainians had exposed to public view the dominant position within the Provisional Government of the 'inner cabinet'. During July, Tsereteli, its only non-freemason, became increasingly disillusioned, gradually developing an antipathy toward the "troika" of Kerensky, Nekrasov and Tereshchenko. He was wary of Kerensky's "subjective inclinations towards strong power." The excluded Kadets were even more critical, charging that "this group concentrated all the power and properly bears all responsibility for the general course of activity of the government." Young, charming, confident, and almost totally indifferent to ideology, the troika were men of adventurous temperament and almost no experience of government.

If Chernov found the program too tame, Tereshchenko felt it was far too radical; like Chernov, he accepted it reluctantly and with determination to subvert it whenever possible. Chernov hoped to use the Soviets to bring pressure to bear on the government, while Tereshchenko intended to use the Allies for the same purpose. This gave Tereshchenko a decided advantage. The moment Chernov tinkered with agrarian reform by administrative regulation, telegrams of protest would arrive from all over Russia. If Tereshchenko ignored the government's official foreign policy, knowledge might be restricted to the diplomatic services of Russia and her Allies.[3]

The government was pledged to invite the Allies to confer on war aims during August, but on July 9, Tereshchenko told Buchanan he hoped the conference would be convened at the beginning of September. However, as Buchanan reported,

It was not so much that he wished it to meet actually during the first days of that month as to be able to announce that it would do so. If this was done date of meeting could always be postponed to suit the convenience of Allied Governments, and as he was very anxious that Minister of War [Kerensky] should attend it, it should meet at a time when Minister of War's presence was not required at the front.

On this basis, it might be postponed until after the war.[4]

In May, the coalition had promised to facilitate an international socialist conference in Stockholm. The new program reiterated that "not a drop of blood of a Russian soldier will be shed for aims alien to the sense of justice of the Russian Democracy," so there was no ostensible reason why the government should withdraw its support for the Stockholm Conference. In reality, the hostility of British and French conservatives to the conference had reached a pitch that threatened the positions of the Western socialist ministers. Despite his own difficulties, Albert Thomas did not wish to do anything to embarrass Kerensky, so he asked Eugène Petit, his personal representative in Petrograd, to feel out Kerensky as to his present attitude toward this conference. Kerensky was overwrought when Petit saw him on July 14, and the intimacy of the occasion may have contributed to his undiplomatic franchise. He told Petit "he had completely lost sight of the question of the conference for several weeks and had not thought about whether it should meet."

Petit was unable to wait for the fuller answer Kerensky promised him before communicating with Thomas. "I have a personal impression," he telegraphed, "that the idea of this conference is clearly in decline in view of present events," and he advised Thomas to "insist with intransigence on the preconditions" Thomas had posed for French participation. These involved assurances that "war guilt" would be discussed at the conference. This would guarantee its failure, since the German Social Democrats were determined not to discuss the issue.[5]

Kerensky, the ambitious diplomat of April, was now unable to answer a simple question about the Stockholm Conference. Yet until July 13, he himself represented the conference's Soviet sponsors in the government. The failure of the offensive had crippled him. Where he had once spoken freely on all aspects of policy, he now seemed incapable of thinking hard about matters outside his own immediate sphere of competence. He relied increasingly on Tereshchenko, who had decided that the war must continue to a victorious conclusion. For him, and hence for Kerensky, only a rapid Allied victory could now save Russia.[6]

The fate of the government was now uncertain. This was partly the result of the Kadet boycott and the Bolshevik mutiny, but some of the blame rests with the ministers themselves. On July 9, they had requested the All-Russian Soviet Executive Committee to release them from its tutelage and to endow the government with dictatorial powers. They had ambitious ideas for a radical restructuring of Russian politics, hoping to obtain a mandate more reliable than that provided by shifting Soviet majorities and the ebb and flow of Milyukov's control over the Kadet Central Committee. Nekrasov and the former Progressists formed a Radical Democratic party to woo the democratically inclined bourgeoisie, but this was a *rara avis* in July 1917 and the experiment was not a success. After his rebuff by the PSR, there was nothing to inhibit Kerensky from supporting the attempts of Breshkovskaya, Argunov, Savinkov, and the Anglo-Russian lawyer and journalist Dr. David Soskice, to form a right-SR faction around the newspaper *Volia Naroda* [People's Freedom]. (French and American money appeared providentially to assist this enterprise.) While more successful than Nekrasov's party, the group were unable to contest Chernov's leadership of the PSR.[7]

Until the July Days, only the Bolsheviks had doubted the government's legitimacy, but as long as the Soviets supported the government, the Bolshevik slogan "All Power to the Soviets!" was self-contradictory. During the July Days Bolshevik demonstrators had cursed the Soviet leaders for refusing to take the power offered to them. As soon as the government began to imprison, and even execute, its opponents, its need for legitimacy became much more urgent. While a majority of Russians continued to approve its policies for the time being—as Lenin conceded—that might change.[8]

On July 9, *Rech'* pointed out that the Duma Committee had played no part in Kerensky's elevation to the Premiership so the government was no longer an "all-national" authority. The writer, probably Milyukov, launched a poisoned dart at Nekrasov, while paying backhanded tribute to Kerensky: "A. F. Kerensky is the last minister of the former composition [of the government] with whose retention in power hopes in the happy outcome of our external and internal difficulties [rest]"[9] The truth was that the Provisional Government had originally been put together by two self-appointed bodies, since when it had become a self-perpetuating and technically irresponsible body.

This nonresponsible authority now found itself at loggerheads with the one institution in the former Russian Empire whose legitimacy was incontestable. The Finnish assembly had been legally summoned by the last Tsar-Grand Duke, democratically elected by free vote of adult Finns of both sexes, and recognized by the Provisional Government. Its decision to assume all the powers of the former Grand

Duke, except defense and foreign affairs, created intolerable embarrassment. On July 11, Kerensky received Carl Enckell once more.

Kerensky stood in Napoleonic pose in the middle of a large hall and cried out in a loud voice. . . . "So there you are, the representative of Finland, which has declared itself independent and wants to break off relations with Russia. . . . Will you force it so far that Russia begins taking military measures against you and closes the frontier between the two countries?

Enckell ignored this threat to starve the Finns into submission and assured Kerensky that he personally thought the *valtalaki* unwise. They agreed that the Finnish assembly should be dissolved and new elections held, but the Provisional Government's embarrassment at its own autocratic behavior is evident from the assertive insecurity of its claim that "With the abdication of the last Emperor, the plenitude of powers pertaining to him . . . could be transferred only to the Provisional Government entrusted by the Russian people with supreme power."[10]

On July 15, Kerensky and Kozmin attended the funeral of the seven Don Cossacks killed by the Bolsheviks during the July Days. As the procession prepared to set out for the Kazan Cathedral and the Alexander Nevsky Monastery, Kerensky stepped forward to say his first words in public since the July Days.

I summon all to sacrifices, to work and order. The Provisional Government is defending the independence and integrity of Free Russia with all its strength. . . . Openly, before you all I declare that any attempts, wherever they may come from, to create anarchy and disorder will be mercilessly repressed in the name of the blood of these innocent victims.[11]

This was the new, chastened Kerensky, his mood somber, his tone authoritarian, his vocabulary increasingly traditional. His uncritical admiration of the masses had now turned into an equally uncritical contempt for all who had followed the Bolsheviks in July. With it came the quite erroneous belief that the soldiers and workers of Petrograd might be cowed by harsh language alone. The adoption of a synthetic authoritarian personality did not come easily to Kerensky and it did not always convince. Legal fictions and the language of Stolypin were no substitute for a truly popular mandate.

Kerensky spent most of early July at GHQ and at the front. With the failure of the offensive, new ideas were required and a conference was therefore summoned to GHQ. Kerensky arrived in Mogilev with Tereshchenko and Baranovsky on July 16. Brusilov and his staff attended, as did the Commanders-in-Chief of the Northern and the Western fronts. Kornilov and Shcherbachev, Commander-in-Chief of Romania, were absent, but both sent telegrams stating their views. In Kornilov's absence, the Southwest front was represented by Savinkov, its Chief Commissar. Generals Alexeyev and Ruzsky were also on hand.

The conference began inauspiciously. When the Prime Minister's train arrived at Mogilev Station, Brusilov was not present. Baranovsky telephoned and instructed him to present himself at the station, whereupon Brusilov explained that his absence was caused by the pressure of work and was not intended as a slight on Kerensky.[12]

The major speech at the conference was made by General Denikin. The Commander-in-Chief of the Western front was an intelligent conservative of modest social origins, who was probably seeking dismissal. He launched a bitter attack, both personal and political, on Kerensky himself:

I have heard that bolshevism has destroyed the army. I deny this. Bolshevism is worms in the festering wound of the army. The army was destroyed by others, by those who recently passed military legislation destructive to the army, by people who do not understand the mode of life and the conditions necessary for the existence of the army. . . . Authority was abolished, the officers were humiliated. Officers up to and including the Commander in Chief were expelled like servants. The Minister of War once made a passing remark on the Northern Front that he could disperse the entire high command within 24 hours. In his speech addressing the soldiers, the Minister of War said: "Under the tsars you were driven into battle by knouts and machine-guns. The commanders led you to slaughter."

I was standing at the foot of the rostrum on which the Minister of War was speaking; I listened, and my heart was wrung at the offense, because what he said was not true.

Denikin demanded the abolition of all changes made in army organization since the Revolution. He also dismissed all thought of a separate peace as "the course of treachery" and he concluded by showing that generals could also be orators:

Lead Russia to truth and brightness under the red banner of freedom, but give us the opportunity to lead our troops under the old banners that have been winnowed with victories, whose tattered ribbons thousands kiss reverently in taking their oath of allegiance to the fatherland and behind which they have marched to victory and glory. . . . Do not fear the remnants of the Autocracy inscribed upon it; they have long ago been erased by our hands. It is you who have stamped them into the dirt, our glorious banners of battle, and it is you who must pick them up if you have a conscience.

Here was the authentic voice of the Russian generals with an eloquence that rivalled Kerensky's own. In a characteristic emotional gesture, Kerensky thanked Denikin for his honesty.[13]

Sincere or not, Denikin's claims were nonsense. Few officers had welcomed the Revolution and they certainly had not erased the remnants of Autocracy with their own hands. Neither the government nor the soldiers could consider the officers corps unconditionally loyal to the Revolution, so the abolition of commissars and committees was out of the question. It was frequently only the commissars who saved the officers from the wrath of their own men.

The other generals gave similar advice in more circumspect language. The government must restore discipline, they said, as though the government wanted anything else. They put forward no program for immediate action, though they did not dispute Kerensky's assertion that "sharp transitions must not occur." The only commander who made coherent and concise suggestions was the absent Kornilov, who had the benefit of Savinkov's advice. Kornilov, in a telegram, requested the restoration of the death penalty for soldiers in the rear, a purge of the officer corps, and the restoration of the officers' monopoly over promotions and demotions. He proposed the integration of the commissars with the officer corps, giving the commissars the right to confirm all death sentences. The committees should deal only with "economic and routine matters." Meetings, card playing, and Bolshevik literature should be suppressed.[14]

Kerensky took exception to Denikin's attacks on himself and he vigorously defended the government's record. He now disavowed the Declaration of the Rights of the Soldier: "I am not defending the Declaration, and had I been the Minister at the time it was drawn up, the Declaration would not have been issued. I am compelled to liquidate many things which I received as a legacy." He tried hard to persuade the commanders that he shared their interest in a disciplined army, but he could not efface the impression produced by millions of copies of the Declaration under his portrait.[15]

Kerensky left the conference with a deplorable impression of the generals. Brusilov seemed lost and Kerensky knew he would have to go. Savinkov's opportunity had arrived. For some time, he had been singing Kornilov's praises, doing his best to convince his fellow commissars that Kornilov was a "sincere democrat." Shortly after the GHQ conference, Kerensky met Savinkov and Filonenko in his train, where Savinkov pressed Kerensky to appoint Kornilov to the Supreme Command. Kerensky had his doubts. He had not forgotten the April Crisis, when Kornilov had proposed shooting at the very crowds that had brought him to the War Ministry. He knew that Kornilov loathed the Soviets, but then, which general did not? At least Kornilov had criticized the Imperial regime before the Revolution and he had discouraged monarchist agitation since. He had shown civic courage and good sense in demanding the cancellation of the offensive. His republicanism had little in common with the desires of the Soviets, but was it so different from Kerensky's chastened views? They also discussed the revival of the coalition, and Savinkov left the meeting convinced that it was only a matter of days before Kornilov became Supreme Commander while he himself became Minister of War.

On July 18, Kerensky nominated Kornilov, who expressed no gratitude for his appointment and qualified his acceptance with the constitutionally anomalous proviso that he would consider himself responsible only to his conscience and the nation as a whole. A bitter conflict erupted over his demand that there should be no interference . . . with his appointment of senior commanders, since Kerensky had already nominated General Cheremisov to the command of the Southwest front vacated by Kornilov's promotion. Cheremisov had done well during the offensive, but Kornilov feared that he was too lenient toward his men and he refused to take over the Supreme Command until Cheremisov's appointment was countermanded. Kerensky later claimed that he opposed this demand and even argued for his revocation of Kornilov's appointment in the government. The inner cabinet would certainly have reminded him that if he dismissed Kornilov there could be no hope for a renewal of the coalition. The upshot was that Kerensky made a bitter enemy of Cheremisov, without gaining a friend in Kornilov.[16]

Kerensky's accounts of July and August 1917 record "a steady diminution of revolutionary chaos and the development of political strength and wisdom," and it is true that the Bolsheviks were quiescent. They had suffered some real casualties on the streets, and one

Bolshevik had been killed when military cadets seized a Bolshevik press. Trotsky, Kollontai and a number of others were in prison, while Lenin had fled to Finland. The remaining "legal" Bolsheviks, led by the ever-prudent Kamenev, kept their heads down in the Soviets, which were now at a low ebb. The moderate socialists were also demoralized by the fear that their support for the government had destroyed working-class solidarity. They were stricken by the nightmare that the class enemy might now crush the Revolution. Nor was Kerensky himself immune from these fears.[17]

Conditions in Petrograd and Moscow were superficially calmer, but according to Pitirim Sorokin, a member of the Prime Minister's secretariat and one of those who prepared the intelligence digests on which Kerensky's optimism was based, "Mingled with telegrams from cities, Semstvo, peasants and workers expressing devotion to the Government are disturbing telegraphic reports of strikes among workmen, riots of soldiers, and anarchistic conditions among the peasants." Workers, cowed by repression, turned back to economic grievances, while peasants found harvest time the most convenient moment for expropriating their landlords.[18]

The struggle was fiercest in the army. Most of the men accepted the new limits to their freedom, though not without petty frictions and expressions of nostalgia for the "conquests of the revolution." In thoroughly Bolshevized units, a murderous struggle broke out: officers and commissars were impaled on the bayonets of their men, or beaten to death with rifle butts. The men were then surrounded by cossacks or bombarded by artillerymen, until they gave up their leaders and returned to sullen obedience. By the end of July, the situation was quieter, but most officers were now convinced that the problem would not go away until the root of all infection, the soviets, were eradicated. They felt a mounting contempt for a government that failed to execute the murderers of their comrades.[19]

Kerensky's optimistic assessments have nothing to say about economics, yet whatever he or Kornilov now did to tame mutiny in the army, it was certain that a deteriorating economic situation would exacerbate social tensions during the autumn and winter. When taxed by General Knox with statistics proving the inevitability of catastrophe, one of Kerensky's closest aides, entering the realms of mystical economics, replied, "You base your pessimism on naked figures, but you do not take into account the wonderful Russian spirit."[20]

Emboldened by the government's isolation, Milyukov reopened his campaign for a war to a victorious conclusion, and for a government that could be relied upon to fight for it. His suggestion that the government was no longer an "all national" authority was followed by the denigration of the surviving Octobrist ministers as "Anarcho-Octobrists." Nekrasov was attacked, ostensibly for failing to keep the trains moving, Chernov was attacked for his agrarian radicalism, Tereshchenko, for his part in the Ukrainian negotiations and for holding back the evidence against Lenin.

Buchanan reported that Kerensky would not have Rodzyanko, Guchkov, or Milyukov back in the government but reported that "if Miliukoff is passed over he will prevent any of his followers from joining." And so it turned out. Kerensky's overtures to individual Kadets were politely rebuffed, and on July 15, the Kadet Central Committee announced its terms for a new Coalition: Chernov, the "arsonist of the countryside," must go, the Zimmerwald formula must be renounced, and there must be more Kadets in the new government. This would prevent party mavericks such as Nekrasov from helping Kerensky to evade Kadet control. Kerensky was already hoping to gain the assent of the SR Central Committee for Chernov's dismissal, but he refused to do so at the behest of the Kadets. He was quite prepared to bargain about policy, but Tsereteli had made enough concessions and he insisted that the government stick to its program.[21]

The troika were stung by Kadet attacks, but Nekrasov's Radical Democrats had little success in weaning the country's best administrators and the officer corps from the Kadets. Such a party could not be excluded from a government of national unity. Tereshchenko had already intimated to Buchanan that "it might soon be possible to eliminate Monsieur Tchernoff who did not inspire him with confidence," so the Kadets were demanding a sacrifice the troika were delighted to make.[22]

Aware that his days as "Village Minister" were numbered, Chernov resolved to nudge the agrarian revolution along while he still could. On July 12, he gained government sanction for a prohibition of all land sales, in order to prevent landowners from concluding fictitious deals to evade eventual expropriation. Four days later, Chernov signed an instruction to the local land committees, this time without government approval, to act as land rent tribunals, arrange the compulsory leasing of draft animals and machinery to poorer peasants when such assets were underutilized, and manage estates which had become unviable. This was practically "a green light to sequester property coveted by the local population."[23]

Chernov's enemies now found other sticks to beat him with. For some time, Colonel Nikitin had been reporting that Chernov had been a German agent. It now appeared that Chernov had written articles for a magazine subsidized by the German government for distribution to Russian prisoners-of-war. The information was leaked to the patriotic daily *Bez lishnykh slov* [Without unnecessary words] just as a new attack was being mounted on the government from the revived State Duma.[24]

On July 18, members of the Duma met in the Library of the Tauride Palace at Rodzyanko's invitation. Purishkevich and Maslennikov castigated Chernov for "provoking" the peasants against their landlords, while Milyukov defended the Kadet refusal to reenter the government and demanded the postponement of the Constituent Assembly. Once more, he tried to drive a wedge into the heart of the government, contrasting Kerensky and Tsereteli favorably with Chernov:

In their time, Tsereteli and Kerensky called themselves Zimmerwaldians; I hope that now they do not call themselves thus. But, within the membership of the Government there is a definite defeatest, a participant of the Zimmerwald Conference—Chernov.[25]

The campaign against Lenin *had* cast a shadow over Zimmerwald, and in one respect Milyukov had his way: Kerensky never found another good word for Zimmerwald, and never again did he publicly call for a peace without annexations or contributions.

Once more, Tereshchenko and Nekrasov solicited Tsereteli's assistance, telling him that they had proofs of Chernov's "treason." Tsereteli was unconvinced and he warned them that he would denounce their proofs as slander. In view of his hostility, they declined to reveal all their evidence until Chernov had resigned, since to do so would have undermined the whole government. Tsereteli fought back: Chernov might leave office for just three days, during which his accusers would have to put up or shut up.

Chernov had failed to spring to Kerensky's defense when he had been slandered at the PSR Congress, and the Prime Minister would have been more than human had he derived no satisfaction from Chernov's difficulties. At the same time, he was still a member of Chernov's party. More important, the support of Zenzinov, Gotz, and Avksentiev was vital to his government, as the PSR was still the most popular party in Russia. He was therefore mortified when Gotz and Zenzinov arrived with an ultimatum: the Provisional Government had three days in which to investigate Chernov's past. If it produced a clean bill of health, Chernov must be readmitted to the government or the SRs would abandon it.[26]

Kerensky was thus placed in an impossible situation: The Kadets were demanding Chernov's dismissal, the SRs were demanding his reinstatement, and Kornilov was demanding the dismissal of Cheremisov and the immediate implementation of his full program. On July 21, therefore, Kerensky resigned.

In view of my inability, despite all my efforts in this direction, to broaden the membership of the Provisional Government in such a way that it would answer the demands of the exceptional historical moment which the country is passing through, I can no longer bear the responsibility before the state [while] remaining true to my conscience and understanding.

He left immediately for Tsarskoe Selo and Grankulla.[27]

Before his departure, Kerensky had spoken to a leading Kadet.

Now look what you Kadets have done! I am obliged to resign. . . . They [i.e., the Kadets themselves] demand that we renounce our declaration. . . . Then the left blames me for conciliating the Kadets. . . . Then Nekrasov and Tereshchenko demand the departure of Chernov. . . . No, they won't accept my resignation. I will form a new cabinet of friends, men personally known to me.

The Kadet was shocked: "Excuse me, that's dictatorship." Kerensky had nothing to add.[28]

Kerensky also saw Emmeline Pankhurst and convinced her that he was a sick man, whose threats must be taken seriously. She told U.S. Ambassador David Francis, who rushed off to find Milyukov. The normally skeptical Milyukov was sufficiently alarmed to put off a trip to Moscow to dissuade Kerensky in person. The Kadet ultimatum was quietly withdrawn.[29]

That evening, Nekrasov and Tereshchenko summoned a joint meeting of the ministers, the Soviet Executive Committee, and the Duma Committee to the Malachite Hall of the Winter Palace. The

Octobrist V. N. Lvov summed up the mood of the overwhelming majority, saying that

He could not imagine how a new government could be formed unless A. F. Kerensky would agree to withdraw his resignation. For A. F. Kerensky is the only man whom the country still trusts and whom the country will follow. If it is impossible to form a strong government at whose centre stands A. F. Kerensky, the country will be ruined.

Tsereteli argued in vain for the accountability of government, but in the end the Kadets, Radical Democrats, Popular Socialist-Trudoviks, SRs, and Mensheviks voted Kerensky full powers to form a new government. In theory he was dictator, but their offer of full powers was really a euphemism for washing their hands of the government, a situation made all the more dangerous by the growing hostility of the army high command. In forming a government of his own choice, Kerensky was threatened with the hostility of all parties should he fail to meet their wishes.[30]

Kerensky left no doubt as to the priorities of his new Coalition. "The national work of the salvation of the country . . . must proceed under conditions and in forms dictated by the severe necessity of continuing the war, supporting the fighting capacity of the army and restoring the economic power of the nation."

The Kadets mitigated their discomfiture at withdrawing their ultimatum by the feeble expedient of accepting only junior ministries for their members. Kerensky reluctantly restored Chernov to the Ministry of Agriculture, but Chernov was more than balanced by the appointment of three right-wing SRs: Avksentiev became Minister of the Interior, while Savinkov and V. I. Lebedev were appointed Kerensky's deputies for the Army and Navy respectively within the Ministry of War.

Savinkov was indignant at Kerensky's failure to honor his promise to make him Minister of War in his own right and he nursed a deep hatred of Chernov. The SR Central Committee was equally taken aback by the appointment of Savinkov, whom they found too militaristic and elitist. (Savinkov was wont to describe Russia as the Congo at the time.) The SRs were also unhappy about the resignation of Tsereteli and agreed to join the government only after forcing Kerensky to make a formal offer to Tsereteli in the presence of Gotz. Tsereteli's growing antipathy to the troika was not his only motive for resigning. He was worried about the erosion of support for Menshevism in the Soviets; experience had confirmed the Menshevik prophecy that the Provisional Government would be a graveyard of reputations.

The Mensheviks were still strongly represented. Skobelev was joined by Nikitin, Kerensky's old comrade from the Lena Commission, and by the old Marxist-Revisionist Prokopovich. Kerensky had hoped to bring Plekhanov into the government, but the Soviet vetoed him as too defencist. Both Milyukov and the Soviet leaders were pleased by the elimination of the last Octobrist ministers. Kartashev, one of the mainstays of the Religious-Philosophical Society, replaced V. N. Lvov as Minister of Religious Affairs. (The post of Procurator of the Holy Synod had been abolished in keeping with the government's secularism.) Kartashev was a man of far greater learning and integrity than V. N. Lvov, but once again Kerensky made a mortal enemy without gaining a very reliable supporter.[31]

◦ Kerensky's commitment to continuing the war should have pleased Russia's European Allies—as it did the Americans. The permanent American diplomats compared rather unfavorably with their British and French opposite numbers, but during May and June, they were augmented by a distinguished American mission under the leadership of Senator Elihu Root. The New York Republican was impressed, and in his final report to Secretary of State Robert Lansing, he recommended the provision of massive sums to combat pacifism in the Russian army—under cover of the YMCA—and to stabilize the economy. It seemed to Root that even if the Russian army undertook no further offensive action, "the advantage to the United States and its Allied would be so great as to justify the expenditure by the United States of the largest sums which it can possibly devote to that purpose."[32]

American benevolence was not shared by the other Allies, which now began to treat the Russian Provisional Government with barely disguised contempt. They were now determined to beat the Germans to their knees with or without Russia. The factors effecting this change of heart included the secret peace feelers of the young Austrian Emperor Karl, the confidence that the United States would tide over shortages of cash and materiel, disappointment with the results of the Russian offensive and most of all, fear of the corrosive effects of peace propaganda on their own men. Public indifference to the socialist conference in Stockholm was now replaced by an open determination to torpedo it.[33]

One casualty of the new hard line was a member of the British War Cabinet, Arthur Henderson—a Labour Party member—who was expelled from the government for refusing to denounce the conference. News of his resignation had not yet reached Petrograd on July 29, when Kerensky and Tereshchenko entertained the ambassadors of Britain, France, and Italy at lunch. The proceedings began civilly enough. Buchanan congratulated Kerensky on the formation of the new government and expressed hopes for a speedy restoration of order. Kerensky was less cordial and mentioned his anxiety about the nonarrival of field guns, promised by Britain. Buchanan now upset Kerensky by trying to suggest that Petrograd should be placed under martial law as a precondition for the delivery of the guns. "Turning to me," Buchanan reported, "he then said in his bad French that if we were going to bargain about guns and did not intend to help Russia we had better say so straight out." Buchanan poured salt on the wound by suggesting that the guns might be better employed "*in Russia's interest*," on the western front.[34]

As Buchanan's genteel insults were uttered, the correspondence between Lloyd George and Henderson was published in London. The Prime Minister suggested that he was merely fulfilling the wishes of the Russian government in opposing the Stockholm Conference, and in the debate on Henderson's resignation he told the Commons that Kerensky had *personally* communicated his opposition to the Stockholm Conference, though this was quite untrue. (Lloyd George's impression was a third-hand report via Petit and Thomas.) In seeking to discredit Henderson in the eyes of the Labour Party, Lloyd George had exposed Kerensky to the wrath of the soviets. Not that Kerensky was blameless. His unguarded, and uncorrected, remarks to Petit had unseated his only friend in the British Cabinet and had exposed Tsereteli to unpleasantness in the Soviet. Kerensky's subsequent statement of sympathy for the Stockholm Conference, which appeared in the *Manchester Guardian* made little impression.[35]

Kerensky's emigré writings betray a curious ambivalence toward the Allies. Kerensky believed that Russia had to fight alongside the Allies for her own internal reasons, but he also felt that the Allies, as democracies, were morally obliged to give unstinting support for Russian democracy. He always maintained that Russia had been loyal, perhaps even too loyal, toward the Allies, and it is true that, apart from a solitary protest at Allied policy in Greece, the Provisional Government made no attempt to play hard out of weakness as General de Gaulle would do in a later war. This was partly a result of inexperience and consequent naïveté about Allied foreign policy.

Kerensky recognized that involuntary fidelity is no virtue, so his books lay a great deal of stress upon the possibility of a separate peace between Russia and the Central Powers in 1917. He went so far as to agree with Lord Beaverbrook that if he had made peace, "We should be in Moscow now."[36]

Toward the end of May 1917, Emperor Karl had written to Wilhelm II accusing him of obstructing a separate peace with Russia by insisting on German annexations in the East. Suppressing his irritation, Wilhelm replied on June 9(22) to refute the charge:

I doubt Kerensky's inclination to enter into negotiations with us. Recently, his behaviour and our intelligence reports rather tend to show that he has become completely subservient to the Entente. I can scarcely promise myself that any success will come of a direct peace offer to the present Provisional Government. Under these circumstances, our efforts must be [directed] to work on the broad masses and to convince them of our willingness for peace.

As a concession, he promised to place an official announcement in the *Norddeutsche Allgemeine Zeitung* indicating German willingness for talks in general terms. The statement appeared, despite the Grimm affair, on the same day as Kerensky's manifesto announcing the offensive.[37]

The Germans were now inclined to put all their money on the Bolsheviks, but Emperor Karl and his foreign minister, Count Czernin, still held out hopes for an accommodation with Kerensky. A couple of weeks after the German announcement, a conversation between a Dutch journalist and a Russian official in Petrograd suggested that the Russians might be willing to talk. Kerensky then authorized the statement that Russia did not support Italian and Serbian aims to partition the Dual Monarchy. The "Russian government is ready to enter a friendly conversation with the Austro-Hungarian government, provided it communicates its propositions immediately."[38]

Czernin was delighted at this apparent "peace proposal of Mr. Kerensky" and told Berlin that he intended to contact Kerensky in

strictest secrecy about a settlement based on a renunciation of annexations by force and provision for averting future wars. In other
words, Czernin was prepared to make an offer, but not a separate
offer, and certainly not an offer of a peace that excluded Germany.

Czernin looked "forward to further developments with excitement" and on July 21, the Dutchman left Stockholm for Petrograd,
promising to return within a month. When he failed to do so, that
seemed to be the end of the affair, but on September 4, Czernin
reported to his ambassador in Stockholm that the Dutchman *had*
returned with a peace offer from the Provisional Government based
on a return to the status quo of 1914. And that was that. When
questions were asked about these feelers a year later, the Austrians
had forgotten all about them.[39]

Kerensky's unpublished notes list another incident: "11.—JUL—
attempt at negotiation about SEP.PEACE *with me*." He kept this
bottled up for forty years before recounting a garbled and misleading
version of it to an old friend in New York.[40] Neither man knew that
a full account of this incident had been published in Finland between
the wars by a key participant.

This intermediary was Kerensky's friend and doctor, Dr. Runeberg. Runeberg recalled that early in August 1917, Dr. Poul Bjerre,
a distinguished Swedish psychiatrist, arrived in Grankulla with an
introduction from Alma Söderhjelm. Bjerre told Runeberg that he
hoped to facilitate peace talks. He would not say exactly how, though
he mentioned a possible plebiscite in Alsace-Lorraine. This suggests
the offer of a general settlement appealing to Russian sentiment,
rather than a separate peace offer from Austria. Runeberg was skeptical of what he took to be a "private initiative," but on August 11,
he saw Kerensky to arrange a meeting. Kerensky later suggested that
had he been Macchiavellian, he would have agreed, but that instead
he threatened to arrest "this person." Runeberg remembered a more
diplomatic response: "Russia is not in a position to make peace proposals, Lloyd George is the only one who can begin to think about
peace. In any case, you must turn to him first." But Kerensky offered
to speak to Tereshchenko and made no objection to a meeting between Bjerre and foreign ministry officials. Runeberg believed that
Tereshchenko saw Bjerre, albeit without result.[41]

Nothing in Runeberg's account leads to the supposition that Kerensky had received an official offer of a separate peace. Kerensky's

loyalty to the Allies is not impugned by it. Yet it was from chance contacts such as these that the fatal legend of a separate peace as a prelude for the suppression of internal opposition had been woven around the ex-Tsarina. This was a risk that Kerensky could not afford in 1917. Hence his long silence and inaccurate memory of the affair.

In July Kerensky's style became perceptibly more 'Bonapartist'. He and Lilya moved into Alexander III's suite on the third floor of the Winter Palace, a move described as *meshchanstvo* (lower-middle-class vulgarity) by Hippius. Now, the red flag was raised and lowered to mark his movements, while the pennant of the Minister of the Navy flapped from his car. He traveled in one of the Tsar's trains, slept in Alexander III's bed, and was photographed at the huge desk used by the Tsars. He was attended with a deference and diligence which was fast ceasing to exist in Russia. His Napoleonic mannerism, the leather-gloved hand clenched across his chest, survived the healing of the wound which had first occasioned it, and his plebeian dress was replaced by smartly tailored officer's tunics. Now he shunned large meetings, finding committees contemptible and mass meetings dangerous and unrewarding. Accustomed to salacious Court gossip, Petrograd society speculated on the identity of Olga's substitute. Was it the actress Timé? Or was it one of the Tsar's daughters? Such gossip was embellished by Bolshevik agitators and retold in the factories where the workers were coming to see the imprisoned Bolsheviks as martyrs.[42]

Early that month, Buchanan had confided in Tereshchenko that he found the ideas of Kerensky and Tsereteli on the war "too much those of idealists." Tereshchenko reassured him. "This was no longer the case with Minister of War"[43] Repin's portrait was painted at about this time. Kerensky's pose is Bonapartist but closer inspection suggests a man sad, even suffering. For those who saw him from close quarters, he had changed little. If Lilya shared his chamber, the incorruptible 'Babushka' shared their suite—and at Kerensky's demand.

His day still began with Breshkovskaya, as unaffected as ever, pouring the tea. His optimism still verged on irresponsibility on occasion, as for example when he ordered that a sleeping cadet guard at the Admiralty go unpunished—or, more seriously, when he commuted death penalties imposed on men at the front without considering the safety of those who had served on the elective courts martial.

When he heard that Bochkaryova had been wounded at the front, Kerensky ordered her a handsome private room. When he arrived to see her, he kissed her on the forehead and presented her with a handsome bouquet, apologizing for the troubles he had given her.[44]

More serious was Kerensky's failure to lay hands on Lenin. Though Trotsky and Alexandra Kollontai were in custody, Lenin and Zinoviev had escaped arrest and, after a few days with Stalin's future in-laws, they found a refuge at Razliv, just across the Finnish border. From there, Lenin wrote obsequious letters to Menshevik newspapers, denying the charges against him. It was easy to refute the charge that he had spied for Germany; denying that his party had received a German subsidy would be more difficult, and he had some trouble with the "constitutional illusions" of some of his own comrades who thought the matter could easily be cleared up if he went to court. The Bolshevik party continued to function. *Pravda* was "definitively" suppressed on July 16, but lesser Bolshevik papers maintained an intermittent existence and Menshevik-Internationalist papers opened their columns to Bolshevik articles.

Kerensky now anticipated a move from the right, and to the fury of the counterintelligence service, he imposed his personal friend, Prof. N. D. Mironov, on them with *carte-blanche* to keep a close watch on possible sponsors of a right-wing coup. The agents, however, frustrated Mironov by tipping off the suspects. Kerensky even attempted to circumvent hostile Allied diplomats by canvassing the sympathy of the Canadians! In short, little had changed and there can be no doubt that this was the way Kerensky wanted it. The Kadets were emboldened to criticize him personally for the first time. He was "merely deputizing for a great man"; his continued popularity was a myth: the country said that he was popular with the army and the army that he was popular in the country. Some days later, Boris Moiseenko admitted to Petit that Kerensky's popularity had indeed begun to wane.[45]

On the last day of July, Kerensky performed his final service for the Romanovs, paying the last of his six visits to Tsarskoe Selo to inspect the security arrangements and to satisfy his personal curiosity about the Imperial couple. His opinion of them did not improve. He still found Nicholas "Not very intelligent, poorly educated and lacking vitality," though he conceded that he "had something of an instinctive knowledge of life." His final impressions of the former

Empress were still less flattering: "an unbalanced, hysterical, morally maimed woman, but strong, earthly, passionate and proud." The inner cabinet now arranged for them to go to Tobolsk in Siberia. It was more peaceful than European Russia and offered the possibility of transit to Japan or the United States, though Tereshchenko admitted to Buchanan that the real motive was Kerensky's fear of monarchist rescue plots. It was Kerensky who overcame the suspicions of the guards: "Remember," he said, "no hitting a man when he is down. Behave like gentlemen, not cads." He had always tried to preserve the Revolution from bloodshed. He must have begun to wonder whether anyone would be as considerate toward him.[46]

13

Statesman or Revolutionary?

For many left-wing Russians, Kerensky was a renegade by August 1917. A campaign of defamation and vilification began that has never ceased. Its principal author was Lenin, for whom Kerensky's new government was "merely a screen for the counterrevolutionary Cadets and the military clique which is in power at present." Soviet authors still echo the judgment that "the Kerensky affair (*Kerenshchina*) is merely a variety of the . . . counterrevolutionary policy of the imperialist bourgeoisie."[1]

This was not how things seemed to those who knew Kerensky. As early as June, Hippius had endorsed Kerensky's desire to continue the war and suppress the Bolsheviks, but, she added, "he has absorbed a sort of revulsion from power, from its indispensably exterior, necessarily coercive methods. He can't, he stops, he becomes afraid." And in August, she wrote even more emphatically: "It is a fact that Kerensky is afraid. Of what? Of whom?"[2] The same impression of vacillation is conveyed by other close observers. It is usually assumed that vacillation equals weakness, yet Kerensky's vacillations were evidence of the tremendous determination with which he pursued the cause of coalition to avert a civil war.

But as August went on, Kerensky became an increasingly tragic figure as his intellect told him to serve the state, while his emotions refused to sever all the bands that still tied him to the revolutionary movement. He was still only thirty-six. Could he, who had saved so many from "Stolypin's necktie," become the new Stolypin? He must have hoped desperately that it would not be necessary.

The initial differences between Kerensky and Kornilov were over-shadowed by Kerensky's attempts to form a new government. Still, it was an ill omen that they became public knowledge at all. Kerensky had been infuriated by the ultimatum presented by Kornilov on his appointment as Supreme Commander-in-Chief in July. Savinkov and Baranovsky had advised him to ignore it, as it probably emanated from "unscrupulous adventurers" in Kornilov's retinue. No one ever explained why this should have sounded reassuring. The settlement worked out by the government's commissar, M. M. Filonenko, left Kornilov feeling that the government had adopted all his demands in principle, and the government was seen to back down over its nomination of General Cheremisov as Kornilov's successor on the Southwest front. This experience encouraged Kornilov to believe that if he pushed hard enough, Kerensky would yield. As Kerensky conceded, "I plead guilty for not having finally insisted upon Kornilov's immediate dismissal, but . . . those were such terrible times, there was sore need of a strong personality at the front."[3]

Savinkov described Kornilov as politically illiterate, while Brusilov made the splenetic jibe that Kornilov had the "brains of a sheep." Kornilov was, of course, unversed in the labyrinthine complexity of the Russian left, but he was no fool. His underground forays in South Asia displayed qualities of stealth and cunning. Like Denikin, he loved the banners, uniforms, and marching songs of the Imperial Russian Army. Like Alexeyev, he believed that the men would show remarkable courage and endurance if led by colorful, intelligent leaders. This made him a social leveler, since he disliked effete aristocrats. Together, these beliefs constitute an unacknowledged political philosophy which becomes overtly partisan when foisted on civilian society. What, after all, was fascism but a combination of hyperbolic patriotism and the military organization of society?[4]

In the spring of 1917, a Society for the Economic Rehabilitation of Russia and a Republican Centre were formed to press for a restoration of order. At first the Society supported Kerensky's attempts to galvanize the army by oratory alone, but as July went on they began to see Kornilov as Russia's future savior. Baranovsky and Prince Tumanov had belonged to the Centre in its early days, but after the July Crisis, its leadership had passed to A. F. Aladin, leader of the Trudoviks in the First Duma. Aladin had attempted unsuccessfully to persuade the British to enroll him as a secret agent, but his return to Russia in the uniform of a British Army translator was almost as useful, earning him the suspicions of the Soviet and a welcome at GHQ. There he encountered V. S. Zavoiko, a relative of the banker Putilov, who had taken on the ostensibly menial duties of Kornilov's orderly, though he was really Kornilov's secretary. Another organization influential at GHQ was the Union of Officers, led by Colonel Novosiltsev, a former Kadet deputy. As the "dissolution" of the army proceeded, this initially nonpartisan body became totally committed to the suppression of the soviets.[5]

The French patriotic press had greeted Kornilov as the author of the offensive even before his promotion to the Supreme Command. Did the Allies support him against Kerensky, as Kerensky himself suspected? Supportive toward Kerensky until mid-July, the British Imperial War Cabinet rapidly lost sympathy with him thereafter. Kerensky's own diplomatic gaffe had helped secure the expulsion of Henderson from the War Cabinet. A hiatus followed as, bereft of clear direction, British representatives in Russia pursued their own courses. At GHQ, General Barter advised all-out support for Kornilov, while doing little to dissuade Kornilov from plotting against Kerensky. Ambassador Buchanan counseled diplomatic moderation. On August 5, General Knox, the British Military Attaché, left for England. The War Cabinet needed to hear from him in person before deciding on a new policy toward Russia.[6]

By late July, Kornilov himself felt that only the militarization of the factories and railways could save Russia. This meant the elimination of the soviets and the suppression of the Bolsheviks. He did not trust Kerensky to go along with all of this and in a confidential interview with General Barter at the very end of July, he expressed the opinion "that Kerensky was an opportunist and that he could not be relied on." Kornilov thought the only chance of reaching an agreement with Kerensky lay in Allied diplomatic pressure.[7]

On August 3, Kornilov arrived in Petrograd to report to the government for the first time since his promotion. He met Kerensky, Tereshchenko, and Savinkov for discussions before the full cabinet meeting. Kerensky warned him that his reports too often resembled ultimata, to which Kornilov replied that they were dictated solely by circumstances, and he showed Kerensky a report including demands which Kerensky felt were sure to destroy the government he had so laboriously reconstructed. In refusing to read them to the whole government, Kerensky was avoiding a trap set by Savinkov, who had informed Milyukov personally of Kornilov's program. Kerensky knew that the barest reference to the militarization of factories and railways would provoke Chernov to resign and denounce the demands to the soviets before they could be implemented. For the time being, the politicians overcame the general and it was agreed that Savinkov and Filonenko would work out a revised program for presentation at a later date.

Kornilov now raised the possibility of changes in the government. Kerensky did his best to convince him that coalition was the only viable form of government, and he asked Kornilov the rhetorical question: "Well, suppose I retire, what would be the outcome?" Kornilov reassured him. Kerensky was still essential in view of his leadership of the "democratic parties," i. e., the socialists. Kerensky's above-party manner obviously did not wash with Kornilov. Kerensky warned him of the dangers of a military dictatorship, which would have to contend with a general strike and a massacre of officers. Kornilov was not intimidated: "I forsee that possibility, but at least those who are left alive will have the soldiers in hand."

It had been agreed that Kornilov would merely report on the state of the fronts at the full meeting of the government, but he went on to answer detailed questions on the capacity of the army for defensive and offensive operations. According to Kornilov, Kerensky then leant toward him and whispered to him to be more careful in talking about such questions. In addition, Kornilov remembered Savinkov passing him a note with a similar warning. Later that day, Savinkov explained that Chernov might inform the Soviet leaders, some of whom might pass on the information to the Germans. (It emerged later that one of Chernov's friends had indeed been a German informant.) Kerensky merely remembered asking Kornilov to be brief, "as was his manner." He denied passing any note from Savinkov and insisted that Kornilov, who was sitting next to him at the meeting, received no note from anyone else either. Subsequently, Kornilov would make much of this alleged incident, yet at the time, he told Barter that his discussions in Petrograd had been "satisfactory."[8]

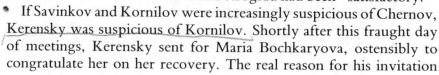 If Savinkov and Kornilov were increasingly suspicious of Chernov, Kerensky was suspicious of Kornilov. Shortly after this fraught day of meetings, Kerensky sent for Maria Bochkaryova, ostensibly to congratulate her on her recovery. The real reason for his invitation

soon appeared. He wanted her to discover whether Kornilov really wanted to restore Tsarism. This delicate mission was quite beyond the ultra-patriotic, open-hearted peasant woman who confessed her mission to Rodzyanko, and then to Kornilov himself. His apoplectic reaction was understandable: "The scoundrel! The upstart! I swear by the honour of an old soldier that I do not want Tsarism restored." And he continued: "The idiot! He can't see that his days are numbered. . . . Tomorrow, Lenine will have his head, and everything will be wrecked."[9]

Kerensky publicly voiced his distrust of Kornilov to the Soviet Executive Committee only the day after Kornilov's visit to Petrograd. The Soviet leaders badly needed reassurance, and Kerensky was greeted coolly at first; but after a while, his unfailing persuasiveness began to melt the ice and he left to warm applause. He reaffirmed his faith in the democratic revolution; the ruin of the revolution meant the ruin of Russia and vice versa. He warned anyone who felt tempted to take power by force: "As long as I stand at the head of the new government, I declare determinedly that I shall not permit any attempts at a restoration, or a return to autocracy or monarchy." This overture to the soviets exasperated the Kadets who saw it as a "political step, toning down, like many things in the last few days, that determined line which it seemed the new government wants to adopt."[10]

It was also bitterly resented by Savinkov, for whom the soviets were the "councils of rats', dogs' and chickens' deputies." Savinkov had succeeded in persuading the Kadets that Kornilov was a martinet, while trying to persuade Kerensky that the general was a "true democrat and staunch republican." He and Filonenko were supposed to reconcile them, but Savinkov's own attitudes made this almost impossible. He felt a European intellectual's condescension for Kornilov's political ideas, but he admired his "Asiatic" military qualities. Savinkov fancied himself a Russian Ludendorff to Kornilov's Hindenburg, and he told Ilya Ehrenburg he despised "our narcissistic women's premier" as a "phrase-monger who nourishes himself on the timbre of his voice." For the time being, he affected to admire the Prime Minister's "noble nature" and he confided to Stepun and the Merezhkovskys that his aim was a Directory of Kerensky, Kornilov, and himself. There can be little doubt as to who would be First Consul. Despite this, the poetess of cold emotion felt that Savinkov's motives were pure, "a genuine love for *Russia* and for her *freedom*."[11]

Savinkov and Kerensky also quarreled about the need for further repression of the Bolsheviks. The party leaders had lain low for most of July, but toward the end of the month they showed signs of renewed activity. From July 26 to August 3, they even convened 270 leading Bolsheviks for the underground Sixth Party Congress in Petrograd, at which time the Inter-District Group, which included Trotsky and Lunacharsky, finally threw in its lot with the Bolsheviks. Lenin was still in Finland and Trotsky in prison, but Savinkov saw this as a golden opportunity to bag many of the leading Bolshevik cadres. His own experience suggested that this might cripple the party. On July 28, the Ministers of War and the Interior were empowered to close all assemblies which endangered the state or its military efforts. On August 2, the same ministers were authorized to arrest and expel from Russia anyone threatening the defense of the state, its internal security or "the freedom conquered by the Revolution."

Kerensky must have refused Savinkov's plea to use these powers against the Bolshevik congress, for Savinkov asked Breshkovskaya to join him in a further attempt. Kerensky was initially cold, suspicious of Savinkov's contacts with Rodzyanko and Milyukov, and then silently noncommittal. When his beloved Babushka begged him to take action, he replied lamely that he did not know where the Bolsheviks were meeting and, in any case, he would have to get Avksentiev's agreement. David Soskice witnessed Breshkovskaya's dramatic response:

suddenly without answering his arguments the grey haired woman bowed to the ground before Kerensky and repeated several times in solemn imploring tones, "I beg thee, Alexander Fyodorovich, suppress the Conference, suppress the Bolsheviki. I beg thee do this, or else they will bring ruin on our country and the revolution." . . . I looked at Kerensky. His pale face grew still whiter. His eyes reflected the terrible struggle that was proceeding within him. He was silent for long, and at last he said in a low voice, "How can I do it?" "Do it, A. F. I beseech thee" and again Babushka bowed to the ground. Kerensky could stand it no longer. He sprang to his feet and seized the telephone.

Fortunately for the Bolsheviks and Kerensky's conscience, Avksentiev was not in his office—to Kerensky's evident relief.[12]

On August 8, Savinkov confronted him again. He had already given Kerensky a list of 50 right-wing and 50 left-wing extremists he wanted arrested and deported. Kerensky endorsed the expulsion of the rightists but only half the socialists. Avksentiev then struck out all the remaining socialists but Trotsky and Kollontai, who were already free on bail. Savinkov then demanded that Kerensky sign that part of the program he and Filonenko had drafted providing for the reestablishment of the death penalty in the rear. Kerensky categorically refused, thereby blocking discussion of the proposal in the cabinet. Kerensky later suggested that his opposition was due solely to the pragmatic consideration that civilians and soldiers in the rear would refuse to impose the death penalty, a view partly shared by Mannerheim, then commander of a Russian cavalry division, who felt that talk of revolutionary courts and the death penalty was "a big bluff." Mannerheim knew Kornilov and his opinion that the Supreme Commander was "dilettante" in approach must be treated seriously. Pragmatic considerations were probably less important than Kerensky's knowledge that the Kadets were primed to support Kornilov, while Chernov was poised to denounce him.[13]

Savinkov regarded Kerensky's obstruction as a breach of the assurances made to him before his entry into the government, and he resigned immediately. At the same time, he decided to circumvent Kerensky's veto by summoning Kornilov to Petrograd. (As Supreme Commander, Kornilov had the right in theory to say what he liked to the whole government.) At first Kornilov refused, pleading a critical situation at the front, but Savinkov overcame these scruples by insisting, untruthfully, that the whole government required his presence.[14]

Kornilov's opinion of the Provisional Government had not improved since his previous visit. On August 7, commissar Fonvizen warned him that the government intended to remove him, and he was warned that the Soviet might have him assassinated, so when Kornilov arrived in the capital on August 10, he drove into the city escorted (at General Barter's suggestion!) by two cars carrying machine guns manned by Caucasian native troops. His temper was not improved when he discovered that Kerensky had ordered him to remain at the front. Collecting a copy of the proposals prepared by Savinkov and Filonenko, he arrived at the Winter Palace, flanked by Rodzyanko and Bochkaryova. His escorts were not admitted to the stormy two-hour session that followed. Kerensky claimed that this was the first time he had heard mention of the militarization of the railroads and ordnance factories, so he could hardly have been expected to recommend them to a plenary session of the government. This was a legalistic evasion, at best, and it did not go down well with Kornilov. The most superficial consideration of the personalities of the protagonists suggests that their matter-of-fact accounts left for history do no justice to the dramatic quality of this encounter. The clash between Russia's most emotional orator and her most swashbuckling general must have been more colorful. Bochkaryova's keyhole account of the two men screaming threats of dismissal and semimutiny at one another is more credible. When Kerensky finally admitted him, Rodzyanko took up where Kornilov had left off, accusing Kerensky of destroying Russia and shouting, "The blood of the country will be on your head," before Kerensky threw them out. Over lunch at Rodzyanko's, Kornilov told his companions that if Kerensky dismissed him, he would "lead the Savage Division, consisting of tribesmen loyal to him, against Kerensky."[15]

That afternoon, Kornilov went off to discover whether Savinkov had doublecrossed him. It took Savinkov some time to calm him down. Kerensky had seen the report, though not quite in its present form, and he certainly knew its substance. With this assurance, Kornilov countersigned the report and agreed to read it to the government. He then returned to the Winter Palace.

Kerensky refused to summon a plenary session of the government and excluded Savinkov, who had now resigned, and pro-Kadet Kartashev from his discussions with the Supreme Commander. He then called in Nekrasov and Tereshchenko to create the illusion that Kornilov was at least addressing a "partial meeting of the Provisional Government." At this meeting, Kerensky's brethren tried, "with the greatest tenderness for the General's feelings," to explain that the militarization of factories and railroads simply would not work: the Tsar's government had tried it and it had failed. Kornilov felt that the ministers were again approving his ideas in principle while refusing to carry them out. Savinkov saw Kornilov off that night and told him just how bad his relations with Kerensky had become. That night, Savinkov read his report to Kartashev at the Merezhkovskys. Hippius saw at once that it could be implemented only over the dead bodies of the Bolsheviks, and many of the moderate socialists in the soviets. Once more, Savinkov had prompted both Kornilov and the Kadets to put more pressure on Kerensky.[16]

Kerensky, whose intuition was not yet totally anesthetized by fame and power, the next morning summoned Savinkov for a dressing-down: "You are a Lenin but of the other side! You're a terrorist! Well then, come and kill me. Are you leaving the government straight away? Now a wide field of political activity is open to you." Savinkov indignantly retorted that he would leave for the front and serve as a common soldier. The cold-blooded terrorist was, of course, a far better actor than the histrionic minister. Kokoshkin then arrived to insist on the immediate implementation of all the measures proposed by Kornilov, failing which he (and the other Kadet ministers) would resign.

Kerensky was distraught, and he complained to Sorokin that "to resign the day before the [Moscow] Conference is simply a crime."

Why these men are demanding immediate militarization of the railroads, ironclad discipline in the army, limitation of Soviet interference in governmental functions, and even, if necessary, dispersal of the Soviet. Briefly, they think a dictatorship may be necessary. This might not be so bad—if only it could be accomplished, but. . . . the thing is absolutely impossible. Where are the forces through which we could execute such a plan? Nowhere. They accuse me of inefficiency, they think I am ambitious for power. Fools! If I could only resign, get away from all this and retire to some quiet village, I would be the happiest man in the world. But to whom could I resign my office? Where is the man? I know they are plotting against the Government. Days ago this same scheme was proposed to me by Savinkov, then by Korniloff, and now Kokoshkin proposes it. God knows, if I could see any possibility of its realization I would welcome it with all my heart. But I know that the first attempt to put it into execution would result in new and more terrible riots.

Kerensky himself could think of no better solution, but hoped that time would bring one. Nor could he accept the idea of stealing the Bolsheviks' clothes. "All this is impossible, too," he lamented, "A separate peace would be shameful. No, no. Better perish with honor than infamy."[17]

Eventually, Kerensky induced Kokoshkin to withdraw his resignation and a full meeting of the government, attended by Chernov, discussed Kornilov's less hair-raising proposals. They clarified the competence of commanders, commissars, and committees in the army and accepted the need for the death penalty in the rear, but deferred its introduction. There would be a total silence in public about the militarization of railroads and factories. It was understood that Kerensky would invite Savinkov to withdraw his resignation, also.

This was the day on which Dr. Runeberg arrived with his "peace offer." Kerensky left Runeberg alone in his study for a while, unaware of Runeberg's inability to control his curiosity. A fishing expedition in Kerensky's wastepaper basket yielded a crumpled sheet of paper, a letter formally accepting Savinkov's resignation. That evening, Savinkov rang Hippius to say that Kerensky had asked him to stay on. He let Kerensky sweat: three days later, he was still insisting that his resignation was irrevocable. That same evening, Kerensky, Breshkovskaya and the ministers entrained for the overnight journey to Moscow.[18]

On July 12, Kerensky had first proposed a conference of all organized forces in the country in Moscow. At that moment, the rump cabinet had stood in obvious need of reinforcement. Kerensky hoped that a conference would renew his mandate for coalition. He had returned to the idea after the formation of the second coalition, but events had moved on. "Putting his hand to his heart," wrote the Kadet *Moskovskie Vedomosti* [Moscow News], "no-one in the population can say exactly what the Moscow Conference ought to give to the country."[19]

The composition of the conference was corporatist rather than democratic. Bankers and industrialists commanded more seats than the Soviets, who found themselves occupying only a part of the sector allotted to socialist organizations, sharing seats with the politically moderate cooperatives. The 488 seats assigned to members of the four former Dumas were nearly a fifth of the total, illustrating graphically how far the schism on the left had eroded the standing of the soviets. In a passage studded with ironic borrowings from the vocabulary of the right, Sukhanov summed up his view of the aims of the Conference:

to suppress the opinion of "the whole Democracy" with the opinion of "the whole country"; for the sake of the final liberation of the "all-national government" from the guardianship of all the workers, peasants, Zimmerwaldists, semi-German, semi-Jewish, hooligan organizations.[20]

Government policies made the Conference even less welcome to the soviets. Chernov's ambiguous circular enlarging the powers of the elected land committees had been followed by one from Tsereteli's Interior Ministry, warning against land seizures. The Finnish assembly had been dissolved. This was followed by a First Instruction to the Ukrainian *Rada*, which broke the spirit—if not the letter—of the agreements reached in June. It defined the borders of the Ukraine as narrowly as possible, reduced the General Secretariat's departments to seven, and insisted that at least four be headed by non-Ukrainians. Kerensky and Tereshchenko had helped to torpedo the Stockholm Conference and their claim that they were putting pressure on the Allies to redefine war aims now looked pretty hollow. The government's emergency powers might be employed with devastating effect without warning. For many socialists, the most ominous change was the announcement that elections to the Constituent Assembly would not, after all, be held in September, but in November. Would it ever meet, they wondered?[21]

Nor were the Kadets satisfied by the government's new line. They were still waiting for the government to apply the legislation adopted with so much fanfare. Nothing would satisfy them but the suppression or elimination of the soviets. On the eve of the Moscow State Conference, some 400 conservative politicians, capitalists, and generals enthusiastically supported Milyukov's demand that the government "immediately and decisively break with all servants of utopia.'" A Soviet historian claims they were secretly addressed by a representative of Kornilov, who warned them that he would oppose his dismissal with "armed conflict." She adds that when the Kadet Central Committee met on August 11, Milyukov expressed the view that only a military dictatorship could save Russia from anarchy, though he hoped this might come through agreement.[22]

On the eve of the Moscow State Conference, all thoughts were on Kornilov, and the right-wing leaders declared: "In the terrible hour of grave suffering, all thinking Russia looks to you with hope and faith." Analogous messages were sent by the Union of Cossacks and the Association of Knights of St. George. A *coup d'état* was widely rumored and Colonel Verkhovsky, Commander-in-Chief of Moscow, concerted plans with the local Soviet. But the Allies were not yet ready to ditch Kerensky. On August 10, French Consul-General

Bertrand warned the Quai d'Orsay that a coup might be in the offing, and British diplomats passed on similar tipoffs the next day. Premier Ribot was sufficiently alarmed to write in person to Ambassador Noulens and Bertrand enjoining the utmost discretion. "It concerns all the Allies that M. Kerensky and Gen. Korniloff [are] equally resolved to form a government capable of energy [in] suppressing all disorders of the sort which weaken the military power of Russia[;] in re-establishing discipline in the nation as in the army."[23]

The mobilization of the right created ideal conditions for the Bolsheviks to pursue "unification from below." The Soviet Executive Committee adopted rules to gag the Bolsheviks and Internationalists, thereby justifying Bolshevik sabotage tactics. The Bolsheviks only narrowly failed to gain the authority of the Moscow Soviet for a general strike, but it went ahead anyway under the aegis of the Central Bureau of Trade Unions. The socialist press claimed that 400,000 workers, a majority of Moscow's working class, took part. Bolshevik factory workers were joined by electricity workers, who stopped the trams and forced the Conference participants to walk to the Bolshoi Theatre. More surprising was the solidarity of waiters and commissionaires. Kerensky felt that the Bolsheviks had only isolated themselves, a view shared by few observers, but Kerensky no longer had to travel by tram or seek refreshment in public restaurants. Besides, there was the evidence of the seventh Council of the PSR, where a resolution condemning the death penalty had been carried over the objections of the Central Committee and Breshkovskaya, who had taken an active part in the debate. The Soviet Executive Committee and Moscow Soviet now set up committees of all the socialist parties to coordinate action in the event of a coup; the Bolsheviks were asked to join them.[24]

On the morning of August 12, Kerensky's train was greeted by Minister Nikitin and Colonel Verhovsky, who reported on security measures for the Conference. After a ministerial meeting in the Kremlin, they proceeded to the Bolshoi Theatre, past jeering crowds of Bolsheviks and through the massed ranks of military cadets. The polarization that met their eyes in the famous white-and-gold auditorium must have made their hearts sink.

the right side of the stalls was filled with the representatives of the four Dumas and the middle-class parties—all respectable people with frock-coats and collars. On the left came the Soviet delegates of the unshaven chin and the working-day shirt, with a fair sprinkling of common soldiers. In the middle, as if crushed between two millstones, came the co-operators and the free professional associations.

The boxes contained the high command and Allied diplomats, though the box provided for the Soviet Executive Committee was ominously vacant. In cutting the soviets down to size, Kerensky had unintentionally cast himself as the leader of the left, an impression reinforced by the absence of Kadet ministers on the platform. The two young adjutants standing to attention behind him provided a less than convincing symbol of military backing.[25]

Kerensky had long spoken in the name of the People and the working masses. Since February, he had appealed to the people on behalf of the Revolution, free Russia, and the French revolutionary motto, Liberty, Equality, and Fraternity. As he opened the Conference, he reconsecrated himself to "the service of the State," warning that the State was "experiencing an hour of deadly danger." The effect was slightly marred when the Soviet Committee members finally arrived, but Kerensky was not to be deflected. "Our aim . . . is the salvation of the State. . . . Now the time has arrived for organization, consolidation, and defense of the rights achieved by the Russian state as such."

In the name of the State, Kerensky promised the successful prosecution of the war and the repression of the "impossible" and "ruinous" demands of the Finns and Ukrainians. He threatened the mutinous with "iron and blood," an unfortunate and misleading reference to the phrase coined by Bismarck in a passage deriding democracy. When he thanked the Allies for turning down offers of a separate peace at Russia's expense, he provoked a scene. The shamefaced socialists refused to stand and join the rest of the auditorium in a standing ovation for the Allied Ambassadors.

He knew that only autocrats and bureaucrats love the State, so he tried to communicate his spiritual conversion to intellectuals and enlisted soldiers. "While still Minister of Justice," he reminded them, "I introduced in the Provisional Government the question of abolishing capital punishment." There was applause, and he continued, "and as Minister of War it was also I who introduced . . . the partial restoration of capital punishment." This time there was even more enthusiasm, especially on the right. At this his sensibilities were affronted. "Who dares applaud when it is a question of capital punishment? Don't you know that at that moment, at that hour, a part of our human heart was killed?" There was dead silence. "But if it is necessary for the preservation of the State, if our words, warning of great trials, do not reach those who demoralize and pervert our army in the rear, we will pluck our heart out, but save the State." His words, pauses and gestures were immensely impressive and the auditorium responded with a roar of sympathetic applause.

The hint of Othello, the suggestion of public suicide, was totally theatrical yet there were few listeners unconvinced that he was totally sincere. What sort of Christian could applaud the death penalty? Later, he hit a false note in describing himself as one of the military, but the speech had made its mark. If Russians would think in ethical rather than political terms, coalition would be saved. What could be more unethical than fratricide?[26]

Before leaving Mogilev, Kornilov told Barter that "a crisis was inevitable unless government took immediate steps demanded by the moderates" (i.e., the Kadets). Barter's estimate was that Kornilov now regarded "action by force" against the government as "indispensable." Kornilov's arrival in Moscow was a triumph. At the station he was fêted by officers, well-dressed ladies, and Kadet politicians with flowers in their hands. Rodichev, who had once excoriated Stolypin in the Duma, now greeted the Supreme Commander with the words: "Come, Leader [*vozhd'*] and save Russia!" Verkhovsky punctured Kornilov's euphoria a little by warning him that any movement would be suppressed, but Kornilov assured him that his supporters would not indulge in armed demonstrations. Kornilov then paid a brief visit to the Chapel of the Iberian Mother of God, the first place at which Russian rulers—and simpler pilgrims—paused on entering Moscow.[27]

That evening, Kornilov received a telephone call with the government's ruling: he could address the Conference on the following day, but he must restrict himself to reporting on the situation at the front. Dissatisfied, Kornilov phoned Kerensky, who explained that the ministers had given comprehensive reports on the state of the army and there should be no sign of disunity. Kornilov insisted on reporting the whole truth as he saw it, and on the measures required in the current situation. The discussion was reopened, actually behind the scenes of the Bolshoi Theatre, on the following day. Kerensky appealed to Kornilov not to set an example of indiscipline. Kornilov finally agreed to stick to the government's brief, provided General Kaledin, Ataman of the Don Cossacks, could say the rest.

The appearance of the small, wiry figure in dress uniform, with his familiar hooded eyes and triangular beard, drew an overwhelming ovation from the right, while the socialists, civilian and soldier, remained glued to their seats. "Soldiers, stand up! Shame!" shouted the right. Kerensky's intervention was adroit: "I request the audience to maintain order and to hear out the first soldier of the Provisional Government with the respect due to him and out of respect for the Provisional Government." Consul-General Bertrand felt that "from that moment, M. Kerensky appeared master of the day." Kornilov's speech had been drafted by Filonenko and Zavoiko, and in the main it limited itself to the topics agreed. Kornilov described cases where men had murdered their commanders, cases of cowardice, and the serious effect on army supplies of disorder in the rear. Kerensky had to check the enthusiasm of the right, which seemed almost to enjoy this catalogue of woes. Kornilov did exceed his brief in referring to a report which he, Savinkov, and Filonenko had presented to the government. He also spoke about order on the railroads in a way vague enough to escape Kerensky's censure while explicit enough to alarm the railroad union. All the same, the right had expected stronger stuff and they were disappointed.[28]

General Kaledin followed with the real manifesto of counter-revolution, demanding the suppression of all the soviets, "strong government," and the abandonment of all "socialist" economic policies. As he enunciated each point, he was cheered by the right and booed and hissed by the left. The cards were now well and truly on the table. From then on, Kerensky kept a tight rein on debate, cutting speakers off ruthlessly when they touched on sensitive topics. Guchkov, Maklakov, and Rodzyanko were all interrupted in this way; Kerensky cannot have minded turning the tables on the former Duma Chairman.[29]

It was Nikolai Chkheidze, Kerensky's old comrade, friend and Masonic brother, who spoke for the Soviet Executive Committee. The disappointments of the Revolution and the personal tragedy of his son's suicide had affected him deeply, and he advanced a variant of the government's program of July 8 without conviction. He demanded no change in the war and no new agrarian legislation, but the national economy must be totally controlled, the rich heavily taxed, counterrevolutionaries weeded out of the army high command, and the nationalities promised "full self-determination" at the end of the war.[30]

Milyukov's contribution was slighter, and more polemical, analyzing the weaknesses of the Provisional Government, vindicating his own conduct, and attacking Chernov once more. He offered Kerensky the conditional support of the Kadets, though this did not extend to passing on Kornilov's tipoff that something serious was scheduled for August 27. Maklakov had a distinct impression that Milyukov had assured Kornilov that the Kadets would mobilize massive support behind him if he should find it necessary to come out against the government.[31]

In winding up the Conference on August 15, Kerensky argued vigorously for conciliation. "The only genuine policy that considers the State." Iron-fisted measures would only provoke civil war. He justified his authoritarian chairmanship by the need to spare the nerves of the army, and he invited the Conference to share his spiritual ordeal:

> I am often told that I have too much faith and that I dream too much. Now, members of the State Conference and citizens of the Russian land, I will not dream any more. I will try to have less faith—it often happens that the Government is blamed for having this boundless faith, the faith in man, in his soul, in his conscience and his reason. . . . If each one of you could glance for just a moment at everything that is happening in the country, if you could take a glance and see everything and understand, you would not be speaking the way you do. Since it must be, so let it be. Let my heart turn to stone, let all the chords of my faith in man die away, let all the flowers of my dreams for man wither and die (Cries of "don't let this happen!") These have been scorned and stamped upon today from this rostrum. Then I will stamp upon them myself. They will cease to be. (Cry: "You cannot do this—your heart will not let you do this!") I will cast away the keys to this heart that loves the people and I will think only of the State.

And, with a few concluding words, he closed the conference.[32]

Kerensky reminded Shingaryov of Tsar Fyodor Ioannovich, the religious and emotional son of Ivan the Terrible, and there was more than a passing similarity between them. Kornilov was out to liberate Kerensky from Soviet influence, as Shuisky had tried to release Fyodor from the grip of Boris Godunov. There were more personal resemblances, too, between Kerensky and A. K. Tolstoy's "Fyodor," the role Kerensky had once dreamed of playing on just such a stage. Verdicts on his performance were mixed. This was the moment when Zinaida Hippius "fell out of love" with him. "He is like a railroad car that has left the rails. He sways, vacillates, painfully and—without any glamour." Allied diplomats were more complimentary; the impressionable General Barter even called his chairmanship "impartial and distinguished."[33]

The rhetoric of the State purveyed by Kerensky, and translated into Marxist jargon by Tsereteli in the Soviet, was followed with keen interest by Lenin. Now without his beard, looking years younger, he was living in a small farm outhouse just outside Petrograd. This unlooked-for holiday gave him the opportunity to make his final serious contribution to Marxist theory, *State and Revolution*. Never finished, it had little impact on events, but it captures Lenin's hopes in the summer and early autumn of 1917. It also offers a benchmark for future Soviet reality more devastating than the critiques of all but the most bilious anti-Communist polemicists. As usual, Lenin struck out to right and left simultaneously. He reminded the Social Democrat Mensheviks that, according to Marx and Engels, the bourgeois state "*cannot* be superseded by the proletarian state . . . through the process of "withering away," but, as a general rule, only through violent revolution." To those who mistook Leninism for anarchism, he put Marx's question: "After overthrowing the yoke of the capitalists, should the workers 'lay down their arms,' or use them against the capitalists in order to crush their resistance?" But what is the systematic use of arms by one class against another if not a 'transient form' of state." The new state would be the "dictatorship of the proletariat" erroneously denounced as premature by Kerensky and the Mensheviks.

Such a state would be perfectly viable:

We, the workers, shall organize large-scale production on the basis of what capitalism has already created, relying on our experience as workers, establishing strict, iron discipline backed up by the state power of the armed workers. We shall reduce the role of state officials to that of simply carrying out our instructions as responsible, revocable, modestly paid "foremen and accountants."

There was an almost lyrical quality about a future,

under which the functions of control and accounting, becoming more and more simple, will be performed by each in turn, will then become a habit and will finally die out as the *special* functions of a special section of the population.[34]

Lenin's hopes were raised by the increasing militancy of the workers and peasants and by the evident disunity of his enemies, though he did not guess how much divided Kerensky from Kornilov. Verkhovsky claimed later that he had urged Kerensky to arrest Kornilov and Kaledin, but that Kerensky rejected the idea. On August 17, Kerensky returned to Petrograd, where his military cabinet lobbied him for Savinkov's reinstatement. Kerensky called Savinkov in for a private meeting at which he admitted that the Moscow Conference had exposed the government's weakness. He accused Savinkov of permitting a counterrevolutionary movement to develop at GHQ and warned that he would not tolerate the emergence of a Directory of the two of them with Kornilov. He made it clear that he was being forced to reinstate Savinkov and reiterated his intention of dismissing Filonenko. Savinkov was adamant in defense of his friend Filonenko, and Kerensky had to back down. Once more, Kerensky assured him that the death penalty would, eventually, be restored in the rear.

Kerensky had hoped for a gentlemanly compromise, but Savinkov consented to remain in office only as a concession, reminding him of his offensiveness at their last meeting. When Savinkov persisted in the face of Kerensky's usual silence, Kerensky smiled oddly. "Yes, I have forgotten everything. It seems that I have forgotten everything. I am a sick man. No, not quite. I have died, I am no more. At that Conference I died. I cannot offend anyone and no one can offend me." That afternoon the ministers reconvened with Savinkov but minus Chernov. Kerensky also agreed that determined measures must be taken against those who had just sabotaged the Kazan ordance dumps.[35]

On August 20, Kerensky met Savinkov for another confidential discussion, whose gravity was underlined by news of the German attack on Riga. Savinkov told Kerensky that his draft of the bill for the restoration of the death penalty was now ready. He claimed that Kerensky then agreed to put Petrograd under martial law and asked him to go to GHQ to arrange for a force to be sent to Petrograd capable of enforcing it. Kerensky also asked Savinkov to see that the Officers' Union was removed from GHQ; Savinkov had himself warned Kerensky that this body was plotting against him. The devious Savinkov probably hoped to kill two birds with one stone, removing hotheads from Kornilov's entourage, while proving his loyalty to the Premier.[36]

Kerensky's recollections of this meeting were different. He *had* discussed the subordination of the Petrograd Military District to the Supreme Command, since the front was now only 250 miles from Petrograd, but *minus the capital itself.* He wanted a force stationed not *in* but *near* the city. At GHQ, Baranovsky did demand the exclusion of Petrograd from the Petrograd Military District, and Kerensky clarified his intentions to Ambassador Noulens on August 24. The government intended to move to Moscow, the "normal" capital of Russia, but not yet. When the government left, Petrograd would fall into Kornilov's zone of competence. The implication was clear: unleashing the tiger on the Bolsheviks was one thing, putting your own head in its mouth quite another.[37]

Baranovsky told Kornilov that he anticipated action of "the most decisive character" against the Bolsheviks and Tereshchenko told Buchanan that an armed force was to be used to suppress them. Nekrasov later publicly confirmed this. Yet Kerensky, absurdly, denied it, claiming that the force was merely to be ready for the suppression of disturbances from any quarter. Tactical considerations apart, this claim follows logically from his assertion that the Bolshevik revival did not begin until the end of August and then only in response to the actions of General Kornilov.[38]

This view does not withstand serious scrutiny. Kerensky knew that on August 18, the Petrograd Soviet had defied Tsereteli in the vote on the death penalty. While Kerensky and Savinkov were discussing the posting of an armed force in (or near) the city, elections were in progress for a city Duma. The results were deeply disappointing for Kerensky. The high rate of abstention was an implicit vote of no confidence in electoral politics. The Bolsheviks had not merely recovered from their defeat in July; they were now in a relatively better position.[39] The detailed results were not available to him when he sent Savinkov to GHQ, but he knew from which quarter to expect "armed demonstrations." Kerensky was taking an

awful gamble with the future of Russian democracy. Kornilov
wanted the suppression of all the soviets, something *all* socialists
were bound to oppose, as well as the repression of the Bolsheviks.

The German attack on Riga seriously embarrassed the Bolsheviks,
who had assured their Latvian comrades that if they refused to support the offensive, the Germans would leave them alone. Latvia's
Bolshevik Social Democrats had just won 41 percent of the votes
for the Riga city Duma and nearly all the seats on the Latvian Riflemen's Executive Committee. The Latvians feared that German occupation would restore the hegemony of their hereditary oppressors,
the Baltic Germans. The Bolsheviks found a scapegoat, remembering—and distorting—the words used by Kornilov at the Moscow
Conference: "Let us not permit the introduction of order in the rear
to depend on the loss of Riga." The impression that Kornilov was
prepared to lose Riga to bring the men to their senses was reinforced
by his accusations of cowardice against the troops. This was certainly
untrue of the Bolshevized Latvian Riflemen, who had their own
reasons for fighting on this occasion. They believed that West Latvia
had been lost by the treachery of the Tsar's generals; now Riga had
been lost through the treachery of Kerensky's. Their cold contempt
for all Russians mounted, and with it the conviction that only Lenin
would do anything for Latvia. Moderate socialist commissars shared
their view that Kornilov was playing a cynical game with the reputation of the northern armies, and Barter was shocked by the "indifference" he found at GHQ to the loss of Riga and the assumption
that it would "increase chance of early military supremacy in conduct
of Russian affairs."[40]

On August 23, the ministers considered Chernov's land bill; the
Kadets filibustered, evidently convinced that time was on their side.
Chernov swallowed his pride to seek an audience with Kerensky to
beg him to get rid of Savinkov and break with the Kadets. They
were out to identify the government with repression so as to facilitate
its removal. From the other side, Zinaida Hippius begged Kerensky
to resign the ministries of War and Navy to Savinkov and accept
elevation to the Presidency of the Republic, a ceremonial post which
might be created for him. (It was probably then that Hippius caught
the glimpse of Kerensky with Lilya in the Winter Palace that so
disgusted her years later. She seems not to have noticed that Lilya was

already carrying Kerensky's child.) Kerensky took this approach more kindly than Chernov's but did nothing about either.[41]

In Mogilev, Savinkov was trying to achieve an understanding with Kornilov. Savinkov evaded Kerensky's eyes and ears, as well as those of Baranovsky and Mironov, by demanding a private conversation with Kornilov. Kornilov was bitter, venting his spleen on Kerensky's weakness, vacillations, and incompetence. Savinkov pointed out that several minor reforms had taken effect since the Moscow Conference, and Kornilov reluctantly conceded that Kerensky's presence in government was still necessary. Savinkov promised that the death penalty law would be approved within days. They agreed that the Third Cavalry Corps should approach Petrograd to deal with expected Bolshevik resistance to the law, and agreed that the soviets should be suppressed if they took the Bolsheviks' part. Such resolute action was bound to destroy Kerensky's role as fulcrum of Russian politics, so Kornilov had no need to discuss ministerial changes. At Savinkov's departure, he promised to serve the government faithfully.[42]

If the meeting ended cordially, it did not eliminate all sources of potential friction. Savinkov wanted to ensure that Prince Bagration's Caucasian Native Cavalry Division would not be attached to the Third Cavalry Corps, forseeing that Russian workers might not take kindly to receiving their "liberty" at the hands of "Tatars." He also tried to veto the appointment of the "bloodthirsty" General A. N. Krymov. They also differed about army committees, which Kornilov now wanted suppressed completely. Savinkov left Mogilev urging Filonenko to restrain Kornilov, under no illusion that the last hope of averting a mutiny by the Supreme Commander lay in Kerensky's dedication to the State.[43]

The Petrograd Special Army, prepared by Kornilov for the suppression of Bolshevism, had begun to assemble before the Moscow Conference. Altogether, there were over 15,000 experienced, well-equipped front-line troops. Even more to the point, these men had not so far shown any vulnerability to Bolshevik propaganda. The British Armoured Car Division was moved up from the Southwest front to support them.

Well aware that the struggle would be political and psychological as well as military, Kornilov was hoping to convene some 3000 sympathetic officers in Petrograd (in addition to 4000 already there to fake a "Bolshevik uprising" to persuade the Special Army, and the Petrograd garrison, that the Special Army was entering the capital only to save the democratic government from German agents).

The neutralization of Bolshevik forces was not neglected. Kerensky had agreed to the forcible closure of the Kronstadt naval garrison before the Moscow Conference but attempts to carry this out had failed. Officers in Kronstadt were now prepared to sink barges to prevent ships crewed by Bolshevik sailors from intervening in Petrograd. It was hoped that the Latvians had been exhausted by the battle for Riga, but there were attempts to bribe some units in Petrograd. Czech and Polish units were earmarked for the suppression of disturbances at the front and in other major cities. Still, these were slender resources for restoring order over an army of ten million and a mobilized working class.[44]

Kornilov was resolved to give Kerensky until August 27 to deliver the goods, and he was confident of Kadet support when the moment arrived. Shortly after the Moscow Conference, Zavoiko had given Aladin a letter for V. N. Lvov. The letter quoted General Lukomsky, Kornilov's Chief-of-Staff, as saying that the Kadets had better quit the government by August 27 "to avoid troubles for themselves." Lvov was still nursing a grudge because Kerensky had replaced him with Kartashev in July, and he was struck by the possibilities suggested by Zavoiko's note. He immediately offered to mediate between Kornilov and Kerensky to avert "whatever it is that is being prepared for August 27." When Aladin accepted his offer, Lvov assumed that he was authorized to do so by Kornilov.[45]

Lvov's excitable efforts effaced hours of poker-faced diplomacy by Savinkov. He arrived in Petrograd on August 22, just as Savinkov was departing for GHQ. He warned Nabokov of what was to happen and redeemed his pledge to Aladin by seeking an interview with Kerensky. Not surprisingly, there is disagreement as to what was said, and Lvov changed his story several times.[46]

In his first, and more reliable, version Lvov claimed that he told Kerensky that the government was now defenseless in the event of a second Bolshevik rising and that it should be strengthened by the addition of certain "social groupings." "I convinced him not to refuse to test the ground for negotiations, to which Kerensky replied to me that for negotiations there must be definite demands and a definite program, and he did not reject my proposal of mediation for such negotiations. With this I went back to Moscow." Lvov now began to act as though he had been given plenipotentiary powers by Kerensky for the reconstitution of the government. Kerensky, who knew Lvov well, ought to have tried harder to dispel this illusion.[47]

There were some mitigating circumstances. Lvov had repeatedly backed Kerensky against Milyukov, for whom he had been obliged to dismiss Lvov. In any case, such approaches were commonplace. Even the patriotic protofascist Purishkevich had gone round to Kerensky's apartment to complain to his family about the mess he was making of the army. Slapping down feelers that might ultimately emanate from Kornilov might trigger the very upheaval he hoped to avert. Less excusable was Kerensky's practice of using intermediaries to smoke out his enemies. He evidently did not believe that he was in immediate danger from Kornilov, for on August 24, he entrusted the Petrograd Military District, minus the city, to Kornilov's command.[48]

V. N. Lvov left Petrograd immediately after his interview with Kerensky on August 22, passing through Moscow, where he alerted Kadet circles there. He met Kornilov at GHQ on August 24, where the Commander-in-Chief asserted that the situation was now so grave that only a dictatorship and martial law would do; perhaps for form's sake he insisted that he did not care for power himself and he would gladly hand it over to any dictator. He mentioned Kerensky, Alexeyev, and Kaledin as possible candidates, but when pressed he agreed that he would prefer to be dictator himself. Lvov convinced him that neither Kerensky nor his ministers were clinging to power and announced that the Premier had given him full authority to negotiate for him. Perhaps Lvov felt this was the only way to avoid catastrophe.[49]

Kornilov expected the existing ministers to resign, while Kerensky and Savinkov came to Mogilev to assume portfolios in the new dictatorial government. Lvov later claimed that he found this suspicious, fearing that Kornilov himself, or possibly Zavoiko, would have Kerensky assassinated. (He could not have known that Baranovsky had warned Kerensky that "they can't stand you at GHQ.") Confident that he was getting his way at last, Kornilov telegraphed Rodzyanko, Maklakov, and Tereshchenko to GHQ for the negotiations. He would hardly have invited Tereshchenko had he intended to murder Kerensky.[50]

The moment Kerensky had dreaded for so long was upon him. He had agreed on August 17 to override his political and ethical principles and his remaining ties with "Democracy" by reintroducing the death penalty. There was no doubt at all that this would make him a renegade in socialist eyes. It was entirely possible that soviet resistance would be such that only force would break it. On August 25–26, Savinkov saw Kerensky three times to get him to sign the bill restoring the death penalty. He was augmented by Tumanov, Yakubovich, and Baranovsky, yet still Kerensky resisted. In desperation, Savinkov saw him alone on August 26 and employed all the force of his powerful personality, accusing Kerensky of ruining Russia with his weak will. Kerensky was sufficiently shaken to agree to sign the bill and read it to the government that night. Savinkov was jubilant. At last, he had averted the clash with Kornilov that had begun to seem inevitable.[51]

Some time during August, a British secret agent arrived in Russia from the United States. This was none other than W. Somerset Maugham, who remembered later:

I went as a private agent, who could be disowned if necessary, with instructions to get in touch with parties hostile to the government and devise a scheme that would keep Russia in the war and prevent the Bolsheviks, supported by the Central Powers, from seizing power.

Meanwhile, General Knox had reached London. By the time he was summoned to the Imperial War Cabinet, Kadet politicians had tipped off both Barter and Buchanan about an impending *coup d'état* involving Kornilov. Lloyd George was away in the north of England, trying to revive flagging working–class enthusiasm for the war, so, with the exception of the South African General Smuts, the cabinet that Knox addressed was an entirely Tory group. They were joined by General Robertson, Chief of the Imperial General Staff, and General MacDonogh, Director of Military Intelligence, both Tories in uniform. For all of them, it was axiomatic that it was up to democracy to prove itself patriotic.

Knox painted a chilling picture of Russian conditions. "The great mass of the soldiers did not want to fight," industrial relations were approaching anarchy, and grain procurements were catastrophic. "If Kerensky were to suggest a separate peace he would have the great majority of the country with him." Knox drew the inescapable conclusion that the Russians were unfit for democracy; "they must be ordered what to do." Kornilov must be given full diplomatic support even though it "might be construed as helping Korniloff to a *coup d'état.*" Concerned with possible American reactions, Foreign Secretary Lord Robert Cecil spelled out that the Allies would be urging "what would, in effect, be the establishment of a Military dictatorship."[52]

The British were too late. A day later, on the early evening of August 26, V. N. Lvov entered Kerensky's study in the Winter Palace for the second time in five days. This time his manner was not so much importunate as imperious. A Bolshevik rising was imminent, the government would find no support, and Kerensky's own life was in danger. An emotional fellow at the best of times, Lvov's manic manner had not been improved by four days and nights without proper sleep. Kerensky's jocose reaction was understandable. "It can't be helped, such is fate," he joked. But Lvov was not to be put off. He was the bearer of a formal offer from Kornilov. The government must transfer its powers to Kornilov and proclaim martial law throughout the country. Kerensky and Savinkov must go to GHQ to assume portfolios in the new government, and without telling the other ministers.[53]

Kerensky was shocked out of his jocosity into a mood only slightly less hysterical than Lvov's:

I did not hesitate for an instant in my acting. I rather felt than understood all the extraordinary seriousness of the situation. . . . Calming myself a little, I deliberately pretended that I had no longer any doubt or hesitation, and that personally I had decided to agree.

Kerensky persuaded Lvov to commit his agreement with Kornilov to paper, omitting only the supposedly secret invitation to Kerensky and Savinkov to assume portfolios in the new government. "As soon as he began to write, my last doubt disappeared. I had only one desire, one over-mastering impulse: to check the madness at the outset, not giving it time to blaze up, and preventing the possible breaking-out of its partisans in Petrograd itself." Everything had fallen into place. The whiff of counterrevolution which had troubled his nostrils since July was no false scent after all. "All, all instantly shone clear in a very brilliant light and merged into one clear picture.

The double game was manifest. Certainly, I could not then prove every point, but I saw everything with extraordinary clarity."[54]

Kerensky would not permit Kornilov to stage a coup against the lawful government. He would save them all, the noble dogmatist Tsereteli and the contemptible trimmer Chernov alike. Martial commissars and internationalist idealists would all be indebted to him once more. But only the whole government had the right to remove the Supreme Commander, and the Kadet ministers were sympathetic to Kornilov. How could he persuade them to dismiss the General in the absence of hard evidence of mutiny?

Lvov knew that an early meeting between Kerensky and Kornilov would reveal his deception and he asked Kerensky whether he would go to GHQ in person. Alerted by something in Lvov's manner, Kerensky replied, "Certainly not. Do you really think that I can be Minister of Justice under Kornilov?" Lvov enthusiastically endorsed this decision, and warned him that a trap awaited him at GHQ! Neither "conspirator" noticed that this exchange cast grave doubts on the sincerity of the "agreement" they had concluded. They agreed to mislead Kornilov on this point by pretending that Kerensky was coming to GHQ. It occurred to Kerensky that they could send this message, and clarify Kornilov's intentions, by using the Hughes apparatus, an early form of teleprinter, located in the War Minister's apartment, just across Palace Square. They agreed to meet there at 8.00 P.M. Lvov then left the Winter Palace to tell Milyukov what was afoot.[55]

Kerensky was ready as arranged, with Prince Lvov's nephew Colonel V. V. Vyrubov, whom he had invited to attend as a witness. Lvov was late so Kerensky decided to go ahead anyway, impersonating Lvov as well as misrepresenting his own intentions, in the conversation with Kornilov. This extraordinary exchange has been preserved:

Kerensky: . . . On the line are Vladimir Nikolaevich Lvov and Kerensky. We beg you to confirm that Kerensky can act in accordance with the information, transmitted by Vladimir Nikolaevich.
Kornilov: . . . Confirming once more that sketch of the situation in which the country and the army seems to me, a sketch, made by me to Vladimir Nikolaevich with a request to report to you, I declare once more, that the events of the last days are those to be observed again imperatively demand an entirely definite decision in the briefest period.

The Trudovik leaders in the Duma. Dzyubinsky and Kerensky in the gardens of the Tauride Palace, 1916.

Kerensky with Mary Gavronsky, Byfleet, 1919. (Asher Gransby)

Kerensky and his Comité pour la Russie, Paris, 1919.
The historian S. P. Melgunov stands behind and to the
right of Kerensky. (Asher Gransby)

Cartoon of Kerensky, 1920,
by "Spat." (Asher Gransby)

ДНИ

RUSSISCHE TAGESZEITUNG für Politik, Wirtschaft und Literatur — DNI

Редакция: Berlin SW 68, Lindenstrasse 3, IV. Hof.   Телефон: Amt Dönhoff 65-10
Контора: Berlin SW 68, Friedrichstrasse 204.   Телефон: Amt Zentrum 28-35, 28-36

20 Pfg.

Адр. для телеграмм: Berlin Colroslag

Редактор принимает от 3 до 4 час. дня
Непринятыя рукописи не возвращаются и ни по
воду их редакция не вступает ни в какую переписку

Прием подписки в гл. конторе и во всех почт. отд. Германии
Прием объявлений в гл. конторе и во всех русск. книжн. маг.
Успехи подписки и объявлений помещены на последней страниц

◄═══ Контора открыта от 9—5 час. ═══►

№ 359 | Воскресенье, 13-го января 1924 г. | III-й г. изд.

В этом номере 10 страниц

Берлин, 12-го января.

Загонщики

Существует одно забавное недоразумение. Многие до сих пор думают, что европейская реакция «боится» большевицкой «революционности». Это ошибочное суждение весьма часто приводит к неправильной тактике, хотя бы, например, в борьбе за и против признания Политбюро — правительства России.

Что капиталистической реакции — в не здоровом капитализму, конечно, — диктатура РКП с ея «русскими варварами» крайне выгодна — это не подлежит никакому сомнению. Ведь не только доморощенные рвачи «капралы», как напоминл во время партийной дискуссии один из ораторов оппозиции, не один только они говорят: «коммунистическое государство» для нас самое лучшее». То же самое твердят, например, постоянно в своих газетах сам Стиннес. «Лучшее» оно, конечно, только в России. Ибо антинациональная власть русского большевизма для чужого «экономического национализма» безграничныя «возможности». Именно, этими возможностями — жирными кусками! — соблазнял недавно Бомбаччи итальянских капиталистов. А другой московский агент, Риболди, для пущего соблазна итальянских консерваторов добавил: «в России больше нет коммунизма». А есть лишь широкое поле для поднятия иностранного капитала.

Господство Зиновьевых в России тем и хорошо для иностранцев, что оно, убивая национальную русскую промышленность, превращает огромную страну в поприще для колониального хищничества. А таким возможностей европейский капитал — кажется, конечно, не «боязнь»!

Но реакции политической господа Зиновьевы, пожалуй, еще более полезны. Не будем возвращаться к тому, что уже случилось, в Баварии, потом в Венгрии, потом в Италии, потом в Болгарии и т. д. Там знают, сделавшись свое дело и «ушли». Посмотрим лучше, как г. г. постащики «планетарной революции» заново собираются действовать в своей привычной роли загонщиков на охоте реакции на красную звезду демократии.

Давно уже не приходилось новому правительству начинать свою работу в столь насыщенной электрической атмосфере, что суждено завтрашнему кабинету Рамзая Макдональда. Все, действительно, черное внутри и вне Англии мобилизуется для посрамления, а затем и уничтожения этой вновь зарождающейся возможности вывести Европу на тот путь действительного мира, который, казалось, стал не возможным после «Октября» и «Версаля».

Правда, перед английскими рабочими двери в святилище власти распахиваются как будто радушно, но, склоняясь с глубоким поклоном преданности и уважения, приветствующие новую власть частично за этим призорным жестом скрывают торжествующую улыбку людей, уже успевших поставить капканы. Тяжелыя двери страшнаго премьерскаго особняка на Downing street должны, по хитроумному плану некоторых, так крепко захлопнуться за Макдональдом, чтобы у почтенных джентльменов из четвертаго сословия охота сюда соваться подгропала надолго.

Вот тут-то загонщики и начинают свою облаву. Во время перваго заседания новой Палаты Общин, — рассказывают газеты, — некий Джонсон, рабочий депутат, стал сначала насвистывать «Красное знамя», а затем учинил скандал совсем в

стиле втородумскаго Пуришкевича только на изнанку.

Почему Джонсон? Кто такой Джонсон?

А об этом мы легко можем узнать из «Известий» от 22 декабря. Здесь в лондонской корреспонденции от 14 декабря, то есть за три недели до учиненнаго скандала, сообщается.

«Левое крыло (рабочей партии) под руководством Уилья, Макстона и Джонсона приобрело власть Макдональда. Эти элементы очень близки к коммунистам и кто знает — не будет ли рабочая партия иметь своего раскола. Процесс разслоения начался и жизнь сделает остальное».

Вот Джонсон и делает «остальное» вместе с Уилья, который уже и избран особым председателем «радикальной оппозиции», образовавшейся внутри рабочей партии.

Разбить единство английскаго рабочаго фронта, как раз перед началом боя, — это значит вернейшим способом подготовить победу не только английской, но и международной реакции.

Думаем, что русский, баварский и прочий опыт в Англии обречен на скандальный провал. Мы в этом более чем уверены. Но ведь в этих самих загонщиках по всюду — слагается вред общественности они выполняют и будут до конца выполнять усердно.

Бояться большевиков в Европе, во всяком случае, приходится не реакции.

Запоздали

Сначала восторгались:
— Ура! возвращаются из деревень рабочие, ушедшие с фабрик и заводов в семнадцатом и восемнадцатом годах...
— Теперь выражают большую тревогу:
— Увы, возвращаются!.. К несчастью.

Радовались, — пока, витая в облаках туманных теорий, полагали, будто «возвращением усилят физическую мощь компартии. Забили тревогу, — когда с заоблачных высот спустились на землю и присмотрелись ближе к тому, что на ней делается. Недавно сами г. Каменев и г. Рыков сочли нужным закрыть о «коротких низких истинах» в противовес возвышающему обману. Истины эти вкратце таковы:

1. Промышленность содержится в значительной мере за счет налогов, взимаемых с крестьянства.

2. Крестьянство же на столько истощено, что мечты о расширении промышленности надо совершенно оставить. «Мы приходим к такому положению, которое может иметь скверныя политическия последствия». И это «положение» обязывает не расширять, а сокращать «государственные» заводы и фабрики.

3. Сокращать, «концентрировать» и «консервировать», разумеется, надо с осторожностью. «Как бы ни смотреть на концентрацию, — заявляет г. Рыков — но деконцентрироваться до того, чтобы закрыть большую часть крупнейших заводов, невозможно по причинам не экономическаго, а политическаго порядка». В частности, — пояснил он — по причинам экономическаго порядка нужно бы закрыть заводы Коломенский, Сормовский, Брянский, Путиловский. Но по соображениям политическим, приходится поддерживать и эти предприятия, ставшия ненужными и в настоящее время и при полном разорении рынка ненужными.

4. Однако, отдавая должное мотивам политическаго порядка, все таки нужно свертывать, сокращать и закрывать... и поэтому рабочих «возвращенцев» в деревню пристроить и некуда ед. Между

тем двигаются не только «возвращенцы». Происходит еще нашествие «заработников» — «крестьянскаго элемента, как выражаются имениные харьковские товарищи, который идет заработка в город». В частности, вот что случилось: «Заработник», как тип из русской деревни исконн двигался в определенные «сезоны» на заработки. Хорошо известно, почему двигался: скудоземье, задержавшее развитие сельско-хозяйственной культуры, создало на необжитых пространствах России противоестественный избыток рабочих сил, который в определенные «сезоны» и выбрасывал на фабрики, на заводы, в города. Октябрьским переворотом возможность фабрично-заводских и городских заработков была взорвана. Движение «заработников» из деревни сразу исчезло. Более того, миллион обсадил фабрично-заводского и городского народа назад в деревню. Там, в деревнях, эти миллион совсем скрылись из поля зрения до 3-х лет.

Появилась опять в городах они начали лишь с 1922 г. Но это были единицы,

десятки, сотни... «Возвращенство», как массовое явление, стало заметно и принудило говорить о себе лишь в конце 1923 года. И тоже самое случилось с «заработниками». Первая — после рекордного «октября» — волна их появилась к концу 1921 г. по причине голода. Это — специальная и острая причина. А как следствие некоторых общих условий «заработники» стали двигаться с 1922 г. И только к осени 1923 г. о них начинают говорить, как о массовом явлении, не менее характерном, чем при самодержавии.

Обе волны — и возвращенская и заработническая — взымаются, таким образом, одновременно. И то же, без сомнения, не случайны.

Все ли сбежавшие из городов возвращаются обратно? Нет, не все. В своем массовом заработке, стало заметно и приму, горожане-рабочие оседли в деревнях прочно и рабочих оседли в деревнях прочно навсегда. Теперь это подтверждают и наблюдатели коммунистической партии. И то же этим осуществившиеся и прочно оседлые? Те, кто помнить, вкрапленных старым словами Успенского «власть земли», — подчиняется неумол

Кончил дело, гуляй смело

Ген. Врангель ждет в Америку.

Карикатура Нова

Above. Kerensky's arrival in the New World, New York, March 1927. (*The New York Times*)

Opposite. Dni, No. 359, 13 January 1924. The cartoon shows General Wrangel being shipped off to America after failing in the Crimea. (British Library Newspaper Collection, Colindale)

Flora Solomon and her son, Peter Benenson, the future founder of Amnesty International. (Peter Benenson)

Kerensky during the Second World War. (Gladys Edds)

Opposite. Lydia Kerensky (née Tritton) at the time of her marriage to Kerensky. (Gladys Edds)

Above. "Nel" goes home. The Kerenskys arrive in Brisbane, Australia, 1945. (*The Courier-Mail*, Brisbane)

"The Professor." Kerensky at Stanford in the 1960s.
(United Press Telephoto, Courtesy Bettman Archive)

[This might simply have referred to the restoration of the death penalty. Kerensky needed better evidence than this.]

Kerensky: [impersonating Lvov] I, Vladimir Nikolaevich ask you: must that definite decision be carried out, about which you asked me to inform Alexander Fyodorovich in complete privacy only?

[This could only refer to the invitation to Savinkov and Kerensky to come to GHQ as members of the new cabinet.]

Kornilov: Yes, I confirm, that I asked you to transmit to Alexander Fyodorovich my insistent request to come to Mogilev.

Kerensky: I, Alexander Fyodorovich. I understand your answer as a confirmation of the words transmitted to me by Vladimir Nikolaevich. It is impossible to do that and leave today. I hope to leave tomorrow. Is Savinkov necessary?

Kornilov: I beg urgently that Boris Viktorovich come with you. What I said to Valdimir Nikolaevich relates to Boris Viktorovich in the same measure. I beg do not postpone your arrival after tomorrow. I ask you to believe that only a consciousness of the responsibility of the moment forces me to ask you so insistently.

As Kerensky heard the Morse Code transcribed from the ribbon, he realized that this would allow the Kadet ministers to claim that Kornilov was acting only in response to an imminent danger from the Bolsheviks. So he asked one last question:

Kerensky: [Are we] to come only in case of outbreaks, about which there are rumours, or in any case?

Kornilov: In any case.

Kerensky: Goodbye, we shall see each other again soon.

Kornilov: Goodbye.

Shortly after the conversation had finished, Lvov appeared. "Have I been a good friend to you, Alexander Fyodorovich?" he asked pathetically. Kerensky asked him to confirm all he had told him in the presence of the deputy chief of the Militia. Lvov did so and was immediately arrested.[56]

This cryptic exchange has inspired an exegetical literature of imposing dimensions. It is amazing and surely rather disgraceful that matters of supreme importance for millions of Russians should have been decided in a conversation consisting entirely of inference and allusion. Kerensky always argued that each had spoken in a code well understood by the other, a point that is hard to accept considering their different motives during the conversation. For Kornilov, this did not matter; he expected to see Kerensky the next day to sort things out. Kerensky was merely looking for evidence on which to convict Kornilov without alerting him to his real intentions. Kornilov could have proven his "innocence" in Kerensky's eyes only by denying all knowledge of Lvov's mission, something he had no reason to do.[57]

That night, the ministers assembled for the decision on the death penalty. Instead, Nekrasov was summoned from the meeting and shown the "evidence," Lvov's note of the "ultimatum" and the tape from the Hughes' apparatus. Kerensky declared: "I will not give up the Revolution to them." He then summoned Savinkov for a less friendly interview: "Your hand's in this, Boris Viktorovich," he began. Savinkov was unconvinced by the evidence though he agreed that Kornilov's apparent conduct was impermissible; he demanded that the conflict should be kept secret until all hope of a settlement had been exhausted. Savinkov's legendary self-control must have been sorely tried and this may have been the first of the two occasions on which he felt he should have killed Kerensky. Reluctantly, Kerensky allowed him to communicate with Kornilov, but began to work out plans for stopping the Special Army with Nekrasov.[58]

Kerensky and Nekrasov then returned to the ministers in the Malachite Hall. Kartashev thought Kerensky was raving. Kerensky demanded that all the ministers place their portfolios at his disposal to allow him a "plenitude of power" in the struggle against the counterrevolution. It gave him the right to get rid of Kornilov on his own authority. Faced with the threat of dictatorship, Kerensky had made himself dictator once more.[59]

On the morning of August 27, the atmosphere at GHQ was cautiously optimistic and Lukomsky informed the Chief of the French Military Mission of the agreement reached between Kornilov and Kerensky. He felt that if the government reneged on it there would be catastrophe and he solicited Allied pressure on Kerensky. Kornilov was therefore astonished to be handed a telegram signed baldly (and improperly) "Kerensky," which relieved him of his command and instructed him to report to Petrograd. In refusing to obey this order, General Kornilov became a mutineer.

General Lukomsky's refusal to take over the Supreme Command confirmed Kerensky's fears of a conspiracy. Savinkov and Maklakov tried to negotiate over the Hughes, but Kerensky decided that no more time could be lost. That same day, he broadcast a radio-tele-gram informing the country of Kornilov's ultimatum and explaining why he assumed dictatorial powers in terms far more revolutionary than any he had used for some time. He ordered General Klembov-sky, Commander-in-Chief of the northern front, to take over as Supreme Comander, declared martial law in Petrograd, and called on the army at the front to carry on fighting the Germans. Rather fatuously, he refused assistance from unofficial sources: "I am taking all necessary measures to protect the liberty and order of the country, and the population will be informed in due time with regard to such measures." His word was once again law. But would anyone obey?[60]

Kornilov did not hide behind the formal irregularity of Kerensky's first telegram. The radio-telegram proved to Kornilov that Kerensky had finally fallen under the influence of the "traitorous" Soviet lead-ers. To retreat before them was tantamount to cowardice in action, and his own counterblast accused Kerensky of lying and provocation. "Russian people, our great land is dying! The hour of death is near!" He broadcast his suspicions of the loyalty of ministers and soviets and urged everyone to fight them. "All, in whom beats a Russian heart, all who believe in God, in the shrines—pray to God for the appearance of a most great miracle, the miracle of the salvation of our native land." He claimed that he was no aristocrat, merely the son of a Cossack peasant; and he swore to bring Russia to victory and to a Constituent Assembly. "Russian people," he concluded, "in your hands is the life of your native land."[61]

14

Reproaches and Slander

The Russian people were still unaware of the conflict between Prime Minister and Supreme Commander as the Special Army advanced on Petrograd unopposed, while Kerensky remained in the Winter Palace, whose splendor masked his isolation from the real Russia. He alone would defend the State against all threats to liberty and order. Never was his republican virtue more explicit or more impervious to social analysis—Marxist or otherwise. Since July, he had surrounded himself with men who paid lip service to the same ideal, and he expected them to support him now. He was bitterly disappointed. Lukomsky's refusal to take over from Kornilov was compounded by the temporizing of Klembovsky. General Denikin, Commander-in-Chief of the Southwest, was more straightforward, seeing in Kornilov's dismissal "the return of the government to the path of systematic disruption of the army, and consequently the ruin of the country." The commanders of the Western and Romanian fronts supported Kornilov also, while General Vasilkovsky, Commander in Petrograd, showed no enthusiasm for his commission and General Polovtsev, humiliated by Kerensky in July, now refused to replace him. Kerensky's military cabinet—Baranovsky included—were appalled by the "misunderstanding." Conscious of their disapproval, Kerensky harangued them, "his small, unusually green eyes anxious and angry, jumped from one to another."[1]

Kerensky's first telegraphed message, on August 27, had not accused Kornilov of treason, and Savinkov still thought a settlement possible. All the same, in a conversation he conducted with Kornilov over the Hughes apparatus that day, Savinkov was more concerned to establish "historical accuracy,"—in other words, to save his skin—than to find a solution. Kornilov was less canny, failing even to comment on the irregularity of Kerensky's telegram of dismissal.[2]

Later that day, the ministers reassembled to hear from Kerensky on the latest developments. Tereshchenko had now returned from GHQ and he urged that both Kerensky and Kornilov should resign in the interest of a peaceful settlement, a suggestion that met with no opposition from the ministers present. Kerensky could hardly have resisted this pressure indefinitely, had the actions of Nekrasov and Kornilov not made the breach definitive. Kerensky had asked Nekrasov to draft a manifesto; in it, Nekrasov called Kornilov a traitor. Russian generals could be called stupid without too much offense, but to call one a traitor was unforgivable. Tereshchenko was horrified when he saw the manifesto. Too late the ministers begged Kerensky not to circulate it.[3]

Even now, most of the ministers refused to accept that the die had been cast. They were reinforced in the early hours of August 28 by General Alexeyev. Several ministers suggested to Alexeyev that he form his own government, or at least join a Directory. If Kerensky's intuition was not what it had been, his tactical agility never deserted him. He himself offered Alexeyev the post of Supreme Commander, but Alexeyev refused when Kerensky adamantly refused to negotiate with Kornilov. Tereshchenko and Savinkov now joined Alexeyev in putting more pressure on Kerensky to negotiate. According to Savinkov, Kerensky now admitted that there might have been a misunderstanding, though Kerensky denied this.[4]

By the morning of August 28, the Petrograd papers had begun to print Nekrasov's manifesto. This gave rise to the feeling in right-wing circles that Nekrasov had been Kerensky's evil genius and Tereshchenko his conscience. Buchanan felt that had Tereshchenko been present in the Winter Palace on the night of August 26–27, "he would have prevented Kerensky pushing matters to a complete rupture, while had he been at Stavka (GHQ), he would have exercised a restraining influence on Korniloff." Nekrasov's actions were compounded by Kornilov's failure to stop his troops. Early on August 28, news came in that they had entered Luga, only 88 miles from Petrograd, without resistance.[5]

It was time for Kerensky to count his friends. They were few and far between and Sorokin discovered Kerensky, "sitting alone in a corner of the Military Staff Headquarters, bowed with chagrin and disappointment. He looked like nothing but a deserted child, helpless and homeless. Yesterday a ruler, today a forsaken idol, he sat face to face with ruin and despair." The ultra-loyal Avksentiev begged the safety of Sorokin's apartment for the night of August 28–29, while even the doggedly faithful Stankevich canvassed the advisability of replacing Kerensky with Savinkov. Kerensky confirms that he was utterly despondent.

I shall never forget the painful long hours of that Monday, and especially of that Monday night. What pressure was I subjected to all that time, resisting while seeing the growing perplexity all round me! This Petrograd atmosphere was rendering still more unbearable one's consciousness that the absence of a Chief at the front, the excesses within the country, and the dislocation of transport might cause at any moment irretrievable consequences to the as yet hardly recuperated mechanism of the State.

His Anglo-Russian secretary, David Soskice, closed a farewell letter to his wife with the pathetic postscript: "I write this though there is little chance that it will ever reach you."[6]
    A pall of silence hung over the Winter Palace and liveried servants looked on blankly as their new chief marched up and down trying to find an outlet in restless physical activity from the strains which beset him, or collapsed from fatigue on the luxurious sofas of the Palace beneath the mocking portraits of Russia's rulers and marshals. He was besieged by sympathizers of Kornilov who sought to reconcile them. A delegation of Cossacks offered to mediate, as did the Kadet Kishkin. Milyukov turned up, accompanied by a mute Alexeyev. Kerensky refused to negotiate with Kornilov but made the suggestion that if "one or another grouping of political leaders considers that it has enough strength behind it, then I am ready to concede power to those persons, and they can negotiate with Kornilov themselves." Milyukov had no intention of falling into the same trap as V. N. Lvov, and he declined the offer. That evening the Allied Ambassadors called on Tereshchenko. For them the unexpected breach came as a crushing disappointment, but Kerensky refused their mediation as he had the others.[7]
    The Soviet Excom had first caught wind of the crisis on the night of August 27–28. Fyodor Dan read out Kerensky's manifesto and

endorsed the measures Kerensky had taken, and he went on to discuss possible political solutions to the crisis. This was rather premature as Kerensky had not even asked for Soviet support. Dan suggested that the Soviet might support a Directory formed by Kerensky alone, but he preferred a new socialist government purged of Kadets and bound to carry out the aborted government program of July 8. The new government should be accountable to a "Democratic Conference," like the Moscow Conference, but shorn of Duma deputies and Kadets.

Despite their ever-present fears of Bonapartism, most socialists were caught off-balance by Kornilov's mutiny. Menshevik reactions ranged from Martov's acid "all directories spawn counterrevolution" to Vainshtein's loyal comment that "the only person who can form a government at this time is Comrade Kerensky." As recently as mid-August, Lenin had mocked rumors of tension between Kerensky and Kornilov as devices to frighten the Bolsheviks into supporting the moderate Soviet leaders. He had even proposed the expulsion from the party of those Bolsheviks who had joined the Moscow Mensheviks and SRs in a committee to oppose counterrevolution. Bolshevik reaction to the conflict was initially cautious. Sokolnikov reiterated Bolshevik demands for radical social reform but did not object to a Democratic Conference and did not press Bolshevik objections to Kerensky's premiership.

Finally, the Executive Committee voted to add a few more socialists to the government and to summon a Democratic Conference. More significant was their almost unanimous demand for the exclusion of the Kadets from government, which would have meant the end of coalition. When their delegates visited Kerensky with this message, he gave them a dusty answer. He knew the mettle of these men and it was not long before he recalled Tsereteli, Gotz, and Chernov to the Winter Palace.

A couple of hours later, they returned to the Smolny Institute to report back to the Committee. Kornilov's manifesto had now been received and they were thoroughly alarmed. Skobelev appealed for trust in Kerensky and Tsereteli informed them that Kerensky insisted on a directory, threatening to resign if this was unacceptable, "since he would not feel the strength to oppose Kornilov's bloc with sufficient energy." Chernov seems to have been genuinely flattered by the thought that his junior party comrade had finally taken his advice and, for the last time, he warmly supported Kerensky, urging his comrades to forget "all quarrels, envy, and malice" and unite around Kerensky in the fight against counterrevolution. Over Lunacharsky's objections, the Soviet resolved to assist Kerensky and to establish its own Committee for Struggle Against Counterrevolution. The Bolsheviks were offered places on the Committee, but after intense and bitter internal debates—Lenin himself was still away in Finland—they limited themselves to collaboration "on a technical and informational basis."[8]

By August 30, there were some 240 committees against counterrevolution throughout Russia. The Petrograd Committee issued propaganda, supervised the distribution of arms to the workers, secured food supplies, and dispatched agitators to meet Kornilov's troops. The railroadmen sabotaged the movement of the Special Army. Paradoxically, the most convincing accounts of resistance to Kornilov stress both the spontaneity of mass action and the crucial organizational role played by the only party which retained a mass following among the urban working class, the Bolsheviks.[9]

When Tsereteli and Gotz returned to the Winter Palace to report on the success of their efforts, they were distressed to discover that Kerensky had already formed a directory without waiting for their support. They were even more shocked by its proposed membership: Kerensky himself and his irreplaceable Masonic brethren, Nekrasov and Tereshchenko, would be joined by Kishkin, a left-wing Kadet who was willing to resign from his party, and Savinkov, just appointed as the new military governor of Petrograd. The Soviet leaders were incensed, but the only concession Kerensky offered was the possible inclusion in his Directory of the Menshevik defencist Nikitin. This did not satisfy them, so Kerensky pretended to shelve his plan. In practice, the "dictator" could, and did, invite whom he liked to help him.[10]

The resourceful Savinkov had gotten the governorship when he came to Kerensky on the morning of August 28 to "confess" that Kornilov had "doublecrossed" him, by sending the Savage Division and General Krymov, and by arresting his friend Filonenko. Savinkov begged Kerensky either to put him on trial for collusion with Kornilov or to appoint him governor. Was this sheer effrontery or was it blackmail? Kerensky must have known that he would hardly emerge unscathed from the trial of his Assistant Minister of War, and at this moment of isolation, he could not afford to pick and chose. Milyukov would later allege that Kerensky had promised to "destroy his soul to save the state, while actually saving his soul and ruining Russia," but the appointment of Savinkov shows that he was still determined to retain his independence of the Soviets and his freedom to suppress Bolshevism.[11]

Savinkov's appointment was the last straw for Chernov, whose disappointment in Kerensky turned to hatred as details of Kerensky's previous dealings with Savinkov began to emerge. Coalition, and its policies, to which he had given his equivocal support for so long, now became forever hateful to him. As he looked back on the months of mental anguish and administrative failure, he resolved, like blind Samson, to pull the tottering edifice to the ground with him, and in his last hours as Minister of Agriculture, he appealed to the peasantry and soldiers for an all-out struggle with the high command. His career in government over, he resigned for good.[12]

By the morning of August 29, the lines were drawn for the full-scale confrontation Kerensky had tried so long to avert. The decision of "the Russian people" was not to Kornilov's liking. The industrialists and Kadet politicians, who had encouraged him, stayed at home. So did the plotters of the fake Bolshevik uprising. Some days later, Maklakov bitterly criticized Milyukov for encouraging Kornilov to believe he would receive mass support from the Kadets. At least Milyukov himself showed courage, writing an editorial for *Rech'* supporting Kornilov's objectives. The printers suppressed it and the Kadet Central Committee packed him off to exile in the Crimea. For months, the right had gone on about the cowardice of the Bolshevized soldiers, yet they had done little to help Kornilov. To be fair, they simply could not resist the tidal wave of popular hostility to anything that smacked of a repetition of the Stolypin reaction.[13]

Kerensky's denunciation of the Supreme Commander ensured that the officers who followed Kornilov would be opposed by the government's commissars and, in the words of a fireeating British officer, "they alone hold the army together." The soldiers of the Special Army had been told that they were going to save the Provisional Government from the Bolsheviks and German spies. Now their commissars—including Filonenko—told them that the officers were leading them against the government "to restore the old regime." They became thoroughly confused and demoralized. A congress of Muslim nationalities was fortuitously meeting in Petrograd, and its delegates had little trouble convincing even the Savage Division that Kornilov's venture was not in their interest. Confident that he had at last secured Kerensky's consent to the movement of the Special Army, Kornilov had neglected to provide it with an independent communications network, and soon the officers were as lost as the men. The railroadmen divided the force into harmless driblets, encircled by Soviet agitators.

Soviets all over Russia hurled threats at Kornilov's sympathizers still at liberty. The solidly defencist Executive Committee of the Southwest front arrested Denikin and his staff, and subjected them to humiliating treatment. Guchkov was arrested by the commissar of the 12th Army. The government lost all control over troop movements in Finland, and when General Oranovsky objected, he and ten others were shot. In Helsinki harbor, the men took over the ships and demanded that the officers condemn Kornilov. Four junior officers who refused were killed.[14]

By midday on August 30, Kornilov's defeat was plain to everyone, but Kerensky still wanted to resolve the conflict with a minimum of bloodshed. This entailed the appointment of a new Supreme Commander who could command everybody's respect. That morning, he went to see General Alexeyev at his apartment. Alexeyev, initially frigid, treated Kerensky to a twenty-minute lecture on the decline of the Russian Army, which he dated from Order No. 1. Kerensky listened, pale and drawn. When he finally replied he said simply: "But Russia, General, we must save her!"

This was an appeal Alexeyev could not resist and Kerensky remembered him saying: "I am at your disposal and I agree to be Chief of Staff of the Supreme Commander under you." Kerensky suggests that he was surprised at this suggestion and that his friend Vyrubov had to urge him to accept. Vyrubov himself recalled that Kerensky's nomination had already been settled before they called on Alexeyev. Kerensky's critics on the left assumed that Kerensky's nomination was merely a screen for the appointment to the Supreme Command of the "Kornilovite" Alexeyev. This underestimates Kerensky's powers of self-persuasion. He genuinely believed that he was the "providential" Supreme Commander.[15]

Kerensky exaggerated the effect of his pathos on Alexeyev, who accepted the post of Chief-of-Staff only on certain conditions. They included permission for Kornilov to communicate with Krymov, the promise that one division of the Third Cavalry Corps should be brought into Petrograd "in case of disorders," permission for the Union of Cossacks to continue their patriotic agitation, and the prohibition of any armed attack on GHQ and any forcible arrest of senior officers. This deal appealled to Kerensky's gentlemanly feelings and he agreed with a good conscience. He failed to anticipate the extent to which a massive resurgence of Bolshevism would take matters out of his hands.

Alexeyev contacted Kornilov and they struck a bizarre agreement: Kornilov would continue to direct the fronts pending Alexeyev's arrival in Mogilev. The man condemned as a "traitor" by his government would thus continue to command its defenses! Alexeyev then set off for Mogilev, confident that he would be able to arrange for Kornilov's genteel detention.[16]

Krymov now arrived in Petrograd under a safe-conduct pass extended by Kerensky. The well-educated cavalryman with the physique of an American football player was, like Kerensky, emotional and subject to fits of depression. His personal life, as well as his career, were in ruins. Kerensky had arranged for Krymov's old friend, General Samarin, to bring him to his study in the Winter Palace, and it was there that the Prime Minister personally interrogated the rather shamefaced general. "Shouts and loud voices were heard through the double doors."

Krymov admitted that he believed in a military dictatorship, but he insisted that on this occasion, he had merely been instructed to defend the government from Bolshevik attack. When asked how he knew the Bolsheviks' intentions, he gave no reply. Kerensky had promised Samarin that he would not arrest Krymov, so Krymov was allowed to go to a friend's apartment, where he shot himself. It now emerged that Krymov was a close friend of Tereschenko, and that he had joined the plot to depose the Tsar the previous winter. To outsiders Krymov's suicide looked like the convenient elimination of an embarrassing witness.[17]

Kerensky now began to doubt the wisdom of the agreement he had concluded with Alexeyev. Suppose Kornilov could put Alexeyev under his sway, and use his prestige against Kerensky himself? At all events, when Alexeyev arrived at Vitebsk, en route for GHQ, he discovered that Kerensky had dispatched an expeditionary force which was actually ahead of him on the line to Mogilev. Alexeyev had some difficulty restraining this force. Kerensky's defense was that he had dispatched the force to protect Alexeyev and the Investigating Commission that was following behind him. When Alexeyev got to GHQ he had another unpleasant suprise in the form of a contumacious message from Verkhovsky in Moscow announcing the departure of another expeditionary force "to put an end to this continuing mockery of common sense." In a conversation by telegraph shortly afterward, Kerensky warned Alexeyev that "volunteer detachments are everywhere being formed to move on GHQ."

On September 1, Kerensky telegraphed Alexeyev again to demand additional firm measures.

In view of the rumors which are rapidly spreading concerning our inaction, and the charge that we are even being intentionally soft, we should arrrest today and no later five or six people. The rumors I referred to are causing disintegration in the army and among the populace.

He added pointedly:

I would ask you most sincerely to see that the essential facts are not presented in a manner unacceptable to the *demos*.

Hours later, Baranovsky reinforced this message:

The Commander-in-Chief demands that General Kornilov and his accomplices shoud be arrested immediately, since any further delay would threaten innumerable calamities. The Democracy is excited without measure and keeps on threatening to break out in an explosion, the consequences of which it is not easy to forsee.[18]

August 30 had been St. Alexander's Day, and Kerensky's desk was loaded with telegrams of congratulation from all corners of Russia, wishing him success in his struggle with Kornilov. For a brief instant, his popularity with the masses seemed restored. That night, he returned to the Ministry of Justice to appoint an extraordinary commission to investigate the mutiny. Kerensky insisted on keeping this investigation secret and extracted corresponding oaths from its participants, but according to Colonel Raupakh, who later broke this oath, the commission was created just after midnight on August 31. Its creation should have been dated August 31, but those present realized that this would look odd when it appeared in the same day's papers. The superstitious Kerensky refused to let it bear the date of his saint's day and wrote August 29 instead, the first of a series of interventions in the commission's proceedings. The commission was led by I. S. Shablovsky, an experienced lawyer, now chief naval prosecutor, aided by Colonels N. P. Ukraintsev and R. R. Raupakh, both military lawyers, and a civilian magistrate. On September 2, they traveled to Mogilev and immediately demanded the transfer of Denikin and his colleagues from Berdichev, where they were threatened with a kangaroo court, or even a lynching. This met with the determined resistance of those now responsible for the Southwest front, who feared an explosion from their own men—and from Kerensky, who had followed the commission to GHQ.

It was in a railroad car in Mogilev that Kerensky fought the decisive battle of his premiership. His opponents were torn between the oaths they had taken to Kerensky and their conviction that Kornilov and Denikin had acted out of patriotism and were entitled to due process of law. The issue was the transfer of Denikin from Berdichev. Commissar Iordansky insisted that Denikin be tried by military-revolutionary court immediately, though no one present doubted that such an elective court would itself risk a lynching if it failed to impose the death penalty. Kerensky tried to overcome the scruples of the commissioners by promising to commute any death sentences, but they were adamant. If Denikin, a mere agent, were guilty, how could Kornilov, the principal, be acquitted? This would breach the basic principles of justice. Raupakh recalled that Kerensky lost control completely. He began browbeating the commission and concluded an hysterical peroration with the ominous words: "I appointed judges and not defenders for General Kornilov and will ensure that my error is corrected." He then stormed from the car.

The commissioners now learned that a court-martial was being convened in Berdichev over their objections. Raupakh had already been alarmed by the disappearance of the GHQ copy of Kerensky's telegram dismissing Kornilov. He believed, mistakenly, that it would show that Kornilov had been sacked illegally—i.e., before Kerensky was legally "dictator." Convinced that Kerensky was the author of a shameless coverup, Raupakh obtained—probably from General Barter–the GHQ copy of the Hughes telegraph conversation between Kerensky and Kornilov of August 26. He took it secretly to Alexeyev, who copied it by hand, and had it printed in the 'patriotic' Moscow paper *Utro Rossii* [Morning of Russia]. By the standards of their caste, Raupakh and Alexeyev had now compounded Kerensky's disgraceful conduct. Raupakh accuses Kerensky of riding roughshod over the principles he had preached for so long, but this was no more inconsistent than for Tsarist officers to break their oaths to place the safety of thirty individuals above *raisons d'état*.[19]

The effects on Kerensky's supporters in the rapidly dwindling middle ground of Russian politics were shattering. The impression created by the conversation—which Kerensky was unable publicly to explain—was that he himself had summoned the Third Cavalry Corps to Petrograd to suppress the Bolsheviks. The Bolsheviks were jubilant. Kornilov and Denikin did not matter. They were after bigger game.

Kerensky responded with renewed attacks on the freedom of the press. During the crisis, he had ordered the closure of two established conservative papers, which had expressed sympathy for Kornilov. Now he ordered the closure of the Bolshevik *Pravda*, which had resurfaced as *Proletarii* [Proletarian] and of *Novaia Zhizn'* [New Life], the journal of his old Menshevik-Internationalist comrades, Gorky and Sukhanov. Gorky had defended Kerensky, in the teeth of all the evidence, in April and in August, but his patience with Kerensky was now gone. Support from the intelligentsia had been almost universal as recently as July, but it was crumbling fast. The pressure for the release of Trotsky, Kollontai, and the other imprisoned Bolsheviks was now irresistible.[20]

Despite left-wing pressure, Kerensky now made a bold attempt to redeem at least some of his pledges to Alexeyev, ordering that the political struggle in the army cease forthwith. The committees must give up the powers they had assumed during the crisis, the men must release the arrested officers and special detachments against the counter-revolution must be disbanded. He resorted, once again, to bluff:

The Army, which during these anxious days has shown complete confidence in the Provisional Government and in me as Prime Minister, and therefore responsible for the fate of the Country, must understand that the salvation of the country lies only in correct organization, in maintaining complete discipline and in the unity of all.

The evasion or nonexecution of these orders would "be suppressed with all force and the guilty will suffer severe punishment." But the soldiers were not trusting anyone in authority and these orders fell on deaf ears.[21]

Savinkov's success in overriding Kerensky's suspicions was short-lived. The last straw came when Kerensky discovered that Filonenko had discussed the reconstitution of the government with Kornilov. From that moment on, Savinkov felt that Kerensky showed "a lack of correctness towards me," while Kerensky dismissed that as a "purely personal question." Quite apart from this exchange of insults, Savinkov was affronted by Kerensky's choice of a new Minister of War. As the first civilian Supreme Commander, Kerensky felt it vital that the new Minister be a military man, but the sole remaining general acceptable to the Soviets was Verkhovsky. Despite trimming to the Soviets, Verkhovsky was offered the post denied Savinkov. Savinkov was even more incensed by the appointment of Admiral Verderevsky as Naval Minister, as he was still under investigation for equivocal conduct during the July Days. Kerensky fully shared Savinkov's opinion of these ministers and allowed them no freedom of action, but Savinkov resigned anyway, to join the swelling multitudes of Kerensky's enemies. He even reingratiated himself with the guillible Merezhkovskys, who had been stunned by his desertion of Kornilov. Since 1900, Gorky and the Merezhkovskys had been the antipodes of the cultural intelligentsia. In spring they had all loved Kerensky; now they were relentless critics.[22]

Three days after the Soviet stymied Kerensky's directory, Nekrasov announced a new government. Kerensky and Tereshchenko retained their portfolios, and Tereshchenko also assumed the deputy premiership in place of Nekrasov himself. The psychiatrist Dr. N. M. Kishkin became Minister of the Interior, replacing the right-wing Avksentiev, who moved over to Agriculture in Chernov's place. Kartashev swallowed his Kornilovite sympathies to retain the management of religious affairs, while Konovalov, another Kadet, returned to the Augean stables of Trade and Industry, displacing the Menshevik S. L. Prokopovich. Kadet representation was thus maintained at its former level. They would be joined by two SRs and three Mensheviks.[23]

Nekrasov's explanation for his own departure convinced nobody. He had, he averred, assumed the deputy premiership for a period of two weeks in July and these were long past. He also worried lest the "legend" of an inner triumvirate of Kerensky, Nekrasov, and Tereshchenko make it more difficult to form a government. Kerensky insisted that Nekrasov was blackballed by the Kadets, who blamed him for carrying out Kerensky's orders "most conscientiously and with rare energy," while Milyukov argues that Nekrasov's fate was sealed when, on August 28, he urged Kerensky to resign.[24] Tereshchenko defined the new government's first priority as defense. "All social reforms must be carried out only in so far as they are dictated by the interests of that defence." The army would be brought back to normality by the lenient treatment of Kornilov's supporters and harsh punishment for those who had opposed him,[25] a logic incomprehensible to all but a small, beleaguered minority of the population. In a sole gesture to majority feeling, the ministers agreed to the immediate proclamation of a republic.

Kerensky was now faced with an unprecedented act of defiance by the SR Central Committee. While the new ministers continued their discussion, Kerensky was summoned to his study to meet Zenzinov and Gotz. They told him that the PSR would not participate in any coalition with the Kadets and that Kerensky himself would cease to represent his party in any such coalition. They also demanded a socialist minister of the Interior. "Suppressing his fury," Kerensky replied that "I personally consider it to be essential to include the Kadets in the goverment as well as all the other democratic parties. . . . As head of a national government I cannot take orders from individual parties."

The embarrassed Zenzinov tried to argue "as a friend," even confessing that he disagreed with the ultimatum. Kerensky cut this obsequious apologia short. Kerensky did not immediately call their bluff, however, and the new government was shelved. Still, it was only a matter of time before men like Gotz and Zenzinov came around.[26]

Both July and August gave birth to an assembly of indeterminate competence whose real function was to renew the government's mandate. It was announced on September 3 that, for the time being, the government would be entrusted to a directory, consisting of Kerensky, Tereshchenko, Verkhovsky, Verderevsky, and Nikitin. In the same manifesto, Russia was proclaimed a Republic, although the Governing Senate, whose members—appointed by the Tsar—still met as Russia's supreme court, contested this. At the same time, a communiqué appeared in the papers. Only a lawyer would have seen that this did not have the same standing as the manifesto announcing the government. It stated that the final determination of the question of a new government was to be transferred to the Democratic Conference, called by the Soviet Central Executive Committee. Had Kerensky finally accepted that his government should be accountable to the Soviets? Was there one last chance that all Russia's socialists, from Kerensky to Lenin, would finally agree to an interim soviet constitution for Russia? Tereshchenko hastened to reassure the Allies: "The Government considers this congress an entirely private affair." His efforts were wasted. Russian stock in the Allied capitals was at rock bottom. In France, the patriotic tide that had brought Ribot to power was about to replace him with Painlevé, while Georges Clemenceau waited his turn.[27]

Allied doubts were fully justified. In a report to the government, Alexeyev concluded sorrowfully that "with an army so disorganized and morally broken, it is impossible to think of extensive active operations." He himself resigned as Chief-of-Staff after a week, convinced that Kerensky had broken his promises to him, and he told reporters that he could not consider Kornilov a criminal and could not stomach the "corruption" of the army and the martyrdom of the officers. Verkhovsky now set to work to reduce the size of Russia's swollen army by discharging the over-40s, disbanding reserve regiments and militia and 60 recently formed divisions. Despite their preference for Kornilov's methods, the Allied attachés felt that these were the only measures "that the country in its present state could stand." They did not blame the men alone. In a comment that prefigures the tragedy of the civil war, Colonel Blair recorded: "There is the inability on the part of the officer class to swallow their pride, turn over a new leaf and try to work with the men."[28]

Kerensky continued to gather the bitter harvest of the Kornilov affair. The diatribes of the far left and right had been unpleasant but expected. Not so was the raking he now received from Chernov, apparently with the sanction of the SR Central Committee. In a series of articles which began in *Delo Naroda* on September 3, the former "village minister" insinuated that Kerensky had plotted with Kornilov and attacked every aspect of the policies pursued by Kerensky since April. Chernov's personal hostility was hardly new, but this public campaign threatened to split the PSR throughout Russia. Two days later, Kerensky replied in the right-SR *Volia Naroda*, pointing

out that Chernov had been a member of the governments whose
record he now chose to attack. He exhumed Chernov's conduct
during the June elections to the SR Central Committee. Breshkovskaya also threw herself into the counterattack. All the efforts of the
party's fixers failed to heal the breach.[29]

The crisis of the PSR was exacerbated by agrarian disorders which
left none in doubt about the chaotic state of agrarian relations. On
September 8, Kerensky issued an order describing the situation: "Information reaches me all the time from the localities about coercive
acts and the rule of anarchy aimed at the solution of various agricultural questions by illegal means." He threatened the perpetrators,
and officials who failed to prosecute them, with three years'
imprisonment.[30]

The language which had overawed Gotz and Zenzinov no longer
impressed the peasants, and on the same day a major agrarian revolt
broke out in the SR stronghold of Tambov Province. Within days,
the movement had engulfed four counties and twenty manor houses
were in ashes. The remaining landlords were warned to get out by
September 20. In excusing his own failure, the district commissar—
almost certainly an old SR—telegraphed: "The transfer of land [to]
the control of the land committees would have prevented excesses.
The struggle is made more difficult by the sympathy of the soldier
mass for the cause of the struggle against private land tenure."

From Kerensky's Volga homeland, once so solid for the PSR, came
warnings of the collapse of trade and industry and the growing influence of the Bolsheviks and left-wing SRs. The four peasants reported killed in Kazan province were four more martyrs for Lenin.
In Kerensky's electoral province of Saratov, the provincial peasant
soviets insisted on the transfer of all the land to the land committees
and demanded a cutback in grain prices, which had been doubled at
the end of August in an attempt to encourage peasants to deliver
grain. Many poorer peasants now found the cost of their seed for
1918 twice what they had got for their harvests of 1917. It was in
this tragic autumn that Kerensky had to order troops to protect
Yasnaya Polyana from the peasants Tolstoy had once idolized.[31]

The grain shortage was critical in such grain-importing areas as
Central Asia and Finland, where economic collapse and national sentiment had sharply reduced Kerensky's initial popularity. Toward
the end of August, Kerensky had been lobbied by Central Asian

Muslims, begging him to exempt the area from the prohibition on land sales pending agrarian reform. He sounded sympathetic on this issue, but soon shifted the conversation to warn them against secessionist ideas, threatening "the most drastic measures" against any nationalist rising. "Return home," he concluded, "and tell those who delegated you that the government remembers their needs; may Turkestan see in my person a defender of its interests." Within days these very people would save Kerensky by dissuading the Savage Division from the march on Petrograd. In the end, it was not the Islamic nationalists who struck, but the new Bolshevik/left-wing SR presidium of the Tashkent Soviet, which cited the government's failure to deal with food supplies as the motive for taking power. Kerensky gave them 24 hours to rescind their decision, promising that troops with machine guns were on their way.[32]

Like the Central Asians, the Finns bitterly resented the collapse of the Russian transport system that had guaranteed them bread in return for industrial exports. Kerensky had continued to give private assurances that he would speak up for Finland's independence, but his government's Juridical Commission would not hear of the idea.[33]

During those September evenings, Kerensky and Lilya must sometimes have gazed past the heavy velvet curtains of his suite across the broad expanse of the Neva toward the heavy classical mass of the Stock Exchange. Beyond it lay the working class districts of the Petrograd Side and Vyborg, where he had once been so popular. In the unseasonably warm February Days, they had come to him in confidence. In this chilly September, he did not need to be told what they thought of him now. Out of sight to the East, a stone's throw from his family's apartment, the new Bolshevik representatives of the Petrograd workers were in possession of one wing of the Smolny Institute. How long would it be until they controlled the All-Russian Executive Committee and with it, the soviets of all Russia?

On August 31, the Petrograd Soviet had accepted the Bolshevik programme thrown out by the All-Russian Committee just four days earlier. The Bolsheviks then demanded the resignation of the Menshevik-SR presidium, which countered by asking for a vote of confidence. The Bolsheviks ingeniously sidestepped this challenge by proposing that all parties receive proportional representation on the presidium, and won a narrow majority. Members of the old presidium then walked out. On September 25, they were replaced by a

Bolshevik-dominated presidium headed by Trotsky who had become a Bolshevik during his detention after the July Days. Kerensky was obliged to resign his honorary vice-chairmanship of the Petrograd Soviet. As the left-wing SRs had just captured the Petersburg Committee of the PSR, his last formal link with the Petrograd workers was severed.[34]

During the Moscow State Conference, Lenin had poured scorn on the suggestion that Kornilov might be plotting a coup and had bitterly criticized those willing to collaborate with the moderate socialists against Kornilov. Since the fall of Riga, he had taken refuge in Helsinki, and he remained there until mid-September. At first, he approved the cautious response of his followers toward Kornilov's mutiny and, in a radical change of tactics, he even suggested that if the Mensheviks and SRs broke with the Kadets and established a government accountable to the Soviets, the Bolsheviks would confine themselves to the role of loyal opposition. Lenin's benevolence toward the moderate socialists did not survive their capitulation to Kerensky, and on the eve of the Democratic Conference, he demanded that: "The Bolsheviks, having obtained a majority in the Soviets of Workers' and Soldiers' Deputies of both capitals, can and *must* take state power into their hands . . ."[35]

The Democratic Conference gathered in the red plush of the Alexandriinsky Theater on September 14. It united delegates of the urban soviets with those of such moderate institutions as elected dumas and zemstvos, army committees, and cooperatives. It guaranteed the moderates a majority. Chkheidze and Avksentiev opened the conference, reminding the delegates of the gravity of the moment. Kerensky addressed the first session himself and at once addressed the suspicions of his comrades:

I cannot speak to the conference of the Democracy, whose will I carried out and with which I created the Russian revolution, until I feel that there is no one here who would cast reproaches and slander against me personally of the kinds that have been heard in recent times.

His audience included Chernov and 89 Bolsheviks, who expressed their sentiments by heckling him throughout his speech. Yet, for most of the audience, the old magic still worked. Kerensky denied that he had sought a co-dictatorship with Kornilov, a defense that was crucial for his future relations with all Russian socialists, but it was a weak performance in comparison with his pleas for the victims of Tsarism.

The inevitable moment of drama came when Kerensky claimed that everyone in the army wanted its reorganization "along the principles of reason and harmonious work of all its elements." "And what of the death penalty, Marat?" came a voice from the floor. Kerensky looked pale, paused for a moment and then replied, at first softly:

> Yes, at the beginning of the revolution the death penalty was abolished, but later, at the demand not only of the commanders but also the public organizations of the front, it was re-introduced.
>
> The front curses and calls to shame those who, in spite of all warnings, were perverting ignorant people, . . . which reached the point of horrifying scenes where young children and nurses were raped by the dozen.
>
> But I say to you . . . when just a single death sentence is signed by me, the Supreme Commander, then I will permit you to curse me.

What did this mean? Was he claiming that the death penalty was not being applied? Wasn't he deserting his subordinates who had passed death sentences in the elective courts-martial? In practice, the death penalty was quietly dropped.

Kerensky closed by warning the Bolsheviks that if they tried a coup, "the roads will be blocked, the troops will not advance,

> and your dispatches will not go out . . . Anyone who dares to plunge a knife into the back of the Russian army, will discover the might of the revolutionary Provisional Government, which governs with the faith and confidence of the whole country.

The left raged, but the Mensheviks and SRs dominated the auditorium and Kerensky left the stage to a stormy ovation, kissing the hand of Vera Figner as he went.[36]

Kerensky's jaunty parting gesture suggested a justified confidence in the ability of his comrades to master the conference. Tsereteli vigorously defended the previous coalitions and insisted that a coalition with Kadets not personally implicated in Kornilov's venture was both possible and necessary. Even Chernov now conceded the principle of coalition, though not with the Kadets—a virtual contradiction in terms, as Kamenev gleefully pointed out. "One cannot substitute Kishkin-Tereshchenko or Nekrasov for the large political party which is the only representative of the bourgeois elements in

Russia." The Bolsheviks were at loggerheads, too, with Trotsky demanding that all power be transferred to the soviets, while Kamenev was happy to settle for "that democracy which is well enough represented here."[37]

After five days of speeches, the conference prepared to vote on the principle of coalition. Lenin was so exasperated by the constitutionalists of his central committee that he left Helsinki for Vyborg on September 17, ready to argue for an insurrection whatever the conference decided. For once, Kerensky shared Lenin's fears. The last thing he wanted was an all-socialist government responsible to the conference or the soviets.

The rollcall vote dragged on for hours in the tense auditorium, complicated by a procedural irregularity: the vote on the substantive motion was taken *before* the amendments. The vote on the principle of coalition carried 766–688. The abstentions included Chernov's. The first amendment proposed the exclusion from coalition of bourgeois elements implicated in the Kornilov affair. This passed overwhelmingly. The second amendment proposing the exclusion of the Kadets, passed 595–483. Chernov appeared to have won in spite of his own peculiar conduct: there would be coalition, but without the Kadets. His triumph was short-lived, however; the presidium ruled that there must now be another vote on the amended resolution. Both left and right wings of the PSR bolted and the amended resolution collected only 183 votes. There were 813 against. "Revolutionary Democracy" had labored for six days to produce a miscarriage.[38]

Lenin was delighted. "The so-called Democratic Conference is over. Thank God, one more farce is behind us and still we are advancing." Kerensky could have written these words himself. He, too, felt he was advancing. He had recovered his freedom of action and he could barely conceal his glee when he met the conference presidium for a short exchange of views on September 20.[39]

The abortion of the Democratic Conference also vindicated Kerensky in his second serious dispute with Tereshchenko, who had been pressing Kerensky to break with the Soviets since the Kornilov affair. On the eve of the conference, he had begged Kerensky to announce his new government before the conference met. Kerensky knew that this would embarrass his Soviet comrades so he refused. After Kerensky's successful appearance on the first day of the conference, Tereshchenko again urged him to announce his own government. Again, Kerensky refused, and Tereshchenko was sufficiently put out to take two days' leave in Moscow. At Tereshchenko's behest, Ambassador Noulens saw Kerensky to express his own anxiety about the Conference and Kerensky's forthcoming discussions with its presidium. Kerensky reassured him. The left block, formed after the Kornilov affair, was now shattered and if the Bolsheviks tried anything, well "the Bolsheviks don't like bayonets."

The formulas which the conference voted may appear awkward for the government, but they are only formulas and basically everything will work out satisfactorily.

He concluded:

My list is ready . . . and I will not modify it. But I shall only publish it after my interview with the delegates so that they have the illusion that they have exerted influence. My cabinet will include some Kadets and representatives of industry.[40]

So he went on, from one oratorical success to another and from one pyrrhic tactical victory after another, as the country evaded his grasp. Infuriated at inflation's erosion of their pay the Railroadmen threatened a general strike for September 23. On the same day, the government declared Tashkent under martial law without any certainty that it could be enforced. On the following day, the Ukrainian General Secretariat threw off the tutelage of the Provisional Government, though the *Rada* was no longer such an awesome opponent since its break with the Bolshevik Kharkov Soviet. On September 23, the Bolsheviks and left-wing SRs won the victory that meant everything to them when the Soviet Executive Committee reluctantly conceded that a second congress of soviets should be convoked on October 20. As Kerensky's new government was announced, the Bolsheviks assumed the leadership of the Petrograd Soviet, and the Moscow electors chose district dumas with a Bolshevik majority. Within the Bolshevik party, there was a furious debate about whether or not to boycott the Council of the Republic or "Pre-Parliament," which would succeed the Democratic Conference. Trotsky and Stalin led the majority. "Trotsky was for the boycott. Bravo, Comrade Trotsky!" wrote Lenin. His own message was predictably violent: "Disperse the Bonapartist gang of Kerensky and *his* fake Pre-Parliament, with this Tsereteli-Bulygin Duma."[41] A so-called third coalition was now put together after less than a week of bargaining between the Democratic Council, the ghostly presidium of the Democratic Conference, on the left, and Tereshchenko and the Kadets not officially implicated in Kornilov's mutiny on the right. On the morning of September 21, Gotz, Avksentiev, Chkheidze, and Tsereteli arrived to see the Premier, hoping to tie the government to a socialist program and make it accountable. One by one, their conditions were withdrawn as Kerensky and Tereshchenko confronted them with their own weakness. There would be a pre-parliament, but the government would not be accountable to it. The prospective Kadet ministers merely offered to inspire themselves "with the democratic point of view which had guided Chkheidze at the Moscow Conference." Tereshchenko brought the socialists to heel with a letter angrily criticizing both government and Soviet:

They had . . . learnt nothing and forgotten nothing. Instead of trying to save Russia, demagogues had thought of nothing but their own party interests and of how to control and impede the Government's action. A counter-revolution, though not necessarily a monarchical one, offered, . . . the only hope of saving the country.

The Kadets declared their solidarity, refusing to join the government if he resigned. Tereshchenko withdrew his resignation on the understanding that the government would not be responsible to any outside body, that one-third of the ministers would be bourgeois, and that socialist reforms would be held over until the Constituent Assembly.

Kerensky had redeemed his pledges to M. Noulens, for the ministry was almost identical with the one announced by Nekrasov on August 30. The existing members of the directory retained their posts, and capital was openly represented by the Chairman of the Moscow Region War Industries Committee and the Chairman of the Moscow Stock Exchange. Ten days later, the right-center SR Maslov was appointed to the vacant Ministry of Agriculture. The breech between Kerensky and Tereshchenko was not entirely healed, however, and it was Konovalov who became deputy premier. The Masonic connection had done Kerensky one last service.[42]

On the day after Kerensky announced the formation of the most bourgeois government since April, the Allied ambassadors called. Kerensky, Tereshchenko, and Konovalov received Sir George Buchanan, M. Noulens, and the Marchese Carlotti in the Winter Palace. As usual, the Americans dodged this unseemly display of Allied heavy-handedness. As senior member, Sir George spoke for all three. He congratulated Kerensky perfunctorily on the formation of a new government, but then his tone changed:

We emphasized the necessity of their organizing all Russia's military and economic forces by the adoption of rigorous measures for the maintenance of internal order, for increasing the output of the factories, for improving the transport services, and for re-establishing strict discipline in the army.

As Tereshchenko translated the note into Russian for Kerensky's benefit, his chief's face turned to stone.

Kerensky suggested that Buchanan was so embarrassed at this confrontation that he blushed and a "moist glimmer" appeared in his eye, while he himself went through a "mental storm":

I had only to accept the Note and issue it to the press with an explanation as to *where, when, how,* and by whom General Kornilov had been helped— and there would have been the end of the "alliance"! In fact, I should have had to provide pretty strong protection for the Allied Embassies pending the departure of the Ambassadors.

He contented himself with the grim hope that Russian public opinion would not misunderstand the note. He then lectured the ambassadors on Russia's contribution to the war effort, on the past tolerance of the Allies toward the Tsarist regime, and on the need for unity. Rising, he offered his hand curtly to each of them and muttered, "Russia is also a great power," before walking off.

Buchanan tried to follow Kerensky, not, as Kerensky supposed, to apologize, but to tell him some even more disagreeable things. In the end, it was agreed that the purpose of the visit would not be made public. Kerensky's suggestion that he might have denounced the alliance to his advantage is quite unconvincing. Tereshchenko and the Kadets would have resigned, denouncing him in turn. The Americans would have cancelled the $450 million worth of credits so far extended, and largely unspent. What could he have said to assuage the wrath of the families of men killed in the June offensive? The denunciation of the alliance would merely have swept him away sooner.[43]

Still, the encounter convinced Kerensky that he must somehow get through to Lloyd George directly. Surely, the Welsh radical and the Central Asian socialist could find a common language. But how could he circumvent the castebound Tories of the Foreign Office, the War Office, and the Allied Press Corps? He had already drafted a personal letter to Lloyd George pledging that "the Russian army will continue to hold the forces of the enemy here," and describing his hopes for a reform of the army over the coming winter, though he warned that the morale and political allegiances of the forces would continue to fluctuate.

Kerensky now decided to underline this message with a secret oral postscript, and on October 1, he summoned Somerset Maugham to the Winter Palace. He complained to the British author-secret agent of the niggardliness of Allied supplies and the harm done to Anglo-Russian relations by "Blimps" such as Colonel Wilton of *The Times*. He also asked that Buchanan be replaced by "someone of the type of M. Thomas." The kernel of his message was, however, a brutally concise and frank summary of the state of the army, which shows that his intuition had lost none of its acuity.

For the last time, Kerensky appealed to Lloyd George to offer the Germans "peace without annexations or compensations," a peace "the Germans will refuse." Then Kerensky could tell his soldiers to fight with some chance of being obeyed:

If something of the sort is not done, then, when the cold weather comes I don't think I shall be able to keep the army in the trenches. I don't see how we can go on. Of course, I don't say that to the people. I always say that we shall continue whatever happens, but unless I have something to tell my army it's impossible.

To keep this message safe (from the Germans or from Teresh-chenko?) Maugham was instructed to write nothing down, an instruction broken only after his arrival in London. The British took every precaution to ensure that the message arrived in total secrecy, sending a destroyer to Christiania to pick Maugham up, but it did not reach Lloyd George until November 18.[44]

The new government still hoped to survive until the Constituent Assembly, and still hoped for some miraculous development to halt the war on terms favorable to Russia, but it lived increasingly from hand to mouth. One day the threatened rail strike was settled amicably, the next the oil workers of Baku stopped work. If the government was unsure, so were its enemies. On September 26 and 27,

Lenin was insisting that this was the last moment for a peaceful revolution that would hand power to the Constituent Assembly. Yet half of his Central Committee still wanted to attend the pre-parliament. Lenin may not always have believed in the plots he ascribed to his enemies, still, the anxiety he expressed to Smilga, the Chairman of the Finnish Soviets, on September 26, was both real and well-founded. "Kerensky at General Headquarters is obviously entering into an understanding—a *business-like* understanding—with the Kornilovites to use troops to put down the Bolsheviks."[45]

Kerensky went to GHQ ostensibly to discuss the forthcoming conference of Allied military commanders in Paris. It was his first opportunity for a full discussion with General Dukhonin, who had replaced Alexeyev as *de facto* Supreme Commander. Kerensky had been impressed by Dukhonin's willingness to work under revolutionary conditions in June, but now they bickered, under the censorious eyes of Allied officers, and Kerensky admits to suffering a nervous collapse for two days. Dukhonin and Verkhovsky had worked out a plan to reduce the size of the army, weed out unreliable elements, and create secret forces to suppress Bolshevism. Dukhonin hoped that Russia would carry on until the Germans were beaten, but the picture he presented was so dismal that Alexeyev, who had been asked to represent Russia at the Allied Conference, refused to take on this humiliating task. Verkhovsky came to the even more depressing conclusion that Russia would soon have to sue for an immediate ceasefire.

The conference was interrupted by a full-scale emergency. The Germans attacked the Estonian islands of Ösel (Saaremaa), Moon (Muhu) and then Dagö (Hiiumaa), straddled across the mouth of the Gulf of Riga. On September 29, a major naval engagement erupted. To general surprise the Bolshevized Baltic Fleet put up stiff resistance—perhaps because their retreat had been cut off. The men of the *Grazhdanin* and the *Slava* fought with particular valor and over twenty German ships were damaged. Nevertheless, the German operation was successful, and by October 6, Petrograd was only 250 miles from German guns.[46]

The panic-stricken Russian Naval Staff asked the British to send a detachment into the Baltic to distract the Germans. Admiral Stanley merely offered a diversion in the North Sea. When Tereshchenko failed to move Buchanan, Kerensky himself took over and the two men wrangled—giving vent to all the disappointment they felt in one another. Buchanan finally advised Kerensky to eradicate Bolshevism, then "he would go down to history, not only as the leading figure of the revolution, but as the savior of his country." Kerensky agreed, but said he could not suppress the Bolsheviks without provocation.[47]

It was to this troublesome alliance that Vladimir Burtsev, the muckraking journalist, now dedicated his newspaper, *Obshchee Delo* [The Common Cause]. Some of the funds behind this venture were French, another installment of the Allied subsidies to defencists, which dwarfed those provided to the Bolsheviks and Ukrainians by the Germans. Its initial editorial proclaimed that it would pursue the truth in the Kornilov affair—a "truth" Burtsev thought he already knew. He simultaneously denounced Kerensky's "cowardice" and "complete lack of character."[48]

The Shablovsky Commission now delivered further crushing blows. Had Kornilov been tried for treason or mutiny, specific charges might have been preferred and proper cross-examination conducted. The trouble was that precisely framed charges might have led to Kornilov's acquittal, a result the left would have found intolerably provocative. In the event, the Commission had traveled to see Kornilov in his comfortable prison, still guarded by his faithful Turkmen, at Bykhov. There, he and other participants in the affair were encouraged to make written statements presenting their actions in the most favorable light and incriminating Kerensky. The "honest" Kornilov admitted that he had worked for a military dictatorship—but so had Kerensky. Of course he had sent the Special Army to Petrograd to put down the Bolsheviks—just as Kerensky had wanted. Kornilov's explanatory note was leaked to Burtsev and published on October 2. It was followed by the testimony of Alexeyev, V. N. Lvov and others, all of which was highly damaging to Kerensky. Kerensky's anger over these leaks never died and to the end of his days, he denied the authenticity of the documents while admitting he knew who had leaked them.[49]

Kerensky must have set Mironov to trace the source of the leaks, and by the time he received the Commission for his own examination on Sunday, October 8, he had a shrewd idea of who this was. The military lawyers had now been augmented by two Soviet representatives, and all of them—plus stenographers—met Kerensky in the same study overlooking Palace Square in which he had interrogated Krymov six weeks earlier. There were moments of real anger. Some members of the Commission found him a refractory witness, which is hardly to be wondered at. He had chosen a secret inquiry to calm public tempers. It had done the opposite, forcing him to keep his mouth shut while others regaled the press with their versions of events. It had buried his reputation as a moderate socialist of integrity, and with it, the authority of the Provisional Government—the sole body he believed capable of leading Russia to the democratically-elected Constituent Assembly. Even he knew that "the poison of doubt was penetrating ever deeper into the very masses of the people."[50]

Kerensky's refusal to submit to proper cross-examination has added to the doubts that persist over his role in the Kornilov affair. Yet if Kerensky was a second Bonaparte, he was now the Napoleon of 1812–1813, vaulting a raging flood, his stilts splintering beneath him.

15

All Necessary Measures

And now it was autumn. Work at factories was put on a part-time basis, tram services were irregular, and rations were reduced. Inside the Winter Palace, there was an atmosphere of impermanence. Patriotism had decreed that the art treasures be evacuated so Kerensky's few remaining petitioners had to squeeze past packed-up paintings and antiques. Many people were disillusioned, exhausted, and apathetic, but there were apocalyptic hopes abroad. As gangs of soldiers smashed the wine stores and got themselves drunk, everyone willed the unbearable moment of transition to pass. But what would replace it? The heaven or hell of the Bolsheviks' new world? A German occupation? Or a resolution by the Constituent Assembly of the problems that had already overwhelmed Russia's democratic politicians?[1]

October 7 dawned bleakly for Kerensky as he read another of Chernov's attacks in *Delo Naroda*. His principal task for the day was the opening of the pre-parliament—the Provisional Council of the Russian Republic. The Tauride Palace was being refurbished for the Constituent Assembly, so the pre-parliament gathered in the Mariinsky Palace before Repin's monumental painting of Nicholas II and his ministers, which was tactfully draped in red sheeting. The ushers and stenographers borrowed from the Duma lent some dignity to the proceedings.

Kerensky's opening address was brief and unemotional. He paid unprecedented tribute to the bravery of the navy, but he admitted the poor state of the army. Anarchy had reached serious proportions and must stop. The food situation alone threatened political and economic disaster. He concluded in terms of unwonted humility: "We, the Provisional Government, invested with full powers, are only the servants of the country, and we ask you to tell us the truth, but only the truth—in all honesty and honor." There was no flamboyant gesture as he handed over the chair to Breshkovskaya. Soon afterward, he left, determined to miss the performance of Leon Trotsky, who had eclipsed him in the hearts of the Petrograd workers.[2]

A far greater intellectual and a distinguished writer, Trotsky shared Kerensky's oratorical and organizational gifts. Like Kerensky, Trotsky found himself speaking words that emerged "in full array from my subconscious." He did not evoke the pathos that made Kerensky's performance so hard to resist, and he was less given to cliché. His speeches had more humour—or at least sarcasm. Released from prison late in September, he immediately became the most prominent Bolshevik. Lenin was still in Finland, Zinoviev and Kamenev were unhappy about Lenin's tactics. Sverdlov was too much the bureaucrat, and Bukharin and Stalin were too young. It was Trotsky who toured the barracks and factories, pouring scorn on Kerensky's Bonapartism and translating Lenin's messages into language which echoed the fears and hopes of his listeners.[3]

With the ceremonies over, Trotsky demanded permission to make a declaration. The ten-minute rule, adopted from the Duma, was sufficient for his purpose. He had come to draw a line between the Bolsheviks and the rest of Russian society. His tone was that of an ambassador declaring war. If Trotsky provoked "scandal," it was his enemies who ran amok, shouting accusations of treason and obscenities. He accused them of frustrating the convocation of the Constituent Assembly, of counting on the "bony hand of hunger" to bring the masses into line, of betraying Petrograd to the Germans. Through the tumult, he concluded:

Petrograd is in danger, the Revolution is in danger, the government is making this danger even worse. Only the people can save themselves and the country. We are turning to the people. Long live an immediate, democratic peace, all power to the Soviets, all land to the people, long live the Constituent Assembly!

As the Bolsheviks left the hall, the question was no longer whether they would take power, but *when*. That night, Lenin arrived in Petrograd.[4]

There was mounting hysteria among the propertied classes, as

General Knox reported: "They one and all state that failing the introduction of discipline on Kornilov's lines, the only salvation is for the Allies to send a force to Russia to put things right."

Days later a Bolshevik paper reported an apoplectic speech by Rodzyanko in Moscow, throwing all discretion to the winds:

Petrograd appears threatened. . . . I say, to hell with Petrograd. . . . People fear our central institutions in Petrograd will be destroyed. To this, let me say that I should be glad if these institutions are destroyed because they have brought Russia nothing but grief.[5]

The dispirited and frequently inquorate sessions of the pre-parliament brought Kerensky little relief, and Avksentiev could only murmur, "On ne pense qu'à la Constituente!" A re-tamed Kadet Central Committee armed Milyukov with a mandate to block all serious decisions by insisting on the cumbersome procedure of the Duma, and when, on October 18, the Mensheviks demanded action against anarchy and counterrevolution, the Kadets had the matter referred to a commission for preliminary analysis.[6]

Lenin and Trotsky had their difficulties, too. The Bolshevik party of 1917 was neither the disciplined corps of professional revolutionaries projected by Lenin in 1902, nor the post-1922 Communist Party, with elections to all significant offices predetermined by lists. Sverdlov did his best to manipulate votes in Lenin's favor, and foreign money may have affected the tone of some Bolshevik papers, but these things are features of parliamentary democracies. The Bolshevik Party of 1917 did impose stiffer conditions for membership than the other parties, but it was in every sense a democratic party—as it had to be to rob the other parties of their supporters.[7]

Unhappily for Lenin, Bolshevik support was far from homogeneous. The party attracted only a small minority of the intelligentsia, but they were disproportionately represented in the higher reaches of the Bolshevik party (as in all the others). Behind the rationalist arguments of Zinoviev and Kamenev against an insurrection, one senses an unspoken fear of the terrible cultural costs of rending the seamless garment of the democratic intelligentsia. The hereditary proletariat of Marxist dogma had been diluted by young and old recruits from the villages, many of them women. They were now persuaded that they could do without the bourgeoisie and were impatient for action, but they were hopelessly lacking in military organization, experience and equipment. However moved they might be by Trotsky's vision of socialist paradise, they needed the support of the 200,000-man Petrograd garrison to challenge the government with success. Few of these men were Bolsheviks, and fewer still had any clear view of the future; but they had shown throughout 1917 that they would not willingly fire on fellow Russians, no matter what their politics.

And now Kerensky's intuition failed him. In the spring, he had appealed to the nobility and compassion of the masses; during the offensive, to their sense of patriotism and shame; after July, to their fear of the Germans and his own threats of ruthless reprisals. By contrast, Lenin went to great lengths to appear harmlessly "anarchist" in public. When Kerensky sought to make the masses fear him, Lenin echoed him. If only the soldiers could be persuaded to believe that Kerensky was a mere avatar of reaction, they would topple him as a matter of self-defense.[8]

On October 7, Lenin rhetorically asked the Petrograd Bolsheviks whether the evidence proved that Kerensky and the Russian, British, and French capitalists *"have conspired* to surrender Petrograd to the Germans and thus stifle the revolution?"

"I think it does" he opined. Four days later, he repeated the warning. Why should the Bolsheviks wait, he asked?

For Kerensky and his Kornilovite generals to surrender Petrograd to the Germans, and thus enter directly or indirectly, openly or secretly, into a conspiracy with *both* Buchanan *and* [Kaiser] Wilhelm for the purpose of completely stifling the Russian revolution.[9]

According to Soviet myth, the crucial decision for insurrection was taken on October 10 by the Bolshevik Central Committee. For conspiratorial reasons they met in Sukhanov's apartment on Vasilievsky Island. Lenin ground down the resistance of Zinoviev and Kamenev. Though the decision committed the Bolsheviks to insurrection, no date was fixed. The minutes include a classic piece of Bolshevik cynicism about free elections: "It is senseless to wait for the Constituent Assembly that will obviously not be on our side, for this will only make our task more involved."[10]

Was Kerensky really the center of a "second Kornilov affair" (*Kornilovshchina*) as Soviet authors still insist? Did he really open the front to the Germans? Did he plot to abandon Petrograd? Did he seriously plan to repress the Bolsheviks by force? Soviet historians allege that the Provisional Government had advance notice of the German attack on the Estonian islands but did nothing to reinforce the positions, a repetition of Kornilov's behavior over Riga. No evidence is given for a myth amply refuted by the contemporaneous reports of Generals Knox and Barter—no friends of Kerensky—describing the government's preparations in detail. One Soviet historian alleges that the Jacobstadt Platzdarm was "treacherously conceded," without citing any evidence at all. He also asserts that after a conference with Kerensky, General Cheremisov ordered an offensive near Wenden in full knowledge of the incapacity of the forces concerned. The "evidence" consists of a third-hand remark by Cheremisov uncharacteristically accepting the blame for this near fiasco. Lenin's allegations of an "Anglo-French-German-Russian imperialist plot" to hand Petrograd to the Germans are arrant nonsense. The fact that the Germans still had their money on the Bolsheviks shows that the Anglo-French and German imperialists were quite unable to concoct any joint plot against the Russian revolution. Far from being in cahoots with Buchanan to sink the Baltic Fleet, Kerensky had just quarrelled with him for declining to save it.[11]

The evacuation of Petrograd was quite another matter. Bolshevism was much stronger there than in Moscow, so the suggestion that the government might leave Petrograd had inevitable political implications, as Kerensky had admitted to Ambassador Noulens in August. There were pragmatic reasons for the evacuation. With the Germans only 250 miles away, contingency plans were vitally necessary. The government had become a burden on a city where bread rations had been cut by a third, with only two days' supply in hand, and where the collapse of the transport system and the coming of winter could only make things worse. The government was not helped by Kadet support for the evacuation, nor by Rodzyanko's inflammatory remarks which convinced many ordinary soldiers and workers that Lenin was right to charge that "Kerensky will surrender Petrograd to the Germans, that is now as clear as daylight. No assertions to the contrary can destroy our full conviction that this is so." Kerensky did his best to nail the lies and half-truths that were engulfing him:

The categorical and determined view of the Provisional Government consists in this: that under no conditions and in no circumstances can there be even a thought that the country would reconcile itself in this matter to even the temporary cession of the center of the state administration.[12]

Lenin was nearer the mark when he asserted that "Russian imperialists" were "standing behind" Kerensky and preparing for the suppression of Bolshevism. On her last visit to Kerensky Bochkaryova found that after the Kornilov affair, he had "cut himself off completely from his friends and acquaintances of the upper classes."By October, some bourgeois leaders had put this behind them. They included Prince Lvov and Bochkaryova's patron, Rodzyanko, who helped to finance secret plans to create "Revolutionary Guards" under the command of General Wrangel. (Disguised as "depots for winter training," these "anti–Maximalist" units were still undetected by the Bolsheviks on October 24.) As for the Navy, even before the Baltic Fleet asserted its right to elect its own officers on October 2, Kerensky had decided to replace its crews once the ice froze. These plans would take months to come to fruition.[13]

At a conference with the high command of the Northern front early in October, Kerensky sanctioned plans for an immediate relocation of forces, involving the reinforcement of the front by Bolshevized armored car units from Petrograd and the marginal reinforcement of "loyal" units in Finland and the capital by forces of Cossacks and infantry and cyclist units from the Southwest front, still relatively free from Bolshevism. Lenin did hear of these changes but felt the numbers involved to be too trivial to affect the balance of power in Petrograd.[14] Lenin's hypocritical charge that Kerensky's plans threatened the Constituent Assembly lacks any basis in evidence, but there was undeniably a new sense of urgency in the government's handling of military matters. Plans for a New Model army of volunteers were discussed during Kerensky's last visit to GHQ on October 14–16 and promulgated into law by the government on the night they were telegraphed to Petrograd. Kerensky had nothing against the Constituent Assembly, but he was now in deadly earnest about the Bolsheviks.[15]

Despite these efforts, the objective appraisals of their agents convinced the Allies that the Russian government must soon make peace. Symptomatic of Russian resentment toward the growing contempt of the Allies was the Gurko incident. King George V, who had twice urged his government to withdraw offers of asylum to his Imperial cousin in the spring, now invited the rebellious and monarchist General Gurko to tea at Buckingham Palace. Kerensky took this as a calculated slap in the face and threatened to send a telegram of sympathy to the Sinn Féin rebels then meeting in Dublin. Tereshchenko tried to appease Buchanan by suggesting that Kerensky had been joking![16]

Following the Kornilov affair, the Russian government had tried to revive the idea of an inter-Allied conference on the war aims and had affected renewed sympathy for the Stockholm Conference. The Allies, absorbed in the hellish struggles in Flanders, agreed merely to discuss the *conduct* of the war, but the moderate socialists in Russia still failed to comprehend Russia's military weakness and Allied diplomatic obduracy. On the day the pre-parliament opened, the Soviet Committee elected Skobelev to supervise Tereshchenko's conduct at the inter-Allied conference and supplied him with a mandate. Though it included the defencist demand for a complete German withdrawal from Russian territory, it also included the demand for a restitution of the German colonies, a plebiscite in Alsace-Lorraine, and an offer of "full self-determination in Poland, Lithuania and Latvia."[17]

This provoked a dreary post-mortem on the whole inconsistent foreign policy of the Provisional Government, as Tereshchenko sought to bring the Soviet to heel once more. He also paid lip service to self-determination, but his affection for the Czechs and South Slavs was matched by an inability to pronounce the word Ukraine. As for the Latvians, currently under German occupation, their independence could not be tolerated partly because of the Russian, German, Polish and Jewish minorities there, but mainly because of Russia's need for an ice-free port on the Baltic Sea. The demand that Austria-Hungary should be dismantled while Russia emerged from the war intact was only marginally less utopian than the Soviet mandate. Returning to the real world, Tereshchenko concluded that Russian difficulties were not so much material as lying "in the psychology of the people." He knew already that the majority of the Petrograd garrison was pro-Bolshevik.

For the last time, the government offered the Soviet a figleaf. Tereshchenko would try to get Skobelev an invitation for the Allied conference provided the mandate was revised and on the understanding that he would supervise Skobelev. Avksentiev and the right-SRs rejected the mandate and forced Skobelev to agree.[18]

Tereshchenko's victory was ruined by the totally unexpected intervention of the Minister of War. Verkhovsky's attempts to resuscitate the government's "democratic" foreign policy had met icy hostility in the government (Kerensky did not trust him enough to let him know of his own secret approach to Lloyd George.), and his attempts to speed up demobilization had been rewarded by the truncation of his ministerial responsibilities. While in public he appeared to be a left-wing general of ambition, he suggested to the Allied Embassies that he stood for order. To Bochkaryara, Verkhovsky seemed "like a man who is drowning, reaching for help."

On October 19, Verkhovsky told the cabinet that "in view of the present attitude toward the question of peace, a catastrophe is inescapable." The other ministers were used to this sort of exaggeration and refused to accept his resignation.

On the following day, Verkhovsky reported on the state of the army to the Kadet Central Committee. "Under such circumstances," he concluded, "it is impossible to fight on and each attempt to prolong the war can only bring the catastrophe closer." Milyukov and Shingaryov attacked him bitterly. Nabokov, who agreed with him, kept his mouth shut in deference to party policy. He also suspected Verkhovsky of staging a provocation on behalf of the Bolsheviks.[19]

That evening, Verkhovsky gave an unscheduled address to a closed session of the joint defense and foreign affairs subcommittees on the horrendous state of the army. It had some three million more mouths to feed. The men were out of control. He wanted 150,000 officers withdrawn from the army for use as internal security troops, the power of the committees to be further reduced, patriotic propaganda stepped up, and so on. For the first and last time, a minister of the Provisional Government declared, "we can not fight." A Bolshevik attack was imminent and in the trenches the men were beginning to demand peace. The government must "take the ground from under their feet, to raise the question of the conclusion of peace ourselves immediately."

As he listened, Tereshchenko's irritation turned to fury. "*C'est une maison de fous*" (It's a madhouse) he muttered, and then he got up to dispute Verkhovksy's facts and refute his conclusions. The army had fought through the winter of 1916 despite the shortage of supplies, American railroad engineers had worked wonders with the Trans-Siberian Railroad, and so on. Verkhovsky backpeddled. He was not asking for an immediate separate peace but for Russia to set a date for general peace negotiations. The Allies would either accept or release Russia from her obligations. He added, quixotically, that should the Allies refuse both options, Russia would have to continue the struggle, even at the cost of a Bolshevik rising and civil war. He repeated that "a strong personal power" was now necessary.[20]

On the evening of October 21, Kerensky received his blundering subordinate in the Winter Palace. Verkhovsky was sent away for two weeks' "rest," suggesting to the public a nonpolitical reason for his erratic behavior, while Quartermaster-General Manikovsky took over the Ministry of War. It was widely rumored that Verkhovsky had been let go for advocating peace. Burtsev's *Obshchee Delo* ignored government appeals not to publish Verkhovksy's report. Mistakenly it suggested that Verkhovsky had demanded a secret *separate* peace, and this provided Kerensky with a welcome pretext for its suppression. Oddly enough, he told the Allied embassies that Verkhovsky had been sacked for plotting a military dictatorship.[21]

Verkhovsky's tactlessness had exposed the futility of Tereshchenko's wrangles with the moderate socialists, had undermined Kerensky's secret diplomacy, and had shown up Kerensky's final attempt to act as the leader of a great power as a hollow sham. Furious at Carlotti's participation in the Allied démarche in September, Tereshchenko had told the pre-parliament that Italy had entered the war with a large appetite and little else. Italian pride now took a beating as the Austro-Germans inflicted the murderous rout of Caporetto, immortalized by Hemmingway. On October 18 Marchese Carlotti asked to see Kerensky in person to demand a diversion on the Eastern front. When Kerensky arrived at the Italian Embassy he offered a diversion in Romania, He was not over-complimentary about the Italian war effort, but he made no attempt to tie Russian aid to a moderation of Italian demands for Austrian territory, which were an insuperable obstacle to a peace settlement with Austria.[22]

Kerensky later alleged that on October 20, Russia received an offer of a separate peace from Austria through the Swedish Embassy in Petrograd. No mention of such an offer has been found in the archives of either the Swedish or the Austro-Hungarian foreign ministries. Count Czernin alleged that persons close to Emperor Karl *were* urging a separate peace on him at this time, and Czernin himself may still have entertained hopes about his own overture to Kerensky.

Kerensky claimed that the defection of Austria was to be followed by the desertion of both Bulgaria and Turkey from the alliance with Germany. It was this danger, he later insisted, that had frightened the German General Staff into triggering the revolt of their "agents," Lenin and Trotsky. He grew fond of this tale in exile, even recommending to Lloyd George that he include it in his memoirs. But Lloyd George refutes these claims, quoting instead Balfour's summary of September 20, 1917. In Balfour's view, the peace feelers from Bulgaria and Turkey had come from rebels inclined to overstate their case, while, "Austria is so tightly bound to Germany, that *as things are at present*, she could do no more for the cause of peace than press moderation upon her arrogant partner."

No one can doubt Emperor Karl's sincerity in working for a general peace throughout 1917, but the presence of a German army in Austria, the intractability of the Hungarian aristocracy, and the aspirations of Czechs, Serbs, Romanians, and Italians—supported increasingly by President Wilson—made a separate peace virtually impossible for Austria.[23] Desperate as the situation of the last Habsburg was, Russia's need for peace was even more pressing. Russian soldiers were now ready to taunt defencist orators by agreeing, "yes, we want a shameful peace." Kerensky's secret appraisal of the morale of the army came from reports of such commissars as Moiseenko who admitted that only free food and lodging still held the men in the trenches. If, as seemed likely, these gave out, the army would simply dissolve.[24]

Kerensky could have responded positively to Austrian offers only by ditching Tereshchenko. Was he still capable of this kind of ruthlessness? Konovalov was doubtful:

You settle everything, you insist on these or those measures, at last you obtain agreement. "So, Alexander Fyodorovich, now it is firm, finally decided, there won't be any changes?" You receive a categorical assurance. You go out of his study and after several hours you learn of some entirely different decision which has already been carried out. The best [you can expect] is that the urgent measure which ought to have been taken now, today, is put off again, new suspicions have occurred or old ones have revived which seemed to have been removed.

The psychiatrist minister Kishkin agreed: "Passivity and indecision are the symptoms of our government's mental illness. . . . Our Prime Minister should be blamed for the whole distressing situation."[25]

In contrast to his lyrical accounts of February and his persuasive accounts of the Kornilov affair, Kerensky's accounts of October are lifeless and stylized. The lighting is lurid; the masses have disappeared; he is face to face with evil. The archfiend is the German General Staff, Lenin its Mephistopheles. Trotsky was "responsible for the technical side of the uprising and also for political agitation," while the role of Kamenev, Kerensky's one-time client was,

to distract the attention of the . . . socialist parties from Lenin's real aims [so] . . . that when Trotsky attacked, the Provisional Government would get no active support from them. . . . This mild, amiable man knew how to tell lies with incredible plausibility. He had a shrewd understanding of the people he was cheating, and he was able to do it with an almost childishly innocent expression on his face.[26]

These remarks probably refer to the role played by Kamenev after October 25. They omit to mention that it was precisely Kamenev, with Zinoviev, who exposed Lenin's plans.

Since early September, Kamenev and Zinoviev, Lenin's closest friend in exile, had resisted all Lenin's appeals for insurrection. They had voted against insurrection at the Central Committee meeting on October 10 and had done all they could to scotch Lenin's hopes that the Northern Regional Soviet congress would initiate insurrection in mid-October. They fed *Novaia Zhizn'* with the accurate summary of Lenin's intentions which was published on October 15, and they tried to persuade the Central Committee to defer the rising until after the Second Congress of Soviets met. When they failed to get their objections to insurrection printed in the Bolshevik press, they had their protest printed in Gorky's paper. In demanding "the expulsion of both blacklegs from the Party," Lenin explained that they had, "*betrayed* to Rodzyanko and Kerensky the decisions of the Central Committee of their Party on insurrection and the decision to conceal from the enemy preparations for insurrection and the date appointed for it."[27]

Lenin's fury was understandable. He had only just persuaded the Bolsheviks on the Military-Revolutionary Committee (MRC) of the Petrograd Soviet to use it as a front for a Bolshevik coup. The warnings of the Bolshevik dissidents did not fall on deaf ears. On October 16, the command of the Petrograd Military District increased the guard on public buildings and ordered the commanders of the artillery schools of Petrograd and the cadet schools in Peterhof and Oranienbaum to bring out their charges. On October 18, General Polkovnikov alerted the garrison to the plans of the Bolsheviks. Thereafter he gave daily warnings through the press that "all necessary measures have already been taken for the suppression of any uprising." Deceived by his experience in July, Kerensky assumed that Bolshevik popularity would evaporate the moment they tried anything. As he told Buchanan: "I only wish that they would come out, and I will then put them down."[28]

The plans for a relocation of forces had met with disobedience and on October 17, General Cheremisov called a joint meeting of delegates of the Northern front and Petrograd garrison to put pressure on the mutineers. The Petrograders arrived with a mandate drafted by Sverdlov and the arguments of Cheremisov and Commissar Voytinsky simply made them more obdurate. Nevertheless, Kerensky's military staff continued to work on the new military legislation and on dispositions for the garrison to meet the Bolshevik rising. Trouble was expected on Sunday, October 22, dubbed the Day of the Petrograd Soviet by the Bolsheviks and left-wing SRs, but familiar to the Cossacks as the anniversary of the liberation of Moscow in 1812. The Cossacks planned a religious procession for the day. On October 21, the garrison delegates gave Trotsky a rapturous reception, promising the Military-Revolutionary Committee its full support, and calling on the coming Second Congress of Soviets to take power and provide "peace, land, and bread for the people." Late that night, the Military-Revolutionary Committee sent out commissars to oust the government's. They informed General Polkovnikov that "henceforth, orders not signed by us are invalid." Polkovnikov threatened to arrest the commissars. By the time Kerensky suspended Verkhovsky, the garrisons of Petrograd, Finland, Estonia, and the Baltic Fleet were all in a state of open insubordination.[29]

Sunday October 22 went off peacefully enough. The Cossacks canceled their procession and the Bolsheviks contented themselves with raising the morale of their supporters. Sukhanov attended a meeting addressed by Trotsky:

All around me was a mood bordering on ecstasy. It seemed as if the crowd, spontaneously and of its own accord, would break into some religious hymn. Trotsky formulated a brief and general resolution. . . .

Who was it for? The crowd of thousands, as one man, raised its hands.
. . .

This was also an occasion for reviling Kerensky. He did not need to
be reminded that Good Friday followed Palm Sunday, and his mood
that day must have been somber. When Polkovnikov failed to convene a conference of garrison delegates, Baranovsky and Voytinsky
were asked to send troops from the Northern front. Konovalov
informed Kerensky that the Military-Revolutionary Committee was
trying to take over the garrison. Kerensky insisted on the immediate
withdrawal of the MRC's order, "in the opposite case," he threatened, "the military powers will take energetic measures for the restoration of the legal order." That night, Kerensky abandoned
Alexander III's suite in the Winter Palace for the General Staff
Building.[30]

Two days remained until the Second Congress of Soviets. Though
everyone expected it to be dominated by the Bolsheviks, Lenin was
frantically anxious for an insurrection *before* the Congress met. He
would not feel secure until Kerensky was under lock and key in the
Peter-Paul Fortress. On October 27, Trotsky gained an important
victory by persuading the gunners in the fortress, overlooking the
Winter Palace, to submit to the Petrograd Soviet. Yet the bulk of
the garrison was still reluctant to take offensive action. Under pressure from Gotz and Bogdanov, the left-SRs on the MRC now forced
their Bolshevik comrades to withdraw any claim to jurisdiction over
the garrison. The Bolsheviks had backed down.[31]

Kerensky thought that he had won. Buoyed by a declaration of
support from the General Army Committee at GHQ, he now pressed
the All-Russian Executive Committee to sanction the arrest of the
Military-Revolutionary Committee. Instead, it was resolved merely
to prosecute them for sedition, return Trotsky and the other parolees
to prison, and suppress the Bolshevik press. (Two right-wing papers
would be shut down to maintain the semblance of fair play.)

General Bagratuni summoned the military cadets and the first Petrograd Women's Battalion to guard duty on Palace Square. At 5.00
AM on October 24, the cadets broke into the presses of the Bolshevik
papers, smashed the plates and sealed the doors. Trotsky was jubilant:
"Kerensky is on the offensive." Hours later, a company of Litovsky

Guards overwhelmed the government's militia picket and reopened the presses.

Again, Kerensky telegraphed the front for additional troops. In a futile attempt to disarm the Latvians, he now authorized the creation of a separate Latvian army corps. The forces in Petrograd seemed adequate for interim police duties. They included 2000 cadets, 200 women soldiers, and 134 unattached officers. Kerensky then returned to the Winter Palace, where David Soskice found him "absolutely undisturbed."

We knew from information received from the military authorities that the Government had the situation well in hand. I watched from Kerensky's windows in the upper floor of the Winter Palace how the loyal troops were taking possession of the bridges across the Neva, leaving one bridge open for the passage of the crowds. We saw the Women's Battalion regulating the movements of the crowds and arresting anyone who showed resistance. We all remembered the insurrection of the Bolsheviks of July 16–18, when, although little effort was made by the Government to resist them, they showed such a poor capacity for organization and such complete absence of any scheme or object that they were easily defeated and covered with ridicule.[32]

Just after midday, Kerensky arrived at the Mariinsky Palace to seek the support of the pre-parliament. In a controlled speech, he cited Lenin's attacks on Kamenev and Zinoviev and some of Trotsky's speeches. The parallels between Bolshevik and right-wing arguments were justification enough for their suppression. In a mirror-image of Lenin's logic, he argued that a rising in the capital was timed to facilitate another German offensive, to forestall the government's new land bill, the departure of the Russian delegation to the Allied Conference in Paris, and the elections of the Constituent Assembly.

Kerensky argued that he had treated the MRC with kid gloves so far, but announced that arrests had now been ordered. The Mensheviks and SR internationalists protested noisily, provoking some of Kerensky's old fire:

Yes, yes, listen, because at the present time, when the State is imperilled by deliberate or unwitting treason and is at the brink of ruin, the Provisional Government, myself included, prefers to be killed and destroyed [rather than to betray] the life, the honor, and the independence of the State.

For the last time, he qualified this statement in an effort to win over those for whom there could be no enemy on the left:

The Provisional Government can be reproached with weakness and extraordinary tolerance, but . . . no one has the right to say . . . that . . . [it] has ever resorted to any kind of repressive measures until there was a threat of immediate danger and peril to the State.

Konovalov handed him an intercepted message from the MRC, alerting the garrison for action. Kerensky held it up as further proof of Bolshevik treason that would play into the hands of the Germans, and the counterrevolution. He concluded his last public speech in Petrograd with an imperious demand for support. Even now, his performance was an immense success, and he departed to an overwhelming ovation.[33]

That afternoon, the telephone lines to the Smolny Institute were cut and some of the bridges were raised. Tram services were curtailed and the street lights failed to come on. Yet on Nevsky, the usual mixture of smart shoppers and theatergoers, cabbies and prostitutes milled about as usual. Many Bolsheviks remembered the July Days with apprehension and were anything but confident. For the impatient Lenin, still in hiding, the delay was intolerable. The Central Committee had still not taken a clear decision for a mass uprising, yet, as he wrote to them, "everything now hangs by a thread. . . . "It would be a disaster, or a sheer formality, to await the wavering vote [of the Congress of Soviets] of October 25. . . . The government is tottering. It must be *given the death-blow* at all costs. To delay action is fatal." In the end, the tension was too much. Slightly disguised, he defied the instructions of his Central Committee and took a tram to Smolny with a lone Finnish comrade.[34]

The party fractions in the pre-parliament had re-assembled. There was universal disapproval of Bolshevik activity, but a total absence of confidence in the government's ability to enforce order impartially. A resolution supporting Kerensky was defeated. Instead, it voted for Dan's Menshevik resolution demanding radical social policies and a new approach for peace and proposing the creation of a committee to supervise the impartial restoration of order.

Kerensky had left the pre-parliament confident of its support, so Dan's resolution came as a bitter disappointment. Dan, flanked by Gotz and Avksentiev, appealed to Kerensky to accept the resolution as the only possible bridge to the Constituent Assembly. For the last time, Menshevik logic was submerged by SR solidarity. Kerensky's threat to resign subdued Avksentiev, and Kerensky turned Dan down flat. The government would deal with the Bolsheviks by itself.[35]

October 25 dawned gray and chilly. Overnight, Lenin had succeeded in persuading the Military-Revolutionary Committee to adopt a more aggressive posture and they now took over the General Post Office, the Telephone Exchange, the Arsenal, and the railroad stations. Regular telephone communication ceased while the government's military communications' system became increasingly unreliable. As the depressing reports came in, Kerensky and Konovalov summoned the ministers for a meeting in the Malachite Hall of the Winter Palace. What had become of the reinforcements from the Northern front? It was agreed that Kerensky would go to meet them and rally their spirits. But how? The stations were in Bolshevik hands and so was the government car pool. Not a single functioning automobile remained at the disposal of the government.

Lieutenant Knirsh was sent to find cars, if necessary from the Allied Embassies. He returned with a Renault borrowed from Kerensky's friend, Prince Sidamon-Eristov, and an American Embassy automobile, complete with Old Glory. Gray with exhaustion, Kerensky struggled for words to console the pathetic garrison of the Winter Palace:

As supreme head of the Provisional Government and Supreme Commander of the army, I know nothing for certain. . . . But, as an old revolutionary, I address you, young revolutionaries, I beg you to remain at your posts and to defend the conquests of the revolution.

But many of his listeners saw him as the man who had "broken the plow on which he was sitting."[36]

Around 11:00 A.M., Kerensky, set off in the Renault with Captain Kozmin, Lieutenants Knirsh and Vinner. The American Embassy car was asked to lead, but the chauffeur refused as he did not know the route. From the arch of the General Staff Building, they sped past St. Isaac's and on to the Mariinsky Palace. Near the Catherine Canal, they halted briefly to avoid a Bolshevik cordon. Then, they were on to Zabalkansky Prospect and southward out of the city. Perhaps foreseeing accusations of cowardice, Kerensky frequently stood to receive the salutes of the men they passed.[37]

They arrived at Pskov after dark. There Baranovsky confirmed that troops were on their way, but advised him to check with Cheremisov. Kerensky was horrified to discover that Cheremisov had no intention of carrying out his instructions. For all his arguments, Cheremisov had an answer. The men would open the front to the Germans if reinforcements were sent to Petrograd, such troops would succumb to Bolshevik agitation themselves, and anyway, the government had already been arrested. Baranovsky later reported that Kerensky had given his "unwilling consent." "Alexander Fyodorovich experienced the agonies of hell from the hopelessness of carrying out what he felt to be his duty."[38]

Voytinsky then arrived with less depressing information and Kerensky realized that Cheremisov had misled him. Equally suspicious of Cheremisov was General P. N. Krasnov, commander of the Third Cavalry Corps, a convinced Kornilovite. He now joined them. This was his first close look at Kerensky:

A face with traces of heavy, sleepless nights. Pale, unhealthy, with an ill-looking skin and swollen red eyes. Clean-shaven like an actor. His head too large for his trunk. Military jacket, breeches, boots with gaiters—all this made him look like a civilian who had got himself up for a Sunday ride. He looks piercingly into your eyes, as if searching for a reply in the depths of the soul and not in the words; short, commanding phrases. He doesn't doubt that what he orders is carried out. . . .

Voytinsky found him on a sofa "in a state of complete prostration," but he soon recovered sufficiently to inform Krasnov that "the whole army stands behind me against those malcontents."[39]

By a malicious irony of fate, the Third Cavalry Corps, which Kerensky proposed to lead into battle, was the very unit sent by Kornilov to overawe Petrograd. Since then they had been dispersed on Kerensky's own instructions. Neither officers nor men entertained very warm feelings for him. At a meeting in Ostrov, a soldier shouted, "They've spilt a bit of our soldiers' blood," while a young officer refused to shake hands with Kerensky, explaining curtly, "I am a Kornilovite!"[40]

Kerensky had lunched hastily in the palace of the ill-fated Emperor Paul in Gatchina on October 25, and he returned there two days later, attended by the unenthusiastic Cossacks. Count Zubov, the acting steward of the palace, offered Kerensky his hospitality hoping to limit any further damage to the artistic treasures there. Kerensky was now in better humor and the Count found him at the billiard table. Cue in hand, Kerensky demanded accommodation for "his suite." Zubov found them rooms along the Kitchen Court but insisted that the Cossacks sleep, traditional style, under the open sky with their horses.

Lieutenant Knirsh, now Kerensky's "administrator," set to with gusto, sending radiotelegrams denying that the government had fallen. Normal telephone communications had been restored and news came from Petrograd that the Bolsheviks were not in full control and that many people were eagerly awaiting Kerensky's return. Yet his forces were slow to gather. The Latvians and the railroad workers impeded the rallying of Kornilovite troops. Krasnov commanded just three Cossack centuries and two guns, though Kerensky insisted that the Petrograd garrison supported him.[41]

During Kerensky's absence from Petrograd, the insurrection had continued to develop. Avksentiev had vainly argued himself hoarse in attempting to sway the garrison on the night of October 24–25. He could not convene the pre-parliament for want of a quorum, so he settled for a meeting of the party leaders in the Council of Elders, a sad echo of Kerensky's frustration in February. When Bolshevik soldiers threatened to shoot them, they passed a motion to disperse, "in view of the impossibility at the present time of calling plenary meetings." They decided to join the self-styled Committee for the Salvation of the Country and the Revolution. Many of the leading SRs had gone to the building of the Executive Committee of the Peasants' Soviets, to forestall its occupation by the left-SRs. The Committee of Salvation decided to gather its supporters at the City Duma that night.[42]

Kerensky's difficulties were shared by his enemies. Antonov-Ovseenko, the bespectacled intellectual charged by Lenin with the conquest of the Winter Palace, failed to meet his deadline. Lenin had insisted that the capture of the government precede the opening of the Soviet Congress at 2:00 P.M., but the Kronstadt sailors failed to arrive before 3:00, giving the lie to leaflets which had already been circulated announcing the capture of the ministers. Bolshevik forces showed little enthusiasm for action and, for a long time, the gunners

in the Peter-Paul Fortress refused to fire on the Winter Palace, making nonsense of Antonov's ultimatum to Konovalov to vacate the
Palace.[43]

Inside the Winter Palace, the gallant Stankevich assured the defenders that "the faith of the army in the present composition of the
Government, headed by the revered Alexander Fyodorovich Kerensky, is unusually strong." The women and cadets were unconvinced and begged the ministers to explain why they were fighting.
The commissar of the government's horse artillery decided to change
sides and absconded with the guns, while the Cossacks began to
mutter about defending "women and Yids" from the "Russian people" outside. After talks with Bolshevik representatives, they
marched out of the Palace early in the evening. This pathetic spectacle
demoralized the ministers. Konovalov was upset, Terehchenko excited, and Tretyakov accused Kerensky of betraying them. Their
decision to wait out their capture in the Malachite Hall owed more
to inertia than heroism.[44]

By 10:40 P.M., Lenin had run out of pretexts for postponing the
Soviet Congress and Dan presided as the packed and excited gathering elected a new All-Russian Central Executive Committee consisting of 14 Bolsheviks, 7 Left-SRs, 3 Mensheviks, and one
Menshevik Internationalist. The defeated SRs and Mensheviks were
angry. Captain Kharash denounced the victors: "The political hyp-
ocrites who control this Congress told us we were to settle the
question of Power—and it is being settled behind our backs, before
the Congress opens!" They walked out to the sound of cannon fire
as Trotsky verbally consigned them to the garbage-heap of history.[45]

That night, the members of the Committee of Salvation marched
from the City Duma toward the Winter Palace. They were halted
by Bolshevik sailors who would neither shoot them nor let them
pass—though one offered to spank them. Prokopovich exclaimed,
"we cannot have our innocent blood upon the hands of these ignorant
men," and they dispersed peacefully, honor satisfied. Further down
Nevsky, the indomitable Olga Kerenskaya was tearing down proclamations announcing the fall of the government. She was arrested by
a Bolshevik crowd but soon released, and the MRC, evidently well-
informed she and her husband lived apart, published an order to
leave her in peace.[46]

At around eleven P.M., the cruiser *Aurora*, searchlights ablaze, opened up on the Winter Palace with thunderous blank rounds. The Peter-Paul Fortress and smaller naval vessels joined in with real ammunition and there was increasing small arms fire across Palace Square. Infiltration and discussion played as large a part in wearing down the garrison as did gunfire, and the role of the latter was psychological as well as murderous. By 2:00 A.M. on October 26, twelve hours late by Lenin's timetable, the Winter Palace had fallen. The hapless ministers were escorted through jeering Bolshevik crowds to detention in the Peter-Paul Fortress.[47]

It was widely alleged that several of the women soldiers were raped, and one young woman did commit suicide. Less well-known was the fact that British diplomatic intervention was successful in protecting the women. The allegation of rape increased revulsion against Kerensky in many circles. His own silence on the women soldiers of 1917 is part of a familiar pattern of patriarchal erasure, the product of collective "masculine" shame.[48]

On the evening of October 27, Kerensky telephoned his friends to say that he would be in Petrograd with loyal troops in the morning. He spoke to Olga and his sister, Elena, at the home of his old friend, Somov. They had gone to bed "reassured and joyful," but the following day was "gray and cloudy" and their spirits wilted. Other witnesses remember the day as fine, but for Olga and the boys, the atmosphere was what counted. When Olga asked a soldier where he was off to, he replied grimly, "to kill Kerensky." Not that all the Bolsheviks' enemies were equally dispirited. There were rumors that the garrison was out of sympathy with the new regime, while in the British Embassy, Buchanan and Noulens met to plan for the stationing of Allied troops in Petrograd after Kerensky's return.[49]

On October 28, Kerensky and Krasnov advanced as far as Tsarskoe Selo, where the small band of disciplined Cossacks confronted a sullen crowd of pro-Bolshevik soldiers. Kerensky could no more resist the urge to save lives than could Prokopovich. He ordered his car between the opposing forces and attempted to win over the Bolsheviks. His address was a fiasco which ended in fraternization. That night, he returned to Gatchina, where Krasnov told him he would have to keep his mouth shut in future.[50]

The Committee of Salvation tried to synchronize an uprising to coincide with Kerensky's arrival, but it was mistimed, and on October 28 came the news that the Moscow Kremlim had been re-taken by anti-Bolshevik forces after a stiff fight. The next day, the Bolsheviks set out to disarm the Petrograd military schools. The "boy heroes" had no choice but to fight or surrender. There was heavy fighting and the cadets were crushed only by the use of artillery. Outraged by the bloodletting, the humanitarians on the Central Committee of the Railroad Union warned both sides that it would deny them trains unless they stopped fighting and begin negotiations for an all-socialist coalition.[51]

The Railroadmen's leader, de Planson visited Kerensky with Chernov on the evening of October 29, to urge him to negotiate with the Bolsheviks. Kerensky reacted with irritation to advice he considered unhelpful. He was supported by Voytinsky, Stankevich, and Gotz, who urged him to go to GHQ to gather loyal troops. They drafted an appeal to the army, warning that "the whole burden of responsibility for delay falls on the procrastinators." At Stankevich's instigation, Kerensky now appointed Avksentiev his successor, just in case.[52]

When Stankevich woke the next morning, he discovered that Kerensky had changed his mind, under the influence of Boris Savinkov. Savinkov seems to been tempted to use his influence with the Cossacks to oust Kerensky as leader of the Third Cavalry Corps, and he may even have considered Kerensky's assassination. (A warning by Zubov had just saved Kerensky from a deranged monarchist.) In the event, Savinkov deferred dealing with Kerensky pending the imminent battle with the Bolsheviks, and appealed for support from such reliable units as the Polish Rifle Division.[53]

By the morning of October 30, Krasnov's command consisted of only nine Cossack centuries, eighteen field guns, an armored car, and an armored train. Baranovsky's frantic efforts in Pskov had been vigorously countered by the Latvians. Krasnov also commandeered two planes from the Gatchina flying schools, which dropped proclamations in Petrograd announcing Kerensky's return.

They rode and drove to the low, sandy hills just seven miles southwest of Petrograd, overlooking the observatory at Pulkovo. The skies were gray and there was a biting wind. Over ten thousand Bolshevik troops were haphazardly dug in behind the scanty cover. The Cossack traditions stood firm, but they could make no headway in the face of withering small arms fire. Eventually, they withdrew.

For the Cossacks, this was the last straw and they began to long for their beloved Don.

Five days of hypertension and insomnia had left Kerensky incapable of coping with the frenetic lobbying to which he was now subjected. Chernov advised him to negotiate with the Bolsheviks, while Savinkov counseled resistance. Stankevich and even Savinkov now accepted that negotiations via the railroadmen might buy time. Savinkov still hoped for Polish assistance. Kerensky was tempted to agree but could not commit himself. Savinkov then left in disgust, while Krasnov began to think of ways of getting his men back to the Don.[54]

As October 31 dawned, there were rumors of approaching loyal troops, but instead Gatchina Palace began to fill up with unfamiliar, hostile faces, a repetition of the technique of infiltration and persuasion which had eroded the garrison of the Winter Palace. Soon, the sailors arrived, under the command of the laughing, bearded Bolshevik Dybenko. Kerensky talked repeatedly about the need for energetic action, though there was no longer any possibility of taking any. He and Kozmin also reminisced about happier times gone by. Sometime before 11:00 A.M., Krasnov warned Kerensky that the Cossacks were discussing the idea of exchanging him for Lenin; the wily Dybenko was encouraging some such deception. Krasnov disingenuously offered Kerensky a Cossack "guard" for direct negotiations with Lenin in Petrograd.

This was, of course, a counsel of death, and Kerensky's aides searched desperately for a way out of the Palace. The Kitchen Court had only one heavily guarded exit, and Kerensky and Lieutenant Vinner, a close political and personal friend, resolved on suicide. At the last moment, the SR military organization came to their assistance, in the guise of a young soldier named Belenky and an SR sailor. Kerensky donned the sailor's uniform as instructed, adding a pair of aviators goggles to mask his features. Belenky led the grotesque figure out through the crowds of fraternizing Cossacks and sailors and through the main gate. There a sympathizer feigned a collapse to distract the Bolshevik soldiers. Kerensky found a car waiting for him at the Chinese Gate of Gatchina village, and they drove off toward Luga at high speed, pursued for a while by shooting monarchists. Kerensky's chauffeur offered to drive the pursuing Bolshevik soldiers, and then simulated a breakdown. The Palace servant who put on Kerensky's greatcoat was beaten and later executed.[55]

The debacle was complete. The Provisional Government had fallen without a serious fight. It had found few mourners and fewer martyrs. The anti-Bolsheviks of Petrograd and Moscow had fought without any commitment to the restoration of the Provisional Government. If there was hostility to Bolshevism, there was no love lost for Kerensky. He himself vacillated to the end, seeming to accept advice from the left and right and acting on neither. By October 31 he was in an appalling state, possibly drugged with tranquilizers as an unfriendly witness suggests. But even in these straits, Kerensky remained true to the principles which had once impelled him into politics. When, on October 29, he was asked to take steps against the Bolsheviks in Gatchina, Kerensky refused. In defeat as in victory, Kerensky's supreme value was the freedom of the individual.[56]

16

Regeneration?

Even the most scrupulous of Soviet historians claims that "as a political activist," Kerensky "died" in November 1917. It would be more accurate to say that he had been "knocked out." Ejected from the center to the periphery of Russian life, for several years he continued to play an active and significant part in Russian politics. As Lenin himself recognized, until his regime asserted its control over every aspect of Russian life, the anti-Bolshevik socialist parties "objectively reserved for themselves the role of a potential political force, despite their organizational weakness and isolation from the popular masses."[1] Many of the intellectual cadres of the PSR regarded Kerensky with admiration still. Had they recovered control he would certainly have regained an honorable niche in Russian life.

Throughout his period in office, Kerensky had sought the support of his party while remaining "above" its disciplines. After his non-election to the Central Committee, he had frequently treated the leaders of the PSR with contempt. In the immediate aftermath of the Bolshevik coup his very physical survival depended on the party's military organization, and at first even Avksentiev, Gotz, and Zenzinov spurned his advice. Eventually, this·humiliating dependency was replaced by a more honorable part in the party's councils and a vital "diplomatic" mission to the West. When Clemenceau and Churchill threw their weight behind the extreme right in Russia, Kerensky appealed to liberal and socialist opinion in Europe. Later, he sought American assistance in an effort to mitigate the barbarities of Admiral Kolchak's counterrevolutionary forces. Finally, he be-

came a key figure in his party's attempts to promote a Third Revolution. Despite the debacle he had suffered—or because of it—he
never stopped trying to restore democracy, as he understood it, to
the Russian people.

It was not just the political circumstances of his life that had
changed. For eight hectic months, he had been besieged by advisers,
petitioners, and even blackmailers, and while he had tried to stay
ahead of events, all too often he had merely reacted to them. Now
he was a petitioner himself. The external pressure on him was gone,
to be replaced by an internal commitment to regain what had been
lost, to atone for his past mistakes and to give the lie to those who
alleged that he had been merely a carpetbagger of the revolution like
Khlestakov in the *Inspector-general*.[2] His Bolshevik (and his reactionary) enemies made this psychologically easier for him by subjecting
him to slander and by persecuting his relatives, friends, and comrades. Yet time moved slowly. The frenetic pace which had sustained
him in 1917 was gone. He compensated by skiing through the snow-
covered forests of Russia and Finland, and later by tramping over
the Weald and the hills of Prague and through the Bois de Boulogne,
ruminating always on Russia and her destiny.

The previous August, Kerensky had told Ambassador Noulens
that the key to the Russian character was to be found in Tolstoy's
Power of Darkness. "It is after touching the depths of the ordeal that
we have known the finest hours of our history." He had no doubt
that Bolshevism was another "power of darkness" which would
pass.[3] Unlike some of his comrades, he did not expect this to happen
spontaneously. The Russian people needed the leadership that only
a nationally respected alternative government could provide. The
resources at his disposal—the pen and the SR courier service—sound
pathetic until one remembers that these were precisely the means
employed to such devastating effect by Lenin after the July Days.

After the fall of the Winter Palace, two institutions remained which
might have become the focus for the re-creation of a viable provisional government. The one that offered most hope was GHQ, where
General Dukhonin, and the Menshevik-led General Army Committee held sway. By November 1, Kerensky had resigned in favor
of Avksentiev and for a week it looked as though an Avksentiev
government might emerge in Mogilev. Kerensky had no intention
of being a passive spectator of this process, but when he begged the

party to let him come to GHQ, they turned him down. In the words of his young SR "minder," V. O. Fabrikant, "all his initiatives conflicted with the panic and helplessness of his political friends, whose position was not, in any case, enviable."[4]

Meanwhile, in Petrograd, the Bolsheviks had still not got round to closing down the ghostly Provisional Government or "Little Council" of assistant ministers, who met under Demyanov at the Ministry of Justice. The majority of civil servants accepted Demyanov's authority, especially as the deputy ministers had forged an entry in the *Zhurnaly zasedanii* (Provisional Government minutes) authorizing them to pay civil service salaries. Otherwise morale was low. Gotz and Avksentiev ignored this "government" and the Moscow Committee of Public Salvation refused to have anything to do with it. Absurdly, Prokopovich, the sole full minister, demanded dictatorial powers and issued orders. When the Bolsheviks cunningly released the socialist ministers as "class comrades," they were exposed to the contempt of the bourgeoisie. To the relief of the ministers, Kerensky's resignation as Premier was confirmed, though he still considered himself a member of the government and even confirmed one of its "laws." This Provisional Government might have offered useful administrative facilities to a government at GHQ. It had no political authority of its own.[5]

While negotiations were going on between Mogilev and the underground in Petrograd, Kerensky set down his own inflammatory appeal to the Russian people:

Come to your senses! Don't you see that your simplicity has been abused and that they have shamelessly deceived you? They promised to give you peace with the Germans within three days, and now the traitors pray for it. But the face of the Russian land is soaked in the blood of your brothers;. ... They promised you bread, but a frightful famine is already beginning its domination, and your children will understand who is killing them. ... This is me speaking to you, Kerensky. Kerensky, whom your leaders have defamed as a "counter-revolutionary" and "Kornilovite," but whom the "Kornilovites" wanted to had over into the hands of the deserter Dybenko and those with him. ... Only now, when the violence and horror of Leninist coercion, his dictatorship with Trotsky, reign, only now has it become clear even to the blind that in the period when I was in power, there was real freedom and genuine democracy. ... Come to your senses or it will be too late and our state will perish. Hunger, unemployment will destroy the happiness of your families and once more we shall return under the yoke of slavery. Come to your senses![6]

The SR Central Committee was not going to have Kerensky upset their delicate negotiations at GHQ, nor upset the delegates to the imminent Second Congress of Peasant Soviets and they sat on this appeal. Time was when Kerensky would have circumvented them by contacting Breshkovskaya and Argunov, the militant defencist editor of *Volia Naroda*, but his paper, though nominally "socialist," soon began to suffer the same repressive treatment as the "bourgeois" press.[7]

The proposed government at GHQ was wrecked both by Allied intransigence and the growing radicalism of the masses. The Allies refused to sanction a Russian ceasefire, and when, on November 17, the Allied Conference, on which the SRs and Mensheviks had pinned so many hopes, finally convened in Paris, Clemenceau's response to British attempts to raise the question was brutal: "Alors. . . . vous voulez que je remercie les gens qui me volent mon portemonnaie?" Dukhonin remained loyal to the Treaty of Paris until three days later, when Bolshevik soldiers beat him to death.[8]

Even before this tragedy, things had continued to go wrong for Kerensky's comrades. On November 7, the General Army Committee reluctantly decided that only Chernov could now command mass loyalty. However, Chernov fluffed his lines once more, refusing to take on the proferred role pending a mandate from a special army congress and from the Peasant Soviets. This gave the Bolshevized Northern front ample time to adopt military counter-measures, while the peasant delegates rebuffed Chernov by electing to the Chair his erstwhile Left-SR pupil, Maria Spiridonova, now leader of a separate party. Naturally, Gotz and Avksentiev had lost interest in the project once it had been associated with Chernov. Instead they now begged 300,000 Rubles from the 'Provisional Government' in Petrograd. The "ministers" sanctimoniously turned down this request and on November 16, the "government" wound up its business, accusing the Committee of Salvation of failing to support the legal government. Kerensky expressed his solidarity with this pathetic declaration.[9]

Dukhonin's murder, and the opening of negotiations at Brest-Litovsk, persuaded the majority of the SR Central Committee that no harm could now come from the publication of Kerensky's appeal in *Delo Naroda*, so far unscathed from Bolshevik repression. To render the message absolutely innocuous, Chernov had it prefaced by an introduction describing it as a "cry of the exhausted and wounded soul of the man, who had played such a major role in the first phase of the Russian revolution." The author betrayed continuing resentment at Kerensky's former popularity:

It was precisely the mob which raised Kerensky so high, the same mob threw him down. Like a child, it broke the toy it had just started playing with. The mob is blind in both its love and its hatred. . . . the adulation with which the mob surrounded Kerensky was always foreign and repulsive to us.

Kerensky, his name trampled in the mud, must now "hide somewhere and wander about" [*skryvat'sia i skitat'sia*]. This phrase was an ironic reference to those "true tsars" of Russian social-utopian legend, who hoped one day to return to free their people.

For Kerensky, this odious note was redeemed by the promise that he would attend the opening of the Constituent Assembly. "At that time, he will account for his activities to the people, who will be able to judge the positive, as well as the negative aspects of A. F. Kerensky's political work."[10]

At the beginning of December, the PSR took advantage of the relative immunity offered by the Second Congress of Peasant Soviets to convene their own Fourth Party Congress. The Peasant Soviets split into two almost equal halves—a pro-Chernov right wing, largely peasants from the villages, and the young peasants in uniform who followed the Left SRs and Bolsheviks. Kerensky's letter of greeting was read to the congress, but Chernov resumed his attacks on Kerensky's policies and his alleged abuse of the party's trust. Kerensky was manfully defended by Lebedev, his former deputy in the Navy Ministry, who insisted that Chernov must share the blame for the policies of the coalition, including the repression of left SRs in July. When Chernov accused him of lying, Lebedev challenged him to a court of arbitration. Lebedev was particularly indignant about Chernov's articles after the Kornilov affair: "These articles knifed Kerensky in the back; they constituted a betrayal of him; it was these articles that sank him." "He already was sunk!" shouted Chernov and his friends.

Zenzinov admitted that Kerensky had ignored the party's discipline and it emerged that Kerensky had ceased to represent the party in the government after July, though this had never been publicly stated. This was typical of the party. It still failed to decide on a strategy for the reconstitution of a legitimate central government, on the action to be taken should the Allies persist in blocking a general armistice, and on what to do should the national minorities reject the limited autonomy they proposed to concede. Everything contentious was left to the Constituent Assembly.[11]

Russia's only democratic elections took place in the second half of November. No final results were ever announced but the provincial list system ensured the election of all the party leaders. Lenin and Trotsky, Spiridonova and Kamkov would be faced by Milyukov, Tsereteli, and Chernov. Of the old-style right, fear of which had rationalized the timidity of the moderate left during 1917, only General Kaledin and the Archbishop of Nizhnii Novgorod were elected. The Ukrainian socialists had proclaimed a Ukrainian People's Republic and their participation was uncertain. The new bourgeois majority in the Finnish assembly did not wait for the Russian Constituent Assembly, but declared Finland independent on November 23.[12]

Kerensky was elected from no fewer than five districts, including Saratov, which he had once represented in the Duma. The SR-Peasant Soviet list won nearly a million votes, but even in this haven of rural radicalism, the Bolsheviks harvested a staggering 225,000 votes. Kerensky's personal popularity was on the wane even here. The "Kerensky Museum" established in his house in Volsk in the Spring was now destroyed by arson. Some voters even scratched his name from an SR list that predated the party schism and included a Left SR he had sent to prison in July.[13]

The PSR rejoiced. They had won some 340 seats out of a national total of 816—more than twice as many as the Bolsheviks—though the expulsion of 40 Left SRs reduced this margin. To create a ruling coalition, the PSR would need another 100 allies. But neither the Kadets nor the Mensheviks, their preferred allies, would reach even 20 seats. The Kadets now represented little more than the urban bourgeoisie, while the Mensheviks were merely the spokesmen for the Jewish and Georgian working classes. The SRs now had to face the uncomfortable fact, evaded by almost all Russian democrats since the 1897 Census, that no Great Russian party could rule Russia democratically on its own. The SRs might get the support of their Ukrainian and Tatar counterparts, but only by compromising over the war and the future constitution of the Russian state.[14] Lenin had every intention of sparing the SRs this agonizing dilemma.

Lenin must surely have sniggered at the SR promise that Kerensky would attend the Constituent. Bolshevik propagandists had impugned Kerensky's manhood, by claiming that he had fled dressed as a nurse; his probity, by claiming that he had embezzled a large quantity of cash; and his democratic principles, by asserting that he had gone to join General Kaledin on the Don. Olga Kerensky protested to the Bolshevik press about the allegation of embezzlement, and she felt it received less prominence thereafter.[15]

Kerensky's kindly peasant hosts in Lyapunov Dvor were not the only people who disbelieved the slanders. In Moscow, an English nurse asked her hosts about Kerensky's fate. They replied confidently:

It may be that he is in hiding, biding his time until the moment is ripe for him to defy the commissaries of Bolshevism. If he is still alive, he will not leave his country in the lurch.

As it became clear that the PSR was incapable of creating an alternative government without him, more began to think of Kerensky.

In those troubled days, many, many people in Russia preserved in the secret [recesses] of their souls the belief that A. F. K. would again accomplish one of those miracles, by which he had saved Russia and the revolution in the most tragic moments of the past year.[16]

Kerensky's hosts, the aunt and uncle of an SR soldier, epitomized those basic decencies of Russian village life to which, he must have hoped, the disorientated rural lads would soon return, to be reminded of their duties by venerable fathers and warm-hearted mothers.[17] Yet he was desperately anxious to move closer to Petrograd, where he could exert more influence over his comrades on the eve of the Constituent Assembly. Eventually, his friends secured the agreement of the Central Committee, probably by representing his move as a prelude to exile. Boris Moiseenko was entrusted with the responsibility for his safety. He recruited Fabrikant to help him.

As Kerensky said his farewells to his benefactors on December 7, they put an ikon of the crucifixion around his neck and blessed him:

"Go, Alexander Fyodorovich, and save Russia!" Kerensky, a super-stitious man, was deeply affected and it was many years before he would part with the ikon. His guards then escorted him to a farm near Oredezh railroad station to meet Moiseenko and Fabrikant. Fabrikant immediately recognized the famous face despite the new beard and moustache. Relieved of the burden of representing the state, Kerensky was once more,

a typical Russian *intelligent*... one of the many Russian idealists, ... with whom I had been educated in the same ideals and aspirations, on the very same books, in the lap of the same great country, with the tender distances of her limitless horizons. It seemed to me that AFK became the political Leader [*vozhd'*] of the Russian intelligentsia, precisely because he ... incorporated everything, by which the soul of the Russian *intelligent* had lived for decades.

They set off on horse sledges, making brief stops at peasant farms, where Kerensky's portrait still hung in places of honor, though he had to cower in dark corners to avoid recognition. Savinkov's ex-wife had given them introductions to SRs in Novgorod and they negotiated the Bolshevik picket on the Volkov Bridge unchallenged. After a freezing journey along the frozen Malaya Vishera river, they arrived at the intended refuge at Shchelkalovo village. The hut was awful: tiny, unheatable, and filthy—and evidently frequented by the local Bolshevik peasants' soviet. For a few days Kerensky had to accept the protection of Dr. Frizen at the Novgorod Psychiatric Hospital.

Better accommodation was soon found at Lyadno, the estate of the well-known Populist family, the Kamenskys, close to the Mos-cow-Petrograd railroad. From there, Kerensky bombarded his com-rades with appeals for insurrection, as Lenin had done in September. The parallel is striking:

A. F. K. considered that it was necessary first to create armed forces which could support the Constituent Assembly *manu militari* in the event of an infringement of it by the Bolsheviks, i.e., that it was necessary to overthrow the regime of the Bolshevik soviets, before the meeting of the Constituent Assembly.

The contorted logic of both men contained a sound grasp of the dynamics of power.[18] Kerensky's view was shared by the SR military commission which began to plan an armed demonstration to support the Constituent. The SR Colonel Keller offered a unit of armored cars and there were half promises from the Semyonovsky and Preobrazhensky Guards. Unhappily for the SRs, morale was weak: no one wanted to be the first to attract the attentions of the Kronstadt sailors and Latvian Riflemen.[19] In the end it was compromised by an incident which brought back painful memories of the insubordinate traditions of the Central Terror.

For some weeks, a small group of SRs and independents, including such past and future friends of Kerensky as Nekrasov and his brother, Boris Sokolov, and Nikolai Martyanov, had been planning Lenin's assassination. On January 1, 1918, they fired four shots at Lenin's car as it passed them on Fontanka Quay. The Bolshevik press incited reprisals. Terrified anti-Bolsheviks denied the reports, hoping to avert a pogrom of the intelligentsia. The armed demonstration was called off.[20]

After a farewell New Year party at Lyadno, Kerensky was escorted back to Petrograd by Fabrikant and three SR guards. His arrival at Nikolaevsky Station coincided with the attack on Lenin. He passed unrecognized through the soldiers clearing snow at the Station and was soon reunited with Olga and the boys, who had survived Bolshevik searches and harassment. He was then hidden in a student's apartment on the Petersburg side.[21] When Zenzinov visited him the next day, Kerensky demanded his ticket for the Constituent. Zenzinov was horrified, but Kerensky pleaded with him: how could he let his supporters down and allow the Bolsheviks to call him a coward? Kerensky claimed that he then put an even more daring plan to Zenzinov. It is worth remembering his repeated public allusions to a ritual suicide during 1917. Had he finally understood that a cause, however noble, that cannot find martyrs, will fail before one, however barbaric, that can?

Zenzinov brought him nothing but disappointments. He could not attend the opening, the armed demonstration was off and, the bitterest blow of all, Chernov was to be proposed as Chairman of the Assembly. For Kerensky, as for the great majority of the Russian intelligentsia, January 5–6, 1918 were days of psychological torture, as Lenin defiled and humiliated the democratic body. In a scene reminding Gorky of Bloody Sunday 1905, Red Guards shot at least nine demonstrators dead and wounded twenty more. The galleries of the Tauride Palace were thoughtfully filled with drunken sailors who periodically looked down their rifle sights at the spokesmen of the majority. Chernov and Tsereteli spoke in terms of urbane Marxist dissent, offering no national or ethical principles to justify resistance. When the Bolsheviks and Left SRs walked out, the majority carried on talking until 3:00 A.M. When their tired guards ordered them to cut things short, they scrambled through "laws" on the land question, peace, and a federal constitution—shot through with the ambiguities that had marked their policies in 1917. There was no attempt to create a new government, no tennis court oath and no Vyborg Manifesto. When the deputies returned to the Tauride Palace the next afternoon, they found the gates of the Tauride Gardens locked; machine guns and artillery behind them. Lenin was no more intimidated by the Constituent than Stolypin had been by the First Duma. That night, Bolshevik sailors dragged Kokoshkin and Shingaryov from hospital beds, where they had been detained because of the state of their health, and beat them to death.

Kerensky was as depressed as his fellow intellectuals. He had himself been slandered and abused. Dybenko had humorously proposed him as Chernov's secretary, while a Siberian SR had equated his orders to shoot mutineers in 1917 to the day's massacre by the Red Guards. "After the dissolution of the Constituent Assembly," Kerensky grimly recorded, "the atmosphere in Petrograd became unbearable. . . . It was therefore decided that I should go to Finland until the situation became clearer." This was a compromise between the Central Committee demand that he go abroad and his own refusal to desert Russia at this terrible moment in her history.[22]

At midnight on January 9, Fabrikant and a "Swedish doctor," accompanied by their "wives," passed through the Bolshevik controls at the Finland Station. The journey to Helsinki passed without incident, and Wolter Stenbäck met them at the Central Station. The Stenbäcks were veterans of the 1905 SR–Finnish Activist alliance and Stenbäck's mother, Sofia, met them joyfully, though they were soon aware of the growing Russophobia of the Finnish bourgeoisie and peasantry. Kerensky appeared in high spirits, bursting into arias and recalling his childhood ambition to become an actor. The Stenbäcks' apartment on Kirkkokatu was impossibly exposed and on Saturday, January 13/26, Kerensky set off with Wolter and his sister, Greta, for a safer refuge. For the third time, he missed a Bolshevik rising by the skin of his teeth, as the Finnish Social Democrats now carried out their own coup and proclaimed a workers' and peasants' government.[23]

The little party finally reached Kullo Gård, a farmhouse near Borgå, belonging to veteran Activists Carl Frankenhäuser and his Russian-speaking wife. As the Finnish Civil War erupted, the Swedish-speaking Borgå district remained a White enclave in southeast Finland, cut off from the Vasa area, where Svinhufvud and Mannerheim were rallying the Finnish Whites. The incognito Kerensky was soon exposed to some embarrassment at a family party, when a lady, who had insisted that she would never forget Kerensky's blue eyes, asked him whether he thought that Kerensky had embezzled 12 million Rubles.[24] After a while, he was moved again, to Illby Gård, the farm of Constantin Boijé, a former Russian officer and Lutheran missionary, whose only Russian book was the Bible he lent Kerensky, another portent of Kerensky's approaching reconciliation with Orthodoxy. In the middle of February, an emissary of the Finnish White government arrived to offer Kerensky a German safe-conduct. Kerensky was incensed. This would put him on a par with Lenin. He sent Boijé's daughter, Maria, to Petrograd to demand permission to return. The PSR refused. He decided to defy them and returned at once to Helsinki. There Lilya joined him for a few days, leaving her cousin the unenviable job of finding their baby daughter a wet-nurse.

The Russophobia of the White Finns offended Kerensky, but he was encouraged by Finnish determination to resist Bolshevism. He felt that the social structure and political traditions of Finland precluded the risk of a repressive military regime.[25] Surely, the Russians could do as well. The situation inside Russia now offered some solid grounds for optimism. The Treaty of Brest-Litovsk had finally been signed, but not without shaking the Bolshevik Party to the core. The alliance with the Left SRs, already strained by their differing attitudes to the peasantry, was now near the breaking point. The proletarian base had been weakened by a massive spontaneous evacuation of the capitals—900,000 from Petrograd alone—as hungry workers sought food and shelter with peasant relatives. Those who remained were increasingly polarized between the fortunates co-opted by the new bureaucracies and those still at the workbench. In March 1918, there was a serious attempt to create a non-Bolshevik organization of workers, whose stated aims included support for the Constituent Assembly.[26]

The right reaped few benefits from the discomfiture of the Bolsheviks. At the end of January 1918, General Kaledin, Ataman of
the Don, committed suicide as Cossacks returning from the front
brought civil war to that region. The Bolsheviks took Rostov, driving the Kadet-sponsored Volunteer Army, under Kornilov, into the
Kuban. On April 13 Kornilov was killed at Ekaterinodar, and Denikin assumed the command. So desperate were the Kadets that
Milyukov traveled to Kiev to seek German assistance.[27]

On January 9, 1918, Kerensky arrived alone and unrecognized in
Petrograd. He found Olga and the boys at his mother-in-law's apartment. He must have been shaken by their poverty, reduced as they
were to scratching a living from a cottage industry in cigarette production,—to the mockery of the Bolshevik press. Kerensky was sent
to stay with Dr. Olga Maximova, a medical colleague of Peshekhonov's wife, and a great admirer of Kerensky's, who lived on
Vasilievsky Island.[28]

The SR leadership made the best of a bad job, keeping Kerensky
busy writing a book on the "least understood and most compromising incident of his Premiership, the Kornilov affair." He was
provided with "all the materials of Procurator Shablovsky's investigating commission." Kerensky's first book is an edited and annotated version of the transcript of his examination by the
commission. Kerensky was candid about his motives in writing this
book—and all his others. "The Great Russian Revolution . . . must
not be shadowed by the smallest doubt as to the honesty of those
who were linked to it in life and death."

Kerensky was now embarrassed by the "goody goody sentimen-
talism" that had once ruled out the assassination of Lenin and Trotsky, though he insisted that Kornilov's proposals to apply the death
penalty to industrial disputes had been unworkable. Kornilov's heroic
death occurred a week after the ostensible date of the book's completion and Kerensky's memorable epitaph described him sympa-
thetically as "a fiery man, loving his country, but fated with his own
hands to prepare the victory of those who hated and despised her!"
His description of the Russian people as "deceived and degraded . . .
dancing and grimacing in a repulsive fool's cap before its cruel master
of Berlin" was intended to justify socialist participation in an anti-
Bolshevik civil war. His preference for persuasion was still in evidence as he urged patriotic Russians not to lose heart:

Do not curse the popular masses; do not desert them. Go to the people with words of *stern truth*; rouse its slumbering conscience, and, sooner than you think, its manliness will revive and rekindle the sacrificial flame of its love of Motherland and Freedom![29]

Kerensky was partly insulated from Russian politics as his comrades had followed the Bolshevik government to Moscow after the Treaty of Brest-Litovsk. He was still in touch with both his families. On one occasion, he offered to take ten year-old Gleb to see his baby half-sister. He could not bring himself to announce the new arrival to Oleg until the very moment of his departure for Moscow. As he went down the stairs for the last time, he turned and stated bluntly, "You have a sister." This was a blow for Oleg, who had continued to hope for a reconciliation between his parents.[30]

Fabrikant and his brother escorted Kerensky onto a sleeping car at the Nikolaevsky Station. When Fabrikant awoke, he was horrified to hear Kerensky and his brother in a row about Chernov's appointment to the Ministry of Agriculture in 1917. Despite this security lapse, Kerensky was soon installed in the apartment of Elizaveta Nelidova-Khenkina near Patriarch's Ponds. Now he could participate directly in the debates of his comrades. He immediately committed himself in support of those arguing for "a war within [to] purchase a renewal of the war on the front." The right SRs had resumed control of the party from Chernov and were able to rescuscitate a shadowy form of coalition, by creating a Union for the Regeneration of Russia, embracing left-Kadets and Mensheviks. Meanwhile, French Consul-General Grenard had been canvassing the possibility of Allied intervention. At its eighth Council, the PSR endorsed this idea conditionally. They demanded that the Allies respect Russian sovereignty and territorial integrity and that their agreements with the Allies have the force of treaties. Avksentiev was despatched to Vologda to invite Ambassador Noulens to accede to these conditions.[31]

This surprising willingness of the Allies to deal with the SRs was dictated by the *de facto* alliance of all the right with the Germans. In the Ukraine, the Germans had replaced the moderate socialists by an authoritarian Hetmanate, while encouraging General Krasnov to proclaim the independence of the neighboring Don Cossacks. Their supplies crossed the Don in support of the officially pro-Allied Volunteer Army. In Finland, the Germans had retaken Helsinki, while Mannerheim had broken the Finnish Reds in Vyborg Castle.[32]

The SR invitation to the Allies was entirely in the spirit of President Wilson's Fourteen Points, which had seen in "the treatment accorded Russia by her sister nations . . . the acid test of their goodwill . . . and of their intelligent and unselfish sympathy." American rhetoric obscured the irony that the SRs, who had once asked Albert Thomas and Buchanan to oust Milyukov, were now demanding military intervention by the Allies—most of whom despised them—while insisting that they keep their noses out of Russian politics.

In reality, intervention had already begun with Trotsky's toleration of a British counterweight in Murmansk to the advancing White Finns and Germans, and with the landing of British and Japanese marines at Vladivostok. When the Czechoslovak legionaries revolted on May 14, Bolshevik authority in Siberia was broken and the outlines of a new anti-Bolshevik front began to appear. Kerensky's closest comrades had a hand in the Czech revolt and on June 8, they themselves overthrew Bolshevik power in Samara, proclaiming a new provisional government called KOMUCH, or the Committee of the Constituent Assembly. In a classic piece of Allied doublethink, the French government welcomed this move, while refusing to recognize it on the grounds that its authority was impaired by the absence of Bolsheviks and Left SRs![33]

Kerensky now appeared to visitors as "a long-haired, bearded man wearing thick blue spectacles," like "the intellectuals of the 1860–70 period. . . . an intelligent and sincere person . . . who might fill the role of a teacher or a preacher." He was welcomed with personal kindness everywhere, but even Babushka Breshkovskaya took him to task for his failures—especially the appointment of Chernov—in 1917. She mentioned others who might have conducted a rapid land reform, as the Armenian SRs had, defusing peasant radicalism in time. Kerensky disagreed. "Any haste, any nervousness under the pressure of appetites sharpened by demagogy would merely have led to such agrarian chaos that it would have taken decades to undo." It was Breshkovskaya who conveyed the news that Kerensky's presence in Samara would embarrass the PSR. Instead, they offered him an important mission in London and Paris—that of securing formal Allied ratification of the terms for intervention. Kerensky was not fooled by the sugar on this pill and it took the combined efforts of all his friends and comrades to break his resistance.[34]

Fabrikant soon persuaded the Serbian mission to enroll Kerensky as a "Serbian officer" due for repatriation; his beard now came off though a fine moustache remained. The British (who had already recruited Admiral Kolchak to their service) were anxious to keep out refugees from Russia, apart from "the better class of people," so Consul-General Wardrop refused to grant a visa. Fabrikant appealed directly to Lockhart who, not wanting Kerensky's death on his conscience, wrote out an unauthorized visa and stamped it with the handstamp of his unofficial mission. Fabrikant escorted Kerensky on the train to Murmansk, from where he boarded a British secret service trawler to Scotland.[35]

The Foreign Office was desperate to "avoid if possible the fact of Kerensky's presence in England being twisted into proof that there is an ill-will to the Bolshevik Government," and Balfour pressed the Americans to grant Kerensky a visa, so that he would be "much less embarrassing to the Allied cause." He got a warmer welcome from Dr. Jacob Gavronsky, head of the press section of the Russian Embassy and a relative of many leading SRs, and from David Soskice. Both felt that Kerensky still had a "great part" to play in Russian affairs and they constituted the nucleus of a "staff" for him. For the following eighteen months, Kerensky lived with Dr. Gavronsky, his wife, Maria, and their young sons, Lev and Asher, in a fine house overlooking Regent's Park. Despite his troubles, he had zest and humor enough to make the little boys love him.[36]

On June 24, 1918, Kerensky was summoned to No. 10 Downing Street to meet Lloyd George. He was fortunate in that the Samara government had grown in authority since his departure from Moscow, while the Bolsheviks were facing increasing difficulties. Kerensky assured Lloyd George that he spoke "for the whole of Russia except the reactionaries and the Bolsheviks." The Prime Minister was impressed by his personality and his "piercing eyes," but dismissed him as "not a man of action." Still, he told the Commons that afternoon of his meeting with an unnamed Russian, describing Kerensky's report of a new anti-German mood in Russia as "full of hope."[37]

Kerensky was in luck. The Labour Party Conference was meeting in the Central Hall, Westminster, attended by Vandervelde, Branting, and Albert Thomas. Henderson offered to present him to the party conference, thereby forcing the Foreign Office to drop its silly embargo on the mention of his name and permitting him to appeal directly to public opinion, appropriately enough during the debate on the termination of the wartime political truce. Without any warning, the platform party made room for "a tall young man with a pale, set, rather heavily powerful face." The comrades stared without any sign of recognition, until Henderson brusquely introduced "M. Kerensky." Most of the delegates continued to stare, then the left hissed and booed while the remainder answered with cheers. Unabashed, Kerensky came forward, Gavronsky beside him to translate his words:

Comrades, I am very much impressed by the reception accorded me by the Conference. . . . I came straight here from Moscow and I do feel it my duty as a statesman, as a man and as a politician, my moral duty, to tell you English people, and the people of the whole world, that the Russian people and the Russian democracy are fighting against tyranny, and they are going to fight to the end. . . . I believe, and I am certain, that the Russian people will shortly join you in the fight for—("Socialism, I hope, sir," shouted a delegate)—for the great cause of freedom.

The "personal impressiveness" of the moment was rather lost in the ferocious wrangle that followed as the left broke all the rules of order to deny Kerensky a hearing, (though the right and center had listened courteously to Litvinov at the preceding conference). Ironically, Kerensky was unable to state that he had come as a member of a fraternal party with a mission sanctioned by its Central Committee. He hinted at this mission to a French correspondent; "a speedy regeneration is possible, but we can't achieve it on our own."

The next day, the battle recommenced with Sylvia Pankhurst moving the suspension of Standing Orders to prevent Kerensky speaking. Vandervelde followed with an encomium on Kerensky that rang through the hall: "what he represented was the most heroic effort ever made to save, while there was still time, the Russian Revolution and the future of Russian democracy."

In the end, the motion to hear Kerensky was overwhelmingly carried and even in a foreign language, "the magic of his personality swept away all the ungenerous bickering." He reminded the party of the sacrifices made by the Russian people, of Bolshevik contempt for democracy, of the current Bolshevik-German alliance, and he asked the Party whether it could "remain a calm spectator of that unheard-of tragedy."[38]

London might cheer, but Allied policy was made in Paris. Thomas urged him to cross the Channel and Lloyd George had given the impression that Kerensky might represent Russia at the forthcoming Inter-Allied Conference. On July 10, Kerensky was received cordially by Clemenceau, though the French leader looked puzzled when reminded of "the French government's promises in Moscow." On Kerensky's second visit, Clemenceau showed him a telegram from U.S. Secretary of State Robert Lansing stating that Kerensky's proposed visit to the U.S. was "undesirable," presumably a reply to Balfour's attempt to get rid of him. Now Kerensky was mystified. When invitations to Russian diplomats and soldiers to participate in Bastille Day celebrations were brusquely withdrawn, Kerensky tried to browbeat Clemenceau. The "Tiger" outfaced him. "La Russie est un pays neutre, qui a conclu la paix séparée avec nos ennemis. Les amis de nos ennemis sont nos ennemis." Why should Russia reap the rewards of a victory for which she had ceased to fight?[39]

The fortunes of Kerensky's comrades rose only to fall once more. Kazan was captured and an advance on Nizhnii Novgorod seemed possible. But on September 10, the nascent Red Army retook Kazan, inflicting a personal as well as a political reverse on Kerensky. The citizens of Samara had greeted the formation of KOMUCH with enthusiasm, but they showed no disposition to fight for the directory, headed by Avksentiev, which replaced it. Kerensky's former adjutant, Lieutenant Vinner, reported that, "as last year everyone was gripped by an epidemic of words and no one could do anything." Except, that is, for the hereditary military caste, whose activities, encouraged by the Allied missions, became more and more threatening. Early in October, the directory was forced to retire to Omsk, where the atmosphere was now violently anti-socialist.[40]

In North Russia, the tragicomic kidnap of SR Prime Minister Chaikovsky revealed the weakness of all the moderate socialist regimes. Kerensky tried to alert his comrades to Allied intentions. "The episode involving you in Archangel" he wrote to Chaikovsky, "may recur at the first convenient moment in Omsk and Samara." The Russian Chargé in London refused to transmit a similar warning to Avksentiev. The SR Central Committee now put its head in the noose by calling for resistance to reaction. Too late. On November 18, 1918, Admiral Kolchak deposed the directory and proclaimed himself "Supreme Ruler" of all Russia.[41]

In view of the failure of his mission, Kerensky had asked the Foreign Office to arrange his return to Russia. He was informed that "military considerations" precluded his return via ports in Allied hands, though of course he could make his own way from Bergen. (This would have meant crossing several hundred miles of German-dominated Finland and Bolshevik North Russia.) On the day Kazan fell, Lloyd George's secretary confirmed that Kerensky could not be transported to Russia, since Britain was determined "not to involve itself in the internal politics of Russia"—a hypocritical perversion of the terms for intervention presented by Kerensky himself. Within a few weeks, they could claim with rather more truth that should Kerensky turn up in Russia, the anti-Bolshevik generals would shoot him.[42]

Kerensky drew attention publicly to the contrast between his treatment and that of Kornilov's one-time "orderly," Zavoiko, who was getting Allied assistance. He broke diplomatic etiquette by quoting Clemenceau's heartless description of Russia as a neutral country that had made a separate peace with the enemy in the Paris *L'Information*, and he protested vigorously at the exclusion of Russia from the forthcoming peace talks. The paper was almost suppressed as a result, and Clemenceau never forgave Kerensky.[43]

Gallic insults and English humbug were distressing but they did not shake his allegiance to the Allies, an allegiance fortified by Bolshevik barbarism. On the day after his last interview with Clemenceau, came the Bolshevik reckoning with the Romanovs. The "execution" of the ineffectual autocrat and his willful consort was probably inevitable, but the murder of their innocent children and doctor was a crime shattering the humanitarian traditions of the intelligentsia and recalling the murder of Boris Godunov's heirs in the seventeenth century. Kerensky had sacrificed his own prestige to save the Romanovs, and during his visits to Tsarskoe Selo he had come to know them as human beings. He felt the massacre personally and sensed that these deaths would be avenged countless times, until the soil of Russia was drenched in the blood of innocents.[44]

Kerensky's own family and comrades were also in the firing line. The Czech revolt had caught Olga and the boys in Ust-Sysolsk (Syktyvkar) in the remote Zyryan (Komi) area of North Russia. The suspicious Bolsheviks briefly clapped them into the Lubyanka, headquarters of the fearful *Cheka* in Moscow. When KOMUCH forces captured Kazan, Vera Baranovskaya was performing there with a group from the Moscow Arts Theatre. Lilya had come to visit her and for a brief, tantalizing moment, she was on friendly territory. Vinner's plan to evacuate her came too late, and when the Red Army recaptured Kazan, they captured Kerensky's second family. At least they were still alive . . . but for how long?[45]

Others were less fortunate. Boris Flekkel was captured and shot by the Bolsheviks near Nizhnii Novgorod. As the deputy head of the *Cheka* put it, "He admitted that he had been Kerensky's secretary—that's enough to be shot for." Another casualty was Kerensky's conservative younger brother, Fyodor. When Red Army units mutinied in Tashkent in January 1919, Fedya was shot "in reprisal." White barbarism was equally brutal. Boris Moiseenko was caught by monarchist officers, including Senator Krashenninikov's son, tortured and shot. It must have taken real courage to open the mail in those days. Yet as mourning gave way to iron resolution, the wonder was that Kerensky retained so much of the sunny resilience of happier days.[46]

By early 1919, the Peace Conference was imminent. When Wilson's proposal for a conference of *all* Russian factions foundered, a Russian Political Conference was organized to support Kolchak in Paris. It comprised Prince G. E. Lvov, the former Imperial foreign minister, Sazonov, Maklakov, and Chaikovsky. Savinkov joined it later. Kerensky was still confined to London by Clemenceau's veto, so he resorted to "summoning" Avksentiev and Zenzinov for instructions. His supporters in Paris—Thomas, Vandervelde, and Edvard Beneš—lobbied the U.S. delegation until, at last, the French relented.[47]

Weeks of enforced politeness to obstructive junior officials in London had not improved his temper and M. S. Margulies found him with

an earthy colour in his face, deep lines on his forehead, screwed-up eyes, he talks immoderately loudly, with a vibrant, sonorous voice, becoming excited in discussion, then walking rapidly round the room singing something.

Kerensky felt vindicated by recent events:

I retired from politics for five months, I thought, something intelligent will replace Bolshevism, I waited and what now? Kolchak is marching without any political thought, without a program. What can you expect? I think that Bolshevism is approaching its final days but there is nothing to replace it with, that's the horror.

Kerensky set about rallying his dispirited comrades. Some reacted with skepticism. "Kerensky still remained the incorrigible idealist, the dreamer, the child of St. Petersburg's white nights with their call for detachment from the realities of life." Others were more impressed. Within days of Kerensky's arrival in Paris, an SR group decided to set up an international association to fight dictatorship in Russia. The struggle with the Political Conference was on.[48]

On May 4, Kerensky was received by a senior American official, probably Colonel House himself. If so, the urbane Texan was quite impressed by Kerensky's arguments that the Bolsheviks could last only "a few months now" and that Kolchak would replace them. "His greatest fear is that Kolchak will inaugurate a regime hardly less sanguinary and repressive than that of the Bolsheviks." The Allies should restore Russian democracy by insisting on conditions as the price of aid to Kolchak. These should include the restoration of civil liberties, a coalition cabinet, leaving the land in the hands of the peasants, returning the right to organize and strike to the workers, and promising to give way, when feasible, to a democratic Constituent Assembly.

When the Big Four convened a fortnight later, Wilson put Kerensky's terms to the others. Well aware of their low opinion of the fallen Russian democrat, Wilson suggested that he would not have accepted Kerensky's view, "unless it happened to tally with information he received elsewhere." This was a mere fig leaf. The views he put were those of "Kerensky and his friends." Lloyd George had come close to recognizing the Bolsheviks only weeks earlier, but now he was reduced to echoing Wilson's, and hence Kerensky's, views. Clemenceau kept his mouth shut. For Kerensky, widely seen as Russia's gravedigger in conservative circles, and as a political corpse by the Bolsheviks, this was a remarkable diplomatic triumph.

At a subsequent meeting, Lloyd George raised the question of Russia's Baltic frontiers.[49] Even more than the disagreements over civil liberties and policy on the rights of peasants and workers, the nationalities question was the Achilles heel of the whole White cause. Chkheidze and Tsereteli were also in Paris, but they were now enemies, refusing even to discuss a federation between Russia and Georgia. The Ukrainians, Finns, Estonians, and Latvians took a similar line. Kerensky was among those who vigorously refused to even consider "negotiations" between "Russia" and the borderlands:

We are all representatives of Russian democracy and not of individual nationalities comprising Russia. We can not betray the tradition of the Russian democracy and conduct negotiations in the name of Great Russia with other nationalities.

A few weeks later, the Russian Whites were poised to capture Petrograd. Behind them stood the victorious Finnish Whites and an Estonian army of 35,000. They would help only if the Russians guaranteed their freedom. Jaan Poska and Anton Piip implored the Russians to offer them something:

If it is impossible to receive written confirmation from Kolchak or from the Political Conference in Paris, then it would be desirable to obtain it at least from Kerensky's government. . . . Finally, in extremis, even Kerensky and Avksentiev and their group of right SRs alone could give such a guarantee.

Kolchak appealled to Mannerheim, but he offered the Finns no more than the Estonians. The Russians were all implacable, the Finns and Estonians stayed put and Petrograd stayed Red.[50]

At the end of May, Kerensky returned to London, muttering about English intrigue and leaving Avksentiev to stem an attempt by Savinkov and Chaikovsky to persuade the Union of Regeneration to reconsider its hostility to Kolchak. Savinkov had ingratiated himself with the Paris exiles by publishing a conciliatory account of the Kornilov affair, suggesting that Kerensky and Kornilov had tragically misunderstood one another. Kerensky would have none of this and he exposed Savinkov's illogicality mercilessly:

he did not explain why, while considering "the hero and patriot" Kornilov a victim of Kerensky, he himself went with Kerensky against Kornilov.[51]

By the end of 1919, it was obvious that the pledges extracted from Kolchak in the early summer had been ignored. Indeed, it came to seem more and more naïve ever to have expected a military dictator, who had dissolved the government established by members of one Constituent Assembly, to summon another. With the incapacity of President Wilson, there was no one to insist that the British and

French grant aid only on the agreed terms. Clemenceau's days were numbered, however, when the French elections of November 1919 returned the nationalistic "Chambre bleu horizon," and in January 1920, Alexandre Millerand replaced Clemenceau at the Hôtel Matignon. A series of personnel changes in the French establishment now occurred, all of them to Kerensky's benefit. When Millerand was elevated to the presidency of the Republic in September 1920, Eugène Petit became Secretary General of the Élysée, while Paléologue was replaced as the head of the French foreign service by Philippe Berthelot, whose Algerian background and literary tastes had much in common with Kerensky's.[52]

The weak link was the French foreign, and later Prime Minister, Leygues, a wealthy and affable southerner, who left foreign affairs largely to Millerand. Beneš had now become Czech Prime Minister, and he was determined to give the Russian democrats another chance to show what they could do. It was a near thing. As Berthelot told Kerensky later, "Leygues était très hésitant. Beneš l'avait persuadé d'accepter votre point de vue."[53]

Kerensky now moved back to Paris, where he stayed in the apartment used as an office for the paper *Pour la Russie* edited by his comrades. Events in Russia now threatened to divide him from his French hosts once more. In April 1920, Wrangel's White army advanced northward from the Crimea. Simultaneously, the Poles attacked from the west, eventually capturing Kiev. They made no secrets of their desire to re-create the ancient Polish-Lithuanian *Rzeczpospolita*. Non-Bolshevik Russians began to think that there might be greater evils than Bolshevism and thousands of Tsarist officers, including General Brusilov, volunteered to help the Red Army clear Russian soil of the hereditary foe. Kerensky was not immune from this mood. His lectures in Paris, at first rather poorly attended, had become an instant success once he began to attack the Poles.[54]

In December 1919, an "Initiative Group of Non-Party Unity" was established to foster a rapprochement of right and center SRs outside Russia. Its founding congress convened in Prague in July 1920 and set up an administrative center to disburse the subsidies channelled to Kerensky by the French government via the Czechs. It would be supervised by a 50-member Council, whose members—with the exception of the odd Masonic Menshevik—were all SRs, with the right SRs in the driver's seat.[55]

For the last time, they appealed to the Third Force, the peasants and disillusioned workers inside Russia. "Bolshevik psychology has been outlived to the end by the working masses of Russia," Kerensky warned. Hatred of Bolshevism was growing and "the bloody, frightful troubles will end with the determined intervention of the people themselves." He sharply reproved those who remembered of the February Revolution only "the grimace of a drunken lout," imploring them to "conquer hatred in yourself and proffer assistance with love to the risen people." (Significantly, he chose the Christian *vosskresshii* rather than the secular revolutionary *vosstavshii* to describe the "risen" people.) He was also heartened by the news that Boris Sokolov had engineered the escape from Russia of Olga and his two sons.[56]

As the Initiative Group gathered in Prague in November, Wrangel's army was evacuated from the Crimea amid scenes anticipating Saigon in 1975. Kerensky, Stalinsky, and Rudnev reported on the work of the Information Kollegiia, which controlled the SR press in Prague, Berlin, and Paris, while Brushvit and Zenzinov described the successes of the communications service in setting up a courier system to Russia. Kerensky and Colonel Makhin reported on the work of the special section, charged with fostering risings inside Russia. Makhin was working on plans for an uprising, while Kerensky masterminded the infiltration of Soviet institutions by a cadre of reliable specialists and workers.[57]

This work rapidly enhanced Kerensky's prestige among the democratic Russian emigrés. Not that they all reacted with enthusiasm. When Prince Lvov was asked whether he approved of Kerensky as future Prime Minister of Russia, he replied, "No, I hope not." Others disagreed and a leading SR told Margulies that he favored Kerensky though he was not sure the idea would command a majority of SRs.[58]

At the end of October, Kerensky was in Harwich to greet Olga, Oleg, and Gleb on their arrival in England. But the clock could not be turned back. He and Olga were divided now not only by Lilya and her daughter, but by the privations Olga had endured while he was living comfortably in England and France. For him, the liberation of Russia came before all else and he was soon back in Paris and Prague, leaving Gavronsky to take care of his family.[59]

The Initiative Group had little appeal for Russian emigrés and none at all for Western public opinion, so early in 1921 an attempt was made to provide the administrative center with more impressive legitimation. On January 8, 33 of the 56 members of the Constituent Assembly outside Russia met in Paris, at the invitation of the Initiative Group. The SR majority elected Avksentiev chairman. Milyukov had repented of his flirtation with Imperial Germany and the White generals and he led a distinguished delegation of five leading Kadets. Chernov withdrew from the proceedings, foreseeing that he would be outnumbered in this "private group." The reference to "national-cultural autonomy" included in the resolution adopted was, of course, traditional Kadet policy. Kerensky summed up the proceedings in characteristically optimistic tone: "We are returning to the path of healthy national and state creativity."[60]

The secret work went on as Kerensky shuttled between Berthelot at the Quai d'Orsay, Beneš, who frequently stayed at the Hôtel Continental, and Kerensky's SR comrades at the Rue Vineuse in Passy. He sent Colonel Voronovich to Constantinople to conduct a spying mission in the Black Sea area. In Tallinn, Chernov negotiated on their behalf with an underground Ingrian organization. Finnish circles were sympathetic. French, Czech and Estonian diplomatic channels were open to them and Czech radio prepared to support a Russian uprising. In *Volia Rossii* [The Freedom of Russia], Kerensky gloated over "the ghastly reality of Soviet existence breathing with the stink of death."[61]

From Russia came reports of discontent as peasants, infuriated by Bolshevik requisitions, refused to deliver food. As the winter drew to a close, revolts in Tambov Province and in Siberia reduced food deliveries to the cities to a trickle and seemed likely to trigger an explosion of resentment among the industrial workers, already seriously alienated from the "dictatorship of the proletariat." As delegates gathered in Petrograd for the Bolshevik Tenth Party Congress, strikes broke out. Then on 28 February 1921 came the thunderbolt for which Kerensky and his comrades had worked and prayed. "Red Kronstadt," the pride of the Bolshevik Revolution, overthrew the authority of the Soviet government and called for freely elected soviets. The Third Force had risen: the Third Revolution was no longer a dream.[62]

The panic-stricken Bolsheviks used every conceivable smear against the Kronstadt rebels, and probably exaggerated the marginal part played by Kerensky's organization in setting off the revolt, but there is no doubt that Kerensky did all he could to sustain it. At the first news from Kronstadt, he dashed from Prague to Paris to seek new funds; the French promised 3 million Francs a month. He then arranged with Beneš for the transmission of the funds to Tallinn. But on March 17, Lenin and Trotsky sent Tukhachevsky's men over the ice to take Kronstadt by storm. The Third Revolution was over. For months, Kerensky and his comrades worked to revive the spirit of revolt in Russia and as late as 1922 there was a suggestion that the British government was considering supporting his activities. Nothing came of these ventures. The concessions made by Lenin had done their work. The civil war was finally over.[63]

Lenin did not intend to let Kerensky off scot free and the *Cheka* sent a certain Captain Korotnev to Paris to seize his papers and assassinate him. Korotnev had little difficulty insinuating himself into the apartment on the Rue Vineuse, but he could not bring himself to carry out his mission. He did make off with the papers, however, and they were published in Moscow in a crude pamphlet blaming Kerensky, Avksentiev, and Chernov for the Kronstadt rising.[64]

This reinforced the charges made by Lunacharsky and Krylenko during the first of the great show trials which took place in 1922, designed to deter any further SR activity in Russia. Abram Gotz and other leading SRs were saddled with the entire responsibility for two years of bloody and costly civil war. This trial was fraught with difficulties for the regime, the least of which was Kerensky's offer to testify in person, which predictably received no answer. The defendants came from a tradition which had specialized in turning political trials into indictments of the regime which had brought the charges. The *Cheka*, now reformed as the GPU, was asked to avoid excessive brutality in its interrogations now that the civil war was over.

Krylenko made some telling points for the prosecution and hectored the accused whenever possible. They did manage to save their dignity, and the stenographic record was not published "for a variety of technical reasons." Kerensky would have been glad to echo words of a defendant quoted by Krylenko: "I consider myself guilty before working class Russia [only] in that I could not struggle with all my strength against the so-called Worker-Peasant Government, but I hope that my time has not yet passed."

The Western socialists responded to the SR trial and the invasion of Georgia by breaking off fraternal ties with the Communist International.[65] For Kerensky, this was small compensation for his emigré status.

17

A Romantic Exile

In 1920, Kerensky had written to comrades in Berlin about his greatest fear:

Whatever must happen will happen, but I cannot accept and I won't accept that I am an emigré. Alas, you often have to do what you don't want to. . . . But perhaps the miracle of a new Regeneration of Russia may occur?— It can not, replies Reason. Yes, it can, it will, my whole essence calmly asserts, it apprehends without logic, it believes in the darkness.

Yet this man, who at forty had lost none of his charm, persuasiveness, and vitality, was destined, like so many others, to drink the poisoned wine of exile to the last drop.[1] Western sympathy for the emigrés was limited. The Bar Councils of Paris and Brussels made no move to admit their Russian colleagues. The emigrés suffered collective social demotion as officers became taxi-drivers, doctors became nurses and lawyers took up clerical work. Kerensky's eminence gave him the dubious advantage of patrons who would see he did not starve, but at heavy cost to his pride. The emigrés were traumatized by their recent experiences and haunted by the faces of those they had abandoned to the Bolsheviks. Deprived of Russia, of that pattern of daily life which had rooted them in reality, they were prone to lose their sense of time and place, their self-respect, and their sense of identity. They suffered from apathy and depression. In his terms, Kerensky was fully justified in giving up such frivolous pursuits as the theater "in mourning" for Russia. At least he was spared an identity crisis. People had only to hear his name to ask whether he was not the former Prime Minister of Russia. Indeed he was, and for the remainder of his life, this was the way he preferred to refer to himself. Others might mock him for it. So what? As the ex-Empress Zita put it many years later, "one is what one is." Had he rejected this label—as Prince Lvov did—Western opinion might have concluded that he was ashamed of his record as Russia's leader. And that he never was.[2]

Tsarist policies had eased the path of the educated emigrés. The alienation of the intelligentsia from autocratic Russia, their sense of being "Europeans" in Russia, made emigration a less drastic metamorphosis than it might have been, though they found it a bitter irony now to be regarded as barbaric "Asiatics" in Europe. Nor did the real Europe live up to their expectations, as they discovered that "the Western Europe whose image lived in the heart of the Russian intelligentsia had never really existed. We imagined that somewhere beyond the far, endless Russian horizon—far from the cruel oppression of Czarism—there were blessed lands of every democratic and humanitarian perfection." At least they would understand the phenomenon of Western "fellow-travelling."[3]

The fascistic tenor of Tsarist policies toward the Jews had also created a large number of "marginal" men and women, semi-exiles before 1917, who now mediated between their unhappy compatriots and their hosts. Kerensky was blessed by the unstinting support of David Soskice and Jacob Gavronsky.

A generation older than Kerensky, David Soskice was the son of a millinery merchant in Berdichev. Driven by official anti-Semitism into the revolutionary movement, he worked with Plekhanov in Switzerland before coming to settle in London. During the 1905 Revolution he was the principal spokesman for the revolutionaries in London, until his brief return to Russia as correspondent of the Liberal *Tribune*. A man of many talents, Soskice ran an import-export business and subsidized *The English Review*, edited by his brother-in-law, Ford Madox Ford. He had returned to Russia in 1917 for *The Manchester Guardian*, where Kerensky had co-opted him to his press office. Soskice transmitted his undying loyalty to Kerensky to his sons, Victor and Frank.[4]

Gavronsky had left Russia to avoid discrimination in his career. Just three years older than Kerensky, he studied medicine in Germany, France, and England and conducted medical research in a laboratory he himself endowed at the London Hospital. He was a colleague of Chaim Weizmann during the war. His young wife, Maria, was the daughter of Isaiah Kalmanovsky, a major shareholder in the Vysotsky Tea Company, which had supplied the tea drunk in every third cup in Russia before the Revolution. The Bolsheviks expropriated his Russian outlets but they could not touch the tea plantations in Ceylon. Gavronsky's brother was an SR member of the Constituent, while his sister was married to Bunakov-Fonda-minsky. In 1917, he had volunteered to organize the Provisional Government's press service in Western Europe, characteristically de-clining any salary. His kindness and largesse never ceased and Ker-ensky could still count on a warm welcome from his surviving son Asher until the end of his life.[5]

Among Kerensky's other Jewish friends were the three remarkable Benenson girls from Baku; Simeon Strunsky, an editor of the *New York Times*; and Eugène Petit's wife, Sofia, née Balakhovskaya. He was also helped by friends from other 'marginal' backgrounds, such as Elena Izvolskaya, daughter of the pre-war Russian Ambassador in Paris, and Fyodor Stepun, a Baltic-German, who had studied in Marburg before the war, before serving in Kerensky's War Ministry in 1917. Incredibly, he was to be helped by yet another member of the extraordinary Baranovsky-Vasiliev sisterhood.[6]

Isolated from the processes that were transforming the lives of his own people, and faced by the growing indifference of all but a few influential right-wing socialists in the West, Kerensky was detested by most of the emigrés. After Wrangel's defeat in 1920, tens of thousands of White Guards flooded into Europe. Most of them re-mained loyal to Wrangel's Russian General Military Union in the hope of getting a last crack at the Bolsheviks. In their political com-plexion, the emigrés closely resembled the makeup of the Fourth Duma.[7]

Young White Guards hunted down the men they blamed for their disinheritance. In 1921, they beat up Guchkov in Berlin, and the following year attempted to assassinate Milyukov, leaving V. D. Nabokov dead instead. After his own move to Berlin in 1922, Ke-rensky felt more at risk from White Guards than from German Com-munists or Soviet agents. He walked with a bodyguard, changed his routes to avoid ambush, and used passwords to enter his own office. These precautions did not avert all unpleasantness. In 1923, two young Russian aristocrats found out where Kerensky was staying. They hired the room next to his and spent the afternoon shouting abuses through the thin partition.[8]

It is unlikely that Elena Biriukova was immune to the bitterness of the White Guards. She had qualified as a doctor in 1918, and when she joined her parents in South Russia, she must have tended the wounded of the White Armies. Then there were the frightful scenes of panic and hysteria at the evacuation and the Darwinian struggle for survival that followed in the refugee camps near Istambul. By the time Kerensky met her again in Paris, her husband had been shot by the Bolsheviks while her father had died in a refugee camp. When Oleg asked Kerensky about his half-sister years later, his father cut him off abruptly, implying that it had been agreed that he had no daughter. Lilya never remarried, but worked as a nurse at a Paris hospital, accepting her hard lot with a good grace until her death in the 1960s. In 1932, the Soviet government allowed Vera to visit her in France, but Vera had only three years to live.[9]

Less numerous but more articulate, the "democratic" emigrés were constantly at one another's throats about who was to blame for the debacle and eagerly scanning one another's writings for hints of appeasement toward the Bolsheviks. In April 1921, Kerensky's campaign to apotheosize the Provisional Government received a rude shock when Nabokov's memoir appeared. Nabokov's attitude was less surprising than Milyukov's endorsement of his "cruel but just characterizations." At the next meeting of members of the Constituent Assembly, Kerensky refused to shake Milyukov's hand. Milyukov, angered, kept his counsel. Kerensky never understood Milyukov's professional pride, his need to render unto history that which was true, while continuing to fight the propaganda war with the Bolshevik Caesars. Kerensky could only speculate that his attitude had something to do with Kadet party intrigue.[10]

While Kerensky looked in vain for reciprocal admiration from Milyukov, he despised Chernov. In 1922, Chernov denounced the heterodoxy of an article on post-Communist economics in the Paris *Sovremĕnnyia Zapiski* [Contemporary Notes] and threatened finally to drive the hated right SRs from his dying party:

We are barbarians to one another. We suspected so long ago. The *Sovremĕnnyia Zapiski* group, having taken the initiative in opening polemical fire on our positions, has confirmed the justice of these suspicions. It is in vain however that Comrade Rudněv supposes that the gulf that divides us merely demonstrates "just how wide are the differences between individual SRs within the party."

The authoritarian tone and implied threat of expulsion—with the possible loss of Czech subsidies—drew an impressive rejoinder from Kerensky, who found Chernov's acceptance of the "barbarian" label "very sick and very serious." Chernov's attack was, he suggested, merely a pretext for an attack on the moderate policies of the Provisional Government in 1917, which he proceeded to defend with an eloquence and conviction that have never been bettered. It was not really so difficult for him to demonstrate the utter futility of Chernov's belated conversion to a kind of anti-Bolshevik Bolshevism, a conversion that would arouse only derision in Russia itself. "Let them call me a barbarian and divorce me thrice," Kerensky concluded, "I shall remain with the old beacons, to which Russia will yet return!"[11]

By the early 1920s, half a million Russians had been drawn to Germany by its proximity to Russia, the tolerance of its government, the relative friendliness of its people, and most important, the low valuation of the Mark, which enabled them to convert their savings or relief payments into a tolerable income there. An added attraction for the intellectuals was the presence of a modern and cheap printing industry, whose superb compositors were familiar with Cyrillic type. Writers stimulated by the Revolution, but chaffing under Soviet censorship also found Berlin ideal, so it attracted both confirmed emigrés and such writers as Alexei Tolstoy, Maxim Gorky, Ilya Ehrenburg, and Boris Pasternak, all with a foot in the Soviet camp.[12]

Soviet literary critics have rather overstressed the role of context and audience in creativity, implying that *all* emigré artists declined in exile. An orator is, however, a linguistic artist, who depends on audience response. Kerensky's technique had drawn on the powerful metaphors of the Russian people and the intimate abstractions of Russia's greatest poets. At his best, he had articulated the feelings of workers and intellectuals. There was little place for these talents in Paris and Berlin.

On October 29, 1922 the first number of the new Russian daily, *Dni* [Days] rolled off the presses of the Social-Democrat *Vorwärts* at 204 Friedrichstrasse. Its impressive list of collaborators included the familiar right SRs, Henderson, Snowden, and Bernstein, and a number of gifted writers, including Andrei Bely, Boris Zaitsev, Alexei Remizov, Vladislav Khodasevich, and Nina Berberova. The driving force behind the venture was Kerensky, ably but unobtrusively assisted by Mikhail Ter-Pogosian. In what proved to be his farewell to the Socialist Revolutionary Party, Kerensky insisted on its independence from "any political party or organization existing either in Russia or abroad." Kerensky tried to encourage the artists but he kept a tight rein on the paper's political content and one dissident, the "anarchizing" Osorgin, was hyperbolically banished as "a real enemy of Russian freedom."

Editorship of a paper qualified Kerensky for a subsidy from the Czechs under the agreement he had himself negotiated in 1920. While he was an excellent organizer, he had never been a writer and writing never came easily to him. His extraordinary handwriting, alternating between spiky assertiveness and impatient fluidity—so unlike the copybook hands of Lenin and Chernov—kept far more secrets than even he intended. It is hard to avoid the suspicion that he had little time for the uninitiated. He overcame his aversion to writing by dictating his editorials "in a loud voice, heard in the far corners of the premises." New contributors were nonplussed by his loud and brusque manner.[13]

Kerensky's preoccupation with Russia did not blind him to events in Western Europe. While much of West European opinion was still willing to give Mussolini the benefit of the doubt, Kerensky wrote: "Fascism is a sick, a very sick phenomenon of the will and aspirations of the broad, semi-conscious masses." In 1923, he attacked the "leader of the Bavarian monarchists, Hitler." His hostility to Nazism was reciprocated and Henry Ford resurrected the reactionary accusation that Kerensky was Jewish, adding some inconsequential absurdities of his own: "His father was a Jew and his mother a Jewess. Adler, the father, died and the mother married a Russian called Kerensky, whose name the boy took." Even in 1923, this was not entirely funny. Two decades later it would have been worth a death sentence in most of Europe.[14]

For Kerensky, as for the rest of the emigrés, Berlin was never more than a backdrop for their own tribulations, "sickly Germany, sickly money, sickly trees of the Tiergarten." After the 1920 Kapp putsch, the monarchists had retired to Munich; after the Hitler "Beer

Hall" putsch in 1923, they became unwelcome even there. When in 1922, the German and Soviet governments signed the Rapallo Treaty to evade the rigors of the Versailles settlement, the left-wing emigrés became equally unwelcome. Economics did the rest. The 1923 inflation transformed Germany into a high-cost economy. The Russians decamped en masse, mostly to France. By 1924, there were 200,000 Russians in France, and Kerensky returned to Passy which would remain his base until the Fall of France in 1940.[15]

During the long hours Kerensky had whiled away at 7 Cambridge Terrace, he had fallen hopelessly in love with Maria Evseyevna Gavronskaya, the wife of his host. A privileged observer felt that this was one of his very few "grandes passions," but the less charitable found it a scandalous abuse of hospitality. Maria—or Mary as she liked to be called—was another petite brunette, a woman of cultivation, personality, and charm but, as a rich man's daughter rather spoiled by never having had to make painful decisions. Kerensky's departure for the Continent only inflamed the passion. Torn between the worship of a romantic hero and her admiration for Gavronsky and her maternal affection for her boys, she became more and more emotional. Nothing disturbed the comradely affection between the two men, however; perhaps this was the strongest indication that the passion was never consummated.

Yet there was hysteria enough. In 1923, things came to a head and Kerensky pressed Olga for a divorce. She erupted in anger. "The time when I was ready to give a divorce without posing any conditions has passed" and she demanded a settlement large enough to complete the boys' education. Olga's demands may have caused the divorce to fail, but perhaps Mary began to realize what she would exchange for the comforts of Cambridge Terrace: trying to sustain a passion for a man obsessed by a cause, eking out an uncertain existence in anonymous lodgings, and communicating in irascible telephone calls with distant European cities.[16]

A decade later, Kerensky was moved to write a poem called *The Breach*, describing a meeting between former lovers. She seeks tender words; he proffers silence. They are reconciled to the passing of their love. Death can then smile joyfully at them.[17]

In 1924, Kerensky was less reconciled. He yearned for love, yet fate had brought him an ultimately joyless marriage, a secretive affair, cut short by the Russian catastrophe, and a frustrated passion. His many disappointments may have blunted his sensibilities for a time. In 1924, he shared his Paris apartment with Sonia Martyanova. She was small and dark like his other loves, but there the resemblance ended. Despite her literary ambitions, there is a hint that she was ethically worlds apart, a cool pragmatist rather than a passionate romantic. She probably dumped Kerensky rather unceremoniously. Worse still, she exchanged him for the noted monarchist, Kirill Zaitsev. Eventually, the Zaitsevs departed for China, to the relief of Kerensky and his friends.[18]

These romantic interludes had little effect on his life in Passy. His elder son well remembered the apartment on the Rue Vineuse, the office of *Dni*, where Kerensky lived both before and after his Berlin period. There was no elevator. The apartment had three rooms, plus kitchen and bathroom. It was characteristically emigré in feeling, always untidy, and bereft of those small touches—photographs, a samovar, or an ikon—that might suggest a home. The only ikon he possessed was the little one round his neck, a constant reminder of the Russia he had lost.

In the mornings, Kerensky devoured the emigré and European press. He was then joined by his principal collaborators, S. M. Soloveychik and Ter-Pogosian, and by Olga Vasilieva, one of the sisterhood, who acted as secretary of *Dni*, despite her own nonpartisan politics. They took turns writing down Kerensky's articles for the paper. Sometimes Ter-Pogosian fed Kerensky in his own apartment. More often, Olga Vasilieva cooked and washed up for them. Kerensky liked fruit, sweets, spaghetti, and rice. To spare his single kidney, he avoided butter, cream, and alcohol. Nor did he smoke. Sometimes they ate out in the bars or restaurants of Passy, where he could indulge his harmless passion for cakes and sweets and where the waiters were happy to reward his charm by addressing him as "Monsieur le Président," a custom that encouraged generous tipping in the Third Republic.

In the evenings there were lectures to be given, or dinners at the homes of French sympathizers, such as Marius Moutet, Socialist Senator for La Drôme. Late evening and night was the time for interminable discussions, when the grim present could be pushed back for a time and the atmosphere of Petersburg's White Nights recaptured by firelight. On doctor's orders, Kerensky completed his day with the cleansing ritual of a very hot bath. Then he curled himself up on the sofa and went to sleep.[19]

Kerensky's obsessions were large enough to embrace cultural and literary interests. He was still estranged from Hippius, who never forgave his "treason" against Kornilov, but he quickly made friends with Marina Tsvetaeva, following her tumultuous reception in Paris in February 1926. Elena Izvolskaya remembered her as "neither eloquent nor pretty; thin, pale, almost emaciated; the oval of her face was narrow, serene, her cropped hair was still fair, but already strewn with gray. She was altogether not beautiful, but icon-like." In the summer and early autumn of 1926, Kerensky spent many hours in her company. Both of them had a fatal propensity to romanticize about others and the liaison was brief. Hippius' malicious suggestion that Kerensky was ruled by sex and Tsvetaeva out to seduce him into a reconciliation with the Kremlin bore little relation to reality.[20]

When the Merezhkovskys set out to re-create an incubator of ideas with their Sunday night soirées, called "The Green Lamp," the following winter, Kerensky insisted on attending, despite Hippius' mockery. Kerensky had developed a thick skin and "could live like an oyster, when people doubted his integrity." He listened to the debates on religion and philosophy and turned a deaf ear to the barbs of the poetess. In the end his stoicism wore her down and in the early 1930s, she extended an olive branch, having "regained [her] senses."[21]

In February 1927—the tenth anniversary of the Revolution—Kerensky arrived in New York harbor on the S. S. *Olympic*. He was welcomed by Kenneth F. Simpson, an active Republican and Assistant U.S. Attorney, and his everlastingly kind wife, Helen. There, too, was Nikolai Vinner, his friend and adjutant in 1917—who was now teaching Russian at Columbia University—and his wife, Ludmila, the younger sister of Olga Vasilieva. Simeon and Manya Strunsky were there, and would see that Kerensky's visit was treated like a royal progress by the *New York Times*, a pleasant contrast with the indifference and hostility of its London counterpart.

Kerensky was in ebullient mood, and he predicted the imminent overthrow of the Soviet system. Adjusting effortlessly to American terminology (or was this Strunsky?) he declared: "The Russian Democrats and Republicans of which I am the leader will never forget how America helped their cause in Russia." The *Times* reporter was impressed by his "tremendously vigorous personality," by the "quick, nervous step of a caged lion" and by the "great emphasis of his voice and gesticulation." The *Times* also praised his poise and moderation and William F. Green, President of the AF of L, arrived to pay his respects.[22]

Kerensky's arrival sent a tremor through the New York Russian colony. Monarchists denounced him as "only an enthusiast" and Communists muttered darkly, but they all planned to attend his gala appearance at the 5000-seat Century Theater on Sunday, February 13. Tickets were soon being sold at three times their face value, and by 1:00 P.M., police reinforcements were needed to control the crowd of 7000 besieging the theater. (Even Eamon De Valera, who had just arrived to embarrass the Irish government, had not attracted as large a crowd.) When the doors were opened at last, the crush was so great that a five-ton bronze candelabrum was wrenched from its stand.

The monarchists had packed the orchestra, while the poorer Communists had secured places in the balcony. They stuck out like storm-stricken patches in a wheat field as the rest of the audience stood to cheer Kerensky's dramatic entrance. A young woman rose to offer him a lavish bouquet, and then slapped him three times in the face. The auditorium erupted in competing hoots and cheers and at least one aristocratic Russian nose was broken by a Gaelic fist. It turned out that Kerensky's assailant had lost her brother and fiancé, young Russian officers in 1917, in incidents she blamed on Kerensky.

Impassive until the uproar subsided, Kerensky then shot out a typical staccato phrase. As he paced up and down the stage, he quelled Monarchist and Bolshevik hecklers with equal assurance, alternately refuting them and drowning them out. Bolshevism, he told them, was "the posthumous grimace of monarchism." Today, Russia stood at a crossroads; either there would be Bonapartism or political democracy. The Russian peasantry would regain its liberty "either by revolution or evolution," though he preferred the latter: "None of us Russian democrats insists on Revolution. Such surgical operations are too costly to the people. . . . We wish to conserve as much as possible the resources, human and material, of our country. We say to the Bolsheviki: 'Surrender voluntarily the liberty you stole from the people!' " Otherwise, "there will be nothing for us to do when the madness of those at the top will provoke the madness of those below. He summoned them to "remember Russia and repent" and warned foreign powers not to take advantage of Russia's temporary weakness.[23]

His triumph was nearly marred by a typical piece of impulsiveness. At a party that night, Kerensky found himself with Flora Solomon, née Benenson, now the wife of a patrician English Zionist handicapped after a riding accident. Tiring of the small talk, she took him home with her despite the Victorian rules of her hotel. As Kerensky hid in the bathroom, Flora implored the manager not to cause scandal. Yet this affair, begun so irresponsibly, became Kerensky's most mature intimate relationship. Plain and red-haired, Flora was Kerensky's intellectual equal. While she would never be as famous, her career in publishing and her pioneering work in labor relations for Marks and Spencer, the chain of English department stores, quite apart from her refusal to keep house for him, ensured her his respect, though her suggestion that she was the only woman in his life between 1927 and 1938 flatters them both.[24]

Kerensky's four months in the United States were the most productive he had spent since leaving Russia. His friends, A. J. Sack, Joseph Shaplen, and Strunsky coaxed and bullied him into reworking his memoirs, with all the resources of the world's greatest newspaper to back them up. When he left New York, his reputation was enhanced and his finances shored up against the troubled years ahead. On Sunday May 8, 1927, the *Times* magazine section carried the first of five installments of his memoirs, written with all the freshness and vitality of the best American journalism of those years. Soon, they became a book. *The Catastrophe* was followed by French and German editions, the latter furnished with a particularly ingratiating foreword. Every educated American and European could now own his or her copy of Kerensky's memoirs. Part of the success of the first chapter of *The Catastrophe* lies in the fact that for once, Kerensky wrote as a witness, rather than as advocate, judge, and jury.[25]

This American publicity did not go uncontested. For some years, D. F. Sverchkov, Kerensky's leading Soviet detractor, a leading Menshevik in the 1905 Petersburg Soviet, had been using the cliché of a meteor to explain Kerensky's early popularity with the Petrograd workers. In 1927, the more powerful medium of the cinema was brought to bear when that gifted propagandist, Sergei Eisenstein, made *October*. N. Popov's polished performance as Kerensky accuractely re-creates his mannerisms, but his "Kerensky," doodling on the monogram of Alexander III until it becomes "Alexander IV," is a peacock—the renegade stereotype in all his simple venality.[26]

Why did Eisenstein spurn Hippius' malign vision of Kerensky debauching his mistress, Mussolini-style, on the cushions of the Winter Palace as "the country fell into the hands of the Bolsheviks"? Perhaps it was just too embarrassing to admit that Elena Biriukova was the sister of Vera Baranovskaya who had just become Soviet Russia's greatest woman film star in Pudovkin's *Mother*.[27] The regime was not yet ready for an assault on the tight-lipped etiquette of the intelligentsia. Besides, if Kerensky could love, the film might degenerate into a Russian *Anthony and Cleopatra*, and there was that dreadful Russian tendency to forgive everything . . .

In the late twenties, Kerensky was sublimely optimistic about the future. France had been able to survive her "shattering political crisis without fascist grimaces or Communist convulsions" thanks to parliamentary democracy. The sense of statehood among the German working class and bourgeoisie was as strong as ever, and just a month before the Wall Street Crash, he greeted the election of a British Labour Government as "a world event of major significance."[28] Stalin's difficulties with the *kulaks* seemed to confirm his claim that the Soviet regime was unviable, though he failed to comprehend Bukharin's warning that Stalin would be a "Genghis Khan": "The rumours of revolution, conversations about coups d'état at court, . . . reflect precisely the new psychology of the country, which economics itself is driving towards politics, the politics of real liberation from dictatorship." On the twelfth anniversary of the Bolshevik October, he warned: "the twelfth hour is the last."[29]

When Stalin's brutality disabused Kerensky of this "Menshevik" delusion, his tone changed sharply: "The Bolshevik dictatorship is systematically and consciously destroying the wellbeing of the Russian countryside, is artificially impoverishing the peasant, is infecting Russia with the fatal bacillus of famine." Desperately, he lobbied the French Socialist Party and the General Confederation of Labor. He went on to Oxford to give an address. At least the nonpolitical English should sympathize with Russian Christians, and he begged them for "moral intervention . . . in defence of the freedom of human conscience." The Soviet Embassy complained and the Labour government and Foreign Office warned him that he would get no more visas unless he kept his mouth shut about Russia. Yet even now, Kerensky espied a silver lining. "The first political result of the complete bankruptcy of the second Stalinist experiment in 100% Communism is an end to every kind of social maximalism."[30]

Now that it was suffering the persecution it had once inflicted on others, Kerensky's view of the Orthodox Church altered and he became a regular churchgoer. Though he found the competing claims of the exiled Metropolitans distasteful, he, and intellectuals like him, had continued the efforts of the Merezhkovskys earlier in the century, though the "Secular Order of the Russian Intelligentsia" to rediscover a "City of God," where Christianity and social justice might be reconciled. Gradually, his reservations about dogma waned, and by 1934 he was able to refer to "Thou, O Lord!" in fully Orthodox terms.[31]

Kerensky was no ideal father but he retained a strong interest in his sons, writing to them frequently and having them stay with him in Paris during the summer. The harsh years of civil war and famine had taught them prudence and they decided on nonpolitical careers. They graduated simultaneously as engineers in 1927. Oleg soon began the successful association with Dorman Long that was to make him one of the world's principal bridge designers. He married Nathalie Bely, the daughter of a prosperous Russian bourgeois family, who were initially cool toward Kerensky. Gleb was slower to settle down and though he quarreled more often with his father, he also helped him by translating two of his books. Kerensky would have preferred them to go into politics, but he mentioned their achievements with unmistakable pride.[32]

As the world depression deepened, fewer and fewer emigrés could afford to support *Dni*, while Beneš came increasingly to doubt the wisdom of supporting enemies of Soviet Russia, when it was becoming Czechoslovakia's least hostile neighbour. *Dni* became a weekly and in 1933 it collapsed altogether.

Hitler's victory came as a frightful shock. Kerensky found some comfort in the fact that it had occurred in "the most cultured country of Western Europe." Now the Europeans would have to stop blaming Russian barbarity for Bolshevism.

On September 12, 1934, Babushka Breshkovskaya died at her home near Prague. Broke and demoralized, Kerensky wrote a desperate appeal to Olga in England. She offered to share her accommodation, but tried to stiffen his pride by reminding him that he was "the man in whom Babushka believed."[33] Kerensky flew to Prague for the funeral in Hvaly cemetery. The harvest was in and the day was bright and warm. There were wreaths from the Masaryks and two trainloads of Czechoslovak deputies from Prague. A Ruthenian Senator and children in Carpathian costume honored Babushka's educational work in Mukachevo. Czechoslovak legionaries, workers' militiamen, and Babushka's ex-pupils formed a guard of honor round the coffin, draped in Czechoslovak and SR banners as a band played the favorite funeral march of the Russian revolutionaries. Babushka herself provided the first address, an ethical testament, read out in Kerensky's beautiful baritone at her request. Through him, she thanked the world which had known her and given her so much, and her friends, "not only here, but also in that future world." Pointing to the railroad lines carrying trains to the East, Kerensky himself prophesied: "One day her dust will return home that way and her name will serve as a symbol of the regeneration of Russia in forgiveness and reconciliation, in love and truth." Chernov followed, predicting that Breshkovskaya would join the pantheon "not merely of the party and the international labour movement, but of the whole of a reborn, renewed humanity."[34]

Though the Gavronskys had now lost much of their wealth, Kerensky's friends still did all they could for him. When Lockhart met Flora Solomon at the Dorchester in 1935, she asked him, on Kerensky's behalf: "Mrs. Salomon [*sic*] says can I get him journalistic work not so much to bring him in money (he has friends who will not let him starve) but to save his moral self-respect."

Though she came to regret it later, it was probably Flora who introduced Kerensky to Madame Thérèse Nadéjine.[35] This Franco-Russian sounding lady was in fact an Australian, born Lydia Ellen Tritton. The Trittons, owners of the largest furniture business in Queensland, had six children, of whom Lydia Ellen, born in 1899, was the fifth child and youngest girl. "Nell" Tritton startled her school friends by changing her name to Nellé. At first it was a giggle but she made it stick. "I would rather be *hated* than *ignored*," she said, and she dragooned her family and friends into dramatics, danced with the Prince of Wales and published an anthology of verses. She had been deeply affected by the sight of the Aussie lads in kakhi departing on their troopships for the war and she yearned to travel to "lands of frozen ice" and "wheat and rice." To her parents' distress, she left home in the early twenties to take up journalism, at first in Sydney, and then in Europe.[36]

Nell read Maria Bashkirtseva's diaries and became infatuated with Russians. In 1927, she married Nikolai Nadezhin, a handsome White Guard, who tried his hand at versifying and singing. He drank, flirted, and made scenes, and then spent whole nights kissing her feet in atonement. She disliked his "Russian egotism" and took work with Kerensky. Nadezhin came and blustered, but Kerensky stood his ground and no blood was shed.[37]

Kerensky knew no English and Nell knew no Russian, so they conversed in fractured French. Her typing was only slightly better than his and she had little patience with routine, but she was well-informed and she could drive a car. Kerensky probably admired her charm, her refined features, luxuriant tresses, and figure, but he did not at first reciprocate her infatuation. Indeed, Flora Solomon claimed that he took advantage of one of his fishing and boating holidays at Annecy to propose to *her*. Though he was still able to help her "retain her curiosity, her desires, her bloom," Flora feared "the tedium of the politician passé," wishing to keep him as he was at Annecy, "the great-hearted man-god," and she turned him down. Nell would later remember him with equal nostalgia: "I have been happy—I have lived with you my Unicorn. Avec toi j'ai bu à la source de la Fontaine de la vie."[38]

Gleb translated *The Crucifixion of Liberty* which appeared in 1934 with Kerensky's first memoir of childhood and youth, "a painful occupation, and even perhaps an unnecessary one," as he modestly put it. With a whole chapter dedicated to an attack on anti-Semitism, this book stands out as a beacon of humanity, especially when contrasted with *The White Sea Canal*, published in the same year by Gorky and others to rationalize twentieth-century slavery. This shameful work even handed ammunition to the Gestapo by showing the leading NKVD jailers as large-nosed Jews. Sadly, Kerensky's outspoken hostility to anti-Semitism failed to arrest the erosion of his friendship with Jewish friends, who considered Stalin a lesser evil than Hitler.[39]

In the mid-thirties, the British Tories were the key to the European balance of power and they cannot have enjoyed a book which associated Nicholas II, who did nothing common or mean in the hands of his Bolshevik tormentors, with the origins of anti-Semitism. In 1935, Sir Bernard Pares provided Kerensky with an ideal opportunity for influencing them by yoking together Kerensky's account of the last years of the Russian Imperial couple with the story of Captain Paul Bulygin, a monarchist who had devoted himself to the study of their massacre after vainly trying to rescue them. In his introduction, Pares lent his immense prestige to Kerensky's claim that he had done all he could to save the Tsar.[40]

The depression might have wrecked Ramsay Macdonald's Labour government, but in the U.S.A., President Franklin Roosevelt and in France Premier Léon Blum continued the struggle for democratic reforms, which Kerensky considered essential. The U.S. Republicans charged that Roosevelt was the "Kerensky of the American revolutionary movement," while the French right warned Blum of "the sad Kerensky experience." Blum's riposte seemed to accept some aspects of the "Kerensky" stereotype, driving the exile to reissue his French memoirs in order to suggest guidelines to "the new experience which is beginning."

In March 1936, Kerensky scored a personal triumph by bringing out the first number of *Novaia Rossiia* [The New Russia]. In his fortnightly comments on current events, he warned Stalin against driving the European right into an anti-Bolshevist crusade by his support for the Spanish Republic, though he had no sympathy for Franco.[41]

Kerensky did approve of Stalin's rehabilitation of Russian nationalism, of romantic love and paternal authority, of classical Russian literature and history. For him Stalin's 1936 Constitution was a concession to popular dislike of dictatorship, part of an attempt to create a "plebiscitarian Caesarism." "It is a *fascisation* of Stalinism which is underway." He greeted the first purges, which eliminated his own enemies, with equanimity: "Stalin depends on the spontaneous urge to a free human life in his struggle with the reactionary survivals of the Leninist-Octobrist epic. That is why all ... of the tendencies opposed to Stalinism, ... are painted with the Trotskyist [brush].[42]

Kerensky could accept the show trials of such old acquaintances as Nekrasov, Sukhanov, and Steklov as politically inevitable attempts by Stalin to pin his own failures on scapegoats. Yet he knew that many innocents were suffering, too. His sister, protected by her medical skills for so long, disappeared during the purges that took place in the wake of the murder (probably at Stalin's instigation) of S. M. Kirov, in 1934. Vladimir Baranovsky's association with both Kerensky and Trotsky ensured his summary execution in the late thirties. All contact with relatives in Russia ceased.[43]

Nor did Stalin's paranoia stop at the borders of the USSR. Successive heads of the Russian Military Union were kidnapped from the streets of Paris, and Trotsky's son and Andres Nín were murdered. No Russian emigré felt safe. The burglary of Trotsky's papers was followed by the theft of Kerensky's. He feared an indirect attack, perhaps on Nell, but there seemed little point in informing the police.[44]

Kerensky, never an unconditional Francophile, now began taking English lessons. On March 1, 1938, he arrived in New York for his second visit, this time as a European democrat: "All European believers in democracy turn their eyes towards the United States," he told waiting reporters, "Here is the strongest and greatest fortress of freedom." He still hoped, however, that the purges in Russia were "the last stage of the evolution of the Bolshevik regime." The day after the Munich agreement, he returned to New York once more. He defended the "appeasement" of Hitler on the grounds it would provide the democracies with time to arm themselves. He rebuked American critics of Britain and France, who were doing the best they could "without the collaboration of the United States and without the support of a strong, free Russia." Flora Solomon also found Kerensky strangely unmoved by the Nazis' infamous *Kristallnacht* pogrom. "Such things are occurring all the time to the Russian people," he explained, but she was not mollified and the quarrel that followed brought their intimacy to an end.[45]

Nell had gone back to Australia, but Kerensky enticed her to a meeting in America by suggesting they might soon be married. She was livid to find the divorce from Olga still pending. "I am deeply wounded that you made me leave my country without reason when you knew. I am not returning to live *comedie de la fiancée* [*sic*]", she stormed. She was soon reassured. On August 21, 1939, they drove across New Jersey with Victor Soskice to Martin's Creek, Pennsylvania, where they were married in the home of Harry A. Stein, Justice of the Peace. The 40-year-old Australian had made the debonair, monocled 58-year-old an associate member of the Anglo-Saxon club at last. The secret was too much for Stein, who rushed off to tell the wire services.[46]

Two days after the wedding, Joachim von Ribbentrop arrived in Moscow to sign the pact that would stun the world and finally lay the Versailles settlement to rest. A new era of apocalyptic convulsions was beginning. Nell's dream of a triumphal entry into Moscow might come true, after all. The liberation of Kerensky's beloved Motherland might not be long delayed.[47]

18

The Long Reprieve

The New York Times gave a prominent position to Kerensky's first statement on World War II. From his point of view it could not have begun under more favorable circumstances. The Hitler-Stalin Pact was both a "betrayal of democracy" and the result of "their common totalitarian character and interests." Most welcome of all, "the unnatural, amoral concept of . . . cooperation between the democracies and the Moscow dictatorship is now definitely shattered." The Polish *casus belli* provided an opportunity for intervention throughout Eastern Europe and, at a dinner a few days later, Kerensky urged the democracies to seek the support of 160 million Russians by fighting not just for "the overthrow of the Hitler regime and the restoration of Poland and Czechoslovakia but also for the liberation of the Russian people from bolshevism." To Russian emigrés impressed by Stalin's easy reacquisition of Russia's 'natural' borders, he opposed the choice "against present-day Russia, for the Russia of the future, for humanity, for the eternal bases of life."[1]

Virtually all Russians supported Stalin's demands for a revision of the Russo-Finnish frontier, but when, in the wake of the Russian invasion, Kuusinen's puppet People's Government of the Finnish Democratic Republic signed a pact with the USSR to be ratified in Helsinki, Kerensky's embarrassment was at an end. On a platform with fellow exiles Oskari Tokoi and Thomas Mann, he could now back "all measures, moral and material," which Roosevelt might take and applaud Tokoi's claim that the Finns, his countrymen, were fighting "not only for their freedom but for the liberty of the entire democratic world."

Kerensky was convinced that the time had come for active involvement in Russian affairs. His son, Gleb, volunteered for the British army in the expectation of being sent to Finland, and in January 1940, Kerensky and Bunakov-Fondaminsky sent Zenzinov to Finland. There can be little doubt that the real purpose of this mission was to see whether the formation of a Free Russian Legion of emigrés and Soviet POWs, which would fight alongside the Finns, was feasible. Mannerheim had other ideas, believing that Finland's sole chance of survival lay in convincing Stalin that the struggle was a national and *not* an ideological one. The appeal, for which Kerensky hoped, was never made.[2]

Kerensky and Nell returned to France early in 1940, just before the end of the "phony war." After the defeat of Finland by Stalin's forces and the German invasion of Norway, Kerensky applied for British visas for Zenzinov, who was in imminent danger of being trapped between Hitler's forces and Stalin's, and for himself. MI5, The British counterintelligence service, opposed the application, as their hands were full with the surveillance of "doubtful aliens," as they termed the anti-Nazi refugees. On the day de Gaulle flew to England, Lockhart—who had saved Kerensky's life in 1918—washed his hands of Kerensky and even tried to avert bad publicity in America by claiming that all visas had been suspended.[3]

Nell actually saved Kerensky from the advancing German forces by driving him away from Paris on June 12. They found themselves in the midst of bombardment on their journey south to the Spanish border. At the Irún crossing, Nell found she could not shake Franco's implacable *Guardias*, who would admit British subjects but not Russian refugees. Still she did not give up. They drove back to St. Jean de Luz, where Nell found a lingering Royal Naval vessel. It was her Anglo-Saxon background (and wealth?) and not his democratic past that saved them. Kerensky unjustly preserved a hostile detachment toward Nell, resenting his second escape from martyrdom. His injustice compounded a trauma in her which never quite healed.[4]

Back under British protection, they were allowed to remain long enough to meet his family until a berth could be found on a transAtlantic liner to New York. On July 12, the Kerenskys arrived in the U.S., to a triumphal welcome extended by the *New York Times*.

Kerensky's statement contrasted England's "strong will" with French defeatism. "Not only the leaders are determined to win, but the humblest workers." Kerensky was also contemptuous of the Comintern's pacificism.[5]

Kenneth Simpson, the Republican candidate from the Seventeenth Congressional District of Manhattan, welcomed the Kerenskys, installing them in his own house at 109 East 91st Street. It looked as though Kerensky would soon have the entrée he needed on Capitol Hill if he was to break down American isolationism. It was not to be. Just three weeks after taking his seat in January 1941, Kenneth Simpson died at 45.[6]

Kerensky shared Stalin's tragic underestimation of Hitler's megalomania, seeing Stalin's assumption of the premiership, in addition to his other positions, in May 1941 as a prelude to the "active participation of Soviet Russia on the side of Germany." However, when Hitler launched Operation Barbarossa, his invasion of the USSR on Sunday, June 22, Kerensky now declared that this "was not the time to be settling accounts with Stalin," but, as in 1914, he demanded concessions from the autocratic regime. Stalin must abolish political commissars, promise to restore Poland, liberate the "OGPU slaves," end the terror and abolish collectivization.[7]

Kerensky was convinced that Stalin's weakness was such that he must now accept his assistance and on July 2, he called on Lord Halifax, the British Ambassador in Washington. He told Halifax that Stalin must be persuaded to announce the restoration of personal liberty and the end of collective farms if Hitler were to be prevented from posing as a liberator. If Stalin did so, Kerensky would back him publicly. He offered to go to Moscow, "no doubt at the risk of his own life." Kerensky did not rely on British intercession but telegraphed Stalin directly. Nothing came of this. Stalin's opinion was probably that of the British Foreign Office, which was already resigned to anti-Bolsheviks' looking to Hitler for liberation, believing that Kerensky counted for nothing.[8]

Kerensky did not give up easily. In the wake of Pearl Harbor, when it looked as though America might focus all its energies on the Pacific war, Kerensky urged Stalin to declare war on Japan to ensure the receipt of American aid. Well into the spring of 1942, Kerensky continued to try for a meeting with Soviet Ambassador Litvinov, the new "democratic" face of the USSR in Washington, but this hope went the way of so many others. Then—perhaps at the State Department's indirect request—he disappeared from public view for two years.[9]

After a few months in the U.S., the Kerenskys scraped together enough to move into a small rented apartment at 1060 Park Avenue, a typical emigré apartment-cum-office in a fashionable neighborhood of New York. Simeon and Manya Strunsky also took them out to New Canaan, Connecticut, about 40 miles northeast of New York, where they had a cottage. The Kerenskys themselves rented one in the Silvermine area, though the landlady was rather put out to find Kerensky felling the trees. In 1942, they found a home just inside the New York State–Connecticut line. It was a two-and-a-half story wooden farmhouse, dating from 1800, though recently restored. It offered plenty of scope for Nell's homemaking talents and it reminded Kerensky of a *dacha*.[10]

Tatiana Pollock, a regular visitor, remembered it well:

On the lawn, under a spreading tree, there was a round table, always set with tea things in the afternoon. There was also a croquet game set up. K was an ardent croquet player and we often had wild games. . . . My husband and K used to have terrific matches and one could hear their voices teasing each other (particularly K's voice which was a very loud one!)

He walked as ever, chatting amiably with the neighbors, and there were swimming parties at the Roton Point Beach Club on Long Island. Casual visitors were captivated by the impression the Kerenskys gave of living a pastoral idyll.[11]

Yet Kerensky's thoughts were never far from the apocalyptic events which, even in the "perverted form" of Hitler's war, were bringing the U.S. and USSR closer together.[12] He shared in the pride of all Russians as the Red Army ground down Hitler's *Wehrmacht* and he traced the sources of Russian strength in her history. His lecture tours, their main source of income, were taking him beyond the Northeastern metropolitan, ivy-league centers to "America's Heartland." His first letter to be written entirely in English came from Texas. Nell was thrilled: "I loved your letter. . . . like having a new beau—Simeon was very impressed & said you'd probably come back with a western accent and wearing a ten-gallon [cowboy] hat."[13]

It was the Polish question that finally impelled him back into the public arena. Sol Levitas, editor of the Social Democratic *New Leader* offered Kerensky space to develop his views, and in January 1944, the *New York Times* carried a letter from Kerensky and Konovalov on the same theme. They urged the Poles to "abandon all claims to any Russian, White Russian, and Ukrainian lands," and Moscow to "abandon all efforts, direct or indirect, to dictate to an independent Poland the course of her internal policy." Yet Kerensky knew that this advice was aimed at two equally deaf sets of ears and the gulf between his public optimism and private doubt widened once more as he muttered to Nell of the coming "catastrophe."[14]

The catastrophe was the term used by Kerensky and his comrades to refer to the final Armageddon-like triumph of Bolshevism, when Russia might become "the butcher of the whole world, assembling explosive materials" from the heightened aspirations of men and women of all races. For Kerensky the ultimate tragic misunderstanding was that most people saw the Russian victories as a vindication of Communism, while he felt they were really the result of Stalin's concessions to Russian nationalism. He saw intimations of the catastrophe in British aid to Yugoslavia's Tito, in the willingness of Beneš and de Gaulle to turn Russian emigrés over to the NKVD, and even in the arrogance of the New York Communists, who got Zenzinov fired from a job with the City College of New York.[15]

Shortly after the Warsaw Rising, Kerensky set out to "determine the line" for the emigrés: "*Vrag izgnan iz predelov SSSR.*" His words seem more effective in Russian, which lacks articles, than the English translation "the Enemy has been chased beyond the borders of the USSR." Stalin's amalgam of patriotism and Communism had secured great advantages for Russia, but Soviet victories did not justify terror. He urged the West to resume ideological struggle with Leninists at home and not with "imaginary Russian predatory imperialism." At the Waldorf-Astoria, he defended Russia's new border with Poland and the annexation of the Baltic States. The Lithuanian Minister cut his arguments to pieces, Polish friends cut him, and he quarreled with many Americans. Even Nell protested that "the Alexander Kerensky I loved was a man of superb integrity who said everywhere '*who does not defend liberty everywhere defends it not at all*'— now for the poor Poles and the others he says something else." He snapped back and complained about the inconstancy of his friends. It was not his finest hour.[16]

Avksentiev and Milyukov had died within weeks of one another in the spring of 1943. Kerensky found it difficult to praise his party comrade, though at Zenzinov's behest he consented to give the memorial meeting "the required character." He much preferred lauding Milyukov's injunction "to be on guard for Russia; whatever she may call herself, selflessly, uncomplainingly and to the last breath." Nor did he make any public reference to Milyukov's posthumous attack on his own comrade, Mark Vishnyak, in which Milyukov virtually accepted the legitimacy of the Soviet regime.[17]

Kerensky was with Vishnyak and Soloveychik in Boulder, Colorado, when in March 1945 the emigrés were rocked by the visit of ex-Ambassador Maklakov, Admiral Verderevsky, and Ter-Pogosian to the Soviet Embassy in Paris. The New York Mensheviks and SRs were aghast, though they accepted the advice of the old Menshevik Boris Nicolaevsky to wait for Kerensky's return before reacting publicly. It soon emerged that the visit was virtually ordered by de Gaulle as a condition for the continued residence of the pre-war emigrés in France. Kerensky was understanding and Ter-Pogosian thanked him for removing "an unbearable moral pain." Kerensky gently reproved Maklakov for suggesting that Stalin's despotic methods had been more successful in wartime than the Provisional Government's libertarianism and he urged Maklakov to continue to beg Stalin for freedom for Russia, even if this meant going down on his knees like the Tver nobility before Nicholas II.[18]

Kerensky's misery was exacerbated by the decline in Nell's health. Early in 1944, she had begun to complain to him, but she was apprehensive lest he "be wild & angry & shout at me." She could not face another winter alone waiting for his barked telephone calls and she thought of returning to Australia to take part in war work, much healthier than "sitting alone thinking of the sorrows of the world & the coming catastrophe." She yearned for the beaches of home, and Kerensky feared she was impugning his manhood. She reproached him gently. "When you don't want me any more my Ala—I fear I won't be desirable any more."[19]

Easter 1944 was a triumph. Ninety guests came out to Vista for *kulich* and *paskha* and it seemed as though "Christ was risen indeed." Yet nothing halted Nell's inexorable decline. After a crisis early in 1945, Kerensky began to look into the possibility of a return to Australia in earnest. As he continued his lecture tour, Nell bombarded him with pathetic complaints, though his friends constantly tried to cheer her up, sometimes successfully.[20] When he returned, they bought a more modest house in Rowayton, nearer New York City, where Nell could gaze at the fishing boats on the Five Mile River. Kerensky struck his new neighbors as "stern looking" as he walked, now with a cane, to the shops.[21]

In October, they left for Australia. When they arrived in Clayfield, Brisbane's upper class suburb, Nell contacted her old friends, "drawing about her the tenuous threads of her past life." The troopships were coming home now, bringing her younger brother Cyril home. Kerensky slept on the veranda outside her room, while nurses tended her day and night. In February 1946, she suffered another stroke and her speech became confused. She still had nightmares about their escape from France. Her last weeks were a joyful Christian transfiguration, in which Kerensky saw a refutation of Tolstoy's chilling view of death in *Ivan Ilyich*. She died on April 10, 1946; she was just 47. As her body was placed in the coffin, she appeared to smile, which Kerensky took to be a "sign from the beyond" of which he felt unworthy.[22]

In public, Kerensky was still confident of "great changes in Russia within a matter of years or even months," but his nerves were shattered, and when Nell's cousin Corbett arranged for him to join a party at Surfers' Paradise, he told his hosts that he expected to share Trotsky's fate. When someone disturbed him at night, he became so distressed that he had to return to Clayfield immediately.[23] His lectures at the University of Melbourne were not a success. From England came the news that though his sons had survived the war, they had finally applied for British nationality. He had survived so many with better claims on life—but to what end?[24]

It was the new emigrés, or Displaced Persons (DPs), who did most to pull him out of his despondency. They bombarded him with desperate appeals for help. One came from the daughter of the servant at Gatchina Palace, executed for assisting his escape in 1917. Another came from his nephew, Paul Olferiev, a Yugoslav POW in Germany, fearing repatriation to Tito's Yugoslavia. Kerensky was able to install Olferiev in New York, where he became one of Kerensky's most devoted friends. After his delayed return to New York, Kerensky began to meet DPs regularly. "For us," he said later, "this meeting with Soviet citizens from DP camps was a long awaited happy meeting with a living Russia." He was delighted to find that they shared his literary interests and political views. In a "purge" which echoed Stalin's more brutal variety, they soon silenced the "fellow-traveling" emigrés in the West.[25]

At first, Kerensky lobbied privately on the DPs' behalf, but by 1947, he felt able to do so openly, and with Professor Michael Karpovich, he endorsed a DP appeal in the *New York Times* begging for them either to be tried for war crimes, or permitted to decide their own future. "If our appeal remains a voice in the wilderness we shall know how to face our Calvary, but for you in the West it will mean an open repudiation of all your best traditions."[26] In England, Oleg took up the cudgels on a committee including the Duchess of Atholl, while his son, young Oleg, twice Treasurer of the Oxford Union, rallied the support of such friends as William Rodgers, and Shirley Brittain (later Williams). They could count on the sympathy of Frank Soskice, now an MP and Solicitor-General in Attlee's Labour government.[27]

Kerensky contributed the proceeds of the sale of the house at Vista to supplement the niggardly rations distributed to the DPs in the camps. In 1947, the Western powers officially ceased forcible repatriation, but many DPs were still being driven "home" by sheer economic necessity. By 1949, U.S. Assistant Secretary of State Dean Rusk was willing to receive Zenzinov and other East European exiles to discuss their plea for aid, which Kerensky had signed on behalf of "Russia." Yet as late as 1955, coercive pressures on the DPs were still permitted in some of the DP camps. U.S. Secretary of State John Foster Dulles and Austria's conservative government promised in the draft Austrian State Treaty to deny relief to "persons who refuse to return to their native countries." In a letter to President Eisenhower, Kerensky called this "the uttermost hypocrisy ever written into a document to become binding international law." In the end, the Soviet government itself bowed to international pressure and unilaterally abrogated the most obnoxious part of the Treaty.[28]

There was nothing to draw Kerensky back to the houses at Vista and Rowayton, so it was with relief that Kerensky accepted Helen Simpson's offer of accommodation, following his return to New York.[29] There he would remain for the next two decades.

The 1947 Truman Doctrine was soon followed by the National Security Act creating the CIA—over the objections of the jealous

FBI Director J. Edgar Hoover and the right-wing isolationists, who feared the liberalism of its predecessor, the wartime OSS. The radical experts of the war years were replaced by Kerensky's friends, Isaac Don Levine and Eugene Lyons and others associated with the *New Leader*, organ of the New York Social Democratic Federation. Robert Shaplen felt that Kerensky had prepared this scenario, by suggesting that, "the Russian people remain our own best fifth column in the Soviet Union, and we must do all we can, with whatever weapons we can grasp, to give them hope that their tyranny might some day end." In the same issue of the *New Leader*, Bertrand Russell argued for the creation of an enlightened world government, under American leadership, by nuclear blackmail, or even war. The mentality of the anti-Nazi struggle was being transposed onto the superficially similar post-war conflict with Stalin.[30]

By early 1949, a CIA nominee, flanked by Levine and Lyons, headed an American Committee for Liberation from Bolshevism Inc. It funded and controlled an American Committee for the Liberation of the Peoples of Russia, which came to administer Radio Liberty. According to Kerensky, the Americans rejected the idea of running their own "Russian action" in favor of supporting the autonomous activity of the emigrés. Tsarist and fascist organizations were barred and the Russians justified their acceptance of American aid, since it came from a country whose policies were "friendly to our country and threaten neither her democratic development, nor her inviolability and independence."[31]

Next, Kerensky announced the formation of a purely emigré League of Struggle for the People's Freedom. He was supported by Zenzinzov, Nicolaevsky and Fedotov. They immediately mounted a diversion at the pro-Soviet World Peace Congress currently meeting in Carnegie Hall. The Russian daily *Novoe Russkoe Slovo* [New Russian Word] found space for a fortnightly Bulletin, edited by Kerensky, and for a Ukrainian language supplement.[32]

The Americans had nudged the reluctant British into letting Kerensky broadcast to Russia on the BBC. After an interval of nine years, Gleb, his Yorkshire-born wife, Mary, and their children, Katherine ('Katya') and baby Steven ('Stepan') met him in Scotland, where Gleb was working on hydropower. On November 24, 1949, for the first time in thirty-two years, Kerensky spoke to his own people. He was sure that "even in the Party, there are men who secretly,

with their souls, suffer with the people." He described his meetings
with the DPs, and in a reference to the Atomic Bomb he accused
Stalin of "stirring up hatred between peoples. . . . This is the devil
playing with fire! This fire once lit can certainly burn Russia if not
the whole civilized world." Yet the opportunity for nuclear blackmail
was running out. Only days earlier, the USSR had exploded its own
bomb.[33]

Kerensky went on to France, where a few old waiters still recognized "Monsieur le Président," but where most of the emigrés
had been compromised by deals with the Nazis or the Communists
or both. With 2.5 million DPs, Germany was once more the center
of the emigration and Kerensky was soon in Munich. He got on
surprisingly well with members of the main emigré organization,
the NTS, or Popular Labor Union. Others criticized them for adventurism and found their internal procedures too close to "demo-
cratic-centralism" for comfort. Kerensky probably felt that they had
as much in common with the methods of the old political freemasonry and he shared their interest in intuitivist philosophy. His
personality impressed them and he responded to their harsh judgment
of his own government's "incompetence and weakness" with en-
gaging humility. "We met Communism for the first time. How is
it that after our experience the most distinguished statesmen of the
world have made mistake after mistake in dealing with Communism
for decades?"[34]

The Ukrainians were a different matter. Disproportionately represented in the new emigration and favored by the leadership of
Galicians who had retained their cultural autonomy longer, they were
insistent on campaigning openly for an independent Ukraine. In
1951, prodded perhaps by the Pentagon, which must have hoped for
the support of the partisan Ukrainian National Army in the event
of war with Russia, the new head of the American Committee insisted on banging Russian and Ukrainian heads together at a congress
in Wiesbaden. To Kerensky's horror, his own League now deserted
him and joined the Ukrainian nationalist boycott of his Ukrainian
federalist friends. From his point of view, the U.S.A. no longer
qualified as a country which did not threaten Russia's "inviolability
and independence," and in December 1954 he denounced the whole
American action in terms pathetically similar to those he had employed against the British in 1918–20.[35] His public protest against

the Austrian State Treaty followed. He was fast becoming an embarrassment to Levine and Lyons. They did not want him running amok.

In the summer of 1955, the venerable Republican ex-President and businessman, Herbert Hoover, invited Kerensky for a meeting to suggest that he take a look at the papers in the Hoover Institution, which he had endowed at Stanford University. The ex-President thought Kerensky might wish to prepare a book on his premiership. This was a project near to Kerensky's heart, and he was overwhelmed by the wealth of material he found at the Institution. Still, he did not reply at once, realizing perhaps that his work with the League had not enhanced his reputation. It would be a pity to trip at life's last hurdle.[36]

Eventually, Kerensky accepted Kuskova's advice that it would be "sinful for a Russian patriot to renounce such work." Apart from which, "without work, and entirely definite work, one could die of boredom," hardly an exaggeration for a man in his mid-seventies. The Institution's Director, C. Easton Rothwell, was keen to produce an anthology of documents to complement the collections on the Bolsheviks published earlier. This would obviate the risk that research students would come to rely on the impressive, but ideologically streamlined, collections on 1905 and 1917 that were under preparation in Moscow.[37]

The Institution chose Kerensky for this task, fully intending him to "present the achievements" of the Provisional Government and "illustrate the political crisis which brought about the overthrow of this government." In view of his age and the need to ensure proper academic standards, it was decided to appoint a co-editor. The choice fell on the prize-winning young American, Robert P. Browder, a pupil of Karpovich, who had just written an appreciative review of Kerensky's role in the February Revolution. Browder collaborated in the selection of documents and successfully insisted on accurate standards of translation, but he could not prevent Kerensky from omitting Kornilov's statement in *Obshchee Delo*, nor from glossing over some arguably disastrous economic decisions taken by the Provisional Government. His task was not an easy one; it left painful memories on both sides.[38]

The three clothbound volumes, entitled *The Russian Provisional Government of 1917*, stand out like three proud men in Lincoln green from the bookshelves of specialist libraries, giving aesthetic pleasure as well as enlightenment. They represent a staggering achievement for a team of only two editors, two assistants, and five translators; though they employed no translators for languages other than Russian (and Ukrainian), they published a larger proportion of documents on the nationalities than the equivalent (but much larger) Soviet collection.[39]

This work whetted Kerensky's appetite for a new book of memoirs aimed at the new, more democratic generations of Europeans and Americans. He also nursed the dream of a history of Russia in Russian—no longer such an impossibility after the relaxation of controls in the USSR following Stalin's death. He had enjoyed his work as a professor at Stanford immensely, and he was popular with his students, and when Rothwell moved on to Mills College, Kerensky taught there, also.[40]

He approached his ninth decade with confidence and in fairly good health, though his sight was rapidly deteriorating. He had lost the sight of one eye and an attempt to save the other was only partly successful. Russian aspirations for freedom, American fumbling, and de Gaulle's demonstration that one could denounce a patriotic general and still be a patriot oneself seemed to vindicate things he had been saying for years, yet his work went slowly. He corresponded with Olga, now living with Gleb and Mary in Southport, to fill in gaps in his memory. He tried to use a dictaphone, but hated it. His book might have come out in 1964, but, as he told his family in England, "I passionately want to see you all while my eye still sees. But what it will be like after a year, even if I have an operation, no one knows. Not even the doctor."[41]

England had lost some of its complacent pomposity along with its Empire and was more welcoming than it had been. Kerensky's eldest son, Oleg, had distinguished himself as one of the world's leading bridge designers, while Gleb had a successful career with English Electric. Young Oleg had joined that select band of writers who had helped to expand the audience for ballet, so long considered an un-English art form. Young Katherine was about to begin a career in nursing. Frank Soskice was now a senior Labour MP and would soon be Home Secretary, while Flora Solomon was still a good friend.

Kerensky was installed in pleasant lodgings in Brighton to finish the book, but he could not function in that kind of isolation and the work remained stalled. It was rescued by George Katkov, now a Fellow of St. Antony's College, Oxford, who brought him to Oxford for a few months in the summer of 1963. He never trusted Katkov, but he got on famously with Max Hayward, who acted as stylistic editor of his memoirs. He also met the Pasternak sisters and was delighted when they showed him their brother's poem "Spring Rain," which ensures that Kerensky will always occupy an affectionate niche in the hearts of at least some educated Russians.[42]

The memoirs were still unfinished when Kerensky returned to New York. This was partly because of Kuskova's indiscretions about the political freemasonry, whose existence could no longer be denied. Finally, in 1965, the New York edition of *Russia and History's Turning Point* was published, to be followed by British, German, and French editions. Copies even trickled into the USSR. The book, an amalgam of memoirs and documents, has an air of "I was right" about it, and it lacks the vitality of his earlier accounts. In truth, he found writing for non-Russians a chore, while he feared he no longer had the right words for Russians.[43]

His last years in New York were not entirely happy. Helen Simpson had only a single room to spare and he found his increasing infirmity demeaning. It was now that he finally fell out with Nina Berberova, who had long endured his acting the irascible stepfather in the vain hope of ultimate recognition as his equal. She then published her acute, but cruel, recollections of him.

Berberova was not the only friend with whom he quarreled, but there were others who stayed friends. Paul Olferiev visited him daily. Elena Izvolskaya even moved in with him for a while to help him with his Russian book, and her admiration for his dignity never wavered. Father Kiselev was a regular visitor and Kerensky was punctilious in his religious observances. When he went to Vancouver, Canada, to promote his book, Gavronsky's son and his family welcomed him with affection. His greatest joy was Elena Ivanoff, his former research assistant at Stanford. When she married without telling him he was furious. Strangely, it brought them closer together and she continued to work for him as a friend. In 1968, she concluded the sale of his papers to the University of Texas, which eased his last years. "When he was nearly blind," remembered Robert Payne, "she was his eyes and ears, his nurse, his pride and his most devoted servant. I thought of it as an intricate and spiritual relationship, very Dostoyevskian, with little possessiveness." There were even occasions when he was able to return the compliment and nurse her.[44]

The year 1967 was a trying one. Joel Carmichael and Robert Payne wrote positively of his life's work, and Stalin's daughter, Svetlana, paid him a warm telephone call. These were the exceptions and he felt engulfed by a flood of tendentious and appeasing fiftieth-anniversary literature. Now virtually blind, he finally admitted, "I shall not see the resurrection of liberty in my land. . . . But you will," he defiantly told the Overseas Press Club. Worse was to come when, in the wake of the invasion of Czechoslovakia, UNESCO resolved to honor the work of the "prominent humanist," Lenin, at a seminar in Tampere, Finland. For Kerensky, this new example of Finnish perfidy and Western appeasement was intolerable. He would do such things.[45]

April 1970 saw Lenin's centenary (and Kerensky's 89th birthday). Kerensky responded with an article for the London *Sunday Telegraph*, putting Lenin's "sickness" (i.e., Bolshevism) down to syphilis. Despite Brezhnev's partial re-Stalinization, Kerensky asserted once more that, "The history of the Russian people has been one straight beam—an arrow towards freedom. . . . Russia has a glorious past and glorious personages to revere and love before whom Lenin stands but as a warped, maimed caricature with a demented mind."

Within days, he fell, breaking his pelvis and dislocating his shoulder. The time had come to die. Not for him the transfiguring pieties of Nell's death. He would meet his Maker as one natural force meets another. It took seven weeks of anger before his spirit triumphed over his emaciated flesh. At 5:45 A.M. on June 11, 1970, he died. Now the world would have to remember Kerensky as well as Lenin.[46]

Yet the world was unsympathetic, even the *New York Times* obituarist accusing him of "naïveté" in 1917, while *Novoe Russkoe Slovo* described him as a "lonely man who could not compromise." In the Soviet Union, most people were surprised to discover that he had only just died, while the nationalist Skuratov implied that he had sought to shape Russia according to "measurements . . . from beyond the clouds." At least Sofia Kallistratova, the "Babushka" of the dissident movement, showed in her spirited defense of Natalya Gorbanevskaya, that there were some in Russia who still shared Kerensky's values. Perhaps the most appreciative comments came from A. N. Artemov, an ex-DP, writing in the NTS journal, *Posev* (The Seed).[47]

On Sunday, June 14, 350 mourners gathered at the Frank Campbell funeral parlor on Madison Avenue in New York for the requiem mass. Levine paid tribute to Kerensky's "love of country, love of humanity, and the greatest of them all, love of freedom." The coffin was then flown to London for the family interrment in a modest grave at Putney Vale Cemetery. In the presence of Olga, his sons and grandchildren, Frank Soskice (Lord Stow Hill) now a frail, limping figure with white hair atop his familiar delicate features and expressive hands, showed what passion and grace could add to dignity. Few men have ever paid such beautiful tribute to Kerensky's real "gift," his ability to make men and women love him. Soskice concluded,

Civilization must always be grateful to him and his Ministers and if, in the end, they could no longer stand, almost alone, against the blizzard, that should not be accounted failure, but rather they should be honoured for their iron will and dauntless courage, a shining beacon light for the future conflicts between the rule of reason and the yoke of dictatorship which may yet afflict mankind.[48]

Notes

Abbreviations

AA   Auswärtiges Amt (Imperial German Foreign Ministry) Papers: Weltkrieg Nr. 2 geheim. Friedensstimmungen und Aktionen zur Vermittlung des Friedens, Library and Records Dept, Foreign and Commonwealth Office, London, and Russland 82, Nr. 2, Bände 43–44, Public Record Office, Kew, London.

AFSR   *Armiia i Flot Svobodnoi Rossii*, [formerly *Russkii Invalid*], Pet: Ministerstvo Voennoe i Morskoe, 1917, daily. (Political editor, F. Stepun).

AK   Aleksandr Fëdorovich Kerenskii (Alexander F. Kerensky).

AK, *Catastrophe*   AK, *The Catastrophe: Kerensky's Own Story of the Russian Revolution*, trans. Joseph Shaplen and A. J. Sack, NY-L: D. Appleton, 1927.

AK, *Crucifixion*   AK, *The Crucifixion of Liberty*, trans. Gleb Kerensky, L: Arthur Baker, 1934.

AK, *Prelude*   AK, *The Prelude to Bolshevism: The Kornilov Rebellion*, L: Unwin, 1919.

AK, *Turning Point*   AK, *The Kerensky Memoirs: Russia and History's Turning Point*, NY: Duell, Sloan and Pearce, 1965; L: Cassell, 1966.

ARR   *Arkhiv Russkoi Revoliutsii*, Berlin, 1921–37, periodical.

Botchkareva, *Yashka*   Maria L. Botchkareva [Bochkarëva], *Yashka: My Life as Peasant, Officer and Exile*, (as set down by Isaac Don Levine), NY: F. A. Stokes, 1919; L: Constable, 1919.

Buchanan, *Mission*   Sir George Buchanan, *My Mission to Russia*, 2 vols. L-NY: Cassell, 1923.

CMRS   *Cahiers du Monde Russe et Soviétique*, Paris, periodical.

FO.371	Foreign Office. Political. British Diplomatic Correspondence, Russia (1917–1918), Soviet Union (1940–1941), Public Record Office, London.
FAT	Fonds Albert Thomas, Archives Nationales, Paris.
Gippius, *Siniaia Kniga*	Zinaida N. Gippius [Hippius], *Siniaia Kniga: Peterburgskii Dnevnik 1914–1918*, Belgrade: Russkaia Biblioteka, 1929.
GDSO	*Gosudarstvennaia Duma, Stenograficheskie otchëty*, SPb-Pet: 1906–1917.
H:ki	Helsinki/Helsingfors
KA	*Krasnyi Arkhiv*, M, 1922–1941, periodical
Kerenskii po DP	*Aleksandr Fëdorovich Kerenskii po materialam Departamenta Politsii*, Pet: Tsentral'nyi Komitet Trudovoi Gruppy, 1917.
Kerensky Family Papers	Papers in the possession of the late Mrs. O. L. Kerensky, the late Dr. O. A. Kerensky, CBE, FRS, Gleb Kerensky and Oleg Kerensky, 1970–1985.
Kerensky Papers	The Papers of A. F. Kerensky, Harry Ransom Humanities Research Center, University of Texas in Austin.
L	London.
LA	Los Angeles.
Lenin, *Works*	Vladimir I. Lenin [Ulianov], *Collected Works*, M: Gospolitizdat & L: Lawrence & Wishart, 1960–70 (45 vols. and index).
Lgd	Leningrad.
M	Moscow.
MAE, v.647–658	Ministère des Relations Étrangères, Série Guerre:1914–1918. Russie: Dossier Général, VII–XVIII (1917), Archive du Ministère des Affaires Étrangères, Quai d'Orsay, Paris.
MdA	K.u.K. Ministerium des Aussern (Austro-Hungarian Foreign Ministry Papers), Haus-, Hof-, und Staatsarchiv, Vienna.
Miliukov, *Istoriia*	Pavel N. Miliukov, *Istoriia vtoroi russkoi revoliutsii*, 3 vols. Sofia: Russkoe-Bolgarskoe Knigoizdatel'stvo, 1st edition, 1921–24.
Miliukov, *Vospominaniia*	P. N. Miliukov, *Vospominaniia 1857–1917*, 2 vols. NY: Chekhov, 1955.
Mints, *Istoriia*	Izaak I. Mints, *Istoriia Velikogo Oktiabria*, 3 vols. M: Nauka, (2d ed.) 1977–79.
NRS	*Novoe Russkoe Slovo*, NY, Daily.
NY	New York City.
NYT	*New York Times*.
NZh	*Novyi Zhurnal*, NY, periodical.
Okhranka	Zagranichnaia Agentura (Paris), Okhrannoe otdelenie, Departament Politsii, Ministerstvo Vnutrennykh Del; Papers now in the Hoover Institution on War, Revolution and Peace, Stanford, Cal.

OLK, "Obryvki"   Ol'ga L'vovna Kerenskaia (née Baranovskaia), "Obryvki iz moikh vospominanii: pobezhdënnye molchat, pobeditelei ne sudiat," typescript, Kerensky Family Papers; also published as Olga Kerenskij, *I Morti non Parlanno: Tre Anni e Mezzo della Mia Vita*, Rome: Edizione Paoline, 1977.

Padenie   P. E. Shchegolev, ed. *Padenie Tsarskogo Rezhima: stenograficheskie otchëty doprosov i pokazanii, dannykh v 1917 g. v Chrezvychainoi Sledstvennoi Komissii Vremënnogo Pravitel'stva*, 7 vols. Lgd-M: Gosudarstvennoe Izdatel'stvo, 1924–27.

Pet   Petrograd/Petersburg.

Petit Papers   Papers of M. Eugène Petit, Property of Mme. A. Laurent, Fontenay-aux-Roses.

"Pokazanie...   "Pokazanie General-ot-Infanterii Lavr [*sic*] Georgievicha
    Kornilova"   Kornilova, dannoe chrezvychainoi sledstvennoi komissii 5 sentiabria 1917 goda", typescript (copy), Papers of Col. R. R. Raupakh, Bakhmeteff Archive, Columbia University Libraries, NY.

Polvinen, *VVS*, v. 1.   Tuomo Polvinen, *Venäjän Vallankumous ja Suomi, v. 1: Helmikuu 1917—Toukokuu 1918*, H:ki: WSOY, 1967.

Radkey, *Agrarian Foes*   Oliver H. Radkey, *The Agrarian Foes of Bolshevism: Promise and Default of the Russian Socialist Revolutionaries, February to October, 1917*, NY: Columbia University Press, 1958.

Rosenberg, *Liberals*   William G. Rosenberg, *Liberals in the Russian Revolution: The Constitutional Democratic Party, 1917–1921*, Princeton, NJ: Princeton University Press, 1974.

RPG   Robert P. Browder and A. F. Kerensky, eds. *The Russian Provisional Government of 1917: Documents*, 3 vols. Stanford, Cal: Stanford University Press, 1961.

RR   A. M. Pankratova et al., eds., *Revoliutsiia 1905–1907 gg. v Rossii: Dokumenty i materialy*, 18 vols. M: Institut Istorii, Akademiia Nauk SSSR, 1955–65.

Sokoloff, *White Nights*,   Boris Th. Sokoloff [B. F. Sokolov], *The White Nights: Pages from a Russian Doctor's Notebook*, NY: Devin-Adair, 1956; reprinted, L: Holborn Publishing Co, 1959.

SPb   St. Petersburg.

Stankevich, *Vospominaniia*   Vladimir B. Stankevich [Vlados Stanka], *Vospominaniia 1914–1919 g.*, Berlin: Ladyzhnikov, 1920.

Stepun, *Byvshee*   Fëdor Stepun, *Byvshee i nebyvsheesia*, 2 vols. NY: Chekhov, 1956.

Sukhanov, *Zapiski*   Nikolai N. Sukhanov [Himmer], *Zapiski o Revoliutsii* (Letopis' Revoliutsii No.1), 7 vols. Berlin-Pet-M: Z. I. Grzhebin, 1922–23.

Tsereteli, *Vospominaniia*   Iraklii G. Tsereteli, *Vospominaniia o fevral'skoi revoliutsii*, 2 vols. Paris-The Hague: Mouton, 1963.

USA, *Papers* (1918 etc.)   USA, Department of State, *Papers Relating to the Foreign Relations of the United States. 1918/1919. Russia*, 4 vols. Washington, DC, 1931–37.

VOSR   A. L. Sidorov et al., eds. *Velikaia Oktiabr'skaia Sotsialisticheskaia Revoliutsiia: Dokumenty i materialy*, 14 vols. M: Institut Istorii, Akademiia Nauk SSSR, 1957–63.

WO.33   War Office. European War: Secret Telegrams, Series E.

WO.106   War Office. Directorate of Military Operations and Intelligence, War Office Papers, Public Record Office, London.

Introduction

1. *Russkii Invalid*, June–July 1917; AK in *NYT*, May 22, 1917; AK, *Catastrophe*, 221–23; A. P. Zhilin, *Poslednee Nastuplenie (iiun' 1917 goda)* (M: Nauka, 1983), 57 ff; photographs, Papers of Asher Gransby, Vancouver; conversations with members of Gloucester Ukrainian Club.
2. Personal communications from Elena Izvolskaya and Robert Payne.

1. Inspector Kerensky's Career

1. Topographical information from I. E. Andreevskii, ed. *Entsiklopedicheskii Slovar'*, 40 vols. (SPb: Brockhaus and Efron, 1890–1903); V. P. Semënov-Tian-Shanskii, *Rossiia: Pol'noe geograficheskoe opisanie nashego otechestva*, 19 vols. (SPb: A. F. Devrien, 1890–1914); Carl Baedeker, *Russia* (Leipzig and L: Baedeker, 1914, reprinted, L and Newton Abbot: David and Charles, 1971); *Bol'shaia Sovetskaia Entsiklopediia* (3d. ed.), A. M. Prokhorov et al., eds. (M: *Sovetskaia Entsiklopediia*, 1970–81), (30 vols and index). For Penza Province, see Semënov, *Rossiia* (1902)2: 7, 117, 166–67, map facing 160, 495–97, 342–43, end-paper map. For an interpretation of Russian history, see Lionel Kochan and Richard Abraham, *The Making of Modern Russia*, (L: Penguin, Macmillan, 1983).
2. G. L. Freeze, *The Russian Levites: Parish Clergy in the Eighteenth Century* (Cambridge: Harvard University Press, 1977), passim; D. Mackenzie Wallace, *Russia* (L: Cassell, 1912), ch. 19, 293–304; for changing views of Nicholas I's reign, Marc Raeff, *Understanding Imperial Russia: State and Society in the Old Regime* (NY: Columbia University Press, 1984), 147–171.
3. AK, *Turning Point*, 4–5; Sergei A. Vasiliev to AK, September 8, 1951, Kerensky Papers, F.129; AK's cousin, Vladimir Kerensky, wrote, *Amerikanskaia Episkopal'naia Tserkov': Eia proiskhozhdenie i sostoianie preimushchestvenno v veroispovednom otnoshenii*, (Kazan': Tsentral'naia Tip., 1908); *Adres-Kalendar' nachal'stvuiushchikh i drugikh dolzhnostnykh lits po vsiem viedomstvam i upravleniiam Rossiiskoi imperii na 1913 g.*, (annual) (SPb: Pravitel'stvuiushchii Senat, 1913), part 1, cc. 1469–70; Friedrich Dukmeyer, "Der junge Kerenski," *Vossische Zeitung*, May 30, 1917; For district schools see "Materialy dlia biografii V. O. Kliuchevskago," *Vasilii Osipovich Kliuchevskii: Biograficheskii ocherk, rechi, proiznesënnyia v torzhestvennom zasedanii 12 noiabria 1911 goda, i materialy dlia ego biografii* (M: Imperatorskoe Obshchestvo Istorii i Drevnostei Rossiiskikh pri Moskovskom Universitete, 1914), part 3, 17–96.
4. M. K. Liubavskii, "Vasilii Osipovich Kliuchevskii (ob. 12 maia 1911 g.)", *Vasilii Osipovich Kliuchevskii . . .*, part 1, 19, 25 ff; ibid., part 3, 97 ff; 347–49.
5. AK, *Turning Point*, 5; V. O. Kliuchevskii, *Pis'ma, Dnevniki, Aforizmy i mysli ob istorii* (M: Nauka, 1968), 432.
6. A. J. Richter ed. and introd., *The Politics of Autocracy: Letters of Alexander II to Prince A. I. Bariatinskii 1857–1864* (Paris–The Hague: Mouton and Co., 1966), 25; P. A. Zaionchkovskii, *Provedenie v zhizn' Krest'ianskoi reformy 1861 g.*, (M: Idz. sotsial'noekonomicheskoi literatury, 1958), 63; W. E. Mosse, *Alexander II*

and the Modernization of Russia (L: English Universities Press 1958), chapter 4, passim.

7. AK, *Turning Point*, 5.

8. S. A. Vasil'ev to AK, Sept. 8, 1951, Kerensky Papers, F.129.

9. *Adres-Kalendar' . . . na 1875 g.*, part 1, c. 425, c. 577; *1879*, part 1, c. 443; *1881*, part 1, c. 443; F. M. Kerenskii, "Drevno-russkie otrechënnye verovaniia i Kalendar' Briusa," *Zhurnal Ministerstva Narodnago Prosveshcheniia*, April 1874, 330–331; AK, *Turning Point*, 5, 7, 17. Kerensky's first wife was astonished at his omission of his favorite sister, Nadya, from his memoirs, perhaps an example of his tendency to repress unhappy incidents, as she died young; cf. Dukmeyer, "Der junge Kerenski." In 1917 and afterwards, anti-Semites alleged that Kerensky's mother's name proved him to be Jewish, e.g. A. Popov ed., "Diplomatiia Vremënnogo Pravitel'stva v bor'be s revoliutsiei," *KA* (1927) 20: 27. Marc Ferro uncriticially repeats the canard that as a Jew, Kerensky was barred from high military rank before the revolution, hence his infatuation with his military role in 1917, Ferro, *October 1917: A Social History of the Russian Revolution*, (L: Routledge & Kegan Paul 1980), 47. But Kerensky's "Adler" grandfather *was* a general!

10. A. N. Naumov, *Iz utselevshikh vospominanii 1868–1917*, 2 vols. (NY: A. K. Naumova and O. A. Kusevitskaia, 1954–55), 1: 20–21; AK, *Turning Point*, 10.

11. Isaac Deutscher, *Lenin's Childhood* (L: Oxford University Press, 1970) 8–11, 27 ff.

12. Naumov, *Iz utselevshikh vospominanii*, 1: 36–38.

13. AK, *Turning Point*, 5–7.

14. Franco Venturi, *Roots of Revolution* (NY: Grosset and Dunlap, 1960), 253 ff.

15. P. A. Zaionchkovskii ed., *Dnevnik D. A. Miliutina*, (M: Gosudarstvennaia ordena Lenina Biblioteka SSSR imeni V. I. Lenina: Otdel rukopisei, 4 vols. 1947–50), 4: 35; P. L. Alston, *Education and the State in Tsarist Russia* (Stanford, Cal: Stanford University Press, 1969), 125 ff.

16. Deutscher, *Lenin's Childhood*, 32–67; N. N. Valentinov, *Encounters with Lenin* (L: Oxford University Press 1968), 51.

17. V. V. Kiriakov, "A. F. Kerenskii," *Niva*, no. 19, May 13, 1917; John Spargo, *Bolshevism, the Enemy of Political and Industrial Democracy* (NY-L: Harper & Row, 1919), 61; AK, *Crucifixion*, 10–11; AK, *Turning Point*, 4.

18. D. F. Sverchkov, *Tri meteora: G. Gapon, G. Nosar', A. Kerenskii*, (Pet: "Priboi," 1921), 152; Sverchkov, *Kerenskii*, (Lgd: "Priboi," 1927), 5.

19. *Adres-Kalendar' . . . na 1890 g.*, part 1, c. 494; AK, *Turning Point*, 8–11, 17; AK, *Crucifixion*, 57.

20. Count K. K. Pahlen, *Mission to Turkestan* (L: Oxford University Press, 1964), 1–21.

21. N. V. Tcharykow, *Glimpses of High Politics 1855–1929*, (L: G. Allen & Unwin, 1931), 157 ff; R. A. Pierce, *Russian Central Asia 1867–1917*, (Berkeley-LA: University of California Press, 1960), 17 ff.

22. Hélène Carrère d'Encausse, "La Politique Culturelle du Pouvoir Tsariste au Turkestan (1867–1917)," *CMRS* (1962) 3 (3): 388–92; Carrère d'Encausse, "Organizing and Colonizing the Conquered Territories," in E. Allworth, ed. *Central*

Asia: A Century of Russian Rule (NY-L: Columbia University Press, 1967), passim; H. Seton-Watson, *The Russian Empire 1801–1917*, (L: Oxford University Press, 1967), 505; Alston, *Education*, 119n.

23. P. A. Zaionchkovskii ed., *Dnevnik Gosudarstvennogo Sekretaria A. A. Polovtsëva*, 2 vols. (M: Nauka, 1966) 2: 17, 107, 475 n4; Dukmeyer, "Der junge Kerenski"; AK, *Catastrophe*, 297–98; K. Oberuchev, *V dni revoliutsii* (NY: Narodopravstvo, 1919), 108–9; Stig Jägerskiöld, *Gustaf Mannerheim*, 8 vols (1964–1981) (H:ki: Albert Bonniers Förlag and Holger Schildts Förlag), vol. 2: *Gustaf Mannerheim, 1906–1917*, 327.

24. Dukmeyer, "Der junge Kerenski;" Dukmeyer, "Mit Kerenski in Turkestan," *Deutsche Revue* (1917) 3: 294–96; AK, *Turning Point*, 15–17; Conversations with Mrs. O. L. Kerensky.

25. AK, *Turning Point*, 14.

26. AK, *Turning Point*, 15–17.

27. Ia. E. Vodarskii, *Naselenie Rossii za 400 let (xvi—nachalo xx vv.)*, (M: Prosveshchenie, 1973), 111 ff; L. K. Erman, *Intelligentsia v pervoi russkoi revoliutsii*, (M: Nauka, 1966), 7 ff.

28. Vera Broido, *Apostles into Terrorists*, (L: Maurice Temple Smith, 1977), 45 ff.

29. AK, *Turning Point*, 17; Conversations with Mrs. Kerensky.

2. A Hesitant Hero

1. AK, Crucifixion, 77 ff; AK, *Turning Point*, 17; AK interviewed by Elena Ivanoff, Oct. 29, 1961, Tape (transcript) no. 5, 1, Kerensky Papers, F.97.

2. AK, *Crucifixion*, 78; AK, *Turning Point*, 20, 72

3. AK, *Turning Point*, 27; AK, 'Istoriia Rossii', 230, typescript, Kerensky Papers, F.7, Gabor Kiss, *Die Gesellschaftspolitische Rolle der Studentenbewegung im vorrevolutionären Russland*, (Munich: Bibliotheca Europae Orientalis 1963) 1: 88; F. Dukmeyer, "Der junge Kerenski", *Vossische Zeitung*, May 30, 1917.

4. AK, *Turning Point*, 22; OLK, "Obryvki," introduction, 2–4; S. A. Kozin, *Bibliograficheskii obzor izdannykh i neizdannykh rabot akademika V. P. Vasil'eva*, (M: Izvestiia AN SSSR, 1931), passim; Conversations with, and personal communications from, Mrs. O. L. Kerensky and Kirill Grigorkoff.

5. AK, *Turning Point*, 21, 24–26; AK, *Crucifixion*, 84–5; AK interviewed by E. Ivanoff, Oct. 29, 1961, Tape 5, 4, Kerensky Papers, F.97; Robert Payne, *The Fortress*, (L-NY: W. H. Allen, 1967), 406.

6. S. S. Ol'denburg, *Tsarstvovanie Imperatora Nikolaia II*, (Belgrade-Munich: Izd. Obshchestva Rasprostraneniia Russkoi Natsional'noi i Patrioticheskoi literatury, 2 vols. [1939–1949]), 1: 162–63; S. Galai, *The Liberation Movement in Russia 1900–1905*, (Cambridge: Cambridge University Press, 1973), 113–14.

7. AK, *Crucifixion*, 100–101; AK, *Turning Point*, 26–27; c.f. D. F. Sverchkov, *Kerenskii* (Lgd: Priboi, 1927), 6.

8. V. M. Chernov, *Pered burei: vospominaniia*, (NY: Chekhov, 1953), 55 ff; Leszek Kołakowski, *Main Currents of Marxism: Its Origins, Growth and Dissolution* (L-NY: Oxford University Press, 1978), vol. 2; *The Golden Age*, 94; *Manifest*

Rossiiskoi Sotsialdemokraticheskoi Rabochei Partii (1898 g.) (Geneva: RSDRP, 1903), 3.

9. A. Potresov, "Evoliutsiia obshchestvenno-politicheskoi mysli v predrevoliutsionnuiu epokhu," in L. Martov et al., eds. *Obshchestvennoe Dvizhenie v Rossii v nachale XX-go veka*, 4 vols. (1909–1912), (SPb: Obshchestvennaia Pol'za, 1909), 1: 590.

10. Chernov, *Pered burei*, 55 ff; AK, *Turning Point*, 29–33.

11. S. L. Frank ed., *Iz istorii russkoi filosofskoi mysli kontsa 19-go i nachala 20-go veka*, (Washington, D.C.: Inter-Language Literary Associates, 1965), 225; N. Losskii, *Obosnovanie Intuitivizma*, (SPb: Zapiski istoriko-filologicheskago fakul'teta imp. Sankt-Peterburgskago universiteta, part 78, 1906), 358 ff; Kołakowski, *Marxism*, 2: 383

12. N. S. Timasheff, introduction to Leon Petrażycki, *Law and Morality* (Cambridge: Harvard University Press, 1955), xx-xxxii; Kołakowski, *Marxism*, 2: 338; L. I. Petrazhitskii, *Vvedenie v izuchenie nrava i nravstvennosti: Osnovy emotsional'noi psikhologii* (SPb: Tip. Iu. N. Erlikh, 1905), vi-x.

13. James H. Billington, *Mikhailovsky and Russian Populism* (L: Oxford University Press, 1958), vii, 178–84.

14. Sokoloff, *White Nights*, 63–64.

15. Lionel Kochan, *Russia in Revolution 1890–1918* (L: Weidenfeld and Nicholson, 1966), part 1, passim.

16. J.H.L. Keep, *The Rise of Social Democracy in Russia* (Oxford, England: Clarendon Press, 1963), 39–66; H. Seton-Watson, *The Russian Empire 1801–1917* (L: Oxford University Press 1967), 561–63.

17. Manfred Hildermeier, *Die Sozialrevolutionäre Partei Russlands: Agrarsozialismus und Modernisierung im Zarenreich (1900-1914)*, (Cologne-Vienna: Böhlau Verlag, 1978), 35-57.

18. Galai, *Liberation Movement*, 127 ff; *Osvobozhdenie*, no. 2, July 2, 1902; AK, *Turning Point*, 41

19. AK, *Turning Point*, 23; P. Scheibert, "Die Petersburger religiös-philosophischen Zusammenkünfte von 1902 und 1903," *Jahrbücher für Geschichte Osteuropas* (1964), NF. 12: 513–560.

20. Galai, *Liberation Movement*, 48, 148–50, 167–69, 195; AK, *Turning Point*, 42

21. AK, *Crucifixion*, 91; Conversations with Mrs. O. L. Kerensky.

22. AK, *Turning Point*, 17, 27; Galai, *Liberation Movement*, 120–22; Conversations with Mrs. Kerensky.

23. AK to Mrs. O. L. Kerensky, Sept. 3, 1963, photographs, Kerensky Family Papers; Conversations with Mrs. Kerensky.

24. Personal communications from Mrs. Kerensky.

25. AK, *Crucifixion*, 90–92; AK, *Turning Point*, 43 ff; Valdo Zilli, *La Rivoluzione Russa del 1905*, (Naples: Istituto italiano per gli Studi Storici in Napoli, 1963), 1: 566ff; E. A. Sviatopolk-Mirskaia, "Dnevnik," *Istoricheskie zapiski* (1965), 77: 240 ff.

26. AK, *Turning Point*, 44; AK, "Istoriia Rossii," 308, Kerensky Papers, F.7.

27. AK, *Turning Point*, 44; OLK, "Obryvki," 157–58; *Burevestnik*, Nov. 20, 1905.

28. L. K. Erman, *Intelligentsiia v pervoi russkoi revoliutsii*, (M: Nauka, 1966), 27–28.

29. AK, *Turning Point*, 22, 60; S. A. Vasil'ev to AK, June 18, 1958 and Vasil'ev, "1905–1906 gody," ms, both in the Kerensky Papers, F.170; B. V. Savinkov, *Memoirs of a Terrorist* (NY: Boni, 1931), 187.

30. *RR*, vol. 1: *Nachalo pervoi russkoi revoliutsii, ianvar'-mart 1905 goda*, M: (1955), 15, 24–27; S. Harcave, *First Blood*, (L: Bodley Head, 1964), 78–79.

31. Harcave, *First Blood*, 81–88; N. S. Trusova ed., "A. M. Gor'kii i Sobytiia 9 ianvaria 1905 goda v Peterburge", *Istoricheskii Arkhiv* (1955), no. 1, 91–116; *Kerenskii po DP*, 5; Sverchkov, Leiberov, and Radkey all accepted this source as both authentic and substantially accurate. I consulted the copy deposited by Prof. Frank Golder in the Hoover Institution.

32. AK, *Turning Point*, 47; AK, *Crucifixion*, 95; c.f. AK, "Istoriia Rossii," 305, Kerensky Papers, F.7; Harcave, *First Blood*, 88–97

33. AK, *Turning Point*, 49–50; Conversations with Mrs. Kerensky.

34. AK, *Turning Point*, 49; Harcave, *First Blood*, 121–22.

35. Harcave, *First Blood*, 122–23; Savinkov, *Memoirs*, 85–86; S. D. Mstislavskii, *Na Krovi*, (Berlin: Polyglotte, 1928), 36; Galai, *Liberation Movement*, 240–250.

36. Vasil'ev, "1905–1906 gody," 4–5.

37. Vasil'ev, "1905–1906 gody," 4–6; AK, *Crucifixion*, 108; AK to Mrs. O. L. Kerensky, Aug. 24, 1959, Kerensky Family Papers; AK, *Turning Point*, 60.

38. Harcave, *First Blood*, ch. 5, passim; Conversations with Mrs. Kerensky.

39. Galai, *Liberation Movement*, 251 ff; L. D. Trotsky, *1905*, (L: Allen Lane, 1972), 83; Vasil'ev, "1905–1906 gody," 7; AK interviewed by Elena Ivanoff, Sept. 30, 1961, Tape No. 3, 3, Kerensky Papers, F.97.

40. S. M. Schwarz, *The Russian Revolution of 1905* (Chicago: University of Chicago Press, 1967), 171 ff; H. D. Mehlinger and J. M. Thompson, *Count Witte and the Tsarist Government in the 1905 Revolution* (Bloomington, Ind.: Indiana University Press, 1972), 112 ff; A. A. Dobrovol'skii ed. *Polnyi Svod Zakonov Rossiiskoi Imperii*, sobr.3-e, (SPb: Zakonovedenie 1912–14), vol. 25, section 1, no. 26656; A. V. Gerasimoff, *Der Kampf gegen die erste russische Revolution*, (Frauenfeld-Leipzig: Huber, 1934), 68–71.

41. AK, *Crucifixion*, 108–9; AK, *Turning Point*, 55–57; *Rech'*, Oct. 17, 1906; Ol'denburg, *Tsarstvovanie . . . Nikolaia II* (1939), 1: 316–33; Trotsky, *1905*, 113–17; M. Novoselev, *Nikolai Ernestovich Bauman, 1873–1905*, (M: "Zhizn' zamechatel'-nykh liudei," 1955), 226–28; *Sbornik Karrikatur velikoi russkoi Revoliutsii*, (Berlin: Verlag von Rosenthal, 1906), 112.

42. *Burevestnik*, Nov. 20, 24; Dec. 8, 1905; Vasil'ev to AK, June 18, 1958, Kerensky Papers, F.170; AK to Mrs. O. L. Kerensky, Aug. 27, 1963, Kerensky Family Papers; AK interviewed by E. Ivanoff, Oct. 20, 1961, Tape no. 5, 8; Tape no. 6, n.d., 2; Kerensky Papers, F.97; AK, *Turning Point*, 59.

43. AK, *Turning Point*, 59; *Burevestnik*, Nov. 24, 1905.

44. *Burevestnik*, Nov. 24, 1905; AK, *Crucifixion*, 115; AK, "Istoriia Rossii," 319, Kerensky Papers, F.7; Galai, *Liberation Movement*, 260; Harcave, *First Blood*, 216 ff; Mehlinger and Thompson, *Count Witte*, 112–24.

45. *Burevestnik*, Nov. 27, 1905; AK interviewed by E. Ivanoff, Tape no. 6, n.d., 1, Kerensky Papers, F.97; AK, *Crucifixion*, 115; Vasil'ev to AK, June 18, 1958, Kerensky Papers, F. 170.

46. Vasil'ev, "1905–1906 gody," 3, 7ff, Kerensky Papers, F.170; AK, *Crucifixion*, 115–16; AK, *Turning Point*, 60; *Kerenskii po DP*, 5–6, 46ff; "A.B.," *Za Kulisami okhrannago otdeleniia* (Berlin: Heinrich Caspari, 1910), 329 ff.
47. AK, *Turning Point*, 60–62.
48. AK, *Turning Point*, 60–62; Savinkov, *Memoirs*, 78, 96, 175–79, 196 ff; V. M. Zenzinov, *Perezhitoe* (NY: Chekhov, 1953), 276–77; V. K. Agafonov, *Zagranichnaia okhranka* (Pet-M: Kniga, 1918), 9–11; Gerasimoff, *Kampf*, 208; Boris Nicolaevsky, *Aseff: The Russian Judas*, (L: Hurst & Blackett, 1934), 100–01.
49. AK, *Crucifixion*, 115; AK, *Turning Point*, 64–67; Vasil'ev, "1905–1906 gody," Kerensky Papers, F.170; *Kerenskii po DP*, 5.
50. AK, *Crucifixion*, 116–18; AK, *Turning Point*, 67–68; *Svod Zakonov Rossiiskoi Imperii*, ed. A. A. Dobrovol'skii (SPb: Zakonovedenie 1913), 4: 693–94.
51. AK, *Turning Point*, 71–72; *Kerenskii po DP*, 6; Nicolaevsky, *Aseff*, 133; Savinkov, *Memoirs*, 323; Gerasimoff, *Kampf*, 77; AK interviewed by E. Ivanoff, Tape No. 6, n.d., 6, Kerensky Papers, F.97.
52. AK, *Turning Point*, 72; *Kerenskii po DP*, 6; Personal communication from Mrs. Kerensky.
53. AK, *Crucifixion*, 118–19; AK, *Turning Point*, 60.
54. A. V. Peshekhonov, *K voprosu ob intelligentsii*, (SPb: Russkoe Bogatstvo, 1906), 30; V. Ropshin [alias B. V. Savinkov], *Kon' blednyi*, (Nice: M. A. Tumanov, 1913), passim.

3. Against the Tide

1. S. D. Mstislavskii, *Na Krovi*, (Berlin: Polyglotte, 1928) gives a fascinating view of the 1905 Revolution from an SR point of view. For popular anti-Semitism, see Maxim Gorky, "The Russian Peasant," in R.E.F. Smith, ed. *The Russian Peasant 1920 and 1984*, (L: Frank Cass, 1977), 18–19.
2. C.f. S. Harcave, *First Blood* (L: Bodley Head, 1964), 216–20.
3. Samuel H. Baron, *Plekhanov, the Father of Russian Marxism*, (L: Routledge and Kegan Paul, 1963), 263–67; V. M. Chernov, *Pered burei*, (NY: Chekhov 1953), 252–53; S. M. Schwarz, *The Russian Revolution of 1905* (Chicago: University of Chicago Press 1967), 167–95; Richard Pipes, *Struve, Liberal on the Right 1905–1944* (Cambridge: Harvard University Press, 1980), 3 ff, 18.
4. H. D. Mehlinger & J. M. Thompson, *Count Witte and the Tsarist Government in the 1905 Revolution* (Bloomington, Ind.: Indiana University Press, 1972), 289 ff.
5. John Biggart, " 'Anti-Leninist Bolshevism': the *Forward* Group of the RSDRP," *Canadian Slavonic Papers* (1981) 23(2): 135; *Protokoly pervago s'ezda Partii Sotsialistov-Revoliutsionerov* (L: PSR, 1906), 9–22.
6. S. S. Ol'denburg, *Tsarstvovanie Imperatora Nikolaia II*, (Belgrade-Munich: Obshchestvo Rasprostraneniia Russkoi Natsional'noi i Patrioticheskoi literatury, 1949)2:350 ff; AK, *Turning Point*, 70, where AK claims to have participated in this demonstration, though his police file suggests he had already been released, *Kerenskii po DP*, 6.

7. *Zemlia i Volia*, no. 2, Feb. 2, 1907.
8. T. Riha, *A Russian European: Paul Miliukov in Russian Politics* (Notre Dame, Ind.-L: University of Notre Dame Press, 1969), 118 ff; *Pamiatnaia Knizhka Sotsialista-revoliutsionera* (Paris: PSR, 1911)1: 56–57; S. A. Vasil'ev, "1905–1906 gody," ms, 9, Kerensky Papers, F.170.
9. *Raboty pervoi Gosudarstvennoi Dumy*, (SPb: izd. SPb-go Komiteta Trudovoi Gruppy, 1906), passim; A. V. Peshekhonov, *V tëmnuiu noch'*, (SPb: Russkoe Bogatstvo, 1909), 18.
10. Riha, *Miliukov*, 113–16
11. AK, *Turning Point*, 73; Peshekhonov, *V tëmnuiu noch'*, 3–30.
12. AK, *Turning Point*, 74–75; AK, *Crucifixion*, 120–21; AK interviewed by Elena Ivanoff, tape No. 6, n.d., 9–10, Kerensky Papers, F.97; OLK, "Obryvki," 11*n*; *Rech'*, Nov. 7, 1906 explains that Sokolov was banned from the Baltic Provinces. For Poska, see R. Kleis et al., eds. *Eesti Entsüklopeedia*, (Tartu: Loodus, 1936), 6: 927.
13. *Revaler Beobachter*, Dec. 16, 17, 20; *RR: Vysshii pod'ëm Revoliutsii 1905–1907 gg.: Vooruzhënnye vosstaniia noiabr'-dekabr' 1905 goda*, A. L. Sidorov, ed. part 4, M (1957), 579 ff, 591.
14. *Revaler Beobachter*, Oct. 30, 1906; *Päewaleht*, Oct. 31, 1906; *Rech'*, Nov. 1, 3, 1906; V. V. Kiriakov [?], Dossier Kerensky, typescript, 2, FAT 94 AP 182, contains the version Kerensky told his friends no later than 1917; Conversations with Mrs. O. L. Kerensky, Dr. O. A. Kerensky, CBE, FRS.
15. Ferdinand Carlsson, "Tallinnas Sajandi Alul," in Hans Kruus, ed. *Punased Aastad: Mälestisi ja dokumente 1905. Aasta liikumisest Eestis*, (Tartu: Eesti Kirjanduse Seltsi Kirjastus, 1932), 1: 168–69; Alma Ast-Ani, "Sotsialistliku Noorsoo keskel enne Revolutsiooni, Tartus ja Viljandimaal 1905–1906," *Punased Aastad*, 1: 49.
16. A. Ia. Avrekh ed., "Revoliutsionnoe dvizhenie v Pribaltike (Noiabr'-Dekabr' 1905 g.)," *Istoricheskii Arkhiv*, (1955), no. 1, 216–17; *Düna Zeitung*, Dec. 2, 3, 5, 6, 1905; *Balss*, Dec. 9, 13, 1905; *Düna Zeitung*, Feb. 2, 1907.
17. *Düna Zeitung*, Feb. 6, 1907; *Balss*, Feb. 6, 1907; Adolfs Blodnieks, *The Undefeated Nation* (NY: Robert Speller, 1960), 142.
18. *Pamiatnaia Knizhka s-ra*, 1: 57–59; AK to Mrs. O. L. Kerensky, July 19, 1962, Kerensky Family Papers.
19. V. V. Kiriakov, introduction to AK, *Izbrannyia rechi*, (Pet: Biblioteka "Solntse Svobody" 1917), 8, and in *Niva*, no. 19, May 13, 1917; N.D. Avksentiev, "Krainie levye v Gosud. Dume," *Severnyia Zapiski* (1914) no. 5, 144; David Lane, *The Roots of Russian Communism* (L: Martin Robertson, 1968), 76–77.
20. Conversations with Mrs. Kerensky; *Rech'*, April 20, 1907.
21. Conversations with Mrs. Kerensky; M. Druskim ed. *50 Oper*, (Lgd: 'Sovetskii Kompozitor', 1960), 200–205.
22. 'Tuchkin' in *Protokoly pervago s'ezda Partii S-R-ov*, 157.
23. *Zemlia i Volia*, No. 4, April 7, 1907
24. H. Seton-Watson, *The Russian Empire 1801–1917*, (L: Oxford UP, 1967), 626–27; A. Levin, "The Shornikova Affair," *American Slavonic and East European Review* (1942–43) 2: 3–16; V. S. Diakin, *Samoderzhavie, Burzhauziia i dvorianstvo v 1907–1911 gg.*, (Lgd: 'Nauka', Leningradskoe otdelenie, 1978), 69; *Pamiatnaia*

Knizhka s-ra, 1: 62–64; Biggart, " 'Anti-Leninist Bolshevism,' " passim; Mary Schaeffer Conroy, *Peter Arkad'evich Stolypin: Practical Politics in Late Tsarist Russia* (Boulder, Colo: Westview Press, 1976), 43 ff.

25. Diakin, *Samoderzhavie*, 28–30; Riha, *Miliukov*, 196–98; Manfred Hagen, *Die Entfaltung Politischer Öffentlichkeit in Russland 1906–1914* (Wiesbaden: Franz Steiner Verlag, 1982), 200–205; D. Mandel, "The Intelligentsia and the Working Class in 1917," *Critique* (1981), no. 14, 68–69; *Trud*, no. 19, Feb 1908.

26. Vera Broido, *Apostles into Terrorists* (L: Maurice Temple Smith, 1977), 62, 68, 100–2; Cathy Porter, *Alexandra Kollontai: A Biography* (L: Virago, 1980), 28, 38, 142 ff.

27. V. V. Rozanov, *Semeinyi vopros v Rossii* (SPb: Tip. M. Merkusheva, 1903), passim; *Rech'*, April 11, 1907; D. A. Lowrie, *Rebellious Prophet: A Life of Nicolai Berdyaev* (NY: Harper, 1960), 105–10; S. Karlinsky, introduction to V. Zlobin, *A Difficult Soul: Zinaida Gippius* (Berkeley-LA-L: Univ. of California Press, 1980), 7 ff; Temira Pachmuss, ed. *Intellect and Ideas in Action: Selected Correspondence of Zinaida Hippius* (Munich: Wilhelm Fink Verlag, 1972), 35–36.

28. Both stories were published in *Shipovnik* (SPb, 1907); L. K. Erman, *Intelligentsiia v pervoi russkoi revoliutsii* (M: Nauka 1966), 334–35.

29. M. Artsybashev, *Sanin* (Nice: Russkaia Tipografiia Ia. E. Kleidmana, 1909), 102–3; Porter, *Kollontai*, 149

30. O. O. Gruzenberg, *Vchera: vospominaniia* (Paris: Dom Knigi, 1938), 41–42; Gruzenberg, *Ocherki i rechi* (NY: Grenich Printing Corp., 1944), 78 ff; *Rech'*, Aug. 18, 1907; Conversations with Boris Elkin and Mrs. Kerensky.

31. OLK, "Obryvki," 125*n*; Iu. Martov, *Zapiski sotsial-demokrata* (letopis' revoliutsii no.4) (Berlin-Pet-M: Grzhebin, 1922), 64, 77–79, 102; S Kamenskii, *Vek minuvshii: (Vospominaniia)* (Paris: I.C.E., 1958), 90; *Rech'*, Oct 19, 1907; S. Galai, *The Liberation Movement in Russia 1900–1905* (Cambridge: Cambridge University Press, 1973), 168, 249, 259. Sokolov's "klichka" is in *Kerenskii po DP*, 50.

32. OLK, "Obryvki," 11*n*; Gruzenberg, *Vchera*, 41–42; A. A. Demianov, "Moia sluzhba pri Vremënnom Pravitel'stve," *ARR* (1921), 4: 63–64.

33. AK, *Turning Point*, 77–80; F. D. Kriukov et al, *Vyborgskii protsess*, (SPb: Obshchestvennaia Pol'za, 1908), 1–2; *Rech'*, Sept. 7, 1907; *Pravo*, Dec. 16, 1907; B. V. Savinkov, *Memoirs of a Terrorist*, (NY: Boni, 1931), 323; *Pravo*, Feb. 18, 1908.

34. *Rech'*, July 24, 1907, Sept. 2, 9, 1907; *Pravo*, July 4, 1910, c. 1716.

35. Gruzenberg, *Vchera*, 7; AK, *Turning Point*, 78–79; Fredrik Ström, *Ryska Revolutionens Historia i Sammandrang* (Stockholm: Ryska Revolutionens Historias Förlag, 1924), 100 ff; *Rech'*, Sept. 20, 1907.

36. *Pravo*, Dec. 16, 1907, c. 3248; Jan. 13, 1908, cc. 118–123; *Rech'* Oct. 19–Nov. 22, 1907.

37. Kriukov, *Vyborgskii protsess*, 1–2; *Rech'*, Sept. 7, 1907.

38. Okhranka, XVI b(3), F1.1B, "Obzor sostoianii Tsentral'nago Komiteta partii sotsialistov-revoliutsionerov k kontsu 1908 goda." (The arbitrary reallocation of the Okhranka papers into thematic files unrelated to the *Vkhodiashchie* and *Vykhodiashchie Zhurnaly* makes it pointless to cite the full original archival references.) A. V. Gerasimoff, *Der Kampf gegen die erste russische Revolution*

(Frauenfeld-Leipzig: Huber, 1934), 173–79; Savinkov, *Memoirs*, 312 ff, 318, 328–48; V. K. Agafonov, *Zagranichnaia okhranka* (Pet-M: "Kniga," 1918), 304–7; S. A. Vasil'ev to AK, March 3, 195?, Kerensky Papers, F.129; Boris Nicolaevsky, *Aseff: The Russian Judas*, (L: Hurst and Blackett, 1934), 26 ff.

39. AK to Mrs. O. L. Kerensky, July 19, 1962, Kerensky Family Papers; Gerasimoff, *Kampf*, 210.

40. OLK, "Obryvki," 84; *Ves' Peterburg na 1905 g.*, (annual), (SPb: Izd. Ves' Peterburg), part 3, 289; *Ves' Peterburg na 1908 g.*, part 3, 339; Sokoloff, *White Nights*, 63–64; Sukhanov, *Zapiski*, 1: 61–63; Conversations with, and personal communications from, Mrs. Kerensky, Dr. O. A. Kerensky and Gleb Kerensky.

41. AK interviewed by Elena Ivanoff, Oct. 29, 1961, Tape no. 5, *n*6, 21–22; Tape no. 6, n.d., 20 ff; *Kerenskii po DP*, 8; *Den'*, March 8, 1917; *Delo Naroda*, April 8, 1917; AK, *Turning Point*, 83–84. Sam Spiegel's film *Nicholas and Alexandra* notwithstanding, Kerensky was not, of course, the conscience of the *Third Duma*.

42. 'Tan' [Prof. V. G. Bogoraz], introduction to *Rechi A. F. Alad'ina v pervom Russkom parlamente* (SPb: Baum, 1906), 6 ff; Chernov, *Pered burei*, 283–84; Lenin, *Works*, 10: 411; *GDSO*, May 30, 1906, c. 847; June 2, 1906, c. 870.

43. Hagen, *Entfaltung*, 313 ff.

44. *Pamiatnaia Knizhka s-ra*, 1: 24–25; M. Hildermeier, "Die Sozialrevolutionäre Partei: Zum Verhältnis von 'individuellem Terror' und wirtschaftlicher Entwicklung," in Dietrich Geyer, ed., *Wirtschaft und Gesellschaft im vorrevolutionären Russland*, (Cologne: Kiepenheuer und Witsch, 1975), 375–77.

45. Okhranka, XVI, 6 (3), F1.1A, No. 204, Agentura to DP, 8(21)/March/1910; XVI, 6 (3), F1.1B, No. 117287, MVD to Agentura, Oct. 31, 1910; XVI, 6 (3), F1.1A, no. 217, Agentura to DP, Feb. 17 (March 1), 1912; *Zemlia i Volia*, no. 25, Feb. 1912; *Pochin*, no. 1, June 1912.

46. V. Ropshin [alias V. V. Savinkov], *Kon' Blednyi*, (Nice: M. A. Tumanov, 1913), 98–112; *Pochin*, No. 1, June 1912; Lowrie, *Berdyaev*, 129–131.

47. Lenin, *Works*, 35: 50–51, 68; Biggart, " 'Anti-Leninist Bolshevism,' " passim; Chernov, *Pered burei*, 292–94, mentions Savinkov and Avksentiev but not his own response; Hildermeier, *Sozialrevolutionäre Partei*, 318 ff.

48. Okhranka, XVII, f.F.2, no. 58, Agentura to DP, Jan. 14(27), 1913.

49. Chernov, *The Great Russian Revolution* (New Haven, Conn: Yale University Press, 1936), 116, 394; Conroy, *Stolypin*, 187 ff.

4. Tribune of the People

1. AK, *Turning Point*, 80–81; *Rech'*, Jan. 17, 18, 1912; *Pravo*, Jan. 15, 1912, c. 124; Feb. 5, 1912, c. 282; March 11, 1912, cc. 580 ff; April 15, 1912, c. 866; April 22, 1912, c. 940; May 6, 1912, c. 1056; *Novoe Vremia*, March 21, 1912.

2. *The Times*, March 19, 20, 1912.

3. *Vsëpoddanneishii otchët chlëna Gosudarstvennago Soveta, Senatora Tainago sovetnika Manukhina po ispol'neniiu VSOCHAISHEE vozlozhennago na nego 27 Aprelia*

1912 goda razsledovanie o zabastovke na Lenskikh promyslakh (SPb: Tip. Shtaba Otd. Korp. Pogranichnoi Strazhi, 1912), 4, 250 ff, 228 ff, 245.

4. *Niva*, April 28, 1912; *Padenie*, 2, 105–113; *GDSO*, April 11, 1912, cc. 1941–53.

5. L. Kochan, *Russia in Revolution* (L: Weidenfeld and Nicholson, 1966), 154; K. F. Shatsillo, "Lenskii rasstrel i tsarskoe pravitel'stvo (po materialam Chrezvychainoi sledstvennoi Komissii Vremënnago Pravitel'stva)," *Bol'shevistskaia pechat' i rabochii klass Rossii v gody revoliutsionnogo pod'ëma*, L. M. Ivanov et al., eds. (M: Nauka, 1965), 386; *Novoe Vremia*, April 19, 1912; V. Nevskii, "K desiatiletiiu Lenskogo rasstrela," *Krasnaia Letopis'* nos. 2–3, 356. See plates 7-8 which were published in *Niva* on Aug. 4, 1912.

6. AK, *Turning Point*, 82–83.

7. *GDSO*, March 19, 1914, c. 1959; *Vsëpoddanneishii otchët . . . Manukhina*, 10 ff, 41 ff; *Prilozhenie*, no. 11, 2–3; *Prilozhenie*, no. 18, 4–7, 175 ff; *The Times*, Dec. 4, 1912.

8. AK, "O tom, chto bylo", *Zavety*, August 1912, no. 5, 83; A. F. Koni, *Na zhiznënnom puti*, 5, (Lgd: Priboi, 1929), 310–12.

9. V. F. Vladimirova, *Sovytiia na Lene v dokumentakh* (M: Partiinoe izdatel'stvo, 1932), 77.

10. AK, *Turning Point*, 83; *Vsëpoddanneishii otchët . . . Manukhina, Prilozhenie* no. 18, passim; AK, "O tom, chto bylo," 82; Lenin, *Works*, 18: 104; *GDSO*, March 19, 1914, c. 1972.

11. *Vsëpoddanneishii otchët . . . Manukhina*, vi; A. A. Dobrovol'skii, ed. *Polnyi Svod Zakonov Rossiiskoi Imperii*, (SPb: Zakonovedenie, 1912–14); 25 (26662), para. 38, *Prilozhenie*; Personal communications from Gleb Kerensky.

12. *Kerenskii po DP*, 8; AK, *Turning Point*, 84–85; V. B. Stankevich, "Mnimyia pobedy i deistvitel'nyia porazheniia," *Sovremënnik* (1912), no. 10, 312.

13. AK, *Turning Point*, 84–85; *Kerenskii po DP*, 8; *Rech'*, Oct. 21, 1912.

14. T. Riha, *A Russian European: Paul Miliukov in Russian Politics* (Notre Dame, Ind.: University of Notre Dame Press, 1969), 199–200; G. A. Hosking, *The Russian Constitutional Experiment: Government and Duma 1907–1914* (Cambridge: Cambridge University Press, 1973), 183–84; M. Hagen, *Die Entfaltung Politischer Öffentlichkeit in Russland 1906–1914* (Wiesbaden: Franz Steiner Verlag, 1982), 311–13; Stankevich, "Itogi i fakty," *Sovremënnik* (1912), no. 11, 305 ff.

15. Stankevich, "Mnimyia pobedy," 307–8; AK, *Turning Point*, 84; *GDSO, Chetvërtyi sozyv, ukazateli*; E. D. Vinogradoff, "The Russian Peasantry and the Elections to the Fourth State Duma," in L. H. Haimson, ed. *The Politics of Rural Russia 1905–1914*, (Bloomington, Ind.: Indiana University Press, 1979), 220; Hagen, *Entfaltung*, 288–89, 295 ff; Personal communications from Mrs. O. L. Kerensky.

16. *Polnyi Svod Zakonov Rossiiskoi Imperii*, otd. 1, no. 26661, para 2, *Prilozhenie*.

17. *GDSO*, Dec. 3, 1912, cc. 182–84; A. A. Demianov, "Moia sluzhba pri Vremënnom Pravitel'stve," *ARR*, (1921), 4: 71.

18. *GDSO*, Dec. 8, 1912, cc. 422–431

19. Demianov, "Moia sluzhba," 71; V. V. Kiriakov, introduction to AK, *Izbrannyia rechi*, (Pet: Biblioteka 'Solntse Svobody,' 1917), 8–9; E. H. Wilcox, "Kerensky and the Revolution," *Atlantic Monthly* (1917) 120: 694–95; Wilcox, *Russia's Ruin*, (L: Chapman & Hall, 1919), 189–190.

20. Wilcox, *Russia's Ruin*, 190, 226–34; B. Wolfe, *Three Who Made a Revolution* (L: Penguin, 1966), 596 ff.
21. Riha, *Miliukov*, 153 ff.
22. L. Schapiro, *The Communist Party of the Soviet Union*, (L: Methuen, 1963), 126–28; N. D. Avksentiev, "Krainie levye v Gosud. Dume," *Severnyia Zapiski* (1914), no. 5, 150.
23. George Katkov, *Russia 1917: The February Revolution*, (L: Longmans, 1967), 163–73; N. N. Iakovlev, *1 avgusta 1914*, (M: Molodaia Gvardiia, 1974), 226 ff.
24. AK, *Turning Point*, 87–89.
25. V. A. Maklakov, "Statement" typescript in French, posted to AK, Oct. 27, 1964, Kerensky Papers, F.160; Barbara T. Norton, "Russian Political Masonry and the February Revolution of 1917," *International Review of Social History* (1983) 28 (part 2): 240–258, argues that the political freemasonry *should* be seen as a continuation of earlier freemasonry.
26. E. D. Kuskova to Lydia Dan, G. Ia. Aronson, *Rossiia nakanune Revoliutsii: Istoricheskie etiudy* (NY: Novoe Russkoe Slovo, 1961), 138–42; A. Blodnieks, *The Undefeated Nation* (NY: Robert Speller and Son, 1960), 142; Ludwik Hass, "Wolnomularstwo Ukraińskie 1917–1921," *Studia z dziejów ZSRR i Europy Środkowej*, 18: 62; Iakovlev, *1 avgusta 1914*, 231.
27. Iakovlev, *1 avgusta 1914*, 229–231; B. F. Livchak, "O Politicheskoi roli masonov vo vtoroi russkoi revoliutsii," *Mezhvuzovskii sbornik nauchnykh trudov*, [Sverdlovsk], (1977) 56: 135–141; I. I. Mints, "Metamorfozy Masonskoi legendy," *Istoriia SSSR*, (1980), no. 4, 107–22. For a possible explanation of the success of Yakovlev, an author whose ideology has more in common with Nazism than Leninism, see Alexander Yanov, *The Russian New Right* (Berkeley-LA: University of California Press, 1978), 39–61. Why did it take Mints so long to reply? Couldn't he get permission, or was he hoping an "Aryan" would do the job? Academician Sakharov was less ceremonious with Yakovlev, see *New York Review of Books*, April 12, 1984.
28. M. M. Ter-Pogosian and Ia. L. [Rubinshtein] to AK, Dec. 26, 1962, Kerensky Papers, F.217.
29. Kuskova in Aronson, *Rossiia nakanune Revoliutsii*, 138–42; V. A. Obolensky in Nathan Smith, "The Role of the Russian Freemasonry in the February Revolution: Another Scrap of Evidence," *Slavic Review* (1968) 27: 606–8.
30. *Kerenskii po DP*, 48; Conversations with Dr. O. A. Kerensky.
31. Communications from, and conversations with, Mrs. Kerensky, Dr. O. A. Kerensky and Gleb Kerensky.
32. *GDSO*, Jan. 23, 1913, cc. 1012, 1019; V. N. Kokovtsov, *Out of My Past* (Stanford, Cal: Stanford University Press, 1935), 324–28, 336–39.
33. *GDSO*, April 29, 1913, cc. 656–68.
34. Schapiro, *Communist Party*, 125 ff; I. Getzler, *Martov: A Political Biography of a Russian Social Democrat* (Melbourne-Cambridge: Melbourne University Press & Cambridge University Press, 1967), 133–37.
35. Okhranka, XVI (3), F1. 1A, No. 1365, Agentura to DP, Aug. 28 (Sept. 10), 1914; F1.1B, No. 102, Agentura to DP, Jan. 22 (Feb. 4), 1913; No. 1998, Agentura to DP, Dec. 27 (Jan. 9), 1914; *Kerenskii po DP*, 9; Lenin, *Works*, 19:

432 ff; 20: 573*n*; 35: 92; AK interviewed by E. Ivanoff, Sept. 30, 1961, no. 3, 7, Kerensky Papers, F.97.

36. Lenin, *Works*, 19: 485–86

37. A. Badayev, *The Bolsheviks in the Tsarist Duma*, (L: Martin Lawrence, 1932), 41; c.f. AK, *Crucifixion*, 221

38. *GDSO*, May 3, 1913, cc. 692–717.

39. *GDSO*, May 3, 1913, cc. 714–17; M. L. Lur'ë ed, "O Lenskom rasstrele," *KA*, 83: 35–36.

40. G. Landau, "Politicheskie zametki," *Severnyia Zapiski* (1913), no. 2, 146–55; *GDSO*, May 15, 1913, cc. 1404–05; May 18, 1913, cc. 1690–1704.

41. *GDSO*, Oct. 29, 1913, cc. 410 ff; *Vestnik prikazchika*, no. 8–9, April 2, 1913; Lenin, *Works*, 19: 580, *n* 117; Aronson, *Rossiia nakanune Revoliutsii*, 43; Aronson, *Revoliutsionnaia Iiunost': Vospominaniia 1903–1917*, (NY: Inter-University Project on the History of the Menshevik Movement), Paper No. 6, Mimeographed, (1961), 109; Aronson, *Rossiia v epokhu revoliutsii: istoricheskie etiudy* (NY: 'Novoe Russkoe Slovo,' 1966), 23.

42. *GDSO*, Oct. 29, 1913, c. 413 ff; For the Ministry of Trade and Industry, see R. B. McKean, *The Russian Constitutional Monarchy, 1907–17*, (Historical Association Pamphlet No. G91, L, 1977), 25; Wolfe, *Three Who Made a Revolution*, 601.

43. M. Samuel, *Blood Accusation* (L: Weidenfeld & Nicholson, 1966), passim; Malamud's novel, *The Fixer* is based on this case.

44. S. Kucherov, *Courts, Lawyers and Trials under the Last Three Tsars*, (NY: Praeger 1953), 293; *GDSO*, Oct. 23, 1913, c. 250; *Pravo*, Nov. 3, 1913, cc. 2550–52.

45. D. Zaslavskii, "Delo advokatov," *Severnyia Zapiski* (1914), no. 6, 179–82; *GDSO*, Dec. 3, 1913, c. 1566.

46. Getzler, *Martov*, 135; Lenin, *Works*, 19: 420 ff, 381–87; 20: 138 ff; Avksentiev, "Krainie levye," 139, 142; Sukhanov, *Zapiski*, 1: 75.

47. *Kerenskii po DP*, 10.

48. Lenin, *Works*, 20: 388–91.

49. Miliukov, *Vospominaniia*, 2: 167; *GDSO*, Nov. 12, 1913, cc. 948–62; Nov. 15, 1913, cc. 1075–95; Nov. 22, 1913, cc. 1245–93; Jan. 14, 1914, cc. 1834–41; Jan. 17, 1914, cc. 1943–49, cc. 1992–93; Jan. 28, 1914, cc. 215–22, cc. 259–64. Hagen, *Entfaltung*, 318–20, overlooks the fact that some deputies were afraid of what would happen to them *after* their immunities expired, though it is true that this did not stop them articulating some working-class demands. Malinovsky's double immunity certainly helped the Bolsheviks to achieve "hegemony" over the Petersburg working class.

50. Riha, *Miliukov*, 209–10; *GDSO*, April 22, 1914, cc. 806–07; Badayev, *Bolsheviks*, 145–48; E. Welle-Strand, *Kerenski: Verdenskrigens homo novus*, (Copenhagen: Nordiske Forfatteres Forlag, 1917), 28; Lenin, *Works*, 19: 505–06; 20: 292.

51. Badayev, *Bolsheviks*, 152; Wolfe, *Three Who Made a Revolution*, 612; *GDSO*, May 7, 1914, cc. 114–17.

52. Wolfe, *Three Who Made a Revolution*, 611–20; Wilcox, *Russia's Ruin*, 191

53. Kucherov, *Courts*, 294–95; *Pravo*, June 15, 1914, cc. 1911–13; Badayev, *Bolsheviks*, 164; M. G. Fleer ed., *Rabochee dvizhenie v gody voiny* (M: Narodnyi Komissariat Prosveshchenia, 1925), 258.

54. *Kerenskii po DP*, 11; AK, *Turning Point*, 126–27.
55. AK, "Moia Rabota vo imia moei Rossii", annotated typescript, Kerensky Papers, F.82; Sukhanov, *Marksizm i Narodnichestvo*, (SPb: 'Sotsialist,' n.d.), passim.
56. AK, "Moia Rabota"; c.f. L. M. Ivanov, "Nekotorye itogi i zadachi izucheniia istorii novogo revoliutsionnogo pod'ëma (1910–1914 gg.)," *Bol'shevistskaia pechat'*, 7 ff; Hagen, *Entfaltung*, 360–63.
57. *GDSO*, March 20, 1913, c. 2397–2400; Nov. 8, 1913, c. 809. This view of progress had been shared by senior Tsarist officials even under the last two tsars, e.g. P. A. Zaionchkovskii ed. *Dnevnik Gosudarstvennogo sekretaria A. A. Polovtsëva* (M: Nauka, 1966), 1: 8–10.
58. *GDSO*, April 16, 1914, cc. 486–87.
59. Kuskova in Aronson, *Rossiia nakanune Revoliutsii*, 139; AK, "Russia on the Eve of World War I," *Russian Review* (1945) 5: 29; L. Haimson, "The Problem of Social Stability in Urban Russia, 1905–1917," *Slavic Review* (1965), 24: 13–17.
60. See T. H. von Laue, *Why Lenin? Why Stalin? A Reappraisal of the Russian Revolution, 1900–1930* (L: Weidenfeld and Nicholson, 1964), passim. Compare the far graver problems that confronted independent India in 1947. To suggest that Stalinism was Russia's "developmental dictatorship" does not prove it was inevitable in 1914. Russia's greatest problem was her German neighbor.
61. Riha, *Miliukov*, 205–08; AK, *Erinnerungen: Vom Sturz des Zarentums bis zu Lenins Staatsstreich* (Dresden: Carl Reissner Verlag, 1928), 7–8; AK, *Crucifixion*, 173.
62. AK, *Crucifixion*, 175; AK, *Turning Point*, 115 ff, 127; AK, "Istoriia Rossi," 426, typescript, Kerensky Papers, F.8.
63. AK, *Turning Point*, 127; AK, "Istoriia Rossii," 427; Conversations with Mrs. Kerensky. None of the biographers of Lenin's politically active sisters place them in the right spot for such a meeting, so perhaps it was the "nonpolitical" Olga whom Kerensky met.

5. Terribly Little Time

1. AK, "Nasha vina", *Severnyia Zapiski* (1913), no. 10, 185, 187; *GDSO*, Dec. 8, 1912, c. 430.
2. Lenin, *Works*, 21: 113–14, 318, 434.
3. AK, "Istoriia Rossii," 426a (mislabeled '226 bis'), typescript, Kerensky Papers, F.8; AK, *Turning Point*, 127–29.
4. AK, "Iz dumskikh vpechatlenii," *Severnyia Zapiski* (1916), no. 1, 187–88.
5. Gippius, *Siniaia Kniga*, 10–11. This diary was carefully edited before publication, see Zinaida N. Gippius, *Pis'ma k Berberovoi i Khodasevichu*, Erika F. Sheikholeslami, ed. (Ann Arbor, Mich: Ardis, 1979), 87. Not even the most careful diarists record the words actually spoken with total accuracy. On the other hand, they retain the atmosphere, which more prosaic accounts omit with equally distorting results. Stankevich, *Vospominaniia*, 19, 24.
6. AK, "Iz dumskikh vpechatlenii," 185.
7. AK, *Crucifixion*, 175–77; AK, "Istoriia Rossii," 429–430; AK, *Turning Point*, 129–31; Miliukov, *Vospominaniia*, 2: 189–91; AK, 'Itogi chetvërtoi sessii', *Severnyia Zapiski* (1916), no. 9, 244.

8. H. Shukman, *Lenin and the Russian Revolution* (L: Batsford, 1966), 58–172; Lenin, *Works*, 21: 14–41; G. V. Plekhanov, *O voine* (Pet: M. V. Popov, 1916), 8; AK, *Crucifixion*, 209–12; I. Menitskii ed., *Revoliutsionnoe Dvizhenie voennykh godov (1914–1917)* (M: Izd. Kommunisticheskoi Akademii, 1925), 131–32; Okhranka, IIe, Fl.1, no. 179021, DP to Agentura, Dec. 26, 1914.

9. *GDSO*, July 26, 1914, passim; *Rech'*, July 27, 1914; a translation of the speeches is given by Frank A. Golder, ed., *Documents of Russian History 1914–1917* (NY-L: The Century Co., 1927), 29–37.

10. AK, *Turning Point*, 135 ff; Miliukov, *Vospominaniia*, 2: 183–94; L. S. Gaponenko, *Rabochii Klass Rossii v 1917 godu* (M: Nauka, 1970), 124–25.

11. A. A. Abramov, "Bor'ba bol'shevistskikh organizatsii protiv sotsialshovinizma i tsentrizma v Rossii (1914–fevral' 1917 g.)", *Voprosy Istorii KPSS* (1963), no. 11, 44 ff; A. L. Sidorov ed., *Revoliutsionnoe dvizhenie v armii i na flote v gody pervoi mirovoi voiny (1914-fevral' 1917)* (M: Nauka, 1966), 19 ff; I. P. Leiberov, "Deiatel'nost' Petrogradskoi organizatsii Bol'shevikov: eë vliianie na rabochee dvizhenie v gody pervoi mirovoi voiny," in A. L. Sidorov, ed. *Pervaia Mirovaia Voina* (M: Nauka, 1968), 283–84.

12. Mints, *Istoriia*, 1: 194–98; E. N. Burdzhalov, *Vtoraia russkaia revoliutsiia*, (M: Nauka, 1967), 1: 13–19; George Katkov, *Russia 1917; the February Revolution* (L: Longmans, 1967), 23–33; Okhranka, F.IIe/Fl.1; for Kamenev, see p. 115 supra; for Sukhanov, see Stankevich, *Vospominaniia*, 22–23.

13. Menitskii, *Revoliutsionnoe Dvizhenie*, 126; Katkov, *February Revolution*, 23–33; Okhranka, F.XVIb (3)/Fl.7, No. 1289, Agentura to DP, Oct. 31 (Nov. 13), 1915; O. H. Gankin and H. H. Fisher eds., *The Bolsheviks and the World War* (Stanford, Cal: Hoover Institution, 1940), 276–77, 343–44; S. V. Tiutiukin, "K voprosu o revoliutsionnom shovinizme v gody pervoi mirovoi voiny," in *Pervaia Mirovaia Voina*, 254 ff.

14. AK interviewed by Elena Ivanoff, Sept. 30, 1961, Tape no. 3 (transcript), 7, Kerensky Papers, F.97.

15. Sukhanov, *Zapiski*, 1: 61, 68–69.

16. *Kerenskii po DP*, 11–12; E. D. Kuskova in G. Ia. Aronson, *Rossiia nakanune Revoliutsii* (NY: 'Novoe Russkoe Slovo', 1961), 139; Stankevich, *Vospominaniia*, 19; At the beginning of the war, Kerensky (with Struve, Shingaryov etc.) was elected to a 15-person commission of the Imperial Free Economic Society to consider the economic consequences of the war. He was also elected chairman of a section providing relief to dependents of the Petrograd training battalions and the unemployed. No wonder the government closed the Society down! *Trudy imperatorskago Vol'nago Ekonomicheskago Obshchestva*, (Sept.-Dec., 1914), nos. 5–6: 7–11, 18.

17. *Kerenskii po DP*, 13–14; Menitskii ed, *Revoliutsionnoe Dvizhenie*, 142–43.

18. Mints, *Istoriia*, 1: 198–201; Miliukov, *Vospominaniia*, 2: 195; *GDSO*, Jan. 27, 1915, cc. 45–49; Jan. 28, 1915, c. 151.

19. *Den'*, April 28, 1915; *Kerenskii po DP*, 14.

20. Mints, *Istoriia*, v.1, 189–94; *Pravo*, Feb. 22, 1915, cc. 537–60; March 3, 1915, cc. 634–36; March 8, 1915, cc. 734–49; March 15, 1915, cc. 823–35.

21. *Den'*, Feb. 14, 1915.

22. *Pravo*, Feb. 22, 1915, c. 544.
23. Lenin, *Works*, 35: 175–76.
24. E. H. Wilcox, *Russia's Ruin* (L: Chapman & Hall, 1919), 191; V. N. Zalezhskii, *Iz vospominanii podpol'shchika* (Kharkov: Proletar, 1931), 123 ff, 131–32; Sukhanov, *Zapiski*, 1: 64.
25. N. Lapin ed., "Progressivnyi blok v 1915–1917 gg.," *KA* (1932) 50–51: 147; *Padenie*, 5: 454.
26. K. F. Shatsillo, " 'Delo' Polkovnikova Miasoedova," *Voprosy Istorii* (1967), no. 4, 103–16; Katkov, *February Revolution*, 119–32.
27. *Kerenskii po DP*, 14–15; Wilcox, *Russia's Ruin*, 190–91; Sidorov ed., *Revoliutsionnoe dvizhenie v armii*, 83, 420n.
28. Aronson, *Rossiia nakanune Revoliutsii*, 140; Conversations with Mrs. O. L. Kerensky.
29. Louis Greenberg, *The Jews in Russia* (New Haven: Yale University Press, 1965), 99–100; J. Frumkin, et al., eds. *Russian Jewry (1860–1917)*, (NY: Thomas Yoseloff, 1966), 65–70.
30. V. Zlobin, *A Difficult Soul: Zinaida Gippius*, Simon Karlinsky, ed. (Berkeley: University of California Press, 1980), 5, 10–14, 39; *Sovremënnik* (1911) no. 1, 8, 11; A. Field, ed., *The Complection of Russian Literature* (L: Penguin, 1971), 175–78.
31. Zlobin, *Difficult Soul*, 42; Gippius, *Siniaia Kniga*, 10–11.
32. Temira Pachmuss, ed. *Intellect and Ideas in Action: Selected Correspondence of Zinaida Hippius*, (Munich: Wilhelm Fink Verlag, 1972), 35 ff;
33. Gippius, *Siniaia Kniga*, 24–26.
34. OLK, "Obryvki," 1–2.
35. M. Florinsky, *The End of the Russian Empire* (NY: Collier, 1961), 102; Katkov, *February Revolution*, 6–8; Mints, *Istoriia*, 1: 82–85; "Die Tereschtschenkos," *Vossische Zeitung*, June 26, 1917.
36. Menitskii ed., *Revoliutsionnoe Dvizhenie*, 304–13; V. S. Diakin, *Russkaia Burzhuaziia i Tsarizm v gody pervoi mirovoi voiny (1914–1917)* (Lgd: Nauka, 1967), 81; *Kerenskii po DP*, 20–21.
37. *Kerenskii po DP*, 17–18; L. M. Shalaginova, "Esery-internatsionalisty v gody pervoi mirovoi voiny," in *Pervaia Mirovaia Voina*; AK interviewed by E. Ivanoff, Oct. 20, 1961, Tape no. 5, 21, Kerensky Papers, F.97; c.f. Leiberov, "O vozniknovenii revoliutsionnoi situatsii v Rossii v gody pervoi mirovoi voiny (iiul'-sentiabr' 1915 g.)," *Istoriia SSSR*, 1964, no. 6, 43.
38. See *n* 14 supra; cf. Shalaginova, "Esery-internatsionalisty," 325.
39. *Kerenskii po DP*, 18–19; Shalaginova, "Esery-internatsionalisty," 325–26; Tiutiukin, "K voprosu o revoliutsionnom shovinizme," 262; Tiutiukin, *Voina, mir, revoliutsiia: Ideinaia bor'ba v rabochem dvizhenii Rossii 1914–1917 gg.* (M: Mysl', 1972), 192–93.
40. Lenin, *Works*, 36: 354–55. However, Alexandrovich told Shlyapnikov that he *was* working with Kerensky "who had renounced his earlier position of national defence," A. G. Shliapnikov, *Kanun semnadtsatogo goda: Vospominaniia i dokumenty o rabochem dvizhenni i revoliutsionnom podpol'ë za 1914–1916 gg.* (M-Pet: Gosudarstvennoe Izd., 1923), part 1, 293.

41. Tiutiukin, "K voprosu o revoliutsionnom shovinizme," 262–63.
42. Miliukov, *Istoriia*, part 1: *Protivorechiia revoliutsii*, 25; Miliukov, *Vospominaniia*, 2: 205; N. Lapin ed., "Progressivnyi blok," *KA* (1932) 52: 148; Riha, *Miliukov*, 225–27.
43. AK, "Itogi chetvërtoi sessii," *Severnyia Zapiski* (1916), no. 9, 244; *GDSO*, July 19, 1915, cc. 110–19.
44. Katkov, *February Revolution*, 76 ff; Gaponenko, *Rabochii Klass*, 124–25; see Z.A.B. Zeman and W.B. Scharlau, *Freibeuter der Revolution: Parvus-Helphand: Eine politische Biographie* (Cologne: Verlag Wissenschaft und Politik, 1964), 191 ff.
45. Lapin ed., "Progressivnyi blok," *KA* (1932), 50–51: 120, 157; AK, *Turning Point*, 139; AK, "Moia Rabota vo imia moei Rossii," typescript, Kerensky Papers, F.82; AK, "Itogi chetvërtoi sessii," 243.
46. V. I. Gurko, *Features and Figures of the Past* (Stanford, Cal: Hoover Institution, 1939), 571–77; Lapin ed., "Progressivnyi blok," passim; Miliukov, *Istoriia*, part 1, 25–27; Katkov, *February Revolution*, 133 ff.
47. *Kerenskii po DP*, 19–20.
48. Mints, *Istoriia*, 1: 303 ff.
49. Wilcox, *Russia's Ruin*, 192; In 1917, a Swedish journalist found a similar *Okhrana* circular in the Helsinki Police HQ, *Social-Demokraten* (Malmö), April 5, 1917
50. Lenin, *Works*, 36: 354–55; 43: 493–94.
51. AK, *Turning Point*, 147.
52. *Padenie*, 7: 183; Anton Karlgren, *Ryska Intervjuer: Studier från Världskrigets Ryssland* (Stockholm: P. A. Norstedt and Söners Förlag, 1916), 49–51; Gippius, *Siniaia Kniga*, 37–38; R.H.B. Lockhart, *The Diaries of Sir Robert Bruce Lockhart*, Kenneth Young, ed. vol. 1: *1915–1938* (L: Macmillan, 1973), 24–25; unfortunately, the published version, edited on grounds of security and privacy, ceases in March 1917, several months before Lockhart's recall to England. The originals have now been lost. Professor Robert P. Browder and Michael Kettle feel they add little to our knowledge of Kerensky in 1917.
53. *Kerenskii po DP*, 20.
54. AK, "Istoriia Rossii," 451, Kerensky Papers, F.8.
55. Katkov, *February Revolution*, 178–79.
56. *Kerenskii po DP*, 22.
57. Katkov, *February Revolution*, 16–19; Tiutiukin, *Voina, mir, revoliutsiia*, 293 *n*69; Leiberov, "Deiatel'nost' Petrogradskoi organizatsii Bol'shevikov," 291–93.
58. *Kerenskii po DP*, 25–27; Tiutiukin, *Voina, mir, revoliutsiia*, 295 *n*100; Leiberov mistakenly cites *Kerenskii po DP* in suggesting that Kerensky backed the workers groups of the CWIC *in 1915*. For Kerensky's undoubted support for them later, see chapter 6.
59. Leiberov, "Deiatel'nost' Petrogradskoi organizatsii Bol'shevikov," 292–93; Katkov, *February Revolution*, 618–20; M. G. Fleer ed., *Rabochee dvizhenie v gody voiny* (M: Tsentrarkhiv, 1925), 269–91; *GDSO*, Feb. 17, 1917, cc. 1516 ff; Okhranka, F.IIe/Fl.3, No. 103568, DP to Agentura, April 5, 1916; G. Petrovich, "Sotsial'no-politicheskoe obozrenie: Rabochie v voenno-promyshlennykh Komitetakh," *Delo* (1916), no. 1, 72.

60. Gankin and Fisher eds., *Bolsheviks and the War*, 344, 329–33; Marc Ferro, *The Russian Revolution of February 1917* (L: Routledge & Kegan Paul, 1972), 332–36; V. M. Chernov, *Pered burei: Vospominaniia* (NY: Chekhov, 1953), 309–10.
61. *Kerenskii po DP*, 26–35; Shalaginova, "Esery-internatsionalisty", 326–27.
62. B. B. Grave, *K istorii klassovoi bor'by v Rossii v gody imperialisticheskoi voiny (iiul' 1914 g.- fevral' 1917 g.): Proletariat i Burzhuaziia* (M-Lgd: Gosudarstvennoe Izd., 1926), 305–6; *Kerenskii po DP*, 35.
63. Shliapnikov, *Kanun semnadtsatogo goda*, part 1, 293; *Kerenskii po DP*, 35.
64. *Kerenskii po DP*, 47 ff; V. V——yi [alias V. V. Kiriakov], *A. F. Kerenskii*, (Pet: Narodnaia Vlast', 1917), 13; V. M. Zenzinov, "Fevral'skie dni," part 2, *NZh* (1955) 35: 220.
65. *Kerenskii po DP*, 39; Gippius, *Siniaia Kniga*, 47.
66. Mints, *Istoriia*, 1: 320; Gippius, *Siniaia Kniga*, 46; Sokoloff, *White Nights*, 7–8; *Kerenskii po DP*, 40–41; *Hufvudstadsbladet*, March 3, 1916.
67. Helsingin Kirurgien Sairaala/Helsingfors Kirurgiska Sjukhuset, "Kliniska Journal" (1916) n532; *Hufvudstadsbladet*, March 31, April 1, 3, 14, 1916; for Krogius, see *Iso Tietosanakirja*, 7th. ed. (H:ki: Otava, 1934), 1934; Conversations with Mrs. Kerensky.
68. *Kerenskii po DP*, 40–42; Örnulf Tigerstedt, *Vastavakoilu iskee: Suomen taistelu neuvostovakoilua vastaan 1919–1939* (H:ki: Otava, 1943), 187–88; *Hufvudstadsbladet*, March 6, 1916.
69. Gippius, *Siniaia Kniga*, 47; Zinaida Hippius, "Green, White, and Flame: A Sort of Afterword," *The Green Ring*, trans. S. S. Koteliansky (L: C. W. Daniel Ltd, 1920), 94 ff.
70. Einar Runeberg, "Nikolain sänky on vapaana," *Suomen Vapaussota* (1935), 10: 222 (reprinted in *Vapaussodan Kertomuksia*, ed. Erkki Räikkönen [H:ki: 'Sanatar', 1938], vol. 3); Börje Thilman, "Bad Grankulla bjöd 'skotsk dusch,' 'medikamentösa bad,' " *Hufvudstadsbladet*, May 10, 1970

6. Citizen Brutus

1. V. Vasil'evskaia, "Zabastovochnoe dvizhenie v Peterburge po agenturnym dannym (1914–1916 gg.)," *Proletarskaia Revoliutsiia* (1923), no. 13, passim; L. S. Gaponenko, *Rabochii Klass Rossii v 1917 godu* (M: Nauka, 1970), 129–31; George Katkov, *Russia 1917: the February Revolution* (L: Longmans, 1967), 88–96.
2. Buchanan, *Mission*, 2: 1–3; N. N. Iakovlev, *1 avgusta 1914* (M: Molodaia Gvardiia, 1974), 166 ff.
3. T. Riha, *A Russian European: Paul Miliukov in Russian Politics*, (Notre Dame, Ind.: University of Notre Dame Press, 1969), 242–59; Raymond Pearson, *The Russian Moderates and the Crisis of Tsarism, 1914–1917* (L: Macmillan, 1977), 90 ff.
4. *GDSO*, June 9, 1916, c. 5017.
5. *GDSO*, June 3, 1916, cc. 4758–80; June 9, 1916, cc. 5048–49. For Prime Minister Stürmer's furious reaction to Kerensky's speech and Rodzyanko's conduct in permitting it, see V. P. Semënnikov ed., *Monarkhiia pered Krusheniem 1914–1917* (M-Lgd: Gosudarstvennoe Izd., 1927), 122–24.

6. *GDSO*, June 3, 1916, c. 4780.

7. M. V. Rodzianko, "Gosudarstvennaia Duma i Fevral'skaia 1917 goda Revoliutsiia", *ARR* (1922) 6, 69; c.f. AK, "Itogi chetvërtoi sessii," *Severnyia Zapiski* (1916), no. 9, 251–52.

8. *Kerenskii po DP*, 42–43; Riha, *Miliukov*, 250–51.

9. *Kerenskii po DP*, 43–44; Alma Söderhjelm, *Min Värld* (Stockholm: Albert Bonniers Förlag, 1931), 3:388.

10. Elena Vsevolodovna Biriukova, née Baranovskaia is identified as "Elena" in Zinaida N. Gippius, Erika F. Sheikholeslami ed. *Pis'ma k Berberovoi i Khodasevichu* (Ann Arbor, Mich: Ardis, 1979), 48, 73; as "Elena Vsevolodovna" in N. N. Vinner to AK, Nov. 11, 1918, ms., Papers of David Soskice, DS/2/1, Box 8, The Soskice Papers, House of Lords Record Office, London; and as the cousin of Gen. Vladimir Baranovsky by General Knox, WO.106.1096, Knox to DMI, Nov. 1, 1917. Her married name and the current rank of her husband were given in *Index. Adressbok och yrkeskalender för Helsingfors* (annual), 1914–1917 (H:ki: Tidnings- och Tryckeri-Aktiebolagets Tryckeri). For Vera Baranovskaia, see I. Vinogradskaia, ed. *Zhizn' i tvorchestvo K. S. Stanislavskogo* (M: Vsërossiiskoe Teatral'noe Obshchestvo, 1971), vol. 2: *1906–1915*, 49, 367; Kh. Abul-Kasymova, ed. *Istoriia Sovetskogo Kino* (M: Iskusstvo, 1969), 1: 287–97; T. Ponomarëva, "Vera Baranovskaia," *Iskusstvo Kino* (1966) no. 5, 73–79.

11. K. Grigorkoff, "Family Tree of the Baranovskys," ms.; Håkon Holmberg ed., "(Keisarillen) Suomen Senaatin talousosaston virkamiehet 1909–1919," *Suomen Sukututkimusseuran vuosikirja* (1965), 38: 125–26.

12. For Hippius' patronage of Savinkov, see Temira Pachmuss, ed. *Intellect and Ideas in Action: Selected Correspondence of Zinaida Hippius* (Munich: Wilhelm Fink Verlag, 1972), 130–31, *n*58.

13. AK to Mrs. O. L. Kerensky, Sept. 3, 1963, Kerensky Family Papers; Conversations and correspondence with the Kerensky family and friends.

14. *Kerenskii po DP*, 43–44.

15. P. G. Galuzo ed., *Vosstanie 1916 goda v Srednei Azii: Sbornik dokumentov* (Tashkent: Gosizdat UzSSR, 1932), 106–11. This collection contains the stenographic record of Kerensky's speeches to the closed Duma sessions of 13 and 15 December 1916 with annotations by Governor-General Kuropatkin; R. A. Pierce, *Russian Central Asia 1867–1917* (Berkeley: University of California Press, 1960), 333–34, *n*50.

16. Galuzo ed., *Vosstanie*, 124.

17. Galuzo ed., *Vosstanie*, 106 ff, 160; E. D. Sokol, *The Revolt of 1916 in Russian Central Asia* (Baltimore: Univ. of Maryland Press, 1954), 80 ff.

18. A. V. Piaskovskii et al. eds. *Vosstanie 1916 goda v Srednei Azii i Kazakhstane: sbornik dokumentov* (M: AN SSSR, 1960), 720, *n*42; Kh. Tursunov, ed. *Vosstanie 1916 goda v Srednei Azii i Kazakhstane* (Tashkent: Gosizdat UzSSR, 1962), 199–201.

19. Galuzo ed., *Vosstanie*, 114, 123, 125.

20. Galuzo ed., *Vosstanie*, 160

21. N. P. Karabchevskii, *Chto glaza moi uvideli* (Berlin: Izd. Ol'gi D'iakovoi i Ko, 1921), vol. 2: *Revoliutsiia i Rossiia*, 119–20; I. V. Gessen, "V dvukh vekakh:

zhiznënnyi otchët," *ARR* (1937), 12: 366; S. P. Mansyrev, "Moi vospominaniia o Gosudarstvennoi Dume," *Istorik i Sovremënnik* (1922) no. 3, 19; *GDSO*, Nov. 1, 1916, c. 29; Personal communication from Mrs. Kerensky.

22. Pierce, *Russian Central Asia*, 333n; *Kerenskii po DP*, 44.
23. *Kerenskii po DP*, 44–46.
24. *Kerenskii po DP*, 46; V. V——yi [alias V. V. Kiriakov], *A. F. Kerenskii*, (Pet: Narodnaia Vlast', 1917), 13–15; AK, *Turning Point*, 484.
25. L. M. Shalaginova, "Esery-internatsionalisty v gody pervoi mirovoi voiny," A. L. Sidorov, ed. *Pervaia Mirovaia Voina* (M: Nauka, 1968), 332.
26. V. M. Zenzinov, "Fevral'skie dni," [part 1,] *NZh* (1953) 34: 190; AK interviewed by Elena Ivanoff, Sept. 30, 1961, tape no. 3, 7–8, Kerensky Papers, F.97; c.f. *Kerenskii po DP*, 46
27. Mansyrev, "Moi vospominaniia," 18–20. Only a minority of the Progressists broke with the block at this point, the majority following in October 1916, Pearson, *Russian Moderates*, 48–49, 114.
28. AK, "Itogi chetvërtoi sessii," 248–53.
29. V. V. Shul'gin, *Dni* (Belgrade: M. A. Suvorin and Co, Novoe Vremia, 1925), 80; AK, *Crucifixion*, 196–99.
30. Miliukov, *Vospominaniia*, 2: 232 ff.
31. *GDSO*, Nov. 1, 1916, cc. 10–48; Pearson, *Russian Moderates*, 115 ff.
32. Gippius, *Siniaia Kniga*, 57; A. G. Shliapnikov, *Kanun semnadtsatogo goda: Vospominaniia i dokumenty o rabochem dvizhenii i revoliutsionnom podpol'ë za 1914–1916 gg.* (M-Pet: Gosudarstvennoe Izd., 1923), part 2, 240–41; *GDSO*, Nov. 3, 1916, c. 67; Nov. 4, 1916, c. 202; B. B. Grave ed., *Burzhuaziia nakanune fevral'skoi revoliutsii* (M-Lgd: Gosudarstvennoe Izd., 1927), 170; E. D. Chermenskii, "IV Gosudarstvennaia Duma i Sverzhenie Samoderzhaviia v Rossii," *Voprosy Istorii* (1969), no. 6, 72–73; Pearson, *Russian Moderates*, 115.
33. *GDSO*, Nov. 19, 1916, cc. 240 ff; Rodzianko, *Le Règne de Raspoutine*, (Paris: Payot, 1928), 273; A. Martynoff, "Die Duma und die Arbeiter in Russland," *Die Neue Zeit* (1917), no. 24, 576.
34. *GDSO*, Dec. 2, 1916; *Prilozhenie*, Dec. 8, 1916, cc. 829–55; A. A. Demianov, "Moia sluzhba pri Vremënnom Pravitel'stve," *ARR*, (1922) 4: 71.
35. L. Haimson, "The Problem of Social Stability in Urban Russia, 1905–1917" *Slavic Review* (1965), 24: 15n; Anna Bourgina-Nicolaevsky was kind enough to confirm Halpern's disclosures; Adolfs Blodnieks, *The Undefeated Nation* (NY: Robert Speller, 1960), 142.
36. Miliukov, *Vospominaniia*, 2: 278–79; F. A. Golder ed., *Documents of Russian History 1914–1917* (NY-L: The Century Co, 1927), 177; *GDSO*, Dec. 13, 1916, c. 1097.
37. AK, "Nechto o demagogii," *Severnyia Zapiski* (1917), no. 1, 194 ff; *GDSO*, Dec. 16, 1916, c. 1178; cc. 1220–26; Miliukov, *Vospominaniia*, 2: 279.
38. Miliukov, *Vospominaniia*, 2: 279 ff; Rodzianko, *Règne de Raspoutine*, 285–86.
39. "Iz vospominanii A. I. Guchkova," *Poslednie Novosti*, Sept. 9–13, 1936; AK, *Turning Point*, 147 ff.
40. G. Ia. Aronson, *Rossiia nakanune Revoliutsii* (NY: Novoe Russkoe Slovo, 1961), 140; AK, "Why the Russian Monarchy Fell," *Slavonic and East European Review* (1929–30) 8: 496 ff.

41. *Kerenskii po DP*, 46; Izaak Babel, *Izbrannoe* (M: Khudozhestvennaia Literatura, 1966), 201–3.
42. Robert Payne, *The Life and Death of Lenin* (L: Weidenfeld & Nicholson, 1964), 271–73; Lenin, *Works*, 23: 177ff, 264.
43. Shul'gin, *Dni*, 127; Rodzianko, *Règne de Raspoutine*, 283–84; A. I. Verkhovskii, *Na trudnom perevale* (M: Voennoe Izd. Min. Oborony SSSR, 1959), 147ff; On this source, see G. Katkov, *Russia 1917: The Kornilov Affair: Kerensky and the Break-Up of the Russian Army* (L: Longmans, 1980), 198–200.
44. Stankevich, *Vospominaniia*, 65.
45. A. G. Shliapnikov, *Semnadtsatyi god* (M: Gosudarstvennoe Izd., 1927), 1: 45; MAE, vol. 647, Ètat-Major de l'Armée: 2ᵉ Bureau: "La Situation Intérieure de la Russie," March 6, 1917; FO.371.2995, Lockhart to Buchanan, Jan, 10, 1917; Katkov, *February Revolution*, 173–77; Chermenskii, "IV Gos. Duma," 65 ff.
46. AK, "Nechto o demagogii," 195, 199, 203; AK, *Crucifixion*, 190 ff.
47. AK, "Moia Rabota vo imia moei Rossii," typescript, Kerensky Papers F.82; FO.371.2995, Lockhart to Buchanan, Jan. 3, 16, 1917.
48. I. Iurenev, " 'Mezhraionka' (1911–1917 gg.)" *Proletarskaia Revoliutsiia* (1924) no. 2 (25): 130–31; Shliapnikov, *Semnadtsatyi god*, 1: 24ff; K. A. Gvozdev, "Pered revoliutsiei" and A. N. Smirnov, "Iz zapisnoi knizhki agitatora," both in *Rabochaia Mysl'*, March 3 (16), 1918; M. Smilg-Benario, *Der Zusammenbruch der Zarenmonarchie* (Zurich-Leipzig-Vienna: Amalthea-Verlag, 1928), 76–77; Tsuyoshi Hasegawa, *The February Revolution: Petrograd 1917* (Seattle: University of Washington Press, 1981), 204–9. Kerensky may have forgotten this episode by 1967, but his papers contain an annotated section of S. P. Melgunov's perceptive article on it in *Golos Minuvshago* (1926), no. 2, 184, Kerensky Papers, F.35. Melgunov ended as a Monarchist but was a member of Kerensky's "Comité pour la Russie" in 1919–20.
49. *Padenie*, 6:285–87; Verkhovskii, *Na trudnom perevale*, 155–56; Grave, *Burzhuaziia*, 180–83; Hasegawa, *February Revolution*, 205.
50. *Padenie*, 5: 249, 260–61; Miliukov, *Vospominaniia*, 2: 285–86; Hasegawa, *February Revolution*, 207.
51. Gippius, *Siniaia Kniga*, 66–67; Shliapnikov, *Semnadtsatyi god*, 1: 48.
52. Hasegawa, *February Revolution*, 208; E. N. Burdzhalov, *Vtoraia russkaia revoliutsiia*, vol. 1: *Vosstanie v Petrograde* (M: Nauka, 1967), 107 ff; GDSO, Feb. 15, 1917, cc. 1345–59; cf. the uncut version in AK, *Izbrannyia rechi* (Pet: Biblioteka "Solntse Svobody," 1917), 35–48.
53. Katkov, *February Revolution*, 248–61; Burdzhalov, *VRR*, vol. 1: *Vosstanie v Petrograde*, 115–18; Hasegawa, *February Revolution*, 210–11.
54. Zenzinov, "Fevral'skie dni," [part 1,] 196–98; AK, *Turning Point*, 188; c.f. Shliapnikov, *Semnadtsatyi god*, 1: 43; Iurenev, " 'Mezhraionka,' " [part 2], 137.
55. GDSO, Feb. 23, 1917, cc. 1649–53.
56. *Padenie*, 2: 261–62; 3: 385; 4: 489–91; Gen. A. I. Spiridovich, *Velikaia Voina i Fevral'skaia Revoliutsiia 1914–1917 gg.*, 3 vols. (NY: Vsëslavianskoe Izd., 1960–62), 3: 52–54, suggests that Protopopov was too frightened to tell the Tsar the true content of Kerensky's speeches; M. N. Pokrovskii introd., *Perepiska Nikolaia i Aleksandry Romanovykh*, 5 vols. (M-Pet: Gosudarstvennoe Izd., 1923–

27), 5: 215; *Syn velikoi russkoi revoliutsii Aleksandr Kerenskii: ego zhizn', politi-cheskaia deiatel'nost' i rechi* (Pet: N. N. Kholmushin, 1917), 4; V. V——yi [alias Kiriakov], *A. F. Kerenskii,* 23.
57. Miliukov, *Vospominaniia,* 2: 272ff; Shul'gin, *Dni,* 124.
58. Sukhanov's remembered words were that Kerensky would soon be "at the head of the state." Sukhanov, *Zapiski,* 1: 64.
59. Lenin, *Works,* 23: 177ff, 264; Katkov, *February Revolution,* 166–73.

7. *Fires of Hope and Aspiration*

1. Fëdor Kriukov, "Obval," *Russkie Zapiski* [formerly *Russkoe Bogatstvo*] (1917) no. 3, 353. Kriukov was politically close to Kerensky early in 1917. For his subsequent tragic career, see Roy A. Medvedev, *Problems in the Literary Biography of Mikhail Sholokhov* (Cambridge: Cambridge University Press, 1977), 78 ff. For this chapter, I have consulted the standard eyewitness accounts, British and French diplomatic correspondence, and the memoirs of foreign journalists who were present. Kerensky's accounts are "Inside the Russian Revolution," *NYT,* May 8, 15, 1927; AK, *Catastrophe,* ch. 1, passim; AK, *Crucifixion,* 230–35; AK, "Istoriia Rossii", typescript, 464 ff, Kerensky Papers, F.8; AK, "Rusalka," typescript, Kerensky Papers, F.33; AK, *Turning Point,* 183 ff. Useful secondary works include those of Burdzhalov, Florinsky, Katkov, Mints, Smilg-Benario, and Hasegawa. S. P. Melgunov, *Martovskie Dni* (Paris: Imp. de Navarre, 1961), 8–10, gives a useful critique of the reliability of the memoirs of Milyukov, Kerensky, Shulgin, and Sukhanov.
2. Tsuyoshi Hasegawa, *The February Revolution: Petrograd 1917,* (Seattle: University of Washington Press, 1981), 232–46; Kriukov, "Obval," 353–59; V. M. Zenzinov, "Fevral'skie dni" [part 1], *NZh,* 1953, 34: 198–99.
3. *GDSO,* Feb. 24, 1917, cc. 1730–32.
4. *GDSO,* Feb. 24, 1917, cc. 1725–30.
5. *Padenie,* 2: 221; 6: 394.
6. Kriukov, "Obval," 360–61.
7. Zenzinov, "Fevral'ski dni" [part 1], 201–4; *Padenie,* 1: 190; Sukhanov, *Zapiski,* 1: 37–44; Hasegawa, *February Revolution,* 247–266.
8. *GDSO,* Feb. 25, 1917, cc. 1756–57.
9. Sukhanov, *Zapiski,* 1: 39–41.
10. Sukhanov, *Zapiski,* 1: 345–51; A. G. Shliapnikov, *Semnadtsatyi god,* (M: Gosudarstvennoe Izd., 1925[?]), 1: 89; E. N. Burdzhalov, *Vtoraia russkaia revoliutsiia,* vol. 1: *Vosstanie v Petrograde* (M: Nauka, 1967), 158–60; Mints, *Istoriia,* vol. 1: *Sverzhenie Samoderzhaviia,* 474 ff.
11. Zenzinov, "Fevral'ski dni", [part 1,] 203; Sukhanov, *Zapiski,* 1: 51–52; Shliapnikov, *Semnadtsatyi god,* 1: 89 ff; Burdzhalov, *VRR,* vol. 1, *Vosstanie v Petrograde,* 159–60.
12. V. V. Shul'gin, *Dni,* (Belgrade: M. A. Suvorin, 1925), 143–46; Miliukov, *Vospominaniia,* 2: 289; MAE, *Russie: Dossier Général,* MAE, vol. 647, Paléologue to MAE, March 11, 1917.

13. Shul'gin, *Dni*, 147–48.
14. Zenzinov, "Fevral'skie dni" [part 1], 204–6; Kriukov, "Obval," 361–63; Sukhanov, *Zapiski*, 1: 53–54, 58; Hasegawa, *February Revolution*, 267–77.
15. Sukhanov, *Zapiski*, 1: 59–60; Zenzinov, "Fevral'ski dni," [part 1,] 207–10; AK, "Inside the Russian Revolution," *NYT*, May 8, 1927; AK, "Why the Russian Monarchy Fell," *Slavonic and East European Review*, (1929–30) 8: 498–99; AK, *Crucifixion*, 236–37; *RPG*, 1: 32; I. Iurenev, " 'Mezhraionka' (1911–1917 gg.)" [part 2], *Proletarskaia Revoliutsiia* (1924), no. 2 (25): 138–39, broadly confirms his group's pessimism.
16. Kriukov, "Obval," 363.
17. *RPG*, 1: 41–42; V. M. Rodzianko, "Gosudarstvennaia Duma i Fevral'skaia 1917 goda Revoliutsiia," *ARR* (1922) 6: 57.
18. G. Katkov, *Russia 1917: The February Revolution* (L: Longmans, 1967), 296 ff; Marc Ferro, "Le Soldat russe en 1917: indiscipline, patriotisme et révolution," *Annales* (1968) 26: 14–39; L. M. Gavrilov and V. V. Kutuzov, "Istoshchenie liudskikh rezervov russkoi armii v 1917 g.," A. L. Sidorov, ed. *Pervaia Mirovaia Voina*, (M: Nauka, 1968), 145 ff.
19. A. L. Sidorov ed., *Revoliutsionnoe dvizhenie v armii i na flote v gody pervoi mirovoi voiny (1914-fevral' 1917)* (M: Nauka, 1965) 278, 281, 293, 302; Hasegawa, *February Revolution*, 278–81.
20. Kriukov, "Obval," 366; Katkov, *February Revolution*, 271–73.
21. OLK, "Obryvki," 3; AK, *Catastrophe*, 1; but cf. *NYT*, May 8, 1927, where he states, "I cannot explain my reaction for I do not remember what was taking place within me in those few moments of conversation over the telephone."
22. Stankevich, *Vospominaniia*, 66, 76; K. A. Gvozdev, "Pered Revoliutsiei," *Rabochaia Mysl'*, March 3 (16), 1918; AK, *Catastrophe*, 1–2, 8; Sokolov told Sukhanov that he had brought the first regiments, Sukhanov, *Zapiski*, 1: 84. (Sokolov was a close personal friend and comrade of the Kerenskys). Peshekhonov saw the Trudovik teacher, Cornet S. F. Znamensky, in uniform at the Tauride Palace early on February 27. A. N. Peshekhonov, "Pervyia nedeli," *Na Chuzhoi Storone* (1923) 1: 261. Zenzinov fails to confirm any role for Kerensky or his friends, suggesting that the Tsar's Manifesto proroguing the Duma "gave the soldiers the address," Zenzinov, 'Fevral'skie dni', [part 2,] *NZh* (1953) 35: 208.
23. AK in *NYT*, May 8, 1927; AK, *Catastrophe*, 11–13; AK, "Moia Rabota vo imia moei Rossii," typescript, Kerensky Papers, F.82; Rodzianko, "Gosudarstvennaia Duma," 59–60.
24. Zenzinov, "Fevral'skie dni" [part 2], 210; *RPG*, 1: 45–47; S. P. Mansyrev, "Moi vospominaniia o Gosudarstvennoi Dume," *Istorik i Sovremĕnnik* (1922) no. 3, 27–28; Miliukov, *Vospominaniia*, 2: 292–93.
25. *RPG*, 1: 44; I. A. Malinovskii, *Partiia narodnoi svobody i revoliutsiia* (Rostov-on-Don: Edinenie [?], 1917), 3; Sukhanov, *Zapiski*, 1: 178–79; AK in *NYT*, May 8, 1927; AK, *Catastrophe*, 16–17.
26. AK, *Catastrophe*, 15–18; Shul'gin, *Dni*, 159–61, 176 ff; V. V——yi [alias V. V. Kiriakov];, *A. F. Kerenskii* (Pet: Narodnaia Vlast', 1917), 23–24; Zenzinov in *Delo Naroda*, March 15, 1917; Zenzinov, "Fevral'skie dni' [part 2], 212; A. A.

Bublikov, *Russkaia Revoliutsiia* (NY: 'Narodopravstvo', 1918), 19; Gen. P. G. Kurlov, *Konets russkogo tsarizma* (M-Pet: Gosudarstvennoe Izd., 1923), 293–95; Col. G. G. Perets, *V tsitadeli russkoi revoliutsii: Zapiski komendanta Tavricheskago Dvortsa, 27 fevralia–23 marta 1917 g.*, (Pet: Prosveshchenie, 1917), 24 ff; S. I. Shidlovskii, *Vospominaniia* (Berlin: Otto Kirchner, 1923), part 2, 54 ff; S. D. Mstislavskii, *Piat' dnei* (Letopis' Revoliutsii No. 3) (Berlin-Pet-M: Z. I. Grzhebin, 1922), 24.

27. Katkov, *February Revolution*, 359 ff; Burdzhalov, *VRR*, vol. 1: *Vosstanie v Petrograde*, 207; Hasegawa, *February Revolution*, 313–47; Zenzinov, "Fevral'skie dni" [part 2], 215–17; Sukhanov, *Zapiski*, 1: 86–89.

28. Peshekhonov, "Pervyia nedeli," 261–64; Sukhanov, *Zapiski*, 1: 126, 129; Kriukov, "Obval," 371–74.

29. Peshekhonov, "Pervyia nedeli," 260–61; AK, *Catastrophe*, 25–26; V. D. Nabokov, "Vremënnoe Pravitel'stvo," *ARR* (1921,) 1: 13–14; Stankevich, *Vospominaniia*, 66; FO.371.2995. Report by Mr. Walpole, April 5, 1917.

30. Shul'gin, *Dni*, 172 ff; A. A. Oznobishin, *Vospominaniia chlëna IV-i Gosudarstvennoi Dumy* (Paris: Izd. E. Sial'skoi, 1927), 35 ff; Nabokov, "Vremënnoe Pravitel'stvo," 13–14; M. I. Tereshchenko to AK, June 26, 1950, Kerensky Papers, F.167; AK, *Catastrophe*, 4ff, 22.

31. AK, *Catastrophe*, 16–27, 53, 58–59; Sukhanov, *Zapiski*, 2: 55; Bublikov, *Russkaia Revoliutsiia*, 20–22; *RPG*, 1: 67; Burdzhalov, *VRR*, vol. 1: *Vosstanie v Petrograde*, 280; My informant on Elena Biriukova's movements prefers to remain anonymous.

32. Sukhanov, *Zapiski*, 1: 84; AK, *Catastrophe*, 34–35.

33. Sukhanov, *Zapiski*, 1: 200–202.

34. MAE, v. 647, Paléologue to MAE, March 18, 1917; FO.371.2995, Walpole's Report; Sukhanov, *Zapiski*, 1: 138–39, 152–53.

35. Shul'gin, *Dni*, 85 ff; Sukhanov, *Zapiski*, 1: 292–95; Zenzinov, "Fevral'skie dni" [part 2], 223–25.

36. Sukhanov, *Zapiski*, 1: 196, 265, 281–91; Shul'gin, *Dni*, 222–23; AK in *NRS*, May 10, 1957; E. D. Kuskova in *NRS*, May 26, 1957. Yurenev claimed that Sokolov was himself a Bolshevik at the time, Iurenev, " 'Mezhraionka' " [part 2], 137; *RPG*, 1: 63*n*; cf. Sukhanov, *Zapiski*, 1: 207; A. I. Verkhovskii, *Na trudnom perevale*, (M: Voennoe Izd. Min. Oborony SSSR, 1959), 220–21; *VOSR: Revoliutsionnoe dvizhenie v Rossii posle Sverzheniia Samoderzhaviia*, 189–90.

37. Miliukov, *Vospominaniia*, 2: 296 ff; Sukhanov, *Zapiski*, 1: 220ff.

38. Sukhanov, *Zapiski*, 1: 220–22, 289–90, 307–09; Mstislavskii, *Piat' dnei*, 60; Zenzinov, "Fevral'skie dni" [part 2], 228.

39. A. A. Demianov, "Moia sluzhba pri Vremënnom Pravitel'stve," *ARR* (1922) 4: 57; Aleksander Hellat, "Revolutsiooni miilitsas," *Mälestused iseseivuse võitluspäivilt*, v.1: *Revolutsioon ja okupatsioon 1917–1918* (Tallinn: Rahvaülikooli Kirjastus, 1927), 109.

40. Sukhanov, *Zapiski*, 1: 297.

41. Miliukov, *Vospominaniia*, 2: 305–10; Sukhanov, *Zapiski*, 1: 272ff.

42. For Plekhanov's views, see Samuel H. Baron, *Plekhanov, The Father of Russian Marxism* (L: Routledge & Kegan Paul, 1963), 96 ff; for their influence on the

"Legal Marxists," see L. Kołakowski, *Main Currents of Marxism: Its Origins, Growth and Dissolution* (L: Oxford University Press, 1978), 2: 362–73.

43. AK, "Moia Rabota vo imia moei Rossii"; AK interviewed by Anatole Mazour, Mills College, California, 1965.

44. Shul'gin, *Dni*, 235–36. Shulgin's belletristic account does not always place events in correct sequence. The only comparable incident Sukhanov records was Kerensky's intervention with the Soviet leadership to permit Rodzianko to collect the Tsar's abdication, Sukhanov, *Zapiski*, 1: 242–48. That Kerensky did all he could to avert a breach cannot be doubted.

45. AK, *Catastrophe*, 57–58; AK, "Moia Rabota vo imia moei Rossii."

46. Sukhanov, *Zapiski*, 1: 297; AK, *Catastrophe*, 57–59; OLK, "Obryvki," 4 ff.

47. *RPG*, 1: 135–36.

48. AK, *Catastrophe*, 57; Miliukov, *Vospominaniia*, 2: 299 ff; Miliukov, "Bol'shoi chelovek: pamiati A. I. Guchkova," *Poslednie Novosti*, Feb. 15, 1936.

49. The first version of the speech is cited after Kiriakov, who claims to have been present, V. V——yi, *A. F. Kerenskii*, 27–29; The second is in *Izvestiia Petrogradskago Soveta Rabochikh i Soldatskikh Deputatov*, March 3, 1917; c.f. *RPG*, 1: 128–29.

50. Zenzinov, "Fevral'skie dni", [part 2,] 230–31; E. H. Wilcox, *Russia's Ruin*, (L: Chapman & Hall, 1919), 195–98.

51. *Izvestiia*, March 3, 1917; Mints, *Istoriia*, 1: 517, cites this report in support of his allegation that Kerensky's speech provoked protests as well as applause. I can find no trace of this. Would the editors have printed such a thing?

52. Sukhanov, *Zapiski*, 1: 314 ff, 328–29; Conversations with Mrs. Kerensky.

53. Miliukov, *Vospominaniia*, 2: 313–19; Miliukov in *Poslednie Novosti*, Feb. 15, 1936; Rodzianko, "Gosudarstvennaia Duma," 61–62; A. I. Guchkov in *Padenie*, 6: 276, and in *Poslednie Novosti*, Sept. 16, 1936; AK in *NYT*, May 8, 1927.

54. Shul'gin, *Dni*, 296–303.

55. Sukhanov, *Zapiski*, 1: 60 ff; A sound appreciation of Kerensky's contribution to the February Revolution is given by Robert P. Browder, "Kerenskij revisited", *Russian Thought and Politics*, (The Hague, 1957), 421–34. For obvious reasons, Kerensky was always guaranteed the enmity of the Leninist left and the authoritarian right. This does not fully explain the success of Sverchkov's meteor image, helped though it was by Kerensky's own reticence about his SR past. Where interest is involved mere evidence will not prevail. Kerensky also offended the rationalist, Westernized intellectuals (the "professorate" of the intelligentsia), who suffered badly from intellectual snobbery and expected a revolutionary leader to be a great theoretician. Nabokov's inability to apprehend Kerensky's calibre mirrored Sukhanov's fatal underestimate of the "gray blur" (Stalin). The Milyukov-Sukhanov deal was a charade—as Kerensky and Stalin clearly saw—whereby the bourgeois intelligentsia would "liberate" capitalism from Tsarist bureaucracy, while the petty-bourgeois intelligentsia *pretended* to oppose them, thereby retaining the leadership of the masses. Their experiment was even shorter lived than Kerensky's—no evidence of superior wisdom. Kerensky's strategy ran the risk of making the united intelligentsia too visible, with tragic results once the masses saw them all as *boorzhooi*. In the Milyukov-

Sukhanov scheme, the intelligentsia are invisible—the better to achieve what both men wanted, the implantation of Western political culture in Russia. It is not hard to understand the attraction of such a scheme to Professor Hasegawa in a country which has twice eradicated "Western" influences. In reality, as Professors Ferro and Keep have reestablished, the intelligentsia *was* an actor in 1917, and Kerensky was their Leader. The emotional, semi-educated rank-and-file intelligentsia (the 'students')—a true product of autocracy—suffered from a political culture inhibiting them from taking any political decisions conflicting with their personal ethics, while permitting them to blame the current autocrat when things went wrong—e.g., Kerensky's nonelection to the Central Committee of the PSR. Kerensky was psychologically typical of this rank-and-file intelligentsia (or don't we read Chekhov?), so he also offended against patriarchy. His enormous success in February was due precisely to his intuition and emotionalism. The generals' memoirs, and even Milyukov's account of the Moscow State Conference, are full of patriarchal reactions. A feminist perception, encouraged by the political "disloyalties" of Anna Milyukova and Galina Flakserman, may complete these connections better than I can. Students looking for conceptual starting points might consult G. Konrád and I. Szelényi, *The Intellectuals on the Road to Class Power: A Sociological Study of the Role of the Intelligentsia in Socialism* (Brighton: Harvester, 1979), (though I have strong reservations about some aspects of their theory) and Dale Spender, *Women of Ideas (and what men have done to them)* (L: Ark, 1983). The relevance of the feminist "erasure" thesis is not affected by Kerensky's sadly patriarchal treatment of his own wife. For Kerensky on his "constituents," see *Dni*, April 12, 1929.

56. Stankevich, *Vospominaniia*, 75; cf. V. A. Maklakov to AK, March 27, 1949, Kerensky Papers, F.120.
57. For contrasting Bolshevik reactions to the association of Kerensky's name with the news of the Revolution, see, G. V. Kuibysheva et al, *Valerian Vladimirovich Kuibyshev: Biografiia* (M: Izd. Politicheskoi Literatury, 1966), 58; and V. Antonov-Saratovskii, "Saratov s Fevralia po oktiabr 1917 g.," *Proletarskaia Revoliutsiia* (1924) no. 2(25): 147. The verse is cited by V. V———yi [Kiriakov], *A. F. Kerenskii*, 3, after *Respublika* (1917) no. 1. This latter publication has eluded me.

8. The People's Minister of Justice

1. *RPG*, 1: 69–70, 135–36; Sukhanov, *Zapiski*, 1: 281–83.
2. FO.371.2995, Report of Mr. Walpole, April 5, 1917; *The Times*, March 16, 19, 20, 1917.
3. FO.371.2995, Buchanan to FO, March 15, 1917.
4. FO.371.2995, Buchanan to FO, March 19, 1917 (Cabinet Green Paper).
5. Claude Anet, *Through the Russian Revolution* (L: Hutchinson & Co, 1917), 47–50; *The Times*, March 17, 1917; Sukhanov, *Zapiski*, 2: 27–35; L. S. Gaponenko, *Rabochii Klass Rossii v 1917 godu* (M: Nauka, 1970), 227 ff.

6. *Rech'*, March 5, 9, 1917; Gaponenko, *Rabochii Klass*, 227 ff.
7. AK, *Catastrophe*, 64–65; see photograph in Anet, *Through the Russian Revolution*, opp. p. 144.
8. *Izvestiia*, March 9, 1917.
9. *Iskry*, March 19, 1917, 88; FO.371.2995, Lockhart to Buchanan, March 21, 1917; MAE, v.647, Engelhard to Paléologue, March 19, 1917; E. N. Burd-zhalov, *Vtoraia Russkaia Revoliutsiia*, vol. 2: *Moskva, Front, Periferiia* (M: Nauka, 1971), 76–77.
10. *The Times*, March 22, 23, 1917.
11. *The Times*, April 5, 1917.
12. AK, "Rusalka," typescript, 2, Kerensky Papers, F.83; M. I. Tereshchenko to AK, June 26, 1950, Kerensky Papers, F.167.
13. T. I. Pol'ner, *Zhiznënnyi put' Kniazia Georgiia Evgenievicha L'vova: Lichnost'. Vzgliady. Usloviia deiatel'nosti* (Paris: Imp. de Navarre, 1932), 5, 231 ff; Tsereteli, *Vospominaniia*, 1: 63–64; V. D. Nabokov, "Vremënnoe Pravitel'stvo," *ARR* (1921), 1: 34–52; Miliukov, *Vospominaniia*, 2: 325ff; M. M. Novikov, *Ot Moskvy do N'iu Iorka: Moia zhizn' v nauke i politike*, (NY: Chekhov, 1952), 260 ff.
14. Nabokov, "Vremënnoe Pravitel'stvo," 32–33.
15. Ibid., 47–49; Marc Ferro, *October 1917: A Social History of the Russian Revolution* (L: Routledge and Kegan Paul, 1980), 59 ff.
16. Nabokov, "Vremënnoe Pravitel'stvo," 34ff, 22–23.
17. Ibid., 45–50; Miliukov, *Vospominaniia*, 2: 325–33.
18. MAE, v.647, Paléologue to MAE, March 18, 1917.
19. FO.371.2995, Buchanan to FO, March 19, 1917; Pol'ner, *Zhiznënnyi put'*, 251.
20. Nabokov, "Vremënnoe Pravitel'stvo," 40; Gippius, *Siniaia Kniga*, 116; FO.371.2995, Buchanan to FO, March 26, 1917; MAE, v.648, Paléologue to MAE, March 24, 1917.
21. Stepun, *Byvshee*, 2:35; Anet, *Through the Russian Revolution*, 85; Florence Farmborough, *Nurse at the Russian Front* (L: Futura Publications, 1977), 246, 261–62.
22. *VOSR: Revoliutsionnoe dvizhenie v Rossii posle Sverzheniia Samoderzhaviia*, 252; *Delo Naroda*, March 15, April 21, 1917.
23. A. A. Demianov, "Moia sluzhba pri Vremënnom Pravitel'stve", *ARR* (1922), 4: 59–60; V. V——yi, [alias V. V. Kiriakov], *A. F. Kerenskii*, (Pet: 'Narodnaia Vlast' ', 1917), 29 ff; Carl Enckell, *Politiska Minnen* (Stockholm: Gebers Förlag, 1956), 1: 82–83; AK interviewed by Elena Ivanoff, Sept. 27, 1961, unnumbered, 6, Kerensky Papers, F.97; Conversations with Mrs. O. L. Kerensky.
24. Demianov, "Moia sluzhba," 60 ff; Aleksander Hellat, "Revolutsiooni miilitsas," *Mälestused iseseivuse võitluspäivilt*, vol. 1: *Revolutsioon ja okupatsioon 1917–1918* (Tallinn: Rahvaülikooli Kirjastus, 1927), 110–11; cf. Nabokov, "Vremënnoe Pravitel'stvo," 31, who insists that he dissuaded Kerensky from an unfortunate appointment.
25. Demianov, "Moia sluzhba," 60–70.
26. Ibid., 73; V. V——yi [Kiriakov], *A. F. Kerenskii*, 36 ff; Werner E. Mosse, "A. F. Kerensky and the Emancipation of Russian Jewry," *Bulletin on Soviet and East European Jewish Affairs* (1970) no. 6, 33–37; *Padenie* 1: v–xxvii; N. P. Karabchevskii, *Chto glaza moi uvideli* (Berlin: Izd. D'iakovoi i Ko., 1921), vol. 2: *Revoliutsiia i Rossiia*, 122–23.

27. *RPG*, 1: 201–3; N. Kadmin, "Otmena smertnoi kazni," *Probuzhdenie*, 1917, no. 5, 252–53; *Novoe Vremia*, March 18, 1917.
28. Oskari Tokoi, *Maanpakolaisen Muistelmia* (H:ki: Tammi, 1959), 182 ff; *Hufvud-stadsbladet*, March 30, April 1, 1917; Keijo Kylävaara, *Vuosi Seitsämäntoista* (H:ki: Helsingin Sanomat, 1967), 67 ff.
29. *Hufvudstadsbladet*, March 30, 1917; Karl H. Wiik, "Dagsanteckningar," ms., 14, Yksityiskokoelmat, Valtion Arkisto, H:ki; "Sosialistien 29.3.1917 jättämän pro-memoria Kerenskille," ms, Työväen Arkisto, H:ki; Väinö Tanner, *Kuinka se oikein tapahtui: Vuosi 1918 esivaiheineen ja jälkiselvittelyineen* (H:ki: Tammi, 1948), 41–42; Tuomo Polvinen, *VVS*, 1: 33–35; *Delo Naroda*, March 19, 1917. For the Estonian and Ukrainian military demonstrations, see Edvard Laaman, *Eesti Iseseivuse Sünd* (Stockholm: Kirjastus Vaba Eesti, 1964), 92; Gippius, *Siniaia Kniga*, 117.
30. V. V——yi [Kiriakov], *A. F. Kerenskii*, 29–30; *Izvestiia*, March 9, 1917.
31. Harold Nicholson, *King George the Fifth* (L: Constable, 1952), 299–302. Nicholson places King George V's constitutionally unusual action in blocking the invitation to the Romanovs in the context of his strategic objective of creating an above-party monarchy; "Dokumenty k 'Vospominaniiam' gen. A. Lukom-skago," Gen. A. Lukomskii, ed. *ARR* (1921) 3: 246 ff; AK, *Crucifixion*, 146–48; AK, *Catastrophe*, 262–67; AK, "The Road to the Tragedy," *The Murder of the Romanovs*, Sir Bernard Pares, ed. (L: Hutchinson, 1935), 121–26; AK interviewed by Anatole Mazour, Mills College, California, 1965. Cf. Marie Klein-michel, *Memoirs of a Shipwrecked World* (L: Brentano's, 1923), 246–48; Count Paul de Benkendorff, *Last Days at Tsarskoe Selo* (L: William Heinemann, 1927), 54–62; Both Monarchists and Communists credit the story that Kerensky went determined to address the ex-Tsar as Nicholas Romanov, but was so charmed that he used Your Imperial Majesty, that Kerensky then secretly repented of overthrowing him, even describing Nicholas II as an ideal "Popular Ruler." This is not mentioned by either Kleinmichel or Benkendorff, who were present at Tsarskoe Selo. However, Kerensky was both sentimental and sensitive enough to know that Nicholas Romanov (with its echoes of Citizen Capet) would sound like a death sentence. It is quite possible that he compromised with Highness. It is equally possible that the ex-Tsar devined and manipulated Kerensky's residual monarchism. V. I. Nazanskii, *Krushenie velikoi Rossii i doma Romanovykh*, (Paris: Knizhnyi magazin E. Sial'skoi, 1930), 200–201; M. K. Kas-vinov, *Dvadtsat' tri stupeni vniz* (M: Mysl', 1979), 359 ff.
32. Sukhanov, *Zapiski*, 2: 131–32; AK, "The Road to the Tragedy," 109; MAE, vol. 648, Paléologue to MAE, March 21, 23, 1917; AK interviewed by Elena Ivanoff, Sept. 27, 1961, no. 7, 6, Kerensky Papers, F.97.
33. Sukhanov, *Zapiski*, 2: 86–88; Nabokov, "Vremënnoe Pravitel'stvo," 36–37; Tsereteli, *Vospominaniia*, 1: 123.
34. *Delo Naroda*, March 28, 1917; Sukhanov, *Zapiski*, 2: 357–60.
35. B. Nikolaevskii, "I. G. Tsereteli i ego Vospominaniia," Tsereteli, *Vospominan-iia*, 1: x–xv; Stepun, *Byvshee*, 2: 53–59; *VOSR: . . . posle Sverzheniia Samoder-zhaviia*, 131–41; Mints, *Istoriia*, vol. 2: *Sverzhenie Vremënnogo Pravitel'stva i Ustanovlenie Diktatury Proletariata*, 73ff; Sukhanov, *Zapiski*, 2: 288–91.

36. M. Ferro, *The Russian Revolution of February 1917* (L: Routledge, 1972), 112–30; John L. H. Keep, *The Russian Revolution: A Study in Mass Mobilization* (L: Weidenfeld, 1976), esp. pp. 162–85; Mints, *Istoriia*, vol. 1. *Sverzhenie Samoderzhaviia*, 716ff.

37. Despite the prominence of the Latvians and Czechs in the Civil War, most Western and Soviet historiography of the Revolution is hopelessly Russocentric, while minority nationalists tend to write exclusively about their own nationality. The exceptions are S. M. Dimanshtein ed., *Revoliutsiia i natsional'nyi vopros* (M: Kommunisticheskaia Akademiia, 1930), and Richard Pipes, *The Formation of the Soviet Union: Communism and Nationalism 1917–1923* (Cambridge: Harvard University Press, 1964), which concentrates on the final phase. For the national units, see Lieutenant-Colonel Henryk Bagiński, *Wojsko Polskie na Wschodzie* (Warsaw: Główna Księgarnia Wójskowa, 1921); Mieczysław Wrzosek, "Polskie formacje wojskowe w Rosji (1914–1920)," in Halina Florkowska-Frančić, ed. in *Polonia wobec Niepodległości Polski w Czasie I Wojny Światowej* (Warsaw: Polska Akademia Nauk, Komitet Badania Polonii, 1979), 195–216; I. I. Beliakovich, "Iz istorii sozdaniia pol'skikh natsional'nykh formirovanii v sostave russkoi armii vo vremia pervoi mirovoi voiny," A. L. Sidorov, ed. *Pervaia Mirovaia Voina*, (M: Nauka, 1968), 158–67; Arnolds Sprekke, *History of Latvia* (Stockholm: M. Goppers, 1951), 327–36; Uldis Ģermanis, *Oberst Vācietis und die lettischen Schützen im Weltkrieg und in der Oktoberrevolution* (Stockholm: Almquist and Wiksell, 1974); John F. N. Bradley, *La Légion Tchécoslovaque en Russie 1914–1920* (Paris: CNRS, 1963); Gerburg Thunig-Nittner, *Die Tschechoslowakische Legion in Russland* (Wiesbaden: Otto Harrassowitz, 1970), A. Tõnisson, "Esimest Eesti Polgust," in *Mälestused iseseivuse võitluspäivilt*, 1: 155ff; M. A. Petrov, "Formirovanie estonskikh natsional'nykh polkov v 1917 g.," *Pervaia Mirovaia Voina*, 170–78; K. Oberuchev, *V dni revoliutsii* (NY: Narodopravstvo, 1919), 98ff; Oleh S. Pidhainy, *The Formation of the Ukrainian Republic* (Toronto-NY: New Review Books, 1966), 1: 63 ff, 120 ff; Jovan M. Jovanović, *Borba za Narodno Ujedinenje 1914–1918* (Belgrade: Getsa Kon A.D., 1935), 116–19.

38. MAE, v.648, Paléologue to MAE, March 20, 1917; MAE, vol. 648, notes of Russian Ambassadors in London and Paris, March 22, 23, 1917; V. S. Vasiukov, *Vneshniaia politika Vremënnogo Pravitel'stva* (M: Mysl', 1966), 28.

39. *RPG*, 2: 1042–43; *VOSR: . . . posle Sverzheniia Samoderzhaviia*, 252–53, 422–24.

40. AK, "Varlaam Levanovich Gelovani," *Severnyia Zapiski*, February 1915, 217–19.

41. FO.371.2995, Buchanan to FO, March 19, 1917; V. V. Shul'gin, *Dni*, (Belgrade: M. A. Suvorin "Novoe Vremia," 1925), 207; USA, *Papers* (1918) 1: 18–20, Winship to Lansing, April 3, 1917.

42. MAE, vol. 648, Gen. Morier to Minister of War, March 27, 1917; Barrère (Rome) to MAE, March 29, 1917; AA, Russland 82, no. 2 (GFM.6. SA Reel 132), Report from Ziese, April 3, 1917; *Vossische Zeitung*, March 31, 1917; *Berliner Tageblatt*, March 31, 1917.

43. *Delo Naroda*, March 25, 1917; MAE, vol. 649, Paléologue to MAE, April 8, 1917; AA, Russland 82, no. 2 (GFM. 6. SA Reel 132), Report on Kerensky, April 26, 1917.

44. *Berliner Tageblatt*, April 4, 7, 1917; *Rech'*, March 23, 1917; Vasiukov, *Vneshniaia politika*, 87.
45. Nabokov, "Vremënnoe Pravitel'stvo," 57–58.
46. Tsereteli, *Vospominaniia*, 1: 62–74.
47. Miliukov, *Vospominaniia*, 2: 344–46; Rex A. Wade, *The Russian Search for Peace: February–October 1917* (Stanford, Cal: Stanford University Press, 1969), 26–32.
48. Nabokov, "Vremënnoe Pravitel'stvo," 59–60; For Miliukov's feelings about his son, see Miliukov, *Vospominaniia*, 2: 196–98.
49. FO.371.2995, Buchanan to FO, April 9, 1917.
50. Tsereteli, *Vospominaniia*, 1: 123; Sukhanov, *Zapiski*, 2: 372–73; Stankevich, *Vospominaniia*, 95.
51. Enckell, *Politiska Minnen*, 1: 81–82.
52. *Hufvudstadsbladet*, April 14, 17, 1917; Wiik, "Dagsanteckningar," 19; *Delo Naroda*, April 1, 5, 1917.
53. K. Ruuskanen, "Kerenski puheilla," *Suomen Vapaussota* (1934), no. 5, 109–11.
54. Johnny Hackman, "En gammal film," *Grankulla Samskola 1907–1957: Festskrift utgiven till skolans 50-årsjubileum i september 1957*, Magnus Hagelstam, ed. (H:ki: Holger Schildts Förlag, 1957), 142; Enckell, *Politiska Minnen*, 1: 82; *Delo Naroda*, April 6, 1917.

9. Ambition and Diplomacy

1. Lenin, *Works*, 23: 288, 292, 303–05, 316, 334.
2. Lenin, *Works*, 23: 406–7, nn124, 126, 127; Z.A.B. Zeman ed., *Germany and the Revolution in Russia 1915–1918* (L: Oxford University Press, 1958), 25–46.
3. Lenin, *Works*, 24: 21–26; Cathy Porter, *Alexandra Kollontai: A Biography* (L: Virago, 1980), 235–36, 240 ff; Stephen E. Cohen, *Bukharin and the Bolshevik Revolution: A Political Biography, 1888–1938* (L: Oxford University Press, 1980), 47–50; Charles Duval, "Iakov Mikhailovich Sverdlov: Founder of the Bolshevik Party Machine," in Ralph C. Elwood, ed. *Reconsiderations on the Russian Revolution*, (Cambridge, Mass: Slavica, 1976), 218; Mints, *Istoriia*, vol. 2: *Sverzhenie Vremënnogo Pravitel'stva. Ustanovlenie Diktatury Proletariata*, 80–81; Alexander Rabinowitch, *Prelude to Revolution: The Petrograd Bolsheviks and the July 1917 Uprising* (Bloomington, Ind.: Indiana University Press, 1968), 32–42.
4. Gippius, *Siniaia Kniga*, 118–20, 130; c.f. V. D. Nabokov, "Vremënnoe Pravitel'stvo," *ARR* (1921), 1: 75, who quotes Kerensky as saying, "Just wait, Lenin himself is coming. . . . then it'll really begin!" Nabokov alleges that Kerensky even thought of going to see Lenin to "reorientate" him.
5. MAE, vol. 650, Paléologue to MAE, April 18, 1917; *Delo Naroda*, April 9, 1917.
6. Sukhanov, *Zapiski*, vol. 3, 140 ff; Gippius, *Siniaia Kniga*, 47.
7. *Delo Naroda*, April 16, 1917; Radkey, *Agrarian Foes*, 127 ff.
8. Sukhanov, *Zapiski*, 3: 149ff.
9. FO.371.2995, Buchanan to FO, March 15, 1917; USA, *Papers* (1918), 1: 18, Lansing to Francis, April 3, 1917; MAE, vol. 650, Paléologue to MAE, March

15, 1917; Maurice Paléologue, *La Russie des Tsars pendant la Grande Guerre* (Paris: Plon, 1922), 3: 303–04.

10. *Delo Naroda*, April 6, 1917; Nabokov, "Vremënnoe Pravitel'stvo," 60.

11. *Rech'*, April 9, 1917; B. W. Schaper, *Albert Thomas: Dertig Jaar Sociaal Reformisme* (Leiden: Universitaire Pers, 1953), 99–124; AK, *Catastrophe*, 270; Albert Thomas, "Journal," typescript, FAT, 94 AP 176; (also published with an introduction by I. Sinanoglou, *CMRS*, [1973] 14: 86–204); A. Thomas, "Meine Mission in Russland im Jahre 1917," *Neue Freie Presse*, May 5, 1928; M. Ter-Pogosian (letter to AK, Dec. 22, 1954), claims to have discovered that neither Paléologue *nor* Thomas had been Masons, Kerensky Papers, F.217.

12. *Delo Naroda*, April 7, 8, 9, 12, 20, 1917.

13. *Delo Naroda*, April 12, 1917; V. G. Arkhangel'skii, *Katerina Breshkovskaia* (Prague-Uzhgorod: Izd. Obshchestva 'Shkol'naia Pomoshch' ' v Uzhgorode, 1938); E. Breshkovskaia, *Hidden Springs of the Russian Revolution* (Stanford, Cal: Stanford University Press, 1931); (for a hostile view, see V. M. Purishkevich, *Dnevnik chlëna Gosudarstvennoi Dumy* [Riga: Natsional Reklama, 1924], 126–28); Ed. Hubel, "Tribunaal ja Sõjatsensor," *Mälestused Iseseivuse võitluspäivilt*, vol. 1: *Revolutsioon ja okupatsioon 1917–1918* (Tallinn: Rahvaülikooli Kirjastus, 1927), 244. Conversations with members of the Kerensky family.

14. Zinaida N. Gippius, *Stikhi: Dnevnik 1911–1921* (Berlin: Slovo, 1922), 69; Temira Pachmuss, *Zinaida Hippius, An Intellectual Profile*, Carbondale, Ill: Southern Illinois University Press, 1971), 194–95; C. Anet, *Through the Russian Revolution*, (L: Hutchinson, 1917), 161–64.

15. *Delo Naroda*, April 20, 1917; *Rech'*, April 20, 1917

16. *Rech'*, April 21, 1917.

17. Miliukov, *Vospominaniia*, 2: 311–12, 339, 354–55; Rex A. Wade, *The Russian Search for Peace: February-October 1917*, (Stanford, Cal: Stanford University Press, 1969), 17. Wade regards Tsereteli as "probably the most important figure in the ruling circles from his return in March until July or August"; Radkey, *Agrarian Foes*, 156 ff.

18. *Rech'*, April 12, 1917; Wade, *Russian Search*, 34–35; *RPG*, 3: 1251–52.

19. V. S. Vasiukov, *Vneshniaia politika Vremënnogo Pravitel'stva*, (M: Nauka, 1966), 90–91; T. G. Masaryk, *Světová Revoluce, za války a ve válce, 1914–1918, vzpomína a uvažuje* (Prague: Orbis, 1925), 189–90.

20. Thomas, "Journal," 8–12.

21. Tsereteli, *Vospominaniia*, 1: 84–85; Miliukov, *Vospominaniia*, 2: 358–60; Nabokov, "Vremënnoe Pravitel'stvo," 63. For the purging of the Bureau of the Soviet Excom, see Sukhanov, *Zapiski*, 3: 160–79.

22. Thomas, "Journal," 13–15.

23. AK, *Catastrophe*, 133–34; *Delo Naroda*, April 13, 1917; MAE, vol. 650, Paléologue to MAE, April 27, 1917; Paléologue, *La Russie des Tsars*, 3: 315–16; Wade, *Russian Search*, 37–38.

24. Nabokov, "Vremënnoe Pravitel'stvo," 63; *Rech'*, April 14, 1917; Wade, *Russian Search*, 38; MAE, vol. 651, Ribot to Paléologue, May 2, 1917.

25. AK, *Catastrophe*, 133–34; Sukhanov, *Zapiski*, 3: 227.

26. Thomas, "Journal," "Visite à M. Kerensky—14/27 avril 1917—11 h. du matin."

27. Sukhanov, *Zapiski*. 3: 224–26; Tsereteli, *Vospominaniia*, 1: 85.
28. Nabokov, "Vremënnoe Pravitel'stvo," 63–64; Miliukov, *Vospominaniia*, 2: 359–60; Thomas, "Journal," 60; AK, *Catastrophe*, 135–37; Buchanan, *Mission*, 2: 123; Wade, *Russian Search*, 24, argues that the Soviet "Star Chamber" was where "the basic decisions" were taken "that were to decide the fate of the revolution from the end of March to October." It depends what you call basic. My impression is that Kerensky and Tereshchenko eluded their control after the July Days.
29. Wade, *Russian Search*, 38–39; Tsereteli, *Vospominaniia*, 1: 87.
30. *Delo Naroda*, April 21, 1917; MAE, vol. 651, Thomas to MAE, May 3, 1917.
31. *Rech'*, April 21, 1917; Paléologue, *La Russie des Tsars*, 3: 329–30; Miliukov, *Vospominaniia*, 2: 361–62.
32. Tsereteli, *Vospominaniia*, 1: 87–90; Sukhanov, *Zapiski*, 3: 262–63.
33. *Novaia Zhizn'*, April 21, 1917; Anet, *Through the Russian Revolution*, 186; AK, *Catastrophe*, 135–37; For Linde, see Sokoloff, *White Nights*, 15–29; Mints, *Istoriia*, vol. 2: *Sverzhenie Vremënnogo Pravitel'stva. Ustanovlenie Diktatury Proletariata*, 203; P. N. Krasnov, "Na vnutrennem fronte," *ARR*, (1921), 1: 105–10; Tsereteli, *Vospominaniia*, 1: 91.
34. Stankevich, *Vospominaniia*, 86; Anet, *Through the Russian Revolution*, 167, 171–72, 181–86; *RPG*, 3: 1240–41; Tsereteli, *Vospominaniia*, 1: 95–96; AK, *Catastrophe*, 297–300; For Kornilov's career, see Gen. A. A. Brusilov, *Moi Vospominaniia*, (Riga: Knigoizd. Mir [1929?]), 241–42; G. Katkov, *Russia 1917: The Kornilov Affair: Kerensky and the Break-Up of the Russian Army* (L: Longmans, 1980), 39–41.
35. Thomas, "Journal," 57–60.
36. Anet, *Through the Russian Revolution*, 169–72; Ariadna Tyrkova-Williams, *From Liberty to Brest-Litovsk* (L: Macmillan, 1919), 86–87; Sukhanov, *Zapiski*, 3: 277 ff; *Rech'*, April 21, 1917.
37. Sukhanov, *Zapiski*, 3: 280–81; *VOSR: Revoliutsionnoe dvizhenie v Rossii v aprele 1917 g.: Aprel'skii Krizis*, 736.
38. Anet, *Through the Russian Revolution*, 172–74; Tsereteli, *Vospominaniia*, 1: 98–105; *Rech'*, April 22, 1917; Miliukov, *Vospominaniia*, 2: 364.
39. Miliukov, *Vospominaniia*, 2: 367–68; Nabokov, "Vremënnoe Pravitel'stvo," 64; T. I. Pol'ner, *Zhiznënnyi put' Kniazia Georgiia Evgenievicha L'vova: Lichnost'. Vzgliady. Usloviia deiatel'nosti* (Paris: Imp. de Navarre, 1932), 248 ff.
40. V. Rakhmetov, ed. "Aprel'skie dni 1917 goda v Petrograde," *KA* (1929) 33: 34–81; Mints, *Istoriia*, vol. 2: *Sverzhenie Vremënnogo Pravitel'stva*, 272; Anet, *Through the Russian Revolution*, 183.
41. Tsereteli, *Vospominaniia*, 1: 124; *Rech'*, April 22, 1917.
42. Thomas, "Journal," 63–64. The secret *Osobye Zhurnaly Vremënnago Pravitel'stva* in the Hoover Institution are no more informative. The decision was probably deferred.
43. Miliukov, *Vospominaniia*, 2: 366, 371 ff; Sukhanov, *Zapiski*, 3: 257; AK, *Catastrophe*, 127–28; Nabokov, "Vremënnoe Pravitel'stvo," 42, 64–65; *RPG*, 3: 1249–51.
44. *RPG*, 3: 1251–52; Miliukov, *Vospominaniia*, 2: 362.
45. V. M. Chernov, *The Great Russian Revolution* (New Haven, Conn: Yale Uni-

versity Press, 1936), 205; *RPG*, 3: 1251 ff; Tsereteli, *Vospominaniia*, 1: 127–33; Sukhanov, *Zapiski*, 3: 397–400.
46. *Rech'*, April 20, May 2, 1917; Tsereteli, *Vospominaniia*, 1: 124–26; AK, *Izbrannyia rechi*, (Pet: Biblioteka 'Solntse Svobody', 1917), 61–64.
47. Miliukov, *Vospominaniia*, 2: 368–69.
48. *RPG*, 3: 1267–68; Miliukov, *Istoriia*, part 1, 108–9.
49. Sukhanov, *Zapiski*, 3: 406–8; Tsereteli, *Vospominaniia*, 1: 136–37.
50. *RPG*, 3: 1276–78.
51. Nabokov, "Vremënnoe Pravitel'stvo," 56; *Delo Naroda*, March 22, 1917.
52. Sukhanov, *Zapiski*, 3: 357–58; V. V. Vyrubov to AK, Jan. 10, 1958, Kerensky Papers, F.172.
53. See *Delo Naroda, Rech'*, and *Izvestiia*; Miliukov, *Vospominaniia*, 2: 369–81; Tsereteli, *Vospominaniia*, 1: 138–68; Sukhanov, *Zapiski*, 3: 408–43; Stankevich, *Vospominaniia*, 129–31; Radkey, *Agrarian Foes*, 174–76; Wade, *Russian Search*, 48.
54. Sukhanov, *Zapiski*, 3: 440.
55. *RPG*, 3: 1276–79.
56. *Izvestiia*, May 5, 6, 7, 1917.

10. Patriotism of a New Type

1. MAE, vol. 648, Paléologue to Ribot, March 27, 1917; USA, *Papers* (1918), 3: xi; A. L. Sidorov, *Finansovoe Polozhenie Rossii v gody pervoi mirovoi voiny, 1914–1917* (M: AN SSSR, 1960).
2. Even the Root Mission posed this question, though only *after* the collapse of Kerensky's July offensive. USA, *Papers* (1918), 1: 145–46, Report of Root to Lansing, August 1917. For Russia's military obligations for 1917, see E. Martynov, ed. "Konferentsiia soiuznikov v Petrograde v 1917 g.," *KA* (1927), 20: 38–55.
3. AK, *Catastrophe*, 207–9; Tsereteli, *Vospominaniia*, 1: 122.
4. Gen. N. N. Golovine, *The Russian Army in the World War* (New Haven, Conn: Yale University Press, 1931), 278–79; A. P. Zhilin, *Poslednee nastuplenie (iiun' 1917 goda)* (M: Nauka, 1983), 30 ff.
5. Stepun, *Byvshee*, 2: 18 ff; Sukhanov, *Zapiski*, 2: 138 ff; Mints, *Istoriia*, vol. 2: *Sverzhenie Vremënnogo Pravitel'stva. Ustanovlenie Diktatury Proletariata*, 319 ff; Lenin, *Works*, 24: 163–65.
6. *RPG*, 2: 848–49; 878–80.
7. L. S. Gaponenko, ed. *Revoliutsionnoe dvizhenie v russkoi armii v 1917 g.* (M: Nauka, 1968), 36.
8. *RPG*, 2: 854, 880–83; Gen. A. I. Denikin, *The Russian Turmoil: Memoirs: Military, Social, and Political* (L: Hutchinson, 1918), 177–88; Gen. B. Gourko, *Memories and Impressions of War and Revolution in Russia, 1914–1917* (L: John Murray, 1918), 299–307; Gen. A. A. Brusilov, *Moi Vospominaniia* (Riga: Mir, [1929?]), 231.
9. Gaponenko ed, *Revoliutsionnoe dvizhenie v russkoi armii*, 61–63; *Obshchee Delo*, Oct. 3, 1917

10. *Russkii Invalid*, May 5, 1917.

11. Tsereteli, *Vospominaniia*, 1: 401–12.

12. *Deklaratsiia prav soldata* (Pet: Ministerstvo Voennoe i Morskoe, 1917); Mints, *Istoriia*, vol. 2: *Sverzhenie Vremënnogo Pravitel'stva*, 323–24; A. Thomas, "Journal," 6–17, FAT 94 AP 176; *VOSR: Revoliutsionnoe dvizhenie v Rossii v maeiiune 1917 g.: Iiun'skaia demonstratsiia*, 231.

13. Gourko, *Memories*, 323. Gourko passed his suspicions of Baranovsky's influence on to General Knox. See WO.106.1096, Knox to DMI, Nov. 1, 1917; Sukhanov, *Zapiski*, 3: 357–58; Stepun, *Byvshee*, 2: 89–94; Gen. P. A. Polovtsëv, *Dni zatmeniia* (Paris: Vozhrozhdenie, 1927), 5 ff; Vl. Maksakov, "Iz zapisnoi knizhki arkhivista: Zapiski A. I. Koz'mina," *KA* (1933), 60: 142 ff; Stankevich, *Vospominaniia*, 143 ff; Conversations with Dr. O. A. Kerensky and Gleb Kerensky.

14. Maksakov, "Zapiski A. I. Koz'mina," 142, 144–45, 151.

15. *RPG*, 3: 1277; Radkey, *Agrarian Foes*, 229 ff. Kerensky told me these unedifying details in 1967. He had previously given a similar account to Prof. Marc Ferro.

16. *Russkii Invalid*, May 5, 10, 1917; *Hufvudstadsbladet*, May 24, 1917. The first public attack on Kerensky in Finland was a leader in *Työmies*, "Suomen vapaus ja Venäjän hallituksen kanta," signed O[tto] V[ille] K[uusinen]. This militant exponent of Finnish independence would later try to snuff it out, see pp. 369–70 supra; Polvinen, *VVS*, 1: 60 ff.

17. *Russkii Invalid*, May 12, 13, 1917; Brusilov, *Moi Vospominaniia*, 212–13; Stepun, *Byvshee*, 2: 72 ff; Mints, *Istoriia*, vol. 2: *Sverzhenie Vremënnogo Pravitel'stva*, 394.

18. K. Oberuchev, *V dni revoliutsii* (NY: Narodopravstvo, 1919), 79–80.

19. Stepun, *Byvshee*, 2: 74–76; A. Thomas, "Journal," vendredi 12/25 mai 1917; cf. Marina Tsvetaeva, *The Demesne of the Swans: Lebedinnyi Stan*, Robin Kemball trans., (Ann Arbor, Mich.: Ardis, 1980), 41. AK, *Catastrophe*, 194–96; Oberuchev, *V dni revoliutsii*, 80–81; Claude Anet, *Through the Russian Revolution* (L: Hutchinson, 1917), 222–25.

20. Florence Farmborough, *Nurse at the Russian Front* (L: Futura Publications, 1977), 269–70.

21. *Russkii Invalid*, May 27, 1917; AK, *Catastrophe*, 202–4; Gourko, *Memories*, 309

22. Uldis Ģermanis, *Oberst Vācietis und die lettischen Schützen im Weltkrieg und in der Oktoberrevolution* (Stockholm: Almquist and Wiksell, 1974), 198–200; *Russkii Invalid*, May 27, 1917. Bolshevik sources allege that he was not entirely successful with the Russians in Riga, either, see D. I. Grazkin, *Okopnaia Pravda* (M: 'Sovetskaia Rossiia', 1958), 124–25.

23. Mints, *Istoriia*, vol. 2: *Sverzhenie Vremënnogo Pravitel'stva*, 394–95; cf. Sukhanov, *Zapiski*, 4: 69–70.

24. Gaponenko ed, *Revoliutsionnoe dvizhenie v russkoi armii*, 571–72; Brusilov, *Moi Vospominaniia*, 233 ff; AK, *Catastrophe*, 193–99; A. I. Verkhovskii, *Na trudnom perevale* (M: Voennoe Izd. Min. Oborony SSSR, 1959), 178 ff.

25. AK, *Catastrophe*, 199–201; Gourko, *Memories*, 310; Denikin, *Russian Turmoil*, 149.

26. MAE, v.653, Notes du Capitaine de Maleisye, 18/31 mai 1917; *Russkii Invalid*, May 30, 1917.

27. Botchkareva, *Yashka*, 149 ff; Boris Solonevich, *Zhenshchina s vintovkoi; Istori-*

cheskii roman [i.e., the slightly fictionalized memoirs of Nina Krylova] (Buenos Aires: [privately printed], 1955); 34 ff; Rech', May 28, 1917.

28. R. H. Bruce Lockhart, Memoirs of a British Agent (NY: Putnam, 1932), 176–77; See also Emmeline Pankhurst's reference to Olga Kerensky in Britannia [formerly The Suffragette], July 13, 1917; Botchkareva, Yashka, 160; Personal communications and conversations. As late as June 25, 1917, Iskry reported that Olga Kerensky would be going as a nurse with Bochkarëva's unit to the front.

29. AK, Catastrophe, 206; Osobye zhurnaly Vremënnago Pravitel'stva, May 21, 1917, Hoover Institution.

30. O. H. Gankin & H. H. Fisher, eds., The Bolsheviks and the World War (Stanford, Cal: Stanford University Press, 1940), 613–20; MAE, vol. 652, Thomas to Ribot, May 19, 1917; MAE, vol. 653, Thomas to Ribot, June 14, 1917; Thomas, "Journal," Journée du 21 mai/3 juin.

31. Russkii Invalid, May 24, 1917.

32. A. Blodnieks, The Undefeated Nation (NY: Robert Speller, 1960), 142; Witold Trzciński, "Uznanie niepodległości Polski przez Rosję," Niepodległość (1933), 8: 301–4; Wiesława Toporowicz, Sprawa Polska w Polityce Rosyjskiej 1914–1917 (Warsaw: Państwowe Wydawnictwo Naukowe, 1973), 154–55, 267ff; AK, Turning Point, 240n; Norman Davies, God's Playground: A History of Poland (New York: Columbia University Press, 1981), 2: 378–87.

33. Hufvudstadsbladet, Oct. 2, 1965; Russkii Invalid, May 24, 1917; Esa Arra, "Alexander Kerenski: Haaveilija vaiko Realisti," Kerenskistä Kekkoseen (Jyväskylä: K. J. Gummerus, 1972), 90; The song "Kerenski se leipoi" was recorded on Valkoisien Armeijan Laulut, Scandia Musikki Oy, SLP 538–1970, (H:ki, 1970); Polvinen, VVS, 1: 67 ff.

34. Gen. A. Tõnisson, "Esimest Eesti Polgust," Mälestused iseseivuse võitluspäivilt, vol. 1: Revolutsioon ja okupatsioon 1917–1918 (Tallinn: Rahvaülikooli Kirjastus, 1927), 155 ff; Theodor Käärik, "Rasformirovatj," Mälestused iseseivuse võitluspäivilt, 1: 153–54; E. Laaman, Eesti Iseseivuse Sünd (Stockholm: Kirjastus Vaba Eesti, 1964), 82–90.

35. T. G. Masaryk, Světová Revoluce, za války a ve válce, 1914–1918, vpomína a uvažuje (Prague: Orbis, 1925), 189; G. Thunig-Nittner, Die Tschechoslowakische Legion in Russland (Wiesbaden: Otto Harrassowitz, 1970) 22; Vojtěch Holoček, "Ohlas Zborova v tisku," in Josef Kopta et al., eds. Zborov: Památník k třicátemu výročí bitvy u Zborova 2. července 1917, (Prague: Čin, 1947), 1965.

36. B. Nolde, La Formation de l'Empire Russe (Paris: Université de Paris) 1953, vol. 3; passim; M. S. Hrushevsky, A History of Ukraine, (New Haven, Conn: Yale University Press, 1941), 521–27; J. S. Reshetar, The Ukrainian Revolution 1917–1920 (Princeton, NJ: Princeton University Press, 1952), 47 ff; O. S. Pidhainy, The Formation of the Ukrainian Republic (Toronto-NY: New Review Books, 1966), 1: 42 ff; S. M. Korolivs'kii, Peremoha Velykoi Zhovtnevoi Sotsialistychnoi Revoliutsii na Ukraínii (Kiev: Vydavnytstvo 'Naukova Dumka', 1967) 78–83.

37. Oberuchev, V dni revoliutsii, 92–96; Pidhainy, Ukrainian Republic, 63–65, 84, 90 ff; Reshetar, Ukrainian Revolution, 60–62; Pravda, June 15, 1917.

38. FO.371.2996, Lockhart to Buchanan, June 11, 1917; c.f. Lockhart, Memoirs, 178–79.

39. *RPG*, 2: 888
40. Radkey, *Agrarian Foes*, 224–33.
41. Eugène Petit to A. Thomas, 14/27 juin 1917, Petit Papers; *Volia Naroda*, June 21, 1917; M. Vishniak, *Dan' proshlomu* (NY: Chekhov, 1954), 283–84; Radkey, *Agrarian Foes*, 225–26.
42. MAE, vol. 653, Thomas to Ribot, June 14, 1917; USA, *Papers* (1918), 1: 145–46, Root to Lansing, August 1917.

11. 'The Supreme Persuader-in-Chief'

1. Sukhanov, *Zapiski*, 4: chapter 4, 198–281; AK, *Catastrophe*, 215–16.
2. *Russkii Invalid*, June 6, 1917; Sukhanov, *Zapiski*, 4: 222–28; Tsereteli, *Vospominaniia*, 1: 238–70; Mints, *Istoriia*, vol. 2: *Sverzhenie Vremënnogo Pravitel'stva. Ustanovlenie Diktatury Proletariata*, 489 ff.
3. Sukhanov, *Zapiski*, 4: 231–32; Tsereteli, *Vospominaniia*, 2: 163–69.
4. Lenin, *Works*, 25: 17 ff; Sukhanov, *Zapiski*, 4: 232–34; AK, *Catastrophe*, 215–16
5. *Russkii Invalid*, June 6, 1917; *RPG*, 3: 1305–6; AK, *Catastrophe*, 216; Sukhanov, *Zapiski*, 4: 229, 234; Robert Payne, *The Fortress* (NY: W. H. Allen, 1967), 410–12.
6. Lenin, *Works*, 25: 29 ff.
7. *Russkii Invalid*, June 11, 1917. Kerensky had also sent Lincoln Steffens with a message to President Wilson asking him to put pressure on Britain and France to offer Germany peace on "Zimmerwaldist" terms (no punishments, no compensation, no annexations). Steffens took this to be a serious peace move, even though Kerensky explained that if Germany refused it, it would raise the morale of the Russian army., see Ella Hicks and Granville Winter eds, *The Letters of Lincoln Steffens* (NY: Harcourt, Brace & Co, 1938) vol. 1: *1889–1919*, 399–400. This is probably the origin of the erroneous allegation that Kerensky asked the Allies for permission to make a *separate* peace. See A.J.P. Taylor, *The First World War. An Illustrated History* (L: Hamish Hamilton, 1963), 142.
8. Alexander Rabinowitch, *Prelude to Revolution: The Petrograd Bolsheviks and the July 1917 Uprising* (Bloomington, Ind: Indiana University Press, 1968), 72–84; Tsereteli, *Vospominaniia*, 2: 226–53; Sukhanov, *Zapiski*, 4: 302–11.
9. Botchkareva, *Yashka*, 169–88; Boris Solonevich, *Zhenshchina s vintovkoi: Istoricheskii roman* [The memoirs of Nina Krylova], (Buenos Aires: [privately printed] 1955), 76–82; Louise Bryant, *Six Red Months in Russia* (L: William Heinemann, 1918), 210–13.
10. *Russkii Invalid*, June 14, 20, 1917; *RPG*, 2: 942.
11. AK, *Catastrophe*, 190; Stankevich, *Vospominaniia*, 151–53; *Russkii Invalid*, June 21, 27, 1917; *AFSR*, July 2, 1917; L. S. Gaponenko ed., *Revoliutsionnoe dvizhenie v russkoi armii v 1917 g.* (M: Nauka, 1968), 240–41, 251–52; *VOSR: Revoliutsionnoe dvizhenie v Rossii v mae-iiune 1917 g.: Iiun'skaia demonstratsiia*, 365–66; General Sir Alfred Knox, *With the Russian Army. 1914–1917* (L: Hutchinson and Co, 1921), 2: 638–39; In the wake of the Kornilov affair, Dziewałtowski was acquitted of incitement to mutiny, *Russkie Vedomosti*, Oct. 5, 1917.

12. *Russkii Invalid*, June 21, 22, 1917; *VOSR:* . . . *Iiun'skaia demonstratsiia*, 367; AK, *Catastrophe*, 219–20.

13. A. I. Denikin, *The Russian Turmoil: Memoirs: Military, Social, and Political* (L: Hutchinson, 1922), 273; Stankevich, *Vospominaniia*, 154 ff; AK, *Catastrophe*, 221–23; J.F.N. Bradley, *La Légion Tchécoslovaque en Russie 1914–1920* (Paris: CNRS, 1963), 53–54; G. Thunig-Nittner, *Die Tschechoslowakische Legion in Russland* (Wiesbaden: Otto Harrassowitz, 1970), 23 ff; WO.33.924, Major Neilson to CIGS, July 4, 1917; Gen. Barter to CIGS, July 9, 1917; A. P. Zhilin, *Poslednee nastuplenie: (iiun' 1917 goda)* (M: Nauka, 1983), 57–60.

14. *Russkii Invalid*, June 29, 1917; Stankevich, *Vospominaniia*, 160; Gaponenko ed., *Revoliutsionnoe dvizhenie v russkoi armii*, 241 ff.

15. Stepun, *Byvshee*, 2: 106–7; Rabinowitch, *Prelude to Revolution*, 97–106; Botchkareva, *Yashka*, 184–88; Thunig-Nittner, *Tschechoslowakische Legion*, 27.

16. *Russkii Invalid*, June 20, 1917, July 1, 1917.

17. *Russkii Invalid*, July 1, 1917; FO.371.2996, Buchanan to FO, July 5, 1917.

18. Stankevich, *Vospominaniia*, 160; *VOSR:* . . . *Iiun'skaia demonstratsiia*, 372–74; Botchkareva, *Yashka*, 189; Solonevich, *Zhenshchina*, 86 ff; *Britannia*, July 13, 1917.

19. Denikin, *Russian Turmoil*, 274; *Russkii Invalid*, June 28, 1917; OLK, "Obryvki," 125n; *VOSR:* . . . *Iiun'skaia demonstratsiia*, 375–76; Stankevich, *Vospominaniia*, 159; Rabinowitch, *Prelude to Revolution*, 149; V. Kamenshchykau, *Za uladu savetau (1917 god na Zakhodnim fronte). Uspaminy*, (Minsk: Dziarzhaunae Vydaventstva BSSR, 1959), 57–58; Zhilin, *Poslednee nastuplenie*, 60–65.

20. J. Reshetar, *The Ukrainian Revolution 1917–1920* (Princeton, NJ: Princeton University Press, 1952), 60 ff; O. S. Pidhainy, *The Formation of the Ukrainian Republic* (Toronto-NY: New Review Books, 1966), 1: 109 ff; Eugène Petit to A. Thomas, 12/25 juillet 1917, 2–3, Petit Papers; Tsereteli, *Vospominaniia*, 2: 133 ff; Several of the Ukrainian leaders were freemasons, while the Kiev Kadets who, unlike Milyukov, endorsed the agreements, were members of the Freemasonry of the Peoples of Russia. See Ludwik Hass, "Wolnomularstwo Ukraińskie 1917–1921," *Studia z dziejów ZSRR i Europy Środkowej*, 18: 57–58, 62.

21. Tsereteli, *Vospominaniia*, 2: 156–59; Petit to Thomas, 12/15 juillet 1917; *Rech'*, July 4, 1917; Ariadna Tyrkova-Williams, *From Liberty to Brest-Litovsk* (L: Macmillan, 1919), 137–41; Rosenberg, *Liberals*, 174–77.

22. Miliukov, *Istoriia*, part 1, 139ff; Tyrkova-Williams, *Liberty to Brest-Litovsk*, 136ff; Rosenberg, *Liberals*, 171–72.

23. Rosenberg, *Liberals*, 78–83.

24. M. V. Vishniak, *Vserossiiskoe Uchreditel'noe Sobranie* (Paris: Sovremennyia Zapiski, 1932), 70–79; AK to *NZh*, April 20, 1953, 9–12; Lionel Kochan, "Kadet Policy in 1917 and the Constituent Assembly," *Slavonic and East European Review* (1967), 45: 183–92

25. Radkey, *Agrarian Foes*, 287, 291–93; AK, *Catastrophe*, 237; Denikin, *Russian Turmoil*, 274–75; Rabinowitch, *Prelude to Revolution*, 144 ff; *Izvestiia*, July 1, 1917; Polvinen, *VVS*, 1: 80–82.

26. *AFSR*, July 6, 1917; *VOSR: Revoliutsionnoe dvizhenie v Rossii v iiule 1917 g.: Iiul'skii Krizis*, 290, 31; Rabinowitch, *Prelude to Revolution*, 192–93; AK to *In-*

ternational Affairs (October 1956) 32: 536–37; For a critical analysis of Lenin's defense, see Adam B. Ulam, *Lenin and the Bolsheviks* (L: Secker and Warburg, 1966), 349.

27. Pidhainy, *Ukrainian Republic*, 123–25; *AFSR*, July 7, 1917; FO.371.2996, Buchanan to Balfour, July 18, 1917; *VOSR*: . . . *Iiul'skii Krizis*, 38–41; Rabinowitch, *Prelude to Revolution*, 187–89; Polvinen, *VVS*, 1: 83.

28. Botchkareva, *Yashka*, 202–4.

29. *AFSR*, July 7, 1917; AK, *Catastrophe*, 240–41; AK, *International Affairs*, October 1956, 536–37; P. A. Polovtsëv, *Dni zatmeniia* (Paris: Vozrozhdenie, 1927), 136 ff.

30. Col. B. V. Nikitine, *The Fatal Years* (L: W. Hodge, 1938), 168 ff. Col. Nikitin had no conception of the limited powers of governments in democratic *Rechtsstaaten*. *Rech'*, July 6, 1917; *Moskovskie Vedomosti*, July 7, 14, 1917; FO.371.2996, Buchanan to FO, July 18, 1917, gives Tereshchenko's version. AK, *International Affairs*, October 1956, 536–38. Polovtsov took his revenge by alleging that when troops arrived at Trotsky's apartment to arrest him, they found him in friendly conversation with Kerensky, see M. S. Margulies, *God interventsii* (Berlin: Grzhebin, 1923), 3: 263.

31. Sukhanov, *Zapiski*, 4:446–48; Nikitine, *Fatal Years*, 170; *Izvestiia*, July 11, 1917.

32. A. I. Guchkov in *Poslednie Novosti*, Sept. 30, 1936; Tsereteli, *Vospominaniia*, 2: 151–55.

33. AK, *Catastrophe*, 239–43; Sukhanov, *Zapiski*, 4: 484–89; Miliukov, *Istoriia*, part 2, 17ff; *RPG*, 3: 1386–89; Radkey, *Agrarian Foes*, 287.

34. Marc Ferro, *October 1917: A Social History of the Russian Revolution* (L: Routledge, 1980), 46–47; AK, *Catastrophe*, 249 ff; AK, "Iz vospominanii," *Sovremënnyia Zapiski* (1929), 38: 251–52; T. I. Pol'ner, *Zhiznënnyi put' Kniazia Georgiia Evgenievicha L'vova: Lichnost'. Vzgliady. Usloviia deiatel'nosti* (Paris: Imp. de Navarre), 1932, 258.

35. *Russkii Invalid*, July 1, 1917; *AFSR*, July 8; FO.371.2996, Buchanan to FO, July 19, July 20, 1917; Nikitine, *Fatal Years*, 184–85.

12. No Longer an Idealist?

1. *VOSR: Revoliutsionnoe dvizhenie v. Rossii v iiule 1917 g.: Iiul'skii Krizis*, 290, 293, 298–303; WO.33.924, Knox to DMI, Aug. 2, 1917; "Pokazanie . . . Kornilova," 2–3; *RPG*, 3:1357–61; AK, *Izdalëka: Sbornik statei (1920–1921 g.)*, (Paris: Povolotskii, 1921), 236; B.V. Savinkov, *K delu Kornilova*, (Paris: Imp. Union, 1919), 5–6. The copy of the document given by Kornilov to the Shablovsky Commission is cited here in preference to he edited version, published in *Obshchee Delo*, Oct. 6, 1917. Kerensky always denied the authenticity of the latter version, though without offering plausible grounds. Eugène Petit, whose veracity Kerensky extols, accepted it as genuine. Under pressure from journalists (and from Kerensky?), Procurator Shablovsky stated that the edited and published version "cannot serve as an incontestable basis for the resolution of the question of the significance of Gen. Kornilov's demonstration, though it fully

describes the role of Gen. Kornilov," *Novoe Vremia*, Oct. 5, 1917. The inaccurate conflation provided by Dr. Katkov is closer to the *Obshchee Delo* text than to the document in the Raupakh Papers, see G. Katkov, *Russia 1917: The Kornilov Affair: Kerensky and the Break-Up of the Russian Army* (L: Longmans, 1980), 166–91.

2. Lenin, *Works*, 25: 219–22; *RPG*, 3: 1386–87; Radkey, *Agrarian Foes*, 285–93; AK, *Turning Point*, 407–8; FO.371.2996, Buchanan to FO, July 22, 1917.

3. *Rech'*, July 25, 1917; *Vossische Zeitung*, June 26, 1917; Rex Wade, *The Russian Search for Peace, February–October 1917* (Stanford, Cal: Stanford University Press, 1969), 97 ff; c.f. J. L. H.Keep, *The Russian Revolution: A Study in Mass Mobilization* (L: Weidenfeld, 1976), 167–68; MAE, Série Guerre 1914–1918. *Russie. Action des Alliées*, G.676, 3934, Tereshchenko to Russian Ambassador, Madrid, Aug. 21, 1917, opposes *any* concession to the Central Powers in the interest of peace. Evidently, the French had access to secret Russian telegrams.

4. *RPG*, 3:1386–87; FO.371.2996, Buchanan to FO, July 22, 1917.

5. E.Petit, "Ma Mission en Russie," ms., carnet XII, 54–56; Petit, "Copie: extraits d'un Télégramme chiffré du 28 juillet," Petit Papers.

6. FO.371.2996, Buchanan to FO, July 27, 1917.

7. *Izvestiia*, July 11, 1917; Petit, "Ma Mission," carnet XIII: 54–56; Radkey, *Agrarian Foes*, 188–91; George F. Kennan, *Soviet-American Relations, 1917–1920*, vol.1: *Russia Leaves the War* (L: Faber and Faber, 1956), 56–57; Barry Hollingsworth, "David Soskice in Russia," typescript, Paper read to the Study Group on the Russian Revolution, University of East Anglia, January 1975.

8. A. Rabinowitch, *Prelude to Revolution: the Petrograd Bolsheviks and the July 1917 Uprising*, (Bloomington, Ind.-L: Indiana University Press, 1968), 187–88; Lenin, *Works*, 25: 183–90.

9. *Rech'*, July 9, 1917.

10. C.Enckell, *Politiska Minnen*, (Stockholm: Gebers Förlag, 1956), 1: 102–4; *RPG* 1: 351–52.

11. *Rech'*, July 16, 1917; Rabinowitch, *The Bolsheviks Come to Power*, (L: New Left Books, 1979), 39–43.

12. *AFSR*, July 11, 13, 14, 1917; AK, *Delo Kornilova* (M: Zadruga, 1918), 9ff; AK, *Prelude*, 33–44; A. A. Brusilov, *Moi Vospominaniia*, (Riga: Mir, 1929), 236–37; B. Gourko, *Memories and Impressions of War and Revolution in Russia, 1914–1917* (L: John Murray, 1918), 321–22.

13. MAE, vol.654, "Rapport de Général Denikine à la réunion des Commandants en chef et des membres du Gouvernement Provisoire"; *RPG*, 2: 989–1010.

14. K.Vendziagol'skii [Wędziagołski], "Savinkov", *NZh* (1962), 68: 192–94; "Pokazanie . . . Kornilova," 1–5.

15. *RPG*, 2: 1003–5.

16. AK, *Delo Kornilova*, 21–26; Savinkov, *K delu Kornilova*, 7–9; Hollingsworth, "David Soskice"; Vendziagol'skii, "Savinkov", 209; *Rech'*, August 3, 1917; General A. I. Denikin, *The Russian Turmoil: Memoirs: Military, Social and Political* (London: Hutchinson, 1920; rpt. Westport, Conn.: Hyperion, 1973), p. 303.

17. AK, *Catastrophe*, 245–46; AK, *Turning Point*, 324; Sukhanov, *Zapiski* vol.5, chapter 1, passim.

18. Pitirim Sorokin, *Leaves from a Russian Diary* (L: Hurst and Blackett, 1927), 76.
19. *VOSR: . . . Iiul'skii Krizis*, 436–39; L.S.Gaponenko, ed. *Revoliutsionnoe dvizhenie v. russkoi armii v 1917 g.*, (M: Nauka, 1968), 340–50.
20. Gen.A.Knox, *With the Russian Army 1914–1917* (L: Hutchinson), 2:669; c.f. AK, *Turning Point*, 324–25.
21. *Moskovskie Vedomosti*, July 14, 1917; FO.371.2296, Buchanan to FO, July 26, 1917; *RPG*, 3:1401–6; Radkey, *Agrarian Foes*, 304–5.
22. FO.371.2996, Buchanan to FO, July 22, 1917.
23. Radkey, *Agrarian Foes*, 296 ff; Keep, *Russian Revolution*, 168.
24. Radkey, *Agrarian Foes*, 121–22; B.V.Nikitine, *The Fatal Years*, (L: W.Hodge, 1938), 77 ff.
25. A.K.Drezen ed., *Burzhuaziia i Pomeshchiki v. 1917 godu*, (M-Lgd: Narodnyi Komissariat Prosveshcheniia, 1932), 195 ff.
26. Radkey, *Agrarian Foes*, 304 ff.
27. *RPG* 3:1416–18; AK, *Catastrophe*, 251–54; For Kerensky's retreat to Tsarskoe Selo, see Count Paul Benkendorff, *Last Days at Tsarskoe Selo* (L: William Heinemann, 1927), 96–97.
28. Petit, "Ma Mission," carnet XIV, 50.
29. *Britannia*, Nov. 16, 1917; David R. Francis, *Russia from the American Embassy: April 1916–November 1918* (NY: G. Scribner's, 1921), 148–50.
30. *AFSR*, July 22, 1917; *RPG*, 3:1418–27; Tsereteli, *Vospominaniia*, 2:381–87; AK, *Catastrophe*, 253.
31. AK, *Catastrophe* 255–56; *RPG*, 3:1427–30; Radkey, *Agrarian Foes*, 312–21; Tsereteli, *Vospominaniia*, 2:372 ff; *Rech'*, July 25, 1917; *AFSR*, July 23, 25, 1917; V.M.Chernov, *The Great Russian Revolution*, (New Haven, Conn: Yale University Press, 1936), 399; AK, *Prelude*, 49.
32. USA, *Papers* (1918), 1:146, Root to Lansing, August 1917.
33. Raymond Poincaré, *Au Service de la France: Neuf Années de Souvenirs*, 11 vols. (Paris: Plon-Nourrit et Cie.), 1926–74, vol.9: *L'Année Trouble 1917*, 86–87; Michael Kettle, *The Allies and the Russian Collapse: March 1917–March 1918* (L: André Deutsch, 1981), ch. 2, passim.
34. Wade, *Russian Search*, 110–12; A.V.Ignat'ev, *Russko-angliiskie otnosheniia nakanune Oktiabr'skoi revoliutsii (fevral'-oktiabr' 1917 g.)* (M: Nauka, 1966), 275 ff; *The Manchester Guardian*, Aug. 11, 13, 14, 15, 16, 17, 1917; Buchanan, *Mission*, 2:162–63; FO.371.2996, Buchanan to FO, Aug. 11, 1917; MAE, v.655, Noulens to Ribot, Aug. 15, 1917.
35. Wade, *Russian Search*, 111–15; Ignat'ev, *Russko-angliiskie otnosheniia*, 280–85; Petit to Thomas, July 28, Aug. 8, 1917, FAT, 94 AP 189; David Lloyd George, *War Memoirs*, 6 vols (L: Nicholson and Watson, 1933–36), 4:1916, 1922; *The Manchester Guardian*, Aug. 14, 1917.
36. AK in *L'Information*, Nov. 14, 1918; AK, *Turning Point*, 432–33; R.H.B. Lockhart, *Diaries of Sir Robert Bruce Lockhart*, Kenneth Young, ed. (L: Macmillan, 1973), 1:175.
37. AA, Weltkrieg, Nr.2 geheim. Friedensstimmungen und Aktionen zur Vermittlung des Friedens, (GFM 2, Serial 4914), Band 41, Kaiser Karl to Kaiser Wilhelm II, June 7, 1917; Band 42, Kaiser Wilhelm II to Kaiser Karl, June 22, 1917;

Norddeutsche Allgemeine Zeitung, June 16, 1917; Ingeborg Meckling, *Die Aussenpolitik des Grafen Czernin* (Vienna: Verlag für Geschichte und Politik, 1969), 244–47.

38. MdÄ, Karton PA I/956—Liasse Krieg 25s, Friedensverhandlungen mit Russland, Hadik to Czernin, July 29, 1917; Wolfdieter Bihl, *Österreich-Ungarn und die Friedensschlüsse von Brest-Litovsk* (Vienna-Cologne-Graz: Hermann Bohlaus Nachf., 1970), 12 ff.

39. MdÄ, Karton PA I/956, L 25s, t., Czernin to Hohenlohe, Aug. 3, 1917; Czernin to Hadik, Aug. 3, 1917; Czernin to Hadik, July 30, 1917; Hadik to Czernin, Aug. 4, 1917; Czernin to Hadik, Sept. 17, 1917; Hadik to Czernin, Sept. 18, 1917.

40. AK, "Predlozheniia mira Germaniei i Avstrii v 1917," typescript, Kerensky Papers, F.83; *RPG*, 2:1161.

41. Dr. Einar Runeberg "Nikolain sänky on vapaana", *Suomen Vapaussota* (1935), no. 10, 222–27.

42. Gippius, *Siniaia Kniga*, 153; P.A.Polovtsëv, *Dni zatmeniia*, (Paris: Vozrozhdenie, 1927), 173–74; Louis de Robien, *Journal d'un Diplomate en Russie (1917–1918)* (Paris: Editions Albin Michel, 1967), 112–13; Stepun, *Byvshee*, 2:153–43; Gustaf von Dardel, *Lyckliga Hov, Stormiga År* (Stockholm: Wahlström & Widstrand, 1953), 83–84; OLK, "Obryvki," 12–15, 15a, 15b.

43. FO.371.2997, Buchanan to FO, July 22, 1917.

44. Louise Bryant, *Six Red Months in Russia* (NY: Heinemann, 1918), 106 ff; Alexander Stashevskii to AK, May 17, 1949, Kerensky Papers, F.134; Botchkareva, *Yashka*, 218.

45. Katkov, *Kornilov Affair*, 34; Rabinowitch, *Bolsheviks Come to Power*, 24–25, 51 ff; Polovtsëv, *Dni zatmeniia*, 180–81; Count Constantine Benckendorff, *Half a Life: The Reminiscenses of a Russian Gentleman* (L: The Richards Press, 1954), 189; *Moskovskie Vedomosti*, July 26, 1917; FO.371.2996, Buchanan to FO, July 22, 1917; Petit to Thomas, 30 juillet/12 août 1917, 10, Petit Papers.

46. AK, *Catastrophe*, 288–89; 271–76; AK, "The Road to the Tragedy," *The Murder of the Romanovs*, Sir Bernard Pares, ed. (L: Hutchinson, 1935), 128 ff; M.K.Kasvinov, *Dvadtsat' tri stupeni vniz*, (M: Mysl', 1979), 387ff; FO.371.3015, Buchanan to FO, July 27, 1917. Buchanan did not make it clear whether Kerensky feared that monarchist plots to liberate the Romanovs would be successful, or whether, in failing, they would merely inflame the masses. I incline to the latter interpretation. Benkendorff suggests that Kerensky allowed the Tsar to think he might be permitted to go to Livadia, *The Last Days of Tsarskoe Selo*, 97–98.

13. Statesman or Revolutionary?

1. Lenin, *Works*, 25:222; N. Ia. Ivanov, *Kontrrevoliutsiia v Rossii v 1917 godu i eë razgrom* (M: Mysl', 1977), 68–69, 95. This claim is so crucial to the self-legitimizing myth of the Soviet ruling *Nomenklatura* that Ivanov is able to treat evidence in a cavalier way as compared with such genuine historians as Burd-

zhalov or Startsev. Ivanov even relies on the American Stalinists, M. Sayers and A. E. Kahn, *The Great Conspiracy against Russia* (NY: Boni and Gaer, 1946). Here are two gems from this muddy source referring to later events: "Most important of all was Trotsky's growing intimacy with the German Military Intelligence" (p.75) and "The trial of the Bloc of Rights and Trotskyites made public for the first time in history the details workings of an Axis Fifth Column" (p.108).

2 .Gippius, *Siniaia Kniga*, 143, 150.

3. AK, *Prelude*, 28–29, *Obshchee Delo*, Oct. 2, 1917; "Pokazanie... Kornilova," 5–6; WO.33.924, Barter to CIGS, Aug. 7, 1917.

4. R. H. B. Lockhart, *The Diaries of Sir Robert Bruce Lockhart*, K. Young, ed. (L: Macmillan, 1973), 1:273; G. Katkov, *Russia 1917: The Kornilov Affair: Kerensky and the Break-Up of the Russian Army* (L: Longmans, 1980, 39ff); S. Jägerskiöld, *Gustaf Mannerheim*, 8 vols. (H:ki: Albert Bonniers Förlag & Holger Schildts Förlag, 1964–81), 2:321; K. Vendziagol'skii [Wędziagolski], "Savinkov," *NZh* (1962) 68:205 ff, 212–13; William J. Oudendijk, *Ways and By-Ways in Diplomacy* (L: Peter Davies, 1939), 228 ff.

5. *RPG* 3:1527 ff; AK, *Prelude*, 79 ff; AK, *Catastrophe*, 315; AK, *Turning Point*, 379 ff; J. D. White, "The Kornilov Affair—A Study in Counter-Revolution," *Soviet Studies* (1968) 20(2):187–205; Katkov, *Kornilov Affair*, 61–63.

6. See *Le Petit Parisien* for June–July 1917; AK, *Catastrophe*, 315; AK, *Crucifixion*, 310–11; M. Kettle, *The Allies and the Russian Collapse, March 1917–March 1918* (L: André Deutsch, 1981), 54–69; Gen. A. Knox, *With the Russian Army 1914–1917* (L: Hutchinson, 1921), 2:677. The head of the British Secret Service in Russia, Samuel Hoare (see WO.33.924, Wilson to CIGS, Feb. 6, 15, 1917) loathed "the demagogue Kerensky," see *The Fourth Seal* (L: William Heinemann, 1930), 302–3. Until British Secret service records are available for public scrutiny, Katkov's summary dismissal of British involvement in the Kornilov affair will lack conviction, Katkov, *Kornilov Affair*, 197. Katkov may be right, if only because the British government, like many others in 1917, was overwhelmed by the speed of the Russian Revolution.

7. "Pokazanie... Kornilova," 6–7; WO.33.924, Barter to CIGS, Aug. 13, 1917. Barter's interview was not accidental. Kornilov made sure the French got the same message, see R. Poincaré, *Au Service de la France: Neuf Années de Souvenirs*, 11 vols. (Paris: Plon Nourrit, 1926–74), 9:345.

8. "Pokazanie... Kornilova," 7–9; B. V. Savinkov, *K delu Kornilova* (Paris: Imp. Union, 1919), 12–13; AK, *Prelude*, 71–77, 91–94; WO.33.924, Barter to CIGS, Aug. 19, 1917.

9. Botchkareva, *Yashka*, 219–22.

10. *AFSR*, Aug. 5, 1917; *Rech'*, Aug. 6, 1917.

11. Stepun, *Byvshee*, 2:144–45; F. Stepun to AK, April 23, 1956, Kerensky Papers, F.134; Vendziagol'skii [Wędziagolski], "Savinkov i Kerenskii," *NZh* (1961–62) 65:242ff; (1962) 68:193; Ilya Ehrenburg, *Sobranie sochinenii v deviati tomakh*, vol. 8: *Liudi, gody, zhizn'* (M: Khudozhestvennaia Literatura, 1968), part 1, 220–221; E. Petit, "Resumé de la conversation que j'eus avec Boris Victorovitch Savinkov gérant du ministère de la Guerre—le lundi 14/27 août 1917," types-

cript, 4, Petit Papers; Gippius, *Siniaia Kniga*, 150–51; Stankevich, *Vospominaniia*, 225–28.

12. Mints, *Istoriia*, vol. 2: *Sverzhenie Vremënnogo Pravitel'stva. Ustanovlenie Diktatury Proletariata*, 578 ff; *VOSR: Revoliutsionnoe dvizhenie v Rossii v iiule 1917 g.: Iiul'skii Krizis*, 326, 329–40; *Rech'*, Aug. 9, 1917; David Soskice, "Savinkoff, Kerensky and Breshkovskaya," typescript, Soskice Papers, DS/2/1, Box 8, House of Lords Record Office, London; Petit, "Resumé," 2–3; Stepun, *Byvshee*, 2:160.

13. Petit, "Resumé," 2–3; Savinkov, *K delu Kornilova*, 13–16; Stepun, *Byvshee*, 2:160; AK, *Prelude*, 2 ff, 60–63, 96–97; A. I. Verkhovskii, *Na trudnom perevale* (M: Voennoe Izd. Min. Oborony SSSR, 1959), 292–94; Jägerskiöld, *Mannerheim*, 2:327.

14. Savinkov, *K delu Kornilova*, 14–15; AK, *Prelude*, 95; "Pokazanie . . . Kornilova," 9–10.

15. WO.33.924, Barter to CIGS, Aug. 22, 1917; "Pokazanie . . . Kornilova," 9–10; AK, *Prelude*, 59–63, 71–74; Botchkareva, *Yashka*, 223–27.

16. "Pokazanie . . . Kornilova," 10–12; Kornilov states that Savinkov and Filonenko had signed the report *before* him and were therefore innocent of the insubordination alleged by Kerensky. Kerensky had not complained when Savinkov had countersigned Kornilov's demands early in July. AK, *Prelude*, 95–97, 101; Savinkov, *K delu Kornilova*, 16; Stepun, *Byvshee*, 2:150–52; Stankevich, *Vospominaniia*, 218–20; Gippius, *Siniaia Kniga*, 153–55.

17. Gippius, *Siniaia Kniga*, 158–59; Petit, "Resumé," 1 ff; AK, *Prelude*, 63–65, 102–3, 106–9; P. Sorokin, *Leaves from a Russian Diary* (L: Hurst and Blackett, 1925), 78–79.

18. *Zhurnal zasedanii Vremënnago Pravitel'stva*, Aug. 11, 1917. Hoover Institution, lists the ministers present without giving any indication of the sensitive matters that were discussed. Gippius, *Siniaia Kniga*, 159; Petit, "Resumé," 4; Dr. Einar Runeberg, "Nikolain sänky on vapaana," *Suomen Vapaussota*, 1935, no. 10, 223 ff.

19. *RPG*, v. 3, 1451; *VOSR: . . . Iiul'skii Krizis*, 327; *Moskovskie Vedomosti*, Aug. 12, 1917; *Rech'*, Aug. 2, 1917; AK, *Turning Point*, 324–25.

20. *VOSR: Revoliutsionnoe dvizhenie v Rossii v Avguste 1917 goda: Razgrom Kornilovskogo Miatezha*, 363; Sukhanov, *Zapiski*, 5:53–56, 147–49.

21. *VOSR: . . . Iiul'skii Krizis*, 207 ff; *VOSR: . . . Razgrom Kornilovskogo Miatezha*, 174–75, 177–78; *RPG*, 3:1451; *RPG*, 1:452–53, 396–97.

22. N. G. Dumova, "Maloizvestnye materialy po istorii Kornilovshchiny," *Voprosy Istorii*, (1968), no. 11, 77ff; Katkov, *Kornilov Affair*, 141–45.

23. *VOSR: . . . Razgrom Kornilovskogo Miatezha*, 360; Verkhovskii, *Na trudnom perevale*, 301–2; MAE, vol. 655, Bertrand to Noulens·and Ribot, Aug. 23, 25, 26, 27, 1917; Ribot to Noulens and Bertrand, Aug. 28, 1917; FO.371.3015, Balfour to Buchanan, Aug. 24, 1917; WO.33.924, Barter to CIGS, Aug. 20, 1917; CIGS to Barter, Aug. 25, 1917.

24. Sukhanov, *Zapiski*, 5:150–59; *VOSR: . . . Razgrom Kornilovskogo Miatezha*, 378 ff; *AFSR*, Aug. 13, 1917; *Russkoe Slovo*, Aug. 13, 1917; *Moskovskie Vedomosti*, Aug. 13, 1917; A. Tyrkova-Williams, *From Liberty to Brest-Litovsk* (L: Mac-

millan, 1919), 207; Gippius, *Siniaia Kniga*, 160; Stepun, *Byvshee*, 2:156; M. Philips Price, *Reminiscences of the Russian Revolution* (L: George Allen and Unwin, 1921), 70–71; Diane Koenker, *Moscow Workers and the 1917 Revolution* (Princeton, N.J.: Princeton University Press, 1981), 124–28.

25. *AFSR*, Aug. 13, 1917; Verkhovskii, *Na trudnom perevale*, 302–4; Stepun, *Byvshee*, 2:153–56; Tyrkova-Williams, *Liberty to Brest-Litovsk*, 205; Sukhanov, *Zapiski*, 5:160; Price, *Reminiscences*, 71; Sorokin, *Leaves from a Russian Diary*, 81–82.

26. *Russkoe Slovo*, Aug. 13, 1917; *RPG*, 3:1457–62; E. H. Wilcox, *Russia's Ruin*, (L: Chapman and Hall, 1919), 204.

27. WO.33.924, Barter to CIGS, Aug. 28, 29, 1917; FO.371.3015, FO to Buchanan, Aug. 24, 1917; Verkhovskii, *Na trudnom perevale*, 304–10; Katkov, *Kornilov Affair*, 59–63, 198–200. Katkov suggests that Verkhovsky's 1959 memoirs should be treated with caution. The picture they convey is, however, substantially similar to that given by Barter in his secret telegrams.

28. "Pokazanie . . . Kornilova," 12–14; cf. *Obshchee Delo*, Oct. 6, 1917; Verkhovskii, *Na trudnom perevale*, 310–12; AK, *Prelude*, 108–10; *RPG*, 3:1474–78; MAE, vol. 655, Bertrand to MAE, Aug. 25, 1917.

29. *RPG*, 3:1478–80, 1489; *Moskovskie Vedomosti*, Aug. 15, 17, 1917; WO.33.924, Barter to CIGS, Aug. 28, 1917.

30. *Delo Naroda*, March 30, 1917; *RPG*, 3:1480–88.

31. *RPG* 3:1493–96; MAE, vol. 656, Noulens to MAE, Sept. 13, 1917; Katkov, *Kornilov Affair*, 141–43.

32. *RPG*, 3:1510–15.

33. *VOSR*: . . . *Razgrom Kornilovskogo Miatezha*, 373; Gippius, *Siniaia Kniga*, 161–63; WO.33.924, Barter to CIGS, Aug. 29, 1917.

34. Adam Ulam, *Lenin and the Bolsheviks* (L: Secker & Warburg, 1966), 352–55; Lenin, *Works*, 25:426.

35. Verkhovskii, *Na trudnom perevale*, 312–13; Gippius, *Siniaia Kniga*, 164–65; Savinkov, *K delu Kornilova*, 17–18; AK, *Prelude*, 247.

36. Savinkov, *K delu Kornilova*, 19; Gippius, *Siniaia Kniga*, 164–65.

37. AK, *Prelude*, 133–35; Katkov, *Kornilov Affair*, 67; MAE, vol. 656, Noulens to MAE, Sept. 6, 1917.

38. "Pokazanie . . . Kornilova," 19; AK, *Prelude*, 154.

39. Radkey, *Agrarian Foes*, 363–64; Rosenberg, *Liberals*, 218–21.

40. U. Germanis, *Oberst Vācietis und die lettischen Schützen im Weltkrieg und in der Oktoberrevolution* (Stockholm: Almquist & Wiksell, 1974), 224–41; "Pokazanie . . . Kornilova," 13–15; Stankevich, *Vospominaniia*, 202–4; W. S. Woytinsky [Voitinskii], *Stormy Passage: A Personal History through Two Russian Revolutions to Democracy and Freedom, 1905–1960* (NY: Vanguard Press, 1961), 343–45; Petit, "Lettre—Rapport, 20 août/ 2 sept. 1917," Petit Papers; WO.33.924, Barter to CIGS, Sept. 4, 1917.

41. *AFSR*, Aug. 24, 1917; Radkey, *Agrarian Foes*, 387; Zinaida N. Gippius, *Pis'ma k Berberovoi i Khodasevichu*, E. F. Sheikholeslami, ed. (Ann Arbor, Mich: Ardis, 1979), 48.

42. "Pokazanie . . . Kornilova," 15–19; cf. *Obshchee Delo*, Oct. 2, 1917; Savinkov, *K delu Kornilova*, 20–22; AK, *Prelude*, 152–47.

43. "Pokazanie . . . Kornilova," 19–21.
44. P. N. Krasnov, "Na vnutrennem fronte," *ARR*, (1921), 1:115; Ivanov, *Kontr-revoliutsiia*, 112–19; Kettle, *The Allies*, 77 ff; WO.33.924, Knox to DMI, Oct. 19, 1917.
45. *VOSR: . . . Razgrom Kornilovskogo Miatezha*, 420, 425–26; *RPG*, 3:1531–33, 1538–41, 1558–60.
46. V. D. Nabokov, "Vremënnoe Pravitel'stvo," *ARR*, (1921), 1:43–45.
47. *VOSR: . . . Razgrom Kornilovskogo Miatezha*, 426, 441; cf. Lvov's 1920 version in *RPG*, 3:1561–62; AK, *Prelude*, 158–61.
48. AK, *Prelude*, 158–62; *VOSR: . . . Razgrom Kornilovskogo Miatezha*, 424–26; Conversations with Dr. O. A. Kerensky.
49. *RPG*, 3:1562; "Pokazanie . . . Kornilova," 21–22; *VOSR: . . . Razgrom Kornilovskogo Miatezha*, 427.
50. AK, *Prelude*, 80; 'Pokazanie . . . Kornilova," 22; *RPG*, 3:1563–67; *VOSR: . . . Razgrom Kornilovskogo Miatezha*, 426–27.
51. Savinkov, *K delu Kornilova*, 23; Gippius, *Siniaia Kniga*, 176ff.
52. W. Somerset Maugham, *The Summing Up* (L: Heinemann, 1938), 202–5. For an anodyne interpretation of Maugham's mission, see Nigel West, *MI6: British Secret Intelligence Service Operations, 1909–45* (L: Weidenfeld, 1983), 13–14; Knox, *With the Russian Army*, 2:676–77; Minutes of the Imperial War Cabinet, CAB.23.4, WC 229, Sept. 7, 1917, Public Record Office, London.
53. AK, *Prelude* 162–72; *VOSR: . . . Razgrom Kornilovskogo Miatezha*, 441–42.
54. AK, *Prelude*, 165–66.
55. AK, *Prelude*, 167–68; Katkov, *Kornilov Affair*, 74ff; *RPG*, 3:1570; Miliukov, *Istoriia*, part 2, 210.
56. *VOSR: . . . Razgrom Kornilovskogo Miatezha*, 443; *RPG*, 3:1571.
57. For conservative views, see L. I. Strakhovsky, "Was there a Kornilov Rebellion?—A Reappraisal of the Evidence," *Slavonic & East European Review* (1955) 33:372ff; Katkov, *Kornilov Affair*, passim. For "socialist" views, see White, "Kornilov Affair," and Ivanov, *Kontrrevoliutsiia*, 58ff. As always, the well-informed and perceptive Tory journalist, Wilcox, provides an excellent summary of the evidence available in 1917–18, *Russia's Ruin*, 293–307. Katkov is right in contending that on August 26, 1917, Kornilov was not knowingly in a state of mutiny, though (even without the benefit of Barter's appraisals), Katkov concedes that "we may presume that Kornilov had certain plans in mind in the event of the government's not taking the desired action," *Kornilov Affair*, 65. By August 27, Kornilov *was* a mutineer and he did not deny it when reproached by Savinkov and Maklakov over the Hughes.
58. F. Stepun to AK, June 3, 1956, Kerensky Papers, F.134; AK, *Prelude*, 195; Capt. George A. Hill, *Go Spy the Land: Being the Adventures of I.K.8 of the British Secret Service* (L: Cassell, 1932), 195–96.
59. Gippius, *Siniaia Kniga*, 176 ff; AK, *Prelude*, 200 ff; V. Vladimirova, *Kontr-revoliutsiia v 1917 g., (Kornilovshchina)*, (M: Rossiiskaia Kommunisticheskaia Partiia, 1924), 142; V. I. Startsev, *Krakh Kerenshchiny* (Lgd: Nauka, 1982), 13–16.
60. MAE, v.656, Gen. Janin to Minister of War, Sept. 9, 1917. This establishes

beyond doubt that the telegram dismissing Kornilov was not sent until after the resignation of the ministers, so Kornilov's telegram of dismissal, though irregular in form, was not actually illegal. "Pokazanie... Kornilova," 25; *RPG*, 3:1572–73; WO.106.1036, "Despatch No. 18. Kornilov's coup d'état," Sept. 15, 1917; Vladimirova, *Kontr-revoliutsiia*, 142.

61. *RPG*, 3:1573; "Pokazanie... Kornilova," 25–26; WO.106.1036, "Despatch No. 18. Appendix D."

14. Reproaches and Slander

1. *VOSR: Revoliutsionnoe dvizhenie v Rossii v avguste 1917 goda: Razgrom Kornilovskogo Miatezha*, 477–48, 454–57; AK, *Prelude*, 224; P. A. Polovtsëv, *Dni zatmeniia* (Paris: Vozrozhdenie, 1927), 183; D. W. Wasiljew [Vasil'ev], *Der letzte Kommandant; Aufzeichnungen des letzten zaristischen Befehlshabers der Peter-Paul-Festung zu Petersburg* (Leipzig-Berlin: Schwarzhäupter-Verlag, 1938), 93–94. Vasiliev has Kerensky weeping, while an old general comments, "Köstliche Tränchen, rührende Tränchen, bitte schön—alten Weibern lauwarm im Wodkagläschen zu servieren!" Vintage patriarchy!

2. *Russkie Vedomosti*, Aug. 29, 1917; B. V. Savinkov, *K delu Kornilova*, (Paris: Imp. "Union," 1919), 25–26; *VOSR:... Razgrom Kornilovskogo Miatezha*, 448–52.

3. Buchanan, *Mission*, 2:178, 182–83; Miliukov, *Istoriia*, part 3, 231–32; "Pokazanie ... Kornilova," 26; *AFSR*, Aug. 30, 1917; *Russkoe Slovo*, Aug. 30, 1917; Savinkov, *K delu Kornilova*, 26. Kerensky vigorously refuted the charge that Nekrasov "destroyed the possibility of an agreement between Kerensky and Kornilov." Nekrasov was merely carrying out orders, but Kerensky admitted, "Nekrasov really did very much towards putting an end to Kornilov's move as promptly as possible. This was his crime for which the Kornilovists could not forgive him!" *Prelude*, 232–34. Buchanan felt that Tereshchenko's absence had left Nekrasov as Kerensky's sole confidant. "It was only after consulting Nekrasoff that Kerensky, in accordance with the latter's advice, decided to denounce Korniloff as a traitor and to demand his resignation," *Mission*, 2:177–78. Then how do we explain Kerensky's treatment of V. N. Lvov? What Nekrasov did was to confirm Kerensky's hope that Kornilov might be denounced *successfully*.

4. *RPG*, 3:1575; *Obshchee Delo*, Oct. 3. 1917; AK, *Prelude*, 232–35; Miliukov, *Istoriia*, part 3, 231–33.

5. Buchanan, *Mission*, 2:178; AK, *Turning Point*, 351–53.

6. P. Sorokin, *Leaves from a Russian Diary* (L: Hurst & Blackett, 1925), 89–90; Stepun, *Byvshee*, 2:176–77; Stankevich, *Vospominaniia*, 234–35; AK, *Prelude*, 224; B. Hollingsworth, "David Soskice."

7. AK, *Prelude*, 218–22, *Obshchee Delo*, Oct. 3, 1917; Miliukov, *Istoriia*, part 3, 249–52; Rosenberg, *Liberals*, 232; G. Katkov, *Russia 1917: The Kornilov Affair: Kerensky and the Break-Up of the Russian Army* (L: Longmans, 1980), 100–101.

8. *VOSR:... Razgrom Kornilovskogo Miatezha*, 476–77; Sukhanov, *Zapiski*, 5:280 ff; Radkey, *Agrarian Foes*, 408–10; A. Rabinowitch, *The Bolsheviks Come to Power*

(L: New Left Books, 1979), 129–35; V. I. Startsev, *Krakh Kerenshchiny*, (Lgd. Nauka, 1982), 24–26.

9. Rabinowitch, *Bolsheviks Come to Power*, 138–44; Marc Ferro: *October 1917: A Social History of the Russian Revolution* (L: Routledge, 1980), 54 ff.

10. *VOSR: . . . Razgrom Kornilovskogo Miatezha*, 192; Sukhanov, *Zapiski*, 5:280ff, 6:9ff; Katkov, *Kornilov Affair*, 1–2, 10.

11. AK, *Turning Point*, 349; AK, *Prelude*, 247–54; Savinkov, *K delu Kornilova*, 27–28; Miliukov, *Istoriia*, part 3, 249–52.

12. Radkey, *Agrarian Foes*, 388–91.

13. *RPG*, 3:1530–46; Rosenberg, *Liberals*, 235–39; MAE, vol. 656, Noulens to Ribot, Sept. 13, 1917, A. I. Verkhovskii, *Na trudnom perevale*, (M: Voennoe Izd. Min. Oborony SSSR, 1959), 332 ff.

14. WO.106.1131, Lieutenant-Colonel, J. F. Neilson, "Report on Northern Front," Aug. 18, 1917; Rabinowitch, *Bolsheviks Come to Power*, 148–49; "Pokazanie . . . Kornilova," 31; *VOSR: . . . Razgrom Kornilovskogo Miatezha*, 462–64, 474 ff; The racist term Asiatics is in ibid, p. 479; L. S. Gaponenko, ed., *Revoliutsionnoe dvizhenie v russkoi armii v 1917 g.* (M: Nauka, 1968), 302–3, 374–75, 395, 590 n192; P. N. Krasnov, "Na vnutrennem fronte," *ARR* (1921), 1:113ff; *AFSR*, Aug. 30, 1917; A. I. Denikin, *The Russian Turmoil: Memoirs: Military, Social, and Political* (L: Hutchinson, 1922), 322 ff.; *RPG*, 3:1581–82; Mints, *Istoriia*, vol. 2: *Sverzhenie Vremënnogo Pravitel'stva. Ustanovlenie Diktatury Proletariata*, 637 ff.

15. AK, *Prelude*, 263; AK, *Turning Point*, 354; V. V. Vyrubov, "Account of the appointment of Alexeev as Chief of Staff to the Supreme C-in-C after the Kornilov affair," in letter to AK, Jan. 10, 1958, Kerensky Papers, F.172.

16. *VOSR: . . . Razgrom Kornilovskogo Miatezha*, 466–68, 631n243; AK, *Prelude*, 263–67; WO.33.924, Barter to CIGS, Sept. 14, 1917; Katkov, *Kornilov Affair*, 105 ff.

17. AK, *Prelude*, 145–52; *RPG*, 3:1587–89; Katkov, *Kornilov Affair*, 106; Startsev, *Krakh Kerenshchiny*, 51–52.

18. Col. R. R. Raupakh, "Vospominaniia," typescript, ch. 5: "Vozstanie Generala Kornilova," 43 ff, Raupakh Papers, Bakhmeteff Archive, Columbia University Library, New York; *Obshchee Delo*, Oct. 3, 1917; Verkhovskii, *Na trudnom perevale*, 339–40; AK, *Prelude*, 263–67, 237–40; *Novoe Vremia*, Oct. 4, 1917; Katkov, *Kornilov Affair*, 111–14.

19. AK to Mrs. O. L. Kerensky, Sept. 19, 1962, Kerensky Family Papers; *AFSR*, Sept. 10, 1917; Raupakh, "Vospominaniia," ch. 5, passim; I have compared this text with Robert von Raupach [alias R. R. Raupakh], *Russische Schatten (Facies Hippocratica)* (Leipzig: Paul List Verlag, 1939), 278 ff. This was published on the eve of the Second World War, with a Nazi introduction. Even had Kerensky known of its existence, legal action would have been impossible. I have not traced the article by Colonel Ukraintsev mentioned by Raupakh (and Katkov). Why did Katkov omit Raupakh's allegations against Kerensky? Because they cast Alexeyev, one of his key witnesses, in an even more "equivocal" light? Or had Kerensky's charm eroded Katkov's hostility during that summer of 1963 at St. Antony's? Kerensky altered the date of at least one other important public document for superstitious reasons, Carl Enckell, *Politiska Minnen* (Stockholm: Gebers Förlag, 1956), 1:126.

20. WO.33.924, Knox to DMI, Sept. 19, 1917, *Rech'*, Sept. 27, 1917; Sukhanov, *Zapiski*, 5:351ff, 6:53ff.
21. WO.106.1036, Blair to DMI, Sept. 15, 1917, Appendix; *VOSR*: . . . *Razgrom Kornilovskogo Miatezha*, 470–741; MAE, vol. 656, Noulens to Ribot, Sept. 12, 1917.
22. AK, *Prelude*, 247–56; Savinkov, *K delu Kornilova*, 28–29; *AFSR*, Sept. 1, 2, 1917; A. I. Verkhovskii, *Rossiia na Golgofe: iz pokhodnago dnevnika 1914–1918 g.* (Pet: Piataia Gosudarstvennaia Tipografiia, 1918), 18; Gippius, *Siniaia Kniga*, 176 ff.
23. *AFSR*, Sept. 1, 1917; *VOSR: Revoliutsionnoe dvizhenie v Rossii v sentiabre 1917 g.: Obshchenatsional'nyi Krizis*, 215–17; Sukhanov, *Zapiski*, 5:346.
24. AK, *Prelude*, 232–35; Buchanan, *Mission*, 2:177–78.
25. *Russkie Vedomosti*, Sept. 1, 1917.
26. AK, *Turning Point*, 408–9; Radkey, *Agrarian Foes*, 409–10; *AFSR*, Sept. 2, 1917.
27. AK, *Prelude*, 221–22; *AFSR*, Sept. 3, 1917; *RPG*, 3:1657–58; *VOSR*: . . . *Obshchenatsional'nyi Krizis*, 219; R. Poincaré, *Au Service de la France: Neuf Années de Souvenirs*, vol. 9, *L'Année Trouble 1917* (Paris: Plon-Nourrit, 1932), 279 ff; D. Ligou, *Histoire du socialisme en France (1871–1961)*, (Paris: Presses Universitaires de France, 1962), 293–97.
28. *RPG*, 3:1620–22; Gaponenko ed, *Revoliutsionnoe dvizhenie v russkoi armii*, 386–87; WO.33.924, Barter to CIGS, Sept. 18, 25, 1917; Verkhovskii, *Rossiia na Golgofe*, 113 ff; Verkhovskii, *Na trudnom perevale*, 290 ff; WO.106.1037, Blair's Despatch encl. with Buchanan to FO, Sept. 29, 1917.
29. *Delo Naroda*, Sept. 3, 1917; *Volia Naroda*, Sept. 5, 1917; Radkey, *Agrarian Foes*, 393 ff.
30. *VOSR*: . . . *Razgrom Kornilovskogo Miatezha*, 191; *VOSR*: . . . *Obshchenatsional'-nyi Krizis*, 221–22; Mints, *Istoriia*, vol. 2: *Sverzhenie Vremënnogo Pravitel'stva*, 723 ff.
31. V. V. Vas'kin and A. G. Gerasimenko. *Fevral'skaia Revoliutsiia v Nizhnem Povol'zhë* (Saratov: Izd. Saratovskogo Universiteta, 1976); *VOSR*: . . . *Obshchen-atsional'nyi Krizis*, 486–87, 490–92, 494–95; *RPG*, 3:1644–45; M. Philips Price, *Reminiscences of the Russian Revolution* (L: Allen & Unwin, 1921), 99 ff; Anne Edwards, *Sonya: the Life of Countess Tolstoy* (L: Hodder & Stoughton, 1981), 445–47.
32. *AFSR*, Aug. 19, 1917; *Narodnoe Slovo*, Aug. 25, 1917; *VOSR*: . . . *Obshchenat-sional'nyi Krizis*, 176–77, 229–30.
33. Enckell, *Politiska Minnen*, 1:101–11; *VOSR*: . . . *Obshchenatsional'nyi Krizis*, 230–31; S. M. Dimanshtein, *Revoliutsiia i natsional'nyi vopros* (M: Kommunistiches-kaia Akademiia, 1930), 3:219–26; Polvinen, *VVS*, 1:87–98.
34. *AFSR*, Sept. 16, 1917; Rabinowitch, *Bolsheviks Come to Power*, 160–62, 174–75; Radkey, *Agrarian Foes*, 440–442.
35. Lenin, *Works*, 25:243–50, 310 ff, 366–73; 26:19 ff; Sukhanov, *Zapiski* 6:44; Rabinowitch, *Bolsheviks Come to Power*, 169–71.
36. *RPG*, 3:1673–79; *VOSR*: . . . *Obshchenatsional'nyi Krizis*, 248–49; Buchanan, *Mission*, 2:189; Sorokin, *Leaves from a Russian Diary*, 92; MAE, vol. 656, Noulens to MAE, Sept. 18, 1917; WO.33.924, Knox to DMI, Nov. 1, 1917; *AFSR*, Sept. 16, 1917; Rabinowitch, *Bolsheviks Come to Power*, 177.

37. Rabinowitch, *Bolsheviks Come to Power*, 178; *AFSR*, Sept. 16, 1917.
38. Radkey, *Agrarian Foes*, 411–18; *AFSR*, Sept. 16–20, 1917; Rabinowitch, *Bolsheviks Come to Power*, 178–84.
39. Lenin, *Works*, 26:43; Radkey, *Agrarian Foes*, 418–19.
40. MAE, vol. 657, Noulens to MAE, Oct. 4, 1917; Kerensky's visit to the presidium of the Democratic Conference, at which he challenged them to create an all-socialist government, was therefore a bluff that he knew they would not call. See, AK, "Fevral' i Oktiabr' ", *Izdalëka: Sbornik statei (1920–1921 g.)*, (Paris: Povolotskii, 1922), 232.
41. *VOSR*: . . . *Obshchenatsional'nyi Krizis*, 321–22, 231; Mints, *Istoriia*, vol. 2: *Sverzhenie Vremënnogo Pravitel'stva*, 953–55; Rabinowitch, *Bolsheviks Come to Power*, 187–89; Lenin, *Works*, 26:57.
42. Buchanan, *Mission*, 2:188–91; MAE, vol. 657, Noulens to MAE, Oct. 6, 7–8, 1917; Radkey, *Agrarian Foes*, 418–19; *AFSR*, Sept. 22–24, 1917; *VOSR*: . . . *Obshchenatsional'nyi Krizis*, 233–36; AK, *Turning Point*. 417–18; Rosenberg, *Liberals*, 244–46.
43. Buchanan, *Mission*, 2:191–94; FO.371.3015, Lindley's Report, Oct. 30, 1917; MAE, v.657, Noulens to MAE, Oct. 9, 11, 1917; Cambon to Noulens, Oct. 18, 1917; AK, *Crucifixion*, 316–19; USA, *Papers* (1918), 3:1 ff.
44. *VOSR: Revoliustionnoe dvizhenie v Rossii nakanune Oktiabr'skogo Vooruzhënnogo Vosstaniia (1–24 oktiabria 1917 g.)*, 204–6; Maugham to Wiseman, ca. Nov. 18, 1917, F60/2/36, Lloyd George Papers, House of Lords Record Office, London; N. West, *M16: British Secret Intelligence Service Operations, 1909–45* (L: Weidenfeld, 1983), 14–15.
45. Mints, *Istoriia*, vol. 2: *Sverzhenie Vremënnogo Pravitel'stva*, 708–17; Lenin, *Works*, 25:366–73; 26: 69; Rabinowitch, *Bolsheviks Come to Power*, 193–94.
46. AK, *Turning Point*, 420–21, 428–29; Stankevich, *Vospominaniia*, 252; Verkhovskii, *Rossiia na Golgofe*, 122–24; Erich von Ludendorff, *Meine Kriegserinnerungen 1914–1918* (Berlin: E. S. Mittler, 1919), 404–6.
47. Buchanan, *Mission*, 2:194–96.
48. *Obshchee Delo*, Sept. 26, 1917; E. Petit, "Lettre Rapport à M. Albert Thomas," Oct. 19, (Nov. 1), 1917, 3–4, Petit Papers.
49. Raupakh, "Vospominaniia," ch. 5: "Vozstanie Generala Kornilova," 58–60; *Obshchee Delo*, Oct. 2, 3, 1917 etc; *RPG*, 3:1600–01; *Novoe Vremia*, Oct. 5, 1917.
50. *Novoe Vremia*, Oct. 10, 1917, AK, *Prelude*, 22–24, 286.

15. All Necessary Measures

1. A. Rabinowitch, *The Bolsheviks Come to Power* (L: New Left Books, 1979), 201; Count Valentin P. Zubov, *Stradnye gody Rossii: Vospominaniia o Revoliutsii (1917–1925)* (Munich: Wilhelm Fink Verlag, 1968), 8–14; V. I. Startsev, "Poslednii den' Vremënnogo Pravitel'stva," *Iz istorii velikoi oktiabr'skoi revoliutsii i sotsialisticheskogo stroitel'stva v SSSR: Sbornik statei*, V. A. Ovsiankin, ed. (Lgd.: Izd, Leningradskogo Universiteta, 1967), 100–102.

2. *Delo Naroda*, Oct. 7, 1917; *AFSR*, Oct. 8, 1917.

3. L. D. Trotsky *My Life*, (L: Penguin, 1971), 307; Isaac Deutscher, *The Prophet Armed: Trotsky 1879–1921* (L: Oxford University Press, 1970), 287–88, 294 ff; A. Ulam, *Lenin and the Bolsheviks* (L: Secker & Warburg, 1966), 359–64.

4. Rabinowitch, *Bolsheviks Come to Power*, 202.

5. WO.106.1037, Despatch No. 19 in Buchanan to FO, Sept. 29, 1917; Rabinowitch, *Bolsheviks Come to Power*, 226.

6. E. Petit, "Lettre Rapport à M. Albert Thomas," Oct. 19 (Nov. 1), 1917, 26–27, Petit Papers; *AFSR* Oct. 24, 1917; F. I. Dan, "K istorii poslednikh dnei Vremënnago Pravitel'stva," *Letopis' Revoliutsii*, 1923, 1:167; Rosenberg, *Liberals*, 167.

7. Rabinowitch, *Bolsheviks Come to Power*, esp. ch. 5; Charles Duval, "Iakov Mikhailovich Sverdlov: Founder of the Bolshevik Party Machine," *Reconsiderations on the Russian Revolution*, Ralph C. Elwood, ed (Cambridge, Mass; Slavica, 1976), 218 ff.

8. M. Ferro, *October 1917. A Social History of the Russian Revolution* (L: Routledge, 1980), 224 ff; J. L. H. Keep, *The Russian Revolution: A Study in Mass Mobilization* (L: Weidenfeld, 1976), part II, 67 ff; A. G. Savraskin ed., *Listovki Petrogradskikh Bol'shevikov*, vol. 3: *1917–1920* (Lgd: Lenizdat, 1957), 90 ff. For an analysis of Bolshevik use of language, see Abram Terz [Andrei Sinyavsky], "The Literary Process in Russia," *Kontinent* (L: Hodder & Stoughton, 1977), 94 ff. Kerensky had been warned. As early as July 15, 1917, *Pravda* had published one of his intimidating speeches which *Delo Naroda* had suppressed.

9. Lenin, *Works*, 26:145, 148, 184.

10. Sukhanov, *Zapiski*, 7:33–35; Rabinowitch, *Bolsheviks Come to Power*, 202–8; Lenin, *Works*, 26:189.

11. N. Ia. Ivanov, *Kontrrevoliutsiia v Rossii v 1917 godu i eë razgrom*, (M: Mysl', 1977), 220 ff; WO.33.924, Knox to CIGS, Oct. 27, 1917; Barter to CIGS, Oct. 27, 1917; A. Drezen ed., "Oktiabr'skaia revoliutsiia v Baltiiskom flote (Iz dnevnika I. I. Rengartena)," *KA*, (1927), 25:47. Rengarten quotes Cherkasky quoting Cheremisov, so we have this quotation at *third* hand (without counting Drezen), Even so, Cheremisov did not blame Kerensky and imputed anti-patriotic motives to no one.

12. WO.33.924, Knox to DMI, Oct. 28, 1917; *Rech'*, Oct. 6, 1917; Lenin, *Works*, 26:186; *AFSR*, Oct. 13, 1917.

13. WO.33.924, Barter to CIGS, Oct. 28, 29, Nov. 6, 1917; FO.371.3016, Buchanan to FO, Oct. 9, 1917. Gen. Baron Peter N. Wrangel, *Always with Honour* (NY: Robert Speller, 1957), 38. Wrangel suggests that he turned down an appointment "realizing that I could be of no service to my country in the existing circumstances." Kerensky himself identifies Wrangel as a key counterrevolutionary throughout 1917. See AK, *Turning Point*, 355, 360.

14. W. S. Woytinsky [Voitinskii], *Stormy Passage: A Personal History through Two Russian Revolutions to Democracy and Freedom, 1905–1960* (NY: Vanguard, 1961), 366–67; Lenin, *Works*: 26: 141.

15. *AFSR*, Oct. 15, 1917.

16. FO.371.3016, Buchanan to FO, Oct. 30, 1917; Stamfordham to Drummond,

FO, Oct. 31, 1917; Buchanan to FO, Oct. 3, 1917; MAE, v.657, Noulens to MAE, Oct. 30, Nov. 7, 1917; Proinsias Mac Aonghusa, Éamon De Valera: Na Blianta Réabhlóideacha, (Dublin: An Clóchomhar, 1981), 38ff.

17. R. Wade, The Russian Search for Peace, February–October 1917, (Stanford, Cal: Stanford University Press, 1969), 133 ff; Buchanan, Mission, 2:198–99; RPG, 2:1128–30.

18. RPG, 2:1130 ff, 1155–56; Wade, Russian Search, 133–36; E. Petit, "Lettre Rapport," Oct. 19 (Nov. 1), 1917, 18.

19. MAE, v. 657, Noulens to MAE, Oct. 18, Nov. 3, 1917; AFSR, Oct. 19, 1917; VOSR: Revoliutsionnoe dvizhenie v Rossii nakanune Oktiabr'skogo Vooruzhënnogo Vosstaniia (1–24 oktiabria 1917 g.), 212–13; A. I. Verkhovskii, Rossiia na Golgofe: Iz pokhodnago dnevnika 1914–1918 g. (Pet: Piataia Gosudarstvennaia Tipografiia), 125 ff; Verkhovskii, Na trudnom perevale, (M: Voennoe Izd. Min. Oborony SSSR, 1959), 354 ff; Botchkareva, Yashka, 245–47; V. D. Nabokov, "Vremënnoe Pravitel'stvo," ARR, (1921), 1:81–83.

20. RPG, 3:1735 ff; VOSR: . . . nakanune Oktiabr'skogo Vooruzhënnogo Vosstaniia, 220–30; Verkhovskii, Rossiia na Golgofe, 124; Verkhovskii, Na trudnom perevale, 389–94; Petit, "Lettre Rapport," Oct. 19, (Nov. 1), 1917, 31; Dan, "K istorii," 169.

21. AFSR, Oct. 22, 24, 1917; Obshchee Delo, Oct. 21, 1917; Verkhovskii, Na trudnom perevale, 395; MAE, vol. 658, Noulens to MAE, Nov. 4, 1917; AK, "Otchislenie gen. Verkhovskago," Izdalëka: Sbornik statei (1920–1921 g.) (Paris: Povolotskii, 1922), 193–94.

22. RPG, 2:1132; cf. Mario Silvestri, Isonzo 1917, (Turin: Giulio Einaudi, 1965), 313–15; AFSR, Oct. 20, 1917; Italy, Ministero degli Affari Esteri, I Documenti Diplomatici Italiani, Quinta Seria: 1914–1918 (Rome: Istituto Poligrafico e Zecca dello Stato, 1983), 9:232–44.

23. A search of the Swedish Utrikesdepartament's files by Inga Offerberg of the Riksarkivet failed to discover any traces of this offer, while Mark Cornwall's search of the files of the Austro-Hungarian Ministerium des Äussern found only the reactions of the ministry to Herman Bernstein's allegations in 1918. For Czernin's views in autumn 1917, see "Rede des Grafen Czernin, Wien, am 2. Oktober 1917," MdÄ, Karton PA I/962; c.f. Graf Ottokar Czernin [Černín] von und zu Chudenitz, Im Weltkrieg, (Berlin-Vienna: Ullstein, 1919), 296–99; Count Arthur Polzer-Hoditz, The Emperor Karl (NY-L: Putnam, 1930), 371–74; Neither Ingeborg Meckling, Die Aussenpolitik des Grafen Czernin (Vienna: Verlag für Geschichte und Politik, 1969), nor Heinz Rieder, Kaiser Karl: Der letzte Monarch Österreich-Ungarns (Munich: Callwey Verlag, 1981), provides the slightest support for Kerensky's story. For Kerensky's versions, see R. H. B. Lockhart, The Diaries of Sir Robert Bruce Lockhart, Kenneth Young, ed. (L: Macmillan, 1973) 1:175, 270–73, and AK, Turning Point, 431–33. Balfour's letter is in David Lloyd George, War Memoirs (L: Nicholson & Watson, 1934), 4:2093–94. The allegation was first published by the patriotic American Herman Bernstein in the Copenhagen Dagens Ekko, on May 17, 1918, shortly after he had met Tereshchenko in Norway. Bernstein had also met Kerensky in the Winter Palace, and he arranged for Kerensky to see Colonel House in 1919. See Herman

Bernstein, *Celebrities of Our Time* (L: Hutchinson, 1925), 170–74; See Louise Bryant on Bernstein in *Six Red Months in Russia*, (NY: George H. Doran, 1918), 265. Bernstein's allegations caused a stir and some perplexity on the Ballhausplatz. See MdÄ, Karton PA I/956—Liasse Krieg, 25s, t Friedensverhandlungen, Hoyos (Oslo) to Burián, June 2, 1918; Franz (Copenhagen) to Burián, June 2, 1918; Burián to Hoyos and Franz, June 4, 1918.

24. Petit, "Lettre Rapport," Oct. 19 (Nov. 1), 1917, 28.

25. Nabokov, "Vremënnoe Pravitel'stvo," 83; Sokoloff, *White Nights*, 97, 166; Petit to M. Hubert, Oct. 19 (Nov. 1), 1917, Petit Papers, 8–9.

26. AK, *Catastrophe*, 321–25. Kerensky's 1927 memoirs have 4 pages on the last 56 days of his government as compared with 76 on the first hundred hours of the February Revolution. His later accounts are fuller. For Kamenev see AK, *Turning Point*, 431.

27. Sukhanov, *Zapiski*, 7:59–67, Lenin, *Works*, 26:225–27; Rabinowitch, *Bolsheviks Come to Power*, 209–23.

28. D. A. Chugaev et al., eds. *Petrogradskii Voenno-Revoliutsionnyi Komitet: Dokumenty i materialy v trëkh tomakh* (M: Nauka, 1966–67), 1:40–41; *VOSR: . . . nakanune Oktiabr'skogo Vooruzhënnogo Vosstaniia*, 260–62; Buchanan, *Mission*, 2:201.

29. Woytinsky, *Stormy Passage*, 366–68; *VOSR: . . . nakanune Oktiabr'skogo Vooruzhënnogo Vosstaniia*, 210–14; *VOSR: Oktiabr'skoe Vooruzhënnoe Vosstanie v Petrograde*, 270–71, 273 ff; Petit, "Lettre Rapport," Oct. 19 (Nov. 1), 1917, 18–19; Rabinowitch, *Bolsheviks Come to Power*, 226 ff, 240–42.

30. Sukhanov, *Zapiski*, 7:91; *AFSR*, Oct. 24, 1917; MAE, vol. 658, Noulens to MAE, Nov. 12, 1917. On Oct. 22, Kerensky was still confident of the loyalty of the troops; Rabinowitch, *Bolsheviks Come to Power*, 242–47; P. N. Maliantovich, "V Zimnem Dvortse 25–26 oktiabria 1917 goda; Iz vospominanii," *Byloe* (1918) no. 12, 111.

31. Lenin, *Works*, 26:234–35; Chugaev ed., *Petrogradskii Voenno-Revoliutsionnyi Komitet*, 1:64–65; Rabinowitch, *Bolsheviks Come to Power*, 247–50.

32. AK, "Gatchina," *Izdalëka*, 195; *VOSR: Oktiabr'skoe Vooruzhënnoe Vosstanie*, 274–75; B. Hollingsworth, "David Soskice"; WO.33.924, Knox to DMI, Nov. 6, 1917; U. Ģermanis, *Oberst Vācietis und die lettischen Schützen im Weltkrieg und in der Oktoberrevolution*, (Stockholm: Almquist and Wiksell, 1974), 259–60; Stankevich, *Vospominaniia*, 258, found Kerensky still confident in victory even after his visit to the pre-parliament.

33. *AFSR*, Oct. 25, 1917; *RPG*, 3:1772ff; AK, "Gatchina," 196; Dan, "K istorii," 171; John Reed, *Ten Days that Shook the World* (NY: Random House, 1960), 91–94.

34. Lenin, *Works*, 26:235; Rabinowitch, *Bolsheviks Come to Power*, 266.

35. *RPG*, 3:1779 ff; Dan, "K istorii," 172–73; Sukhanov, *Zapiski*, 7:134 ff; Reed, *Ten Days*, 84–87; Stankevich, *Vospominaniia*, 259–60; AK, "Gatchina," 197–99.

36. Stankevich, *Vospominaniia*, 260; S. L. Maslov, "Kak zaniali Zimnyi dvorets,", *Delo Naroda*, Oct. 29, 1917; Maliantovich, "V Zimnem Dvortse," 112–15; I. I. Mints, ed. "Poslednie Chasy Vremënnogo Pravitel'stva (Dnevnik ministra Liverovskogo)," *Istoricheskii Arkhiv* (1960), no. 6, 40–41; AK, "Gatchina," 201–4; E. Petit, "Lettre Rapport de M. Petit au Ministre de l'Armement," Oct. 31,

(Nov. 13), 1917, 1–2; B. Solonevich, *Zhenshchina s vintovkoi* [the memoirs of Nina Krylova] (Buenos Aires: [privately printed], 1955), 158; V. I. Startsev, "Begstvo Kerenskogo," *Voprosy Istorii* (1966), no. 11, 204–5.

37. Mints ed., "Poslednie Chasy," 40–41; Savraskin ed., *Listovki*, 1:112; AK, "Gatchina," 204; Startsev, "Begstvo Kerenskogo," 205. In his film *October*, director Sergei Eisenstein shows Kerensky standing up in the car.

38. AK, "Gatchina," 206; *VOSR: Oktiabr'skoe Vooruzhënnoe Vosstanie*, 603 ff; Startsev, "Begstvo Kerenskogo," 205.

39. Woytinsky, *Stormy Passage*, 375; AK, "Gatchina," 207–8; *VOSR: Oktiabr'skoe Vooruzhënnoe Vosstanie*, 605; P. N. Krasnov, "Na vnutrennem fronte," *ARR* (1921), 1:149–50.

40. Woytinsky, *Stormy Passage*, 380–83; AK, "Gatchina," 208; Krasnov, "Na vnutrennem fronte," 130–36, 152–54.

41. Zubov, *Stradnye gody*, 15–21; AK, "Gatchina," 209–10, 214; Krasnov, "Na vnutrennem fronte," 155–56.

42. Sukhanov, *Zapiski*, 7:207–9; Oliver H. Radkey, *The Sickle under the Hammer: The Russian Socialist Revolutionaries in the Early Months of Soviet Rule* (NY: Columbia University Press, 1963), 19ff.

43. V. A. Antonov-Ovseenko, "Baltflot v dni Kerenshchiny i Krasnogo Oktiabria," *Velikaia Oktiabr'skaia Sotsialisticheskaia Revoliutsiia: Sbornik Vospominanii Uchastnikov Revoliutsii v Petrograde i Moskve* (M: Gosudarstvennoe Izd. Politicheskoi Literatury, 1957), 197 ff; Rabinowitch, *Bolsheviks Come to Power*, 280 ff.

44. Stankevich, *Vospominaniia*, 261–65; Maliantovich, "V Zimnem Dvortse," 116 ff; Mints ed., "Poslednie Chasy," 41 ff; A. Sinegub, "Zashchita Zimnago Dvortsa," *ARR* (1922) 4:134, 152, 165; Maria Bochkarnikova, "Boi v Zimnem Dvortse," *NZh* (1962) 68:215–16; M. Levin, ed., "Iz zapisnoi knizhki arkhivista: Poslednie chasy Vremënnogo Pravitel'stva v 1917 g." [Notes of P. L. Pal'chinskii], *KA* (1933), 56:137; Startsev, "Poslednii den'," 102–15.

45. *RPG*, 3:1793–98; Reed, *Ten Days*, 120–31; Deutscher, *Prophet Armed*, 312–14; Rabinowitch, *Bolsheviks Come to Power*, 278–80.

46. Reed, *Ten Days*, 135–37; Bryant, *Six Red Months*, 120; OLK, "Obryvki," 20–24; Chugaev ed., *Petrogradskii Voenno-Revoliutsionnyi Komitet*, 3:225.

47. Sinegub, "Zashchita," 147–71; Mints ed., "Poslednie Chasy," 45–47; Rabinowitch, *Bolsheviks Come to Power*, 285ff.

48. P. Sorokin, *Leaves from a Russian Diary* (L: Hurst and Blackett, 1925), 101–3; Marie Kleinmichel, *Memories of a Shipwrecked World* (L: Brentano's, 1923), 266–67; Solonevich, *Zhenshchina*, 164–65, suggests that some were raped, though Krylova did not witness any such incident herself, c.f. Bochkarnikova, "Boi v Zimnem Dvortse," 220. Ariadna Tyrkova-Williams found them safe, *From Liberty to Brest-Litovsk* (L: Macmillan, 1919), 256–59; Buchanan, *Mission*, 2:208, claims that Knox saved them, while Bryant also found them safe soon afterwards, *Six Red Months*, 213–19. Neither Rodzyanko nor Kerensky found it worth mentioning the women in their memoirs.

49. OLK, "Obryvki," 25–27; Stankevich, *Vospominaniia*, 267–68; MAE, vol. 658, Noulens to MAE, Nov. 10, 1917.

50. Krasnov, "Na vnutrennem fronte," 161; AK, "Gatchina," 212–18; Zubov,

Stradnye gody, 23; Gregory P. Tchebotarioff, *Russia, My Native Land: A U.S. Engineer Reminisces and Looks at the Present* (NY: privately printed [?], 1964), 122; FO.371.3018, Buchanan to FO, Nov. 25, 1917, enc. Report for DMI from Knox; cf. Reed, *Ten Days*, 254.

51. Radkey, *Sickle under the Hammer*, 18ff; Woytinsky, *Stormy Passage*, 383–84; James Bunyan and H. H. Fisher, eds. *The Bolshevik Revolution 1917–1918: Documents and Materials*, (Stanford, Cal: Stanford University Press, 1934), 155 ff.

52. V. A. Veiger-Redemeister, "S Kerenskim v Gatchine," *Proletarskaia Revoliutsiia* (1923), no. 9 (21):85; Bunyan and Fisher, *Bolshevik Revolution*, 159 ff; *RPG*, 3:1809–10; Stankevich, *Vospominaniia*, 273–80; G. Semenov [Vasil'ev], *Voennaia i boevaia rabota Partii Sotsialistov-Revoliutsionerov za 1917–1918 gg.* (Berlin: G. German, 1922), 6; AK, "Gatchina," 219–20.

53. Krasnov, "Na vnutrennem fronte," 161–63; Woytinsky, *Stormy Passage*, 383; Capt. G. Hill, *Go Spy the Land: Being the Adventures of I.K.8 of the British Secret Service* (L: Cassell, 1932), 195–96; Zubov, *Stradnye gody*, 21–23; Stankevich, *Vospominaniia*, 275.

54. Krasnov, "Na vnutrennem fronte," 161–72; Ģermanis, *Oberst Vācietis*, 265–69; AK, "Gatchina," 216–17, 220–21; Woytinsky, *Stormy Passage*, 384; Zubov, *Stradnye gody*, 23; Veiger-Redemeister, "S Kerenskim," 88–89; Radkey, *Sickle under the Hammer*, 45–46; Semenov, *Voennaia i boevaia rabota*, 7; Stankevich, *Vospominaniia*, 280–81.

55. AK, "Gatchina," 222–24; Krasnov, "Na vnutrennem fronte," 172–75; Veiger-Redemeister, "S Kerenskim," 90–94; Semenov, *Voennaia i boevaia rabota*, 7ff; Zubov, *Stradnye gody*, 25–26; V. O. Fabrikant, "A. F. Kerenskii v Rossii posle Oktiabr'skago Perevorota", typescript copy, 6–7, Kerensky Family Papers, see ch. 16, *n*4; Woytinsky, *Stormy Passage*, 387–90; A. F. Podozerova to AK, Jan. 30, 1948, Kerensky Papers, F.165; Startsev, "Begstvo Kerenskogo," 205–6.

56. Zubov, *Stradnye gody*, 22; Semenov, *Voennaia i boevaia rabota*, 9; Radkey, *Sickle under the Hammer*, 46–47; Stankevich, *Vospominaniia*, 272; AK, "Gatchina", 211–12; Veiger-Redemeister, "S Kerenskim," 85.

16. Regeneration?

1. V. I. Startsev, "Begstvo Kerenskogo," *Voprosy Istorii* (1966) no. 11, 206; Iu. A. Shchetinov, *Krushenie melkoburzhuaznoi kontrrevoliutsii v Sovetskoi Rossii (konets 1920–1921 g.)* (M: Izd. Moskovskogo Universiteta, 1984), 41.

2. For Kerensky as Khlestakov, see the right-wing pasquinade, Vatrantsev [sic], *Russkaia Revoliutsiia ili Velikii Khlestakov* (Kharbin: Tipo-lit. Shtaba okhrannoi strazhi, 1919).

3. MAE, vol. 656, Noulens to MAE, Sept. 18, 1917, cf. Gippius, *Siniaia Kniga*, 219, where she calls Bolshevik rule *"vlast' t'my."*

4. O. H. Radkey, *The Sickle Under the Hammer: The Russian Socialist Revolutionaries in the Early Months of Soviet Rule* (NY: Columbia University Press, 1963), 73–74; Stankevich, *Vospominaniia*, 284 ff; V. O. Fabrikant, "A. F. Kerenskii v Rossii posle Oktiabr'skago Perevorota," typescript copy, 7, Kerensky Family

Papers. To shield his friends, Kerensky refused to set down a detailed account of his months underground until long afterward, see *NYT*, March 3, 1927. His earliest detailed account is the Russian typescript, AK, "V Popdol'ë," Kerensky Papers, F.72. As translated, this became chapter 25 of AK, *Turning Point*. Fabrikant's more detailed and accurate account seems not to have been available to Kerensky when he wrote his own version. He was also unaware that his Finnish hosts had already identified themselves. Fabrikant's account was first given verbally to Margulies during the Civil War, see M. S. Margulies, *God interventsii* (Berlin, Grzhebin, 1923), 2:92–93.

5. M. Fleer, ed. "Vremënnoe Pravitel'stvo posle Oktiabria," *KA*, (1924), no. 6, 200–08; A. A. Demianov, "Zapiski o podpol'nom Vremënnom Pravitel'stve," *ARR* (1922) 7:34–36; *Delo Naroda*, Nov. 24, 1917.

6. *Delo Naroda*, Nov. 22, 1917; AK, *Turning Point*, 452–53.

7. Radkey, *Sickle Under the Hammer*, 77ff, 167ff; AK, *Turning Point*, 451–52.

8. Buchanan, *Mission*, 2:221–26, 233 ff; Raymond Poincaré, *Au Service de la France: Neuf Années de Souvenirs*, vol. 9: *L'Année Trouble 1917* (Paris: Plon-Nourrit, 1932), 277–396; Radkey, *Sickle under the Hammer*, 85–88.

9. Radkey, *Sickle Under the Hammer*, 73–84; Demianov, "Zapiska," 49; Fleer ed., "Vremënnoe Pravitel'stvo," 209; *Delo Naroda*, Nov. 17, 24, 1917.

10. *Delo Naroda*, Nov. 22, 1917.

11. AK, *Turning Point*, 449–51, Radkey, *Sickle Under the Hammer*, 163ff, 196, 203ff, 229, 241–43.

12. O. H. Radkey, *The Election to the Russian Constituent Assembly of 1917* (Cambridge, Mass: Harvard University Press, 1950); I. S. Malchevskii ed., *Vsërossiiskoe Uchreditel'noe Sobranie*, (M-Lgd: Gosizdat, 1930), 113–38; Radkey, *Sickle Under the Hammer*, 280 ff.

13. Radkey, *Election*, 119–20; Radkey, *Sickle under the Hammer*, 303–4; AK interviewed by Elena Ivanoff, Oct. 20, 1961, tape no. 5, 23, Kerensky Papers, F.97; Conversations with Mrs. O. L. Kerensky.

14. Mark V. Vishniak, *Vsërossiiskoe Uchreditel'noe Sobranie* (Paris: "Sovremënnyia Zapiski," 1932), 90–92; Malchevskii, *Vsërossiiskoe Uchreditel'noe Sobranie*, 115; Radkey, *Sickle under the Hammer*, 306 ff. 456–57.

15. A. G. Savraskin ed., *Listovki Petrogradskikh Bol'shevikov*, 3:*1917–1920* (Lgd: Lenizdat, 1957), 112 ff. In 1938, Mikhail Zoshchenko revived the allegation of peculation in "Bezslavnyi konets," *Rasskazy 1937–1938* (Lgd: "Sovetskii pisatel,' " 1938), 182, 228. In view of the date he should not be judged too harshly. Less defensible is the repetition by the *Bol'shaia Sovetskaia Entsiklopediia* (3d. ed.), A. M. Prokhorov et al. eds. (M: Sovetskaia Entsiklopediia, 1973), 12:160, of the allegation that Kerensky fled to the Don. For refutations, see OLK. "Obryvki," 13–14; V. P. Zubov, *Stradnye gody Rossii: Vospominaniia o Revoliutsii (1917–1925)*, (Munich: Wilhelm Fink Verlag, 1968), 26; Fabrikant, "A. F. Kerenskii v Rossii," 19. From a Soviet point of view, Kerensky *was* technically guilty of embezzlement, since he took government money to Gatchina to pay his troops. Kollontai's attempts to have Countess Panina tried on similar charges were an embarrassing failure, though they kept the feminists divided. Whose idea was that?

16. Florence Farmborough, *Nurse at the Russian Front* (L: Futura, 1977), 349; Fabrikant, "A. F. Kerenskii v Rossii," 1.

17. For the "peasant matrix," see Radkey, *Sickle under the Hammer*, 218.

18. Fabrikant, "A. F. Kerenskii v Rossii," 3–14; AK, "V Podpol'ë," 5–12; AK, *Turning Point*, 463–65.

19. B. F. Sokolov, "Zashchita Vsërossiiskogo Uchreditel'nago Sobraniia," *ARR* (1924), 13:49 ff; G. Semënov [Vasil'ev], *Voennaia i boevaia rabota Partii Sotsialistov-Revoliutsionerov za 1917–1918 gg.* (Berlin: G. German, 1923), 9–13; Radkey, *Sickle under the Hammer*, 370 ff.

20. P. Sorokin dismissed the assassination attempt as a "tire burst," though he must have known better, see *Leaves from a Russian Diary* (L: Hurst & Blackett, 1925), 123; Compare Sokolov's conflicting accounts in "Zashchita," 33, 46–48, and in Sokoloff, *White Nights*, 139–40, 146–53; M. Sonkin, *Vystrel' na Fontanke: Iz Khroniki sem'desiat' piatoi komnaty Smol'nogo* (Lgd: Lenizdat, 1968) gets it about right. This was confirmed by the surviving participant, N. N. Martianov to AK, n.d., *Kerensky Papers*, F.161; Radkey, *Sickle Under the Hammer*, 328–49, 364–77.

21. Fabrikant, "A. F. Kerenskii v Rossii," 15–16; AK, "V Podpol'ë," 12–13; AK, *Turning Point*, 465–66. For Bolshevik harassment of Kerensky's family and friends, see OLK, "Obryvki," 28–32; Sukhanov, *Zapiski*, 1:64; Pëtr Malkov, *Zapiski Komendanta Moskovskogo Kremlia* (M: Molodaia Gvardiia, 1961), 84–86.

22. Fabrikant, "A. F. Kerenskii v Rossii," 15–20; AK, "V Podpol'ë," 14–17 (and addenda 2–5); AK, *Turning Point*, 466–72; Sokolov, "Zashchita," 58 ff; Adam Ulam, *Lenin and the Bolsheviks* (L: Secker & Warburg, 1966), 394–98; Lenin, *Works*, 26:437–41; *Novaia Zhizn'*, Jan. 6, 1918; *Delo Naroda*, Jan. 5, 7, 12, 1918; Vishniak, *Vsërossiiskoe Uchreditel'noe Sobranie*, 98–116; Malchevskii, ed., *Vsërossiiskoe Uchreditel'noe Sobranie*, 3–25, 37–53, 56, 64, 67–70, 110–12; B. Nicolaevsky, Introduction to Tsereteli, *Vospominaniia* 1:xvi–xx; V. M. Chernov, *Pered burei* (NY: Chekhov, 1953), 367–68; Rosenberg, *Liberals*, 282–83; Radkey, *Sickle under the Hammer*, 381–95.

23. Fabrikant, "A. F. Kerenskii v Rossii," 20–30; AK, "V Podpol'ë," 17–18; AK, *Turning Point*, 472–73; Sofia Stenbäck, "Minnesanteckningar," 4, typescript, Wolter Stenbäcks Samling, Kapsel 1, Handskriftsavdelningen, Åbo Akademis Bibliotek; cf. Sofia Stenbäck, *Idyll och drama: Anteckningar och brev Greta Dahlström*, ed. (Eckenäs/Tammisaari: Eckenäs Tryckeri Aktiebolags Förlag, 1967), 168–70; Wolter Stenbäck, "Venäjän kuuluisen mies Suomessa piilossa Vapaussodan aikana," *Suomen Vapaussota* (1932), no. 4, 87–88 (reprinted as "Kerenski Suomessa" in E. Räikkönen, ed. *Vapaussodan Kertomuksia*, (H:ki: Sanatar, 1934) 1:300–301. For the Stenbäcks in 1905, see B. V. Savinkov, *Memoirs of a Terrorist* (NY: Boni, 1931), 239–46. For the Finnish revolution, see Eino Jutikkala and Kauko Pirinen, *A History of Finland* (Espoo: Weilin and Göös, 1979), 215–16.

24. Fabrikant, "A. F. Kerenskii v Rossii," 31; Wolter Stenbäck, "Venäjän kuuluisen mies," 87–88; Carl Frankenhäuser in *Hufvudstadsbladet*, Jan. 28, 1958.

25. Ibid.; AK, "V Podpol'ë," 18–20; AK, *Turning Point*, 473–74; Fabrikant, "A. F. Kerenskii v Rossii," 31; Personal communication.

26. Edward H. Carr, *The Bolshevik Revolution 1917–1923*, (L: Macmillan, 1963–

66), vols. 2 and 3; Radkey, *Sickle under the Hammer*, 275–76; M. S. Bernshtam, ed., "Narodnoe Soprotivlenie Kommunizmu v Rossii: Nezavisimoe Rabochee dvizhenie v 1918 godu: dokumenty i materialy," *Issledovaniia Noveishei Russkoi Istorii*, (Paris: YMCA Press, 1981–82), 2:2–3.

27. Rosenberg, *Liberals*, 308–20; Peter Kenez, *Civil War in South Russia, 1918* (Berkeley-LA: University of California Press, 1971), 45–116.

28. AK,"V Podpol'ë," 20–22; AK, *Turning Point*, 474–75; OLK, "Obryvki," 32–41; Fabrikant, "A. F. Kerenskii v Rossii," 32.

29. Fabrikant, "A. F. Kerenskii v Rossii," 32; AK, *Delo Kornilova*, (M: Zadruga, 1918), v; AK, *Prelude*, 23, 107–8, 287.

30. AK, "V Podpol'ë," 24; Conversations with Kerensky family and friends.

31. Fabrikant, "A. F. Kerenskii v Rossii," 32–42; AK, "V Podpol'ë," 23–31; AK, *Turning Point*, 475–81; Margulies, *God interventsii*, 2:92–93; Stankevich, *Vospominaniia*, 308–11; M. V. Vishniak, *Gody emigratsii 1919–1969: Parizh-N'iu Iork: Years of Emigration 1919–1969* (Stanford, Cal: Hoover Institution, 1970), 14 ff; N. V. Krylenko, *Za piat' let: 1918–1922 gg.: obvinitel'nye rechi po naibolee krupnym protsessam, zaslushannym v Moskovskom i verkhovnom revoliutsionnykh tribunalakh* (M-Pet: Gosudarstvennoe Izd., 1923), 154; M. Levidov, *K istorii soiuznoi interventsii v Rossii* (Lgd: Priboi, 1925), 116 ff; V. Vladimirova, " 'Rabota' eserov v 1918 godu," *KA*, 1927, No. 1 (20), 153. When the French decided to ignore their pledges, Noulens not only denied giving them, but even claimed that "j'avais prescrit à mes agents de Moscou de les [the centre-left in Moscow] assurer de ma sympathie," Joseph Noulens, *Mon Ambassade en Russie Soviétique 1917–1919*, (Paris: Plon, 1933), 2:107. Lockhart gave a different picture: "Early in June M. Noulens, the French Ambassador, read, through the medium of the French Consul-general at Moscow, a *note verbale* to the various counter-revolutionary leaders at Moscow, in which it was stated that Allied intervention on a large scale would take place before the end of June." Lockhart felt that these assurances triggered Savinkov's revolt at Yaroslavl, which might have caused the Bolshevik regime to collapse had Allied units arrived in time. R. H. B. Lockhart, "Memorandum on the Internal Situation in Russia," Nov. 1, 1918, Box C(110), F2, 283–427, Milner Papers: Great War Papers 1914–1918, Bodleian Library, Oxford (Property of New College).

32. John S. Reshetar, *The Ukrainian Revolution, 1917–1920* (Princeton, NJ: Princeton University Press, 1952), 145 ff; Kenez, *Civil War in South Russia, 1918*, 92 ff; P. N. Krasnov, "Vsëvelikoe Voisko Donskoe," *ARR* (1922), 5:202; Stig Jägerskiöld, *Mannerheim*, vol. 3: *Gustaf Mannerheim 1918* (H:ki: Albert Bonniers Förlag, 1967).

33. Vishniak, *Vsërossiiskoe Uchreditel'noe Sobranie*, chs. 6–7, 117–58; Vishniak, *Gody emigratsii*, 32–33; Gerburg Thunig- Nittner, *Die Tschechoslowakische Legion in Russland* (Wiesbaden: Otto Harrassowitz, 1970), 45–76; Vladimirova, " 'Rabota' eserov," 154 ff; V. G. Boldyrev, *Direktoriia, Kolchak, Interventy* (Nikolaevsk-on-Amur: Sibkraiizdat, 1925), 28–29; Lockhart to FO, April 2, 1918, B109, Milner Papers; G. K. Gins, *Sibir', Soiuzniki i Kolchak* (Peking: Tipo-Litografiia Russkoi Dukhovnoi Missii, 1921), 1 (part 1): 132ff; Chernov, *Pered burei*, 369–74.

34. Sorokin, *Leaves from a Russian Diary*, 143; AK, "Fevral' i Oktiabr'," *Izdalëka: Sbornik statei (1920–1921 gg.)* (Paris: Povolotskii, 1922), 236 ff; Fabrikant, "A. F. Kerenskii v Rossii," 42–43; For the Armenian land reform, see M. M. Ter-Pogosian, "Vospominaniia o Revoliutsii 1917 goda," interview no. 15, Radio Liberty, 1964, Oral History Research Office, Columbia University Libraries.

35. Fabrikant, "A. F. Kerenskii v Rossii," 43–45; AK, "V Podpol'ë," 34–42; AK, *Turning Point*, 481–85; FO.371.3020, Memorandum of HM Inspector under the Aliens Act, Dec. 21, 1917; Interdepartmental Conference of Dec. 20, 1917; FO to Buchanan, Dec. 23, 1917; R. H. B. Lockhart, *Memoirs of a British Agent* (NY-L: Putnam, 1932), 278; D. Francis, *Russia from the American Embassy* (NY: Scribner's, 1932), 277–78, 194–95; *The Daily Mail* (Kingston-upon-Hull), Nov. 14, 1964.

36. Richard H. Ullman, *Anglo-Soviet Relations 1917–1921* 3 vols. (Princeton, NJ: Princeton University Press, 1961–72) 1:208–10; FO.371.3020, "Private meeting of officials and public men at the Russian Embassy forwarded to DMI by Under Secretary of State for Foreign Affairs," Dec. 29, 1917; Balfour to Gavronsky, Jan. 3, 1918; AK, *Turning Point*, 485–89, 512; Personal communication from Asher Gransby.

37. "Interview between the Prime Minister and Mr. Kerensky at 10 Downing Street, 24 June 1918," typescript, B 124, Fl (1–181), Milner Papers. Kerensky's meetings with Lloyd George's secretary, Philip Kerr, and with Lord Milner, are mentioned in B 124, F 1 (1–181) and in B 281, Lord Milner, "Diary for 1918," Milner Papers. Ullman, *Anglo-Soviet Relations*, 1:209–10; 107 *House of Commons Debates*, 5S, London 1918, c. 784; AK, *Turning Point*, 489–92.

38. *Report of the Eighteenth Annual Conference of the Labour Party*, (L: The Labour Party, 1918), 35 ff, 54–57, 59–61; *The Manchester Guardian*, June 27, 28, 1918; *The Daily News*, June 28, 1918; *Le Petit Parisien*, June 28, 1918.

39. *Manchester Guardian*, July 1, 1918; S. P. Mel'gunov, *N.V. Chaikovskii v gody grazhdanskoi voiny* (Paris: Rodnik/La Source, 1929), 55–57; AK, "Ce que fut la politique des Alliées en Russie," *Pour la Russie*, Jan. 17, 1920; AK, *Turning Point*, 492–97; Noulens was furious at the agitation of Kerensky's friends, see Noulens, *Mon Ambassade*, 2:107–8.

40. Boldyrev, *Direktoriia*, 35–53; I. M. Maiskii, *Demokraticheskaia Kontrrevoliutsiia* (M-Pet: Gosudarstvennoe Izd., 1923), 256ff; N. N. Vinner to AK, Nov. 11, 1918, DS/2/1, Box 8, Soskice Papers, House of Lords Record Office.

41. AK, "Ce que fut la politique des Alliées"; Vishniak, *Vsërosiiskoe Uchreditel'noe Sobranie*, 202–3n; Boldyrev, *Direktoriia*, 93–120; V. M. Zenzinov ed., *Gosudarstvennyi perevorot Admirala Kolchaka v Omske 18 noiabria 1918 goda: Sbornik dokumentov*, (Paris: Tip. N. Rurakhovskago, 1919), 9ff; FO.371.3020, FO to Sir. C. Greene, Dec. 29, 1917.

42. J. Y. Simpson, FO, to AK, Aug. 30, 1918 (copy), FAT 94 AP 182; AK, *Crucifixion*, 312; Vishniak, *Vsërossiiskoe Uchreditel'noe Sobranie*, 200–201; AK in *The Daily News*, Oct. 15, 1918; AK, "Ce que fut la politique des Alliées."

43. *The Daily News*, Oct. 15, 1918; *L'Information*, Sept. 5, Nov. 14, 1918; AK to Albert Thomas, Nov. 8, 1918; Thomas to AK, Dec. 2, 1918, FAT 94 AP 407. AK, *Turning Point*, 505–7, and hence Vishniak, *Gody emigratsii*, 20, give a slightly garbled version of this incident.

44. AK, "The Road to Tragedy," *The Murder of the Romanovs*, Sir Bernard Pares, ed. (L: Hutchinson, 1935), 137–53.

45. OLK, "Obryvki," 41–50, 56–80; N. N. Vinner to AK, Nov. 11, 1918.

46. Sukhanov, *Zapiski*, 1:293n; B. F. Sokolov, "Pamiati Borisa Flekkelia," *Volia Rossii*, Nov. 25, 1920; Zenzinov ed., *Gosudarstvennyi perevorot*, 175; N. N. [sic], "Krasnyi terror v Turkestane," *Volia Rossii*, Dec. 7, 1920; OLK, "Obryvki," 110–13, 115–16; Gavronsky to Thomas [?], Sept. 13, 1918, FAT 94 AP 182.

47. Vishniak, *Gody emigratsii*, 11, 22; Herman Bernstein, *Celebrities of Our Time* (L: Hutchinson, 1925), 173–74; Margulies, *God interventsii*, 1:348; 2:11, 38; Sokoloff, *White Nights*, 262–63. For Kerensky's visa, see FAT 94 AP 407.

48. Margulies, *God interventsii*, 2:46–47, 53; Sokoloff, *White Nights*, 263.

49. Margulies, *God interventsii*, 2:71, 79, 82–83; "Memorandum of conversation with Mr. Alexander Kerenski," May 4, 1919: Notes of a Meeting held at President Wilson's House in the Place des États Unis, May 19, 1919, USA, *Papers* (1919), 1937, 337–38, 340–54; AK, *Turning Point*, 517 ff.

50. Margulies, *God interventsii*, 1:332; 2:43, 45, 73, 90; Vishniak, *Gody emigratsii*, 30–31, cf. AK, Avksentiev, Zenzinov, Argunov, Rogovsky, Minor, B. Sokolov, Slonim, "Memorandum on the question of Nationalities" undated (1919), DS/2/1, Box 8, Soskice Papers; J. F. N. Bradley, *Civil War in Russia 1917–1920* (L: Batsford, 1975), 150–52.

51. B. V. Savinkov, *K delu Kornilova* (Paris: Imp. Union, 1919), 24; AK, "Iz stat'i— 'Legenda o g. Savinkove'. O vozstanii gen. Kornilova," *Izdalëka*, 173 ff; Margulies, *God interventsii*, 2:73, 76. For a fuller statement of Kerensky's views on British policy, see AK, *Allied Policy towards Russia* (L: The Labour Party [?], 1920).

52. *Dictionnaire Biographique du Mouvement Ouvrier Français*, Jean Maitrou et al., eds. (Paris: Les Éditions Ouvrières, 1976), 14:98–103; Jacques Chastenet, *Les Années d'Illusions 1918–1931*, vol. 5 of *Histoire de la Troisième République* (Paris: Hachette, 1960), 77–78, 80 ff; Zinaida N. Hippius, *Between Paris and St. Petersburg: Selected Diaries of Zinaida Hippius*, Temira Pachmuss, ed. (Urbana-Chicago, Ill: University of Illinois Press, 1975), 238, n56; J. Balteau et al., eds. *Dictionnaire de Biographie Française*, (Paris: Librairie Letouzey et Ané, 1954), 6:199–200.

53. Chastenet, *Années*, 70; František Nečásek and Jan Pachta eds., *Dokumenty o protisovětských piklech Československé Reakce*, (Prague: Státní Nakladatelství politické literatury, 1954), 113: Shchetinov, *Krushenie*, 114–15; Vishniak, *Gody emigratsii*, 78–80. Kerensky defended his acceptance of French and Czech aid in *Dni*, Sept. 5, 1923, but he could publish no detailed account without betraying his Western sponsors and his underground comrades in Russia. The scanty information available was published in two installments, (1) by the Soviet government in its campaign against the SRs in 1922, and (2) by Czech Stalinists anxious to discredit Masaryk and Beneš in the 1950s; see Libuše Škornová, *Nejedleho Kritika Benešovy zahraniční politiky k SSSR* (Prague: Státní Nakladatelství politické literatury, 1954), 18 ff. This unsatisfactory situation is redeemed only partly by Vishniak's admission that the documents published in Moscow were, at least, authentic.

54. On Feb. 11, 1920, Gavronsky told John Spargo that Kerensky was still living in London, and on May 29, 1920 that he was "staying at present" in Paris, John Spargo Papers, Bailey/Howe Library, University of Vermont; Margulies, *God interventsii*, 3:72, Bradley, *Civil War*, 134 ff.

55. *Rabota eserov zagranitsei: po materialam Parizhskogo arkhiva eserov* (M: "RSFSR," 1922), 1 ff. (The official anonymity of this publication suggests that Vladimirova—or whoever the editor was—still feared SR reprisals.) These were the papers stolen by Captain Korotnev, Vishniak, *Gody emigratsii*, 78. (The Menshevik Mason was Ia. L. Rubinshtein); Václav Král, *O Masarykově a Benešově Kontrarevoluční politice* (Prague: Státní Nakladatelství politické literatury, 1953), 102. N. N. Martianoff told me that he had himself collected money from Dr. Papoušek, Masaryk's secretary, at the Hradčany.

56. AK, "Tret'ia sila," *Volia Rossii*, Oct. 17, 1920; OLK, "Obryvki," 130 ff; Sokoloff, *White Nights*, 286–91, is inaccurate, e.g., in suggesting that Kerensky met the family in Reval (Tallinn).

57. *Rabota eserov*, 3, 7; Table mat showing Prague, autographed by AK, Avksentiev et al, Papers of Asher Gransby.

58. Margulies, *God interventsii*, 3:258, 261–62.

59. OLK, "Obryvki;" Dr. O. A. Kerensky, "Reminiscences of 1917/18," typescript, Nov. 1979, Kerensky Family Papers.

60. *Biulleten' soveshchaniia chlënov Uchreditel'nago Sobraniia*, Jan. 12, 15, 22, 26; Feb. 1, 1921; Vishniak, *Gody emigratsii*, 55–65; L. K. Shkarenkov, *Agoniia beloi emigratsii*, (M: Mysl', 1981), 37–38; John Spargo to AK, Jan. 13, 1921, John Spargo Papers; *Rabota eserov*, 18.

61. *Rabota eserov*, 8 ff; AK, "Veianie smerti," *Izdalëka*, 62–63. Kerensky was capable of a much more serious analysis of Soviet reality. For an acute analysis of the role of trade unions under Communism, based on the critical use of Soviet sources, see AK, *Soviet Russia in the Autumn of 1919* (L: Twentieth Century Press, 1920), 17–18.

62. Sorokin, *Leaves from a Russian Diary*, 263–67; O. H. Radkey, *The Unknown Civil War in Soviet Russia: A Study of the Green Movement in the Tambov Region 1920–1921* (Stanford, Cal: Stanford University Press, 1976), 3 ff; Victor Serge, *Memoirs of a Revolutionary, 1901–1941* (L.: Oxford University Press, 1963), 122–33; *Pravda o Kronshtadte* (Prague: 'Volia Rossii' [i.e. Kerensky's comrades], 1921).

63. *Rabota eserov*, 14–16, 20–23; Nečásek and Pachta eds., *Dokumenty*, 119–22; Vishniak, *Gody emigratsii*, 66; Lenin, *Works*, 32:43–159; 5:42, 272–75; Robin Bruce Lockhart to AK, April 10, 1967, Kerensky Papers, F.134.

64. *Dni*, Sept. 5, 1923; Vishniak, *Gody emigratsii*, 79–80; Lord Stow Hill interviewed in 1970. The pamphlet is *Rabota eserov*, see n55.

65. Vishniak, *Gody emigratsii*, 80–82, 86–92; Marc Jansen, *Een Showproces onder Lenin: Het vorspeel van de Grote Terreur*, (Haarlem: De Haan, 1980), 117; A. I. Solzhenitsyn, *The Gulag Archipelago 1918–1956* (L: Collins/Fontana, 1974), 1:354–67; Krylenko, *Za piat' let*, 4, 103; Serge, *Memoirs*, 163ff; F. Claudín, *The Communist Movement. From Comintern to Cominform*, (L: Penguin, 1975), 145 ff,150.

17. A Romantic Exile

1. AK to comrades in Berlin [copy], Feb. 18, 1920, Kerensky Papers, F.84; Simon Karlinsky and Alfred Appel Jr. eds., *The Bitter Air of Exile: Russian Writers in the West 1922–1972* (Berkeley: University of California Press, 1977), epigraph and introduction, 5–9.
2. Personal communications from the Kerensky family. For emigré mockery, see e.g. G. Katkov, *Russia 1917: The Kornilov Affair: Kerensky and the Break-Up of the Russian Army* (L: Longmans, 1980), 143. The classic study of the pre–1917 emigration is E. H. Carr, *The Romantic Exiles* (L: Penguin, 1933). W. Chapin Huntington, *The Homesick Million: Russia-out-of-Russia* (Boston: The Stratford Co, 1933), provides a vivid snapshot of the emigrés in the early 30s. Robert C. Williams, *Culture in Exile: Russian Emigrés in Germany 1881–1941*, (Ithaca, NY-L: Cornell UP, 1972), uses German archives and psychology in an illuminating study. Hostile, but competent, is Vítězslav Čech, "Ruská Emigrace a Pomocná Akce Československé Buržoasie v dvacátých letech," *Knižnice Odborných a Vědeckých Spisů Vysokého Učení Technického v Brně*, Svazek B–2, 1967, 45–63; Pierre [P. E.] Kovalevsky, *La Dispersion Russe à travers le Monde et son Rôle Culturel* (Chauny, Aisne: A. Baticle, 1951), catalogues the remarkable achievements of the emigrés. His student Tilghman B. Koons' doctoral dissertation, "Histoire des doctrines politiques de l'émigration russe (1919–1939)," Thèse. Université de la Sorbonne, W. univ. (1952) (14), provides a competent description of the emigrés in France. L. K. Shkarenkov, *Agoniia beloi emigratsii* (M: Mysl', 1981), is concise but tendentious, reinforcing by default the impression that a less barbaric regime could eventually have regained the allegiance of most of the emigrés (though not Kerensky). Karlinsky and Appel, *Bitter Air*, is an indispensable introduction to emigré literature, while Temira Pachmuss' encyclopedic notes to Hippius' writings are invaluable, see Z. N. Hippius, *Between Paris and St. Petersburg: Selected Diaries of Zinaida Hippius*, (Urbana-Chicago: University of Illinois Press, 1975); Z. N. Hippius, *Intellect and Ideas in Action: Selected Correspondence of Zinaida Hippius*, T. Pachmuss, ed. (Munich: Wilhelm Fink Verlag, 1972). Kerensky's political passions are illuminated by Mark. V. Vishniak, *Gody emigratsii 1919–1969: Parizh-N'iu Iork: Years of Emigration 1919–1969* (Stanford, Cal: Hoover Institution, 1970), and his personal and political life by Nina Berberova, *The Italics are Mine* (L: Longmans, 1969) and in Russian, 2d. ed. *Kursiv Moi* (NY: Russica Publishers Inc., 1983).
3. AK, *Crucifixion*, 301.
4. B. Hollingsworth, "David Soskice"; Conversations with Victor Soskice and Frank Soskice (Lord Stow Hill).
5. J. O. Gavronsky, "Result of Clinical Investigations Based on the Methods of Aberhalden," *The Lancet*, June 16, 1914; Dr. Chaim Weizmann, testimonial, Aug. 1, 1917; Ukaz Vremënnago Pravitel'stva, Sept. 2, 1917; Dr. Gavronsky's diplomatic passport, Sept. 5(18), 1917; Politcheskoe Upravlenie Voennago Ministerstva, "Ot kakago libo voznagrazhdeniia . . . otkazyvaius'," Sept. 6, 1917; *Jewish Chronicle*, Oct. 19, 1934; "Jacob Ossip Gavronsky," typescript c.v., 1938 [?]; "Jacob Ossip Gavronsky, MRCS, LRCP, MD," typescript obituary, 1948;

Wissotzky House: Promise and Fulfillment, [promotional literature] (Tel Aviv, n.d.); Papers of Asher Gransby, Vancouver; Personal communications from Asher Gransby.

6. Manya Harari [née Benenson], *Memoirs 1906–1969* (L: Harvill, 1972), 9 ff; Flora Solomon [née Benenson] and Barnett Litvinoff, *Baku to Baker Street: the Memoirs of Flora Solomon* (L: Collins, 1984); Conversation with Countes Fira Ilinska (née Benenson), 1970; Personal communication from Peter Benenson. For Strunsky, see *NYT*, Feb. 6, 1948; Personal communication from Tatiana Pollock. Personal communications from Elena Izvolskaya; Stepun, *Byvshee*, 1:93 ff; Williams, *Culture in Exile*, 162–74; Hippius, *Intellect and Ideas*, 129, *n*54; Hippius, *Between Paris and St. Petersburg*, 238, *n*56; Information on the Vasilieva sisters was provided by Dr. O. A. Kerensky and K. Grigorkoff.

7. General Baron Peter N. Wrangel, *Always with Honour* (NY: Robert Speller, 1957), 338 ff; Shkarenkov, *Agoniia*, 23–36, 72–73; Koons, "Histoire," 81–82, 88–92; Williams, *Culture in Exile*, 173–81, 213–17.

8. *Golos Rossii*, Jan. 7, 1921; Williams, *Culture in Exile*, 208–12, 236; R. H. B. Lockhart, *Memoirs of a Secret Agent* (NY: Putnam, 1932), 180.

9. Personal communications from Dr. O. A. Kerensky and K. Grigorkoff; T. Ponomarëva, "Vera Baranovskaia," *Iskusstvo Kino* (1966), no. 5, 79.

10. Vishniak, *Gody emigratsii*, 67–68.

11. Vishniak, *Gody emigratsii*, 67–68; AK, "Fevral' i Oktiabr'," *Izdalëka: Sbornik statei (1920–1921 g.)* (Paris: Povolotskii, 1922), 226, 228 ff; For the collapse of Chernov's pretensions to represent the SR underground, see Shkarenkov, *Agoniaa*, 42 ff, 165.

12. Williams, *Culture in Exile*, 111–40; Koons, "Histoire," 74–75.

13. *Dni*, Oct. 29, 1922 etc.; Berberova, *Italics*, 305; George Popoff, *Ich sah die Revolutionäre: Moskauer Erinnerungen und Begegnungen während der Revolutionsjahre* (Bern: Verlag Schweizerisches Ostinstitut), 1967, 31–32. For the polemic with Ossorgin, see *Dni*, Oct. 28, 30; Nov. 11, 1925. Kerensky's overreaction deprived the paper of a gifted writer.

14. *Dni*, Nov. 1, 1922, Sept. 28, 1923; Henry Ford, *Der internationale Jude* (Leipzig: Hammerverlag, 1922) 1:183–84. (Ford later disclaimed authorship of this appalling work.) C.f. Kasinov's assertion that Kerensky had to "accommodate himself to the views and tastes of that extreme reactionary milieu to which he adhered and from which he depended," M. K. Kasvinov, *Dvadtsat' piat' stupeni vniz* (M: Mysl', 1979), 235–37, i.e., Czech Social-Democrats, *New York Times* readers and British Tories. But perhaps Kasvinov was only a "moderate" Communist?

15. Čech, "Ruska emigrace," 47; Williams, *Culture in Exile*, 237–38; Berberova, *Italics*, 167; Koons, "Histoire," 76.

16. Zinaida N. Gippius, *Pis'ma k Berberovoi i Khodasevichu*, E. F. Sheikholeslami, ed. (Ann Arbor, Mich: Ardis, 1979), 48; AK to Mrs. O. L. Kerensky, Nov. 25, 1922, Dec. 7, 1922; A. M. Onu to Mrs. Kerensky, April 13, 1923; Mrs. Kerensky to A. M. Onu, April 14, 1923; Mrs. Kerensky to AK [copy], Dec. 11, 1923, Kerensky Family Papers; Conversations with the Kerensky family and friends.

17. AK, "Razryv," typescript, Kerensky Papers, F.5.

18. Personal communications; Sonia Zaitseva later published three children's books: *Detskimi glazami na mir: Povest' iz zhizhni Peterburgskoi devochki* (Kharbin: K. I. Zaitsev, 1937); *Put' cherez mir* (Shanghai: K. I. Zaitsev, 1946); and *U poroga v mir*, (2d. posthumous edition), (Shanghai: Kiosk Kafedral'nago Sobora, 1947). For Father Kirill Zaitsev's opinions, see *Pamiati posledniago Tsaria*, Shanghai: Kiosk Kafedral'nago Sobora, 1948.

19. Huntington, *The Homesick Million*, 174–76; Dr. O. A. Kerensky, "Answers to Abraham's Questions," ms, April 21, 1983; Hippius, *Intellect and Ideas*, 460, n5; Berberova, *Italics*, 310; Lord Stow Hill, "Alexander Kerensky" (Obituary), *Survey*, (1970), no.77, 208.

20. Hippius, *Between Paris and St. Petersburg*, 228, 246; Ariadna Efron, *Stranitsy vospominanii* (Paris: Lev, 1969), 159–60; Elena Izvol'skaia, "Ten' na Stenakh (O Tsvetaevoi)," *Opyty*, (1954), no. 3, 152–53; Simon Karlinsky, *Marina Cvetaeva*, (Berkeley-LA: University of California Press, 1966), 53 ff; In 1924, Tsvetaeva sent Kerensky autographed copies of *Remeslo* and *Tsar'-Devitsa*, Kerensky Family Papers; Gippius, *Pis'ma k Berberovoi i Khodasevichu*, 48–49, 64.

21. Temira Pachmuss, Introduction to Hippius, *Between Paris and St. Petersburg*, 49; Hippius, *Intellect and Ideas*, 415; Gippius, *Pis'ma k Berberovoi i Khodasevichu*, 73; Temira Pachmuss, *Zinaida Hippius: An Intellectual Profile* (Carbondale & Edwardsville, Ill: Southern Illinois University Press, 1971), 237, 280, 439, n 43; Dr. O. A. Kerensky, "Answers".

22. *NYT*, March 2, 3, 4, 13, 14, 1927; AK to Mrs. O. L. Kerensky, March 25, 1927, Kerensky Family Papers, C.f. V. M. Zenzinov, *Zheleznyi Skrezhet: Iz amerikanskikh vpechatlenii* (Paris: La Presse Française et Étrangère, 1927), 15 ff.

23. *NYT*, March 2, 3, 14, 15, 1927.

24. Flora Solomon, *Baku to Baker Street*, 134–35. Space obliges me to give shorter shrift to the celebrated "Sisters Karamazov" than they deserve. Their own memoirs are inimitable.

25. *NYT*, May 8, 15, 22, 29; June 5; July 3, 1927; AK, *Catastrophe*, vi, 1–76; AK, *La Révolution Russe* (Paris: Payot, 1928); AK, *Erinnerungen: Vom Sturz des Zarentums bis zu Lenins Staatsstreich* (Dresden: Carl Reissner Verlag, 1928), 7ff, 19, 21–22.

26. D. F. Sverchkov, *Try meteora: G. Gapon, G. Nosar', A. Kerenskii*, (Pet: Priboi, 1921); Sverchkov, *A. F. Kerenskii* (Lgd: Priboi, 1927). A leading member of the 1905 Petersburg Soviet, Sverchkov was in exile when Kerensky was earning his spurs; his use of the meteor image may have been sincere. Sergei Eisenstein, *Izbrannye proizvedeniia v shesti tomakh*, (M: Iskusstvo, 1971), 6:72–79; Thorold Dickinson and Catherine De la Roche, *Soviet Cinema* (L: Falcon Press, 1948), 130–31.

27. Gippius, *Pis'ma k Berberovoi i Khodasevichu*, 48; Ponomarëva, "Vera Baranovskaia," 76–78.

28. *Dni*, March 11, 1926; March 9, 1929.

29. *Dni*, Jan 20, April 12, March 17, Sept. 8, Nov. 10, 1929.

30. *Dni*, Dec. 29. 1929, Jan. 19, Feb. 9, Feb. 16, May 18, 1930; AK, *The Communist Dictatorship and Religion* (Oxford: The Alden Press, 1930), 8; R. H. B. Lockhart,

The Diaries of Sir Robert Bruce Lockhart, Kenneth Young, ed. (L: Macmillan, 1973) 1:175.

31. *Dni*, Jan 20, April 12, Oct. 28, 1925; G. P. Fedotov, "I. I. Fondaminskii v Emigratsii," *NZh*, (1948), no. 18, 318; Hippius, *Between Paris and St. Petersburg*, 239, *n*69, 240, *n*72; *Novyi Grad* (1931), no. 1, 3 ff; Nicholas Berdyaev, *Dream and Reality: An Essay in Autobiography* (L: Geoffrey Bles, 1950), 279–81; AK, "Molitva o Babushke," Kerensky Papers, F.5; Personal communication from Elena Izvolskaya.

32. Personal communications; Lockhart, *Diaries*, 1:174–75.

33. Berberova, *Italics*, 358 ff; Shkarenkov, *Agoniia*, 115; Koons, "Histoire," 80; AK, "Vo vlast' illiuzii," *Sovremënnyia Zapiski* (1934), 56:359–74; *Dni*, April 9, 1933; Mrs. O. L. Kerensky to AK [copy], Oct. 1, 1934.

34. AK, "K. K. Breshkovskaia" [Obituary], *Sovremënnyia Zapiski* (1934), 56:397; V. G. Arkhangel'skii, *Katerina Breshkovskaia*, (Prague: Izd. Obshchestva 'Shkol'naia Pomoshch'), 1938, 205–12.

35. Personal communications; Lockhart, *Diaries*, 1:318–19.

36. I am indebted to *The Courier-Mail*, Brisbane, and the Somerville House Old Girls' Association, Brisbane, for assisting my enquiries into Kerensky's Australian connections. Gladys Edds (née Tritton), "Family History," typescript, July 7, 1983; F. W. Tritton to Mrs. Helen Simpson, May 2, 1944, Papers of Mrs. Simpson; J. Cyril and Heather Tritton interviewed in London, 1983; Personal communications from Joan Priest, Jesse Jackson, Dr. Kurt Aaron, OBE, Grace Copp, Orma Fry, Colin Hughes; See also, Lydia E. "Nellé" Tritton, *Poems*, (Brisbane: privately printed, 1920), 17, 19; *The Queenslander*, May 29, 1926; Photographs belonging to Grace Copp.

37. Berberova, *Italics*, 308; *Western Mail*, March 31, 1927; Personal communications from Joan Priest, Grace Copp, Mary Burgum, J. Cyril Tritton, Dr. O. A. Kerensky; See also N. Nadezhin, *Izbrannye Stikhotvoreniia* (L: Nadéjine [i.e. the author], 1954).

38. Nina Christesen, "A Russian Migrant," in Patricia Grimshaw and Lynne Strahan eds., *The Half-Open Door*, (Sydney: Hale and Iremonger, 1982), 72; Lydia Kerensky to AK, "between Jan. 28 and Feb. 1, 1945," Feb. 3, Feb. 14, 1945, Kerensky Papers, F.191; Personal communication from Jesse Jackson; Flora Solomon, *Baku to Baker Street*, 164, though other observers feel their intimacy ended earlier.

39. AK, *Crucifixion*, 55; ch. 5: "The Czar and the Jews," 65–76; M. Gorky et al, *Belomorsko-Baltiiskii Kanal imeni Stalina: Istoriia Stroitel'stva* (M: Gosudarstvennoe Izd. 'Istoriia fabrik i zavodov', 1934), see photographs on pp. 51, 78, 102, 119, 213, 222, 295. The normally alert Solzhenitsyn fails to note the significance of the incidence of Jewish NKVD men, A. I. Solzhenitsyn, *The Gulag Archipelago* (L: Collins/Fontana, 1976), 2:71 ff; Flora Solomon, *Baku to Baker Street*, 174–75.

40. Captain Paul Bulygin, *The Murder of the Romanovs: The Authentic Account*, Sir Bernard Pares, ed. (L: Hutchinson, 1935), including AK, "The Road to the Tragedy."

41. *NYT* Oct. 16, 1936, *NYT*, Editorial, Oct. 20, 1936; *Novaia Rossiia*, March 8,

Aug. 1, Nov. 1, 15, 1936; AK, *L'Expérience Kérenski*, (Paris: Payot, 1936), 7–9, 176–83; Personal communication from Elena Izvolskaya.

42. *Novaia Rossiia*, March 8, Sept. 15, 1936. Though Kerensky did hope that Yagoda's appointment would end the purges, *Novaia Rossiia*, Oct. 1, 1936.

43. Lockhart, *Diaries*, 1:271; A. P. Danilovskii, "Otdel'nye etapy zhiznénnogo puti In.Put.Soobshch.N. V. Nekrasov" [*sic*], roneo, Kerensky Papers, F.129; Simon Wolin, "The 'Menshevik' Trial of 1931," in L. H. Haimson, ed., *The Mensheviks: from the Revolution of 1917 to the Second World War* (Chicago: University of Chicago Press, 1974), 394–402; Roy Medvedev, *Let History Judge: The Origins and Consequences of Stalinism* (L: Spokesman, 1972), 110 ff; AK to Mrs. O. L. Kerensky, Dec. 5, 1936, April 8, 1937; OLK, "Obryvki," 120; Conversation with Paul Olferiev, 1970.

44. V. L. Burtsev, *Bol'shevistskie gangstery v Parizhe: Pokhishchenie Generala Millera i Generala Kutepova* (Paris: Izd. avtora, 1939); Berberova, *Italics*, 336–37; Nina Berberova, *Zheleznaia zhenshchina: Rasskaz o zhizni M. I. Zakrevskoi-Benkendorf-Budberg, o nei samoi i eë druz'iakh* (NY: Russica, 1981), 275; Victor Serge, *Memoirs of a Revolutionary, 1901–1941* (L: Oxford University Press, 1963), 326–45.

45. Hippius, *Intellect and Ideas*, 517, *n*14; *NYT*, Feb. 28, March 3, April 24, Oct. 11, 23, 1938; Flora Solomon, *Baku to Baker Street*, 174–75.

46. The divorce was handled for Kerensky by Messrs Marcel Bourgeois, Kerensky Family Papers; *The Courier-Mail*, March 10, Aug. 23, 1939; Lydia Kerensky to AK, July 21, 1939, Kerensky Papers, F.191; *NYT*, Aug. 22, 27, 1939.

47. *The Courier-Mail*, Aug. 23, 1939 carried the news of the Kerensky-Tritton wedding *and* the Hitler-Stalin Pact. Some of Kerensky's predictions are in "Tezisy," ms., Nov. 22, 1940, Kerensky Papers, F.82, eg. "The democratization or totalization [*sic*] of the entire Europo-Asiatic-Afr. Continent (if not the whole world) will be the obligatory consequence of this war." I am indebted to Richard Davies of the Leeds Russian Archive for helping decipher this document.

18. The Long Reprieve

1. *NYT*, Sept. 17, 21, Oct. 6, 22, Nov. 13, 1939; *Novaia Rossiia*, Oct. 1, Nov. 1, 1939.

2. Anthony F. Upton, *Finland 1939–1940* (L: Davis-Poynter, 1974), 11–44, 46–50; Alexander Werth, *Russia at War 1941–1945* (L: Barrie and Rockliff, 1964), 67–68; *NYT*, Dec. 4, 13, 1939; Oskari Tokoi, *Maanpakolaisen Muistelmia* (H:ki: Tammi, 1959), 381–83, mentions Herbert Hoover's support, but not Kerensky's; V. M. Zenzinov, *Vstrecha s Rossiei: Kak i chëm zhivut v Sovetskom Soiuze: Pis'ma v Krasnuiu armiiu 1939–1940* (NY: Zenzinov, 1944), 11–12, 22; Personal communication from Gleb Kerensky; Jukka Nevakivi, *The Appeal that was Never Made: The Allies, Scandinavia and the Finnish Winter War 1939–1940*, (L: C. Hurst, 1976), 174; S. Jägerskiöld, *Mannerheim* (H:ki: Holger Schildts Förlag), 6:197, 77 ff; Mannerheim himself thanked the volunteers, but mentioned no Russians, see C. G. E. Mannerheim, *The Memoirs of Marshal Mannerheim* (L: Cassell, 1953), 358–59. The topic is still too sensitive for proof or disproof.

3. *NYT*, Feb. 2, 1940; AK and I. I. Fondaminskii to Zenzinov (telegram), May 8, 1940, Zenzinov Papers, Bakhmeteff Archive, Columbia University Libraries, New York; FO.371.24856, Lockhart to Maclean, May 24, 1940; AK to Lockhart, May 7, 1940; Lockhart to Maclean, June 9, 1940.

4. Nina Berberova, *The Italics are Mine* (L: Longmans, 1969), 309–10; A. J. Smithers, *Dornford Yates: A Biography* (L: Hodder and Stoughton, 1982), 184; *NYT*, Aug. 13, 1940; Lydia Kerensky to AK, April 5, 1944, Kerensky Papers, F.191; Personal communication from Lorraine Jarrett.

5. FO.371.24856, Lockhart to Maclean, July 6, 1940; Maclean to Parkin, July 6, 1940, FO Minutes, July 29, 1940; Parkin to Davies; Maclean to Parkin, June 29, 1940; Lockhart to Maclean, Sept. 21, 1940; *NYT*, June 29, Aug. 13, 1940.

6. *NYT*, Jan 26, 1941; Lydia Kerensky to AK, Feb. 1, 1941, Kerensky Papers, F.191.

7. For Stalin's assumption of the premiership, see E. Gnedin, *Iz istorii otnoshenii mezhdu SSSR i fashistskoi Germaniei: Dokumenty i sovremënnye Kommentary* (NY: Khronika, 1977); *NYT*, May 7, June 23, 28, 1941.

8. FO.371.29591, Halifax to FO, July 2, 1941; Minutes by Maclean, Coote, and Warner, July 4; by Eden, July 5, 1941; AK to Joseph Stalin, March 2, 1942, telegram [copy], Kerensky Papers, F.149.

9. *NYT*, Dec. 9, 1941; Lydia Kerensky to AK, March 2, 1942, Kerensky Papers, F.191; E. D. Kuskova to AK, May 5, 1944, Kerensky Papers, F.217.

10. The New York apartments are mentioned in AK to Zenzinov, Sept. 11, 1941, Zenzinov Papers; Lydia Kerensky to AK, March 15, 1944, and "between Jan. 28 and Feb. 1, 1945," Kerensky Papers, F.191. I am indebted to *The New Canaan Advertiser*, the New Canaan Historical Society and Ewing S. Walker for facilitating my enquiries into Kerensky's connection with the area. For the house in Silvermine, see AK to Zenzinov, Sept. 11, 1941, Zenzinov Papers; Personal communications from Helen G. Bristow, Mr. & Mrs. John McGinley and Tatiana Pollock. The house in Vista was featured in *American Home Magazine*, June 1939; AK to Mrs. Peter Davis, Dec. 19, 1958, Papers of William Garnett, Vista; Lydia Kerensky to AK, 'samedi' 1942, n.d., and Feb. 16, 1945, Kerensky Papers, F.191; Frederick W. Tritton to Mrs. Helen Simpson, May 2, 1944, Papers of Mrs. Simpson; *The New Canaan Advertiser*, April 18, 1946, June 25, 1970; Personal communications from William Garnett, Collette De Silvers and Tatiana Pollock.

11. Personal communications from Tatiana Pollock and Mrs. John Somers; Zenzinov to AK, Sept. 11, 1941, Zenzinov Papers.

12. AK, "Tezisy," ms., Kerensky Papers, F.82.

13. AK to Zenzinov, Dec. 4, 1943, Zenzinov Papers; Lydia Kerensky to AK, Nov. 22, 1943, Kerensky Papers, F.191.

14. AK, "O rizhskom mire" and "Stydnoe," *Izdalëka: Sbornik statei (1920–1921 g.)* (Paris: Povolotskii, 1922), 112 ff; *Dni*, Jan. 19, 1930; AK, "Vo vlast' illiuzii," *Sovremënnyia Zapiski*, 1934, vol. 56; Lydia Kerensky to AK, Nov. 24, 1943, March 3, 1944, Kerensky Papers, F.191; *NYT*, Jan. 14, 1944. For 'Katyn', see Werth, *Russia at War*, 661–67; Louis Fitzgibbon, *Katyn Massacre*, (L: Corgi, 1977), passim.

15. *Novyi Grad*, 1931, No. 1, 4; Zenzinov to AK, Aug. 6, Sept. 17, 1943, Zenzinov Papers; Lydia Kerensky to AK, March 29, 1944, Kerensky Papers, F.191; E. D. Kuskova to AK, May 5, 1944, Oct. 18, 1946, Kerensky Papers, F.217. For de Gaulle's motives, see Brian Crozier, *De Gaulle* (L: Methuen, 1973), 1:302–16; For Beneš' prudence, see W. P. Crozier, *Off the Record: Political Interviews 1933–1943*, A. J. P. Taylor, ed. (L: Hutchinson, 1973), 374.

16. AK, "Vrag izgnan iz predelov SSSR", typescript, Nov. 13, 1944, Zenzinov Papers; *NYT*, Dec. 16, 17, 1944; B. Nikolaevskii to AK, March 31, 1946, Kerensky Papers, F.134; Lydia Kerensky to AK, Feb. 14, 18, 22, 1945; Helen Simpson to Lydia Kerensky, Jan. 24, 1945, Kerensky Papers, F.191.

17. V. M. Chernov, "N. D. Avksent'ev v Molodosti"; M. M. Karpovich, "Pamiati N. D. Avksent'eva"; AK, "P. N. Miliukov"; M. Aldanov, "Pamiati P. N. Miliukova", all in *NZh*, (1943), no. 5; Zenzinov to AK, March 11, April 9, 1943; L. G. Shkarenkov, *Agoniia beloi emigratsii* (M: Mysl', 1981), 187–89; M. V. Vishniak, *Gody emigratsii 1919–1969: Parizh-N'iu Iork: Years of Emigration 1919–1969: Paris-New York* (Stanford, Cal: Hoover Institution, 1970), 192–96.

18. Zenzinov to AK, March 15, 1945; AK to Zenzinov, March 19, 1945, Zenzinov Papers; *NRS*, March 7, 1945; Lydia Kerensky to AK, March 8, 1945, Kerensky Papers, F. 191; Vishniak, *Gody emigratsii*, 190–91; AK to Zenzinov, Sept. 1, 1943, Aug. 21, 1945; AK to V. A. [Maklakov], July 7, 1945 [copy], Zenzinov Papers.

19. Lydia Kerensky to AK, March 14, 19, 24 [telegram], 27, 1944, Kerensky Papers, F.191; AK to Lydia Kerensky, March 18, 1944, Kerensky Papers, F.190.

20. Lydia Kerensky to AK, April 4, 5; March 29, 1944; between Jan. 28 and Feb. 1, 1945, Feb. 3, 14, 1945, Kerensky Papers, F.191; AK to Lydia Kerensky, April 5, 1944; AK to Mrs. F. W. Tritton, Feb. 5, 1945, Kerensky Papers, F.191.

21. *Norwalk Land Records* 357:171–73; 306:490–94. Personal communications from Ruth and Stephen Boski (who checked the Land Records for me) and from Tatiana Pollock. Kerensky felt inhibited by the rules of hospitality from criticizing the societies that sheltered him, except in relation to their policies towards Russia. His private letters and conversations show him fully aware of all their major failings. For example, on Aug. 23, 1945, he wrote to Oleg about the corruption of *the victors*, who "had used on the vanquished NOT their democratic, but alien totalitarian rules and to a degree unprecedented in history," Kerensky Family Papers.

22. AK to Zenzinov, Oct. 6, 17, 18, 1945, Jan. 20, 1946, Zenzinov Papers; *The Daily Telegram* [Sydney], Nov. 12, 1945; *The Courier-Mail*, Nov. 14, 1945, April 11, 1946; *The Telegraph* [Brisbane], Nov. 14, 1945; AK to Nina Berberova, April 17, 1946, Berberova, *Kursiv Moi: Avtobiografiia* (NY: Russica, 1983), 1:355–57 (it does not appear in the English edition); Personal communications from Oleg Kerensky Jr., Noel Busch, Nina Berberova, Orma Fry, Lorraine Jarrett, and J. Cyril and Heather Tritton.

23. *The Telegraph* [Brisbane], Nov. 14, 1945; Personal communications from Dr. J. L. C. Laahz. Corbett Tritton later became secretary to Prime Minister Menzies.

24. Personal communications from Nina Christesen, Dr. O. A. Kerensky, Gleb Kerensky, Oleg Kerensky Jr.

25. A. F. Podozerova to AK, Jan. 3, 1948, Kerensky Papers, F.105; Personal communications from, and conversations with, Paul Olferiev. In 1936, Kerensky had briefly visited Yugoslavia to help his sister Anna sort out her divorce, AK to Gleb Kerensky, May 8, 1936, AK to Mrs. O. L. Kerensky, April 8, 1937, Kerensky Family Papers; AK, "Broadcast to Russia", Nov. 24, 1949, Disc, BBC Sound Archives; printed in *NRS*, Dec. 4, 1949 and *New Leader*, Dec. 24, 1949; E. D. Kuskova to AK, Oct. 4, 18, 1946, Kerensky Papers, F.217.

26. *NYT*, Jan. 24 ,1947; Victor Soskice told me that Kerensky had successfully interceded with Eleanor Roosevelt to stop NKVD agents intimidating Soviet DPs in America. See also, Nikolai Tolstoy, *Victims of Yalta* (L: Hodder & Stoughton, 1977).

27. Conversations with Lord Stow Hill; Personal communications from Oleg Kerensky Jr., Dr. O. A. Kerensky; Professor Sergei Utekhin interviewed by Professor Barbara Norton, 1983.

28. Julius Epstein, *Operation Keelhaul: The Story of Forced Repatriation from 1944 to the Present* (Old Greenwich, Conn: Devin-Adair, 1973), 119 ff, 218–19; *NRS*, May 22, 1949; Kuskova to AK, Nov. 17, 1955, Kerensky Papers, F.217.

29. Zenzinov to AK, July 7, 1946, Zenzinov Papers; Personal communications from Oleg Kerensky Jr., Tatiana Pollock.

30. The genesis of the CIA and the question of nuclear blackmail are such live issues that detachment is difficult. My resources did not permit me to follow this up in U.S. government archives. Sidney Hook to AK, Oct. 20, 1949, Kerensky Papers, F.134; *New Leader*, Sept. 4, 1948. For Eugene Lyons, see Lyons, *Assignment in Utopia* (L: G. G. Harrap, 1938), 3 ff, 37 ff; Lyons, *Our Secret Allies: The Peoples of Russia* (L: Arco, 1954). Lyons was subsequently a director of *Reader's Digest*. In 1945–46, Kerensky was resolutely opposed to "nuclear blackmail," see AK to Oleg A. Kerensky, Feb. 11, 1946, Kerensky Family Papers.

31. *NYT*, Sept. 30, 1954; AK, "Otkrytoe pis'mo M. E. Vainbaumu," *NRS*, Dec. 19, 1954; Zenzinov to AK, July 17, Nov. 14, 1949, Zenzinov Papers.

32. *NRS*, March 12, 27, 1949.

33. *Glasgow Evening News*, Oct. 3, 1949; AK, "Broadcast to Russia," *NRS*, Dec. 4, 1949; Personal communications from Gleb Kerensky. For the FO's squirming, see R. H. B. Lockhart, *The Diaries of Sir Robert Bruce Lockhart*, Kenneth Young, ed. (L: Macmillan, 1980), 2:708–09.

34. Nina Berberova, *Italics*, 309–10; Zenzinov to AK copy, Nov. 14, 1949, Zenzinov Papers; *NTS: Union of Russian Solidarists*, (Frankfurt/M: NTS, 1961), 21–22, 32–33; A. N. Artëmov, *Ideologiia solidarizma i eë Razvitie* (Frankfurt/M; NTS, 1952), 5 ff; V. Ianovskii, "Diskussiia ob Amerikanskom Komitete," *NRS*, Jan. 11, 1955; Kuskova in *NRS*, March 7, 1953; Jan. 21, 22, 1955; A. N. Artëmov, "A. F. Kerenskii i sud'by demokratii," *Posev*, July 1970, 55–56; Personal communication from A. N. Artëmoff.

35. M. Kovalevs'kii, *Opozytsiini rukhy v Ukraïni i natsional'na polityka SSSR (1920–1954)*, (Munich: Doslydy i Materialy; Seriia 2), (tsyklostylevi vydannia) no. 26, (Institut dlia Vyvchannia Istoriï i Kul'tury SSSR, 1954), 65 ff; John A. Armstrong, *Ukrainian Nationalism 1939–1945* (NY: Columbia University Press, 1963), 290–321; *NRS*, Jan. 4, Feb. 7, 15, 1953, Jan. 1, 1955; AK to Zenzinov,

Dec. 30, 1951; Zenzinov to AK, April 8, Dec. 18, 1952 (b), Zenzinov Papers; Kuskova to V. A. Maklakov [copy], Sept. 29, 1953[?], Kerensky Papers, F.217. The crucial exchange was in *NRS*, Dec. 19, 29, 1954.

36. AK to Herbert Hoover, Sept. 21, 1955, Box 243, Folder 1D, Kerensky, Alexander; C. Easton Rothwell to AK, June 27, Dec. 19, 1955; W. Sworakowski to AK, Nov. 21, 1955, Box 247, Folder 1D, Provisional Government, A. Kerensky, Series T–16, W. S. Sworakowski: Administrative and Curatorial Records, 1946–1977, Hoover Institution Files, Stanford. Kerensky had already asked Tereshchenko to write a book with him, Tereshchenko to AK, June 26, 1950, Kerensky Papers, F.167.

37. Kuskova to AK, Dec. 21, 1955, Kerensky Papers, F.217; J. Bunyan and H. H. Fisher, *The Bolshevik Revolution 1917–1918* (1934); O. H. Gankin and H. H. Fisher, *The Bolsheviks and the World War* (1940); *Revoliutsiia 1905–1907 gg. v Rossii* (1955–65); *Velikaia Oktiabr'skaia Sotsialisticheskaia Revoliutsiia* (1957–63).

38. *RPG*, 1:vii; Robert P. Browder won The Honorable Mention for the George Louis Beer Prize of the AHA for *The Origins of Soviet-American Diplomacy* (Princeton, N.J.: Princeton University Press, 1953); R. P. Browder, "Kerenskij Revisited", *Russian Thought and Politics* (Festschrift for Michael Karpovich), v.6 of *Harvard Slavic Studies* (The Hague, 1957), 421–34; Browder to Rothwell, March 8, 1958, Box 247, Folder 1D, Hoover Institution Files; Personal communications from Elena Ivanoff, Ella Wolfe, Prof. Robert P. Browder; Anna Bourguina-Nicolaevsky interviewed in 1970.

39. *RPG*, passim; Robert S. Call checked the files of the Hoover Institution and Stanford University Press for administrative details. The comparison is made with the first three volumes of *VOSR*, which are of comparable size.

40. Personal communications from Elena Ivanoff and C. Easton Rothwell.

41. Countess Fira Ilinska interviewed in 1970; Personal communications from Elena Ivanoff; AK to Mrs. O. L. Kerensky, Aug. 24, 1959, July 19, 1962, July 5, 1963, Aug. 27, 1963, Kerensky Family Papers.

42. AK to Sir Frank Soskice, May 18, 1963, FS/KER/1, Soskice Papers, House of Lords Record Office, London; "O. A. Kerensky: Curriculum Vitae"; *The Times*, June 26, 1984; AK to Mrs. O. L. Kerensky, Aug. 16, 1963, Kerensky Family Papers. Oleg Kerensky Jr. wrote regularly on ballet for *The Daily Mail* and the *New Statesman*, before publishing a series of books. Josephine Pasternak, " 'Ich bestand darauf, Blutvergiessen zu vermeiden.' Erinnerungen an Alexander Kerenski," *Der Monat*, 1982, No. 3, 50–51; Max Hayward to AK, May 22, 1964, Kerensky Papers, F.33; Conversations with Max Hayward, Dr. George Katkov, Ronald Higley and Dr. Harold Shukman.

43. G. Ia. Aronson, *Rossiia nakanune Revoliutsii* (NY: Novoe Russkoe Slovo, 1961), 138–42; AK, "La franc-maçonnerie en Russie," *Le Contrat Social* (1965), no. 6, 356–58. It is understandable that one of those who objected most strongly to these revelations, which partly confirmed the "Judaeo-Masonic myth" exploited so savagely by Russian and German anti-Semites, was one of the *few* Jewish members of the Political free-masonry. Ia. L. [Rubinstein] to AK, Nov. 15, 1959, Kerensky Papers, F.217; Alexander Yanov, *The Russian New Right*, (Berkeley-LA: University of California Press, 1978), 79 ff, 131, suggests that

Rubinstein's fears were not misplaced. For official Soviet and 'dissident' reactions to Kerensky's last memoirs, see S. L. Titarenko, "Obzor: Memuary 'cheloveka s togo sveta' (O knige A. F. Kerenskogo 'Rossiia i povorotnyi punkt istorii'," *Voprosy Istorii* (1967), no. 12, 189–95; A. Skuratov, "Vospominaniia meteora," *Veche*, 1970, no. 2, (reprinted in *Arkhiv Samizdata*, No. 680, Radio Liberty); Personal communications from Elena Izvolskaya and Elena Ivanoff.

44. Berberova, *Italics*, 315–16; Paul Olferiev and Countess Fira Ilinska interviewed in 1970; Personal communications from Oleg Kerensky Jr., Elena Ivanoff, Dr. O. A. Kerensky; Letter from Robert Payne, Dec. 22, 1982.

45. Joel Carmichael, "Kerensky," *The Russian Revolution: The CBS Legacy Collection* (NY: Macmillan, 1967), Robert Payne, *The Fortress* (NY: W. H. Allen, 1967), 405 ff; Svetlana Allilueva, *Tol'ko odin god* (L: Hutchinson, 1969), 364–65; AK, "Address to Overseas Press Club," New York, Nov. 5, 1967, typescript, Papers of Elena Ivanoff; AK, "The Truth About Lenin," with a note by David Floyd, *Sunday Telegraph*, April 19, 1970.

46. AK, "The Truth About Lenin"; Interview with Countess Ilinska; Personal communications from Elena Ivanoff, Dr. O. A. Kerensky; *NYT*, June 12, 1970 If anything, Russian history appears to follow cycles rather than straight lines, see Alexander Yanov, "The Drama of the Time of Troubles 1725–30," *Canadian-American Slavic Studies* (1978), 12, (1):1–59; This does not mean that Russians lack the desire for greater personal liberty, see Alexander I. Solzhenitsyn, *The Mortal Danger: How Misconceptions about Russia Imperil the West* (L: Bodley Head, 1980).

47. *NYT*, June 12, 1970; *NRS*, June 12, 1970; Skuratov's review of Kerensky's memoirs appeared as he died; For Sofia Kallistratova's defense of Natalia Gorbanevskaya, see *Khronika tekushchikh sobytii*, Aug. 31, 1970, (reprinted, Amsterdam: Fond imeni Gertsena, 1979), 456–74.

48. *NRS*, June 14, 16, 1970; *NYT*, June 15, 1970; Isaac Don Levine, "Tribute to Alexander Kerensky, Premier of Democratic Russia in 1917, at Memorial Services June 14, 1970, introduced by Hon. F. Edward Hébert, Louisiana, House of Representatives," *Congressional Record*, 91st Congress, 2nd Session, June 16, 1970; Lord Stow Hill [Sir Frank Soskice], "Alexander Kerensky (Obituary)," *Survey*, (Autumn 1970), 207–8; Conversations with the Kerensky family.

Index of Names

Subject Index